D0516782

A
SPEAKER'S
SOURCEBOOK
FOR
LATTER-DAY
SAINTS

The following collections of quotes from LDS Church Leaders
are available in special, low-priced gift editions
at LDS bookstores or from ASPEN BOOKS:

Great Thoughts From Latter-day Prophets
Great Thoughts For Success & Happiness
Great Thoughts For Missionaries
Great Thoughts For Latter-day Saint Youth
Great Thoughts For Latter-day Saint Sisters
Never, Ever, Ever Give Up: Thoughts on Overcoming

A SPEAKER'S SOURCEBOOK

FOR

LATTER-DAY SAINTS

3,000 Quotes
by LDS Church Leaders

Compiled by Aspen Books

ASPEN
BOOKS

A Speaker's Sourcebook for Latter-day Saints

©1991, 1998, 1999, 2001 by Aspen Books
All rights reserved.
Printed in the United States of America.

No part of this book covered by copyrights hereon may be
reproduced or copied by any means without written permission
of the publisher,
Aspen Books, 801-974-0414.

ISBN 1-56236-201-1

Fourth Printing

Cover design by Jeremy Wright
based on original design by Stewart Anstead

Acknowledgement

In appreciation to the editors at ASPEN BOOKS, Peggy Duckworth, Curtis Taylor, and Stan Zenk, and to Marc Garrison for support and direction.

Contents

Preface

The *LDS Speaker's Sourcebook* contains over 3,000 statements, mostly by leaders of the Church of Jesus Christ of Latter-day Saints, arranged into 287 topics. These statements provide supportive and instructional material for teachers, parents, and gospel students.

The quotations were selected for clarity, conciseness, and relevance to the topic. Our search for quotes began with recent general conference talks and widened to include all conference addresses and other important works. Original sources have been listed when possible. Also, when available, references from the *Ensign* have been listed rather than *Conference Reports*, providing easier access for the average member of the Church. Some sources were not available at press time; we hope to remedy this in future editions.

Though most of these quotes are concerned with inspirational themes, some declarations of doctrine are included; generally we have reserved strictly doctrinal statements for a forthcoming volume, *The LDS Speaker's Doctrinal Sourcebook*.

In our year's work on this volume, we have been touched by the words of our prophets. It is our hope that these teachings will give understanding and strength to all who study them. And thus, we hope that the words of the prophets will continue to touch the lives of Saints everywhere.

The editors

List of Abbreviations

CR	*Conference Report*
DBY	*Discourses of Brigham Young*, John A. Widtsoe, comp., Salt Lake City: Deseret Book Co., 1954
DFTP	*Doctrines From The Prophets*, Alma P. Burton, comp., Salt Lake City: Bookcraft, 1970
GD	*Gospel Doctrine*, Joseph F. Smith, Salt Lake City: Deseret Book Co., 1975
HC	*History of the Church*, 7 vols., 2nd edition, Salt Lake City: Deseret Book Co., 1967
IE	*Improvement Era*
JD	*Journal of Discourses*, 26 vols., Liverpool, England: Albert Carrington [and others], 1853-1886
MS	*Millenial Star*
OAT	*Of All Things*, Gary P. Gillum, ed., Salt Lake City: Signature Books, 1981
TETB	*Teachings of Ezra Taft Benson*, Ezra Taft Benson, Salt Lake City: Bookcraft, 1988
TLS	*Teachings of Lorenzo Snow*, Clyde J. Williams, comp., Salt Lake City: Bookcraft, 1984
TPJS	*Teachings of the Prophet Joseph Smith*, Joseph Fielding Smith, comp., Salt Lake City: Deseret Book Co., 1976
TSWK	*Teachings of Spencer W. Kimball*, Edward L. Kimball, Salt Lake City: Bookcraft, 1982

Aaronic Priesthood

I desire to impress upon you the fact that it does not make any difference whether a man is a priest or an Apostle, if he magnifies his calling. A priest holds the keys of the ministering of angels. Never in my life, as an Apostle, as a Seventy, or as an elder, have I ever had more of the protection of the Lord than while holding the office of a priest. The Lord revealed to me by visions, by revelations, and by the Holy Spirit, many things that lay before me. (Quoted by Gordon B. Hinckley, *Ensign*, May 1988, p. 45.)

— *Wilford Woodruff*

I want to emphasize that the holding of the Aaronic Priesthood, and the exercise of its power, is not a small or unimportant thing. The bestowal of these keys in this dispensation was one of the greatest and most significant things incident to the entire Restoration. It was the first bestowal of divine authority in this, the dispensation of the fullness of times. It is the priesthood of God, with authority to act in the name of the Savior of mankind. (*Ensign*, May 1988, p. 46.)

— *Gordon B. Hinckley*

It is time for the Aaronic Priesthood to come of age. The rod of iron leading to the tree of life for you, our young men, may well be the implementation of the complete and full work of the Aaronic Priesthood. As we marshal your forces in your true identity as deacons, teachers, and priests in the holy Aaronic Priesthood, we mobilize an army of Israel such as has never been known before in the Church. Your numbers are legion. I believe you will be expected to perform the most important work in this dispensation, with the exception of the work done by the Prophet Joseph Smith. (*Ensign*, November 1987, p. 30.)

— *Vaughn J. Featherstone*

The fact that it is called the lesser priesthood does not diminish at all the importance of the Aaronic Priesthood. The Lord said it is necessary to the Melchizedek Priesthood. (See D&C 84:29.) Any holder of the higher priesthood should feel greatly honored to perform the ordinances of the Aaronic Priesthood, for they have great spiritual importance. (*Ensign*, November 1981, pp. 30-31.)

— *Boyd K. Packer*

When you priests of the Aaronic Priesthood administer the sacrament, you are doing what Jesus did while He was yet in the flesh, and which He also did when He ministered among the Nephites following His resurrection.

When you, as a priest, kneel at the sacrament table and offer up the prayer, which came by revelation, you place the entire congregation under covenant with the Lord. Is this a small thing? It is a most important and remarkable thing. (*Ensign*, May 1988, p. 46.)

— *Gordon B. Hinckley*

The Aaronic Priesthood Trains Future Leaders

No young man should aspire to a calling, but as surely as you are sitting in this priesthood meeting tonight, many of you will preside over wards, stakes, missions, quorums, and, of course, your own families. Priesthood training, my brethren, starts when a young man is ordained a deacon in the Aaronic Priesthood. You Aaronic Priesthood bearers need to understand that you are in training. . . . Train hard. Get ready. The Church needs you. The world needs you. The Lord needs you. (*Ensign*, May 1985, pp. 41, 43.)

— *M. Russell Ballard*

You young men must be worthy and realize what a privilege you have to pass the bread and water, the emblems of the Lord's love for all of us. Think of the blessings you offer— hope, love, joy, forgiveness, freedom, and everlasting life. What a contrast to so many youth who today pass other types of white substances and other kinds of liquids that bring gloom and failure, captivity and death in the deceitful guise of happiness! Oh, the goodness and mercy of our God as he overcomes the cunning of the evil one! (*Ensign*, May 1989, p. 37.)

— *John H. Groberg*

See also PRIESTHOOD, YOUNG MEN

——— Abortion ———

Abortion Sheds Innocent Blood

The woman's choice for her own body does not validate choice for the body of another. The expression "terminate the pregnancy" applies literally only to the woman. The consequence of terminating the fetus therein involves the body and very life of another. These two individuals have separate brains, separate hearts, and separate circulatory systems. To pretend that there is no child and no life there is to deny reality. . . . Approximately twenty-two days after the two cells have united, a little heart begins to beat. At twenty-six days the circulation of blood begins.

Scripture declares that the "life of the flesh is in the blood" (Lev. 17:11). Abortion sheds that innocent blood. (*Ensign*, May 1985, p. 13.)

— *Russell M. Nelson*

Abortion, the taking of life, is one of the most grievous of sins. We have repeatedly affirmed the position of the Church in unalterably opposing all abortions, except in two rare instances: When conception is the result of forcible rape and when competent medical counsel indicates that a mother's health would otherwise be seriously jeopardized. (*Ensign*, November 1976, p. 4.)

— *Spencer W. Kimball*

As loud voices argue on, let us remember that those who advocate abortion have already been born! (*Ensign*, November 1984, p. 31.)

— *Russell M. Nelson*

I thank the Father that His Only Begotten Son did not say in defiant protest at Calvary, "My body is my own!" I stand in admiration of women today who resist the fashion of abortion, by refusing to make the sacred womb a tomb! (*Ensign*, May 1978, p. 10.)

— *Neal A. Maxwell*

Like all the diseased doctrines of the devil, [abortion] is pleasing unto the carnal mind. (*Ensign*, May 1978, p. 77.)

— *Spencer W. Kimball*

Too many wives are working in order that the couple may have its own home, a car, color television, or extensive vacation trips. Children for such couples are an unwanted handicap and a needless expense.

We shudder as we read in Leviticus of the sacrifices of idol worshipers of that time who fed their children into the fiery maw of the iron god, Molech. Is . . . [it] any less repulsive to God, as modern people through abortion offer the sacrifice of their children to their idol of selfish materialism? (*Ensign*, May 1979, p. 73.)

— *Theodore M. Burton*

We decry abortions and ask our people to refrain from this serious transgression. (*Ensign*, November 1975, p. 6.)

— *Spencer W. Kimball*

———— **Abuse** ————

A physician revealed to me the large number of children who are brought to the emergency rooms of local hospitals in your city and mine. In many cases guilty parents provide fanciful accounts of the child falling from his high chair or stumbling over a toy and striking his head. Too frequently it is discovered that the parent was the abuser and the innocent child the victim. Shame on the perpetrators of such vile deeds. God will hold such strictly accountable for their actions. (*Ensign,* May 1990, p. 53.)

— *Thomas S. Monson*

If we could recognize the true greatness of women, we would not treat them as we sometimes do. The world often uses and abuses women. Holders of the priesthood should honor good women in and out of the Church as true sisters, not as objects and sources of service or pleasure. Our consideration for women should spring from esteem for the daughters of Zion and an awareness of their true identity more than from a concern with their functions and roles. . . .

Any form of physical or mental abuse to any woman is not worthy of any priesthood holder. (*Ensign,* May 1988, pp. 36, 37.)

— *James E. Faust*

It ill becomes any man who holds the priesthood of God to abuse his wife in any way, to demean or injure or take undue advantage of the woman who is the mother of his children, the companion of his life, and his companion for eternity if he has received that greater blessing. (*Ensign,* November 1982, p. 77.)

— *Gordon B. Hinckley*

Let no Latter-day Saint parent ever be guilty of the heinous crime of abusing one of Christ's little ones! (*Ensign,* May 1978, p. 5.)

— *Spencer W. Kimball*

Strife in families leads to wife abuse and child abuse. This comes through personal selfishness. It is so common in the world that we find it creeping into the Church. (*Ensign,* May 1979, p. 74.)

— *Theodore M. Burton*

The safety and protection of each person, especially children, should be a concern for all of us. We can be instrumental in assisting in the protection of each other by being aware of potential dangers and being willing to do our part to thwart those who would injure, steal, or abuse any person, young or old. (*Ensign,* November 1982, p. 65.)

— *Marvin J. Ashton*

Achievement

Keep in mind the challenging fact that your aim is not to get ahead of others, but to surpass yourself; to begin today to be the person you want to be. (*CR*, April 1968, p. 100.)

— *Hugh B. Brown*

Present levels of performance are not acceptable either to ourselves or to the Lord. In saying that, I am not calling for flashy, temporary differences in our performance levels, but a quiet resolve on the part of General Authorities, Regional Representatives of the Twelve, stake presidents, bishops, mission presidents, and branch presidents to do a better job—to lengthen our stride. (*Ensign*, November 1974, p. 117.)

— *Spencer W. Kimball*

The desire to achieve has been placed in us by a loving Creator who honors our free agency but nonetheless beckons to us to do well. (*Ensign*, November 1977, p. 73.)

— *Marvin J. Ashton*

The happy life is not ushered in at any age to the sounds of drums and trumpets. It grows upon us year by year, little by little, until at last we recognize that we have it. It is achieved . . . by a body of work done so well that we can lift our heads with assurance and look the world in the eye. (Address, Brigham Young University, May 19, 1970.)

— *Thomas S. Monson*

The word *can't* is false doctrine in the Mormon Church. (*CR*, 1972, p. 107.)

— *Paul H. Dunn*

The work of the world is not done by intellectual geniuses. It is done by men of ordinary capacity who use their abilities in an extraordinary manner. (*CR*, October 1972, p. 107.)

— *Gordon B. Hinckley*

Action

An enterprising turkey gathered the flock together and, following instructions and demonstrations, taught them how to fly. All afternoon they enjoyed soaring and flying and the thrill of seeing new vistas. After the meeting, all of the turkeys walked home.

It is not our understanding of the principles of the gospel that brings the blessings of heaven. But the living of them. (*Ensign*, May 1990, p. 82.)

— *Merlin R. Lybbert*

As we grow and increase in knowledge and in the testimony of the Spirit of God, we must also grow and increase in labor and effort for the advancement of the work of God or we will lose the Spirit of God. It is not a knowledge that God lives that will save us, it is keeping the commandments of God. (*MS, 59:133.*)

— *Heber J. Grant*

Consecration Brings Value to our Daily Acts
A piece of silver always has a certain value as it passes from hand to hand; it is weighed and we sell it in the market place; but, when that piece of silver is coined into a dollar, it receives the stamp of government service; it becomes a coin of the realm and it moves from hand to hand to accomplish the work of the realm. So, every act of man, the moment it is fitted into the great plan, the plan of salvation, receives spiritual coinage, and passes from hand to hand, from mind to mind, to accomplish the great work of God. (*CR*, April 1922, p. 97.)

— *John A. Widtsoe*

Establish specific objectives, and move steadily toward them. A rudder won't control a drifting boat; it must be underway. Similarly, you need to be moving forward to gain control of your life. (*Ensign*, May 1990, p. 75.)

— *Richard G. Scott*

I have been impressed with the *urgency* of doing. Knowing is not enough; we must apply. Being willing is not enough; we must do. (*Ensign*, November 1984, p. 23.)

— *Russell C. Taylor*

It is in the doing that the real blessing comes. *Do it!* That's our motto. (*Ensign*, May 1979, pp. 100-101.)

— *Spencer W. Kimball*

It is through our own efforts and decisions that we earn our way in this life. While the Lord will magnify us in both subtle and dramatic ways, he can only guide our footsteps when we move our feet. Ultimately, our own actions determine our blessings or lack of them.

— *Marion G. Romney*

Love of God is something that requires action, for men cannot have faith in God, nor love him, unless they are acting in his cause, with their whole heart constantly thinking of him and giving of their physical strength in love. (*CR*, April 1948, p. 147.)

— *Joseph L. Wirthlin*

Ours is the active, not the passive part. Man is to act, and not to be acted upon. We are to take possession, and not to be taken possession of. (*OAT*, p. 111.)

— *Hugh Nibley*

The religion of Christ itself is not so much a set of ideas as it is a set of activities. The purpose of the Church is to help us translate the principles of the Gospel of Christ into constructive, meaningful human experience. (*CR*, April 1971, p. 35.)

— *Sterling W. Sill*

The sin that will cleave to all the posterity of Adam and Eve is that they have not done as well as they know how. (*JD*, 2:129.)

— *Brigham Young*

They who secure eternal life are doers of the word as well as hearers. (*JD*, 14:37.)

— *Brigham Young*

To work out one's salvation is not to sit idly by dreaming and yearning for God miraculously to thrust bounteous blessings into our laps. It is to perform daily, hourly, momentarily . . . the immediate task or duty at hand, and to continue happily in such performance as the years come and go, leaving the faults of such labors either for self or for others to be bestowed as a just, beneficent Father may determine. (*CR*, April 1957, p. 7.)

— *David O. McKay*

While the Lord will magnify us in both subtle and dramatic ways, he can only guide our footsteps when we move our feet. (*Ensign*, May 1981, p. 91.)

— *Marion G. Romney*

See also INITIATIVE, LIVING THE GOSPEL, PROCRASTINATION

"And they straightway left their nets, and followed him." (See Matt. 4:18-22.) How descriptive, how powerful, how rewarding when properly applied in human conduct.

We invite all to serve the Savior and walk in His paths straightway. There is an urgency for all of us who have this knowledge of His divinity to act upon it without hesitation or delay. The time is now. (*Ensign*, May 1983, p. 30.)

— *Marvin J. Ashton*

───── Adversity ─────

Behold your little ones. Pray with them. Pray for them and bless them. The world into which they are moving is a complex and difficult world. They will run into heavy seas of adversity. They will need all the strength and all the faith you can give them while they are yet near you. While they are young, pray with them that they may come to know that source of strength which shall then always be available in every hour of need. Said Isaiah of old, "All thy children shall be taught of the Lord; and great shall be the peace of thy children." (Isaiah 54:13.) (*Ensign*, November 1978, p. 20.)

— *Gordon B. Hinckley*

Death and adversity come to us all, but so does life everlasting! (*Ensign*, November 1987, p. 95.)

— *Joy F. Evans*

Every burden on the back can become a gift in the hand. (*Ensign*, May 1982, p. 96.)

— *Elaine Cannon*

For the faithful, our finest hours are sometimes during or just following our darkest hours. (*Ensign*, May 1984, p. 22.)

— *Neal A. Maxwell*

Just as a flood-lighted temple is more beautiful in a severe storm or in a heavy fog, so the gospel of Jesus Christ is more glorious in times of inward storm and of personal sorrow and tormenting conflict. (*CR*, April 1965, p. 16.)

— *Harold B. Lee*

Many of you may have severe trials, that your faith may become more perfect, your confidence be increased, and your knowledge of the powers of heaven be augmented; and this before your redemption takes place. If a stormy cloud sweep over the horizon of your course . . . if the cup of bitter suffering be offered and you be compelled to partake—if Satan is let loose among you, with all his seductive powers of deceiving and cunning craftiness—if the strong relentless arm of persecution is against you, then, in that hour lift up your heads and rejoice that you are accounted worthy to suffer with Jesus, the Saints, and holy prophets, and know that the period of your redemption approaches. (*MS*, 13:364.)

— *Lorenzo Snow*

Here then is a great truth. In the pain, the agony, and the heroic endeavors of life, we pass through a refiner's fire, and the insignificant and the unimportant in our lives can melt away like dross and make our faith bright, intact, and strong. In this way the divine image can be mirrored from the soul. It is part of the purging toll exacted of some to become acquainted with God. In the agonies of life, we seem to listen better to the faint, godly whisperings of the Divine Shepherd. (*Ensign*, May 1979, p. 53.)

— *James E. Faust*

No pang that is suffered by man or woman upon the earth will be without its compensating effect . . . if it be met with patience. (Quoted by Spencer W. Kimball, *Speeches of the Year, 1955-56*, Provo: Brigham Young University, 1956, pp. 5-6.)

— *James E. Talmage*

One of the advantages of having lived a long time is that you can often remember when you had it worse. I am grateful to have lived long enough to have known some of the blessings of adversity. (*Ensign*, May 1990, p. 85.)

— *James E. Faust*

The conquering of adversity produces strength of character, forges self-confidence, engenders self-respect, and assures success in righteous endeavor. (*Ensign*, November 1981, p. 11.)

— *Richard G. Scott*

The nearer a person approaches the Lord, a greater power will be manifested by the adversary to prevent the accomplishment of His purposes.

— *Orson F. Whitney*

There is a divine purpose in the adversities we encounter every day. They prepare, they purge, they purify, and thus they bless. (*Ensign*, May 1979, p. 59.)

— *James E. Faust*

We learn obedience, as the Savior did, by the things which we suffer. . . . Sometime in the eternities to come, we will see that our trials were calculated to cause us to turn to our Heavenly Father for strength and support. Any affliction or suffering we are called upon to bear may be directed to give us experience, refinement, and perfection.

— *Delbert L. Stapley*

Words of an Unknown Martin Handcart Company Pioneer

We suffered beyond anything you can imagine and many died of exposure and starvation, but did you ever hear a survivor of that company utter a word of criticism? Not one of that company ever apostatized or left the Church, because everyone of us came through with the absolute knowledge that God lives, for *we became acquainted with him in our extremities.*

I have pulled my handcart when I was so weak and weary from illness and lack of food that I could hardly put one foot ahead of the other. I have looked ahead and seen a patch of sand or a hill slope and I have said, I can go only that far and there I must give up, for I cannot pull the load through it. I have gone on to that sand and when I reached it, the cart began pushing me. I have looked back many times to see who was pushing my cart, but my eyes saw no one. I knew then that the angels of God were there.

Was I sorry that I chose to come by handcart? No. Neither then nor any minute of my life since. *The price we paid to become acquainted with God was a privilege to pay,* and I am thankful that I was privileged to come in the Martin Handcart Company. (*Relief Society Magazine,* January 1948, p. 8.)

— Related by David O. McKay

Age

Among us, I am happy to say, old age is honorable, and regarded as a blessing from the Lord. It is our duty to desire to live long upon the earth, that we may do as much good as we possibly can. I esteem it a great privilege to have the opportunity of living in mortality. The Lord has sent us here "for a wise and glorious purpose," and it should be our business to find out what that purpose is and then to order our lives accordingly. (*TLS,* p. 94.)

— Lorenzo Snow

The older we get and the longer we labor in the Church the more there is that we can do. There is no need for any person in this Church to have an empty hand or an empty heart. (*CR,* April 1952, p. 31.)

— George Q. Morris

I have commenced to feel the infirmities of increasing age and years; and so many of us now, after these many years of toil, have to struggle with the going down sun of our earthly existence. But we have the consolation of knowing that our mortal body will not always impede our progress, we shall not forever suffer its inconveniences; we are gladdened in the hope of either laying down this mortal tabernacle or undergoing that welcome change which will free us from all afflictions and annoyances. And we hail the day when we shall be free from sorrow and death, to forever rejoice in the joys of everlasting lives. (*JD*, 19:59-60.)

— *Orson Hyde*

May we suggest eight areas in which we can make the most of our senior years:

1. Work in the temple and attend often.
2. Collect and write family histories.
3. Become involved in missionary service.
4. Provide leadership by building family togetherness.
5. Accept and fulfill Church callings.
6. Plan for your financial future.
7. Render Christlike service.
8. Stay physically fit, healthy, and active. (*Ensign*, November 1989, pp. 4-6.)

— *Ezra Taft Benson*

To those in your mature years. "Press forward with a steadfastness in Christ, having a perfect brightness of hope, and a love of God and of all men" (2 Ne. 31:20). Continue to be living testimonies of the gospel as you share your faith, love, and wisdom. You are sorely needed in the mission field. What lives you will bless as you accept the call to serve! There is so much for you to do in the holy temples. Don't retire from active service in the Lord's kingdom. You are needed! (*Ensign*, November 1986, p. 26.)

— *George I. Cannon*

You are as young as your faith, as old as your doubt, as young as your self-confidence, as old as your fear, as young as your hope, as old as your despair. (*Ensign*, November 1983, p. 25.)

— *Paul H. Dunn*

See also LIFE

Agency

Free agency, given us through the plan of our Father, is the great alternative to Satan's plan of force. With this sublime gift, we can grow, improve, progress, and seek perfection. Without agency, none of us could grow and develop by learning from our mistakes. (*Ensign*, November 1987, p. 35.)

— *James E. Faust*

Free agency is the impelling source of the soul's progress. It is the purpose of the Lord that man become like him. In order for man to achieve this it was necessary for the Creator first to make him free. (*CR*, April 1950, p. 32.)

— *David O. McKay*

God has given to all men an agency and has granted to us the privilege to serve him or serve him not, to do that which is right or that which is wrong, and this privilege is given to all men irrespective of creed, color or condition. The wealthy have this agency, the poor have this agency, and no man is deprived by any power of God from exercising it in the fullest and in the freest manner. This agency has been given to all. This is a blessing that God has bestowed upon the world of mankind, upon all his children alike. (*JD*, 24:175.)

— *Joseph F. Smith*

God loves us and believes in us and has done and will do anything he can to help us, but he will not impose on our free agency. (*Ensign*, November 1983, p. 21.)

— *Marion D. Hanks*

Individual self-government lies at the root of all true and effective government, whether in heaven or on earth. (*DBY*, p. 355.)

— *Brigham Young*

My independence is sacred to me—it is a portion of that same Deity that rules in the heavens. There is not a being upon the face of the earth who is made in the image of God, who stands erect and is organized as God is, that should be deprived of the free exercise of his agency so far as he does not infringe upon others' rights, save by good advice and a good example. (*JD*, 10:191.)

— *Brigham Young*

Next to the bestowal of life itself, the right to direct that life is God's greatest gift to man. . . . Freedom of choice is more to be treasured than any possession earth can give. (*CR*, April 1950, p. 32.)

— *David O. McKay*

One of the fundamental doctrines of revealed truth is that in the Garden of Eden, God endowed man with free agency. The preservation of this free agency is more important than life itself. Indeed, the independence to act for oneself is life, for without it "there is no existence." (D&C 93:30.) It is, therefore, clear that everything which militates against man's enjoyment of this endowment persuades not to believe in Christ, for he is the author of free agency.

— *Marion G. Romney*

I think back just a few years when I was sixteen-years old and a printing apprentice. A fellow apprentice was totally engrossed in motorcycles. In those days, we rode British motorcycles, and he had an AJS-350.

One sunny summer's day, he said to me, "Would you like to come for a ride on my motorcycle?" That seemed to be a good idea. In those days we didn't wear any protective clothing, and, thus very lightly clad, I became the passenger on his motorcycle. He weaved through the streets of Norwich and then came to a long, straight road. He leaned back and said to me, "Have you ever traveled at one hundred miles an hour?"

I said, "No."

He said, "Well, you're going to."

I said, "We don't have to."

He began to rev the motorcycle, and the motorcycle roared forward. The skin on my face pulled tight, and the clothing blew as we went past ninety-eight to one hundred miles an hour. I determined that day that never again would I let somebody else control my life. (*Ensign*, May 1990, p. 42.)

— *Kenneth Johnson*

Perhaps the greatest discovery of my life, without question the greatest commitment, came when finally I had the confidence in God that I would loan or yield my agency to him— without compulsion or pressure, without any duress, as a single individual alone, by myself, no counterfeiting, nothing expected other than the privilege. In a sense, speaking figuratively, to take one's agency, that precious gift which the scriptures make plain is essential to life itself, and say, "I will do as you direct," is afterward to learn that in so doing you possess it all the more. (*Speeches of the Year*, Provo: Brigham Young University, 1971, pp. 1-7.)

— *Boyd K. Packer*

The Council . . . said, . . . "Who will redeem the earth, who will go forth and make the sacrifice for the earth and all things it contains?" The Eldest Son said: "Here am I" and then he added, "Send me." But the second one, which was "Lucifer, [a] Son of the Morning," said, "Lord, here am I, send me, I will redeem every son and daughter of Adam and Eve that lives on the earth, or that ever goes on the earth." "But," says the Father, "that will not answer at all. I give [unto] each and every individual his agency; all must use that in order to gain exaltation in my kingdom; inasmuch as they have the power of choice they must exercise that power. They are my children; the attributes which you see in me are in my children and they must use their agency. If you undertake to save all, you must save them in unrighteousness and corruption." (*DBY*, pp. 53-54.)

— *Brigham Young*

We are separated from God in order that we may *voluntarily* return to him. (*Ensign,* April 1975, p. 14.)

— *Arthur Henry King*

While we are free to choose, once we have made those choices, we are tied to the consequences of those choices. (*Ensign,* November 1988, p. 7.)

— *Russell M. Nelson*

See also CHOICES, FREEDOM, PLAN OF SALVATION, PROBATION

——— **America** ———

For centuries the Lord kept America hidden in the hollow of His hand until the time was right to unveil her for her destiny in the last days. . . .
In the Lord's due time His Spirit "wrought upon" Columbus, the pilgrims, the Puritans, and others to come to America. . . .
Our Father in Heaven planned the coming forth of the Founding Fathers and their form of government as the necessary great prologue leading to the restoration of the gospel. (*Ensign,* November 1987, p. 4.)

— *Ezra Taft Benson*

If we would make the world better, let us foster a keener appreciation of the freedom and liberty guaranteed by the government of the United States as framed by the founders of the nation.(*CR,* October 194, 104.)

— *David O. McKay*

Next to being one in worshipping God, there is nothing in this world upon which this Church should be united than in upholding and defending the Constitution of the United States. (*CR,* October 1939, p. 105.)

— *David O. McKay*

So far as I am concerned the flag of the United States is the flag of Almighty God. Old Glory to me stands for everything that the gospel of Christ stands for, because Old Glory was raised up because there was to be a restoration of the gospel. I cannot separate my flag and my religion. I would fight for my flag as I would fight for my religion. (*BYU Speeches of the Year,* February 20, 1968, p. 10.)

— *Mark E. Peterson*

The Almighty raised up [this nation] by the power of his omnipotent hand, that it might be possible in the latter days for the kingdom of God to be established in the earth.

His hand has been over this nation, and it is his purpose and design to enlarge it, make it glorious . . . to the end that those who are kept in bondage and serfdom may be brought to the enjoyment of the fullest freedom and liberty of conscience possible for intelligent men to exercise in the earth. (*GD*, p. 409.)

— *Joseph F. Smith*

The true destiny of America is *religious*, not political; it is *spiritual*, not physical. (*CR*, October 1968, p. 106.)

— *Alvin R. Dyer*

This nation, founded on principles laid down by men whom God raised up, will never fail. . . . I have faith in America; you and I must have faith in America, if we understand the teachings of the gospel of Jesus Christ. (*Ye Are the Light of the World*, Salt Lake City: Deseret Book Co., 1974, p. 351.)

— *Harold B. Lee*

Those men who laid the foundation of this American government and signed the Declaration of Independence were the best spirits the God of heaven could find on the face of the earth. They were choice spirits . . . noble spirits before God. (*CR*, April 1898, pp. 89-90.)

— *Wilford Woodruff*

The Constitution of the United States is a glorious standard; it is founded in the wisdom of God. It is a heavenly banner; it is to all those who are privileged with the sweets of its liberty, like the cooling shades and refreshing waters of a great rock in a thirsty and weary land. It is like a great tree under whose branches men from every clime can be shielded from the burning rays of the sun. (*HC*, 3:304.)

— *Joseph Smith*

In the 1940s while serving as the executive officer of the National Council of Farmer Cooperatives in Washington, D.C., I saw in a Hilton Hotel a placard depicting Uncle Sam, representing America, on his knees in humility and prayer. Beneath the placard was the inscription, "Not beaten there by the hammer and sickle, but freely, responsibly, confidently. . . . We need fear nothing or no one save God."

That picture has stayed in my memory ever since; America on her knees in recognition that all our blessings come from God! America on her knees out of a desire to serve the God of this land by keeping his commandments! America on her knees, not driven there in capitulation to some despotic government, but on her knees freely, willingly, gratefully! This is the sovereign remedy to all of our problems and the preservation of our liberties. (*Ensign*, November 1976, p. 35.)

— *Ezra Taft Benson*

To me, the Constitution of the United States of America is just as much from my Heavenly Father as the Ten Commandments. (*CR*, April 1948, p. 182.)

— *George Albert Smith*

See also CITIZENSHIP, GOVERNMENT

———— Anger ————

A man in such a mental state that the anger itself does him more harm than the condition which aroused his anger, and in reality, . . . he suffers more form the vexation than he does from the acts that aroused that vexation. I wonder how long it will take us to realize that in matters of temper nothing can bring us damage but ourselves. (Address, Brigham Young University, October 12, 1965.)

— *David O. McKay*

A man who cannot control his temper is not very likely to control his passion, and no matter what his pretensions in religion, he moves in daily life very close to the animal plane. (*IE*, June 1958, p. 407.)

— *David O. McKay*

Anger itself does more harm than the condition which aroused anger. (*CR*, April 1958, p. 5.)

— *David O. McKay*

If a man does not control his temper, it is a sad admission that he is not in control of his thoughts. He then becomes a victim of his own passions and emotions, which lead him to actions that are totally unfit for civilized behavior, let alone behavior for a priesthood holder. (*Ensign*, November 1986, p. 47.)

— *Ezra Taft Benson*

If I am an angry man, it is my duty to pray for charity, which suffereth long and is kind. (*MS*, 56:261.)

— *George Q. Cannon*

Resentment and anger are not good for the soul. They are foul things. (*Ensign*, May 1988, p. 63.)

— *Marvin J. Ashton*

The moment a man or a woman becomes angry they show a great weakness. (JD, 4:98.)

— *Wilford Woodruff*

The only vulnerable place in our armor is where we ourselves leave it exposed, because God has armed us at all points. He has made us impervious to outside attacks. But when we boil inside, destruction waits upon us. (*CR*, April 1898, p. 26.)

— *Brigham Young*

There should be no yelling in the home unless there is a fire.

— *David O. McKay*

Whenever you get red in the face, whenever you raise your voice, whenever you get "hot under the collar," or angry, rebellious, or negative in spirit, then know that the Spirit of God is leaving you and the spirit of Satan is beginning to take over. (*CR*, October 1974, p. 77.)

— *Theodore M. Burton*

See also CONTENTION

———— Apostasy ————

A friend . . . wished to know whether we . . . considered an honest difference of opinion between a member of the Church and the authorities of the Church was apostasy. . . . We replied that we had not stated that an honest difference of opinion between a member of the Church and the authorities constituted apostasy; . . . but we could not conceive of a man publishing those differences of opinion, and seeking by arguments, sophistry and special pleading to enforce upon the people to produce division and strife, and to place the acts and counsels of the authorities of the Church, if possible, in a wrong light, and not be an apostate, for such conduct was apostasy as we understood the term. We further said that while a man might honestly differ in opinion from the authorities through a want of understanding, he had to be exceedingly careful how he acted in relation to such differences, or the adversary would take advantage of him, and he would soon become imbued with the spirit of apostasy, and be found fighting against God and the authority which He had placed here to govern His Church. (Quoted by Ezra Taft Benson, *CR*, April, 1969, p. 12.)

— *George Q. Cannon*

Omission of duty leads to apostasy. (*JD*, 11:108.)

— *Brigham Young*

I'm thinking of a five-year-old boy who fell out of bed during the night and came crying to his mother's bedside. To her question, "Why did you fall out of bed?" he replied, "I fell out because I wasn't in far enough!"

It has been my experience over the years that, generally speaking, those who fall out of the Church are those who aren't in far enough. (*Ensign*, November 1983, p. 63.)

— *Marvin J. Ashton*

It was only after the death of Christ's apostles that revelation ceased. The pure doctrines Christ taught became diluted with the philosophy of the world, and profane innovations appeared in the ordinances of the Church. Eventually, that which had once been clear and understandable became mythical and confusing. Confusion is the field where Satan operates to deceive and lead mankind astray. Jesus and His apostles predicted a "falling away" (see 2 Thess. 2:1-4), which did occur, and Christianity entered a long night of darkness. (*Ensign*, May 1977, p. 22.)

— *Delbert L. Stapley*

No true Latter-day Saint will ever take a stand that is in opposition to what the Lord has revealed to those who direct the affairs of his earthly kingdom.

No Latter-day Saint who is true and faithful in all things will ever pursue a course, or espouse a cause, or publish an article or book that weakens or destroys faith. (*Ensign*, November 1984, p. 84.)

— *Bruce R. McConkie*

Many have said to me, "How is it that a man like you, who understood so much of the . . . Doctrine and Covenants, should fall away?" I told them not to feel too secure, but to take heed lest they also should fall; for I had no scruples in my mind as to the possibility of men falling away.

I can say, in reference to the Quorum of the Twelve, to which I belonged, that I did not consider myself a whit behind any of them, and I suppose that others had the same opinion; but, let no one feel too secure; for, before you think of it, your steps will slide. You will not then think nor feel for a moment as you did before you lost the Spirit of Christ; for when men apostatize, they are left to grovel in the dark. . . .

The next question is, "How and when did you lose the Spirit?" I became jealous of the Prophet, and then I saw double, and overlooked everything that was right, and spent all my time in looking for the evil; and then, when the Devil began to lead me, it was easy for the carnal mind to rise up, which is anger, jealousy, and wrath. I could feel it within me; I felt angry and wrathful; and the

Spirit of the Lord being gone, as the scriptures say, I was blinded, and I thought I saw a beam in brother Joseph's eye, but it was nothing but a mote, and my own eye was filled with the beam. (*JD*, 5:206.)

— *Thomas B. Marsh*

Small and simple things can be negative and destructive to a person's salvation. A series of seemingly small but incorrect choices can become those little soul-destroying termites that eat away at the foundations of our testimony until, before we are aware, we may be brought near to spiritual and moral destruction. . . . Satan will use small and simple things to lead us into despair and misery. (*Ensign*, May 1990, pp. 7,8.)

— *M. Russell Ballard*

That man who rises up to condemn others, finding fault with the Church, saying that they are out of the way, while he himself is righteous, then know assuredly, that that man is in the high road to apostasy; and if he does not repent, will apostatize, as God lives. (*HC*, 3:385.)

— *Joseph Smith*

The Church is little, . . . injured by persecution and calumnies from ignorant, misinformed or malicious enemies. A greater hindrance to its progress comes from faultfinders, shirkers, commandment-breakers, and apostate cliques within its own ecclesiastical and quorum groups. (*CR*, October 1967, p. 9.)

— *David O. McKay*

There is a superior intelligence bestowed upon such as obey the gospel with full purpose of heart, which if sinned against, the apostate is left naked and destitute of the Spirit of God. . . . When once that light which was in them is taken from them, they become as much darkened as they were previously enlightened. (*TPJS*, p. 67.)

— *Joseph Smith*

See also RESTORATION

——— **Arts** ———

Every accomplishment, every polished grace, every useful attainment in mathematics, music, and in all sciences and art belong to the Saints. (Quoted by Spencer W. Kimball, *Ensign*, July 1977, p. 3.)

— *Brigham Young*

It is important to enhance one's appreciation of the arts and culture which are of the very substance of our civilization. Can anyone doubt that good music is godly or that there can be something of the essence of heaven in great art? Education will increase your appreciation and refine your talent. (*Ensign,* November 1985, p. 89.)

— *Gordon B. Hinckley*

The story of Mormonism has never yet been written nor painted nor sculpted nor spoken. It remains for inspired hearts and talented fingers yet to reveal themselves. They must be faithful, inspired, active Church members to give life and feeling and true perspective to a subject so worthy. (*Ensign,* July 1977, p. 5.)

— *Spencer W. Kimball*

We will yet have Miltons and Shakespeares of our own. God's ammunition is not exhausted. His brightest spirits are held in reserve for the latter times. In God's name and by his help we will build up a literature whose top shall touch heaven, though its foundations be low in earth. (*The Contributor,* 9:300.)

— *Orson F. Whitney*

—— Atonement ——

Before the Crucifixion and afterward, many men have willingly given their lives in selfless acts of heroism. But none faced what the Christ endured. Upon Him was the burden of all human transgression, all human guilt. . . .

He, by choice, accepted the penalty for all mankind for the sum total of all wickedness and depravity; for brutality, immorality, perversion, and corruption; for addiction; for the killings and torture and terror—for all of it that ever had been or all that ever would be enacted upon this earth.

In choosing, He faced the awesome power of the evil one who was not confined to flesh nor subject to mortal pain. That was Gethsemane!

How the Atonement was wrought, we do not know. No mortal watched as evil turned away and hid in shame before the light of that pure being.

All wickedness could not quench that light. When what was done was done, the ransom had been paid. Both death and hell forsook their claim on all who would repent. Men at last were free. Then every soul who ever lived could choose to touch that light and be redeemed.

By this infinite sacrifice, through this atonement of Christ, all mankind may be saved by obedience to the laws and ordinance of the gospel. (*Ensign,* May 1988, p. 69.)

— *Boyd K. Packer*

Contemplation of the Atonement—by which I am assured of resurrection and given opportunity, through faith and repentance and faithfulness unto the end, to obtain remission of my sins—moves me to the most intense gratitude and appreciation of which my soul is capable, and I respond unstintingly to the theme: "Oh, it is wonderful that he should care for me, Enough to die for me." ("I Stand All Amazed," *Hymns*, no. 80.) (*Ensign*, May 1982, p. 9.)

— *Marion G. Romney*

I seldom use the word *absolute*. It seldom fits. I use it now—twice. Because of the Fall, the Atonement was absolutely essential for resurrection to proceed and overcome mortal death.

The Atonement was absolutely essential for men to cleanse themselves from sin and overcome the second death, which is the spiritual death, which is separation from our Father in Heaven. For the scriptures tell us, seven times they tell us, that no unclean thing may enter the presence of God. (*Ensign*, May 1988, p. 70.)

— *Boyd K. Packer*

If the things of this world are all an empty show, "a tale told by an idiot, full of sound and fury, signifying nothing," what is important? The atonement of Jesus Christ—that is the one supreme reality of our life upon this earth! (*OAT*, p. 6.)

— *Hugh Nibley*

Man by reason of anything that he himself could do or accomplish, could only exalt himself to the dignity and capability of man and therefore it needed the atonement of a god before man, through the adoption, could be exalted to the godhead.

— *John Taylor*

Man unquestionably has impressive powers and can bring to pass great things by tireless efforts and indomitable will. But after all our obedience and good works, we cannot be saved from the effect of our sins without the grace extended by the atonement of Jesus Christ. . . .

Man cannot earn his own salvation. (*Ensign*, November 1988, p. 67.)

— *Dallin H. Oaks*

No mortal being had the power or capability to redeem all other mortals from their lost and fallen condition, nor could any other voluntarily forfeit his life and thereby bring to pass a universal resurrection for all other mortals.

Only Jesus Christ was able and willing to accomplish such a redeeming act of love.

We may never understand nor comprehend in mortality *how* He accomplished what He did, but we must not fail to understand *why* He did what He did.

Everything He did was prompted by His unselfish, infinite love for us. (*Ensign*, November 1983, p. 6.)

— *Ezra Taft Benson*

Not only did Jesus come as a universal gift, He came as an individual offering with a personal message to each one of us. For each one of us He died on Calvary and His blood will conditionally save us. Not as nations, communities or groups, but as individuals. (*Juvenile Instructor*, 64:697.)

— *Heber J. Grant*

Nothing compares in any way in importance with the most transcendent of all events as the atoning sacrifice of our Lord. It is the most important single thing that has ever occurred in the entire history of created things; it is the rock foundation upon which the gospel and all other things rest. Indeed, our prophet Joseph Smith said, "All things which pertain to our religion are only appendages to it."

— *Bruce R. McConkie*

The atonement of the Master is the central point of world history. Without it, the whole purpose for the creation of earth and our living upon it would fail. (*IE*, December 1953, p. 942.)

— *Marion G. Romney*

The most important doctrine I can declare, and the most powerful testimony I can bear, is of the atoning sacrifice of the Lord Jesus Christ. His atonement is the most transcendent event that ever has or ever will occur from creation's dawn through all the ages of a never-ending eternity.

— *Bruce R. McConkie*

The principal question before us is not do we comprehend the atonement, but do we accept it. (*CR*, April 1956, p. 112.)

— *George Q. Morris*

The Savior bought us with his blood. We belong to him, whether we know it or not; everybody does. He has a right to tell us what to do; he has a right to punish when we violate the laws he has given; he has the right to reward when we are obedient. (Address, Brigham Young University, May 14, 1957.)

— *Joseph Fielding Smith*

Think of it! When [the Lord's] body was taken from the cross and hastily placed in a borrowed tomb, he, the sinless Son of God, had already taken upon him not only the sins and temptations of every human soul who will repent, but all of our sickness and grief and pain of every kind. He suffered these afflictions as we suffer them, according to the flesh. He suffered them all. He did this to perfect his mercy and his ability to lift us above every earthly trial. (Alma 7:11-12.) (*Ensign*, May 1988, p. 16.)

— Howard W. Hunter

Those who exercise faith in the sacred name of Jesus Christ and repent of their sins and enter into his covenant and keep his commandments (see Mosiah 5:8) can lay claim on the atoning sacrifice of Jesus Christ. Those who do so will be called by his name at the last day. (*Ensign*, May 1985, p. 82.)

— Dallin H. Oaks

We are . . . indebted to Jesus, for by his atonement he not only satisfied the demands of the law of justice, but he made effective the law of mercy, by which men may be redeemed from spiritual death. For, while they are not responsible for mortal death, they are responsible for spiritual death, which shuts them out from the presence of God. (*Ensign*, May 1982, p. 8.)

— Marion G. Romney

When Adam fell, the change came upon all other living things and even the earth itself became mortal, and all things including the earth were redeemed from death through the atonement of Jesus Christ.

— Joseph Fielding Smith

See also JESUS CHRIST, REPENTANCE

——— Attitude ———

At the center of our agency is our freedom to form a healthy attitude toward whatever circumstances we are placed in! (*Ensign*, November 1976, p. 14.)

— Neal A. Maxwell

Attitude is an important part of the foundation upon which we build a productive life. In appraising our present attitude, we might ask: "Am I working to become my best self? Do I set worthy and attainable goals? Do I look toward the positive in life? Am I alert to ways that I can render more and better service? Am I doing more than is required of me?"

Remember, a good attitude produces good results, a fair attitude fair results, a poor attitude poor results. We each shape our own life, and the shape of it is determined largely by our attitude. (*Ensign*, May 1981, p. 86.)

— M. Russell Ballard

Proper attitude in this crisis-dominated world is a priceless possession. Never before is it more important for all of us to move forward with conviction. We may be behind, but we are not losing if we are moving in the right direction. (*CR*, October 1974, p. 56.)

— *Marvin J. Ashton*

To dig a straight furrow, the plowman needs to keep his eyes on a fixed point ahead of him. That keeps him on a true course. If, however, he happens to look back to see where he has been, his chances of straying are increased. The results are crooked and irregular furrows. . . . Fix your attention on your . . . goal[s] and never look back on your earlier problems . . . . If our energies are focused not behind us but ahead of us—on eternal life and the joy of salvation—we assuredly will obtain it. (*Ensign*, May 1987, p. 17.)

— *Howard W. Hunter*

When I'm on the Lord's side, keeping the basic commandments, I esteem myself as a worthy child of God, and I find I am very positive. (*Ensign*, May 1979, p. 29.)

— *Hartman Rector, Jr.*

See also OPTIMISM

Balance

If a man achieves worldly success and does not blend into his life a program of self-improvement to bring about a sensible balance, he no doubt will end up as a failure. (*CR*, October 1972, p. 26.)

— *John H. Vandenberg*

Often the lack of clear direction and goals can waste away our time and energy and contribute to imbalance in our lives. A life that gets out of balance is much like a car tire that is out of balance. It will make the operation of the car rough and unsafe. Tires in perfect balance can give a smooth and comfortable ride. So it is with life. The ride through mortality can be smoother for us when we strive to stay in balance. Our main goal should be to seek "immortality and eternal life" (Moses 1:39). With this as our goal, why not eliminate from our lives the things that clamor for and consume our thoughts, feelings, and energies without contributing to our reaching that goal? (*Ensign*, May 1987, p. 16.)

— *M. Russell Ballard*

See also GOALS, PERSPECTIVE, PRIORITIES

—— Baptism ——

Baptism is a sign to God, to angels, and to heaven that we do the will of God, and there is no other way beneath the heavens whereby God hath ordained for man to come to Him to be saved, and enter into the kingdom of God, except faith in Jesus Christ, repentance, and baptism for the remission of sins . . . ; Then you have the promise of the gift of the Holy Ghost. (*HC*, 4:555.)

— *Joseph Smith*

Baptism is the primary ordinance of the gospel. It is the gate through which all come into the Church. It is so important that it is performed not only for the living but also for the dead, because those who are beyond the veil of death cannot move forward on the way to eternal life without this ordinance having been administered in their behalf. (*Ensign*, May 1988, p. 46.)

— *Gordon B. Hinckley*

Baptism means immersion in water, and it is to be administered by one having authority, in the name of the Father, and of the Son, and of the Holy Ghost. Baptism without divine authority is not valid. It is a symbol of the burial and resurrection of Jesus Christ and must be done in the likeness thereof, by one commissioned of God, in the manner prescribed, otherwise it is illegal and will not be accepted by him nor will it effect a remission of sins, the object for which it is designed, but whosoever hath faith, truly repents, and is "buried with Christ in baptism" by one having divine authority, shall receive a remission of sins and is entitled to the gift of the Holy Ghost by the laying on of hands. (*JD*, 19:190.)

— *Joseph F. Smith*

The baptism of water, without the baptism of fire and the Holy Ghost attending it, is of no use; they are necessarily and inseparably connected. An individual must be born of water and the Spirit in order to get into the kingdom of God. (*HC*, 6:316.)

— *Joseph Smith*

There is but one way in which men can receive salvation, exaltation, and glory, and that is through the order of baptism and the ordinances connected therewith. No mortal man or woman will ever receive celestial glory unless he or she has been baptized, receiving this ordinance personally or by proxy. (*DFTP*, p. 49.)

— *Lorenzo Snow*

When I [was] baptized for the remission of my sins, the feeling that came upon me was that of pure peace, of love and of light. I felt in my soul that if I had sinned—and surely I was not without sin—that it had been forgiven me; that I was indeed cleansed from sin; my heart was touched, and I felt that I would not injure the smallest insect beneath my feet. I felt as if I wanted to do good everywhere to everybody and to everything. I felt a newness of life, a newness of desire to do that which was right. There was not one particle of desire for evil left in my soul. I was but a little boy . . . but this was the influence that came upon me, and I know that it was from God, and was and ever has been a living witness to me of my acceptance of the Lord. (*CR*, April 1898, p. 66.)

— *Joseph F. Smith*

See also GOSPEL PRINCIPLES, ORDINANCES, REPENTANCE

——— Beauty ———

As truly as we must face unpleasant realities all of our days, let us recognize and praise the thousands of beauties of life around us. (*Ensign*, May 1987, p. 73.)

— *Paul H. Dunn*

Beauty is whatever gives joy. (*OAT*, p. 122.)

— *Hugh Nibley*

Man's machinery makes things alike; God's machinery gives to things which appear alike a pleasing difference. . . . Endless variety is stamped upon the works of God's hand. There are no two productions of nature, whether animal, vegetable, or mineral, that are exactly alike, and all are crowned with a degree of polish and perfection that cannot be obtained by ignorant man in his most exquisite mechanical productions. (*JD*, 9:369-70.)

— *Brigham Young*

Said Frank Lloyd Wright, "Beauty is the highest expression of morality." Morality is also the highest expression of beauty—and without these there is ugliness everywhere. (*Ensign*, May 1971, p. 12.)

— *Richard L. Evans*

To truly reverence the Creator, we must appreciate his creations. We need to plan to take time to observe the marvels of nature. Today, we can easily become surrounded by brick buildings and asphalt surfaces that shelter us from real life around us. Plan to share with your family the miracle of buds changing to fragrant blossoms. Take time to sit on a hillside and feel the tranquillity of the evening when the sun casts its last golden glow over the horizon. Take time to smell the roses. (*Ensign*, May 1988, p. 59.)

— *M. Russell Ballard*

See also CREATION

————— **Belief** —————

All things are possible to them that believe. Surely we must believe in a thing before we can desire it. And God does grant unto men according to their desire. (*Ensign*, May 1979, p. 29.)

— *Hartman Rector, Jr.*

Belief, humble belief, is the foundation of all righteousness and the beginning of spiritual progression. It goes before good works, opens the door to an eternal store of heavenly truth, and charts the course to eternal life. (*A New Witness for the Articles of Faith*, Salt Lake City: Deseret Book Co., 1985, p. 21.)

— *Bruce R. McConkie*

Faith, the first principle of the gospel, begins with *belief*. What man can conceive, he can achieve. (*Ensign*, May 1979, p. 29.)

— *Hartman Rector, Jr.*

I believe all that God ever revealed, and I never hear of a man being damned for believing too much; but they are damned for unbelief. (*HC*, 6:477.)

— *Joseph Smith*

The believer is a literalist with a mind open to infinite possibilities. (*OAT*, p. 4.)

— *Hugh Nibley*

See also FAITH

————— **Bible** —————

I love the Bible, both the Old and the New Testaments. It is a source of great truth. It teaches us about the life and ministry of the Master. From its pages we learn of the hand of God in directing the affairs of His people from the very beginning of the earth's history. It would be difficult to underestimate the impact the Bible has had on the history of the world. Its pages have blessed the lives of generations. (*Ensign*, November 1986, p. 78.)

— *Ezra Taft Benson*

In what part of the Bible do you find what we are to do this year or the next? This will be part of a new Bible, for when it takes place it will be written, and then that will be a Bible, . . . Men have been opposed to the Book of Mormon because it was a new Bible. The poor fools did not know that wherever there was a true Church there was revelation, and that wherever there was revelation there was the word of God to man and materials to make Bibles of. (*JD*, 5:266.)

— *John Taylor*

Students everywhere have been led to the conclusion that the Flood story and the Garden of Eden motifs in ancient records of many people discredit the Bible by showing it to be just another primitive presentation of old myths. What it discredits, however, is their concept of what the Bible should be—a unique, perfect, absolutely complete, flawless source of all knowledge, a thing which the Bible itself never claims for a moment. (*OAT*, p. 43.)

— *Hugh Nibley*

The Bible, when it is understood, is one of the simplest books in the world, for, as far as it is translated correctly, it is nothing but truth, and in truth there is no mystery save to the ignorant. (*JD*, 14:136.)

— *Brigham Young*

There are no people on the earth that quibble so little about the Bible as do the Latter-day Saints. (*CR*, April 1903, p. 31.)

— *J. Golden Kimball*

When it is read reverently and prayerfully, the Holy Bible becomes a priceless volume, converting the soul to righteousness. Principal among its virtues is the declaration that Jesus is the Christ, the Son of God, through whom eternal salvation may come to all. (*Ensign*, May 1983, p. 86.)

— *The First Presidency*

——— Blessings ———

A blessing always carries with it a responsibility. (*CR*, October 1954, p. 38.)
— *J. Reuben Clark, Jr.*

Every good and perfect gift comes from the Father of Light, who is no respecter of persons, and in whom there is no variableness, nor shadow of turning. To please him we must not only worship him with thanksgiving and praise but render willing obedience to his commandments. By so doing, he is bound to bestow his blessings; for it is upon this principle (obedience to law) that all blessings are predicated. (*IE*, December 1917, p. 104.)
— *Joseph F. Smith*

Everything I hold dear and precious in my heart, I can trace to my membership in The Church of Jesus Christ of Latter-day Saints.
— *Robert L. Backman*

In very large measure each of us holds the key to the blessings of the Almighty upon us. If we wish the blessing, we must pay the price. (*Ensign*, November 1984, p. 90.)
— *Gordon B. Hinckley*

The Lord's blessings are the fruits of obedience to the laws on which they are predicated. (*Ensign*, May 1988, p. 25.)
— *Angel Abrea*

The purposes of the Lord in our personal lives generally are fulfilled through the small and simple things, and not the momentous and spectacular. (*Ensign*, May 1990, p. 6.)
— *M. Russell Ballard*

We should look to the Lord for our blessings because, among other reasons, he owns everything. (*Ensign*, May 1979, p. 30.)
— *Hartman Rector, Jr.*

If the Latter-day Saints will walk up to their privileges and exercise faith in the name of Jesus Christ and live in the enjoyment of the fullness of the Holy Ghost constantly day by day, there is nothing on the face of the earth that they could ask for that would not be given to them. The Lord is waiting to be very gracious unto this people and to pour out upon them riches, honor, glory, and power, even that they may possess all things according to the promises he has made through his apostles and prophets. (*JD*, 11:114.)

— *Brigham Young*

See also COMMANDMENTS, GOD'S LOVE, GRATITUDE, OBEDIENCE

——— Book of Mormon ———

Aristotle . . . [said] that a good book must have a calculated structure and development which gives a unified impact from beginning to end. By this standard the Book of Mormon is not only a "good book"; it is a classic. In spite of the fact that it is written by a series of prophets who had different styles and different experiences, in spite of the fact that it has some unabridged materials mixed with others that have been greatly condensed, in spite of the fact that it has unique and irregular chronological sequences, it is a classic book—Aristotle's kind of book: unified, whole, verses fitting with verses, chapters fitting with chapters, books fitting with books. It has these ideal qualities because it is the clear, compelling word of God, revealed through his chosen prophets. (*Ensign*, September 1976, p. 8.)

— *Jeffrey R. Holland*

Do eternal consequences rest upon our response to this book? Yes, either to our blessing or our condemnation.

Every Latter-day Saint should make the study of this book a lifetime pursuit. Otherwise he is placing his soul in jeopardy and neglecting that which could give spiritual and intellectual unity to his whole life. There is a difference between a convert who is built on the rock of Christ through the Book of Mormon and stays hold of that iron rod, and one who is not. (*Ensign*, May 1975, p. 65.)

— *Ezra Taft Benson*

Few men on earth either in or out of the Church, have caught the vision of what the Book of Mormon is all about. Few are they among men who know the part it has played and will yet play in preparing the way for the coming of Him of whom it is a new witness. . . . The Book of Mormon shall so affect men that the whole earth and all its peoples will have been influenced and governed by it. . . . There is no greater issue ever to confront mankind in modern times than this: Is the Book of Mormon the mind and will and voice of God to all men? (*Millennial Messiah*, Bruce R. McConkie, Salt Lake City: Deseret Book Co., 1982, pp. 159, 170, 179.)

— *Bruce R. McConkie*

Five Reasons to Read the Book of Mormon

1. It is approved by the highest authority in the universe, the Lord himself. . . . After the Prophet Joseph had translated that part of the record which he had been told to translate, the Lord said: . . . "and as your Lord and your God liveth it is true," (D&C 17:6) . . .

2. It will sustain you against attacks being made by the modernistic against that other great scripture, the Bible. The Book of Mormon is not only a new witness for God; it is also a witness to the truth of the Bible. . . .

3. We shall be judged by what is written in it. Moroni says that the very reason the book has been given to us is that we may know the "decrees of God." (Ether 2:11.) . . .

4. Unless we read, study, and learn the principles which are in the Book of Mormon, we, the . . . teachers of this church, cannot comply with [the] direction to teach them. (D&C 42:12.) . . .

5. We will fill and refresh our minds with a constant flow of that "water" which Jesus said would be in us, " . . . a well of water springing up into everlasting life," (John 4:14). We must obtain a continuing supply of this water if we are to resist evil and retain the blessings of being born again. (CR, April 1949, p. 41.)
    — *Marion G. Romney*

I bless you with increased *understanding* of the Book of Mormon. I promise you that from this moment forward, if we will daily sup from its pages and abide by its precepts, God will pour out upon each child of Zion and the Church a blessing hitherto unknown. (*Ensign,* May 1986, p. 78.)
— *Ezra Taft Benson*

I feel certain that if, in our homes, parents will read from the Book of Mormon prayerfully and regularly, both by themselves and with their children, the spirit of that great book will come to permeate our homes and all who dwell therein. The spirit of reverence will increase; mutual respect and consideration for each other will grow. The spirit of contention will depart. Parents will counsel their children in greater love and wisdom. Children will be more responsive and submissive to the counsel of their parents. Righteousness will increase. Faith, hope, and charity—the pure love of Christ—will abound in our homes and lives, bringing in their wake peace, joy, and happiness. (*Ensign,* May 1980, p. 67.)
— *Marion G. Romney*

I intend to take Moroni as my guide to the present world situation. Why him? Moroni and his father are the principal definitive editors of the Book of Mormon. They not only compiled and edited; they went through and picked out things they felt would be important for us; then they evaluated that and applied it to us—explained everything to us. (*OAT*, p. 86.)

— Hugh Nibley

I remember reading [the Book of Mormon] with one of my lads when he was very young. On one occasion I lay in the lower bunk and he in the upper bunk. We were each reading aloud alternate paragraphs of those last three marvelous chapters of Second Nephi. I heard his voice breaking and thought he had a cold, but we went on to the end of the three chapters. As we finished he said to me, "Daddy, do you ever cry when you read the Book of Mormon?"

"Yes, Son," I answered. "Sometimes the Spirit of the Lord so witnesses to my soul that the Book of Mormon is true that I do cry."

"Well," he said, "that is what happened to me tonight." (*CR*, April 1949, p. 41.)

— Marion G. Romney

In a day when many are challenging the divinity of Jesus Christ or doubting the reality of his atonement and resurrection, the message of that second witness, the Book of Mormon, is needed more urgently than ever. (*Ensign*, November 1988, p. 66.)

— Dallin H. Oaks

Just as the New Testament clarified the long misunderstood message of the Old, so the Book of Mormon . . . reiterate[s] the messages of both testaments in a way that restores their full meaning. (*OAT*, p. 77.)

— Hugh Nibley

Let us consider the miracle of the translation of the Book of Mormon by the Prophet Joseph Smith, with Oliver Cowdery acting as his scribe.

After the 116 pages were lost when Martin Harris was allowed to take them home, the real translation began on April 7, 1829, two days after Oliver Cowdery arrived in Harmony, Pennsylvania, to serve as the Prophet's scribe. By May 15, five weeks later, they had reached the account of the Savior's ministry to the Nephites as contained in 3 Nephi, chapter 11.

By June 11 they had translated the last plates of Mormon, and it was on June 11 that the Prophet applied for a copyright. By June 30 the book was finished—from start to finish, no more than eighty-five days in translation time. However, with all that went on during these eighty-five days, it is apparent there were only sixty to sixty-five days in which the actual translation could have occurred.

Remember that during that time the Prophet moved from Harmony to Fayette, made several trips for supplies, received and recorded thirteen sections of the Doctrine and Covenants, restored the Aaronic and Melchizedek priesthoods, converted and baptized several people, and on and on. They had no time to consult libraries to study the content. There was no time to revise or refine, no time to cross-reference dates or intervals, and details. Instead, the text came, as Oliver recorded, day after day, uninterrupted, as the words fell from the Prophet's mouth.

This was an astonishing achievement! The text came through final copy, one time, dictated and left as it stood with only minor stylistic editing to this day. It is no simple book dashed off from the top of a young man's head, but reflects the best of a thousand years of colonization and inspiration. (*Ensign*, May 1989, pp. 14-15.)

— *L. Tom Perry*

Let us take the Book of Mormon, which a man took and hid in his field, securing it by his faith, to spring up in the last days, or in due time; let us behold it coming forth out of the ground, which is indeed accounted the least of all seeds, but behold it branching forth, yea, even towering, with lofty branches, and Godlike majesty, until it, like the mustard seed, becomes the greatest of all herbs. And it is truth, and it has sprouted and come forth out of the earth, and righteousness begins to look down from heaven, and God is sending down his powers, gifts and angels, to lodge in the branches thereof. (*HC*, 2:268.)

— *Joseph Smith*

Men can get nearer to the Lord, can have more of the spirit of conversion and conformity in their hearts, can have stronger testimonies, and can gain a better understanding of the doctrines of salvation through the Book of Mormon than they can through the Bible. . . . There will be more people saved in the kingdom of God—ten-thousand times over—because of the Book of Mormon than there will be because of the Bible. (Book of Mormon Symposium, BYU, August 1978.)

— *Bruce R. McConkie*

No member of this Church can stand approved in the presence of God who has not seriously and carefully read the Book of Mormon, . . . (*CR*, October 1961, p. 18.)

— *Joseph Fielding Smith*

Now, we have not been using the Book of Mormon as we should. Our homes are not as strong unless we are using it to bring our children to Christ. Our families may be corrupted by worldly trends and teachings unless we know how to use the book to expose and combat the falsehoods in socialism, organic evolution, rationalism, humanism, etc. Our missionaries are not as effective unless they are "hissing forth" with it. Social, ethical, cultural, or educational converts will not survive under the heat of the day unless their taproots go down to the fullness of the gospel which the Book of Mormon contains. . . . Do eternal consequences rest upon our response to this book? Yes, either to our blessing or our condemnation.

Every Latter-day Saint should make the study of this book a lifetime pursuit. Otherwise he is placing his soul in jeopardy and neglecting that which could give spiritual and intellectual unity to his whole life. (*Ensign*, May 1975, p. 65.)

— *Ezra Taft Benson*

Perhaps no other book has been denounced so vigorously by those who have never read it as has the Book of Mormon. (*Ensign*, May 1986, p. 59.)

— *Boyd K. Packer*

Perhaps there is nothing that testifies more clearly of the importance of this modern book of scripture than what the Lord Himself has said about it.

By His own mouth He has borne witness (1) that it is true (D&C 17:6), (2) that it contains the truth and His words (D&C 19:26), (3) that it was translated by power from on high (D&C 20:8), (4) that it contains the fullness of the gospel of Jesus Christ (D&C 20:9; 42:12), (5) that it was given by inspiration and confirmed by the ministering of angels (D&C 20:10), (6) that it gives evidence that the holy scriptures are true (D&C 20:11), and (7) that those who receive it in faith shall receive eternal life (D&C 20:14). (*Ensign*, November 1986, p. 4.)

— *Ezra Taft Benson*

Salvation itself is at stake in this matter. If the Book of Mormon is true—if it is a volume of holy scripture, if it contains the mind and will and voice of the Lord to all men, if it is a divine witness of the prophetic call of Joseph Smith—then to accept it and believe its doctrines is to be saved, and to reject it and walk contrary to its teaching is to be damned. (*Ensign*, November 1983, p. 72.)

— *Bruce R. McConkie*

Sunday, 28.—I spent the day in the Council with the Twelve Apostles at the house of President Young, conversing with them upon a variety of subjects. Brother Joseph Fielding was present, having been absent four years on a mission to England. I told the brethren that the Book of Mormon was the most correct of any book on earth, and the keystone of our religion, and a man would get nearer to God by abiding by its precepts, than by any other book. (*HC*, 4:461.)

— *Joseph Smith*

That book was brought forth by the power of God, and translated by the gift of the Holy Ghost; and, if I could make my voice sound as loud as the trumpet of Michael, the Archangel, I would declare the truth from land to land, and from sea to sea, and the echo should reach every isle, until every member of the family of Adam should be left without excuse. For I do testify that God has revealed himself to man again in these last days, and set his hand to gather his people upon a goodly land, and, if they obey his commandments, it shall be unto them for an inheritance. (*History of Joseph Smith*, Lucy Mack Smith, Salt Lake City: Bookcraft, 1958, p. 204.)

— *Lucy Mack Smith*

The Book of Mormon has not been, nor is it yet, the center of our personal study, family teaching, preaching, and missionary work. Of this we must repent. (*Ensign*, May 1986, pp. 5-6.)

— *Ezra Taft Benson*

The Book of Mormon is a literary and a religious masterpiece, and is far beyond even the fondest hopes or abilities of any farm boy. It is a modern revelation from end to end. It is God-given. (*Ensign*, November 1977, p. 2.)

— *Mark E. Petersen*

The Book of Mormon is tough. It thrives on investigation. You may kick it around like a football, as many have done; and I promise you it will wear you out long before you ever make a dent in it. (*OAT*, p. 73.)

— *Hugh Nibley*

The Book of Mormon is not on trial—the people of the world, including the members of the Church, are on trial as to what they will do with this second witness for Christ. (*Ensign*, November 1984, p. 8.)

— *Ezra Taft Benson*

The Book of Mormon is the great, the grand, the most wonderful missionary that we have. (*CR*, April 1937, p. 126.)

— *Heber J. Grant*

The Book of Mormon claims to be a divinely inspired record, written by a succession of prophets who inhabited ancient America. It professes to be revealed to the present generation for the salvation of all who will receive it, and for the overthrow and damnation of all nations who reject it.

The book must be either *true* or *false*. If true, it is one of the most important messages ever sent from God to man, affecting both the temporal and eternal interests of every people under heaven to the same extent and in the same degree that the message of Noah affected the inhabitants of the old world. If false, it is one of the most cunning, wicked, bold, deep-laid impositions ever palmed upon the world, calculated to deceive and ruin millions who will sincerely receive it as the word of God, and will suppose themselves securely built upon the rock of truth until they are plunged with their families into hopeless despair.

The nature of the message in the Book of Mormon is such, that if true, no one can possibly be saved and reject it; if false, no one can possibly be saved and receive it. (*Orson Pratt's Works, 1845-51,* reprint, Salt Lake City: Deseret New Press, 1945, p. 107.)

— *Orson Pratt*

The Book of Mormon must be reenthroned in the minds and hearts of our people. We must honor it by reading it, by studying it, by taking its precepts into our lives and transforming them into lives required of the true followers of Christ. (*Ensign,* November 1986, p. 80.)

— *Ezra Taft Benson*

The Book of Mormon teaches, both by what it is and what it says, that Jehovah will never forget us. (*Ensign,* September 1976, p. 10.)

— *Jeffery R. Holland*

The Book of Mormon was prepared by divine assignment for the blessing and enlightenment of all those who receive it. . . .

The Book of Mormon contains messages that were divinely placed there to show how to correct the influence of false tradition and how to receive a fulness of life. It teaches how to resolve the problems and challenges that we face today that were foreseen by the Lord. In that book he has provided the way to correct the serious errors of life, but this guidance is of no value if it remains locked in a closed book. (*Ensign,* November 1988, p. 76.)

— *Richard G. Scott*

The Lord has revealed the need to reemphasize the Book of Mormon to get the Church and all the children of Zion out from under condemnation—the scourge and judgment. (See D&C 84:54-58.) This message must be carried to the members of the Church throughout the world. (*Ensign,* May 1986, p. 78.)

— *Ezra Taft Benson*

There are three great reasons why Latter-day Saints should make the study of the Book of Mormon a lifetime pursuit.

The *first* is that the Book of Mormon is the keystone of our religion. . . . the keystone of our testimony, the keystone of our doctrine, and the keystone in the witness of our Lord and Savior.

The *second* . . . is that it was written for our day. . . .

The *third* . . . [is] it helps us draw nearer to God . . . more than any other book. . . . (*Ensign,* November 1986, pp. 5-7.)

— *Ezra Taft Benson*

There is a power in the book [of Mormon] which will begin to flow into your lives the moment you begin a serious study of the book. You will find greater power to resist temptation. You will find the power to avoid deception. You will find the power to stay on the strait and narrow path. The scriptures are called "the words of life" (see D&C 84:85), and nowhere is that more true than it is of the Book of Mormon. When you begin to hunger and thirst after those words, you will find life in greater and greater abundance. (*Ensign*, November 1986, p. 7.)

— *Ezra Taft Benson*

To the Children of the Church

How pleased I am to hear of your love for the Book of Mormon. *I* love it too, and Heavenly Father wants you to continue to learn from the Book of Mormon every day. It's Heavenly Father's special gift to you. By following its teachings, you will learn to do the will of our Father in Heaven. (*Ensign*, May 1989, pp. 81-82.)

— *Ezra Taft Benson*

To the Young Men of the Church

Young men, the Book of Mormon will change your life. It will fortify you against the evils of our day. It will bring a spirituality into your life that no other book will. It will be the most important book you will read in preparation for a mission and for life. A young man who knows and loves the Book of Mormon, who has read it several times, who has an abiding testimony of its truthfulness, and who applies its teachings will be able to stand against the wiles of the devil and will be a mighty tool in the hands of the Lord. ("To the Young Men of the Priesthood," pamphlet, The Church of Jesus Christ of Latter-day Saints, 1986, pp. 3-4.)

— *Ezra Taft Benson*

We must flood the earth with the Book of Mormon—and get out from under God's condemnation for having treated it lightly. (See D&C 84:54-58.) . . . I do not know fully why God has preserved my life to this age, but I do know this: That for the present hour He has revealed to me the absolute need for us to move the Book of Mormon forward now in a marvelous manner. You must help with this burden and with this blessing which He has placed on the whole Church, even all the children of Zion. (*Ensign*, November 1988, pp. 5,6.)

— *Ezra Taft Benson*

[The Book of Mormon] was written for our day. Mormon, who compiled it, saw us in vision and was directed to put into the book those things God felt we would especially need in our time. . . . Not only should we know what history and faith-promoting stories it contains, but we should understand its teachings. If we really did our homework and approached the Book of Mormon doctrinally, we could expose the errors and find the truths to combat many of the current false theories and philosophies of men. . . .

I have noted within the Church the difference in discernment, in insight, conviction, and spirit between those who know and love the Book of Mormon and those who do not. That book is a great sifter. (*New Era*, May 1975, p. 19.)

— *Ezra Taft Benson*

[The Book of Mormon] was written for us—for our day. Its scriptures are to be likened unto ourselves.

— *Ezra Taft Benson*

See also SCRIPTURE STUDY, SCRIPTURES

—— Brotherhood ——

A single, struggling individual may be stalled with his heavy load even as he begins to climb the hill before him. To reach the top unaided is an impossibility. With a little help from fellow travelers he makes the grade and goes on his way in gratitude and rejoicing. (Quoted by Marvin J. Ashton, *Ensign*, May 1988, p. 64.)

— *David O. McKay*

If we are to be the Savior's disciples, if we are to become like him, then we must serve one another, then we must assume responsibility to help with one another's needs, then we must assist each other through the thorny pathways of life. (*Ensign*, May 1981, p. 81.)

— *H. Burke Peterson*

One of the things the gospel of Jesus Christ tells us is that our brotherhood with men on this planet is not a mere biological brotherhood but a kind of brotherhood that lets me know that I have an accountability, for my relationships will be perpetuated far beyond today, far beyond here, and far beyond now. (*New Era*, February 1975, p. 35.)

— *Neal A. Maxwell*

A boy was extended an invitation to visit his uncle who was a lumberjack up in the Northwest. . . . [As he arrived] his uncle met him at the depot, and as the two pursued their way to the lumber camp, the boy was impressed by the enormous size of the trees on every hand. There was a gigantic tree which he observed standing all alone on the top of a small hill. The boy, full of awe, called out excitedly, "Uncle George, look at that big tree! It will make a lot of good lumber, won't it?"

Uncle George slowly shook his head, then replied, "No, son, that tree will not make a lot of good lumber. It might make a *lot* of lumber but not a lot of *good* lumber. When a tree grows off by itself, too many branches grow on it. Those branches produce knots when the tree is cut into lumber. The best lumber comes from trees that grow together in groves. The trees also grow taller and straighter when they grow together."

It is so with people. We become better individuals, more useful timber when we grow together rather than alone. (*CR*, April 1965, pp. 54-55.)

— *Henry D. Taylor*

Sustaining One Another

It is no small thing to "sustain" another person. The word literally means to "uphold" or, if you prefer, to "hold up." When we sustain life, we nourish it, we keep it going. When we sustain a friend or a neighbor or a stranger in the street, we give support, we share strength, we provide help. We hold each other up under the weight of present circumstance. We bear one another's burdens under the heavy personal pressures of life. (*Ensign*, November 1989, p. 25.)

— *Jeffrey R. Holland*

The voice of the Almighty called us . . . , to form a union and a lovely brotherhood, in which we should love one another as we love ourselves. When we depart from this purpose, the Spirit of God withdraws from us to the extent of that departure.

— *Lorenzo Snow*

We *can* reach out to help one another as neighbors and associates, extending even beyond our own brothers and sisters in the Church, to assist any in trouble or want wherever they may be. There is so much of sorrow in the world. There is so much of loneliness and fear. There is so much of hate and bitterness, of man's inhumanity to man.

Let us as Latter-day Saints cultivate a spirit of brotherhood in all of our associations. Let us be more charitable in our judgments, more sympathetic and understanding of those who err, more willing to forgive those who err, more willing to forgive those who trespass against us. Let us not add to the measure of hatred that . . . sweeps across the world. (*Ensign*, November 1985, p. 85.)

— *Gordon B. Hinckley*

We must remember that those mortals we meet in parking lots, offices, elevators, and elsewhere are that portion of mankind God has given us to love and to serve. It will do us little good to speak of the general brotherhood of mankind if we cannot regard those who are all around us as our brothers and sisters. (*Ensign*, August 1979, p. 5.)

— *Spencer W. Kimball*

We speak of the fellowship of the Saints. This is and must be a very real thing. We must never permit this spirit of brotherhood and sisterhood to weaken. We must constantly cultivate it. It is an important aspect of the gospel. (*Ensign*, May 1983, p. 80.)

— *Gordon B. Hinckley*

See also FELLOWSHIPPING, LOVE, SERVICE, UNITY

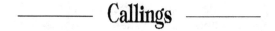

Callings

Christ is the great prototype where priesthood is concerned, . . . the Father swears with an oath that his Son shall inherit all things through the priesthood, so he swears with an oath that all of us who magnify our callings in that same priesthood shall receive all that the Father hath. (*Era*, December 1970, p. 27.)

— *Joseph Fielding Smith*

Considerations of church position and title are of little consequence to Latter-day Saints whose eyes are directed toward God's glory. Their concern is focused on the opportunities for service that church callings present, rather than on gaining personal notoriety. Such members, who serve competently and quietly, regardless of whether they are the "highest" or the "least" in the kingdom, are probably those that the Apostle Paul had in mind when he wrote, "And those members of the body [meaning the Church], which we think to be less honorable, upon these we bestow more abundant honour." (1 Cor. 12:23.) (*Ensign*, November 1989, p. 28.)

— *Marlin K. Jensen*

I can do anything I am set apart to do, if I have the spirit of my appointment and am humble and prayerful. (*CR*, April 1918, p. 133.)

— *J. Golden Kimball*

Some of us do our work as if we had blinders on our eyes. We see only our own little narrow track. We catch nothing of the broader vision. Ours may be a small responsibility in the Church. It is good to fulfill that responsibility with diligence. And it is also good to know how that responsibility contributes to the great overall program of the growing kingdom of God. . . .

We must never lose sight of the greater picture, the large composite of the divine destiny of this work. It was given us by God our Eternal Father, and each of us has a part to play in the weaving of its magnificent tapestry. (*Ensign,* November 1989, pp. 52, 53.)

— Gordon B. Hinckley

We counsel you to accept callings in the Church and to serve faithfully in the positions to which you are called. Serve one another. Magnify your callings. As you do so, you will be the means of blessing others and you will increase in spirituality. (*Ensign,* May 1984, p. 7.)

— Ezra Taft Benson

When I was a missionary in London fifty years ago, my companion and I would shake hands in the morning and say to one another, "Life is good." Life in the service of the Lord is good. It is beautiful. It is rewarding. (*Ensign,* November 1984, p. 86.)

— Gordon B. Hinckley

When we qualify ourselves by our worthiness, when we strive with faith nothing wavering to fulfill the duties appointed to us, when we seek the inspiration of the Almighty in the performance of our responsibilities, we can achieve the miraculous. (*Ensign,* May 1988, p. 43.)

— Thomas S. Monson

See also MAGNIFY CALLINGS

Careers

Continue to invest in your personal development. Expand your occupational horizons by constant study. . . . Look to your present job as a stepping-stone along your career path. Take time to think. The dimensions of most jobs are constrained only by the mind of the uncreative worker. I like what one businessman counseled: "If at first you *do* succeed, try something harder!!" (*Ensign,* May 1982, p. 78.)

— J. Richard Clarke

Do not ever belittle anyone, including yourself, nor count them, or you, a failure, if your livelihood has been modest. Do not ever look down on those who labor in occupations of lower income. There is great dignity and worth in any honest occupation. Do not use the word *menial* for any labor that improves the world or the people who live in it. (*Ensign,* May 1982, p. 84.)

— Boyd K. Packer

Honorable Employment

May I suggest a definition of "honorable employment." Honorable employment is honest employment. Fair value is given and there is no defrauding, cheating, or deceit. Its product or service is of high quality, and the employer, customer, client, or patient receives more than he or she expected. Honorable employment is moral. . . . It involves nothing that would undermine public good or morality. Honorable employment is useful. It provides goods or services which make the world a better place. Honorable employment is also remunerative. It provides enough income so that we may be self-sufficient and able to support our families, while leaving us enough time free to be good fathers and church workers. (*Ensign,* November 1975, pp. 122-23.)

— *Howard W. Hunter*

The employment we choose should be honorable and challenging. Ideally, we need to seek that work to which we are suited by interest, by aptitude, and by training. A man's work should do more than provide adequate income; it should provide him with a sense of self-worth and be pleasurable—something he looks forward to each day. (*Ensign,* November 1975, p. 122.)

— *Howard W. Hunter*

The Lord is not so concerned about what we study or what profession we follow as long as it is an honest living. (*Ensign,* May 1978, p. 29.)

— *Eldred G. Smith*

When young men come to me for advice in choosing their life's work or their careers, I always tell them that they should choose something they will enjoy doing, and then do the very best they can and be honest, honorable, and upright in their dealings and in the kingdom of God and his righteousness, knowing that all these other things will be added unto them. (*CR,* October 1977, p. 64.)

— *N. Eldon Tanner*

See also WORK

——— Caring ———

George Bernard Shaw once wrote, "The worst sin towards our fellow creatures is not to hate them, but to be indifferent to them." Indifference can be one of the most hurtful ways of behavior. (*Ensign,* May 1988, p. 62.)

— *Marvin J. Ashton*

How many times have we observed a benevolent act performed by someone and asked ourselves, "Why didn't I think of that?" Those who do the deeds we would have liked to do seem to have mastered the art of awareness. They have formed the habit of being sensitive to the needs of others before they think of themselves. (*Ensign,* November 1981, p. 81.)

— *J. Richard Clarke*

Indifference can bring great tragedy into our souls, whether it be indifference to the laws of the land, the laws of God, or the rights and privileges of each other. (*CR,* October 1953, p. 28.)

— *Thorpe B. Isaacson*

Our Savior cares for all of his sheep. What a tribute it is to be recognized as one who cares. (*Ensign,* November 1987, p. 22.)

— *Marvin J. Ashton*

There is one thing more serious than merely to not believe, and that is to not care. (*CR,* October 1955, p. 46.)

— *Sterling W. Sill*

See also CHARITY, LOVE, SERVICE

—— Challenges ——

All crosses are easier to carry when we keep moving. (*Ensign,* November 1976, p. 14.)

— *Neal A. Maxwell*

Difficulties are just God's errands. If we are sent upon them, it is an evidence of his confidence. Therefore, let us be glad, be happy, for it is a way of being wise. (*Ensign,* November 1986, p. 89.)

— *Ardeth G. Kapp*

I'm reminded of the little child who came to her daddy and said, "Give me something *hard* to do." So he thought of things she could do, but she would say, "No, daddy, that isn't hard enough. I want something hard to do." He was carrying his briefcase into the house, and he said, "Well, carry this; this will be very hard to carry." She grabbed hold. Oh, boy, it was heavy! She said, "I think I can." She struggled and staggered until she finally got it to the house. We all like to feel that we have met the challenge of something hard to do. (*Ensign*, May 1982, p. 94.)

— *Dwan J. Young*

In the 110-meter hurdles race, runners must jump over hurdles placed in their path. The hurdles are not there so that a runner will come to them and stop and, discouraged, go back to the starting line. They are not there to make him crash. The beauty and excitement of this race is to jump over the hurdles, to overcome the obstacles.

If we understand the importance of the obstacles in our individual lives, we begin to see them in a positive light as true challenges to overcome. (*Ensign*, May 1990, p. 79.)

— *Horacio A. Tenorio*

It was meant to be that life would be a challenge. To suffer some anxiety, some depression, some disappointment, even some failure is normal.

Teach our members that if they have a good, miserable day one in a while, or several in a row, to stand steady and face them. Things will straighten out.

There is great purpose in our struggle in life. (*Ensign*, May 1978, p. 93.)

— *Boyd K. Packer*

Today there are sisters in many places living in poverty, with hunger and disease taken for granted and with infant mortality high and life expectancy low. In some places fewer than 50 percent of the adult population can read or write; 70 percent of these adults are women.

There are those who have no pure water—some who have no water at all except that which they carry on their heads, often for long distances. There are some who live in the shadow of war. What gives these sisters the courage to endure? As with the pioneers, it is their faith that their Father will come, their faith in the gospel of Jesus Christ. (*Ensign*, November 1987, pp. 92-93.)

— *Joy F. Evans*

We are children of the noble birthright, who must carry on in spite of our fore-determined status to be broadly outnumbered and widely opposed. Challenges lie ahead for the Church and for each member divinely charged toward self-improvement and service.

How is it possible to achieve the "impossible"? Learn and obey the teaching of God. (*Ensign*, May 1988, p. 34.)

— *Russell M. Nelson*

With an understanding of God's plan of salvation, we know that the rejoicing, the striving, the suffering, the tutoring, and the enduring experiences of life all play their part in an intelligible process of helping us, if we will, to become, as the Savior beckoningly invited, "even as I am." (3 Ne. 27:27.) (*Ensign,* May 1984, p. 22.)

— Neal A Maxwell

[After quoting the story from 3 Nephi 14:24-27 which tells of the two men who built houses, one upon sand and the other upon rock:]

Did you note that the rain descended and the floods came and the winds blew upon *both* houses? Just because we follow the word of the Lord does not mean we will suffer no ill winds; it does mean that we will spiritually survive them! (*Ensign,* November 1987, p. 74.)

— L. Aldin Porter

See also ADVERSITY, OPPOSITION, PROBLEMS, TRIALS

——— Character ———

An upright character is the result only of continued effort and right thinking, the effect of long-cherished association with Godlike thoughts. (*CR,* October 1953, pp. 10-11.)

— David O. McKay

As a child grows physically by eating regularly at intervals, by breathing fresh air constantly, by resting at stated intervals, so character is built by little things, by daily contacts, by an influence here, a fact or truth there. (*DFTP,* p. 74.)

— David O. McKay

Character is a positive thing. It is not protected innocence but practiced virtue, it is not fear of vice, but love of excellence.

— Hugh B. Brown

Character is the one thing we make in this world and take with us into the next. (*CR,* April 1966, p. 128.)

— Ezra Taft Benson

Character is woven quietly from the threads of hundreds of correct decisions (like practice sessions). When strengthened by obedience and worthy acts, correct decisions form a fabric of character that brings victory in time of great need. (*Ensign*, May 1989, p. 37.)

— *Richard G. Scott*

I am under the strongest impression that the most valuable consideration, and that which will be of the most service when we return to the spirit world, will be that of having established a proper and well-defined character as faithful and consistent Latter-day Saints in this state of probation.

— *Lorenzo Snow*

It takes independence of mind, honesty of heart, faith in God, and firmness of character to live the life of a Latter-day Saint.

— *Wilford Woodruff*

Knowing everything that might be done is knowledge; knowing what is right to do is wisdom; doing it is character. (Address, Brigham Young University, May 11, 1954, p. 8.)

— *Delbert L. Stapley*

Noble character is like a treasured porcelain made of select, raw materials, formed with faith, carefully crafted by consistent righteous acts, and fired in the furnace of uplifting experience. It is an object of great beauty and priceless worth. (*Ensign*, November 1981, pp. 11-12.)

— *Richard G. Scott*

Our character, as Latter-day saints, should be preserved inviolate, at whatever cost or sacrifice. Character approved of God is worth securing, even at the expense of a lifetime of constant self-denial. (*JD*, 26:368.)

— *Lorenzo Snow*

When a man by his course in life has acquired a character that is spotless, it is a priceless jewel, and nothing should induce him to barter it away. If the wicked try to bring a blemish or cast a stain upon it, their efforts will not be successful. They may throw their mud, but it will not stain the garments of the pure and holy. (*JD*, 13:218.)

— *Brigham Young*

Your character is yours alone to build. No one can injure your character but you. (*Ensign*, May 1981, p. 42.)

— *David B. Haight*

See also INTEGRITY, RIGHTEOUSNESS, THOUGHTS

Charity

All of us, I am sure, will find time to shed our tears. It may be in sorrow and lamentation that we have not measured more nearly to the standard of the Lord's expectation in our concern and compassion for each other—that in learning and speaking much about Him we have never been suffused with the warmth of His loving heart, have never really been His disciple in matters that meant so much to Him.

Our tears will be tears of gladness and rejoicing if somehow, amidst all the exhortation and admonition, all the searching and the seeking and the running to and fro, we have begun to understand what He meant when he asked of us, "What do ye more than others?" and have lifted our lives therefore to greater concern for each other, to more forgiving and comforting and confirming of our love toward the sorrowing soul, to more honesty and diligence, to more fairness and kindness, and to more joy and rejoicing in the ward where we live when a beloved son or daughter comes home again. (*Ensign*, November 1976, p. 33.)

— *Marion D. Hanks*

And what is charity in its true sense? It is the pure love of Christ which helps us to love both God and our fellowmen. (*Ensign*, May 1977, p. 75.)

— *Mark E. Petersen*

For charity there is no bookkeeping, no deals, interests, bargaining or ulterior motives; charity gives to those who do not deserve, and expects nothing in return; it is the love God has for us, and the love we have for little children, of whom we expect nothing, but for whom we would give everything.

— *Hugh Nibley*

For me I feel close to the Savior when I can do in a small way for someone else, what He would do if He were there. In a way, that's what being an instrument is all about . . . to make it possible for His love to reach more of His children. (Quoted by Barbara W. Winder, *Ensign*, November 1985, p. 96.)

— *Mary Ellen Edmunds*

God accomplishes His purposes heart to heart. (*Ensign*, November 1982, p. 12.)

— *David B. Haight*

Having compassion on those who are hurting for whatever reason and then translating the response of the heart into the needed act is truly ministering as God would have us do. . . .

We must recognize that life is a precious gift, that trust and tenderness are fragile, that we must love and serve one another, must encourage one another, forgive one another—all this not once, but over and over again. Then perhaps we shall be remembered among those on the right hand of the Lord when he shall come in his glory. (*Ensign,* May 1989, pp. 73, 75.)

— *Joy F. Evans*

In a world and society where Satan is launching his most vicious attacks ever on the children of men, we have no greater weapon than pure, unselfish, Christlike love. (*Ensign,* May 1977, p. 69.)

— *H. Burke Peterson*

It is easy to do things for our own families and loved ones, but to give of our substance for the stranger who is in need is the real test of our charity and love for our fellowmen.

— *N. Eldon Tanner*

Let everyone labor to prepare himself for the vineyard, sparing a little time to comfort the mourners; to bind up the broken-hearted; to reclaim the backslider; to bring back the wanderer; to re-invite into the kingdom such as have been cut off, by encouraging them to lay to while the day lasts, and work righteousness, and, with one heart and one mind, prepare to help redeem Zion, that goodly land of promise, where the willing and obedient shall be blessed. Souls are as precious in the sight of God as they ever were; and the Elders were never called to drive any down to hell, but to persuade and incite all men everywhere to repent, that they may become the heirs of salvation. (*HC,* 2:229.)

— *Joseph Smith*

Let us unite and pray with all the energy of heart, that we may be sealed by [the] bond of charity; that we may build up this latter-day Zion, that the kingdom of God may go forth, so that the kingdom of heaven by come. (*Ensign,* May 1978, p. 81.)

— *Spencer W. Kimball*

Tears came to my eyes when I read of a mere boy in one of our eastern cities who noticed a vagrant asleep on a sidewalk and who then went to his own bedroom, retrieved his own pillow, and placed it beneath the head of that one whom he knew not. Perhaps there came from the precious past the welcome word: "Inasmuch as ye have done it unto one of the least of these my brethren, ye have done it unto me" (Matthew 25:40).

I extol those who, with loving care and compassionate concern, feed the hungry, clothe the naked, and house the homeless. He who notes the sparrow's fall will not be unmindful of such service. (*Ensign,* November 1987, p. 68.)

— *Thomas S. Monson*

The efficacy of our prayers depends on how we care for one another. (*Ensign*, November 1980, p. 93.)

— *Marion G. Romney*

The final analysis of Mormon and Moroni was that the fatal weakness of the Nephites was lack of charity. (*OAT*, p. 89.)

— *Hugh Nibley*

The plight of the homeless is a repudiation of the greatness of our nation. I commend most warmly those who with a compelling spirit of kindness reach out to those in distress, regardless of whom they might be, to help and assist, to feed and provide for, to nurture and to bless. As these extend mercy, I am confident that the God of heaven will bless them, with His own mercy. I am satisfied that these who impart so generously will not lack in their own store, but that there will be food on their tables and a roof over their heads. (*Ensign*, May 1990, p. 70.)

— *Gordon B. Hinckley*

The royal law of love is of sacred significance in the Lord's program for his people—an element as vital as any other in the gospel. It is inseparable from them and the spirit of them. (*Ensign*, November 1988, p. 64.)

— *Marion D. Hanks*

The world today speaks a great deal about love, and it is sought for by many. But the pure love of Christ differs greatly from what the world thinks of love. Charity never seeks selfish gratification. The pure love of Christ seeks only the eternal growth and joy of others. (*Ensign*, November 1986, p. 47.)

— *Ezra Taft Benson*

Too often, charity is extended to another when his actions or conduct are acceptable to us. The exhibition of charity to another must not be dependent on his performance. If should be given because of who we are—not because of how we behave. (*Ensign*, May 1981, p. 82.)

— *H. Burke Peterson*

We should sow within our hearts the seed of charity, the pure love of Christ. He is the perfect model of charity. His total life, particularly his atoning sacrifice, is a lesson in charity. His every act reflects absolute, unequivocal love for all mankind and for each one of us. His example teaches us that charity means subordinating personal interests willingly and gladly for the good of others. I believe our progress toward exaltation and eternal life depends upon how well we learn and live the principle of charity. Charity must become a fundamental state of mind and heart that guides us in all we do.

— *Joseph B. Wirthlin*

Zion consists of the pure in heart—those who are sanctified and whose garments are washed white through the blood of the Lamb. These are they who take charity as a mantle and serve others out of a pure heart.

— *Spencer W. Kimball*

See also BROTHERHOOD, CARING, KINDNESS, LOVE, SERVICE, TEMPORAL LAW, TEMPORAL WELFARE

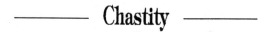

Chastity

As long as the stars shine in the heavens and the sun brings warmth to the earth and so long as men and women live upon this earth, there must be this holy standard of chastity and virtue. (Area Conference, October 1974.)

— *Spencer W. Kimball*

Boys and girls, God bless you to keep your lives unpolluted, that you may go in prayer to God and ask him to guide you in choosing your mates, and when chosen, that you will both so live that you can enter the house of God, and if he were present and asked you about your lives, you could answer him honestly, "Yes, we are clean." A marriage begun on that basis, will bring you the happiness, the sweetest joy known in this life, or throughout eternity. (*Gospel Ideals*, The Improvement Era, Salt Lake City: Deseret Book Co., 1976, pp. 465-66.)

— *David O. McKay*

Chastity before marriage and faithfulness after marriage are cardinal ingredients for the full flowering of sacred love between husband and wife. Chastity nurtures and builds feelings of self-worth and indemnifies against the destruction of self-image. (*Ensign*, May 1981, p. 9.)

— *James E. Faust*

Chastity is like money in the bank. As you save yourself you are *saving* the joy of belonging to one and only one. (*Ensign*, November 1981, p. 72.)

— *Paul H. Dunn*

In the Church and kingdom of god, chastity will never be out of date, regardless of what the world may do or say. So we say to you, young men and women—maintain your self-respect. Do not engage in intimacies that bring heartache and sorrow. You cannot build happy lives on immorality. (*Ensign,* November 1977, p. 31.)

— *Ezra Taft Benson*

Humanity will rise or fall through its attitude toward the law of chastity. (*CR,* April 1969, p. 62.)

— *Mark E. Petersen*

Chastity is the source of virile manhood, the crown of beautiful womanhood, the foundation of a happy home, and the ultimate and perfect standard underlying all spiritual progression. (*Ensign,* November 1989, p. 40.)

— *Robert L. Backman*

Man is endowed with appetites and passions for the preservation of his life and the perpetuation of his kind. These, when held under proper subjection, contribute to his happiness and comfort; but when used for mere gratification, lead to misery and moral degradation. (*CR,* October 1959, p. 69.)

— *David O. McKay*

Movies and television often portray premarital sex as an appropriate expression of love between a man and a woman. This is a lie. Sex outside of marriage becomes an expression of selfishness, lack of self-control, and lack of concern for the other person. These actions will bring you unhappiness and are condemned by God. (*Ensign,* May 1989, p. 42.)

— *Russell C. Taylor*

The rewards for virtue and the consequences of unchastity are dramatically portrayed in the lives of Joseph and David.

Joseph, though a slave in Egypt, stood true under pressure of the greatest temptation. As a reward he received the choicest blessings of all the sons of Jacob: he became the progenitor of the two favored tribes of Israel. Most of us take pride in being numbered among his posterity.

David, on the other hand, though highly favored of the Lord . . . , yielded to temptation. His unchastity led to murder, and as a consequence, he lost his families and his exaltation (see D&C 132:39). (*Ensign,* May 1979, p. 42.)

— *Marion G. Romney*

That the Church's stand on morality may be understood, we declare firmly and unalterably, it is not an outworn garment, faded, old-fashioned, and threadbare. God is the same yesterday, today, and forever, and his covenants and doctrines are immutable; and when the sun grows cold and the stars no longer shine, the law of chastity will still be basic in God's world and in the Lord's church. Old values are upheld by the Church not because they are old, but rather because through the ages they have proved right. It will always be the rule. (*Ensign,* November 1980, p. 94.)

— *Spencer W. Kimball*

The value of moral cleanliness is beyond compare. It cannot be bought by silver or gold, but the price we pay in personal righteousness is of inestimable worth, and will do more to bring about that eternal happiness for which we seek than almost anything else. (*Ensign,* July 1975, p. 3.)

— *N. Eldon Tanner*

There appears to be something beyond and above the reasons apparent to the human mind why chastity brings strength and power to the peoples of the earth, but it is so.

— *Joseph F. Smith*

See also MORALITY, PURITY, VIRTUE

Cheerfulness

Be cheerful in all that you do. Live joyfully. Live happily. Live enthusiastically, knowing that God does not dwell in gloom and melancholy, but in light and love. (*New Era,* September 1979, p. 42.)

— *Ezra Taft Benson*

Be happy in that which you do. Cultivate a spirit of gladness in your homes. Subdue and overcome all elements of anger, impatience, and unbecoming talk one to another. Let the light of the gospel shine in your faces wherever you go and in whatever you do. (*Ensign,* November 1984, p. 86.)

— *Gordon B. Hinckley*

Good cheer is best shared by those who will discard fear, cheerfully accept what comes and use it wisely, become converted, obey the commandments of God, avoid self-deceit and rationalization.

Being of good cheer makes it possible for us to turn all of our sunsets into sunrises.

With good cheer, carrying our cross can be our ladder to happiness. (*Ensign,* May 1986, p. 68.)

— *Marvin J. Ashton*

May God help us to be of good cheer, for this is the forerunner feeling which preceded that glorious condition when our joy will be full! (See D&C 93:34.) (*Ensign,* November 1982, p. 68.)

— *Neal A. Maxwell*

The thing you should have in your mind, and which you should make a motto in your life, is this: Serve God faithfully, and be cheerful. . . . And out of that cheerfulness may arise many good gifts. The Lord has not given us the gospel that we may go around mourning all the days of our lives. (*TLS,* p. 61.)

— *Lorenzo Snow*

When Jesus comes into our lives, cheer lights the way. (*Ensign,* May 1986, p. 68.)

— *Marvin J. Ashton*

With God's help, good cheer permits us to rise above the depressing present or difficult circumstances. It is a process of positive reassurance and reinforcement. It is sunshine when clouds block the light. (*Ensign,* May 1986, p. 66.)

— *Marvin J. Ashton*

See also ATTITUDE, HAPPINESS, JOY, OPTIMISM

———— Children ————

Children, being pure and holy, teach us something of our heavenly home. (*Ensign,* November 1989, p. 91.)

— *Joanne B. Doxey*

No gift bestowed upon us is so precious as children. They are proof that God still loves us. They are the hope of the future. (*Ensign,* May 1987, p. 80.)

— *James E. Faust*

Next to eternal life, the most precious gift that our Father in Heaven can bestow upon man is his children.

— *David O. McKay*

There is a story of a group of Relief Society sisters making candy called "divinity" at the home of one of the sisters. Two little boys in the family were allowed to eat all of the divinity they could scrape from the spoons, pans, and bowls. It was the weekend of general conference and, as the family listened to the talks, one of the speakers said, "There is a spark of divinity in each of us." One of the little boys jumped up and said, "A spark of divinity? Wow, I'm full of it!"

Yes, children are full of divinity. Surely the angels attend them. (*Ensign,* November 1987, p. 90.)

— *Joanne B. Doxey*

Our most precious possessions are not our abundant harvests, nor our orchards yielding luscious fruit, nor our waterways, nor our million miles of paved highways, nor our oil wells, nor our rich mines of copper, silver and gold, not even of uranium—our most precious possessions, our treasures of eternity, are our children. (*CR,* October 1954, p. 8.)

— *David O. McKay*

When we realize just how precious children are, we will not find it difficult to follow the pattern of the Master in our association with them. (*Ensign,* May 1990, p. 53.)

— *Thomas S. Monson*

See also CHILD-REARING, PARENTHOOD

——— Child-Rearing ———

A successful parent is one who has loved, one who has sacrificed, and one who has cared for, taught, and ministered to the needs of a child. If you have done all of these and your child is still wayward or troublesome or worldly, it could well be that you are, nevertheless, a successful parent. Perhaps there are children who have come into the world that would challenge any set of parents under any set of circumstances. Likewise, perhaps there are others who would bless the lives of, and be a joy to, almost any father or mother. (*Ensign,* November 1983, p. 65.)

— *Howard W. Hunter*

As parents, we should remember that our lives may be the book from the family library which the children most treasure. Are our examples worthy of emulation? Do we live in such a way that a son or a daughter may say, "I want to follow my dad," or "I want to be like my mother"? Unlike the book on the library shelf, the covers of which shield the contents, our lives cannot be closed. Parents, we truly are an open book. (*Ensign,* November 1988, p. 70.)

— *Thomas S. Monson*

Before we can teach our children, we must understand and live the principles ourselves. It is vital that the child learn from our example that what we say and what we live are the same. (*Ensign*, November 1983, p. 86.)

— Dwan J. Young

By commandment, parents in this Church are to teach their children faith in Christ, repentance, baptism, and the gift of the Holy Ghost (see D&C 68:25). (*Ensign*, May 1987, p. 81.)

— James E. Faust

Children must learn obedience, and parents must exact obedience from them. Love your children, let them know that you love them; but remember that it is no favor to a child to let him do things he should not do. (*CR*, October 1977, p. 74.)

— N. Eldon Tanner

Discipline is organized love, and children develop properly in an atmosphere of love, with adequate guidelines to shape their lives and their habits. More children are punished for mimicking their parents than ever for disobeying them. We should *be* what we want to *see*. (*Ensign*, November 1990, p. 12.)

— LeGrand R. Curtis

Don't Give Up the Wayward Child

You parents of the willful and the wayward! Don't give them up. Don't cast them off. They are not utterly lost. The Shepherd will find his sheep. They were his before they were yours—long before he entrusted them to your care; and you cannot begin to love them as he loves them. They have but strayed in ignorance from the Path of Right, but God is merciful to ignorance. Only the fullness of knowledge brings the fullness of accountability. Our Heavenly Father is far more merciful, infinitely more charitable, than even the best of his servants, and the Everlasting Gospel is mightier in power to save than our narrow finite minds can comprehend. (*CR*, April 1929, p. 110.)

— Orson F. Whitney

Every child, with few possible exceptions, is the product of a home, be it good, bad, or indifferent. As children grow through the years, their lives, in large measure, become an extension and a reflection of family teaching. If there is harshness, abuse, uncontrolled anger, disloyalty, the fruits will be certain and discernible, and in all likelihood they will be repeated in the generation that follows. If, on the other hand, there is forbearance, forgiveness, respect, consideration, kindness, mercy, and compassion, the fruits again will be discernible, and they will be eternally rewarding. They will be positive and sweet and wonderful. (*Ensign*, May 1990, p. 70.)

— Gordon B. Hinckley

For your own sake, for the love that should exist between you and your [children] . . . when you speak or talk to them, do it not in anger, do it not harshly, in a condemning spirit. Speak to them kindly; get them down and weep with them if necessary and get them to shed tears with you if possible. Soften their hearts; get them to feel tenderly toward you. Use no lash and no violence, but argue, or rather reason-approach them with reason, with persuasion and love unfeigned. (*GD*, p. 316.)

— *Joseph F. Smith*

I cannot help wondering about parents who adopt the attitude with their children, "do as I say, not as I do" with respect to using harmful substances, going to inappropriate movies, and other questionable activities. Children often take license from their parents' behavior and go beyond the values the parents wish to establish. There is one safe parental rule: do not just avoid evil, avoid the very appearance of evil (see 1 Thessalonians 5:22). (*Ensign*, November 1986, p. 10.)

— *James E. Faust*

If our people will . . . teach their children the principles of the gospel, not only by precept but by example, you are going to see a people such as the world has never before beheld, for the children brought up in righteousness will be fit to meet the Lord when He comes in power and great glory. (*CR*, April 1943, p. 61.)

— *Charles A. Callis*

Mothers and fathers and children need the experience of bearing their testimonies and expressing their love for our Father in heaven and Jesus Christ. Testimony-bearing is not restricted to the chapel. The family room can be the ideal setting for some very sensitive spiritual experiences. Happy memories are made by appointment, and parents need to plan special spiritual events to create spiritual experiences. Happy memories are made by appointment, and parents need to plan special spiritual events to create spiritual memories in their homes. (*Ensign*, November 1990, p. 13.)

— *LeGrand R. Curtis*

Parents should govern their children by faith rather than by the rod, leading them kindly by good example into all truth and holiness. (*JD*, 12:174.)

— *Brigham Young*

Sister McKay and I stood one day, I believe it was at San Diego [zoo], watching a mother monkey with a new born babe. She was guarding it, her quick eye watching the other monkeys in the cage; but the little babe was free to do just as it pleased, hopping around, weak in its infancy, getting hold of the bars, starting to climb. When it would reach a certain place, the mother would reach up and bring it back. When it got into a danger point, that mother instinctively guarded it and said, "Back this way." And then the babe was free again, but only within certain limits.

I said to Sister McKay, "There is a lesson of life in guiding children." (*CR*, September 1950, p. 165.)

— *David O. McKay*

Not one child in a hundred would go astray if the home environment, example and training, were in harmony with the truth in the gospel of Christ, as revealed and taught to the Latter-day Saints. Fathers and mothers, you are largely to blame for the infidelity and indifference of your children. You can remedy the evil by earnest worship, example, training, and discipline in the home. (*IE*, December 1904, p. 135.)

— *Joseph F. Smith*

Single Parenthood

If you are a single parent, make friends with others in similar situations and develop friendships with married couples. Counsel with your priesthood leaders. Let them know of your needs and wants. Single parenthood is understood by the Lord. He knows the special challenges that are yours. . . . He loves you and will bless and sustain you. This I know. (*Ensign*, November 1988, p. 97.)

— *Ezra Taft Benson*

The most important teachings in the home are spiritual. Parents are commanded to prepare their sons and daughters for the ordinances of the gospel: baptism, confirmation, priesthood ordinations, and temple marriage. They are to teach them to respect and honor the Sabbath day, to keep it holy. Most importantly, parents are to instill within their children a desire for eternal life and to earnestly seek that goal above all else. (*Ensign*, November 1982, pp. 60-61.)

— *Ezra Taft Benson*

Those who do too much *for* their children will soon find they can do nothing *with* their children. So many children have been so much *done for* they are almost *done in.* (*CR*, April 1975, p. 150.)

— *Neal A. Maxwell*

Some years ago in our ward fast and testimony meeting a young father proudly gave a name and a blessing to his first child. Afterwards the father stood to bear his testimony. He expressed thanks for this, his first son. He then said in a rather perplexed way that since the little fellow didn't seem to understand anything they said, he wished he knew just how to communicate with him. "All we can do," said he, "is hold him, cuddle him, gently squeeze him, kiss him, and whisper thoughts of love in his ear."

After the meeting I went up to the new father and said that in his testimony he had given us a success pattern for raising healthy children. I hoped he would never forget it; even as his children grew to maturity I hoped he would continue the practice. (*Ensign*, May 1977, p. 68.)

— *H. Burke Peterson*

What we need today are parents who are converted to the gospel of Jesus Christ; who are willing to apply it, believe it, and use it; who pay an honest tithing; who are honest with their neighbors and debtors; who actually sustain the authorities of the Church; and who teach the gospel to their children in such a way that the children will love the Lord. We need parents with courage, who will stand up and speak up for the right, who are actively involved in government of all levels; parents who are modest in dress, speech, and conduct; parents who are not ashamed of the gospel of Jesus Christ; parents who teach their children that we do have a Father in heaven, that we are his spirit children, that he has placed us here on earth for a great and glorious purpose, that he loves us, that he has given us commandments along with our free agency, that we will receive rewards and judgments based on our own actions; parents who accept all of the commandments as having come from God, to be obeyed for that reason if for no other; parents who have no other gods before the Lord, who do not commit adultery, who do not steal, who do not covet their neighbor's wife or husband, who do not bear false witness against their neighbor; parents who love the Lord their God with all their heart, and with all their soul, and with all their mind, and who love their neighbor as themselves. (*Era*, June 1970, p. 47.)

— *Victor L. Brown*

When we give our children of our own time, we are giving of our presence, a gift that is always noticed. (*Ensign*, May 1978, p. 5.)

— *Spencer W. Kimball*

The most precious gift a man and woman can receive is a child of God, and that the raising of a child is basically, fundamentally, and most exclusively a *spiritual* process. . . .

The first and most important inner quality you can instill in a child is *faith in God*. The first and most important action a child can learn is *obedience*. And the most powerful tool you have with which to teach a child is *love*. (*Ensign*, May 1983, p. 78.)

— *L. Tom Perry*

You fathers and mothers, put Him first in your lives, and in your hearts. Teach your children of the Lord; . . . Teach them of His love and the great blessings he has for each of them as they desire and live worthy and go to His house. . . .

The finest thing you parents can do for your children is to love one another and put God first in your hearts and lives. It will strengthen your home and safeguard your family. (*Ensign*, November 1982, p. 28.)

— *Rex C. Reeve*

Wise discipline reinforces the dimensions of eternal love. (*Ensign*, January 1974, p. 23.)

— *James E. Faust*

Young parents, prepare yourselves that your children may be properly taught in the ways of the Lord. Teach them faith in the living God. Teach them to pray always, and teach them to keep the laws and commandments the Lord has given us to live by.

— *O. Leslie Stone*

Your children may or may not choose to follow you—but the example you give is the greatest light you will hold before your children. You are accountable for that light. (Quoted by H. Burke Peterson, *Ensign*, October 1977, p. 88.)

— *Ezra Taft Benson*

[We must teach children] by faith rather than by the rod, leading them kindly by good example into all truth and holiness. (*JD*, 12:174.)

— *Brigham Young*

See also CHILDREN, FAMILY, FATHERHOOD, HOME, MOTHERHOOD, PARENTHOOD

——— **Choices** ———

A wise father, speaking to his son, placed the question of choice in a direct setting. He counseled, "Son, if you ever find yourself in a place you shouldn't ought to be—*get out!*" Good advice for a son. Good advice for a father, too. (*Ensign*, May 1989, p. 44.)

— *Thomas S. Monson*

Given the freedom to choose, we may, in fact, make wrong choices, bad choices, hurtful choices. And sometimes we do just that, but that is where the mission and mercy of Jesus Christ comes into full force and glory. He has taken upon himself the burden of all the world's risk. He has provided a mediating atonement for the wrong choices we make. He is our advocate with the Father and has paid, in advance, for the faults and foolishness we often see in the exercise of our freedom. (*Ensign,* November 1989, p. 18.)

— *Howard W. Hunter*

Every time we make choices in our lives, we should weigh the ultimate effect our decisions will have on our goal of attaining eternal life. . . .

When we stand at the crossroads of life and must make a decision whether to go to the great and spacious building of the world's ways or to walk the straight and narrow path that leads to eternal life, we must realize that we cannot travel *both* roads—although sometimes we try. It is difficult to come back, but we can; and our greatest satisfaction will more than likely come from taking the lonelier road which is less traveled.

May the Lord bless us as we make our decisions in life to constantly keep our goal of eternal life in view. (*Ensign,* November 1988, pp. 10, 11.)

— *Robert D. Hales*

Our freedom to choose our course of conduct does not provide personal freedom from the consequences of our performances. God's love for us is constant and will not diminish, but he cannot rescue us from the painful results that are caused by wrong choices. (*Ensign,* November 1990, p. 20.)

— *Marvin J. Ashton*

Private choices are not private; they all have public consequences. . . . Our society is the sum total of what millions of individuals do in their private lives. (*Ensign,* May 1987, p. 80.)

— *James E. Faust*

We are like children walking a path in the rain. We can walk in or around the mud of life as we desire, but with our choices come the consequences. And we are rapidly becoming what we are choosing to be for all eternity. (*Ensign,* November 1983, p. 88.)

— *Elaine Cannon*

With absolute certainty, choices of good and right lead to happiness and peace, while choices of sin and evil eventually lead to unhappiness, sorrow, and misery. (*Ensign,* November 1989, p. 75.)

— *Joseph B. Wirthlin*

Standards of the Church have been given to us to protect us and to help us grow spiritually. When the pioneers ended a day's journey, each night they checked their wagons for any needed repairs. They united in prayer for continued guidance and protection and took a reading of both distance and direction to see how far they had traveled and make sure they were on the right trail. We would do well to follow the same pattern today. A good measurement to ask concerning every important decision is whether or not this decision will move you toward or away from making and keeping sacred covenants and preparing for the ordinances of the temple. (*Ensign*, November 1990, p. 95.)

— *Ardeth G. Kapp*

The course of our lives is not determined by great, awesome decisions. Our direction is set by the little day-to-day choices which chart the track on which we run. (*CR*, October 1972, p. 106.)

— *Gordon B. Hinckley*

The crucial test of life, . . . does not center in the choice between fame and obscurity, not between wealth and poverty. The greatest decision of life is between good and evil. (*Ensign*, November 1980, p. 21.)

— *Boyd K. Packer*

See also AGENCY

——— Church ———

Every phase of [the Church] seems to me applicable to the welfare of the human family. When I consider the quorums of priesthood, I see in them an opportunity for developing that fraternity and brotherly love which is essential to the happiness of mankind. In these quorums and in the auxiliaries of the Church, I see opportunities for intellectual development, for social efficiency. In the judicial phase of the Church I see ample means of settling difficulties, of establishing harmony in society, of administering justice, and of perpetuating peace among individuals and groups. In the ecclesiastical organization, I see an opportunity for social welfare such as cannot be found in any other organization in the world. . . .

I know of nothing else in the world that can even approach Christ's Church as an anchor for the soul. (Quoted by James M. Paramore, *Ensign*, May 1988, p. 12.)

— *David O. McKay*

I want to say to every man that there is within the Church an opportunity for the expression of every legitimate desire that should be in the heart of men. (*CR*, October 1919, p. 103.)

— *Stephen L Richards*

Others may insist that *this* is not the true church. That is their privilege. But to claim that it does not exist anywhere, that it does not even *need* to exist, is to deny the scriptures. (See Eph. 4:5, 13; Acts 3:21.) . . .

We did not invent the doctrine [that this is] the only true church. It came from the Lord. Whatever perception others have of us, however presumptuous we appear to be, whatever criticism is directed to us, we must teach it to all who will listen. (*Ensign*, November 1985, p. 82.)

— *Boyd K. Packer*

The Church is an organized body of true believers; it is the congregation of those who have accepted the holy gospel; and the gospel is the plan of salvation. . . . The Church is the vehicle through which the Lord's affairs on earth are regulated and through which salvation is made available to all who believe and obey. (*Ensign*, November 1981, p. 48.)

— *Bruce R. McConkie*

The Church is engaged in the greatest work in all the world—saving the souls of our Father's children. It is important that each member know his or her duties and be dedicated and committed in carrying them out in a manner that is pleasing to the Lord. . . . [and] that we marshall all the resources and get them working together in a correlated way so the Church can reach its full potential in helping the Lord bring to pass the immortality and eternal life of man. Our goal is perfection for all of God's children who will listen, accept, and live the gospel. (*Ensign*, November 1976, p. 31.)

— *William H. Bennett*

The Church is like a great caravan—organized, prepared, following an appointed course, with its captains of tens and captains of hundreds all in place.

What does it matter if a few barking dogs snap at the heels of the weary travelers? Or that predators claim those few who fall by the way? The caravan moves on.

Is there a ravine to cross, a miry mud hole to pull through, a steep grade to climb? So be it. The oxen are strong and the teamsters wise. The caravan moves on.

Are there storms that rage along the way, floods that wash away the bridges, deserts to cross, and rivers to ford? Such is life in this fallen sphere. The caravan moves on.

Ahead is the celestial city, the eternal Zion of our God, where all who maintain their position in the caravan shall find food and drink and rest. Thank God that the caravan moves on! (*Ensign*, November 1984, p. 85.)

— *Bruce R. McConkie*

The Church is the official organization of baptized believers who have taken upon themselves the name of Christ. (See D&C 10:67-69, 18:20-25.) . . .

The Church is the way by which the Master accomplishes His work and bestows His glory. Its ordinances and related covenants are the crowning rewards of our membership. While many organizations can offer fellowship and fine instruction, only His church can provide baptism, confirmation, ordination, the sacrament, patriarchal blessings, and the ordinances of the temple—all bestowed by authorized priesthood power. (*Ensign*, May 1990, p. 18.)

— *Russell M. Nelson*

The Church provides all of the teachings of the Savior.

The Church exercises the authority from heaven, beginning with a prophet of God and extending down to every family.

The Church provides the saving ordinances of the gospel, including holy, eternal endowments and sealings in the house of God, a fullness of all that the Father has.

The Church provides brotherhood and sisterhood with others, wherever they are upon this earth. . . . It is a refuge from the world, with watchcare and accountability for every member.

The Church helps us to overcome selfishness and uncertainty by serving others in dozens of ways over a lifetime. . . .

The Church is a way of life and has established organizations and cultural and developmental opportunities for ourselves and our children that are the envy of this world. Loving leaders and teachers provide warmth, security, activities, music, theater, and athletics, as well as the teachings of the Savior to help us to learn how to love Him, to try to be like Him and serve others. (*Ensign*, May 1988, p. 11.)

— *James M. Paramore*

The earth will never be left again without the Church of Christ established upon it. (*CR*, April 1908, p. 17.)

— *Francis M. Lyman*

This Church has the seeds of immortality in its midst. It is not of man, nor by man—it is the offspring of Deity. It is organized after the pattern of heavenly things, through the principles of revelation: by the opening of the heavens; by the ministering of angels, and the revelations of Jehovah. It is not affected by the death of one or two or fifty individuals. It possesses a priesthood after the order of Melchizedek, having the power of an endless life, "without beginning of days, or end of years." It is organized for the purpose of saving this generation, and generations that are past. It exists in time and will exist in eternity. This Church fail? No! (*Times and Seasons*, 5:744.)

— *John Taylor*

This is the church of our Lord Jesus Christ, and it does indeed bring forth fruit worthy of him. Its growth will continue unabated because of the faith of its members and because more men and women are discovering the golden threads of truth, hope, and salvation as they learn gospel principles and are "nourished by the good word of God, to keep them in the right way, . . . relying . . . upon the merits of Christ, who [is] the author . . . of their faith" (Moroni 6:4). (*Ensign*, May 1988, p. 21.)

— *David B. Haight*

We are either for the Church or we are against it. We either take its part or we take the consequences. We cannot survive spiritually with one foot in the Church and the other in the world. It's either the Church or the World. We must make a choice. (*CR*, October 1974, p. 44.)

— *Bruce R. McConkie*

The Church is for man, not man for the Church. (*CR*, October 1945, p. 160.)

— *Ezra Taft Benson*

We proclaim the objects of this organization to be, the preaching of the gospel in all the world, the gathering of scattered Israel, and the preparation of a people for the coming of the Lord. (*Messages of the First Presidency of The Church of Jesus Christ of Latter-day Saints*, James R. Clark, comp., Salt Lake City: Bookcraft, 1965-75, 4:145.)

— *Joseph F. Smith*

[Jesus Christ] established His church to serve as a refuge from the world, where the Saints could learn about Him and His truths and His ways and could learn to love and serve each other. (*Ensign*, November 1990, p. 63.)

— *James M. Paramore*

See also CHURCH PROGRAMS, KINGDOM OF GOD, LATTER-DAY WORK

—— Church Programs ——

Church programs strengthen individuals and families. Our success, individually and as a church, will largely be determined by how faithfully we focus on living the gospel in the home. Only as we see clearly the responsibilities of each individual and the role of families and homes can we properly understand that priesthood quorums and auxiliary organizations, even wards and stakes, exist primarily to help members live the gospel in the home. Then we can understand that people are more important than programs, and that the Church programs should always support and never detract from gospel-centered family activities. (*Ensign*, May 1978, p. 101.)

— *Spencer W. Kimball*

Church sports activities have a unique central purpose much higher than the development of physical prowess, or even victory itself. It is to strengthen faith, build integrity, and develop in each participant the attributes of his maker. (*The Church Sports Official*, video tape, produced by The Church of Jesus Christ of Latter-day Saints.)

— *The First Presidency*

I hope we will always remember that the Church is a support to the family. The Church does not and must not seek to displace the family, but is organized to help create and nurture righteous families as well as righteous individuals. (*Ensign*, May 1981, p. 45.)

— *Spencer W. Kimball*

If loving, inspired instruction and example are not provided at home, then our related efforts for success in and around Church programs are severely limited. It is increasingly clear that we must teach the gospel to our families personally, love those teachings in our homes, or run the risk of discovering too late that a Primary teacher or priesthood adviser or seminary instructor *could* not do for our children what we *would* not do for them. (*Ensign*, May 1983, p. 36.)

— *Jeffrey R. Holland*

It takes a Zion people to make a Zion society, and we must prepare for that.

During the past few years a number of resources have been set in place in the Church to help us. New editions of the scriptures . . . . More temples . . . . The consolidated meeting schedule . . . . A special home evening manual . . . . A new hymnal . . . . And so the list goes on and on. We have received much help. We don't need changed programs now as much as we need changed people! (*Ensign*, May 1986, p. 4.)

— *Ezra Taft Benson*

Nobody changes the principles and doctrines of the Church except the Lord by revelation. But methods change as the inspired direction comes to those who preside at a given time. . . . You may be sure that your brethren who preside are praying most earnestly, and we do not move until we have the assurance, so far as lies within our power, that what we do has the seal of divine approval. (*Ensign*, January 1971, p. 10.)

— *Harold B. Lee*

People must always count more than programs. (*Ensign*, May 1988, p. 62.)

— *Marvin J. Ashton*

Procedures, programs, and policies are developed within the Church to help us realize gospel blessings according to our individual capacity and circumstances. Under divine direction, these policies, programs, and procedures may be changed from time to time as necessary to fulfill gospel purposes. . . .

In the scriptures we discover that varying institutional forms, procedures, regulation, and ceremonies were utilized—all divinely designed to implement eternal principles. The practices and procedures change; the principles do not. (*Ensign*, November 1984, p. 64.)

— *Ronald E. Poelman*

The simplicity in the principles of the gospel of Jesus Christ should be matched by simplicity in our church administration and programs. (*Ensign*, May 1983, p. 84.)

— *Neal A. Maxwell*

——— Citizenship ———

It is our duty to concentrate all our influence to make popular that which is sound and good, and unpopular that which is unsound. (*HC*, 5:286.)

— *Joseph Smith*

Let us resolve to be exemplary Saints and good citizens, and to rear our youth so that they will, in their day, courageously carry and pass on the torch of liberty to the next generation. (*Ensign*, November 1987, p. 102.)

— *Ezra Taft Benson*

Sustain the government of the nation wherever you are, and speak well of it, for this is right, and the government has a right to expect it of you so long as that government sustains you in your civil and religious liberty, in those rights which inherently belong to every person born on the earth. (*DFTP*, pp. 227-28.)

— *The First Presidency*

We are under the United States. But the United States is not the kingdom of God. It does not profess to be under his rule, nor his government, nor his authority. . . . Very well, what is expected of us? That we observe its laws, that we conform to its usages, that we are governed by good and wholesome principles, that we maintain the laws in their integrity and that we sustain the government.

And we ought to do it. . . . We ought to pray . . . for those that are in authority, that they may be led in the right way, that they may be preserved from evil, that they may administer the government in righteousness, and that they may pursue a course that will receive the approbation of heaven. (*JD*, 21:68.)

— *John Taylor*

We do appeal to all men and women, realizing the responsibility resting upon them, to seek God our heavenly Father to guide them politically as well as religiously, and to stand for right and for those things that are for the good of this nation. (*CR*, October 1928, p. 9.)

— *Heber J. Grant*

We have been blessed with the light of the gospel to lead us and to guide and direct our lives. Through our understanding and study of the scriptures, we have a knowledge of the laws of the Lord by which we should govern our earthly conduct. With this great blessing comes an obligation to be a part of the communities in which we live. Our influence should be felt to safeguard the moral standard in the villages, in the towns, and in the cities where our homes are located in all parts of the world. I challenge you to become involved in lifting the moral standards of the communities where your homes are. (*Ensign*, May 1977, p. 61.)

— *L. Tom Perry*

We must become involved in civic affairs. As citizens of this republic we cannot do our duty and be idle spectators. (*Ensign*, November 1987, p. 102.)

— *Ezra Taft Benson*

See also AMERICA, FREEDOM, GOVERNMENT

——— Commandments ———

Brothers and sisters, this is the work of the Lord. We deal with many things which are thought to be not so spiritual; but all things are spiritual with the Lord, and he expects us to listen, and to obey, and to follow the commandments. And I beg of you—all of us—that we live the commandments of the Lord. (*Ensign*, May 1977, p. 7.)

— *Spencer W. Kimball*

Every commandment of God is spiritual in nature. There are no carnal commandments. We have learned this from modern revelation. While the commandments have effect upon the body and temporal things they are all in essence spiritual. The Word of Wisdom is spiritual. It is true that it enjoins the use of deleterious substances and makes provision for the health of the body. But the largest measure of good derived from its observance is in increased faith and the development of more spiritual power and wisdom. Likewise, the most regrettable and damaging effects of its infractions are spiritual, also. Injury to the body may be comparatively trivial to the damage to the soul in the destruction of faith and the retardation of spiritual growth. So I say, every commandment involves a spiritual growth. (*CR*, April 1949, p. 141.)

— *Stephen L Richards*

Commandments are *loving counsel from a wise Father.* Our understanding and concept of God as a loving and personal Heavenly Father allows us no other definition. He gives us commandments for one reason only—because he loves us and wants us to be happy. (*Ensign*, November 1981, p. 72.)

— *Paul H. Dunn*

In answer to the question, "Shouldn't the commandments be rewritten?," someone thoughtfully replied, "No, they should be reread." (*CR*, April 1967, p. 9.)

— *Richard L. Evans*

It has always seemed somewhat paradoxical to me that we must constantly have the Lord *command* us to do those things which are for our own good. (*Ensign*, November 1982, p. 93.)

— *Marion G. Romney*

It isn't the Lord who withholds himself from us. It is we who withhold ourselves from him because of our failure to keep his commandments. (*CR*, October 1966, p. 117.)

— *Harold B. Lee*

Keeping the commandments . . . is at once a demonstration of our intelligence, our knowledge, our character, and our wisdom. (*CR*, October 1950.)

— *Stephen L Richards*

We cannot keep all the commandments without first knowing them, and we cannot expect to know all, or more than we now know unless we comply with or keep those we have already received. (*TPJS*, p. 256.)

— *Joseph Smith*

The Book of Mormon contains the history of a people who over the course of a thousand years demonstrated the fruits of righteousness and of wickedness. Whenever they kept the Lord's commandments, they prospered in the land; when they were disobedient, they fell into wickedness, war, famine, and enslavement. Time and time again we read of families, tribes, and whole nations keeping the Lord's commandments and making covenants with him and being blessed by his Spirit. Because of righteousness, they prospered both spiritually and temporally. When they did not keep his commandments, they deteriorated both temporally and spiritually. (*Ensign,* May 1981, p. 90.)

— *Marion G. Romney*

We should know that the Lord will not give us commandments beyond our power to observe. He will not ask us to do things for which we lack the capacity. Our problem lies in our fears and in our appetites. (*Ensign,* November 1985, p. 83.)

— *Gordon B. Hinckley*

When I was younger, I lived to play basketball. It was on my mind constantly. I spent countless hours practicing. Gradually I began to go through the moves automatically, without thinking about them. Physically and mentally I had become conditioned to do certain things by instinct. I had practiced them until they became natural to me.

In like manner, we keep the commandments and teachings of the gospel in order to condition us spiritually. (*Ensign,* May 1979, p. 70.)

— *Loren C. Dunn*

When we break the commandments, we close ourselves to God's influence and open ourselves to Satan's influence. (*Ensign,* May 1988, p. 82.)

— *Joseph B. Wirthlin*

[God] never has—he never will institute an ordinance or give a commandment to his people that is not calculated in its nature to promote that happiness which he has designed, and which will not end in the greatest amount of good and glory to those who become the recipients of his law and ordinances.

— *Joseph Smith*

"My word is my law, saith the Lord." He has a right to require one thing today and another thing tomorrow, and the latest word that comes from him is the word that his people must obey.

— *Albert E. Bowen*

See also BLESSINGS, LAWS, OBEDIENCE

——— Commitment ———

Commitment . . . is a binding, but happy, response to duty. It is at once peaceful yet compelling, for it obligates one to action. It is essential to the good life. It is doing what everyone *can* do. (*Ensign,* May 1979, p. 60.)

— *James M. Paramore*

Commitment is a word that cannot stand alone. We must always ask, "Committed to what?" . . . If we profess to be Latter-day Saints, let us be committed to living like Latter-day Saints, using Jesus Christ as our master teacher. (*Ensign,* November 1983, pp. 61, 63.)

— *Marvin J. Ashton*

He who invites us to follow will always be out in front of us with His Spirit and influence setting the pace. He has charted and marked the course, opened the gates, and shown the way. He has invited us to come unto Him, and the best time to enjoy His companionship is straightway. We can best get on the course and stay on the course by doing as Jesus did—make a total commitment to do the will of His Father. (*Ensign,* May 1983, pp. 30-31.)

— *Marvin J. Ashton*

In this work there must be commitment. There must be devotion. We are engaged in a great eternal struggle that concerns the very souls of the sons and daughters of God. We are not losing. We are winning. We will continue to win if we will be faithful and true. We *can* do it. We *must* do it. We *will* do it. There is nothing the Lord has asked of us that in faith we cannot accomplish. (*Ensign,* November 1986, p. 44.)

— *Gordon B. Hinckley*

The ability to stand by one's principles, to live with integrity and faith according to one's belief—that is what matters, that is the difference between a contribution and a commitment. That devotion to true principle—in our individual lives, in our homes and families, and in all places that we meet and influence other people—that devotion is what God is ultimately requesting of us. (*Ensign,* May 1990, p. 61.)

— *Howard W. Hunter*

Contention The danger of our becoming lukewarm is not from without—the danger is within. (*CR,* April 1903, p. 55.)

— *Reed Smoot*

The difference between those who are committed and those who are not is the difference between the words *want* and *will*. For example, "I want to pay tithing, but our funds are so limited," or "I want to go to sacrament meeting if I have time," or "I will go to sacrament meeting." . . .

To reap the full benefits of life, we must fill our days with commitment to worthy goals and principles. There is no other way. As these commitments lead us to action, we will find added growth and dimension which will guide us towards a productive life here on earth and open the door for eternal life with our Father in Heaven. (*Ensign*, November 1983, p. 63.)

— *Marvin J. Ashton*

There is, in fact, no such thing as neutrality where the gospel is concerned. (*Ensign*, November 1984, p. 84.)

— *Bruce R. McConkie*

See also CONSTANCY, ENDURANCE, FAITHFULNESS, PERSISTENCE, VALIANCY

——— Compassion ———

Let us have compassion upon each other, and let the strong tenderly nurse the weak into strength, and let those who can see guide the blind until they can see the way for themselves. (*JD*, 10:213.)

— *Brigham Young*

Now if we could just learn to live the Golden Rule and let compassion and the kind of love of which our Savior spoke control our actions, we would automatically obey all of the other commandments. (*Ensign*, November 1977, p. 44.)

— *N. Eldon Tanner*

One may have many talents and knowledge but never acquire wisdom because he does not learn to be compassionate with his fellow man.

We will never approach godliness until we learn to love and lift. Indifference to others and their plight denies us life's sweetest moments of joy and service. (*Ensign*, November 1988, p. 17.)

— *Marvin J. Ashton*

When we get emotionally and spiritually involved in helping a person who is in pain, a compassion enters our heart. It hurts, but the process lifts some of the pain from another. We get from the experience a finite look into the Savior's pain as He performed the infinite Atonement. Through the power of the Holy Ghost, a sanctification takes place within our souls and we become more like our Savior. (*Ensign*, November 1990, p. 9.)

— *Glenn L. Pace*

With most of our personal suffering the world goes on about us as if nothing out of the ordinary were happening. However, within the bonds of . . . the Church, hopefully it will be different.

One of our daughters and her family recently suffered a tragedy. Their house burned down, leaving little in the place of all their worldly possessions. The blessing was that . . . all were safe. And they felt great comfort from their ward and neighborhood, who rallied around with food, clothing, and offers of help. Such a blessing it is to belong to "the household of God" (Ephesians 2:19). No one simply turned away or sailed calmly on.

For this family, as for others who experience trials and grief, love and help were extended, along with priesthood blessings and the assurance from the Father of us all that . . . "thine adversity and thine afflictions shall be but a . . . moment" (D&C 121:7).

May we never be indifferent, . . . to the suffering of others. May we be sensitive to those about us who are hurting for whatever reason. (*Ensign*, November 1987, p. 95.)

— *Joy F. Evans*

See also CHARITY, LOVE, SERVICE

Conscience

A God-given conscience will not let us rest until our duty is done. (*CR*, October 1964, p. 96.)

— *Robert L. Simpson*

All men who have moved the world have been men who would stand true to their conscience. (*CR*, October 1908, p. 110.)

— *David O. McKay*

Live so as to have a quiet conscience. (*CR*, April 1954, p. 85.)

— *Richard L. Evans*

Many modern professors of human behavior advocate as a cure to an afflicted conscience that we simply ignore the unwanted messages. They suggest that we change the standard to fit the circumstances so that there is no longer conflict, thus easing the conscience. The followers of the divine Christ cannot subscribe to this evil and perverse philosophy with impunity. For the troubled conscience in conflict with right and wrong, the only permanent help is to change the behavior and follow a repentant path. (*Ensign*, November 1986, p. 10.)

— *James E. Faust*

The ball, or Liahona—which is interpreted to mean a compass—was prepared by the Lord especially to show unto Lehi the course which he should travel in the wilderness. Wouldn't you like to have that kind of a ball—each one of you—so that whenever you were in error it would point the right way . . . ?

That, . . . you all have. The Lord gave to every . . . person, a conscience which tells him every time he starts to go on the wrong path. He is always told if he is listening; but people can, of course, become so used to hearing the messages that they ignore them until finally they do not register anymore.

. . . But if we will remember that everyone of us has the thing that will direct him aright, our ship will not get on the wrong course and suffering will not happen and bows will not break and families will not cry for food—if we listen to the dictates of our own Liahona, which we call the conscience. (*Ensign*, November 1976, p. 79.)

— *Spencer W. Kimball*

The first condition of happiness is a clear conscience. (*Gospel Ideals*, The Improvement Era, Salt Lake City: Deseret Book Co., 1976, p. 498.)

— *David O. McKay*

There is a way by which persons can keep their consciences clear before God and man, and that is to preserve within them the Spirit of God, which is the spirit of revelation to every man and woman. It will reveal to them, even in the simplest of matters, what they shall do, by making suggestions to them. . . . This is the grand privilege of every Latter-day Saint. We know that it is our right to have the manifestations of the Spirit every day of our lives. (*CR*, April 1899, p. 52.)

— *Lorenzo Snow*

See also LIGHT OF CHRIST

Consecration

Another temptation . . . is placing improper emphasis on the obtaining of material possessions. For example, we may build a beautiful, spacious home that is far larger than we need. We may spend far too much to decorate, furnish, and landscape it. And even if we are blessed enough to afford such luxury, we may be misdirecting resources that could be better used to build the kingdom of God or to feed and clothe our needy brothers and sisters. . . . Many of us have made sacred covenants to live the laws of sacrifice and consecration. But when the Lord blesses us with riches and affluence, we may give little thought to how we should use these blessings to help build up His church. (*Ensign,* November 1990, p. 65.)

— *Joseph B. Wirthlin*

Every man who has property and means should so live as to obtain wisdom to know how to use them in the best possible way to promote the welfare of his family and his fellowmen and in building the kingdom of God. (*Ensign,* May 1979, p. 39.)

— *Franklin D. Richards*

I rejoice in the gospel, and I feel that if there is anything of earth that the Lord has given me control of, I would like to put it where he wants it. I want to help forward his work in every possible way, not only by my means and my ability, but by whatever I have; for I want celestial glory. I crave that with all my heart. I feel as though, with God's help, I would make any sacrifice to obtain it, and obey any law, be it ever so high, so far revealed.

— *George Q. Cannon*

Let us go forth and do precisely as we are told; and just as fast as we increase, so will we have to use that spiritual knowledge which is given unto us in a way that will aid in building up the kingdom of God: and it is just so with what little property and means you have got; it must all be upon the altar. You must get rid of this little, mean, nasty spirit, and walk in the light of God. Let your minds expand, and be on hand for every duty that is placed upon you. (*JD,* 5:66.)

— *Lorenzo Snow*

The main purpose of the Doctrine and Covenants, you will find, is to implement the Law of Consecration. . . . This law, the consummation of the laws of obedience and sacrifice, is the threshold of the celestial kingdom, the last and hardest requirement made of men in this life.

— *Hugh Nibley*

One of the last, subtle strongholds of selfishness is the natural feeling that we "own" ourselves. Of course we are free to choose and are personally accountable. Yes, we have individuality. But those who have chosen to "come unto Christ" soon realize that they do not "own" themselves. Instead, they belong to Him. We are to become consecrated along with our gifts, our appointed days, and our very selves. Hence, there is a stark difference between stubbornly "owning" oneself and submissively belonging to God. (*Ensign*, November 1990, p. 16.)

— *Neal A. Maxwell*

Since . . . God owns the earth and all that is in it, any payments made by men to him are the purest token payments, given not because he needs them but as a gesture acknowledging his ownership. (*OAT*, p. 127.)

— *Hugh Nibley*

The law of tithing is a lower law, and was given of God. But the law of tithing does not forbid us obeying a higher law, the law of celestial union in earthly things. And the fact that we do not feel satisfied in simply obeying the law of tithing shows that it is a lesser law. Do you feel justified simply in obeying the law of tithing? Why, then, do you contribute to our temples . . . , and to this object and that, in thousands of ways, after you have properly and justly complied with the law of tithing? In these contributions you are acting just as God designed you should act—by the light of the Holy Ghost that is in you. (*JD*, 20:368.)

— *Lorenzo Snow*

We are not our own, we are bought with a price, we are the Lord's; our time, our talents, our gold and silver, . . . and all there is on this earth that we have in our possession is the Lord's. (*DBY*, p. 176.)

— *Brigham Young*

Zion can only be built up by the law that God revealed for that purpose, which is the law of consecration—not the law of tithing. The law of tithing was instituted because the people could not abide the greater law. If we could live up to the law of consecration, then there would be no necessity for the law of tithing, because it would be swallowed up in the greater law. The law of consecration requires all; the law of tithing only requires one-tenth. (*MS*, 56:386.)

— *Joseph F. Smith*

See also EYE SINGLE, SACRIFICE

Constancy

Progressing through life is like running a marathon. . . . [It] requires a good start and a strong, consistent effort all of the way to the finish. (*Ensign*, November 1989, p. 73.)

— *Joseph B. Wirthlin*

There are no *instant* Christians, but there are *constant* Christians! (*Ensign*, November 1976, p. 14.)

— *Neal A. Maxwell*

To be cheerful when others are in despair, to keep the faith when others falter, to be true even when we feel forsaken—all of these are deeply desired outcomes during the deliberate, divine tutorials which God gives to us—because he loves us. (*Ensign*, November 1982, p. 67.)

— *Neal A. Maxwell*

We see about us constant change. Even the pace of life itself has speeded up. Sometimes it seems that the world is undergoing such throes of change that people are disoriented, not knowing what is of value. Right and wrong, however, are as they always were. The principles of the gospel are unaltered. All of men's evil-speaking and all of men's evil acting cannot alter one jot or tittle of the commandments of God.

The forces of good are clearly and continually under attack. There are times when it seems the world is almost drowning in a flood of filth and degradation. And I want to cry out, "Hold on! Hold on to what is right and true. Therein is safety. Don't let yourself be swept away." (*Ensign*, November 1978, p. 5.)

— *Spencer W. Kimball*

We should send our roots deep into the soil of the gospel. We should grow, flourish, flower, and bear good fruit in abundance despite the evil, temptation, or criticism we might encounter. We should learn to thrive in the heat of adversity.

— *Joseph B. Wirthlin*

When you are in the line of your duty, it is like standing in front of a line of posts, and every post is in line. But step one step aside, and every post looks as though it were not quite in line. The farther you get away from that straight line, the more crooked the posts will appear. It is the straight and narrow path of duty that will lead you and me back to the presence of God. (*CR*, October 1935, p. 5.)

— *Heber J. Grant*

Where the Lord plants us, there we are to stand: when He requires us to exert ourselves for the support of these holy principles, that we are to do; that is all we need to trouble ourselves about; the rest our Heavenly Father will take care of. (*JD*, 5:323.)

— *Lorenzo Snow*

See also DETERMINATION, ENDURANCE, PERSEVERANCE, PERSISTENCE, VALIANCY

——— Contention ———

Another face of pride is contention. Arguments, fights, unrighteous dominion, generation gaps, divorces, spouse abuse, riots, and disturbances all fall into this category of pride.

Contention in our families drives the Spirit of the Lord away. It also drives many of our family members away. Contention ranges from a hostile spoken word to worldwide conflicts. The scriptures tell us that "only by pride cometh contention." (Prov. 13:10.) (*Ensign*, May 1986, p. 6.)

— *Ezra Taft Benson*

As we dread any disease that undermines the health of the body, so should we deplore contention, which is a corroding canker of the spirit. (*Ensign*, May 1989, p. 68.)

— *Russell M. Nelson*

How important it is to know how to disagree without being disagreeable. (*Ensign*, May 1978, p. 8.)

— *Marvin J. Ashton*

I . . . challenge . . . every woman who is a wife to set the tone of that which is spoken in the home. It was said of old that "a soft answer turneth away wrath." (Prov. 15:1.) . . .

There is so much of argument in the homes of the people. It is so destructive. It is so corrosive. It leads only to bitterness, heartbreak, and tears. How well advised we would be, each of us, when there is tension, when there is friction, when there is affliction, to speak with consoling words in the spirit of meekness. (*Ensign*, November 1984, p. 91.)

— *Gordon B. Hinckley*

Let us not become so intense in our zeal to do good by winning arguments or by our pure intention in disputing doctrine that we go beyond good sense and manners, thereby promoting contention, or say and do imprudent things, invoke cynicism, or ridicule with flippancy. In this manner, our good motives become so misdirected that we lose friends and, even more serious, we come under the influence of the devil. (*Ensign*, November 1987, p. 35.)

— *James E. Faust*

Letting off steam always produces more heat than light. (*Ensign*, November 1989, p. 84.)

— *Neal A. Maxwell*

Suggestions for Alleviating Contention
1. Pray to have the love of God in your heart.
2. Learn to control your tongue.
3. Don't allow emotions to take over; rather, reason together.
4. Refuse to get embroiled in the same old patterns of argument and confrontation.
5. Practice speaking in a soft, calm voice. (*Ensign*, May 1978, p. 9.)

— *Marvin J. Ashton*

We thank God for those who are calm instead of contentious. . . .
Contention is a tool of the adversary. Peace is a tool of our Savior. . . .
Contention stops progress. Love brings eternal progression.

Where contention prevails, there can be no united effort in any purposeful direction. . . .

Argument and debate must be supplanted by calm discussion, study, listening, and negotiation. . . .

We should learn to talk together, listen together, pray together, decide together, and avoid all forms of possible contention. We must learn to curb anger. Satan knows that when contention begins, orderly progress is thwarted. (*Ensign*, November 1987, pp. 21-22.)

— *Marvin J. Ashton*

See also ANGER

Conversion

Being converted to the gospel of Jesus Christ means to walk in a newness of life. It means learning to yield to the Spirit and responding to the things that the Lord expects us to respond to. It means caring for and serving others with deep, considerate feelings rather than pursuing the natural desires of our own lives. (*Ensign*, November 1988, p. 21.)

— *Robert E. Sackley*

I was in a meeting not long ago and I asked how many were converts. Probably 50-percent raised their hands. I said, "I advise the rest of you to get converted." . . . In the years that have passed, and they are many, I have continued to be a convert to The Church of Jesus Christ of Latter-day Saints, and for that I thank God. (Fireside Address, Brigham Young University, October 8, 1967.)

— *Hugh B. Brown*

In one who is wholly converted, desire for things inimical to the gospel of Jesus Christ has actually died, and substituted therefore is a love of God with a fixed and controlling determination to keep his commandments. (*IE*, December 1963, p. 1065.)

— *Marion G. Romney*

One is converted when he sees with his eyes what he ought to see; when he hears with his ears what he ought to hear; and when he understands with his heart what he ought to understand—then he is converted. And what he ought to see, hear, and understand is truth—eternal truth—and then practice it. (*New Era*, February 1971, p. 3.)

— *Harold B. Lee*

Somebody recently asked how one could know when he is converted. The answer is simple. He may be assured of it when by the power of the Holy Spirit his soul is healed. When this occurs, he will recognize it by the way he feels, for he will feel as the people of Benjamin felt when they received remission of sins. The record says, " . . . the Spirit of the Lord came upon them, and they were filled with joy, having received a remission of their sins, and having peace of conscience." (Mosiah 4:3.) (*IE*, December 1963, p. 1066.)

— *Marion G. Romney*

The Lord has graciously provided the means for conversion even in the most simple and humble of circumstances. Unfortunately, some of us look beyond the mark and depend too much on buildings, budgets, programs, and activities for conversion rather than on the small and simple things that are central to the gospel. We need not look beyond our own hearts to experience the sweet spiritual feelings promised to those who obey God. That is why a new member in the most humble conditions can experience the gospel as deeply as a lifetime member who was raised in the shadow of Church headquarters. (*Ensign*, May 1990, p. 6.)

— *M. Russell Ballard*

True conversion to the gospel of Jesus Christ produces a compelling influence for good. It makes one more agreeable to live with, more kindly, more tolerant of others; less prone to criticize or find fault; more apt to strive for the better things in life, shunning the base and carnal; seeking always to restrain sordid inclinations, and replacing them with gentle and righteous ones. (*The Challenge*, Alvin R. Dyer, Salt Lake City: Deseret Book Co., 1977, p. 68.)

— *Alvin R. Dyer*

When there throbs in the heart of an individual Latter-day Saint a great and vital testimony of the truth of this work, he will be found doing his duty in the

Church. He will be found in his sacrament meetings. He will be found in his priesthood meetings. He will be found paying his honest tithes and offerings. He will be doing his home teaching. He will be found in attendance at the temple as frequently as his circumstances will permit. He will have within him a great desire to share the gospel with others. He will be found strengthening and lifting his brethren and sisters. It is conversion that makes the difference. (*Ensign*, May 1984, p. 99.)

— *Gordon B. Hinckley*

See also SPIRITUAL REBIRTH, TESTIMONY

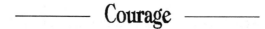

Courage

After we have done all we could do for the cause of truth, and withstood the evil that men have brought upon us, and we have been overwhelmed by their wrongs, it is still our duty to stand. We cannot give up. We must not lie down. Great causes are not won in a single generation. To stand firm in the face of overwhelming opposition, when you have done all you can, is the courage of faith. The courage of faith is the courage of progress. Men who possess that divine quality go on; they are not permitted to stand still if they would. They are not simply the creatures of their own power and wisdom; they are instrumentalities of a higher law and a divine purpose. (*GD*, p. 119.)

— *Joseph F. Smith*

Courage is acting in spite of fear. (*CR*, April 1967, p. 117.)

— *Howard W. Hunter*

Courage, not compromise, brings the smile of God's approval. (*Ensign*, November 1986, p. 41.)

— *Thomas S. Monson*

We need not become paralyzed with fear of Satan's power. He can have no power over us unless we permit it. He is really a coward, and if we stand firm, he will retreat. (*Ensign*, November 1987, p. 35.)

— *James E. Faust*

See also DISCOURAGEMENT, VALIANCY

—— Covenants ——

A covenant is a bond; a solemn agreement. It involves at least two individuals, and, of course, both parties must abide by the conditions of the covenant in order to make it effective and binding. The gospel in its fullness, as it has been restored, is the new and everlasting covenant of God. The new and everlasting covenant embodies all covenants, bonds, and obligations that are required of the Lord for peace in the world, for peace in the hearts of men, and for the salvation and exaltation of man. (*CR*, April 1955, p. 28.)

— *ElRay L. Christiansen*

A covenant is a mutual exchange of enforceable promises. . . .

Gospel covenants are made between God and man. The terms are stipulated by the Lord. Gospel covenants have been given to us by revelation. He has given us those covenants and ordinances that are essential to bring us back into his presence. (*Ensign*, May 1984, pp. 24-25.)

— *A. Theodore Tuttle*

A periodic review of the covenants we have made with the Lord will help us with our priorities and with balance in our lives. This review will help us see where we need to repent and change our lives to ensure that we are worthy of the promises that accompany our covenants and sacred ordinances. Working out our own salvation requires good planning and a deliberate, valiant effort. (*Ensign*, May 1987, p. 14.)

— *M. Russell Ballard*

Several years ago I installed a stake president in England. . . . He had an unusual sense of direction. He was like a mariner with a sextant who took his bearings from the stars. I met with him each time he came to conference and was impressed that he kept himself and his stake on course.

Fortunately for me, when it was time for his release, I was assigned to reorganize the stake. It was then that I discovered what that sextant was and how he adjusted it to check his position and get a bearing for himself and for his members.

He accepted his release, and said, "I was happy to accept the call to serve as stake president, and I am equally happy to accept my release. I did not serve just because I was under *call*. I served because I am under *covenant*. And I can keep my covenants quite as well as a home teacher as I can serving as stake president."

This president understood the word *covenant*. (*Ensign*, May 1987, p. 24.)

— *Boyd K. Packer*

If I do something under covenant, I'm doing it for two reasons. One is to serve the Master—pure obedience—and the other is for myself. It's easy to understand if you've ever experienced being blessed that way. I can't bless myself. I can only lay hands on you and you on me. The Lord never consecrates a world to himself. He gives it to his children, who consecrate it to him, and he accepts that consecration and in turn consecrates it to his Father. That's why doing things under covenant will always purify and sanctify us, rather than cursing us by making us more selfish and more greedy. (*Ensign*, February 1979, pp. 13-14.)

— *R. Quinn Gardner*

If we will keep our covenants, our covenants will keep us spiritually safe. (*Ensign*, May 1987, p. 71.)

— *Neal A. Maxwell*

Keeping our covenants should make a difference in the way we live, the way we act, the way we speak, the way we dress, the way we treat each other. If we "always remember him," we will "always have his Spirit to be with us." (Moro. 4:3.) Then with that Spirit we will be viewed by the world as distinct and different in happy ways. (*Ensign*, November 1989, p. 91.)

— *Joanne B. Doxey*

May the Lord bless us to understand the significance of our temple covenants, and instill these principles in the lives of many others, especially in our children, so they will live the commandments of the Lord. (*Ensign*, November 1987, p. 101.)

— *Ezra Taft Benson*

The sacrament prayers—dictated by the Lord himself—should keep us constantly reminded of the gospel covenants we have entered into with the Lord. (*Ensign*, May 1981, p. 44.)

— *Marion G. Romney*

When a covenant is made between two men or parties, it is usual for each party or man to have a voice in the contract and its various stipulations. This is not the case with a covenant coming to man from the Lord. It is the duty of man to accept all the provisions of such a sacred covenant established for his eternal benefit.

Man does not have the right to change in any sense whatever, or reject in the slightest degree any part of a covenant which the Lord presents for his benefit and salvation. (*Doctrines of Salvation*, Bruce R. McConkie, comp., Salt Lake City: Bookcraft, 1956, 1:154.)

— *Joseph Fielding Smith*

Ordinances and covenants become our credentials for admission into His presence. To worthily receive them is the quest of a lifetime; to keep them thereafter is the challenge of mortality. (*Ensign,* May 1987, p. 24.)

— *Boyd K. Packer*

See also OBEDIENCE, ORDINANCES, TEMPLE ENDOWMENT

——— Creation ———

Heaven was the prototype of this beautiful creation when it came from the hand of the Creator and was pronounced "good." (*JD,* 23:175.)

— *Joseph F. Smith*

How comforting and reassuring it is each day as we behold the wonders of the universe and this beautiful world on which we live. We can see His hand in the matchless order with which the heavenly bodies move and the delicate beauty of the flowers and trees and other growing things, all of them bearing silent witness of His existence. (*Ensign,* November 1982, p. 26.)

— *Rex C. Reeve*

It is impossible for me to describe the beauty of the earth. It is a breathtaking, awe-inspiring, spiritual experience to view the earth from space while traveling at twenty-five times the speed of sound. I could also look into the blackness of the vacuum of space and see billions of stars and galaxies millions of light-years away. The universe is so vast as to be impossible to comprehend. But I did comprehend the hand of God in all things. I felt his presence throughout my seven days in space. I know that God created this earth and the universe. I know that we are his children wherever we live on the earth, without regard to our nationality or the color of our skin. Most important, I know that God lives and is the Creator of us all. (Quoted by M. Russell Ballard, *Ensign,* May 1988, p. 58.)

— *Jake Garn*

It is not so easy to put the spirit of life into things. Man can make the body, but God alone can create the spirit. You have heard, . . . of the scientist who took a grain of wheat into its component parts, and found that it contained so much lime, so much silica, so much of this element and that, and then he took other parts, corresponding thereto, brought them together by means of his chemical skill, and produced a grain of wheat so exactly similar to the other that the natural eye could not detect any difference between them. But there was a difference, a vast difference, and it was demonstrated when he planted the two grains. The one that

God made sprang up, and the one that man made stayed down. Why? Because the man-made grain of wheat had no spirit—only a body, and the body without the spirit is dead. Man cannot breathe into the body of things the breath of life; that is a function and prerogative of Deity. (*CR*, April 1917, p. 42.)

— *Orson F. Whitney*

Men and women in all parts of the world have a desperate need to take time from their demanding routines of everyday life and to quietly observe God's miracles taking place all around them. Think of what would happen if all of us took time to look carefully at the wonders of nature that surround us and devoted ourselves to learning more about this world that God created for us! . . .

Truly, the heavens and the earth and all things in them evidence the handiwork of God, their Creator. (*Ensign*, May 1988, p. 57.)

— *M. Russell Ballard*

The heavens declare the glory of God, and the firmament showeth His handiwork; and a moment's reflection is sufficient to teach every man of common intelligence, that all these are not the mere productions of *chance*, nor could they be supported by any power less than an Almighty hand. (*TPJS*, p. 56.)

— *Joseph Smith*

The special creation of this earth was a vital part of the plan of salvation. It had a particular purpose. It was no afterthought. Neither was it an accident of any proportion, nor a spontaneous development of any kind.

It was the result of deliberate, advance planning and purposeful creation. The Divine Architect devised it. The Almighty Creator made it and assigned to it a particular mission. (*Ensign*, May 1983, p. 63.)

— *Mark E. Petersen*

This earth, after wading through all the corruptions of men, being cursed for his sake and not permitted to shed forth its full lustre and glory, must yet take its proper place in God's creation; be purified from that corruption under which it has groaned for ages and become a fit place for redeemed men, angels, and God to dwell upon.

— *John Taylor*

We are the children of God. He is the Father of our spirits. We have not come from some lower form of life, but God is the Father of our spirits, and we belong to the royal family, because He is our Father. (*CR*, April 1946, p. 125.)

— *George Albert Smith*

See also BEAUTY, ENVIRONMENT

——— Criticism ———

Criticism is a *destroyer* of self-worth and esteem. (*Ensign*, May 1990, p. 83.)
— *H. Burke Peterson*

Disparagement of others should not exist within our ranks, for each of us is struggling to move forward. A helping hand should be extended to lift one another over the shoals along the rocky shore near which our ship must sail. (*Ensign*, May 1989, p. 77.)
— *Royden G. Derrick*

I remember a grandmother who had been widowed early in her life and was moving out of her home. Her granddaughter, about to be married herself, was carefully helping her pack the boxes of dishes and the faded towels. "See that sewing machine over there in the corner?" the grandmother asked. "Your grandfather always left his hat there when he came home in the evening. I used to scold him all the time about it. 'Just put your hat on the hook,' I'd say. 'Why does your hat always have to be on the sewing machine messing everything up?' Then one day he got pneumonia and died, leaving four little children and me to miss him for a lifetime. How many times through the years I've thought, What I'd give to see that hat on the sewing machine, placed there by his own hand!"
Like the grandmother in this story, we often let trifles cloud our vision. . . . We sometimes nag the people we love the best over little inattentions, small faults, mere nothings in the whole scheme of things. Instead of treasuring the all-too-rare moments we have with our dear ones, we pick at faults, imagined or otherwise. (*Ensign*, November 1977, p. 24.)
— *Paul H. Dunn*

Positive criticism is feedback given with the purpose of helping another person to grow and to develop. This is both helpful and needful and is generally accepted and appreciated.
Negative criticism is intended to hurt and often to defame and to destroy. This caustic communication is cruel, and it tends to crush the character of all of those about whom it is directed. King Benjamin urged his people to "not have a mind to injure one another, but to live peaceably." (Mosiah 4:13.) (*Ensign*, November 1988, pp. 23, 24.)
— *L. Lionel Kendrick*

Restrain your tongues in criticism of others. It is so easy to find fault. It is so much nobler to speak constructively. (*Ensign*, November 1981, p. 98.)
Gordon B. Hinckley

The more perfect one becomes, the less he is inclined to speak of the imperfections of others. (*CR*, April 1956 p. 114.)

— *ElRay L. Christiansen*

Your criticism may be worse than the conduct you are trying to correct. (*Ensign*, November 1987, p. 35.)

— *James E. Faust*

See also CONTENTION, JUDGING

Death

Death is a graduation day—and a time of assessment to see what we have become. (*Ensign*, November 1976, p. 46.)

— *Sterling W. Sill*

Death is a mere comma, not an exclamation point! (*Ensign*, May 1983, p. 11.)

— *Neal A. Maxwell*

Death of a loved one is the most severe test that you will ever face, and if you can rise above your griefs and if you will trust in God, then you will be able to surmount any other difficulty with which you may be faced. (*New Era*, August 1971, pp. 4-9.)

— *Harold B. Lee*

Since the creation of man, no fact of life has been so certain as death with the close of mortality. When the last of life's breath is drawn, there is a finality comparable to no other finality. . . . Life is sacred, and death is somber. Life is buoyant and hopeful. Death is solemn and dark. It is awesome in its silence and certainty. . . .

But death is not final. Though it seems so when its dark shroud overshadows mortal life, to those who accept the Christ and His eternal mission there is light and comfort, there is assurance, there is certainty. (*Ensign*, May 1988, pp. 65-66.)

— *Gordon B. Hinckley*

The death of a child is especially poignant, or that of a young person, or of a needed father or mother. We do miss those who die. No matter how many friends or family members one has, the loss of one beloved person is difficult.

One great difference for us is our added knowledge that death is not permanent, that families can be forever. The understanding we have of the reality of the

Resurrection makes the waiting endurable and purposeful. Indeed, "sweet is the peace the gospel brings" (*Hymns*, 1985, no. 14). (*Ensign*, November 1987, p. 93.)
— *Joy F. Evans*

Death, though bitter to observe, is not the end, but is, rather, only another graduation from which we go on to a better life. (*Ensign*, May 1988, p. 65.)
— *Gordon B. Hinckley*

The message of the resurrection is the most comforting, the most glorious ever given to man; for when death takes a loved one from us, we can look into the open grave and say, he is not here; he is alive. (As quoted in *Ensign*, October 1972, p. 33.)
— *David O. McKay*

The more I have to do with genealogical work, the more difficulty I have with that word *dead*. I know of no adequate substitute. I suppose *departed* would suit me as well as any. I have had too many sacred experiences, of the kind of which we never speak lightly, to feel that the word *dead* describes those who have gone beyond the veil. (*Ensign*, May 1987, p. 25.)
— *Boyd K. Packer*

The only difference between the old and young dying is, one lives longer in heaven and eternal light and glory than the other, and is freed a little sooner from this miserable, wicked world. (*HC*, 4:554.)
— *Joseph Smith*

While mortals mourn "a man is dead," angels proclaim "a child is born." (*JD*, 12:180.)
— *Heber C. Kimball*

When men are prepared, they are better off to go hence. . . . The spirits of the just are exalted to a greater and more glorious work; hence they are blessed in their departure to the world of spirits. Enveloped in flaming fire, they are not far from us, and know and understand our thoughts, feeling, and motions, and are often pained therewith. (*TPJS*, p. 326.)
— *Joseph Smith*

We shall turn round and look upon it [the valley of death] and think, when we have crossed it, why this is the greatest advantage of my whole existence, for I have passed from a state of sorrow, grief, mourning, woe, misery, pain, anguish and disappointment into a state of existence where I can enjoy life to the fullest extent as far as that can be done without a body. My spirit is set free, I thirst no more, I want to sleep no more, I hunger no more, I tire no more, I run, I walk, I labor, I go, I come, I do this, I do that, whatever is required of me, nothing like pain or weariness, I am full of life, full of vigor, and I enjoy the presence of my Heavenly Father. (*JD,* 17:142.)

— *Brigham Young*

Where the true Saints are concerned there is no sorrow in death except that which attends a temporary separation from loved ones. Birth and death are both essential steps in the unfolding drama of eternity. (*Ensign,* November 1976, p. 107.)

— *Bruce R. McConkie*

See also PLAN OF SALVATION, RESURRECTION

——— Debt ———

A man cannot be comfortable spiritually who is in bondage financially. (*CR,* October 1904, p. 18.)

— *Richard R. Lyman*

Be prompt in everything, and especially to pay your debts. (*DBY,* p. 303.)

— *Brigham Young*

Get out of debt and keep out of debt, and then you will be financially as well as spiritually free. (*CR,* October 1903, p. 5.)

— *Joseph F. Smith*

I place economy among the first and most important virtues, and debt as the greatest of dangers to be feared. (*CR,* October 1949, p. 100.)

— *Joseph L. Wirthlin*

One of the best ways that I know of to pay my obligations to my brother, my neighbor, or business associate, is for me first to pay my obligations to the Lord. I can pay more of my debts to my neighbors, if I have contracted them, after I have met my honest obligations with the Lord, than I can by neglecting the latter; and you can do the same. . . . First meet your just obligations to God, and then meet your obligations to your fellowmen. (*CR,* April 1903, p. 2.)

— *Joseph F. Smith*

See also FINANCIAL STRENGTH, MONEY

——— Deception ———

There are those who claim authority from some secret ordinations of the past. Even now some claim special revealed authority to lead or to teach the people. Occasionally they use the names of members of the First Presidency or of the Twelve or of the Seventy and imply some special approval of what they teach.

There have been too many names presented, too many sustaining votes taken, too many ordinations and settings apart performed before too many witnesses; there have been too many records kept, too many certificates prepared, and too many pictures published in too many places for any one to be deceived as to who holds proper authority. Claims of special revelation or secret authority from the Lord or from the Brethren are false on the face of them and really utter nonsense!

The Lord never operated that way; these things were not done in a corner (see Acts 26:26); there is light on every official call and every authorized ordination, and it has always been that way. . . .

If someone approaches you individually or invites you to very private meetings, claiming to have some special calling, whatever you do, follow Paul's counsel—"from such turn away." (*Ensign*, May 1985, p. 34.)

— *Boyd K. Packer*

All inspiration does not come from God. (See D&C 46:7.) The evil one has the power to tap into those channels of revelation and send conflicting signals which can mislead and confuse us. There are promptings from evil sources which are so carefully counterfeited as to deceive even the very elect. (See Matt. 24:24.)

Nevertheless, we can learn to discern these spirits. Even with every member having the right to revelation, the Church can be maintained as a house of order. (*Ensign*, November 1989, p. 14.)

— *Boyd K. Packer*

I testify that if a man will maintain his own spirituality—by praying without ceasing, by studying and pondering the scriptures continually, and by obeying his leaders and the light and truth that he presently understands—

He will not be deceived. (*Ensign*, May 1982, p. 27.)

— *Gene R. Cook*

Lips can speak honeyed words while hearts are black and foul. (*IE*, August 1963, p. 658.)

— *Spencer W. Kimball*

The eye, the ear, the hand, all the senses may be deceived, but the Spirit of God cannot be deceived; and when inspired with that Spirit, the whole man is filled with knowledge, he can see with a spiritual eye, and he knows that which is beyond the power of man to controvert. (*JD*, 16:46.)

— *Brigham Young*

The humble followers of the divine Master need not be deceived by the devil if they will be honest and true to their fellow men and women, go to the house of the Lord, receive the sacrament worthily, observe the Sabbath day, pay their tithes and offerings, offer contrite prayers, engage in the Lord's work, and follow those who preside over them. (*Ensign*, November 1987, p. 36.)

— *James E. Faust*

The Savior said that the very elect would be deceived by Lucifer if it were possible. He will use his logic to confuse and his rationalizations to destroy. He will shade meanings, open doors an inch at a time, and lead from purest white through all the shades of gray to the darkest black. (*Ensign*, November 1980, p. 94.)

— *Spencer W. Kimball*

See also DISCERNMENT, FALSE DOCTRINE, SATAN

Decisions

Make certain decisions only once. . . . We can make a single decision about certain things that we will incorporate in our lives and then make them ours—without having to brood and re-decide a hundred times what it is we will do and what we will not do. (*Ensign*, May 1976, p. 46.)

— *Spencer W. Kimball*

When we seek inspiration to help make decisions, the Lord gives gentle promptings. These require us to think, to exercise faith, to work, to struggle at times, and to act. Seldom does the whole answer to a decisively important matter or complex problem come all at once. More often, it comes a piece at a time, without the end in sight. (*Ensign*, November 1989, p. 32.)

— *Richard G. Scott*

You can make every decision in your life correctly if you can learn to follow the guidance of the Holy Spirit. (*CR*, October 1961, p. 60.)

— *Marion G. Romney*

See also CHOICES, INSPIRATION

——— Desires ———

By the power of the Holy Ghost and with the eye of faith, we have glimpsed and we can look forward to the fruit of the gospel. That is the desire of our hearts. And wanting it will give us the power to keep going, with great diligence and patience. (*Ensign*, May 1988, p. 41.)

— *Henry B. Eyring*

Desire is the pilot of the soul. (Address, Brigham Young University, November 1, 1965.)

— *Sterling W. Sill*

If the desire is strong enough, performance is assured. (*Ensign*, May 1979, p. 29.)

— *Hartman Rector, Jr.*

It is not by words, particularly, nor by actions, that men will be judged in the great day of the Lord; but, in connection with words and actions, the sentiments and intentions of the hearts will be taken, and by these will men by judged. (*JD*, 8:10.)

— *Brigham Young*

Our desires, be they spiritual or temporal, should be rooted in a love of the Lord. (*Ensign*, May 1988, p. 4.)

— *Ezra Taft Benson*

Our pleasures depend often more upon the qualities of our desires than upon the gratification [of our desires.]

— *Joseph F. Smith*

You and I will be judged not only for our actions, but also for the desires of our hearts. (*Ensign*, November 1988, p. 15.)

— *Marvin J. Ashton*

"And again, I say unto the poor, ye who have not and yet have sufficient, that ye remain from day to day; I mean all you who deny the beggar, because ye have not; I would that ye say in your hearts that: I give not because I have not, but if I had I would give." (Mos. 4:24.)

It is my feeling that, after all is said and done, it will be the intent of the heart by which we shall be judged. (*Ensign*, May 1985, p. 67.)

— *H. Burke Peterson*

——— Determination ———

I do not believe that any man lives up to his ideals, but if we are striving, if we are working, if we are trying, to the best of our ability, to improve day by day, then we are in the line of our duty. If we are seeking to remedy our own defects, if we are so living that we can ask God for light, for knowledge, for intelligence, and above all for his Spirit, that we may overcome weaknesses, then I can tell you, we are in the straight and narrow path that leads to life eternal. Then we need have no fear. (*CR*, April 1909, p. 111.)

— *Heber J. Grant*

In others we see the "finished" product—but we don't always see the process: the practicing, the learning, the long labor, the giving up of other things, the arduous and seemingly almost endless endeavor. To arrive at what we really want—or at what is really worth wanting—we must deeply desire—a desire that includes a dedicated pursuit of purpose, and not just a "wish is were." Wherever or whatever we want to be, we ought to be on our way—for time will go—and all there is of it is ours.

— *Richard L. Evans*

[All] who are laboring in the improvement cause should be true to themselves, and when they resolve to accomplish something, they should labor cheerfully and with a determination until the promise to themselves has become a reality. ("The Nobility of Labor," reprinted in *Ensign*, March 1972, p. 68.)

— *Heber J. Grant*

[Christ] was perfect and sinless, not because he had to be, but rather because he clearly and determinedly wanted to be. (*Ensign*, November 1976, p. 19.)

— *Howard W. Hunter*

See also COMMITMENT, CONSTANCY, PERSISTENCE, VALIANCY

——— Discernment ———

Every Latter-day Saint should . . . live so near the Lord that they should know his voice and the voice of his shepherds or servants for themselves. (*MS*, 25:123.)

— *George Q. Cannon*

Experience is the best teacher of discernment. (*Ensign*, May 1985, p. 29.)

— *Robert D. Hales*

Spiritual Guides for Teachers of Righteousness

I would like to suggest eight standards against which a person can measure his own teaching of the gospel as well as the doctrines taught by others, to help him unravel illusions and discern the truth.

1. Not only will the teacher teach the truth, but the Spirit of the Lord will accompany the truth *and* the teacher. (See D&C 50:17-22.) . . .
2. The teacher will be in accord with the General Authorities as a group and with his local leaders. . . .
3. The teacher of righteousness will teach from the holy scriptures and will teach that which is taught and confirmed by the Holy Ghost. (See D&C 52:9.) He will not "teach for doctrines the commandments of men." (JS—H 1:19.) . . .
4. The teacher will teach in simplicity, according to the true needs of the people, basic gospel doctrines like faith, repentance, and prayer, which all men can apply. (See D&C 19:31; Al. 26:22.) He will not look beyond the mark by exaggerating, by teaching in the fringe areas, by expanding on the scriptures, or by teaching exotic extremes in any principle, . . .
5. The teacher will speak in the light of day. (Moro. 7:15, 18-19.) He will not speak of secret doctrines, of special elite groups "in the know," or of secret ordinations. (See Jacob 4:13; D&C 42:11.) . . .
6. The teacher will treat all those being taught as like unto himself, not esteeming himself above his brethren. (See Jacob 2:17.) . . .
7. The teacher of righteousness will be anxious to glorify the Lord. He will refuse to assume any glory unto himself. . . .
8. The teacher himself will be in the process of continual personal repentance. (See Moro. 8:26.) He will be an example of meekness, charity, pure motives, dependence on the Lord. He will not just be teaching the doctrine, but also applying it. (See D&C 41:5; 52:15-16.) . . . (*Ensign*, May 1982, pp. 26-27.)

— *Gene R. Cook*

The highest type of discernment is that which perceives in others and uncovers for them their better natures, the good inherent within them. (*CR*, April 1950, p. 162.)

— *Stephen L. Richards*

See also DECEPTION, FALSE DOCTRINE

——— Discipleship ———

Discipline makes the disciple, not knowledge. (Address, Missionary Training Center, Provo, Utah, March 1980.)

— *R. Quinn Gardner*

Emulate the Savior in your life by serving and consecrating, by overcoming temporally so that you might more fully achieve spiritually. (*Ensign*, November 1977, p. 79.)

— *Spencer W. Kimball*

God does not begin by asking us about our ability, but only about our availability, and if we then prove our dependability, he will increase our capability! (*Ensign*, July 1975, p. 7.)

— *Neal A. Maxwell*

It is true that some have actually seen the Savior, but when one consults the dictionary, he learns that there are many other meanings of the word *see*, such as coming to know Him, discerning Him, recognizing Him and His work, perceiving His importance, or coming to understand Him.

Such heavenly enlightenment and blessings are available to each of us. (*Ensign*, November 1990, p. 61.)

— *David B. Haight*

Let us learn our duty. Let us, in the performance of our duty, follow in the footsteps of the Master. As you and I walk the pathway Jesus walked, let us listen for the sound of sandaled feet. Let us reach out for the Carpenter's hand. Then we shall come to know Him. He may come to us as one unknown, without a name, as by the lake side He came to those men who knew Him not. He speaks to us the same words, "Follow thou me" (John 21:22), and sets us to the task which He has to fulfill for our time. He commands, and to those who obey Him, whether they be wise or simple, He will reveal Himself in the toils, the conflicts, the sufferings that they shall pass through in His fellowship; and they shall learn by their own experience who He is. (*Ensign*, May 1986, p. 39.)

— *Thomas S. Monson*

Men captained by Christ will be consumed in Christ. . . .
Their will is swallowed up in His will. (See John 5:30.)
They do always those things that please the Lord. (See John 8:29.)
Not only would they die for the Lord, but more important they want to live for Him.

Enter their homes, and the pictures on their walls, the books on their shelves, the music in the air, their words and acts reveal them as Christians.

They stand as witnesses of God at all times, and in all things, and in all places. (See Mosiah 18:9.)

They have Christ on their minds, as they look unto Him in every thought. (See D&C 6:36.)

They have Christ in their hearts as their affections are placed on Him forever. (See Alma 37:36.) . . .

In Book of Mormon language, they "feast upon the words of Christ" (2 Ne. 32:3), "talk of Christ," "rejoice in Christ," "are made alive in Christ" (2 Ne. 25:25-26), and "glory in [their] Jesus" (see 2 Ne. 33:6).

In short, they lose themselves in the Lord, and find eternal life. (See Luke 17:33.) (*Ensign*, November 1985, pp. 6-7.)

— *Ezra Taft Benson*

That man is greatest and most blessed and joyful whose life most closely approaches the pattern of the Christ. This has nothing to do with earthly wealth, power, or prestige. The only true test of greatness, blessedness, joyfulness is how close a life can come to being like the Master, Jesus Christ. He is the right way, the full truth, and the abundant life. (*Ensign*, December 1988, p. 2.)

— *Ezra Taft Benson*

The Lord has outlined the steps we should follow to draw near unto him: seek through the scriptures, ask through prayer, knock through obedience. (*Ensign*, November 1985, p. 90.)

— *J. Thomas Fyans*

The meaning of complete salvation is that we become like the Savior in word and thought and deed. We can measure our progress toward salvation merely by determining how Christlike we are. If we are not becoming more like Him in our everyday living, we are not advancing toward salvation as we should. . . .

What is the process by which this is done? It is by developing within our own selves the very traits of character which make Him what He is. . . . We need to develop Christlike hearts. We must have a change deep within us. (*Ensign*, November 1982, p. 16.)

— *Mark E. Petersen*

The foundation and guiding light for all our decisions is the gospel of Jesus Christ and His message to the world. The teachings of Christ must be embedded in our desire to choose the right and in our wish to find happiness. His righteous life must be reflected in our own actions. The Lord not only teaches love, He *is* love. He not only preached the importance of faith, repentance, baptism, and the gift of the Holy Ghost, He *lived* accordingly. His life reflected the gospel that He preached. There was and is total harmony between His thoughts and His actions. (*Ensign,* May 1990, p. 25.)

— *Hans B. Ringger*

The Lord expects more of the disciple than ordinary response to need, to opportunity, to commandment. He expects more humility, more hearkening, more repenting, more mercy and forgiving and faith, more service and sacrifice. . . .

Manifest your discipleship in civility, in gentility and tender compassion, in kindness and consideration, in patience and forbearance and refusal to condemn, in forgiveness and mercy. (*Ensign,* November 1976, p. 32.)

— *Marion D. Hanks*

Sincerely striving to follow Jesus will try our faith and our patience— sometimes sorely. (See Mosiah 23:21.) Even with all its travail, however, it is the trek of treks. (*Ensign,* November 1988, p. 31.)

— *Neal A. Maxwell*

To love and care for others is a decision. It is the answer to the Lord's exhortation, "Come follow me." (*Ensign,* May 1990, p. 26.)

— *Hans B. Ringger*

True disciples are those who go beyond simply believing. They act out their belief. (*Ensign,* May 1985, p. 30.)

— *James E. Faust*

We need more men and women of Christ who will always remember Him, who will keep His commandments which He has given them. The greatest yardstick of success is to see how closely you can walk each moment in His steps. (*TETB,* p. 463.)

— *Ezra Taft Benson*

We need not suppose that we can serve two masters. If we try, we may be sure of one thing—that our master will *not* be the Christ, for He will not accept us on those terms. (*Ensign,* May 1982, p. 16.)

— *Mark E. Petersen*

[The Lord's] gospel is a gospel of love—love for God and love for one another. He directs us to follow his example. Our discipleship is measured by how well we comply. (*Ensign,* May 1988, p. 59.)

— *M. Russell Ballard*

See also EYE SINGLE, HEROES, JESUS CHRIST, SAINTS, SERVICE

——— Discouragement ———

At the moment of depression, if you will follow a simple program, you will get out of it. Get on your knees and get the help of God, then get up and go find somebody who needs something that you can help them with. Then it will be a good day. (Address, Brigham Young University, September 27, 1966.)

— Marion D. Hanks

Discouragement is not the absence of adequacy but the absence of courage. (*Ensign*, November 1976, p. 16.)

— Neal A. Maxwell

Do not doubt your abilities. Do not delay your worthy impressions. With God's help, you cannot fail. He will give you the courage to participate in meaningful change and purposeful living. (*Ensign*, May 1983, p. 32.)

— Marvin J. Ashton

If the Apostle Peter had become discouraged at his manifest failure to maintain the position that he had taken to stand by the Savior under all circumstances, he would have lost all; whereas, by repenting and persevering he lost nothing but gained all, leaving us too to profit by his experience. (*JD*, 20:191.)

— Lorenzo Snow

It is easy to get discouraged. It is easy to quit, but you mustn't fail. You remember how Nephi went into an impossible situation and couldn't get the plates. His brothers couldn't. They couldn't buy them. They couldn't bribe them out of the hands of Laban. They couldn't force their way in, and their lives were hanging on a thread. In spite of all that, here comes one boy, unarmed, who walks into a city through a wall that was closed to him, through gates that couldn't be opened, into a garden that was impenetrable, into a vault that was locked, among soldiers that couldn't be bypassed, and comes out with his arms full of records to keep his posterity and others from perishing in unbelief. He did the impossible. But nothing is impossible to the Lord. (Address, Salt Lake Monument Park Stake, September 16, 1958.)

— Spencer W. Kimball

One of Satan's most powerful tools is discouragement. Whisperings of "you can't do it," "you're no good," "it's too late," "what's the use?" or "things are hopeless" are tools of destruction. (*Ensign*, May 1988, p. 63.)

— Marvin J. Ashton

Satan is ever present, trying to destroy our glory and remove our crown. One of his most powerful tools is discouragement. . . . Don't let your discouragement make Satan rejoice. (*Ensign,* May 1984, p. 11.)

— *Marvin J. Ashton*

Satan wants us to feel unequal to our worldly tasks. If we turn to God, He will lead us through our darkest hours. (*Ensign,* November 1980, p. 60.)

— *Marvin J. Ashton*

See also CHALLENGES, COURAGE, ENDURANCE, OPTIMISM, SELF-PITY

——— Dissension ———

Destructive criticism of the officers of the Church or its doctrines is sure to weaken and bring an eventual end to one's testimony if persisted in. (*CR,* October 1944, p. 45.)

— *Spencer W. Kimball*

The adversary has no stronger weapon in his possession for the downfall of our Heavenly Father's children than murmuring. (Address, Brigham Young University, December 9, 1969, p. 7.)

— *Marvin J. Ashton*

The Church is little, if at all, injured by persecution from ignorant, misinformed or malicious enemies. A greater hindrance to its progress comes from faultfinders, shirkers, commandment-breakers, and apostate cliques within its own ecclesiastical and quorum groups. (*Era,* December 1967, p. 35.)

— *David O. McKay*

To desert, defect, give up, resign, surrender, renounce, abdicate, yield, apostatize, withdraw, back out, abandon—each of these words has almost the same meaning. We could find one for every situation in our lives where we might vacillate when facing what is called duty—duty to country, duty to church, duty to family, duty to oneself, duty to God. . . . but the message stands: do not abandon, for the Lord lives. He is our Savior and Redeemer; . . . When we consider that we are, as individuals, looking at two powers, the Church and the world, good and evil, truth and error, how can we avoid being torn apart when we know these powers are moving in opposite directions? We put both feet in the Church and prepare ourselves to be engaged totally and forever. (*Ensign,* November 1981, pp. 52, 53.)

— *Charles Didier*

———— Doctrine ————

I assure you there is, underlying the programs and activities of this church, a depth, and breadth, and height of doctrine that answers the questions of life. (*Ensign*, November 1983, p. 18.)

— *Boyd K. Packer*

The building up of the Church will surely be enhanced if all Church leaders will teach the pure, simple, doctrinal truths that bring the children of God to a spiritual understanding. . . . Every leader should strive to motivate the people to good words by teaching the doctrines of the kingdom. The scriptures are our text, for "in them ye think ye have eternal life." (John 5:39.) From them we glean the truths that will open to us a clear understanding of man's eternal possibilities. (*Ensign*, May 1986, pp. 14-15.)

— *M. Russell Ballard*

True doctrine, understood, changes attitudes and behavior. (*Ensign*, November 1986, p. 17.)

— *Boyd K. Packer*

We are convinced that our members are hungry for the gospel, undiluted, with its abundant truths and insights. . . . There are those who have seemed to forget that the most powerful weapons the Lord has given us against all that is evil are His own declarations, the plain simple doctrines of salvation as found in the scriptures. (Regional Representatives' Seminar, 1 October 1979, p. 6, quoted by Ezra Taft Benson, *Ensign*, May 1986, p. 81.)

— *Harold B. Lee*

You never heard me preach a doctrine but what has a natural system to it, and, when understood, is as easy to comprehend as that two and two equal four. (*JD*, 4:202.)

— *Brigham Young*

[The] doctrines [of Jesus Christ] are like glistening diamonds with many dimensions, displaying their verity and beauty, facet by facet, depending on the faith and preparation of the beholder. (*Ensign*, November 1988, p. 33.)

— *Neal A. Maxwell*

Who is to declare the doctrine of the Church? It is well established by revelation and practice that the current President of the Church and his counselors have the keys to declare the doctrine of the Church. The investiture of this authority comes from revelation. The Presidency are constituted "a quorum . . . to receive the oracles for the whole church." (D&C 124:126.) Of this authority, President Stephen L Richards stated: "They [the Presidency] are the supreme court here on earth in the interpretation of God's law" (*CR*, October 1938, pp. 115-16). (*Ensign*, November 1985, p. 9.)

— *James E. Faust*

See also FALSE DOCTRINE, GOSPEL PRINCIPLES, SCRIPTURES, TRUTH

————— Doctrine and Covenants —————

I consider that the Doctrine and Covenants, our testament, contains a code of the most solemn, the most Godlike proclamation ever made to the human family. (*JD*, 22:146.)

— *Wilford Woodruff*

I wish that I had the ability to impress upon the Latter-day Saints the necessity of searching the commandments of God, the revelations from the Lord, the Creator of heaven and earth, as contained in the Doctrine and Covenants. If we as a people would live up to those wonderful revelations that have come to us, we would be a bright and shining light to all the wide world. (*CR*, October 1927, p. 4.)

— *Heber J. Grant*

The book of Doctrine and Covenants is given for the Latter-day Saints expressly for their everyday walk and actions. (*DBY*, p. 128.)

— *Brigham Young*

If we will put [the revelations in the Doctrine and Covenants] into practice, . . . we will know the truth and there shall be no weapon formed against us that shall prosper. There shall be no false doctrines, no teaching of men that will deceive us. . . . If we will search these revelations then we will be fortified against errors and we will be made strong. (*CR*, October 1931, p. 17.)

— *Joseph Fielding Smith*

The book of Doctrine and Covenants contains some of the most glorious principles ever revealed to the world, some that have been revealed in greater fullness than they were ever revealed before to the world; and this, in fulfillment of the promise of the ancient prophets that in the latter times the Lord would reveal things to the world that had been kept hidden from the foundation thereof; and the Lord has revealed them through the Prophet Joseph Smith. (*CR*, October 1913, p. 9.)

— *Joseph F. Smith*

I consider that the Doctrine and Covenants, our testament, contains . . . the most solemn, the most Godlike proclamations ever made to the human family. (*JD*, 22:146.)

— *Wilford Woodruff*

Section 1 of the Doctrine and Covenants is the Lord's preface to the book. The Doctrine and Covenants is the only book in the world that has a preface written by the Lord Himself. (*Ensign*, November 1986, p. 79.)

— *Ezra Taft Benson*

No man has ever lived upon the face of the earth outside the Redeemer of the world that has given as much revealed truth to the world as the Prophet Joseph Smith. How could anyone read the Doctrine and Covenants, and study it, and think that Joseph Smith wrote it? (*Ensign*, November 1976, p. 66.)

— *LeGrand Richards*

The Book of Mormon and the Doctrine and Covenants are bound together as revelations from Israel's God to gather and prepare His people for the second coming of the Lord. . . .

The Book of Mormon and the Doctrine and Covenants testify of each other. You cannot believe one and not the other. . . .

The Doctrine and Covenants is the binding link between the Book of Mormon and the continuing work of the Restoration through the Prophet Joseph Smith and his successors. . . .

The Book of Mormon brings men to Christ. The Doctrine and Covenants brings men to Christ's kingdom. . . .

The Book of Mormon is the "keystone" of our religion, and the Doctrine and Covenants is the capstone, with continuing latter-day revelation. The lord has placed His stamp of approval on both the keystone and the capstone. (*Ensign*, May 1987, p. 83.)

— *Ezra Taft Benson*

The Doctrine and Covenants is a glorious book of scripture given directly to our generation. It contains the will of the Lord for us in these last days that precede the second coming of Christ. It contains many truths and doctrines not fully revealed in other scripture. Like the Book of Mormon, it will strengthen those who carefully and prayerfully study from its pages. (*Ensign*, November 1986, p. 80.)

— *Ezra Taft Benson*

See also SCRIPTURE STUDY, SCRIPTURES

——— Doubt ———

Darkness cannot be taken into a lighted room any more than doubt can be created in a heart where faith exists. (*CR*, April 1970, p. 47.)

— *Delbert L. Stapley*

Doubt is spiritual poison that stunts eternal growth. (*Ensign*, November 1979, p. 71.)

— *Richard G. Scott*

The Holy Ghost will help us solve crises of faith. The Spirit of the Holy Ghost can be a confirming witness, testifying of heavenly things. Through that Spirit, a strong knowledge distills in one's mind, and one feels all doubt or questions disappear. (*Ensign*, May 1989, p. 33.)

— *James E. Faust*

See also BELIEF, FAITH

——— Drug Abuse ———

Avoid drugs of all kinds, as you would avoid the very gates of hell. (*CR*, October 1967, p. 115.)

— *Hugh B. Brown*

Everyone who partakes of these illicit drugs has on his hands some of the blood of those who have been killed or wounded in the fight to stop the cultivation and exportation of these destructive products. (*Ensign*, November 1989, p. 50.)

— *Gordon B. Hinckley*

I am convinced that [drug] use is an affront to God. He is our Creator. We are made in his image. These remarkable and wonderful bodies are His handiwork.

Does anyone think that he can deliberately injure and impair his body without affronting its Creator? . . .

Can anyone doubt that the taking of these mind- and body-destroying drugs is an act of unholiness? Does anyone think that the Spirit of God can dwell in the temple of the body when that body is defiled by these destructive elements? . . .

Let no member of this church, man or boy, girl or woman, fall prey to this frightful scourge. Some things are right; some are wrong. You know this as well as do I. God grant you the strength to stand free from this enslavement and from the personal holocaust of destruction which inevitably follows. (*Ensign*, November 1989, p. 51.)

— *Gordon B. Hinckley*

If we abuse our body with habit-forming substances, or misuse prescription drugs, we draw curtains which close off the light of spiritual communication.

Narcotic addiction serves the design of the prince of darkness, for it disrupts the channel to the holy spirit of truth. At present, the adversary has an unfair advantage. Addiction has the capacity to disconnect the human will and nullify moral agency. It can rob one of the power to decide. . . .

Teach your children to obey the Word of Wisdom. It is their armor and will protect them from habits which obstruct the channels of personal revelation. (*Ensign*, November 1989, p. 14.)

— *Boyd K. Packer*

Many today, both among the impoverished and the elite, profess to have had all forms of religious experience while they were under the influence of drugs. For the life of me I cannot understand how any sane man or woman could presume that to deaden their natural God-given senses would enable them to have a religious experience. The ecstasy of religious experience comes from a clean soul, and only as we clean up our lives and avoid the downdrags of drugs and other forms of deadening of the human intellect and soul are we going to be successful in what we undertake to do. (Fireside Address, Brigham Young University, October 8, 1967.)

— *Hugh B. Brown*

Some have used as an alibi the fact that drugs are not mentioned in the Word of Wisdom. What a miserable excuse. There is likewise no mention of the hazards of diving into an empty swimming pool or of jumping from an overpass onto the freeway. (*Ensign*, November 1989, p. 50.)

— *Gordon B. Hinckley*

The noble attributes of reason, integrity, and dignity, which distinguish men and women from all other forms of life, are often the first to be attacked by drugs and alcohol. . . . We are free to take drugs or not. But once we choose to use a habit-forming drug, we are bound to the consequences of the choice. Addiction surrenders later freedom to choose. Through chemical means, one can literally become disconnected from his or her own will! (*Ensign*, November 1988, p. 7.)

— *Russell M. Nelson*

We hope our people will eliminate from their lives all kinds of drugs so far as possible. (*Ensign*, November 1974, p. 6.)

— *Spencer W. Kimball*

See also HEALTH, WORD OF WISDOM

Education

If we will not lay to heart the rules of education . . . and continue to advance from one branch of learning to another, we never can be scholars of the first class and become endowed with the science, power, excellency, brightness, and glory of the heavenly hosts, and unless we are educated as they are, we cannot associate with them. (*JD*, 10:226.)

— *Brigham Young*

In our Church we teach that "the glory of God is intelligence." We believe also that the glory of man is likewise intelligence. With this in mind, we are strong advocates of education. (*Ensign*, November 1975, p. 65.)

— *Mark E. Petersen*

The mere stuffing of the mind with a knowledge of facts is not education. The mind must not only possess a knowledge of the truth, but the soul must revere it, cherish it, love it as a priceless gem; and this human life must be guided and shaped by it in order to fulfill its destiny. (*GD*, p. 269.)

— *Joseph F. Smith*

We encourage our people to study and prepare to render service with their minds and with their hands.

Some are inclined toward formal university training, and some are inclined toward practical vocational training. We feel that our people should receive that kind of training which is most consistent with their interests and talents. Whether it be in the professions, the arts, or the vocations; whether it be university or vocational training, we applaud and encourage it. (*CR*, October 1977, p. 5.)

— *Spencer W. Kimball*

What, then, is true education? It is awakening a love for truth, a just sense of duty, opening the eyes of the soul to the great purpose and end of life. It is not teaching the individual to love the good for personal sake, it is to teach him to love the good for the sake of the good itself; to be virtuous in action because he is so in heart; to love and serve God supremely, not from fear, but from delight in His perfect character. (*Instructor*, August 1961, p. 253.)

— *David O. McKay*

When a man is full of the light of eternity, then the eye is not the only medium through which he sees, his ear is not the only medium by which he hears, nor the brain the only means by which he understands. When the whole body is full of the Holy Ghost, he can see behind him with as much ease, without turning his head, as he can see before him. . . . It is not the optic nerve alone that gives the knowledge of surrounding objects to the mind, but it is that which God has placed in man—a system of intelligence that attracts knowledge, as lights cleaves to light, intelligence to intelligence, and truth to truth. It is this which lays in man a proper foundation for all education.

— *Brigham Young*

Why does [the Lord] want us to be a well-educated, well-informed people? So that we can be intellectually as well as spiritually prepared to go out and teach the gospel in all the world, and fit into the various customs and cultures of the peoples of the world. We must become educated in languages, cultures, and customs so that we may make a truly effective approach wherever we go.

— *Mark E. Petersen*

See also KNOWLEDGE, LEARNING, TEACHING, TRUTH

Endurance

By seeing life's experiences through to the end, on our small scale, we can finally say, as Jesus did on the cross, "It is finished." (John 19:30.) We, too, can then have "finished [our] preparations," having done the particular work God has given each of us to do. (D&C 19:19; see also John 17:4.) However, our tiny cup cannot be taken from us either. For this reason have we come unto the world. (See John 12:27.) (*Ensign*, May 1990, p. 35.)

— *Neal A. Maxwell*

Daily, constantly, we choose by our desires, our thoughts, and our actions whether we want to be blessed or cursed, happy or miserable. One of the trials of life is that we do not usually receive immediately the full blessing for righteousness or the full cursing for wickedness. That it will come is certain, but ofttimes there is a waiting period that occurs, . . . During this testing time the righteous must continue to love God, trust in His promises, be patient, and be assured. (*Ensign,* May 1988, p. 6.)

— *Ezra Taft Benson*

Are there times in our lives when we think we have been forsaken by God, or by our fellow men, or by our families? Those are the moments when we have to turn to Christ and endure. (*Ensign,* November 1985, p. 20.)

— *Robert D. Hales*

Enduring, or carrying on, is not just a matter of tolerating circumstances and hanging in there, but of pressing forward. I know that's what most of us find difficult—to endure joyfully. (*Ensign,* November 1989, p. 36.)

— *Marvin J. Ashton*

Greatness is best measured by how well an individual responds to the happenings in life that appear to be totally unfair, unreasonable, and undeserved. Sometimes we are inclined to put up with a situation rather than endure. To endure is to bear up under, to stand firm against, to suffer without yielding, to continue to be, or to exhibit the state or power of lasting. (*Ensign,* November 1984, p. 22.)

— *Marvin J. Ashton*

Knowing a lot is not enough. We have heard moving stories of wandering Arabs who have died of thirst in the night only a few feet from water. He who has not gone all the way cannot drink. (*OAT,* p. 139.)

— *Hugh Nibley*

Let us hold fast to the iron rod. The Savior urged us to put our hand to the plow without looking back. In that spirit we are being asked to have humility and a deep and abiding faith in the Lord and to move forward—trusting in him, refusing to be diverted from our course, either by the *ways* of the world or the *praise* of the world. (*Ensign,* May 1980, p. 81.)

— *Spencer W. Kimball*

Things we cannot solve, we must survive. (*Ensign,* November 1987, p. 18.)

— *Boyd K. Packer*

We are called or chosen to be righteous, holy beings; and let us remember that the time for being chosen because we have been righteous will come after a while, and happy will be that individual who has so lived up to his privileges as to be among the chosen ones. If we wish to attain to this great blessing we must live for it, and not be neglectful in regard to the things of God. We must apply our religion in our daily lives. (*JD*, 12:233.)

— *Daniel H. Wells*

We must endure to the end; we must keep the commandments after baptism; we must work out our salvation with fear and trembling before the Lord; we must so live as to acquire the attributes of godliness and become the kind of people who can enjoy the glory and wonders of the celestial kingdom. (*Ensign*, November 1971, p. 5.)

— *Joseph Fielding Smith*

When in situations of stress we wonder if there is any more in us to give. We can be comforted to know that God, who knows our capacity perfectly, placed us here to succeed. No one was foreordained to fail or to be wicked. When we have been weighed and found wanting, let us remember that we were measured before and we were found equal to our tasks; and, therefore, let us continue, but with a more determined discipleship. When we feel overwhelmed, let us recall the assurance that God will not over-program us; he will not press upon us more than we can bear. (*Speeches of the Year, 1978*, Provo: Brigham Young University Press, 1979, p. 156.)

— *Neal A. Maxwell*

See also ADVERSITY, CHALLENGES, FAITHFULNESS, PERSEVERANCE, VALIANCY

───── Enemies ─────

All we have to do is to go onward and upward, and keep the commandments of our Father and God; and he will confound our enemies. (*JD*, 19:50.)

— *Brigham Young*

It is not our business to fight our enemies. . . . They are our brethren and sisters and God have mercy upon them. That should be our prayer. (*CR*, October 1899, pp. 28-29.)

— *Lorenzo Snow*

The work in which we are unitedly engaged is one of no ordinary kind. The enemies we have to contend against are subtle and well skilled in maneuvering; it behooves us to be on the alert to concentrate our energies, and that the best feelings should exist in our midst; and then, by the help of the Almighty, we shall go on from victory to victory. (*TPJS*, p. 179.)

— *Joseph Smith*

There are enemies to the work of the Lord, as there were enemies to the Son of God. There are those who speak only evil of the Latter-day Saints. There are those—and they abound largely in our midst—who will shut their eyes to every virtue and to every good thing connected with this latter-day work, and will pour out floods of falsehood and misrepresentation against the people of God. I forgive them for this. I leave them in the hands of the just Judge. . . .

I ask mercy for my enemies—those who lie about me and slander me, and who speak all manner of evil against me falsely. In return, I beseech God my heavenly Father to have mercy upon them; for those who do it, not knowing what they are doing, are only misguided, and those who are doing it with their eyes open certainly need, most of all, the mercy, compassion and pity of God. (*GD*, pp. 337, 339.)

— *Joseph F. Smith*

See also OPPOSITION, PERSECUTION, WICKEDNESS

Entertainment

Communities have a responsibility to assist the family in promoting whole-some entertainment. What a community tolerates will become tomorrow's standard for today's youth. (*Ensign*, November 1982, p. 60.)

— *Ezra Taft Benson*

Consider the difference in children who are cuddled and snuggled by parents at bedtime as they listen to stories from good books, and then kneel at their bedside in prayer, as compared to those who go to bed after having viewed a violent television program. (*Ensign*, November 1977, p. 72.)

— *Marvin J. Ashton*

Far too much [television] programming is not wholesome and uplifting but is violent, degrading, and destructive to moral values. This kind of television offends the Spirit of the Lord; therefore, I express a word of warning and caution about such programming. (*Ensign*, May 1989, p. 78.)

— *M. Russell Ballard*

Parents, . . . rigidly monitor the selection of television programs, movies, video-cassettes, music, and other forms of entertainment for your family. . . . Foster in your homes a love of knowledge through uplifting literature; wholesome books; selective movies and television; classical and exemplary popular music; entertainment that uplifts and edifies the spirit and mind. (*Ensign*, November 1984, p. 72.)

— *David B. Haight*

Television is out of control in some homes; the set is rarely turned off, regardless of the programming. Some programs are filthy and evil and are poisoning the minds of God's children today. Likewise, many movies and video-tapes are blatantly corrupt and evil, making their viewers insensible to the promptings of the Spirit. (See Hel. 4:24.) Satan has made the television and film media among his most effective tools to destroy minds and souls. . . .

Despite the concerns I have expressed, many uplifting and inspiring programs are available at little or no cost on television, film, and videotape. I speak for wisdom and balance in accepting the good and rejecting the evil. (*Ensign*, November 1988, p. 36.)

— *Joseph B. Wirthlin*

The Book of Mormon declares that "every thing which inviteth and enticeth to do good, and to love God, and to serve him, is inspired of God." And "whatsoever thing persuadeth men to do evil, and believe not in Christ, and deny him, and serve not God, then ye may know with a perfect knowledge it is of the devil." (Moro. 7:13, 17.)

Let us use that standard to judge what we read, the music we hear, the entertainment we watch, the thoughts we think. Let us be more Christlike. (*Ensign*, May 1986, p. 78.)

— *Ezra Taft Benson*

The desire for profitable gain and popularity in the entertainment world has unmasked in the most appealing way all of the evils of the human race. The most revolting practices and perversions have been masqueraded and even urged upon our inexperienced young people by some seeking to seductively merchandise the evil side of human behavior. Consciences seem seared with a hot iron; spiritual cells seem closed. (*Ensign*, May 1981, p. 8.)

— *James E. Faust*

Whatever you read, listen to, or watch makes an impression on you. . . . Don't be afraid to walk out of a movie, turn off a television set, or change a radio station if what's being presented does not meet your Heavenly Father's standards. In short, if you have any question about whether a particular movie, book, or other form of entertainment is appropriate, don't see it, don't read it, don't participate. (*Ensign*, November 1990, p. 46.)

— *Thomas S. Monson*

Why do people feel guilty about TV? What is wrong with it? Just this: it shuts out all the wonderful things of which the mind is capable, leaving it drugged in a state of thoughtless stupor. (*OAT*, p. 109.)

— *Hugh Nibley*

"A survey of influential television writers and executives in Hollywood has shown that they are far less religious than the general public. . . . While nearly all of the 104 Hollywood professionals interviewed had a religious background, 45 percent now say they have no religion, and of the other 55 percent only 7 percent say they attend a religious service as much as once a month.

"This group has had a major role in shaping the shows whose themes and stars have become staples in our popular culture" (*Los Angeles Times*, 19 Feb. 1983, part 2, page 5).

These are the people who, through the medium of entertainment, are educating us in the direction of their own standards, which in many cases are diametrically opposed to the standards of the gospel. (*Ensign*, November 1983, pp. 45-46.)

— *Gordon B. Hinckley*

Environment

Do you know that the soil can be sanctified by the tithing of its products? The land can be sanctified. There is a relationship between the elements and forces of nature, and the actions of men.

— *James E. Talmage*

Let me love the world as he loves it, to make it beautiful, and glorify the name of my Father in heaven. It does not matter whether I or anybody else owns it, if we only work to beautify and make it glorious, it is all right. (*JD*, 2:308.)

— *Brigham Young*

The soil, the air, the water are all pure and healthy, do not suffer them to become polluted with wickedness. Strive to preserve the elements from becoming contaminated by the filthy wicked conduct and sayings of those who pervert the intelligence God has bestowed upon the human family. (*JD*, 8:79.)

— *Brigham Young*

There is only so much property in the world. There are the elements that belong to this globe, and no more. We do not go to the moon to borrow; neither send to the sun or any of the planets; all our commercial transactions must be confined to this little earth, and its wealth cannot be increased or diminished. And though the improvements in the arts of life which have taken place within the memory of many now living are very wonderful, there is no question that extravagance has more than kept pace with them. (*JD*, 13:304.)

— *Brigham Young*

The greatest acts of the mighty men . . . [have been disastrous.] Before them the earth was a paradise, and behind them a desolate wilderness. (*TPJS*, p. 248, text in brackets by Hugh Nibley in essay, "Brigham Young on the Environment.")

— *Joseph Smith*

We recommend to all people that there be no undue pollution, that the land be taken care of and kept clean to be productive and to be beautiful. (*CR*, April 1975, p. 5.)

— *Spencer W. Kimball*

See also BEAUTY, CREATION

Envy

Am I an envious man? It is my duty to seek for charity, which envieth not. (*MS*, 56:261.)

— *George Q. Cannon*

If we are poor, and have not as much as our neighbor possesses, do not envy him, and do not worry about it. . . . There is an eternity before us, . . . and what we do not gain today we will gain tomorrow, or some other time. (*CR*, April 1901, p. 3.)

— *Lorenzo Snow*

[God] does not want the poor to envy the rich. That is just as great a sin on their part as for the rich to oppress them. They must not envy the rich; they must not look on their brethren and sisters and envy them that which they have. That is sinful, that is wrong, and the man or woman who indulges in it, indulges in a wrong spirit.

— *George Q. Cannon*

—————— Eternal Life ——————

Eternal life is an inherent quality of the creature, and nothing but sin can put a termination to it. (*JD*, 10:22.)

> — *Brigham Young*

Eternal life is the name of the kind of life God lives. It consists, first, of the continuation of the family unit in eternity, and second, of an inheritance of the fullness of the glory of the Father. (*Ensign*, November 1977, p. 34.)

> — *Bruce R. McConkie*

Eternal life is the quality of life which God himself enjoys. The gospel plan, authored by the Father and put into operation by the atonement of Jesus Christ, brings eternal life within the reach of every man. The Lord gave this assurance when he said, " . . . if you keep my commandments and endure to the end you shall have eternal life, . . . " (D&C 14:7). (*CR*, October 1965, p. 20.)

> — *Marion G. Romney*

Immortality comes to us all as a free gift by the grace of God alone, without works of righteousness. Eternal life, however, is the reward for obedience to the laws and ordinances of His gospel. (*Ensign*, November 1989, p. 61.)

> — *David B. Haight*

Just imagine what it's like to be an Olympic champion! Imagine the feeling of having that medal placed around your neck as you stand on the victory platform. It's a feeling I can't describe. But let's realize one more thing. We can all have an experience infinitely greater than that. If we prove worthy, we will return to our Heavenly Father's presence. (*Ensign*, May 1985, p. 40.)

> — *Peter Vidmar*

To obtain life eternal one must so humble and purify himself that he in fact receives through the power of the Holy Ghost a personal witness that God is his Eternal Father and that Jesus Christ is God's Son and our personal Savior as well as the Redeemer of the world. (*Ensign*, November 1981, p. 15.)

> — *Marion G. Romney*

We are called mortal beings because in us are seeds of death, but in reality we are immortal beings, because there is also within us the germ of eternal life. (*JD*, 23:169.)

> — *Joseph F. Smith*

We are called mortal beings because in us are seeds of death, but in reality we are immortal beings, because there is also within us the germ of eternal life. (*JD*, 23:169.)

— *Joseph F. Smith*

We are living for eternity and not merely for the moment. (*GD*, p. 277.)

— *Joseph F. Smith*

Weakness is [our] present condition, glory [our] everlasting birthright. (*OAT*, p. 108.)

— *Hugh Nibley*

[The] distinction between *eternal life*, as received by the faithful, and *immortality*, obtained by both the faithful and unfaithful, is shown in the words of the Lord to Moses: "For behold, this is my work and my glory—to bring to pass the immortality *and* eternal life of man." The conjunction clearly separates the two thoughts. It explains that the Lord is giving to the vast majority of men, those who will not be obedient, the blessing of immortality; and to those who will serve him, the blessing of eternal life. (*The Way to Perfection*, 2d ed., Salt Lake City: Genealogical Society of Utah, 1935, p. 329.)

— *Joseph Fielding Smith*

Our time here is but one phase of an eternal existence. (*Ensign*, November 1989, p. 61.)

— *Dean L. Larsen*

The world we seek offers to its inhabitants unfading glory, immortal renown, and dominions of continued increase, where families grow into nations, nations into generations, generations into worlds, worlds into universes.

— *Lorenzo Snow*

See also EXALTATION, PLAN OF SALVATION

———— **Evil** ————

Every person who desires and strives to be a saint is closely watched by fallen spirits that came here when Lucifer fell, . . . Those spirits are never idle; they are watching every person who wishes to do right and are continually prompting them to do wrong. (*JD*, 7:239.)

— *Brigham Young*

I think we will witness increasing evidence of Satan's power as the kingdom of God grows stronger. I believe Satan's ever-expanding efforts are some proof of the truthfulness of this work. In the future the opposition will be both more subtle and more open. It will be masked in greater sophistication and cunning, but it will also be more blatant. We will need greater spirituality to perceive all the forms of evil and greater strength to resist it. But the disappointments and setbacks to the work of God will be temporary, for the work will go forward (see D&C 65:2). (*Ensign,* November 1987, p. 33.)

— *James E. Faust*

All good things are counterfeited. (*CR,* October 1931, p. 66.)

— *Rulon S. Wells*

It is not good practice to become intrigued by Satan and his mysteries. No good can come from getting close to evil. Like playing with fire, it is too easy to get burned: "The knowledge of sin tempteth to its commission" (Joseph F. Smith). The only safe course is to keep well distanced from him and any of his wicked activities or nefarious practices. The mischief of devil worship, sorcery, casting spells, witchcraft, voodooism, black magic, and all other forms of demonism, should be avoided like the plague. (*Ensign,* November 1987, p. 33.)

— *James E. Faust*

Many of us blame Satan for a great deal for which he is not responsible—poor devil. If Satan and his hosts were bound today and no longer able to work personally upon the earth, evil would go on for a long time, because he has very able representatives in the flesh. (*CR,* October 1914, p. 104.)

— *James E. Talmage*

There are two powers on the earth and in the midst of the inhabitants of the earth—the power of God and the power of the devil. In our history we have had some very peculiar experiences. When God has had a people on the earth, it matters not in what age, Lucifer, the son of the morning, and the millions of fallen spirits that were cast out of heaven have warred against God, against Christ, against the work of God, and against the people of God. And they are not backward in doing it in our day and generation. Whenever the Lord set his hand to perform any work, those powers labored to overthrow it. (*Deseret Evening News,* 17 October 1896.)

— *Wilford Woodruff*

Yes, there is a conspiracy of evil. The source of it all is Satan and his hosts. He has a great power over men to "lead them captive at his will, even as many as would not hearken" to the voice of the Lord. (Moses 4:4.) His evil influence may possible, he would deceive the very elect. As the second coming of the Lord approaches, Satan's work will intensify through numerous insidious deceptions. (*Ensign*, May 1978, p. 33.)

— *Ezra Taft Benson*

We are here in this wicked world, a world shrouded in darkness, principally led, directed, governed, and controlled, from first to last, by the power of our common foe . . . the devil. Lucifer has almost the entire control over the whole earth, rules and governs the children of men, and leads them on to destruction.

— *Brigham Young*

While virtue, by choice, *will not* associate with filth, evil *cannot* tolerate the presence of light. (*CR*, October 1973, p. 24.)

— *Boyd K. Packer*

See also DECEPTION, OPPOSITION, SATAN, WICKEDNESS

——— Exaltation ———

Exaltation is the highest of three degrees of glory in the celestial kingdom. The celestial kingdom is the highest of three kingdoms in the realm of immortality. Exaltation is earned by accepting Jesus Christ and His divine sonship and following His precepts. (*Ensign*, May 1989, p. 76.)

— *Royden G. Derrick*

Here, then, is eternal life—to know the only wise and true God; and you have got to learn how to be Gods yourselves, . . . the same as all gods have done before you, namely, by going from one small degree to another, and from a small capacity to a great one; from grace to grace, from exaltation to exaltation, until you attain to the resurrection of the dead, and are able to dwell in everlasting burnings, and to sit in glory, as do those who set enthroned in everlasting power. . . .

[You] shall be heirs of God and joint heirs with Jesus Christ. What is it? To inherit the same power, the same glory and the same exaltation, until you arrive at the station of a God, and ascend the throne of eternal power, the same as those who have gone before. (*TPJS*, pp. 346-47.)

— *Joseph Smith*

After a person has faith in Christ, repents of his sins, and is baptized for the remission of his sins and receives the Holy Ghost, (by the laying on of hands) . . . then let him continue to humble himself before God, hungering and thirsting after righteousness, and living by every word of God, and the Lord will soon say unto him, Son, thou shalt be exalted. When the Lord has thoroughly proved him, and finds that the man is determined to serve Him at all hazards, then the man will find his calling and election made sure, then it will be his privilege to receive the other Comforter, which the Lord hath promised the Saints, as is recorded in the testimony of St. John. (*TPJS*, p. 150.)

— *Joseph Smith*

As man now is, our God once was; as now God is, so man may be. (*Biography of Lorenzo Snow*, Eliza R. Snow, Salt Lake City: Deseret Book Co., 1884, p. 46.)

— *Lorenzo Snow*

One of the beautiful things to me in the gospel of Jesus Christ is that it brings us all to a common level. It is not necessary for a man to be a president of a stake, or a member of the Quorum of the Twelve, in order to attain a high place in the celestial kingdom. The humblest member of the Church, if he keeps the commandments of God, will obtain an exaltation just as much as any other man. . . . In as far as we observe to keep the laws of the Church we have equal opportunities for exaltation. (*CR*, October 1933, p. 25.)

— *George Albert Smith*

Our individual exaltation depends upon our proving to the Lord that we will at all hazards and under all circumstances faithfully discharge the trust he has placed in us. (*CR*, October 1974, p. 103.)

— *Marion G. Romney*

Then I would exhort you to go on and continue to call upon God until you make your calling and election sure for yourselves, by obtaining this more sure word of prophecy, and wait patiently for the promise until you obtain it. (*HC*, 5:389.)

— *Joseph Smith*

We are becoming exalted today by the acts we perform, by the thoughts we think, and by the words we speak.

— *Hugh W. Pinnock*

See also ETERNAL LIFE, PLAN OF SALVATION, PROGRESSION, RIGHTEOUSNESS, SALVATION

———— Example ————

If our words are not consistent with our actions, they well never be heard above the thunder of our deeds. (*Ensign*, November 1982, p. 43.)

— *H. Burke Peterson*

If we make the claim to hold the truth, it is obligatory upon every Latter-day Saint so to live, that when the people of the world come, in answer to the call, to test the fruit of the tree, they will find it wholesome and good. (*Gospel Ideals*, The Improvement Era, Salt Lake City: Deseret Book Co., 1976, p. 5.)

— *David O. McKay*

Live so that others will want to know Christ because they know you. (Address, Missionary Training Center, Provo, Utah, March 1980.)

— *R. Quinn Gardner*

Of all lessons, the living lesson is the best. Children are surprisingly shrewd in detecting inconsistencies between the instructions and habits of their instructors. Besides, the teacher who seeks to live up to his own advice not only benefits his scholars, but his teachings exert a salutary influence upon himself, and he profits by his own lessons.

— *John Taylor*

One of mother's grandsons said he had watched with wonderment as his tiny daughter paged through her storybook, moistening her first finger to turn the pages as she had seen her daddy do as he read his books. Actually, she was moistening the finger on her left hand and turning the pages with the finger on her right hand! But that only served to emphasize both the power of example and the fact that she, like all the rest of us, is yet learning. (*Ensign*, May 1979, p. 74.)

— *Marion D. Hanks*

Parents and leaders, I am convinced that most youth will respond when they see no faltering, wavering, or weakening on our part. (*Ensign*, November 1990, p. 94.)

— *Ardeth G. Kapp*

The way we live outweighs any words we may profess to follow. (*CR*, October 1974, p. 25.)

— *Delbert L. Stapley*

You cannot lift another soul until you are standing on higher ground than he is. You must be sure if you would rescue the man, that you yourself are setting the example of what you would have him be. You cannot light a fire in another soul unless it is burning in your own soul. (*CR,* April 1973, p. 178.)

— *Harold B. Lee*

You exert a certain degree of influence, and be it ever so small, it affects some person or persons, and for the results of the influence you exert you are held accountable. You, therefore, whether you acknowledge it or not, have assumed an importance before God and man that cannot be overlooked. (*JD,* 18:299.)

— *Lorenzo Snow*

See also CHILD-REARING, LEADERSHIP, TEACHING

Excellence

If a man is to drive the plow, let him do it well; if only to cut bolts, make good ones; if to blow the bellows, keep the iron hot. It is our attention to our daily duties that makes us men. (Quoted by H. Burke Peterson, (*Ensign,* November 1977, p. 87.)

— *Brigham Young*

If another gymnast trains six hours a day, I can't train twelve hours a day. Twelve hours a day in a gym just isn't healthy! But I can train six hours and fifteen minutes a day. This is where giving it that little extra and going the extra mile makes the difference.

In whatever you want to improve upon, whether it be schoolwork, athletics, music, or studying the scriptures, just give a little extra—every day. (*Ensign,* May 1985, pp. 38-39.)

— *Peter Vidmar*

Life is a competition not with others, but with ourselves. We should seek each day to live stronger, better, truer lives; each day to master some weakness of yesterday; each day to repair a mistake; each day to surpass ourselves. (*Ensign,* May 1981, p. 42.)

— *David B. Haight*

We have a moral obligation to exercise our personal capabilities of mind, muscle, and spirit in a way that will return to the Lord, our families, and our society the fruits of our best efforts. To do less is to live our lives unfulfilled. It is to deny ourselves and those dependent upon us opportunity and advantage. We work to earn a living, it is true; but as we toil, let us also remember that we are building a life. Our work determines what that life will be. (*Ensign*, May 1982, p. 77.)

— *J. Richard Clarke*

Striving can be more important than arriving. If you are striving for excellence—if you are trying your best day by day with the wisest use of your time and energy to reach realistic goals—you are a success. (*Ensign*, May 1984, p. 11.)

— *Marvin J. Ashton*

The pursuit of excellence should be the major work of our lives. (*Ensign*, November 1976, p. 29.)

— *William H. Bennett*

We must do more than ask the Lord for excellence; there must be effort before there is excellence.

— *Spencer W. Kimball*

See also GREATNESS, MAGNIFY CALLINGS, PROGRESSION, SELF-MASTERY

——— Experience ———

So many spiritual outcomes require saving truths to be mixed with time, forming the elixir of experience, that sovereign remedy for so many things. (*Ensign*, May 1990, p. 34.)

— *Neal A. Maxwell*

Through the body the experiences of earth are made the possession of the spirit. (*CR*, April 1926, p. 108.)

— *John A. Widtsoe*

What we do with what happens to us is more important than what happens to us. (*Speeches of the Year*, Provo: Brigham Young University, 1975, p. 24.)

— *Marvin J. Ashton*

Eye Single

How should we spend the money and the information that God has given us[?] The answer is simple—for the glory of God. Our eye should be single to the glory of God. That is what we have left the other life for and come into this. We should seek to promote the interests of the Most High God, . . . Inasmuch as we act today and tomorrow, this week and next week, in the interest of God, and have our eye single to His glory, there can be no failure. (*Deseret Weekly*, 48:637.)

— *Lorenzo Snow*

I suppose in the day of judgment the question won't be so much what did you do or where did you serve, but rather, did you serve me with all your heart? did you put me first in your life? . . .

We need to grow in respect and reverence and love of God, the Father, and His Son, Jesus Christ. This can come as we desire and seek. It will not come automatically, but we as individuals, free to choose, must desire and seek and pray and ask. It must grow from the deep feelings in our hearts. (*Ensign*, November 1982, p. 28.)

— *Rex C. Reeve*

If we seek first the kingdom of God, all good things will be added. (*TPJS*, p. 256.)

— *Joseph Smith*

Let us realize that we are not to live to ourselves, but to God; by so doing the greatest blessings will rest upon us both in time and eternity. (*TPJS*, 179.)

— *Joseph Smith*

We must put God in the forefront of everything else in our lives. . . . When we put God first, all other things fall into their proper place or drop out of our lives. (*Ensign*, May 1988, p. 4.)

— *Ezra Taft Benson*

When our eyes are fixed on God's glory, we feel the majesty of His creations and the grand scope of His work on this earth. We feel humble to be participants in His latter-day kingdom. If we pause and quietly reflect on our role an all of this, we will come to know that placing our egos and our vain ambitions on the sacrificial altar is one of the most important offerings we can ever make. (*Ensign*, November 1989, p. 28.)

— *Marlin K. Jensen*

Yielding one's heart to God signals the last stage in our spiritual development. Only then are we beginning to be fully useful to God! (*Ensign*, May 1985, p. 71.)

— *Neal A. Maxwell*

See also CONSECRATION, FAITHFULNESS, LOOK TO GOD, LOVE GOD, TRUST IN GOD, WILLINGNESS

—— Failure ——

If there is one person . . . who is discouraged because of failure . . . to obtain his ideals or some special goal and who is just about ready to give up because of continued loss and discouragement, let him remember . . . that the line between failure and success is so fine that often a single extra effort is all that's needed to bring victory out of apparent defeat.

— *Paul H. Dunn*

Not failure, but low aim is often our greatest sin. (Address, Brigham Young University, October 24, 1967, p. 5.)

— *LeGrand Richards*

We must not fail, individually, for if we fail, we fail twice—for ourselves and for those who could have been helped, if we had done our duty. (*Ensign*, July 1976, p. 75.)

— *Neal A. Maxwell*

See also DISCOURAGEMENT, OPTIMISM, SUCCESS

—— Faith ——

A man must rise by his own efforts and walk by faith. (*Ensign*, May 1983, p. 32.)

— *Marvin J. Ashton*

By faith all things are possible with God and with man. (*MS*, 57:609.)

— *Joseph F. Smith*

Faith is the realization that the Lord can help us with all things. Faith is the ability to do what we are prompted to do, and when we are prompted to do it.

. . . Faith is the ability to live the laws of God that control the blessings we are in need of. . . . Faith is the ability to act "as if." . . . Faith is the ability to be charitable and to believe in people. . . . Faith is the ability to allow ourselves to be guided by the priesthood. (*Ensign*, May 1981, pp. 25-26.)

— *Loren C. Dunn*

Faith can live in neither isolation nor disuse. When you take away works, faith dies. (*Ensign*, March 1971, p. 35.)

— *Sterling W. Sill*

Faith in God develops a personal love for Him which is reciprocated through his blessings to us in times of need. (*Ensign*, November 1982, p. 26.)

— *Rex D. Pinegar*

Faith is a gift of God bestowed as a reward for personal righteousness. It is always given when righteousness is present, and the greater the measure of obedience to God's laws the greater will be the endowment of faith. (*Mormon Doctrine*, Bruce R. McConkie, Salt Lake City: Bookcraft, 1966, p. 264.)

— *Bruce R. McConkie*

Faith is a gift of God; it is the fruitage of righteous living. It does not come to us by our command but is the result of doing the will of our Heavenly Father. (*CR*, October 1913, p. 103.)

— *George Albert Smith*

Faith is nurtured through knowledge of God. It comes from prayer and feasting upon the words of Christ through diligent study of the scriptures. (*Ensign*, May 1988, p. 34.)

— *Russell M. Nelson*

Faith is the first great governing principle which has power, dominion, and authority over all things. (*Lectures on Faith*, N. B. Lundwall, comp., Salt Lake City: N. B. Lundwall, 1.)

— *Joseph Smith*

I heard Joseph Smith say . . . in preaching to the Twelve in Nauvoo, that the Lord would get hold of their heartstrings and wrench them, and that they would have to be tried as Abraham was tried. Well, some of the Twelve could not stand it. They faltered and fell by the way. It was not everybody that could stand what Abraham stood. And Joseph said that if God had known any other way whereby he could have touched Abraham's feelings more acutely and more keenly, he would have done so. It was not only his parental feelings that were touched. There was something else besides. He had the promise that in him and in his seed all the nations of the earth should be blessed; that his seed should be multiplied as the stars of the heaven, and as the sand upon the seashore. He had looked forward through the vista of future ages and seen, by the spirit of revelation, myriads of his people rise up through whom God would convey intelligence, light and salvation to a world. But in being called upon to sacrifice his son it seemed as though all his prospects pertaining to posterity were to come to naught. But he had faith in God, and he fulfilled the thing that was required of him. Yet we cannot conceive of anything that could be more trying and more perplexing than the position in which he was placed. (*JD,* 24:264.)

— *John Taylor*

Faith without works being dead, it is evident that living faith . . . is that which not only believes in God, but acts upon that belief. It is not only the cause of action, but includes both cause and action. Or in other words, it is belief or faith made perfect by works. (*DFTP,* p. 174.)

— *John Taylor*

Great buildings were never constructed on uncertain foundations. Great causes were never brought to success by vacillating leaders. The gospel was never expounded to the convincing of others without certainty. Faith, which is of the very essence of personal conviction, has always been, and always must be, at the root of religious practice and endeavor. (*Ensign,* November 1981, p. 6.)

— *Gordon B. Hinckley*

In all that we do we must cultivate faith. Increased faith is the touchstone to improved church performance. (*Ensign,* May 1984, p. 99.)

— *Gordon B. Hinckley*

In faith, we plant the seed, and soon we see the miracle of the blossoming. Men have often misunderstood and have reversed the process. They would have the harvest before the planting. (*Ensign,* October 1978, p. 74.)

— *Spencer W. Kimball*

It was faith, the simple faith of a fourteen-year-old boy, that took him into the woods that spring morning. It was faith that took him to his knees in pleading for understanding. The marvelous fruit of that faith was a vision glorious and beautiful, of which this great work is but the extended shadow.

It was by faith that he kept himself worthy of the remarkable manifestations which followed in bringing to the earth the keys, the authority, the power to reestablish the church of Jesus Christ in these latter days. It was by faith that this marvelous record of ancient peoples, this testament which we call the Book of

Mormon, was brought forth by the gift and power of God. (*Ensign,* November 1983, p. 52.)

— *Gordon B. Hinckley*

Obedience to the laws and ordinances of the gospel is essential to obtain faith in the Lord Jesus Christ. (*Ensign,* May 1990, p. 39.)

— *Robert D. Hales*

Somewhere between youth and growing up many of us lose that simple faith of a child. Who puts out the light in our eyes and replaces it with the dull film through which most of us see the world and our place in it? Perhaps it is because our lives sometimes hold more frustration than we think we can bear. We get all caught up in the thick of thin things. (*Ensign,* May 1979, p. 8.)

— *Paul H. Dunn*

There is no danger of any man or woman losing his or her faith in this Church if he or she is humble and prayerful and obedient to duty. I have never known of such an individual losing his faith. By doing our duty faith increases until it becomes perfect knowledge. (*CR,* April 1934, p. 131.)

— *Heber J. Grant*

Undaunted faith can stop the mouths of lions, make ineffective the fiery flames, make dry corridors through beds of rivers and seas. Unwavering faith can protect against deluge, terminate drouths, heal the sick, and bring heavenly manifestations. Indomitable faith can help us live the commandments and thereby bring blessings unnumbered with peace, perfection, and exaltation in the kingdom of God. (*CR,* October 1952, p. 51.)

— *Spencer W. Kimball*

We're not going to survive in this world, temporally or spiritually, without increased faith in the Lord—and I don't mean a positive mental attitude—I mean downright solid faith in the Lord Jesus Christ. That is the one thing that gives vitality and power to otherwise rather weak individuals. (*Ensign,* November 1986, p. 73.)

— *A. Theodore Tuttle*

When a man works by faith he works by mental exertion instead of by physical force.

— *Joseph Smith*

What is the difference between just ordinary prayer and a prayer of faith? As we consider that question, the difference is immediately apparent. The difference is *faith*, and what is faith? Of course, there are many definitions of faith, but one definition is "a strong belief plus *action*." It is not perfect knowledge, but real faith lets a man *act* as if he knows it is true when he really doesn't. Therefore, faith in a real sense is power—power to act and perform without actual knowledge. (*Ensign*, January 1974, pp. 106-7.)

— *Hartman Rector, Jr.*

What the world needs today more than anything else is an implicit faith in God, our Father, and in Jesus Christ, His Son, as the Redeemer of the world. (*CR*, April 1935, p. 9.)

— *Heber J. Grant*

When all is said and done, the only real wealth of the Church is the faith of its people. (*Ensign*, November 1985, p. 50.)

— *Gordon B. Hinckley*

Wherever in life great spiritual values await man's appropriation, only faith can appropriate them. (*CR*, October 1969, p. 106.)

— *Hugh B. Brown*

[Sometimes] the Lord . . . responds . . . to prayer by *withholding an answer* when the prayer is offered. Why would He do that?

He is our perfect Father. He loves us beyond our capacity to understand. He knows what is best for us. He sees the end from the beginning. He wants us to act to gain needed experience:

When He answers *yes*, it is to give us confidence.

When He answers *no*, it is to prevent error.

When He *withholds an answer*, it is to have us grow through faith in Him, obedience to His commandments, and a willingness to act on truth. We are expected to assume accountability by acting on a decision that is consistent with his teachings without prior confirmation. We are not to sit passively waiting or to murmur because the Lord has not spoken. We are to act. (*Ensign*, November 1989, p. 32.)

— *Richard G. Scott*

See also BELIEF, KNOWLEDGE

—————— Faithfulness ——————

A worthy daily prayer is one asking for the power to be faithful under all circumstances. (*Ensign*, November 1980, p. 60.)

— *Marvin J. Ashton*

Knowing our religion to be true, we ought to be the most devoted people on the face of the earth to the cause we have embraced. Knowing as we do that the gospel we have received promises all our hearts can wish or desire, if we are faithful, we ought to be very faithful, devoted, energetic, and ambitious in carrying out the designs and wishes of the Lord, as he reveals them from time to time through His servants. We ought not to be lukewarm, or negligent in attending to our duties, but with all our might, strength, and souls we should try to understand the spirit of our calling and nature of the work in which we are engaged. (*JD*, 12:146.)

— *Lorenzo Snow*

Loyalty . . . requires the ability to put away selfishness, greed, ambition and all of the baser qualities of the human mind. You cannot be loyal unless you are willing to surrender. (*CR*, April 1950, p. 180.)

— *J. Reuben Clark, Jr.*

Please don't nag yourself with thoughts of failure. Do not set goals far beyond your capacity to achieve. Simply do what you can do, in the best way you know, and the Lord will accept of your effort. (*Ensign*, November 1989, p. 96.)

— *Gordon B. Hinckley*

There is only one cure for the evils of this world, . . . and that is faith in the Lord Jesus Christ, and . . . obedience to [His] commandments. (*IE*, December 1963, p. 1110.)

— *Mark E. Petersen*

We must not be *nearly* dependable, but *always* dependable. Let us be faithful in the little things, as well as the big ones. (*Ensign*, April 1974, p. 5.)

— *N. Eldon Tanner*

See also CONSTANCY, OBEDIENCE, RIGHTEOUSNESS, VALIANCY

False Doctrine

Among the Latter-day Saints, the preaching of false doctrines disguised as truths of the gospel, may be expected from people of two classes, and practically from these only; they are:

First—The hopelessly ignorant, whose lack of intelligence is due to their indolence and sloth, who make but feeble effort, if indeed any at all, to better themselves by reading and study; those who are afflicted with a dread disease that may develop into an incurable malady—laziness.

Second—The proud and self-vaunting ones, who read by the lamp of their own conceit; who interpret by rules of their own contriving; who have become a law unto themselves, and so pose as the sole judges of their own doings. These are more dangerously ignorant than the first.

Beware of the lazy and the proud; their infection in each case is contagious; better for them and for all when they are compelled to display the yellow flag of warning, that the clean and uninfected may be protected. (*Juvenile Instructor*, 41:178.)

— *Joseph F. Smith*

I would like to warn all of you . . . to be aware of those who cast doubt, the "doubt-sowers" I term them.

They will lead you to the perdition of doubt, the abyss of destruction. They know not the truth. They think they know it. They try to persuade you that you should follow them. But do not follow them in the expressions of doubt, nor accept what they say to you in making known to you those teachings. They are false, I repeat. (Fireside Address, December 11, 1960.)

— *J. Reuben Clark, Jr.*

It is not the *belief* in a false notion that is the problem, it is the *teaching* of it to others. In the Church we have the agency to believe whatever we want to believe about whatever we want to believe. But we are not authorized to teach it to others as truth. (*Ensign*, May 1985, p. 35.)

— *Boyd K. Packer*

Jesus foretold that in our day there would be false Christs and false prophets, meaning that false religions bearing his name would arise, and that false doctrines and false religions bearing his name would arise, and that false doctrines and false teachers would be everywhere. (*Ensign*, May 1977, p. 12.)

— *Bruce R. McConkie*

Tests for Recognizing False Doctrine
1. What do the standard works have to say about it?
2. What do the Latter-day Presidents of the Church say on the subject—particularly the living President?
3. The Holy Ghost—the test of the Spirit. By the Spirit we "may know the truth of all things."

When any teaching or doctrine is in conflict with or contrary to one or all of three requirements, it must be set aside as false.

— *Ezra Taft Benson*

There is an adversary who has his own channels of spiritual communication. He confuses the careless and prompts those who serve him to devise deceptive, counterfeit doctrine, carefully contrived to appear genuine. (*Ensign*, November 1984, p. 66.)

— *Boyd K. Packer*

You needn't worry about being deceived, for the prophet Moroni wrote, "By the power of the Holy Ghost you may know the truth of all things." (Moro. 10:5.) You have the receiving set within you to distinguish false doctrine from true doctrine. Follow the steps outlined by the Savior in the Beatitudes and your receiving set will become finely tuned. Then pray to God in sincerity for an answer and your receiving set will work. This is God's way for us to discern the truth. (*Ensign*, May 1977, p. 58.)

— *Royden G. Derrick*

See also APOSTASY, DECEPTION, DISCERNMENT, DOCTRINE

———— **Family** ————

I can assure you that the greatest responsibility and the greatest joys in life are centered in the family, honorable marriage, and rearing a righteous posterity. (*Ensign*, May 1988, p. 52.)

— *Ezra Taft Benson*

In a profound sense, a family is not alone. When it is consecrated to the Lord's work, his Spirit will always be with them. (*Ensign*, November 1981, p. 85.)

— *Barbara B. Smith*

Let love, peace, and the Spirit of the Lord, kindness, charity, sacrifice for others, abound in your families. Banish harsh words, . . . and let the Spirit of God take possession of your hearts. Teach to your children these things, in spirit and power. . . . Not one child in a hundred would go astray, if the home environment, example and training, were in harmony with . . . the gospel of Christ. (*IE*, December 1904, p. 135.)

— Joseph F. Smith

It is important for us to cultivate in our own family a sense that we belong together eternally, that whatever changes outside our home, there are fundamental aspects of our relationship which will never change. (*CR*, October 1974, p. 161.)

— Spencer W. Kimball

A Formula for Successful Families

This, then, is the tried and proven formula for rearing successful families. I commend the formula to you.

1. Successful families have love and respect for each family member. Family members know they are loved and appreciated.
2. Strong families cultivate an attribute of effective communication. They talk out their problems, make plans together, and cooperate toward common objectives.
3. Fathers and mothers in strong families stay close to their children. They talk.
4. Successful families try to work together toward solutions instead of resorting to criticism and contention. They pray for each other, discuss, and give encouragement.
5. Strong families support each other.
6. Successful families do things together: family projects, work, vacation, recreation, and reunions.
7. Successful parents have found that it is not easy to rear children in an environment polluted with evil. Therefore, they take deliberate steps to provide the best of wholesome influences. Moral principles are taught. Good books are made available and read. Television watching is controlled. Good and uplifting music is provided. But most importantly, the scriptures are read and discussed.
8. In successful Latter-day Saint homes, parents teach their children to understand faith in God, repentance, baptism, and the gift of the Holy Ghost.
9. Family prayer is a consistent practice in [successful] families. (*Ensign*, May 1984, pp. 6-7.)

— Ezra Taft Benson

Love is the very essence of family life. Why is it that the children we love become so frequently the targets of our harsh words? Why is it that these children who love their fathers and mothers sometimes speak as if with daggers that cut to the quick? "There is beauty all around," *only* "when there's love at home." (*Hymns*, 1985, no. 294.) (*Ensign*, May 1989, p. 67.)

— *Gordon B. Hinckley*

Let families put themselves in possession of all the good they can—be in a position to do right, and be continually in the path to exaltation and glory. (*JD*, 5:316.)

— *Lorenzo Snow*

Family Prayer
Family prayer is the greatest deterrent to sin, and hence the most beneficent provider of joy and happiness. The old saying is yet true: "The family that prays together stays together." (*Ensign*, November 1988, p. 69.)

— *Thomas S. Monson*

Family Prayer
I know of no single activity that has more potential for unifying our families and bringing more love and divine direction into our homes than consistent, fervent family prayer. . . .

I appeal with all the fervor of my soul to every family in the Church, every family in the nation, every family in the world, to organize your priorities so that God is first in your lives and to show this by having regular family prayer. (*Ensign*, May 1982, p. 50.)

— *John H. Groberg*

Family Traditions
Build traditions in your families that will bring you together, for they can demonstrate your devotion, love, and support for one another. For each of the members of your family, these events would include blessings of children, baptisms, other priesthood ordinances, graduations, missionary farewells, homecomings, and, of course, marriages. If distance, missions, or ill health prevent personal reunions, write one of those special letters that will be treasured in family histories. Sharing these occasions as a family will help us build a foundation established upon a rock. (*Ensign*, May 1985, p. 23.)

— *L. Tom Perry*

Look around you, and you will soon discover that the greatest joy in this life, and the most comforting hope for the eternities to come, is found in the uniting of eternal family units. Whether we are married or single, we are a part of a family which can be eternal. (*Ensign*, May 1989, p. 14.)

— *L. Tom Perry*

Nothing can surpass the inner security of having one's family committed to God. (*Ensign*, May 1979, p. 61.)

— *James M. Paramore*

Oh! God, let me not lose my own. I can not afford to lose mine, whom God has given to me and whom I am responsible for before the Lord, and who are dependent upon me for guidance, for instruction, for proper influence. . . . The Lord help me to save my own, so far as one can help another. I realize I cannot save anybody, but I can teach them how to be saved. I can set an example before my children how they can be saved, and it is my duty to do that first. I owe it more to them than to anybody else in the world. Then, when I have accomplished the work I should do in my own home circle, let me extend my power for good abroad just as far as I can. (*GD*, p. 462.)

— *Joseph F. Smith*

Only when parents and children work together for the same high objective—to put home and family first—can the home be preserved as God intended. (*Ensign*, May 1990, p. 10.)

— *Rex D. Pinegar*

Our Heavenly Father has organized us into families for the purpose of helping us successfully meet the trials and challenges of life. The home also exists to bless us with the joys and privileges of family associations. Our family is our safety place, our support network, our sanctuary, and our salvation. (*Ensign*, May 1990, p. 9.)

— *Rex D. Pinegar*

The family is far and away the greatest social unit, the best answer to human problems, in the history of mankind. (*Ensign*, May 1987, p. 82.)

— *James E. Faust*

The family is the cornerstone of civilization and no nation will rise above the caliber of its homes. The family is the rock foundation of the Church. We therefore call on the head of every household to strengthen the family. (*Ensign*, May 1984, p. 6.)

— *Ezra Taft Benson*

The Lord organized the whole program in the beginning with a father who procreates, provides, and loves and directs, and a mother who conceives and bears and nurtures and feeds and trains. The lord could have organized it otherwise but chose to have a unit with responsibility and purposeful associations where children train and discipline each other and come to love, honor, and appreciate each other. The family is the great plan of life as conceived and organized by our Father in Heaven. (*Ensign*, May 1984, p. 12.)

— *Spencer W. Kimball*

The time will come when only those who believe deeply and actively in the family will be able to preserve their families in the midst of the gathering evil around us. (*Ensign*, November 1980, p. 4.)

— *Spencer W. Kimball*

The family is one of God's greatest fortresses against the evils of our day. (*Ensign*, May 1986, p. 43.)

— *Ezra Taft Benson*

There is more of a connection than many realize between the order and purpose of the universe and the order and harmony which exists in a happy and good family. (*Ensign*, November 1978, p. 105.)

— *Spencer W. Kimball*

Throughout the ages, evil forces have attacked the family. Why do you suppose Satan is so obsessed with its dissolution? Because it stands for everything he wants and cannot have. He cannot be a husband, a father, or a grandfather. He cannot have posterity now or ever. Satan cannot even keep those he has led away from God. He has no eternal kingdom or inheritance. (*Ensign*, May 1989, p. 60.)

— *J. Richard Clarke*

We come to this earth charged with a mission: to learn to love and serve one another. To best help us accomplish this, God has placed us in families, for he knows that is where we can best learn to overcome selfishness and pride and to sacrifice for others and to make happiness and helpfulness and humility and love the very essence of our character. (*Ensign*, May 1982, p. 50.)

— *John H. Groberg*

See also CHILD-REARING, FATHERHOOD, HOME, MARRIAGE, MOTHERHOOD

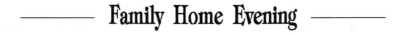

Family Home Evening

If the Saints obey this counsel [to have regular Family Home Evening], we promise that great blessings will result. Love at home and obedience to parents will increase. Faith will be developed in the hearts of the youth of Israel, and they will gain power to combat the evil influences and temptations which beset them. (*Ye are the Light of the World*, Salt Lake City: Deseret Book Co., 1974, p. 82.)

— *Harold B. Lee*

If you will gather your children around you once a week and instruct them in the gospel, they will not go astray. (Quoted by David B. Haight, *CR*, April 1972, p. 132.)

— *Joseph F. Smith*

Regarding our home evenings, an evening home with the family or an evening out to some place of interest with your family only partly solves the need of the home evening. Basically important is the teaching of the children the way of life that is vitally important. Merely going to a show or a party together, or fishing, only half satisfies the real need, but to stay home and teach the children the gospel, the scriptures, and love for each other and love for their parents is most important. (*Ensign*, November 1977, p. 4.)

— *Spencer W. Kimball*

Teach your families in family home evening, teach them to keep the commandments of God, for therein is our safety in these days! (*CR*, April 1973, p. 181.)

— *Harold B. Lee*

The prophets have taught repeatedly that families should teach one another the gospel, preferably in a weekly family home evening. This family practice, if we are not very careful, can slowly drift away from us. We must not lose this special opportunity to "teach one another the doctrine of the kingdom" (D&C 88:77), which will lead families to eternal life. (*Ensign*, November 1988, p. 15.)

— *M. Russell Ballard*

This "Home Evening" should be devoted to prayer, singing hymns, songs, instrumental music, scripture reading, family topics and specific instructions on the principles of the Gospel, and on the ethical problems of life, as well as on the duties and obligations of children to parents, the home, the Church, society and the Nation. (*Ye are the Light of the World*, Salt Lake City: Deseret Book Co., 1974, p. 82.)

— *Harold B. Lee*

———— Fasting ————

Do not go beyond what is wise and prudent in fasting and prayer. The Lord can hear a simple prayer offered in faith, in half a dozen words, and he will recognize fasting that may not continue more than twenty-four hours just as readily and as effectually as he will answer a prayer of a thousand words and fasting for a month. (*CR*, October 1912, pp. 133-34.)

— *Joseph F. Smith*

Failing to fast is a sin. In the 58th chapter of Isaiah, rich promises are made by the Lord to those who fast and assist the needy. Freedom from frustrations, freedom from thralldom, and the blessing of peace are promised. Inspiration and spiritual guidance will come with righteousness and closeness to our Heavenly Father. To omit to do this righteous act of fasting would deprive us of these blessings. (*The Miracle of Forgiveness*, Salt Lake City: Bookcraft, 1969, p. 98.)

— *Spencer W. Kimball*

Fasting brings spiritual blessing. The law of the fast is another test. If we merely go without food to supply welfare funds, it is much of the letter, but in real fasting, for spiritual blessings, come self-mastery and increased spirituality. (*TSWK*, p. 145.)

— *Spencer W. Kimball*

Fasting gives you confidence to know that your spirit can master appetite. . . . and helps to protect against later uncontrolled cravings and gnawing habits. (*Ensign*, November 1985, pp. 30-31.)

— *Russell M. Nelson*

How many here know the origin of [fast] day? Before tithing was paid, the poor were supported by donations. They came to Joseph and wanted help, in Kirtland, and he said there should be a fast day, which was decided upon. It was to be held once a month, as it is now, and all that would have been eaten that day, of flour, or meat, or butter, or fruit, or anything else, was to be carried to the fast meeting and put into the hands of a person selected for the purpose of taking care of it and distributing it among the poor. (*JD*, 12:115.)

— *Brigham Young*

In a sincere fast, we are given an open invitation by the Lord to draw close to him, to open our hearts to him, to feel his Spirit and pure love. It's a time to recommit to obeying his commandments. (*Ensign*, May 1989, p. 41.)

— *Russell C. Taylor*

It is not a burden to refrain from two meals a month and give the value thereof to assist in caring for the poor. It is, rather, a blessing. Not only will physical benefits flow from the observance of this principle, but spiritual values also. Our program of the fast day and the fast offering is so simple and so beautiful that I cannot understand why people everywhere do not take it up. (*Ensign*, November 1985, p. 85.)

— *Gordon B. Hinckley*

The law of the fast benefits both those who fast and those who stand in need. . . . In addition to providing the means for taking care of the poor among us, fasting is a principle of power which helps us to individually achieve righteous purposes in our lives. (*CR*, October 1977.) (*Ensign*, November 1977, p. 82.)

— *Victor L. Brown*

The law of the fast has three great purposes. First, it provides assistance to the needy through the contribution of fast offerings, consisting of the value of meals from which we abstain. Second, a fast is beneficial to us physically. Third, it is to increase humility and spirituality on the part of each individual. (*Ensign*, May 1986, p. 31.)

— *L. Tom Perry*

There is [a] spiritual strength derived from the subjecting of the physical appetite to the will of the individual. "He who reigns within himself and rules passions, desires, and fears is more than king." If there were no other virtues in fasting but gaining strength of character, that alone would be sufficient justification for its universal acceptance. (*CR*, April 1932, p. 65.)

— *David O. McKay*

To discipline ourselves through fasting brings us in tune with God, and fast day provides an occasion to set aside the temporal so that we might enjoy the higher qualities of the spiritual. As we fast on that day we learn and better understand the needs of those who are less fortunate. (*Ensign*, November 1985, p. 74.)

— *Howard W. Hunter*

[By fasting] we are losing nothing financially; we are blessing ourselves physically; and we are gaining greater spiritual power to withstand the temptations that we meet in life; and, best of all, [in giving to the poor] we are practicing the very essence of our religion.

— *David O. McKay*

We wish to remind all the Saints of the blessing that come from observing the regular fast and contributing as generous a fast offering as we can, and as we are in a position to give. Wherever we can, we could give many times the value of the meals from which we abstained. This principle of promise, when lived in the spirit thereof, greatly blesses both giver and receiver. Upon practicing the law of the fast, one finds a personal well-spring of power to overcome self-indulgence and selfishness. (*Ensign*, May 1978, p. 80.)

— *Spencer W. Kimball*

See also OFFERINGS

Fatherhood

A boy needs a father who will correct him when necessary, but beyond that, one who will love him, and like him, and accept him regardless of his performance: a father who may treat a teenager like an adult, but not expect him to act like one. It takes quite a dad to look beyond the actions of boyhood and see the potential of manhood—and even more important, for him to get a glimpse of eternity. (*Ensign*, November 1982, p. 44.)

— *H. Burke Peterson*

A busy father, businessman, and Church leader told me a few years ago that he loved his family so much that he made this commitment: he would give several nights each week and part of every Saturday to them. They were programmed into his schedule. . . . Then , though fatigue, business, Church, and other requirements pressed him every day, he followed this commitment. For him, it was an irrevocable obligation, a looked-for pleasure to be with and nurture his family. He did what every father *could and must do.* (*Ensign*, May 1979, p. 61.)

— *James M. Paramore*

A family should grow up with the comforting assurance that so long as Dad possesses a sound mind and a strong body, he will continue to magnify his talents and develop his career. He will do his best in his preparation and make his performance such that he can provide comfortably for his family unit.

Fathers, be honest in your business dealings. Be loyal to your employers. Determine to be the best in your chosen field of endeavor. Each day make a full effort to be more productive than you were the day before. I challenge you to be leaders in your chosen professions and occupations. (*Ensign*, May 1977, p. 61.)

— *L. Tom Perry*

A father's duty is to make his home a place of happiness and joy. He cannot do this when there is bickering, quarreling, contention, or unrighteous behavior. The powerful effect of righteous fathers in setting an example, disciplining and training, nurturing and loving is vital to the spiritual welfare of his children. . . . Remember your sacred calling as a father in Israel—your most important calling in time and eternity—a calling from which you will never be released. (*Ensign*, November 1987, pp. 50, 51.)

— *Ezra Taft Benson*

As the patriarch in your home, you have a serious responsibility to assume leadership in working with your children. You must help create a home where the Spirit of the Lord can abide. Your place is to give direction to all family life. You should take an active part in establishing family rules and discipline. (*Ensign*, November 1987, p. 50.)

— *Ezra Taft Benson*

Brethren, . . . If you will keep your [children] close to your heart, within the clasp of your arms; if you will make them . . . feel that you love them . . . and keep them near to you, they will not go very far from you, and they will not commit any very great sin. But it is when you turn them out of the home, turn them out of your affection . . . that [is what] drives them from you. . . .

Fathers, if you wish your children to be taught in the principles of the gospel, if you wish them to love the truth and understand it, if you wish them to be obedient to and united with you, love them! and prove . . . that you do love them by your every word and act to[ward] them. (*GD*, pp. 282, 316.)

— *Joseph F. Smith*

A father can do no greater thing for his children than to let them feel that he loves their mother. (Quoted by Gordon B. Hinckley, *CR*, April 1971, p. 82.)

— *David O. McKay*

Father's Blessings

It is the right of every father and his duty as patriarch of his own family to give a father's blessing to his children, and it is our hope that every father will give a sacred blessing to each of his children, especially as they are leaving home to go to school or on missions or to be married, which blessing should then be noted in the individual's private journal. (*Ensign*, November 1977, p. 4.)

— *Spencer W. Kimball*

Fatherhood is leadership—the most important kind of leadership. It has always been so; it always will be so. Father, with the assistance and counsel and encouragement of your eternal companion, you preside in the home. It is not a matter of whether you are the most worthy or best qualified, but it is a matter of law and appointment. You preside at the meal table, at family prayer. You preside at family home evening. And, as guided by the Spirit of the Lord, you see that your children are taught correct principles. It is your place to give direction relating to all of family life. You give fathers' blessings. You take an active part in establishing family rules and discipline. As a leader in your home, you plan and sacrifice to achieve the blessing of a unified and happy family. To do all of this requires that you live a family-centered life. (*Father, Consider Your Ways*, pamphlet, Salt Lake City: The Church of Jesus Christ of Latter-day Saints, 1973, pp. 4-5.)

— *Spencer W. Kimball*

Brethren, we all know fatherhood is not an easy assignment, but it ranks among the most imperative ever given, in time or eternity. We must not pull away from our children. We must keep trying, keep reaching, keep praying, keep listening. We must keep them "within the clasp of our arms." (*Ensign*, May 1983, p. 38.)

— *Jeffrey R. Holland*

Fatherhood is not a matter of station or wealth; it is a matter of desire, diligence, and determination to see one's family exalted in the celestial kingdom. If that prize is lost, nothing else really matters. (*Ensign*, May 1981, p. 36.)

— *Ezra Taft Benson*

Fathers everywhere, consider the gift of love you can give your children when you are worthy and you lay your hands upon their heads to pronounce inspired father's blessings as the family patriarch. They will feel a continuing outpouring of your love, which will keep them close to you and to the Lord. You will not have to "seek them out" later. (*Ensign*, November 1986, p. 27.)

— *Gardner H. Russell*

God established that fathers are to preside in the home. Fathers are to provide, love, teach, and direct. (*Ensign*, May 1984, p. 6.)

— *Ezra Taft Benson*

Heads of families should always take the charge of family worship, and call their family together at a seasonable hour, and not wait for every person to get through with all they may have to say or do. . . . By so doing we shall obtain the favor of our Heavenly Father, and it will have a tendency to teach our children to walk in the way they should go. (*HC*, 4:309.)

— *Joseph Smith*

If you ever secure a union in any family in Zion, . . . you have got to bind that family together in one, and there has got to be the Spirit of the Lord in the head of that family, and he should possess that light and that intelligence which, if carried out in the daily life and conduct of these individuals, will prove the salvation of that family, for he holds their salvation in his hands. (*JD*, 4:243.)

— *Lorenzo Snow*

It becomes the duties of fathers in Israel to wake up and become saviors of men, that they may walk before the Lord in that strength of faith, and that determined energy, that will insure them the inspiration of the Almighty to teach the words of life to their families. (*JD*, 4:158.)

— Lorenzo Snow

No man is too rich or too poor to play with his children. (Quoted by L. Tom Perry, *Ensign*, November 1977, p. 64.)

— Bryant S. Hinckley

The men ought to be more fatherly at home, possessing finer feelings in reference to their wives and children, . . . more kindly and godlike. When I go into a family I do admire to see the head of that family administering to it as a man of God, kind and gently, filled with the Holy Ghost and with the wisdom and understanding of heaven. (*JD*, 12:148.)

— Lorenzo Snow

There is nothing that can take the place of a listening father. His ears and heart must both be in tune. There is no substitute. (*Ensign*, November 1977, p. 87.)

— H. Burke Peterson

We will be effective as fathers only as our lives reflect what we wish to teach. . . . Remember fathers, you are always teaching—for good or for ill. (*Ensign*, November 1977, p. 88.)

— H. Burke Peterson

When the father of a family wishes to make a Zion in his own house, he must take the lead in this good work, which it is impossible for him to do unless he himself possesses the Spirit of Zion. Before he can produce the work of sanctification in his family, he must sanctify himself, and by this means God can help him to sanctify his family. (*JD*, 9:283.)

— Brigham Young

With few exceptions, righteous sons and daughters who have attained eternal blessings are not just physically begotten by their fathers. They are spiritually regenerated by the examples and teachings of their fathers.
Great fathers lead their children to Christ. (*Ensign*, May 1981, p. 36.)

— Ezra Taft Benson

See also CHILD-REARING, FAMILY, MANHOOD, PARENTHOOD, PATRIARCHAL ORDER, PRIESTHOOD

———— Fear ————

Fear is the devil's first and chief tool. (*CR*, April 1950, p. 127.)

— *John A. Widtsoe*

Most fears in the end are fears of oneself and can be conquered by bringing in the Lord as an ally. (*Ensign*, April 1975, p. 16.)

— *Arthur Henry King*

Peace will replace fear in men's hearts when they listen to the counsel of God's prophet and accept and follow the principles of the restored gospel of Jesus Christ. (*CR*, April 1966, p. 140.)

— *Franklin D. Richards*

Preparing ourselves and our families for the challenges of the coming years will require us to replace fear with faith. We must be able to overcome the fear of enemies who oppose and threaten us. The Lord has said, "Fear not, little flock; do good; let earth and hell combine against you, for if ye are built upon my rock, they cannot prevail." (D&C 6:34.) (*Ensign*, 1989, p. 35.)

— *M. Russell Ballard*

So long as men are under the law of God, they have no fears. (*TPJS*, p. 373.)

— *Joseph Smith*

What a tragedy it is in our lives when we are afraid to try, afraid to make decisions, afraid to trust the Lord . . . Fear . . . can be conquered if we will but have faith and move forward with purpose. (*Ensign*, May 1979, p. 69.)

— *Marvin J. Ashton*

When fear becomes unbearable, rebuke it in the name of Christ. All evil and darkness must depart when that holy name is named. Then remember the promises made to you by the priesthood; claim the fulfillment of those promises and cling to the iron rod, the word of God. Offer up a prayer, rebuke your fears in Christ's name, and turn over and go to sleep! (*Relief Society Magazine*, October 1920.)

— *Susa Young Gates*

See also FAITH, TRUST IN GOD, WORRY

—— Fellowshipping ——

Brothers and sisters, we must ever keep in mind that missionary work throughout the world requires great sacrifice, and all of this sacrifice, effort, and exhaustive preparation of missionaries may be in vain if those who accept the gospel do not receive a loving and warm welcome by the members of the Church. . . .

Elder Devere Harris of the First Quorum of the Seventy told me of a recent visit he made to a long-established ward in Utah. He said, "I entered there as a stranger and tried every way that I knew to strike up a conversation, or to say hello, or to be kind, or to be greeted, or to be known. Everyone ignored me; nobody would speak to me—no one!

"Finally, a man recognized me. He said, 'Oh, Elder Harris.' The bishop turned around and said, 'What did you say?' The brother said, 'This is Elder Harris of the Fist Quorum of the Seventy.'

"Well, things changed. It wasn't long before I was asked to sit on the stand; they wondered if I wouldn't like to bear my testimony. After the meeting, many people shook my hand. As I left, I thought, 'What a tragedy! A gray-haired man who was unknown walks into a meeting. Nobody recognizes him, nobody says hello, nobody is kind. Then, because of his Church position, everybody changes and wants to be friendly.'" (*Ensign*, November 1988, pp. 28, 29.)

— *M. Russell Ballard*

I believe we members do not have the option to extend the hand of fellowship only to relatives, close friends, certain Church members, and those selected non-members who express an interest in the Church. Limiting or withholding our fellowship seems to me to be contrary to the gospel of Jesus Christ. The Savior offered the effects of his atoning sacrifice to all mankind. (*Ensign*, November 1988, p. 28.)

— *M. Russell Ballard*

When people are taught and then fellowshipped with warmth and continued interest until they are integrated into the mainstream of the Church, they are "remembered and nourished by the good word of God, to keep them in the right way." (Moro. 6:4.) (*Ensign*, November 1988, p. 84.)

— *David B. Haight*

See also BROTHERHOOD, FRIENDSHIP, REACTIVATION, SHARING THE GOSPEL, UNITY

Financial Strength

Financial strength is realized by keeping God's commandments, by the payment of an honest tithe, by developing habits of work, by being thrifty and living within one's income, as well as by using one's means wisely. (*Ensign*, May 1979, p. 39.)

— *Franklin D. Richards*

If there is any one thing that will bring peace and contentment into the human heart, and into the family, it is to live within our means, and if there is any one thing that is grinding, and discouraging and disheartening it is to have debts and obligations that one cannot meet. (*Relief Society Magazine*, 19:302.)

— *Heber J. Grant*

See also DEBT, MONEY, TITHING

First Vision

Following the First Vision, the Prophet Joseph Smith was persecuted unmercifully for the rest of his life and died as a martyr at thirty-eight years of age; yet he never wavered in declaring what he knew to be the truth. He knew that if he denied what he had said, the persecution would cease; yet he stood firm. (See JS—H 1:25.)

— *Royden G. Derrick*

Once or twice in a thousand years a new door is opened through which all men must enter if they are to gain peace in this life and be inheritors of eternal life in the realms ahead.

Once or twice in a score of generations a new era dawns: the light from the east begins to drive the darkness of the earth from the hearts of men.

Now and then in a peaceful grove, apart from the gaze of men, heaven and earth share a moment of intimacy, and neither are ever thereafter the same. Such a moment occurred on that beautiful, clear morning in the spring of 1820 in a grove of trees near Palmyra, New York.

Man asked and God answered.

Joseph Smith saw the Father and the Son. (*Ensign*, November 1975, p. 18.)

—*Bruce R. McConkie*

The First Vision is the very foundation of this Church, and it is my conviction that each member of this Church performs his duty in direct ratio to his personal testimony and faith in the First Vision. HOW WELL DO YOU BELIEVE THIS STORY? No man having heard the Joseph Smith testimony can, in good conscience, remain on neutral ground.

— *Robert L. Simpson*

The one prayer which impressed me was when Joseph Smith went into the woods to pray. He had read, "If any of you lack wisdom, let him ask of God, that giveth to all men liberally, . . . and it shall be given." If *any of you* lack wisdom, ask of God and you will receive your answer. Pray with faith, not wavering. "For he that wavereth is like a wave of the sea driven with the wind and tossed." (James 1:6.)

God the Father and his Son, Jesus Christ, appeared to Joseph—actually appeared to him—and told him they had a work for him to do. He had talked to God; God heard his prayers; his prayers were answered. (*Ensign*, May 1981, p. 50.)

— *N. Eldon Tanner*

There has been no event more glorious, more controversial, nor more important in the story of Joseph Smith than this vision. It is possibly the most singular event to occur on the earth since the Resurrection. (*Ensign*, May 1984, p. 67.)

— *James E. Faust*

This first revelation, often referred to as "the First Vision," had a far-reaching effect. First, it was a flat contradiction of the assumption that revelation had ceased and that God no longer communicated with man. Second, it reaffirmed the truth that man indeed was created in the image and after the likeness of God. Third, it left no doubt and verified that the Father and the Son are two separate and distinct persons, being one, only in unity of purpose and of will. (*Ensign*, May 1978, p. 38.)

— *Henry D. Taylor*

We testify that this restored gospel was introduced into the world by the marvelous appearance of God the Eternal Father and his Son, the resurrected Lord Jesus Christ. That most glorious manifestation marked the beginning of the fulfillment of the promise of Peter, who prophesied of "the times of restitution of all things, which God hath spoken by the mouth of all his holy prophets since the world began," this in preparation for the coming of the Lord to reign personally upon the earth (Acts 3:21). (From Sesquicentennial Proclamation, *Ensign*, May 1980, p. 52.)

— *The First Presidency*

What resulted from the First Vision, which opened the prophesied dispensation of the fullness of times?

1. The Book of Mormon, another witness for Christ, was received.
2. The priesthood, or authority to perform saving ordinances, was restored, including the sealing powers of the priesthood.
3. The Church of Jesus Christ was again organized on the earth.
4. Revelations came to the Prophet Joseph Smith for the building of the kingdom of God upon the earth, declaring the universal salvation of mankind.
5. Keys, principles, and powers were restored for the carrying out of the three great missions of the Church—the preaching of the gospel, the means of perfecting the Saints, and temples and ordinances therein for the redemption of the living and the dead. (*Ensign*, May 1984, p. 68.)

— *James E. Faust*

What was learned from the First Vision?

1. The existence of God our Father as a personal being, and proof that man was made in the image of God.
2. That Jesus is a personage, separated and distinct from the Father.
3. That Jesus Christ is declared by the Father to be his Son.
4. That Jesus was the conveyer of revelation as taught in the Bible.
5. The promise of James to ask of God for wisdom was fulfilled.
6. The reality of an actual being from an unseen world who tried to destroy Joseph Smith.
7. That there was a falling away from the Church established by Jesus Christ—Joseph was told not to join any of the sects, for they taught the doctrines of men.
8. Joseph Smith became a witness for God and his Son, Jesus Christ. (*Ensign*, May 1984, p. 68.)

— *James E. Faust*

[The First Vision] opened the marvelous work of restoration. It lifted the curtain on the long-promised dispensation of the fulness of times.

For more than a century and a half, enemies, critics, and some would-be scholars have worn out their lives trying to disprove the validity of that vision. Of course they cannot understand it. The things of God are understood by the Spirit of God. There had been nothing of comparable magnitude since the Son of God walked the earth in mortality. Without it as a foundation stone for our faith and organization, we have nothing. With it, we have everything. (*Ensign*, November 1984, p. 53.)

— *Gordon B. Hinckley*

See also JOSEPH SMITH, RESTORATION

———— **Forgiveness** ————

Blessed is he or she who avoids being offended. (*Ensign,* May 1988, p. 62.)
> — *Marvin J. Ashton*

Ever keep in exercise the principle of mercy, and be ready to forgive our brother on the first intimations of repentance, and asking forgiveness; and should we even forgive our brother, or even our enemy, before he repent or ask forgiveness, our Heavenly Father would be equally as merciful unto us. (*HC,* 3:383.)
> — *Joseph Smith*

Forgiveness is in advance of justice, when there is repentance. (Quoted by Heber J. Grant, *CR,* October 1920, p. 7.)
> — *John Taylor*

Forgiveness of others for wrongs—imaginary or real—often does more for the forgiver than for the forgiven. (*Ensign,* November 1983, p. 60.)
> — *H. Burke Peterson*

Has somebody offended you in the Church? You may hold resentment if you wish, say nothing to him, and let resentment canker your soul. If you do, you will be the one who will be injured, not the one who you think has injured you. You will feel better and be far happier to follow the divine injunction: If you have aught against your brother, go to him. (*DFTP,* p. 194.)
> — *David O. McKay*

Latter-day Saints who harbor a feeling of unforgiveness in their souls are more guilty and more censurable than the one who has sinned against them. Go home and dismiss envy and hatred from your hearts; dismiss the feeling of unforgiveness; and cultivate in your souls that spirit of Christ which cried out upon the cross, "Father, forgive them; for they know not what they do." (*CR,* October 1902, pp. 86-87.)
> — *Joseph F. Smith*

I want to speak of a weakness that has thwarted the spiritual growth of men through the ages. It has affected young and old, rich and poor. Its onward roll is not limited by national boundaries, or race, or creed, or social standing. It affects some who appear to be strong. It affects many who are weak. It affects some who appear to be strong. It affects many who are weak. It poisons the spirit of a person to the point that one is hobbled by its debilitating power. It has the power to drag people to the depths of hell; yet, when released from its hold, they may soar to celestial heights. It has kept many from rising to their full potential. It has been a roadblock to the talented and to the favored. It is one of the most effective tools of Satan. We are speaking of an unforgiving and unforgetting spirit. (*Ensign*, November 1983, p. 59.)

— *H. Burke Peterson*

If we always remember our Savior, we will forgive and forget grievances against those who have wronged us. (*Ensign*, May 1988, p. 31.)

— *Dallin H. Oaks*

If we have been wronged or injured, forgiveness means to blot it completely from our minds. To forgive and forget is an ageless counsel. "To be wronged or robbed," said . . . Confucius, "is nothing unless you continue to remember it." (*Ensign*, November 1977, p. 48.)

— *Spencer W. Kimball*

In relationships where there is forgetting and forgiving, joy and trust are nurtured. (*Ensign*, May 1990, p. 84.)

— *H. Burke Peterson*

Those of us who cannot forgive and forget break the bridges over which we must pass. (*Ensign*, May 1979, p. 68.)

— *Marvin J. Ashton*

Too often we make repentance more difficult for each other by our failure to forgive one another. (*Ensign*, May 1982, p. 29.)

— *Ronald E. Poelman*

We ought to say in our hearts, let God judge between me and thee, but as for me I will forgive. (*CR*, October 1902, p. 86.)

— *Joseph F. Smith*

What is our response when we are offended, misunderstood, unfairly or unkindly treated, or sinned against, made an offender for a word, falsely accused, passed over, hurt by those we love, our offerings rejected? Do we resent, become bitter, hold a grudge? Or do we resolve the problem if we can, forgive, and rid ourselves of the burden?

The nature of our response to such situations may well determine the nature and quality of our lives, here and eternally. (*Ensign*, January 1974, p. 20.)

— *Marion D. Hanks*

One of the most Godlike expressions of the human soul is the act of forgiveness. . . . Forgiveness is mortality's mirror image of the mercy of God. (*Ensign*, November 1989, p. 66.)

— *Dallin H. Oaks*

[This] is my counsel to you. If you have festering sores, a grudge, some bitterness, disappointment, or jealousy, get hold of yourself. You may not be able to control things out there with others, but you can control things here, inside of you.

I say, therefore: John, leave it alone. Mary, leave it alone.

. . . Purge and cleanse and soothe your soul and your heart and your mind.

It will then be as though a cloudy, dirty film has been erased from the world around you; and though the problem may remain, the sun will come out. The beam will have been lifted from your eyes. There will come a peace that surpasseth understanding. (*Ensign*, November 1977, pp. 60-61.)

— *Boyd K. Packer*

See also JUDGING, MERCY, REPENTANCE, REVENGE, WEAKNESSES

——— Freedom ———

Among the immediate obligations and duties resting upon members of the Church today, and one of the most urgent and pressing for attention and action of all liberty-loving people, is the preservation of individual liberty. Freedom of choice is more to be treasured than any possession earth can give. (*CR*, April 1950, p. 32.)

— *David O. McKay*

Freedom is based on truth, and no man is completely free as long as any part of his belief is based on error. (*Ensign*, May 1978, p. 14.)

— *N. Eldon Tanner*

Freedom is not a self-preserving gift. It has to be earned, and it has to be protected. (*Speeches of the Year*, Provo: Brigham Young University, 1971, pp. 1-7.)

— *Boyd K. Packer*

Freedom must be continually guarded as something more priceless than life itself. (*CR*, April 1953, p. 40.)

— *Ezra Taft Benson*

Let us remember that it is against the will of God that any one of us should be in bondage—in any way—neither to sin nor to addiction nor to debt. (*Ensign*, May 1981, p. 63.)

— *Mark E. Petersen*

Those men who laid the foundation of this American government and signed the Declaration of Independence were the best spirits the God of heaven could find on the face of the earth. They were choice spirits . . . noble spirits before God. (*CR*, April 1898, p. 89.)

— *Wilford Woodruff*

We are free not because any government has given us our liberty—we are free not because we have received that power and that right from any human source; we are free because God made us free. (*CR*, April 1930, p. 70.)

— *Rulon S. Wells*

We are witnessing today remarkable events occurring throughout the world: evidence of the strength of man's desire for freedom. The history of man's mortal experience would indicate that the desire to be free has spiritual roots.

There is an innate, overwhelming, compelling desire to be free. This desire seems to be more precious than life itself. . . . Most of us will not be called to help nations organize newly found freedoms, but all of us can be involved by making certain the light of freedom burns brightly within our own souls. We can be certain that, by our actions, we are examples of how freedom should be enjoyed. (*Ensign*, May 1990, p. 20.)

— *L. Tom Perry*

We deem it a just principle, . . . that all men are created equal, and that all have the privilege of thinking for themselves upon all matters relative to conscience. (*TPJS*, p. 49.)

— *Joseph Smith*

See also AGENCY, AMERICA, CITIZENSHIP

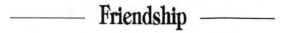

Friendship

We need to reach out and extend our friendship to others regardless of whether they are interested in the gospel or not. We must not be too selective in identifying those we feel are worthy or appreciative of our attention. The spirit of true Christian fellowship must include everyone. . . .

Years ago while walking up main street with his father, Elder LeGrand Richards, then the Presiding Bishop of the Church, tipped his hat and greeted everyone. Upon arrival at their destination, President George F. Richards, then the President of the Council of the Twelve, said, "Son, do you know all those people?" Bishop Richards responded, "Yes, Daddy, I know them all—all but their names." (*Ensign*, November 1988, pp. 29, 30.)

— *M. Russell Ballard*

Cultivate our Savior and Redeemer Jesus Christ as your friend above all. Being his friend will without exception lift your vision and bring you comfort, guidance, peace, and, yes, even the companionship of other true friends. (*Ensign*, May 1990, p. 45.)

— *Malcolm S. Jeppsen*

Do you know how to recognize a true friend? A real friend loves us and protects us.

In recognizing a true friend we must look for two important elements in that friendship:

A true friend makes it easier for us to live the gospel by being around him.

Similarly, a true friend does not make us choose between his way and the Lord's way. (*Ensign*, May 1990, p. 40.)

— *Robert D. Hales*

Friendship is like Brother Turley in his blacksmith shop welding iron to iron; it unites the human family with its happy influence. (*HC*, 5:517.)

— *Joseph Smith*

If my life is of no value to my friends it is of none to myself. (*HC*, 6:549.)

— *Joseph Smith*

Look closely at your friends. Cultivate good friends. They're so valuable. Remember the Savior valued his friends so highly that he would lay down his life for them. (*Ensign*, May 1990, p. 45.)

— *Malcolm S. Jeppsen*

See also BROTHERHOOD, FELLOWSHIPPING, UNITY

Genealogy

Through family history we discover the most beautiful tree in the forest of creation—our family tree. Its numerous roots reach back through history, and its branches extend throughout eternity. Family history is the expansive expression of eternal love. It is born of selflessness. It provides opportunity to secure the family unit forever. (*Ensign*, May 1989, p. 60.)

— *J. Richard Clarke*

The greatest responsibility in this world that God has laid upon us is to seek after our dead. Those Saints who neglect it . . . do it at the peril of their own salvation. (*TPJS*, p. 193.)

— *Joseph Smith*

We cannot be made perfect without our progenitors, neither can they be perfected without us, and they are as much dependent upon us as we are dependent upon them. We can build temples, they cannot; it is not their province to administer in them at present, but it is ours, and we are called upon to do so. They are interested in our welfare, they are our fathers, we are their children; they are laboring there, we here, for our mutual salvation and exaltation in the kingdom of God. (*JD*, 17:374.)

— *John Taylor*

What about you? Have you prayed about your own ancestors' work? Set aside those things that don't really matter in your life. Decide to do something that will have eternal consequences. . . . This is a spiritual work, a monumental effort of cooperation on both sides of the veil where help is given in both directions. It begins with love. Anywhere you are in the world, with prayer, faith, determination, diligence, and some sacrifice, you can make a powerful contribution. Begin now. I promise you that the Lord will help you find a way. And it will make you feel wonderful. (*Ensign*, November 1990, p. 7.)

— *Richard G. Scott*

See also TEMPLE WORK

Gifts of the Spirit

If any of us are imperfect, it is our duty to pray for the gift that will make us perfect. Have I imperfections? I am full of them. What is my duty? To pray to God to give me the gifts that will correct these imperfections. If I am an angry man, it is my duty to pray for charity, which suffereth long and is kind. Am I an envious man? It is my duty to seek for charity, which envieth not. So [it is] with all the gifts of the Gospel. They are intended for this purpose. No man ought to say, "Oh, I cannot help this; it is my nature." He is not justified in it, for the reason that God has promised to give strength to correct these things, and to give gifts that will eradicate them. (*MS*, 56:261.)

— George Q. Cannon

Because faith is wanting, the fruits are. No man since the world was had faith without having something along with it. The ancients quenched the violence of fire, escaped the edge of the sword, women received their dead, etc. By faith the worlds were made. A man who has none of the gifts has no faith; and he deceives himself, if he supposes he has. Faith has been wanting, not only among the heathen, but in professed Christendom also, so that tongues, healings, prophecy, and prophets and apostles, and all the gifts and blessings have been wanting. (*TPJS*, p. 270.)

— Joseph Smith

I rejoice . . . that every Latter-day Saint, every humble son and daughter of God that has embraced the gospel and become a member of the Church of Jesus Christ of Latter-day Saints has received the witness of the Holy Spirit, that the gift of tongues, the gift of prophecy, of healing, and other gifts and blessings, are found in the Church, and are not confined to men that hold responsible positions in the Church. (*CR*, April 1901, p. 64.)

— Heber J. Grant

Let us review some of the less-conspicuous gifts: the gift of asking; the gift of listening; the gift of hearing and using a still, small voice; the gift of being able to weep; the gift of avoiding contention; the gift of being agreeable; the gift of avoiding vain repetition; the gift of seeking that which is righteous; the gift of not passing judgement; the gift of looking to God for guidance; the gift of being a disciple; the gift of caring for others; the gift of being able to ponder; the gift of offering prayer; the gift of bearing a mighty testimony; and the gift of receiving the Holy Ghost.

We must remember that to every man is given a gift by the Spirit of God. It is our right and responsibility to accept our gifts and to share them. God's gifts and powers are available to all of us. (*Ensign*, November 1987, p. 20.)

— Marvin J. Ashton

The gifts of the Gospel are given to strengthen the faith of the believer. (*JD*, 10:24.)

— Brigham Young

The gifts [of the spirit] are not in evidence today, except for one gift, which you notice people ask for—the gift of healing. . . .

As for other gifts—how often do we ask for them? How earnestly do we seek for them? We could have them if we did ask, but we don't. "Well, who denies them?" Anyone who doesn't ask for them. (*OAT*, p. 5.)

— *Hugh Nibley*

The physical characteristics that we inherit from our parents are obvious. The spiritual characteristics we inherit from our heavenly parents have to be developed. You have been born with all the godlike gifts that Christ has. They are within you, but you have to choose to cultivate and develop them. Spiritual growth doesn't just happen without our best efforts. (*Ensign*, November 1989, pp. 87-88.)

— *Elaine L. Jack*

The spiritual gifts are the signs which follow those that believe; they are the miracles and healings performed in the name of the Lord Jesus; they include marvelous outpourings of truth and light and revelation from God in heaven to man on earth. (*Ensign*, November 1977, p. 33.)

— *Bruce R. McConkie*

See also HOLY GHOST, SPIRIT OF THE LORD

See also TALENTS

Giving

Mother taught me that we have an obligation to give, that others don't owe us a living, and that more joy comes from giving than receiving.

As a child, I desired a birthday party. I invited all of my friends to come—it wasn't even near my birthday—and I carefully instructed them to each bring me a dime. When Mother heard of my trick, she immediately gave me a scolding, sat me down, and carefully explained why what I did was not right. Then she went with me to each of my friends so that I could apologize. It was an embarrassing lesson, but one I have never forgotten. (*Ensign*, November 1987, p. 95.)

— *Barbara W. Winder*

Never did the Savior give in expectation. I know of no case in his life in which there was an exchange. He was always the giver, seldom the recipient. Never did he give shoes, hose, or a vehicle; never did he give perfume, a shirt, or a fur wrap. His gifts were of such a nature that the recipient could hardly exchange or return the value. His gifts were rare ones: eyes to the blind, ears to the deaf, and legs to the lame; cleanliness to the unclean, wholeness to the infirm, and breath to the lifeless. His gifts were opportunity to the downtrodden, freedom to the oppressed, light in the darkness, forgiveness to the repentant, hope to the despairing. His friends gave him shelter, food, and love. He gave them of himself, his love, his service, his life. The wise men brought him gold and frankincense. He gave them and all their fellow mortals resurrection, salvation, and eternal life. We should strive to give as he gave. To give of oneself is a holy gift. (*The Wondrous Gift*, Salt Lake City: Deseret Book Co., 1978, p. 2.)

— *Spencer W. Kimball*

Only by voluntarily giving, out of an abundant love for his neighbor, can one develop that charity characterized by Mormon as the "pure love of Christ." (Moro. 7:47.) (*Ensign*, November 1981, pp. 92-93.)

— *Marion G. Romney*

Thanksgiving to be truly thanksgiving, is first thanks, then giving. (Address, Brigham Young University, November 23, 1965.)

— *John H. Vandenberg*

There is an interdependence between those who have and those who have not. The process of giving exalts the poor and humbles the rich. In the process, both are sanctified. (*Ensign*, November 1982, p. 93.)

— *Marion G. Romney*

There is an interdependence between those who have and those who have not. The process of giving exalts the poor and humbles the rich. In the process, both are sanctified. The poor, released from the bondage and limitations of poverty, are enabled as free men to rise to their full potential, both temporally and spiritually. The rich, by imparting of their surplus, participate in the eternal principle of giving. Once a person has been made whole or self-reliant, he reaches out to aid others, and the cycle repeats itself. (*Ensign*, November 1982, p. 93.)

— *Marion G. Romney*

See also CHARITY, SERVICE

——— Goals ———

As you define your goals and plan for their achievement, ponder the thought: The past is behind—learn from it; the future is ahead—prepare for it; the present is here—live in it. (*Ensign*, May 1989, p. 43.)

— *Thomas S. Monson*

A prerequisite for "doing" is goal setting. Actions are preceded by thoughts and planning. All of us must take charge of our own lives. We must evaluate the choices that are open to us, and then we must act positively on our own decision. An old proverb states, "A journey of one thousand miles begins with the first step." (*Ensign*, May 1983, p. 31.)

— *Marvin J. Ashton*

Do not make small goals because they do not have the magic to stir men's souls.

— *Spencer W. Kimball*

Every landing field is also a runway for a new take-off. We must resist the temptation to abide upon arriving at an intermediate goal. There can be no loitering on life's airfield. One must get on the plane or be left behind. (Address, Brigham Young University, May 24, 1962, p. 3.)

— *Hugh B. Brown*

Goals are good. Laboring with a distant aim sets the mind in a higher key and puts us at our best. (Regional Representatives' Seminar, April 3, 1974.)

— *Spencer W. Kimball*

To reach a goal you have never before attained, you must do things you have never before done. (*Ensign*, May 1990, p. 76.)

— *Richard G. Scott*

Set . . . goals that you can reach. Set goals that are well balanced—not too many not too few, and not too high not too low. Write down your attainable goals and work on them according to their importance. Pray for divine guidance in your goal setting. (*Ensign*, May 1987, p. 14.)

— *M. Russell Ballard*

The scriptural advice, "Do not run faster or labor more than you have strength" suggests paced progress, much as God used seven creative periods in preparing man and this earth. There is a difference, therefore, between being "anxiously engaged" and being overanxious and thus underengaged. (*Ensign*, November 1976, pp. 10-11.)

— *Neal A. Maxwell*

We must have goals to make progress, and it's encouraged by keeping records. Progress is easier when it is timed, checked, and measured. Goals should always be made to a point that will make us reach and strain. The key goals we could have are goals to become perfect in certain elements in the perfection of our character, the things we carry with us after this life. (Regional Representatives' Seminar, April 3, 1974.)

— *Spencer W. Kimball*

When we set goals, we are in command. Clearly understood goals bring our lives into focus just as a magnifying glass focuses a beam of light into a burning point. Without goals our efforts may be scattered and unproductive. (*TETB*, p. 384.)

— *Ezra Taft Benson*

Goals are stars to steer by, not sticks to beat yourself with.

— *Barbara B. Smith*

You should look ahead now and decide what you want to do with your lives. Fix clearly in your mind what you want to be one year from now, five years, ten years, and beyond. . . . Write your goals and review them regularly. Keep them before you constantly, record your progress, and revise them as circumstances dictate. Your ultimate goal should be eternal life—the kind of life God lives, the greatest of all the gifts of God. (*Ensign*, November 1989, p. 73.)

— *Joseph B. Wirthlin*

See also BALANCE, PRIORITIES, PROGRESSION

God

God himself was once as we are now, and is an exalted man, and sits enthroned in yonder heavens! That is the great secret. If the veil were rent today, and the great God who holds this world in its orbit, and who upholds all worlds and all things by his power, was to make himself visible—I say, if you were to see him today, you would see him like a man in form—like yourselves in all the person, image, and very form as a man. (*HC*, 6:305.)

— *Joseph Smith*

If any of us could now see the God we are striving to serve—if we could see our Father who dwells in the heavens, we should learn that we are as well acquainted with him as we are with our earthly father; and he would be as familiar to us in the expression of his countenance and we should be ready to embrace him and fall upon his neck and kiss him, if we had the privilege. And still we, unless the vision of the Spirit is opened to us, know nothing about God. You know much about him, if you did but realize it. And there is no other one item that will so astound you, when your eyes are opened in eternity, as to think that you were so stupid in the body. (*JD*, 8:30.)

— *Brigham Young*

It is the first principle of the gospel to know for a certainty the character of God, and to know that we may converse with Him as one man converses with another. (*TPJS*, p. 345.)

— *Joseph Smith*

More mortals die in ignorance of God's true character than die in actual defiance of Him. (*Ensign*, November 1987, p. 30.)

— *Neal A. Maxwell*

The more I try to unravel the mysteries of the world in which we live, the more I come to the conception of a single overruling power—God. (Quoted by N. Eldon Tanner, *Ensign*, May 1978, p. 15.)

— *Henry B. Eyring*

There is a God in heaven who is infinite and eternal. He has all power, all might, and all dominion. There is no power he does not possess and no truth he does not know. Every good thing dwells in him independently in its eternal fullness. He is the Creator, Upholder, and Preserver of all things. His name is Elohim, and he is our Father in heaven, the literal Father of the spirits of all men. He has a body of flesh and bones as tangible as man's, and is in fact a resurrected and glorified Person. The name of the kind of life he lives is eternal life; and eternal life, by definition and in its nature, consists of life in an eternal family unit and of the possession of the fullness of the glory and power of the Father. (*Ensign*, May 1977 p. 12.)

— *Bruce R. McConkie*

We admit that God is the great source and fountain from whence proceeds all good; that he is perfect intelligence, and that his wisdom is alone sufficient to govern and regulate the mighty creations and worlds which shine and blaze with such magnificence and splendor over our heads, as though touched with his finger and moved by his Almighty word.

— *Joseph Smith*

We know, because the lord has revealed it in this our day, that we are the spirit children of an exalted, glorified Being, a Holy Man who has a body of flesh and bones and who is our Father in heaven.

We know that the name of the kind of life He lives is *eternal life* and that it consists of living in the family unit and of possessing all power, all might, and all dominion. (*Ensign*, November 1976, p. 106.)

— *Bruce R. McConkie*

See also HEAVENLY FATHER

———— God's Love ————

As we step back and try to understand this love of God, we are astounded by its profound impact. At its center is the reality of a literal Father in Heaven whose love for His children knows no bounds. All truths, wisdom, power, goodness, and love He desires to share with His children, whom He created and sent to earth. He would have us reach up and know Him as a Father, as one who forgives, as a helper, as friend, as lawgiver—as one anxious to grant to every man the full opportunity of His love and potential and ultimately the blessing to one day become like Him. (*Ensign*, May 1981, p. 53.)

— *James M. Paramore*

God knows and loves us all. We are, every one of us, his daughters and his sons, and whatever life's lessons may have brought us, the promise is still true: "If any of you lack wisdom, let him ask of God, that giveth to all men liberally, and upbraideth not; and it shall be given him." (James 1:5.) (*Ensign*, November 1988, p. 60.)

— *Howard W. Hunter*

In the many trials of life, when we feel abandoned and when sorrow, sin, disappointment, failure, and weakness make us less than we should ever be, there can come the healing salve of the unreserved love in the grace of God. It is a love that forgives and forgets, a love that lifts and blesses. It is a love that sustains a new beginning on a higher level and thereby continues "from grace to grace." (D&C 93:13.) (*Ensign*, November 1976, p. 59.)

— *James E. Faust*

Life has its share of some fear and some failure. Sometimes things fall short, don't quite measure up. Sometimes in both personal and public life, we are seemingly left without strength to go on. Sometimes people fail us, or economies and circumstance fail us, and life with its hardship and heartache can leave us feeling very alone.

But when such difficult moments come to us, I testify that there is one thing which will never, ever fail us. One thing alone will stand the test of all time, of all tribulation, all trouble, and all transgression. One thing only never faileth—and that is the pure love of Christ. (*Ensign*, November 1989, p. 26.)

— *Jeffrey R. Holland*

God our Father, Jesus, our Elder Brother and our Redeemer, and the Holy Ghost, the Testator, are perfect. They know us best and love us most and will not leave one thing undone for our eternal welfare. (*Ensign*, May 1988, p. 5.)

— *Ezra Taft Benson*

Enoch, to whom the Lord revealed so much, praised God amid His vast creations, exclaiming reassuringly, "Yet thou art there" (Moses 7:30).

This same special assurance can see each of us through all the seasons and circumstances of our lives. A universal God is actually involved with our small, individual universes of experience! In the midst of His vast dominions, yet He numbers us, knows us, and loves us perfectly. (See Moses 1:35; John 10:14.) (*Ensign*, November 1987, p. 30.)

— *Neal A. Maxwell*

Not long ago, one of my children said, "Dad, sometimes I wonder if I will ever make it." The answer I gave to her is the same as I would give to you if you have had similar feelings. Just do the very best you can each day. Do the basic things and, before you realize it, your life will be full of spiritual understanding that will confirm to you that your Heavenly Father loves you. When a person knows this, then life will be full of purpose and meaning. . . . (*Ensign*, May 1987, p. 16.)

— *M. Russell Ballard*

Sometimes, we foolishly recite facts about the Father and the Son, mechanically, and—forgive us—preach to them, preen before them, and display our ignorance and pride. Yet they continue to love us perfectly, each one of us, individually. Yes, they are all-powerful and all-knowing; their works extend eternally, yet their love for each of us is personal, knowing, uncompromising, endless, perfect. . . .[They] will never fail us—never in all eternity. (*Ensign*, May 1988, p. 61.)

— *Richard G. Scott*

There is something grand in the consideration of the fact that the Lord loves us with a most ardent love. The love that a woman exercises toward her offspring cannot equal the love that God exercises toward us. He never leaves us. He is always before us, and upon our right hand and our left hand. Continually He watches over us. (*CR*, October 1898, p. 2.)

— *Lorenzo Snow*

See also HEAVENLY FATHER, LOOK TO GOD, TRUST IN GOD

Goodness

All I can offer the world is a good heart and a good hand. (*HC*, 5:498.)

— *Joseph Smith*

Each of us has more opportunities to do good and to be good than we ever use. (*Ensign*, August 1979, p. 7.)

— *Spencer W. Kimball*

Human development . . . consists of both refusing to do evil and choosing to do good. (*Ensign*, July 1976, p. 72.)

— *Neal A. Maxwell*

One of the best qualities in any of the sons and daughters of God, whatever their circumstance, is a determination to become better. Since we all have a need to improve, we should always be willing to recognize goodness and encourage improvement in everyone. (*Ensign*, November 1989, p. 66.)

— *Dallin H. Oaks*

The idea is not to do good because of the praise of men, but to do good because in doing good we develop godliness within us; and this being the case, we shall become allied to godliness, which will in time become part and portion of our being. (*JD*, 23:192.)

— *Lorenzo Snow*

See also PERFECTION, PROGRESSION, RIGHTEOUSNESS

Gospel

A man having the map of the United States in his possession would be considered foolish if he supposed he possessed the United States; and because a man may have the old and new testament in his possession, it does not argue that he has the gospel. (*JD*, 7:362.)

— *John Taylor*

Every dimension of the gospel is relevant to one or more of our social and political problems in our time. (*New Era*, February 1975, p. 38.)

— *Neal A. Maxwell*

Every principle of the gospel has been revealed to us for our individual advancement and for our individual perfection. (*MS*, 66:169.)

— *Heber J. Grant*

Every world problem may be solved by obedience to the principles of the gospel of Jesus Christ. . . .

— *David O. McKay*

I have felt that I might best serve by encouraging and helping all members to feel the necessity of keeping the simple doctrines of the gospel simple. I strongly feel that the gospel was given to us in a simple, plain, and clear manner. My mission president taught us that the gospel of Jesus Christ is beautifully simple and simply beautiful. The tendency of many is to complicate these lovely, simple requirements that the Lord has given to us. (*Ensign*, May 1988, p. 28.)

— *Glen L. Rudd*

Mormonism is an enigma to the world. . . . it is beyond the reach of natural philosophy. It is the philosophy of heaven; it is the revelation of God to man. It is philosophical, but it is heavenly philosophy, and beyond the ken of human judgment, beyond the reach of human intelligence. They cannot grasp it; it is as high as heaven; what can they know about it? It is deeper than hell; they cannot fathom it. It is as wide as the universe; it extends over all creation. It goes back into eternity and forward into eternity. It is associated with the past, present, and future. It is connected with time and eternity, with men, angels, and Gods, with beings that were, that are, and that are to come. (*JD*, 15:25.)

— *John Taylor*

That which is of man must be modified and changed to meet the demands of various ages in which mankind lives, but that which is of God will endure, as the gospel of Jesus Christ, as revealed through the Prophet Joseph Smith, has endured the scrutiny of critics, the discoveries and the light of science in our day and time. (*CR*, October 1901, p. 53.)

— *Abraham O. Woodruff*

The gospel for me is not complex. It is a beautiful and simple pattern, a constant source of strength, a wellspring of faith. (*Ensign*, May 1982, p. 44.)

— *Gordon B. Hinckley*

The gospel embraces principles that dive deeper, spread wider, and extend further than anything else that we can conceive. The gospel teaches us in regard to the being and attributes of God; it also teaches us our relationship to that God and the various responsibilities we are under to him as his offspring; it teaches us the various duties and responsibilities that we are under to our families and friends, to the community, to the living and the dead; it unfolds to us principles pertaining to futurity. . . . and prepares us for an exaltation in the eternal world. There is something grand, profound and intellectual associated with the principles of the gospel as it stands connected with the salvation and exaltation of man. (*JD*, 16:369-70.)

— John Taylor

The gospel is a way of life. Its purpose is to help us become like Christ. (*Ensign*, May 1982, p. 15.)

— Mark E. Petersen

The gospel is *faith in the Lord, Jesus Christ*. This implies a willingness to accept His doctrine and take upon us His name, being obedient to His commandments. *The gospel is repentance* and a cleansing from all iniquity. *It is baptism* whereby we have made the covenant and promise. It is the right to have the *companionship of the Holy Ghost*, . . . *The gospel is the scriptures*. . . . *The gospel is prayer, humility, teachableness, charity*. It is *commitment* and it is *covenant* and *ordinances*. It is also *blessings*. (*Ensign*, May 1982, p. 72.)

— W. Grant Bangerter

The gospel is our being here. (*OAT*, 3.)

— Hugh Nibley

The gospel is so very simple when we understand it properly. It is always right, it is always good, it is always uplifting. (*Ensign*, November 1984, p. 18.)

— L. Tom Perry

The gospel of Christ is more than "the power of God unto salvation;" it is the power of God unto exaltation, and was instituted as such before this earth rolled into existence, before Adam fell, and consequently before man had need of redemption and salvation. It is the way of eternal progress, the path to perfection, and has been upon earth in a series of dispensations reaching like a mighty chain from the days of Adam down to the present time. (*CR*, April 1920, p. 122.)

— Orson F. Whitney

The gospel stands as true for those who reject it as for those who accept it—both will be judged by it. (*CR*, October 1974, p. 127.)

— Boyd K. Packer

The gospel of Jesus Christ is God's pattern for righteous living and eternal life. It makes possible goal-setting and lofty priorities. Satan and his advocates will constantly try to deceive and entice us into following their patterns. If we are to achieve daily safety, exaltation, and eternal happiness, we need to live by the light and truth of our Savior's plan. All salvation revolves around our Savior. (*Ensign*, November 1990, p. 20.)

— *Marvin J. Ashton*

The gospel is the *way* to salvation, and surely there is no other way. Mortals will get there through the gospel of Jesus Christ, or they will not receive salvation, meaning eternal life.

The word *gospel* means literally "glad tidings" or "good news." . . .The gospel is, . . . the good news about Jesus Christ and his atoning sacrifice for our sins and the original transgression that took place in the Garden of Eden. (*Ensign*, November 1985, p. 74.)

— *Hartman Rector, Jr.*

The gospel of Jesus Christ is a divine and perfect plan. It is composed of eternal, unchanging principles, laws, and ordinances which are universally applicable to every individual regardless of time, place, or circumstance. Gospel principles never change. (*Ensign*, November 1984, p. 64.)

— *Ronald E. Poelman*

The greatest appeal of the gospel in every age has been that it is frankly wonderful—one glorious surprise after another. (*OAT*, p. 6.)

— *Hugh Nibley*

The lifeline of the greatest security and trust [is] the gospel of Jesus Christ. That lifeline is secured in the hands of God. If I would hold to it and live by it, it would hold me secure to eternal life. (*Ensign*, November 1985, p. 40.)

— *Rex D. Pinegar*

The Lord wishes to establish a closer and more intimate relationship between Himself and us; He wishes to elevate us in the scale of being and intelligence, and this can only be done through the medium of the everlasting gospel which is specially prepared for this purpose. (*JD*, 23:193.)

— *Lorenzo Snow*

The mission of the Gospel of Jesus Christ [is] to make evil-minded men good and to make good men better. (*MS*, October 1961, p. 469.)

— *David O. McKay*

The purpose of the gospel of Jesus Christ is to prepare us for the celestial kingdom. The Lord has revealed to us that there are other kingdoms of glory and other kingdoms not of glory; but in order that men might be prepared for the celestial kingdom he sent his Only Begotten Son into the world. (*CR*, April 1934, p. 28.)

— *George Albert Smith*

See also CHURCH, DOCTRINE, GOSPEL PRINCIPLES, LATTER-DAY WORK, TRUTH

——— Gospel Principles ———

It takes as much intelligence for one to assimilate the principles of the gospel as it does for one to understand the complicated formulas of science. An understanding of the gospel is a quest and must be pursued through study, thought, and prayer. (*Ensign*, November 1984, p. 62.)

— *Royden G. Derrick*

The love of God, faith, hope, and charity, and the gospel of Jesus Christ, with all the ordinances thereof, with the Holy Priesthood, which has power both in heaven and on the earth, and the principles which have been revealed for the salvation and exaltation of the children of men—are principles you cannot annihilate. They are principles that no combination of men can destroy. They are principles that can never die. . . . Republics may be destroyed, kingdoms overthrown, empires broken up, thrones cast down, the sun may be turned to darkness, the moon to blood, the stars may fall from heaven, and heaven and earth itself may pass away, but not one jot or tittle of these principles will ever be destroyed. (*JD*, 22:342.)

— *Wilford Woodruff*

The principles which compose the gospel—and not merely the first principles, but all that have been or will ever be revealed are self-existent and everlasting in their nature. They have existed from all eternity, and will endure all eternities to come. (Quoted by Harold B. Lee, *CR*, April 1959, p. 68.)

— *Orson F. Whitney*

These great God-given gifts are the unshakable cornerstones which anchor The Church of Jesus Christ of Latter-day Saints, as well as the individual testimonies and convictions of its members: (1) the reality and the divinity of the Lord Jesus Christ as the Son of God; (2) the sublime vision given the Prophet Joseph Smith of the Father and the Son, ushering in the dispensation of the fullness of times; (3) the Book of Mormon as the word of God speaking in declaration of the divinity of the Savior; and (4) the priesthood of God divinely conferred to be exercised in righteousness for the blessing of our Father's children. (*Ensign*, November 1984, p. 53.)

— *Gordon B. Hinckley*

The principles of the restored gospel are so plain, so clear, so compassionate, so endowed with beauty, so graced with love unfeigned, as to be imprinted with the indisputable impress of the Savior himself. (*Ensign*, May 1981, p. 9.)

— *James E. Faust*

Times and seasons may change, revolution may succeed revolution; thrones may be cast down; and empires be dissolved; earthquakes may rend the earth from center to circumference; the mountains may be hurled out of their places, and the mighty ocean be moved from its bed, but amidst the crash of worlds and the crack of matter, truth, eternal truth, must remain unchanged, and those principles which God has revealed to his saints be unscathed amidst the warring elements, and remain as firm as the throne of Jehovah. (*Times and Seasons*, 5:744.)

— *John Taylor*

[God] has revealed to us in these later days the principles by which we may prosper, by which we may perfect ourselves, by which we may rise from the fallen condition in which we are, to the condition we must reach in preparation for the return of the Redeemer to the world. (*Ensign*, November 1976, p. 38.)

— *Marion G. Romney*

The principles of the gospel are timeless and timely and supply precise answers for our present need. (*Ensign*, November 1983, p. 84.)

— *Barbara B. Smith*

See also DOCTRINE, LAWS, TRUTH

Gossip

Gossip is the worst form of judging. The tongue is the most dangerous, destructive, and deadly weapon available to man. (*CR*, October 1972, p. 56.)

— *N. Eldon Tanner*

Slander is poison to the soul. (*CR*, April 1953, p. 16.)

— *David O. McKay*

How damaging is a habit that permits faultfinding, character assassination, and the sharing of malicious rumors! Gossip and caustic comments often create chains of contention. (*Ensign*, November 1986, p. 15.)

— *Marvin J. Ashton*

If your neighbors talk about you, and you think that they do wrong in speaking evil of you, do not let them know that you ever heard a word, and conduct yourselves as if they always did right, and it will mortify them, and they will say, "We'll not try this game any longer." (*JD*, 19:70.)

— *Brigham Young*

Talk about battles yet to be fought! Back-biting and evil-speaking head the list! (*CR*, October 1945, p. 131.)

— *David O. McKay*

See also CONTENTION, CRITICISM, JUDGING, WORDS

———— Government ————

Every government not ordained of God, . . . will, in its time, crumble to the dust and be lost in the fog of forgetfulness, and will leave no history of its doings. (*JD*, 14:91.)

— *Brigham Young*

I support the doctrine of separation of church and state as traditionally interpreted to prohibit the establishment of an official national religion. But this does not mean that we should divorce government from any formal recognition of God. To do so strikes a potentially fatal blow at the concept of the divine origin of our rights and unlocks the door for an easy entry of future tyranny. If Americans should ever come to believe that their rights and freedoms are instituted among men by politicians and bureaucrats, then they will no longer carry the proud inheritance of their forefathers, but will grovel before their masters seeking favors and dispensations, a throwback to the feudal system of the Dark Ages. (*CR*, October 1968, pp. 17-20.)

— *Ezra Taft Benson*

Man is superior to government and should remain master over it, not the other way around. (*TETB*, p. 680.)

— *Ezra Taft Benson*

Man was made to be free, to rule and to have dominion. And this does not mean a dominion to be gained by military power or by brute force but by the power of love, unselfishness and understanding. (*CR*, October 1941, p. 27.)

— *Richard R. Lyman*

No government may remain strong by ignoring the commandments given to Moses on Mount Sinai. (*CR*, October 1976, p. 7.)

— *Spencer W. Kimball*

The government of God has always tended to promote peace, unity, harmony, strength and happiness; while that of man has been productive of confusion, disorder, weakness, and misery. (*HC*, 5:61.)

— *Joseph Smith*

We believe that no man or set of men, of their own wisdom and by their own talents, are capable of governing the human family aright. (*JD*, 9:9.)

— *John Taylor*

See also AMERICA, CITIZENSHIP, FREEDOM

——— Gratitude ———

As gratitude is absent or disappears, rebellion often enters and fills the vacuum. . . . I refer to rebellion against moral cleanliness, beauty, decency, honesty, reverence, and respect for parental authority.

A grateful heart is a beginning of greatness. It is an expression of humility. It is a foundation for the development of such virtues as prayer, faith, courage, contentment, happiness, love, and well-being. (*Ensign*, May 1990, p. 86.)

— *James E. Faust*

If a person wants to enjoy the Spirit of the Lord, let him, when something of a disagreeable nature comes along, think how worse the circumstance might be, . . . Always cultivate a spirit of gratitude. It is the duty of every Latter-day Saint to cultivate a spirit of gratitude.

— *Lorenzo Snow*

Gratitude is twin sister to humility; pride is a foe to both. The man who has come into close communion with God cannot fail to be thankful; for he feels, he knows, that for all he has and all he is, he is indebted to the Supreme Giver; and one would think that there is no need of commandment in the matter of thanksgiving. Yet we find that because of man's propensities toward forgetfulness and selfishness the Scriptures abound in admonitions to render thanks unto the Lord. (*Sunday Night Talks*, Salt Lake City: Deseret Book Co., 1931, p. 483.)

— *James E. Talmage*

Great men have always recognized the greatness of god and their dependence upon him, and they have with regularity rendered to him gratitude and thanksgiving. (*Ensign*, November 1982, p. 50.)

— *Marion G. Romney*

Hold fast to the blessings which God has provided for you. Yours is not the task to gain them, they are here; yours is the part of cherishing them. (*Church News*, 14 June 1969, p.2.)

— *J. Reuben Clark, Jr.*

It has been said that the sin of ingratitude is more serious than the sin of revenge. With revenge, we return evil for evil, but with ingratitude, we return evil for good. (*Ensign*, November 1989, p. 24.)

— *W. Eugene Hansen*

It is perfectly evident . . . that to thank the Lord in all things is not merely a courtesy, it is a *commandment* as binding upon us as any other commandment. (See D&C 59:5-7.) (*Ensign*, November 1982, p. 50.)

— *Marion G. Romney*

Pray in thanksgiving. In many countries, the homes are barren and the cupboards bare—no books, no radios, no pictures, no furniture, no fire—while we are housed adequately, clothed warmly, fed extravagantly. Did we show our thanks by the proper devotion on our knees last night and this morning and tomorrow morning?

Ingratitude, thou sinful habit! (*TSWK*, p. 120.)

— *Spencer W. Kimball*

Thankfulness is measured by the number of words; gratitude is measured by the nature of our actions. (*CR*, October 1955, p. 4.)

— *David O. McKay*

There isn't a word in all the English language with more magic in it than the word gratitude. Love makes fertile the soil for things to blossom and to grow, and love begins with gratitude. (*Ensign*, March 1971, p. 53.)

— *Geraldine P. Anderson*

Think to thank. In these three words are the finest capsule course for a happy marriage, a formula for enduring friendship, and a pattern for personal happiness. (*Pathways to Perfection*, Thomas S. Monson, Salt Lake City: Deseret Book Co., 1974, p. 254.)

— *Thomas S. Monson*

We should confess His hand in all things. Ingratitude is one of our great sins. (*Ensign*, May 1977, p. 33.)

— *Ezra Taft Benson*

You could have an experience with the gift of the Holy Ghost today. You could begin a private prayer with thanks. You could start to count your blessings, and then pause for a moment. If you exercise faith, and with the gift of the Holy Ghost, you will find that memories of other blessings will flood into your mind. If you begin to express gratitude for each of them, your prayer may take a little longer than usual. Remembrance will come. And so will gratitude. (*Ensign*, November 1989, p. 13.)

— *Henry B. Eyring*

See also BLESSINGS, HUMILITY

——— Greatness ———

Greatness is measured by men in many ways. It is generally equated with size, cost, quantity, and position. God, however, has a better way, . . . In [his] eyes, greatness is equated with light, truth, goodness, and service. (See D&C 93:39; Matt. 23:11.) (*Ensign*, May 1990, p. 62.)

— *Carlos E. Asay*

Greatness of life is won only when men regulate and order the affairs and acts of their lives by an understanding of the great spiritual purpose of man's existence. (*CR*, April, 1922, p. 27.)

— *John A. Widtsoe*

He that would be great, let him be good, studying the interests of the whole—becoming the servant of all.

— *Lorenzo Snow*

To do one's best in the face of the commonplace struggles of life, and possibly in the face of failures, and to continue to endure and persevere with the ongoing difficulties of life—when those struggles and tasks contribute to the progress and happiness of others and the eternal salvation of one's self—this is true greatness. (*Ensign*, May 1982, p. 19.)

— *Howard W. Hunter*

That man is most truly great who is most Christlike.

What you sincerely in your heart think of Christ will determine what you are, will largely determine what your acts will be. (*CR*, April 1951, p. 93.)

— *David O. McKay*

Those things which we call extraordinary, remarkable, or unusual may make history, but they do not make real life.

After all, to do well those things which God ordained to be the common lot of all mankind, is the truest greatness. To be a successful father or a successful mother is greater than to be a successful general or a successful statesman. (*Ensign*, May 1982, p. 19.)

— *Howard W. Hunter*

—————— Habits ——————

Being fettered with habits and mistakes of misconduct relegates a person to being a victim of his errors. (*Ensign*, May 1979, p. 69.)

— *Marvin J. Ashton*

Good habits are developed in the workshops of our daily lives. It is not in the great moments of test and trial that character is built. That is only when it is displayed. The habits that direct our lives and form our character are fashioned in the often uneventful, commonplace routine of life. (*CR*, October 1974, p. 25.)

— *Delbert L. Stapley*

I am grateful that it is never too late to change, to make things right, to leave old activities and habits behind. (*Ensign*, November 1986, p. 10.)

— *James E. Faust*

On Bad Habits

The things which we do not begin, we do not have to stop.

— *J. Reuben Clark, Jr.*

I have known good men, decent men, both in and out of the Church who, because of some bad habit, prevented greater happiness and progress from occurring in their lives. One of these good men who saw the great merits of the Church, though he never joined, said to me on one occasion, with cigar in hand, "Ezra, what is your redeeming vice?" It was the first time I had ever heard such an expression. Brothers and sisters, from the Lord's view, there are *no* redeeming vices—only redeeming virtues! (*Ensign*, May 1979, p. 32.)

— *Ezra Taft Benson*

It appears that we do not change when we die (see Alma 34:32, 34), which means that if we are addicted to drugs, bad habits, and evil desires when we go out of this life, those influences will probably follow us. Therefore, repentance and forgiveness, . . . are our whole duty here in mortality. (See Eccl. 12:13.) (*Ensign*, November 1985, p. 76.)

— *Hartman Rector, Jr.*

It is contrary to the order of heaven for any soul to be locked into compulsive, immoral behavior with no way out!

It *is* consistent with the workings of the adversary to deceive you into believing that you *are*.

I gratefully acknowledge that transgressions, . . . yield to sincere repentance. I testify with all my soul that the doctrine of repentance is true and has a miraculous, liberating effect upon behavior. (*Ensign*, November 1986, p. 18.)

— *Boyd K. Packer*

This example suggests how your habit[s] can be overcome.

Suppose a small child were to run in front of your car. What would you do? Careful analysis of each step taken will teach you how to overcome your serious habit[s]:

First your mind decides to stop. Nothing else can happen until that decision is made.

Then you take your foot off the accelerator. Can you imagine stopping a car with one foot on the accelerator and the other on the brake?

Finally you firmly apply the brake.

The same pattern is followed to overcome your entrenched habit[s]. Decide to stop what you are doing that is wrong. Then search out everything in your life that feeds the habit, such as negative thoughts, unwholesome environment, and your companions in mischief. Systematically eliminate or overcome everything that contributes to that negative part of your life. Then stop the negative things permanently. (*Ensign*, May 1990, p. 75.)

— *Richard G. Scott*

Who among us hasn't felt the chains of bad habits? These habits may have impeded our progress, may have made us forget who we are, may have destroyed our self-image, may have put our family life in jeopardy, and may have hindered our ability to serve our fellowmen and our God. So many of us tend to say, "This is the way I am. I can't change. I can't throw off the chains of habit."

Lehi warned his sons to "shake off the chains" (2 Ne. 1:23) because he knew that chains restrict our mobility, growth, and happiness. They cause us to become confused and less able to be guided by God's Spirit. (*Ensign*, November 1986, pp. 13-14.)

— *Marvin J. Ashton*

See also SELF-MASTERY, THOUGHTS

——— Happiness ———

All happiness, all success, all glorious achievement rest with the individual. He can make a heaven or a hell upon the earth. (*TETB*, p. 457.)

— *Ezra Taft Benson*

Ask any people, nations, kingdoms, or generations of men the question, and they will tell you they are seeking for happiness, but how are they seeking for it? . . . By serving the devil as fast as they can, and almost the last being that the children of men worship, and the last being whose laws they want to keep are the laws of the God of heaven. They will not worship God nor honor his name, nor keep his laws, but blaspheme his name, from day to day, and nearly all the world are seeking for happiness by committing sins, breaking the law of God, and blaspheming his name and rejecting the only source whence happiness flows.

If we really understood that we could not obtain happiness by walking in the paths of sin and breaking the laws of God, we should then see the folly of it, every man and every woman would see that to obtain happiness we should go to work and perform the works of righteousness, and do the will of our Father in heaven, for we shall receive at His hand all the happiness, blessings, glory, salvation, exaltation, and eternal lives that we ever do receive, either in time or eternity. (JD, 4:192.)

— *Wilford Woodruff*

Happiness and peace are found when we are in harmony with ourselves, with God, and with our fellowmen. (*Ensign*, November 1985, p. 96.)

— *Barbara W. Winder*

Make others happy, and you will be happy yourself. . . . I have heard Brother Heber C. Kimball state that when he was very much downhearted, he would find somebody worse than himself, and endeavor to comfort him up, and by so doing he would comfort himself, and increase in spirit and in life.

— *Lorenzo Snow*

Happiness comes from understanding and living the teachings of the Lord. It comes from not being critical of ourselves when we don't accomplish all we want to do. (*Ensign*, May 1988, p. 61.)

— *Richard G. Scott*

Happiness comes from within, and not from without. (*CR*, October 1966, p. 39.)

— *Milton R. Hunter*

Happiness is a byproduct of helping others. No man ever finds happiness by thinking of himself. True happiness comes when we lose ourselves in the service of others—when we are merciful to our fellowmen. (*Ensign*, May 1977, p. 58.)

— *Royden G. Derrick*

Happiness is the object and design of our existence; and will be the end thereof, if we pursue the path that leads to it; and this path is virtue, uprightness, faithfulness, holiness, and keeping all the commandments of God. (*HC*, 5:134-35.)

— *Joseph Smith*

I have never seen happier people than those who have repented. (*CR*, October 1940, p. 35.)

— *Stephen L Richards*

I wish to testify that, by the power and gift of the Holy Ghost, we can know what to do and what not to do to bring happiness and peace to our lives. (*Ensign*, May 1989, p. 31.)

— *James E. Faust*

If you would find happiness and joy, lose your life in some noble cause. A worthy purpose must be at the center of every worthy life. (*Ensign*, May 1986, p. 54.)

— *Jack H. Goaslind*

One who practices pure religion soon discovers it is more rewarding to lift a man up than to hold him down. Happiness is bound up with helpfulness. (*Ensign*, November 1982, p. 65.)

— *Marvin J. Ashton*

In obedience there is joy and peace unspotted, unalloyed; and as God has designed our happiness . . . He never will institute an ordinance or give a commandment to His people that is not calculated in its nature to promote that happiness which He has designed, and which will not end in the greatest amount of good and glory to those who become the recipients of his law and ordinances. (*HC*, 5:135.)

— *Joseph Smith*

Our eternal happiness will be in proportion to the way that we devote ourselves to helping others. (*CR*, October 1936, p. 71.)

— *George Albert Smith*

Much of the happiness of this life consists in having something worthy to do and in doing it well. (Quoted by H. Burke Peterson, *Ensign*, November 1977, p. 87.)

— *Brigham Young*

Our yearnings for happiness were implanted in our hearts by Deity. They represent a kind of home-sickness, for we have a residual memory of our premortal existence. They are also a foretaste of the fullness of joy that is promised to the faithful. (*Ensign*, May 1986, pp. 52-53.)

— *Jack H. Goaslind*

Striving for happiness is a long, hard journey with many challenges. It requires eternal vigilance to win the victory. You cannot succeed with sporadic little flashes of effort. Constant and valiant living is necessary. (*Ensign*, May 1986, p. 53.)

— *Jack H. Goaslind*

The key to happiness is to get the spirit and keep it. (*CR*, October 1961, p. 61.)
— *Marion G. Romney*

The Lord wants us to be happy. He will do His part if we will do our part. The Christlike life is the life that brings true happiness. There is no true happiness without God. (*TETB*, p. 339.)

— *Ezra Taft Benson*

The person who enjoys the experience of the knowledge of the Kingdom of God on the earth, and at the same time has the love of God within him, is the happiest of any individuals on the earth. . . .

Where is happiness, real happiness? Nowhere but in God. By possessing the spirit of our holy religion, we are happy in the morning, we are happy at noon, we are happy in the evening; for the spirit of love and union is with us, and we rejoice in the Spirit because, it is of God, and we rejoice in God, for he is the giver of every good thing. Every Latter-day Saint, who has experienced the love of God in his heart, after having received the remission of his sins, through baptism, and the laying on of hands, realizes that he is filled with joy, and happiness, and consolation. He may be in pain, in error, in poverty, or in prison, if necessity demands, still, he is joyful. This is our experience, and each and every Latter-day Saint can bear witness to it. (*DBY*, pp. 235-36.)

— *Brigham Young*

The truly happy people are those who have faith in the Lord and keep the laws of the gospel, those who forget self in their desire and effort to bless others. (*CR*, April, 1975, p. 44.)

— *Joseph Anderson*

There are seeds of happiness planted in every human soul. Our mental attitude and disposition constitute the environment in which these seeds may germinate. (*CR*, October 1934, p. 92.)

— *David O. McKay*

There is no real happiness in having or getting, but only in giving. (*CR*, April 1967, p. 104.)

— *N. Eldon Tanner*

True happiness is not made in getting something. True happiness is becoming something. (*Ensign*, November 1983, p 61.)

— *Marvin J. Ashton*

When the Spirit of God burns in your soul, you cannot be otherwise than happy. (*CR*, April 1950, p. 169.)

— *George Albert Smith*

See also JOY, OBEDIENCE

Health

Physical well-being is not only a priceless asset to one's self—it is also a heritage to be passed on. With good health all the activities of life are greatly enhanced. A clean mind in a healthy body enables one to render far more effective service to others. it helps one provide more vigorous leadership. It gives our every experience in life more zest and more meaning. Robust health is a noble and worthwhile attainment. (*TETB*, p. 479.)

— *Ezra Taft Benson*

Good health is often a matter of good judgement.

— *Marion D. Hanks*

The condition of the body limits, largely, the expression of the spirit. (*A Rational Theology*, 5th ed., Salt Lake City: Deseret Book Co., 1967, p. 171.)

— *John A. Widtsoe*

The healthy man, who takes care of his physical being, has strength and vitality; his temple is a fit place for his spirit to reside. (*IE*, April 1955, p. 221.)

— *David O. McKay*

The state of our health affects every facet of our life—our feeling of personal well-being, our approach to work, our social interactions—even our service to the Lord. Our physical health goals should be—
1. To obey the Word of Wisdom;
2. To maintain proper weight and endurance through regular exercise, adequate rest, and a balanced diet;
3. To improve or maintain personal and home sanitation;
4. To practice preventative measures to preserve good health;
5. To learn and practice home health skills. (*Ensign*, November 1978, pp. 77-78.)

— *Barbara B. Smith*

There is a close relationship between physical health and spiritual development. . . . When one's physical health is impaired by disobedience to God's eternal laws, spiritual development will also suffer. (*CR*, October 1967, p. 74.)

— *Delbert L. Stapley*

Your physical body is a magnificent creation of God. It is his temple as well as yours, and must be treated with reverence. (*Ensign*, November 1985, p. 30.)

— *Russell M. Nelson*

The condition of the physical body can affect the spirit. That's why the Lord gave us the Word of Wisdom. He also said that we should retire to our beds early and arise early (see D&C 88:124), that we should not run faster than we have strength (see D&C 10:4), and that we should use moderation in all good things. In general, the more food we eat in its natural state and the less it is refined without additives, the healthier it will be for us. Food can affect the mind, and deficiencies in certain elements in the body can promote mental depression. A good physical examination periodically is a safeguard and may spot problems that can be remedied. Rest and physical exercise are essential, and a walk in the fresh air can refresh the spirit. Wholesome recreation is part of our religion, and a change of pace is necessary, and even its anticipation can lift the spirit. (*Ensign*, November 1974, p. 66.)

— *Ezra Taft Benson*

See also WORD OF WISDOM

———— Heavenly Father ————

God created the earth in all its magnificent glory, not as an end in itself, but for us, his children. Indeed, we are his children, his offspring, and he is the Father of our spirits. (*Ensign*, May 1988, p. 58.)

— *M. Russell Ballard*

I believe without equivocation or reservation in God, the Eternal Father. He is my Father, the Father of my spirit, and the Father of the spirits of all men. He is the great Creator, the Ruler of the Universe. He directed the creation of this earth on which we live. In His image man was created. He is personal. He is real. He is individual. He has "a body of flesh and bones as tangible as man's" (D&C 130:22). . . . I worship Him "in spirit and in truth." I look to Him as my strength. I pray to Him for wisdom beyond my own. I seek to love Him with all my heart, might, mind, and strength. His wisdom is greater than the wisdom of all men. His power is greater than the power of nature, ... His love is greater than the love of any other, for His love encompasses all of His children, and it is His work and His glory to bring to pass the immortality and eternal life of His sons and daughters of all generations (see Moses 1:39). (*Ensign*, November 1986, pp. 49-50.)

— *Gordon B. Hinckley*

Of all the creations of God, men and women are the ones that are to become as he is. We are his children. He has given us a plan, a model, and teachings that will help us gain his attributes. (*Ensign*, May 1982, p. 81.)

— *Barbara B. Smith*

Our Father in heaven is not an umpire who is trying to count us out. He is not a competitor who is trying to outsmart us. . . . He is a loving Father who wants our happiness and eternal progress and who will help us all he can if we will but give him the opportunity to do so with obedience and humility, and faith and patience. (Quoted by N. Eldon Tanner, *CR*, October 1967, p. 51.)

— Richard L. Evans

The Father *is* the one true God. *This* thing is certain: no one will ever ascend above Him; no one will ever replace Him. Nor will anything ever change the relationship that we, His literal offspring, have with Him. He is Elohim, the Father. He is God. Of Him there *is* only one. We revere our Father and our God; we *worship* Him. (*Ensign*, November 1984, p. 69.)

— Boyd K. Packer

My thoughts go out in gratitude to that loving Father, the Father of us all, who stands with arms outstretched, cheering us on, asking us to come home to him and to his beloved Son, our Savior. (*Ensign*, May 1990, p. 43.)

— Clinton L. Cutler

There is no salvation in worshiping a false god—neither a cow; nor a crocodile; nor a cedar post; nor even a spirit essence, without body, parts, or passions, that fills the immensity of space.

True believers worship that Holy Being who "made heaven, and earth, and the sea, and the fountains of waters." (Rev. 14:7.)

He is the Father of spirits with whom we dwelt before the foundations of the earth were laid. He is our Father in Heaven, who ordained and established a plan of salvation by which his spirit children might advance and progress and become like him.

He is a Holy Man, a personage of tabernacle, having a body of flesh and bones; and he created mortal man in his own image, "male and female created he them." (Gen. 1:27.)

He is a glorified and exalted being in whom all fullness and perfection dwell, who knows all things and has all power, all might, and all dominion. (*Ensign*, November 1984, p. 82.)

— Bruce R. McConkie

See also GOD

Heritage

There should be no doubt what our task is today. If we truly cherish the heritage we have received, we must maintain the same virtues and the same character of our stalwart forebears—faith in God, courage, industry, frugality, self-reliance, and integrity. We have the obligation to maintain what those who pledged their lives, their fortunes, and sacred honor gave to future generations. (*Ensign*, November 1976, p. 35.)

— *Ezra Taft Benson*

As members of this glorious church, we share a rich heritage. We literally stand on the shoulders of the giants of faith, vision, and spirit who preceded us.

When we honor them and their many sacrifices, we preserve their achievements and the principles and values for which they stood. And it provides us a wonderful way in which to praise God! (*Ensign*, November 1987, p. 73.)

— *L. Tom Perry*

My father used to say: "The true way to honor the past is to improve upon it." (*Ensign*, July 1976, p. 4.)

— *N. Eldon Tanner*

Someone has said that from the altars of the past we should take the flame and not the ashes. There are those who stir in the ashes and find themselves covered with soot and grime. They get cinders in their eyes, and no longer see by the light of faith. They miss the purpose of it all. (*Ensign*, May 1984, p. 105.)

— *Boyd K. Packer*

See also GENEALOGY, PARENTS

—————— Heroes ——————

There are hidden heroines and heroes among the Latter-day Saints—"those of the last wagon" whose fidelity to duty and devotion to righteousness go unnoticed by anyone except the One whose notice really matters. (*Ensign*, November 1989, p. 65.)

— *Dallin H. Oaks*

We all need heroes to honor and admire; we need people after whom we can pattern our lives. For us Christ is the chiefest of these. (*Ensign*, May 1979, p. 47.)

— *Spencer W. Kimball*

See also EXAMPLE, GREATNESS

—— Holy Ghost ——

An intelligent being, in the image of God, possesses every organ, attribute, sense, sympathy, affection, of will, wisdom, love, power and gift, which is possessed by God himself. But these are possessed by man in his rudimental state in a subordinate sense of the word. Or, in other words, these attributes are in embryo, and are to be gradually developed. They resemble a bud, a germ, which gradually develops into bloom, and then, by process, produces the mature fruit after its own kind. The gift of the Holy Ghost adapts itself to all these organs or attributes. It quickens all the intellectual faculties, increases, enlarges, expands, and purifies all the natural passions and affections, and adapts them by the gift of wisdom to their lawful use. It inspires virtue, kindness, goodness, tenderness, gentleness, and charity. It develops beauty of person, form and features. It tends to health, vigor, animation, and social feeling. It develops and invigorates all the faculties of the physical and intellectual man. It strengthens, invigorates, and gives tone to the nerves. In short, it is, as it were, marrow to the bone, joy to the heart, light to the eyes, music to the ears, and life to the whole being. (*Key to Theology,* Parley P. Pratt, Salt Lake city: Deseret Book Co., 1978, pp. 101-2.)

— *Parley P. Pratt*

I believe in the Holy Ghost as a personage of spirit who occupies a place with the Father and the Son, these three comprising the divine Godhead. . . .

The Holy Ghost stands as the third member of the Godhead, the Comforter promised by the Savior who would teach His followers all things and bring all things to their remembrance, whatsoever He had said unto them (see John 14:26.)

The Holy Ghost is the Testifier of Truth, who can teach men things they cannot teach one another. . . . "by the power of the Holy Ghost ye may know the truth of all things" (Moroni 10:4-5.) (*Ensign,* November 1986, p. 51.)

— *Gordon B. Hinckley*

I can promise you that the spirit is a whole lot more anxious to help you than you are to be helped. (Address, Mission Home, Salt Lake City, June 1975.)

— *S. Dilworth Young*

No man can receive the Holy Ghost without receiving revelations. The Holy Ghost is a revelator. (*TPJS,* p. 328.)

— *Joseph Smith*

Let us learn to be always enlightened with the powerful understanding of the need for a constant change of heart, that the light and power of the Holy Ghost can penetrate us always to make us better fathers and mothers, husbands and wives, sons and daughters, more diligent workers—with a dream and a vision to touch the lives of all of our Heavenly Father's children and to bring about the final revolution to all the people of this world . . . (*Ensign*, November 1984, p. 29.)

— *F. Enzio Busche*

In simple terms, the gift of the Holy Ghost is an enhanced spiritual power permitting those entitled thereto to receive it, to receive a greater knowledge and enjoyment of the influence of Deity. (*Ensign* May 1989, p. 33.)

— *James E. Faust*

At one time the Prophet Joseph visited the President of the United States, and the President asked him the difference between his church and other churches, and the Prophet said, "We have the Holy Ghost." (*Ensign*, November 1977, p. 22.)

— *LeGrand Richards*

No person whose soul is illuminated by the burning Spirit of God can in this world of sin and dense darkness remain passive. He is driven by an irresistible urge to fit himself to be an active agent of God in furthering righteousness and in freeing the lives and minds of men from the bondage of sin. (*CR*, October 1941, p. 89.)

— *Marion G. Romney*

Now, if you have the Holy Ghost with you, . . . I can say unto you that there is no greater gift, there is no greater blessing, there is no greater testimony given to any man on earth. You may have the administration of angels; you may see many miracles; you may see many wonders in the earth; but I claim that the gift of the Holy Ghost is the greatest gift that can be bestowed upon man. (*DFTP*, p. 229.)

— *Wilford Woodruff*

Perhaps no promise in life is more reassuring than that promise of divine assistance and spiritual guidance in times of need. It is a gift freely given from heaven, a gift that we need from our earliest youth through the very latest days of our lives. (*Ensign*, November 1988, p. 59.)

— *Howard W. Hunter*

The gift of the Holy Ghost confers upon one, as long as he is worthy, the right to receive light and truth. . . .

One is born again by actually receiving and experiencing the light and power inherent in the gift of the Holy Ghost. (*Ensign*, May 1977, p. 44.)

— *Marion G. Romney*

There is a difference between the Holy Ghost and the gift of the Holy Ghost. Cornelius received the Holy Ghost before he was baptized, which was the convincing power of God unto him of the truth of the Gospel, but he could not receive the gift of the Holy Ghost until after he was baptized. Had he not [been baptized], the Holy Ghost which convinced him of the truth of God, would have left him. (*HC,* 4:555.)

— *Joseph Smith*

The comforting Spirit of the Holy Ghost can abide with us twenty-four hours a day: when we work, when we play, when we rest. Its strengthening influence can be with us year in and year out. That sustaining influence can be with us in joy and sorrow, when we rejoice as well as when we grieve.

The Holy Ghost is the greatest guarantor of inward peace in our unstable world. (*Ensign,* May 1989, pp. 32-33.)

— *James E. Faust*

God does not send thunder if a still, small voice is enough. (*Ensign,* November 1976, p. 14.)

— *Neal A. Maxwell*

The doctrine is what the doctrine is, and the concepts are what the concepts are. It is of no moment whatever that they spread confusion among uninspired worshippers . . . or among intellectuals whose interest in religion is purely academic and who rely on the power of the mind rather than the power of the Spirit for understanding.

Gospel truths are known and understood only by the power of the Spirit. Eternal life—which is to know God—is such an infinitely great reward that men must study, ponder, and pray, with all their hearts, to gain the needed knowledge. (*Devotional and Fireside Speeches,* Provo: Brigham Young University, 1985, p. 51.)

— *Bruce R. McConkie*

The gift of the Holy Ghost by the laying on of hands cannot be received through the medium of any other principle than the principle of righteousness, for if the proposals are not complied with, it is of no use, but withdraws. (*HC,* 3:379.)

— *Joseph Smith*

The Holy Ghost is a person, a spirit, the third member of the Godhead. He is a messenger and a witness of the Father and the Son. He brings to men testimony, witness, and knowledge of God the Father, Jesus Christ His Son, and the truths of the gospel. He vitalizes truth in the hearts and souls of men. (*Ensign,* May 1977, pp. 43-44.)

— *Marion G. Romney*

The gift of the Holy Ghost is a priceless possession and opens the door to our ongoing knowledge of God and eternal joy. (*Ensign,* November 1989, p. 61.)

— *David B. Haight*

The gift of the Holy Ghost is the right to the constant companionship of that member of the Godhead based on faithfulness. It is the right to receive revelation, to see visions, to be in tune with the Infinite. (*Ensign,* November 1977, p. 33.)

— *Bruce R. McConkie*

The Holy Ghost bears witness of the truth and impresses upon the soul the reality of God the Father and the son Jesus Christ so deeply that no earthly power or authority can separate him from that knowledge. . . .

I would rather have every person enjoy the Spirit of the Holy Ghost than any other association, for they will be led by that Spirit to light and truth and pure intelligence, which can carry them back into the presence of God. (*Ensign,* May 1989, pp. 31, 33.)

— *James E. Faust*

The Lord's formula for receiving the Spirit is to get on our knees and communicate with him. Tell him what we are going to do—make commitments with him—outline our program—and then get up off our knees and go and *do* precisely what we have told him we would do. In the *doing,* the Spirit comes. (*Ensign,* January 1974, p. 107.)

— *Hartman Rector, Jr.*

The things of God are known only by the power of his Spirit. God stands revealed or he remains forever unknown. No man can know that Jesus is the Lord but by the Holy Ghost. (*Ensign,* May 1981, p. 77.)

— *Bruce R. McConkie*

Though a man should say but a few words, and his sentences and words be ever so ungrammatical, if he speaks by the power of the Holy Ghost, he will do good. (*JD,* 8:120.)

— *Brigham Young*

To have the companionship of the Holy Ghost, you must be clean; and to be clean, you must keep the commandments of God. (*Ensign,* November 1990, p. 94.)

— *Ardeth G. Kapp*

We can tell when the speakers are moved upon by the Holy Ghost only when we, ourselves, are moved upon by the Holy Ghost. In a way, this completely shifts the responsibility from them to us to determine when they so speak . . . the

Church will know by the testimony of the Holy Ghost in the body of the members, whether the brethren in voicing their views are moved upon by the Holy Ghost; and in due time that knowledge will be made manifest. (*Church News,* July 31, 1954.)

— *J. Reuben Clark, Jr.*

When our minds are set upon the things of this world rather than on the things of the kingdom of God, we cannot have the manifestations of the Holy Ghost. (*Church News,* November 4, 1961, p. 14.)

— *Joseph Fielding Smith*

We had a very grievous case that had to come before the high council and the stake presidency which resulted in the excommunication of a man who had harmed a lovely young girl. After nearly an all-night session which resulted in that action, I went to my office rather weary the next morning to be confronted by a brother of this man whom we had had on trial the night before. This man said, "I want to tell you that my brother wasn't guilty of that thing which you charged him with."

"How do you know he wasn't guilty?" I asked.

Because I prayed, and the Lord told me he was innocent," the man answered.

I asked him to come into the office and we sat down, and I asked, "Would you mind if I asked you a few personal questions?" and he said "Certainly not."

"How old are you?"

"Forty-seven."

"What Priesthood do you hold?" He said he thought he was a teacher. "Do you keep the Word of Wisdom?" and he said "Well, no." He used tobacco, which was obvious.

"Do you pay your tithing?"

He said, "No"—and he didn't intend to as long as that blankety-blank-blank man was the Bishop if the Thirty-Second Ward.

I said, "Do you attend your Priesthood meetings?"

He replied, "No, sir!" and he didn't intend to as long as that man was bishop. "You don't attend your sacrament meetings either?"

"No, sir."

"Do you have your family prayers?" and he said no.

"Do you study the scriptures?" He said well, his eyes were bad and he couldn't read very much.

I then said to him: "In my home I have a beautiful instrument called a radio. When everything is in good working order we can dial it to a certain station and pick up a speaker or the voice of a singer all the way across the continent or sometimes on the other side of the world, bringing them into the front room as though they were almost speaking there. But, after we had used it for a long time, there were some little delicate instruments or electrical devices on the inside called radio tubes that began to wear out. When one of them wears out, we get a kind of a static—it isn't so clear. Another wears out, and if we don't give it attention it fades in and out. . . . If we don't give that attention, and another one wears out—well, the radio sits there looking quite like it did before, but something has happened on the inside. We can't get any singer. We can't get any speaker.

"Now" I said, "you and I have within our souls something like what might be said to be a counter-part of those radio tubes. We might have what we call a 'Go-to-Sacrament-Meeting' tube, 'Keep-the -Word-of-Wisdom' tube, 'Pay-Your-Tithing' tube, 'Have-Your-Family-Prayers' tube, 'Read-the-Scriptures' tube, and, as one of the most important, that might be said to be the master tube of our whole soul, the 'Keep-Yourselves-Morally-Clean' tube. If one of these becomes worn out by disuse or is not active—we fail to keep the commandments of God—it has the same effect upon our spiritual selves that that same worn out instrument in the radio in my home has upon the reception that we otherwise could receive from a distance.

"Now, then," I said, "fifteen of the best living men in the Pioneer Stake prayed last night. They heard the evidence and every man was united in saying that your brother was guilty. Now, you, who do none of these things, you say you prayed, and you got an opposite answer. How would you explain that?"

Then this man gave an answer that I think was a classic. He said, "Well, President Lee, I think I must have gotten my answer from the wrong source." And you know that's just as great a truth as we can have. We get our answer from the source of the power we list to obey. If we're keeping the commandments of the Devil, we'll get the answer from the Devil. If we're keeping the commandments of God, we'll get the commandments from our Heavenly Father for our direction and for our guidance. (*Speeches of the Year*, Provo: Brigham Young University Press, 1952, pp. 4-6.)

— *Harold B. Lee*

What a great and powerful friend is this gift of the Holy Ghost! Certainly all who will turn to the Savior and abide by his laws will be healed by this Spirit (3 Ne. 9:13). They will have the mind of Christ (1 Cor. 2:16), they will be "partakers of the divine nature" (2 Pet. 1:4), they will begin to have the image of Christ in their countenances (Al. 5:14). Truly the gospel comes, as Paul said, not only in word "but also in power," the sanctifying, cleansing, soul-enlarging power of the Holy Spirit (1 Thess. 1:5). (*Ensign* May 1979, p. 79.)

— *Loren C. Dunn*

What a privilege it is to serve in the kingdom of God. In this work it is the Spirit that counts—wherever we serve. I know I must rely on the Spirit. Let us obtain that Spirit and be faithful members of the Church, devoted children and parents, effective home teachers, edifying instructors, inspired ward and stake leaders. (*Ensign*, May 1986, p. 77.)

— *Ezra Taft Benson*

There is nothing as important as having the companionship of the Holy Ghost. Those who first receive this endowment and who then remain in tune with this member of the Eternal Godhead will receive a peace and a comfort that passeth all understanding; they will be guided and preserved in ways that are miraculous; they will be instructed until they receive all truth; they will sanctify their souls so as to dwell spotless before the Sinless One in his everlasting kingdom. (*A New Witness For The Articles Of Faith*, Salt Lake City: Deseret Book Co., 1985, p. 253.)

— *Bruce R. McConkie*

Will the Holy Ghost deceive any man? It will not. When a man speaks as he is moved upon by the Holy Ghost, it is the spirit of inspiration; it is the word of God; it is the will of God. It cannot lie; it cannot deceive. It leads into all truth, and reveals to man the will of his Maker. (*MS*, 51:786.)

— *Wilford Woodruff*

See also GIFTS OF THE SPIRIT, REVELATION, SPIRIT OF THE LORD

——— Home ———

A true Mormon home is one in which if Christ should chance to enter, he would be pleased to linger and to rest. (*Gospel Ideals*, The Improvement Era, Salt Lake City: Deseret Book Co., 1976, p. 169.)

— *David O. McKay*

Brethren, there is too little religious devotion, love and fear of God, in the home; too much worldliness, selfishness, indifference and lack of reverence in the family, or these never would exist so abundantly on the outside. (*IE*, December 1904, p. 135.)

— *Joseph F. Smith*

Encourage good music and art and literature in your homes. Homes that have a spirit of refinement and beauty will bless the lives of your children forever. (*Ensign*, November 1987, p. 51.)

— *Ezra Taft Benson*

Every home has both body and spirit. You may have a beautiful house with all the decorations that modern art can give or wealth bestow. You may have all the outward forms that will please the eye and yet not have a home. It is not home without love. It may be a hovel, a log hut, a tent, a wickiup, if you have the right spirit within, the true love of Christ, and love for one another . . . you have the true life of the home that Latter-day Saints build and which they are striving to establish.(*CR*, 1907, p. 63.)

— *David O. McKay*

Family Prayer

I am convinced that one of the greatest things that can come into any home to cause the boys and girls in that home to grow up in a love of God and in a love of the gospel of Jesus Christ is to have family prayer; not for the father of the family alone to pray, but for the mother and for the children to do so also, that they may partake of the spirit of prayer and be . . . in communication with the Spirit of the Lord. (*CR*, October 1923, pp. 7-8.)

— *Heber J. Grant*

Family Scripture Study

In our homes . . . it is our duty, to call our families together to be taught the truths of the Holy Scriptures. In every home children should be encouraged to read the word of the Lord, as it has been revealed to us in all dispensations. . . . not only read it in our homes, but explain it to our children, that they may understand the dealings of God with the peoples of the earth. (*CR*, April 1914, p. 12.)

— *George Albert Smith*

Home and family. What sweet memories surge up in our breasts at the mere mention of these cherished words! . . . As revealed through the Prophet Joseph Smith, the glorious concept of home and the enduring family relationship lies at the very basis of our happiness here and hereafter. I trust you will make your happiness secure. (*Church News*, June 4, 1947, p. 5.)

— *Ezra Taft Benson*

Good homes are still the best source of good humans. (*Ensign*, October 1974, p. 71.)

— *Neal A. Maxwell*

From Abraham sprang two ancient races represented in Isaac and Ishmael. The one built stable homes, and prized its land as a divine inheritance. The other became children of the desert, and as restless as its ever shifting sands upon which their tents were pitched. . . .

The disposition among the Saints to be moving about ought to be discouraged. . . . let the home be erected with the thought that it is to be a family abiding place from one generation to another, that it is to be a monument to its founder and an inheritance of all that is sacred and dear in home life. Let this be the Mecca to which an everlasting posterity may make its pilgrimage. The home, a stable and pure home, is the highest guarantee of social stability and permanence in government. (*IE*, 38:144-46.)

— *Joseph F. Smith*

Home is really only the feeling between husband and wife—how they feel about one another and God. Home isn't the house, for the house can still be there when home is gone. (*Ensign*, November 1982, p. 27.)

— *Rex C. Reeve*

Home life, home teaching, parental guidance is the panacea for all the ailments, a cure for all diseases, a remedy for all problems. (*CR*, April 1965, p. 65.)

— *Spencer W. Kimball*

Home should be a happy place because all work to keep it that way. It is said that happiness is homemade, and we should endeavor to make our homes happy and pleasant places for us and our children. A happy home is one centered around the teachings of the gospel. This takes constant, careful effort by all concerned. (*Ensign*, November 1990, p. 12.)

— *LeGrand R. Curtis*

How beautiful is that home where lives a man of godly manner, who loves those for whose nurture he is responsible, who stands before them as an example of integrity and goodness, who teaches industry and loyalty, not spoiling his children by indulging their every wish, but rather setting before them a pattern of work and service which will underpin their lives forever. How fortunate is the man whose wife radiates a spirit of love, of compassion, of order, of quiet beneficence, whose children show appreciation one for another, who honor and respect their parents, who counsel with them and take counsel from them. Such home life is within the reach of all who have cultivated in their hearts a resolution to do that which will please their Father in Heaven. (*Ensign*, May 1985, p. 50.)

— *Gordon B. Hinckley*

I speak to fathers and mothers everywhere with a plea to put harshness behind us, to bridle our anger, to lower our voices, and to deal with mercy and love and respect one toward another in our homes. (*Ensign*, May 1990, pp. 70-73.)

— *Gordon B. Hinckley*

In this age of selfishness and greed, of birth control and barrenness, of easy divorce, broken homes, and juvenile delinquency, in this age of cheap amusements, idleness and lack of discipline, it is well to search for basic values, to call attention to the fact that the home is the nation's most fundamental institution and that mothers are the first professors in that character-building school. (Quoted by O. Leslie Stone, *Ensign*, November 1976, p. 60.)

— Hugh B. Brown

In homes where high ideals and gospel values are maintained, it is parents, not teachers, who lay the foundation of character and faith in the hearts of their children. If the training a child should receive in the home is neglected, neither the Church nor the school can compensate for the loss. (*Ensign*, May 1990, p. 10.)

— Rex D. Pinegar

No other success can compensate for failure in the home. The poorest shack in which love prevails over a united family is of greater value to God and future humanity than any other riches. In such a home God can work miracles and will work miracles. (*CR*, April 1964, p. 5.)

— David O. McKay

One day a young son, just married, invited his father to visit him and his bride in their new home. The young son took the father from room to room and showed him the furnishings, the paintings on the walls and so forth, and the father said, "This is lovely. I congratulate you, but, Son, I have looked in vain for anything that indicates that you have a place here for God."

In writing about it later, the young man said, "I went through the rooms later, and I found that Father was right."

Let us go back to our homes and see whether the spirit of our homes is such that if an angel called, he would be pleased to remain.

— David O. McKay

Our church buildings are not the only places where we can worship. Our homes should also be places of devotion. It would be well if each day we could "go home to church." There should be no other place where the Spirit of the Lord is more welcome and more easily accessible than in our own homes. (*Ensign*, November 1989, p. 63.)

— Dean L. Larsen

Our homes are next to the temple in sacredness. They are an uplifting refuge, in which we instruct our families as to what the Lord expects of us. (*Ensign*, May 1983, p. 74.)

— Ted E. Brewerton

Remember always that the most important of the Lord's work you and I will ever do will be within the walls of our own homes. (Published text of 1973 motion picture, "Strengthening the Home," p. 7.)

— Harold B. Lee

Some years ago a fire erupted in the middle of the night and completely destroyed a family's home. A neighbor came by to console a seven-year-old, not knowing that he was about to be taught a great principle. "Johnny, it's sure too bad your home burned down." Johnny thought a moment and then said, "Oh, that's where you're mistaken, Mr. Brown. That was not our home; that was just our house. We still have our home, we just don't have any place to put it right now."

What a great principle taught by a child about home. (*Ensign*, May 1984, p. 30.)

— *Gene R. Cook*

The home is an institution of learning, of loving—to develop the capacities of each of its members to live in accordance to the laws of God. (*Ensign*, May 1979, p. 61.)

— *James M. Paramore*

The home is the laboratory of our lives, and what we learn there largely determines what we do when we leave there. (*Ensign*, November 1988, p. 69.)

— *Thomas S. Monson*

The home is the seedbed of Saints. (*Ensign*, May 1978, p. 5.)

— *Spencer W. Kimball*

The home is where we learn what is right, what is good, and what is kind. It is the first school and the first church. (*Ensign*, November 1976, p. 60.)

— *O. Leslie Stone*

The home may not be expert in plasma physics, we leave that to the universities. But it should be expert in teaching true self-identity as a child of God. (*Ensign*, May 1979, p. 10.)

— *G. Homer Durham*

There is no substitute for the home. Its foundation is as ancient as the world, and its mission has been ordained of God from the earliest times. . . .

There can be no genuine happiness separate and apart from the home, and every effort made to sanctify and preserve its influence is uplifting to those who toil and sacrifice for its establishment. There is no happiness without service and there is no greater service than that which converts the home into a divine institution, and which promotes and preserves family life. (*Gospel Doctrine*, Joseph F. Smith, Salt Lake City: Deseret Book Co., 1975, p. 300.)

— *Joseph F. Smith*

Our homes should be among the most hallowed of all earthly sanctuaries. (*Ensign*, November 1977, p. 11.)

— *James E. Faust*

Pure hearts in a pure home are always in whispering distance of Heaven. (*Church News*, 7 Sept. 1968, p. 4.)

— *David O. McKay*

We can make our houses homes and our homes heavens.

— *Spencer W. Kimball*

You can do a great deal to create in your home an atmosphere of peace and hominess and reverence and tranquility and security. You can do this without much to live on. Or you can create something angular and cold and artificial. In a thousand different ways your youngsters will be influenced by the choice you make. You can set the tone. It can be quiet and peaceful where quiet and powerful strength can grow, or it can be bold and loud and turn the mainspring of tension a bit tighter in the little children as they are growing up, until at last, that mainspring breaks. (*Speeches of the Year*, Provo: Brigham Young University Press, p. 8.)

— *Boyd K. Packer*

[Our homes should be] the strong place to which children can come for the anchor they need in this day of trouble and turmoil. (*His Servants Speak*, R. Clayton Brough, comp., Bountiful, Utah: Horizon, 1975, p. 154.)

— *Harold B. Lee*

See also FAMILY

Home Teaching

God called us [as Home Teachers] to watch over and help people in all their struggles for physical and spiritual well-being. He called us to help by the Spirit. He called us to teach by the Spirit. He called us to live what we teach. He called us to bear testimony. He called us to love. (*Ensign*, May 1988, p. 39.)

— *Henry B. Eyring*

Home teaching and visiting teaching are vehicles for saving souls when done the right way with the right intent.

— *Joseph B. Wirthlin*

Home teaching is an inspired program.

It is the heart of caring, of loving, of reaching out to the one—both the active and the less active.

It is priesthood compassionate service.

It is how we express our faith in practical works.

It is one of the tests of true discipleship.

It is the heart of the activation effort of the Church.

It is a calling that helps to fulfill the scriptural injunction "Out of small things proceedeth that which is great." (D&C 64:33.)

There is no greater Church calling than that of a home teacher. (*Ensign*, May 1987, p. 50.)

— *Ezra Taft Benson*

Home teaching, properly functioning, brings to the house of each member two priesthood bearers divinely commissioned and authoritatively called into the service by their priesthood leader and bishop. These Home Teachers—priesthood bearers—carry the heavy and glorious responsibility of representing the Lord Jesus Christ in looking after the welfare of each Church member. They are to encourage and inspire every member to discharge his duty, both family and Church. (*Ensign*, March 1973, pp. 12-13.)

— *Marion G. Romney*

I can remember, as if it were yesterday, growing up as a young boy in Whitney, Idaho. We were a farm family, and when we boys were out working in the field, I remember Father calling to us in a shrill voice from the barnyard: "Tie up your teams, boys, and come on in. The ward teachers are here." Regardless of what we were doing, that was the signal to assemble in the sitting room to hear the ward teachers.

These two faithful priesthood bearers would come each month either by foot or by horseback. We always knew they would come. I can't remember one miss. And we would have a great visit. They would stand behind a chair and talk to the family. They would go around the circle and ask each child how he or she was doing and if we were doing our duty. Sometimes Mother and Father would prime us before the ward teachers came so we would have the right answers. But it was an important time for us as a family. They always had a message, and it was always a good one.

We have refined home teaching a lot since those early days in Whitney. But it is still basically the same. The same principles are involved: caring, reaching out, teaching by the Spirit, leaving an important message each month, and having a concern and love for each member of the family. (*Ensign*, May 1987, p. 51.)

— *Ezra Taft Benson*

I was called and ordained to act as a teacher to visit the families of the Saints. I got along very well till I found that I was obliged to call and pay a visit to the Prophet. Being young, only about seventeen years of age, I felt my weakness in visiting the Prophet and his family in the capacity of a teacher. I almost felt like shrinking from duty. Finally I went to his door and knocked, and in a minute the Prophet came to the door. I stood there trembling, and said to him:

"Brother Joseph, I have come to visit you in the capacity of a teacher, if it is convenient for you."

He said, "Brother William, come right in, I am glad to see you; sit down in that chair there and I will go and call my family in."

They soon came in and took seats. He then said, "Brother William, I submit myself and family into your hands," and then took his seat. "Now Brother William," said he, "ask all the questions you feel like."

By this time all my fears and trembling had ceased, and I said, "Brother Joseph, are you trying to live your religion?"

He answered, "Yes."

Then I said, "Do you pray in your family?"

He said, "Yes."

"Do you teach your family the principles of the gospel?"

He replied, "Yes, I am trying to do it."

"Do you ask a blessing on your food?"

He answered, "Yes."

"Are you trying to live in peace and harmony with all your family?"

He said that he was.

I turned to Sister Emma, his wife, and said, "Sister Emma, are you trying to live your religion? Do you teach your children to obey their parents? Do you try to teach them to pray?"

To all these questions, she answered, "Yes. I am trying to do so."

I then turned to Joseph and said, "I am now through with my questions as a teacher; and now if you have any instructions to give, I shall be happy to receive them."

He said, "God bless you, Brother William; and if you are humble and faithful, you shall have power to settle all difficulties that may come before you in the capacity of a teacher."

I then left my parting blessing upon him and his family, as a teacher, and took my departure. (*Juvenile Instructor*, 27:491-92.)

— *William Cahoon*

Priesthood visitors are to be watchmen on the tower. I'm not sure but what we've arrived at a time when we ought to be thinking of a new name instead of *teacher* attached to the Priesthood visitors. The word *teaching* suggests that they are to go there to teach a gospel message, and that primarily isn't what we expect the home teachers of today to do. They are home visitors; they are Priesthood home visitors to inquire into the health of the family and to see if they are doing their family duties, and if they are assuming their Church responsibilities. (Regional Representatives Seminar, April 3, 1969.)

— Harold B. Lee

Properly performed, home teaching is the Lord's way of making all of the blessings of the gospel available to all the members of his kingdom.

— Bruce R. McConkie

The Lord's formula for receiving the Spirit is to get on our knees and . . . tell him what we are going to do . . . and then get up off our knees and go and *do* precisely what we have told him we would do. In the *doing*, the Spirit comes.

I cannot say that I love to home teach *until* I get to the first home, and then I do love it because I then get the spirit of a home teacher because I am acting like a home teacher—doing what a home teacher does. (*Ensign*, January 1974, p. 107.)

— Hartman Rector, Jr.

There is no greater Church calling than that of a home teacher. There is no greater Church service rendered to our Father in Heaven's children than the service rendered by a humble, dedicated, committed home teacher. (*Ensign*, May 1987, p. 50.)

— Ezra Taft Benson

We do not visit the active just to "visit," or the less active just to get them out to church, although that may be part of what happens. In essence, we visit to help the heads of those homes, male or female, to become the spiritual leaders in their homes, to lead their families to Christ, to pray, to fast, and to read the scriptures together. If that happens in our visits, all else will take care of itself. (*Ensign*, November 1988, pp. 37,38.)

— Gene R. Cook

[Home teaching is] a program so vital that, if faithfully followed, it will help to spiritually renew the Church and exalt its individual members and families. (*Ensign*, May 1987, p. 48.)

— Ezra Taft Benson

See also PRIESTHOOD, PRIESTHOOD QUORUMS, SERVICE

Honesty

Do we understand the gravity of the sin of dishonesty? It is not only unchristian, it is anti-Christian—it is anti-Mormon—it is anti-Christ!

Whether it be lying, or cheating, or robbery or deception; whether it is in the home, in business, in sports, or in the classroom; dishonesty is completely foreign to the teachings of Jesus. (*Ensign,* May 1982, p. 15.)

— Mark E. Petersen

Honesty is more than a policy. It is a happy way of life. (*Ensign,* May 1982, p. 11.)

— Marvin J. Ashton

Honesty is not only the best policy, it is the only policy! (*Ensign,* November 1987, p. 15.)

— David B. Haight

It is binding upon us today, and I want to say to you that the punishment that is meted out to those who are dishonest, when they are apprehended and hailed before the courts of the land, is insignificant when compared with the spiritual punishment that befalls us when we transgress the law of honesty. (*DFTP,* p. 242.)

— George Albert Smith

It is with great alarm that we read newspaper accounts and hear daily media reports that describe the decline of moral decency and the erosion of basic ethical conduct. They detail the corrupting influence of dishonesty, from small-time, childish stealing or cheating to major embezzlement, fraud, and misappropriation of money or goods.

Headlines and feature stories dramatically demonstrate the need for honesty and integrity in family relationships, in business affairs, and in the conduct of government officials and religious ministries. (*Ensign,* November 1987, p. 14.)

— David B. Haight

Simple truth, simplicity, honesty, uprightness, justice, mercy, love, kindness, do good to all and evil to none, how easy it is to live by such principles! A thousand times easier than to practice deception! (*JD,* 14:76.)

— Brigham Young

Those who are honest are fair and truthful in their speech, straightforward in their dealings, free of deceit, and above stealing, misrepresentation, or any other fraudulent action. Honesty is of God and dishonesty of the devil; the devil was a liar from the beginning. (*Ensign*, May 1988, p. 81.)

— Joseph B. Wirthlin

The only security lies in individual, personal honesty. The law cannot make people honest. (*CR*, October 1938, p. 66.)

— Albert E. Bowen

See also INTEGRITY, LYING

—————— Hope ——————

Hope is light. It is a light within us that pierces the darkness of doubt and discouragement and taps into the light of all creation—even the Savior . . . . Christ is the true hope that is in all men. (See D&C 88:50.) (*Hope*, Salt Lake City: Deseret Book Co., 1988, pp. 46-47.)

— John H. Groberg

If you don't have hope, you either don't have the Holy Ghost or you aren't listening to him, for it states clearly, "which Comforter filleth with hope and perfect love." (Moro. 8:26.) (*Hope*, Salt Lake City: Deseret Book Co., 1988, pp. 53-54.)

— John H. Groberg

In a world where materialism, cynicism, and hopelessness exists, we share the message of greatest hope—the gospel of Jesus Christ. (*Ensign*, November 1983, p. 41.)

— David B. Haight

That is the nature of hope. We do all we can, and then the Lord stretches forth his hand and touches our lives with light and courage and, most of all, hope. (*Ensign*, November 1986, p. 86.)

— Dwan J. Young

The daily work of the Lord involves changing hopeless to hopeful—for all of us. And it is for us to find at last that in the midst of winter we have within us an invincible summer. In a world filled with adversity we can reach for joy. (*Ensign*, May 1982, p. 95.)

— Elaine Cannon

The Lord wants us to be filled with hope—not just because it points us to a brighter tomorrow, but because it changes the quality of our lives today. *Hopeless* may be the saddest word in our language. Despair is the enemy of our souls. It can paralyze us, halt our progress, and cause us to lose our way. But hope awakens us like a light shining in the darkness. . . .

We can endure all things when our hope is centered in one who will never fail us—our Savior, Jesus Christ, who is the light of the world. (*Ensign*, November 1986, p. 86.)

— *Dwan J. Young*

We have a hope in Christ here and now. He died for our sins. Because of him and his gospel, our sins are washed away in the waters of baptism; sin and iniquity are burned out of our souls as though by fire; and we become clean, have clear consciences, and gain that peace which passeth understanding. (See Philippians 4:7.)

But today is just a grain of sand in the Sahara of eternity. We have also a hope in Christ for the eternity that lies ahead; otherwise, as Paul said, we would be "of all men most miserable." (1 Cor. 15:19.) (*Ensign*, November 1978, p. 71.)

— *Spencer W. Kimball*

We must not lose hope. Hope is an anchor to the souls of men. Satan would have us cast away that anchor. In this way he can bring discouragement and surrender. But we must not lose hope. The Lord is pleased with every effort, even the tiny, daily ones in which we strive to be more like Him. Though we may see that we have far to go on the road to perfection, we must not give up hope. (*TETB*, p. 398.)

— *Ezra Taft Benson*

We testify of Christ. Our hope is in Christ. Our salvation is in Christ. Our efforts, hopes, and desires to build up the kingdom of God on earth are centered in and through His holy name. (*Ensign*, November 1982, p. 10.)

— *David B. Haight*

See also LOOK TO GOD, OPTIMISM, TRUST IN GOD

Human Rights

If it has been demonstrated that I have been willing to die for a "Mormon," I am bold to declare before heaven that I am just as ready to die in defending the rights of a Presbyterian, a Baptist, or a good man of any other denomination; for the same principle which would trample upon the rights of the Latter-day Saints would trample upon the rights of the Roman Catholics, or of any other denomination who may be unpopular and too weak to defend themselves.

It is a love of liberty which inspires my soul—civil and religious liberty to the whole of the human race. Love of liberty was diffused into my soul by my grandfathers while they dandled me on their knees. (*HC*, 5:498.)

— *Joseph Smith*

As members of Christ's true church we must stand firm today and always for human rights and the dignity of man who is the literal offspring of God in the spirit. (*Ensign*, May 1979 p. 7.)

— *Spencer W. Kimball*

Besides the preaching of the Gospel, we have another mission, namely, the perpetuation of the free agency of man and the maintenance of liberty, freedom and the rights of man. (*JD*, 9:340.)

— *John Taylor*

In my feelings I am always ready to die for the protection of the weak and oppressed in their just rights. (*HC*, 6:57.)

— *Joseph Smith*

The scriptures and the prophets have taught us clearly that God, who is perfect in his attributes of justice, "is no respecter of persons" (see Acts 10:34). . . . We had full equality as his spirit children. We have equality as recipients of God's perfected love for each of us. (*Ensign*, November 1979, p. 102.)

— *Spencer W. Kimball*

We believe that all men are the children of the same God, and that it is a moral evil for any person or group of persons to deny any human being the right to gainful employment, to full educational opportunity, and to every privilege of citizenship, just as it is a moral evil to deny him the right to worship according to the dictates of his own conscience. . . . We call upon men everywhere, both within and outside the Church, to commit themselves to the establishment of full civil equality for all of God's children. Anything less than this defeats our high ideal of the brotherhood of man. (*CR*, October, 1963, p. 91.)

— *Hugh B. Brown*

We should learn to have a great and good opinion of human life, for all are made in the image of God and have a divinity and destiny. (*CR*, April 1952, p. 55.)

— *Levi Edgar Young*

See also FREEDOM, TOLERANCE

Humility

A contrite heart is a fertile field for planting the seeds of truth. In such a field they come to fruition in a knowledge, understanding, and conviction of the great concepts of life which defy the reason and philosophy of the arrogant and self-sufficient who will not stoop to the methods of the humble. (*CR*, April 1939.)

— *Stephen L Richards*

A monk is said to have built a tower sixty feet high and three feet wide. On a certain day he would climb up to the top of the tower and pray, and the words of his prayers were generally about like this, "Oh, God, where art thou?" No answer. "Oh, God, where art thou?" No answer. Finally when he had exhausted someone's patience, there came a voice and it said, "I am down among the people." You have to be humble. Our wealth, our affluence, our liberties, all that we possess must never make us feel above anyone. We must always keep in mind a deep sincerity, a great humility, and a total dependence upon the Lord. (Address, Salt Lake Monument Park Stake, September 16, 1958.)

— *Spencer W. Kimball*

How easy it is for man to believe that temporal success has been achieved by his own skills and labor. Everything good comes from the Lord. . . .

It pleases God to have us humbly recognize his powers and his influence in our accomplishments rather than to indicate by words or innuendo that we have been responsible for remarkable achievements. . . .

Humility must be our foundation if the goodness of the Lord is to continue to come to and from us. (*Ensign*, May 1990, p. 66, 67.)

— *Marvin J. Ashton*

Humility is not a feeling of awe and reverence and personal unworthiness in the presence of overpowering majesty. . . . Plain humility is reverence and respect in the presence of the lowest, not the highest, of God's creatures. Brigham Young said he often felt overawed in the presence of little children or any of his fellow-men—for in them he saw the image of his maker. (*OAT*, p. 154.)

— *Hugh Nibley*

Humility is the precious, fertile soil of righteous character. It germinates the seeds of personal growth. When cultivated through the exercise of faith, pruned by repentance, and fortified by obedience and good works, such seeds produce the cherished fruit of spirituality. (See Alma 26:22.) Divine inspiration and power then result. Inspiration is to know the will of the Lord. Power is the capability to accomplish that inspired will. (See D&C 43:15-16.) Such power comes from God after we have done "all we can do." (2 Ne. 25:23.) (*Ensign*, November 1981, p. 12.)

— Richard G. Scott

Humility responds to God's will—to the fear of his judgments and to the needs of those around us. To the proud, the applause of the world rings in their ears; to the humble, the applause of heaven warms their hearts. (*Ensign*, May 1986, p. 7.)

— Ezra Taft Benson

Humility is royalty without a crown,
Greatness in plain clothes,
Erudition without decoration,
Wealth without display,
Power without scepter or force,
Position demanding no preferential rights,
Greatness sitting in the congregation,
Prayer in closets and not in corners of the street,
Fasting in secret without publication,
Stalwartness without a label,
Supplication upon its knees,
Divinity riding an ass. (*IE*, August 1963, p. 704.)

— Spencer W. Kimball

I firmly believe that no man who honestly bows down every day of his life and supplicates God in sincerity for the light of his Holy Spirit to guide him will ever become proud and haughty. On the contrary, his heart will become filled with meekness, humility, and childlike simplicity. (*DFTP*, p. 246.)

— Heber J. Grant

If the Lord was meek and lowly and humble, then to become humble one must do what he did in boldly denouncing evil, bravely advancing righteous work, courageously meeting every problem, becoming the master of himself and the situations about him, and being near oblivious to personal credit. (*IE*, August 1963, p. 636.)

— Spencer W. Kimball

Sometimes in our enthusiasm for the gospel, we cast our pearls indiscriminately, and we might even be tempted to enhance the luster of our pearl of great price by placing it in a much too attractive setting. This may only detract from the true value of our pearl. Our pearl will stand on its own, with all its beauty and simplicity. We do not need to enhance it with bright and flashy things that will only bring antagonism and conflict to the Church. We need to speak less about our accomplishments and, by our actions, show which kingdom we seek. (*Ensign*, November 1989, p. 72.)

— *L. Tom Perry*

The Lord has not chosen the great and learned of the world to perform His work on the earth. . . . but humble men devoted to His cause . . . , men who are willing to be led and guided by the Holy Spirit, and who will of necessity give the glory unto Him knowing that of themselves they can do nothing. (*Deseret Weekly*, 57:513.)

— *Lorenzo Snow*

We are all beggars . . . (see Mosiah 4:19), beggars rescued by the Creator of the universe who lived humbly as a person "of no reputation." (Philip. 2:7.) In contrast, we are sometimes so anxious about our personal images, when it is His image we should have in our countenances. (See Alma 5:14.) (*Ensign*, November 1988, p. 31.)

— *Neal A. Maxwell*

We can choose to be humble . . . by conquering enmity toward our brothers and sisters, esteeming them as ourselves, and lifting them as high or higher than we are. . . . by receiving counsel and chastisement. . . . by forgiving those who have offended us. . . . by rendering selfless service. . . . by going on missions and preaching the word that can humble others. . . . by confessing and forsaking our sins and being born of God. . . . by loving God, submitting our will to His, and putting Him first in our lives.

Let us choose to be humble. We can do it. I know we can. (*Ensign*, May 1986, pp. 6-7.)

— *Ezra Taft Benson*

We walk today in the sunlight of goodwill. The Church is widely respected and honored. The virtue of our people and the integrity of our efforts have come to be recognized and appreciated.

Let us be grateful. But let us not be boastful. Let us rather be thankful and humble, as becomes those who are the beneficiaries of such rich blessings from the Almighty. (*Ensign*, May 1982, p. 44.)

— *Gordon B. Hinckley*

See also GRATITUDE, PRIDE

───── Hypocrisy ─────

I am not sorry, nor do I regret on account of the near approach of fiery ordeals. The Church, no doubt, needs purifying. We have hypocrites among us, milk-and-water Saints, those professing to be Saints, but doing nothing to render themselves worthy of membership; and too many of us have been pursuing worldly gains, rather than spiritual improvements, have not sought the things of God with earnestness. (*JD*, 26:367-68.)

— *Lorenzo Snow*

I love that man better who swears a stream as long as my arm yet deals justice to his neighbors and mercifully deals his substance to the poor, than the long, smooth-faced hypocrite. (*HC*, 5:401.)

— *Joseph Smith*

No man can stand in this Church, or retain the Spirit of God and continue in a course of hypocrisy for any length of time. (*JD*, 18:84.)

— *George Q. Cannon*

See also HONESTY, INTEGRITY

───── Idleness ─────

Idleness in any form produces boredom, conflict, and unhappiness. It creates a vacancy of worth, a seedbed for mischief and evil. It is the enemy of progress and salvation. (*Ensign*, May 1982, p. 78.)

— *J. Richard Clarke*

To be slothful, wasteful, lazy and indolent . . . is unrighteous. (*DBY*, p. 303.)

— *Brigham Young*

We must purge our hearts of the love of ease; we must put out from our lives the curse of idleness. God declared that mortal man should earn his bread by the sweat of his brow. That is the law of this world. (*CR*, April 1937, p. 26.)

— *J. Reuben Clark, Jr.*

See also WORK

———— Individuality ————

Each of us comes into this world separately, one by one. This is not an accident. I think it's the Lord's way of reminding us of the infinite worth of each soul. (*Ensign*, May 1982, p. 93.)

— Dwan J. Young

We are immortal beings. That which dwells in this body of ours is immortal, and will always exist. Our individuality will always continue. Eternities may begin, eternities may end, and still we shall have our individuality. Our identity is insured. We will be ourselves and nobody else. Whatever changes may arise, whatever worlds may be made or pass away, our identity will always remain the same; and we will continue improving, advancing, and increasing in wisdom, intelligence, power, and dominion, worlds without end. (*CR*, April 1901, p. 2.)

— Lorenzo Snow

We are not saved as congregations nor as groups, but we are saved as we come into the world as individuals, and the Lord's purpose is to save the individual, each being precious in his sight. (*CR*, April 1957.)

— David O. McKay

See also MAN, SELF-WORTH

———— Initiative ————

Certainly one of our God-given privileges is the right to choose what our attitude will be in any given set of circumstances. We can let the events that surround us determine our actions—or we can personally take charge and rule our lives, using as guidelines the principles of pure religion. (*Ensign*, November 1982, p. 63.)

— Marvin J. Ashton

Forced obedience yields no blessings. (*Ensign*, May 1988, p. 59.)

— Richard G. Scott

The power is in us wherein we are agents unto ourselves, and that we should not wait to be commanded in all things, and he that is compelled in all things is a slothful and not a wise servant. We should have the ambition, we should have the desire, we should make up our minds that, so far as the Lord Almighty has given to us talent, we will do our full share in the battle of life. It should be a matter of pride that no man shall do more than you will do, in proportion to your ability, in forwarding the work of God here upon the earth. (*IE*, October 1939, p. 585.)

— *Heber J. Grant*

It is the business of those who profess to be engaged in His work to move on, to go forward, and that too without murmuring or having to be urged. So long as there remains a step forward to be taken, that step should be taken. . . . There is no standing still with the Latter-day Saints.

— *Lorenzo Snow*

We have been provided divine attributes to guide our destiny. We entered mortality not to float with the moving currents of life, but with the power to think, to reason, and to achieve. (*CR*, October 1967, p. 74.)

— *Thomas S. Monson*

You know that it is one peculiarity of our faith and religion never to ask the Lord to do a thing without being willing to help him all that we are able; and then the Lord will do the rest. (*DBY*, p. 43.)

— *Brigham Young*

See also ACTION, LIVING THE GOSPEL, PROCRASTINATION

Inspiration

Each one of us is the architect of his own fate, and he is unfortunate indeed who will try to build himself without the inspiration of God; without realizing that he grows from within, not from without. (*CR*, October 1963, p. 7.)

— *David O. McKay*

I want to advise this people, if the Lord ever does give you an inspiration, for heaven's sake write it down and remember it. (*CR*, April 1927, p. 53.)

— *J. Golden Kimball*

Inspiration can be the spring of every person's hope, guidance, and strength. It is one of the magnificent treasures of life. It involves coming to the infinite knowledge of God. (*Ensign*, May 1980, p. 14.)

— *James E. Faust*

Inspiration comes more as a feeling than as a sound. (*Ensign*, November 1979, p. 20.)

— *Boyd K. Packer*

One of the most fruitful sources of spiritual education lies in the thoughts which arise in our own hearts. (*CR*, October 1906, p. 66.)

— *George F. Richards*

Only through cleanliness and purity of thought, of word, and of action may we enjoy to perfection the inspiration of the Lord. (*Treasures of Life*, Clare Middlemiss, comp., Salt Lake City: Deseret Book Co., 1962, p. 233.)

— *David O. McKay*

Perspiration must precede inspiration. (Second Century Address, Brigham Young University, p. 8.)

— *Spencer W. Kimball*

Some answers will come from reading the scriptures, some from hearing speakers. And, occasionally when it is important, some will come by very direct and powerful inspiration. The prompting will be clear and unmistakable. (*Ensign*, November 1979, p. 21.)

— *Boyd K. Packer*

The Holy Ghost communicates with the spirit through the mind more than through the physical senses. This guidance comes as thoughts, as feelings, through impressions and promptings. It is not always easy to describe inspiration. The scriptures teach us that we may "feel" the words of spiritual communication more than hear them, and see with spiritual rather than with mortal eyes.

The patterns of revelation are not dramatic. The voice of inspiration is a still voice, a small voice. There need be no trance, no sanctimonious declaration. It is quieter and simpler than that. (*Ensign*, November 1989, p. 14.)

— *Boyd K. Packer*

The Latter-day Saints are safe as long as they listen to the voice of inspiration. (*CR*, April 1899, p. 10.)

— *Matthias F. Cowley*

There is a still small voice telling us what is right, and if we listen to that still small voice we shall grow and increase in strength and power, in testimony and in ability not only to live the gospel but to inspire others to do so. (*IE*, December 1937, p. 735.)

— *Heber J. Grant*

There's a fine balance between agency and inspiration. We're expected to do everything in our power that we can, and then to seek an answer from the Lord, a confirming seal that we've reached the right conclusion; and sometimes, happily, in addition, we get added truths and knowledge that we hadn't even supposed. (Address, Brigham Young University, February 27, 1973.)

— *Bruce R. McConkie*

When we receive an impression in our *heart*, we can use our *mind* either to rationalize it away or to accomplish it. Be careful what you do with an impression from the Lord. (*Ensign*, November 1989, p. 31.)

— *Richard G. Scott*

See also HOLY GHOST, LOOK TO GOD, REVELATION

——— Integrity ———

Complete and constant integrity is a great law of human conduct. There need to be some absolutes in life. There are some things that should not ever be done, some lines that should never be crossed, vows that should never be broken, words that should never be spoken, and thoughts that should never be entertained. (*Ensign*, May 1982, p. 48.)

— *James E. Faust*

Do not write a check with your tongue that your actions cannot cash.

— *Neal A. Maxwell*

I like to think of reputation as a window, clearly exhibiting the integrity of one's soul. It is through this integrity of thought and integrity of conduct that we become pure and holy before the Lord. It is in this state that we can be most effective in serving our fellowmen. (*CR*, October 1975, p. 60.)

— *O. Leslie Stone*

Integrity is the core of our character. Without integrity we have a weak foundation upon which to build other Christlike characteristics. (*Ensign*, November 1988, p. 23.)

— *L. Lionel Kendrick*

Integrity means always doing what is right and good, regardless of the immediate consequences. It means being righteous from the very depth of our soul, not only in our actions but, more importantly, in our thoughts and in our hearts. Personal integrity implies such trustworthiness and incorruptibility that we are incapable of being false to a trust or covenant. (*Ensign*, May 1990, p. 30.)

— *Joseph B. Wirthlin*

Integrity is the value we set on ourselves. It is a fulfillment of the duty we owe ourselves. An honorable man or woman will personally commit to live up to certain self-imposed expectations. They need no outside check or control. They are honorable in their inner core. (*Ensign*, May 1982, p. 47.)

— *James E. Faust*

No matter what a man is thought of by his fellow men, . . . if he is true, God is his friend, and he is rich indeed. (*CR*, October 1907, p. 60.)

— *David O. McKay*

Perhaps the surest test of an individual's integrity is his refusal to do or say anything that would damage his self-respect.

— *Thomas S. Monson*

The foundation of a noble character is integrity. (*CR*, April 1964, p. 6.)

— *David O. McKay*

The rewards of integrity are immeasurable. One is the indescribable inner peace and serenity that come from knowing we are doing what is right; another is an absence of the guilt and anxiety that accompany sin. (*Ensign*, May 1990, p. 33.)

— *Joseph B. Wirthlin*

We have heard sermons and exhortations upon honesty, trust, righteousness, dependability, truthfulness, kindness, justice, mercy, love, fidelity, and many other principles of right living.

When one has integrated all of these attributes within his being, when they become the moving force of all his thoughts, actions, and desires, then he may be said to possess integrity, which has been defined as "a state or quality of being complete, undivided, or unbroken; moral soundness, honesty and uprightness." (*Ensign*, May 1977, p. 14.)

— *N. Eldon Tanner*

When one is loyal to the truth, we say he is a person of integrity. When one is loyal to the truth under intense opposition, we say he is a person of *great* integrity. (*Ensign*, November 1984, p. 63.)

— *Royden G. Derrick*

See also HONESTY, HYPOCRISY, VALIANCY

—— Intellectualism ——

If the gospel is only for the learned, how few there are of us who could have any use for it. (*CR*, April 1934, p. 93.)

— *J. Reuben Clark, Jr.*

Jacob speaks of people who placed themselves in serious jeopardy in spiritual things because they were unwilling to accept simple, basic principles of truth. They entertained and intrigued themselves with "things that they could not understand." [Jacob 4:14.] They were apparently afflicted with a pseudo-sophistication and a snobbishness that gave them a false sense of superiority over those who came among them with the Lord's words of plainness. They went beyond the mark of wisdom and prudence and obviously failed to stay within the circle of fundamental gospel truth which provides a basis for faith. (*Ensign*, November 1987, p. 11.)

— *Dean L. Larsen*

One activity which often leads a member to be critical is engaging in inappropriate intellectualism. While it would seem the search for and discovery of truth should be the goal of all Latter-day Saints, it appears some get more satisfaction from trying to discover new uncertainties. I have friends who have literally spent their lives, thus far, trying to nail down every single intellectual loose end rather than accepting the witness of the Spirit and getting on with it. In so doing, they are depriving themselves of a gold mine of beautiful truths which cannot be tapped by the mind alone.

Elder Faust describes this type of intellectual as "a person who continues to chase after a bus even after he has caught it." We invite everyone to get on the bus before it's out of sight and you are left forever trying to figure out the infinite with a finite mind. In the words of Elijah, "How long halt ye between two opinions? If the Lord be God, follow him." (1 Kgs. 18:21.) (*Ensign*, May 1989, p. 26.)

— *Glenn L. Pace*

See KNOWLEDGE, TRUTH

—— Intelligence ——

How foolish it is for men . . . to lay aside God, and think that they can progress, and be smart and intelligent without him. . . . Franklin possessed great

information relating to natural laws. He drew the lightning from the clouds but he could not have done that if there had not been lightning in the clouds. (*JD*, 10:275.)
— *John Taylor*

Intelligence is the power to meet conditions and circumstances and overrule them for our mutual benefit and blessing. (*CR*, April 1936, p. 28.)
— *Antoine R. Ivins*

Pure intelligence comprises not only knowledge but also the power to properly apply that knowledge. (*GD*, p. 58.)
— *Joseph F. Smith*

Satan possesses knowledge, far more than we have, but he has not intelligence or he would render obedience to the principles of truth and right. . . . Pure intelligence comprises not only knowledge, but also the power to properly apply that knowledge. (*GD*, p. 58.)
— *Joseph F. Smith*

The gospel of Jesus Christ . . . recognizes the intelligence in man. It seeks through education to develop that intelligence, to expound the principles of life, to investigate and understand the secrets which nature and the universe hold. (*CR*, April 1928, p. 31.)
— *Stephen L Richards*

See also KNOWLEDGE, LIGHT OF CHRIST, TRUTH

——— Jesus Christ ———

As absolute as the certainty that you have in your hearts that tonight will be followed by dawn tomorrow morning, so is my assurance that Jesus Christ is the Savior of mankind, the light that will dispel the darkness of the world, through the gospel restored by direct revelation to the Prophet Joseph Smith. (Quoted by Gordon B. Hinckley, *Ensign*, November 1981, p. 7.)
— *David O. McKay*

Faith in the Lord Jesus Christ requires belief in him. That is, acceptance as truth of all that has been revealed concerning him and his mission. For example: That he is the firstborn spirit son of God; that he was chosen and ordained in the great heavenly council to be our Redeemer; that he came to earth in the meridian of time as the Only Begotten of God in the flesh, lived a sinless life, taught the gospel, suffered in Gethsemane, died on the cross, was buried, rose again the third day, and ascended into heaven; that through his victory over death he brought about universal resurrection; and that through his atonement he implemented the merciful plan of salvation whereby men may be forgiven of their sins, which forgiveness creates in them pure hearts and clean hands. (*Look to God and Live*, Salt Lake City: Deseret Book Co., 1975, pp. 263, 264.)

— *Marion G. Romney*

How wondrous is the story of the great Creator, the mighty Jehovah, who condescended to come to earth as the babe born in Bethlehem of Judea, who walked the dusty paths of Palestine teaching and healing and blessing, who gave His life on Calvary's painful cross, and who rose from Joseph's tomb, appearing to many on two continents—the resurrected Lord of whom we read in the testament of the Old World, the Bible, and in the testament of the New World, the Book of Mormon, as well as in the sure word of modern revelation.

We have read these, and the Spirit has borne witness in our hearts so that we too can testify that Jesus Christ is the resurrection and the life, and that he that liveth and believeth in Him shall never die (see John 11:25-26). (*Ensign*, May 1988, p. 66.)

— *Gordon B. Hinckley*

I believe in the Lord Jesus Christ, the Son of the eternal, living God. I believe in Him as the Firstborn of the Father and the Only Begotten of the Father in the flesh. I believe in him as an individual, separate and distinct from His Father. . . .

I believe that in His mortal life He was the one perfect man to walk the earth. I believe that in his words are to be found that light and truth which, if observed, would save the world and bring exaltation to mankind. . . .

I believe that through His atoning sacrifice, the offering of His life on Calvary's Hill, He expiated the sins of mankind, relieving us from the burden of sin if we will forsake evil and follow Him. I believe in the reality and the power of His resurrection. . . .

None so great has ever walked the earth. None other has made a comparable sacrifice or granted a comparable blessing. He is the Savior and the Redeemer of the world. I believe in Him. I declare His divinity without equivocation or compromise. I love Him. I speak His name in reverence and wonder. I worship Him as I worship His Father, in spirit and in truth. I thank Him and kneel before His wounded feet and hands and side, amazed at the love He offers me. (*Ensign*, November 1986, pp. 50-51.)

— *Gordon B. Hinckley*

I found myself one evening in the dreams of the night, in that sacred building, the Temple. After a season of prayer and rejoicing, I was informed that I should

have the privilege of entering into one of those rooms, to meet a glorious Person-age, and as I entered the door, I saw, seated on a raised platform the most glorious Being my eyes ever have beheld, or that I ever conceived existed in all the eternal worlds. As I approached to be introduced, he arose and stepped towards me with extended arms, and he smiled as he softly spoke my name. If I shall live to be a million years old, I shall never forget that smile. He took me into his arms and kissed me, pressed me to His bosom, and blessed me, until the marrow of my bones seemed to melt! When He had finished, I fell at His feet, and as I bathed them with my tears and kisses, I saw the prints of the nails in the feet of the Redeemer of the world. The feeling that I had in the presence of Him who hath all things in His hands, to have His love, His affection, and His blessings was such that if I ever can receive that of which I had but a foretaste, I would give all that I am, all that I ever hope to be, to feel what I then felt! (*The Faith of Our Pioneer Forefathers*, Bryant S. Hinckley, Salt Lake City: Deseret Book Co., 1956, pp. 226-27.)
— Melvin J. Ballard

Christ is our pattern, our guide, our prototype, and our friend. We seek to be like him so that we can always be with him. (*Ensign*, May 1979, p. 47.)
— Spencer W. Kimball

Do we fully realize that Jesus is to be the center of our lives? Only the Savior can be our Savior, and that relationship is always personal. We go to him alone. He accepts us that way only.

— Hugh W. Pinnock

I know that Jesus Christ is the Son of the living God and that he was crucified for the sins of the world.

He is my friend, my Savior, my Lord, my God. (*Ensign*, November 1978, p. 73.)

— Spencer W. Kimball

I testify that the name of Jesus Christ is the only name under heaven whereby men may be saved and that all men, everywhere, must be brought to a knowledge of this truth if they are to receive the great, eternal exaltation provided by a gracious and loving Father. (*Ensign*, May 1990, p. 25.)

— David B. Haight

I witness that Jesus Christ is the only name under heaven whereby one can be saved! (See D&C 18:23.)

I testify that He is utterly incomparable in what He *is*, what He *knows*, what He has *accomplished*, and what He has *experienced*. Yet, movingly, He calls us His friends. (See John 15:15.)

We can trust, worship, and even adore Him without any reservation! As the only Perfect Person to sojourn on this planet, there is none like Him! (See Isa. 46:9.)

In *intelligence* and *performance*, He far surpasses the individual and the composite *capacities* and *achievements* of all who have lived, live now, and will yet live! (See Abr. 3:19.)

He rejoices in our genuine goodness and achievement, but any assessment of where we stand in relation to Him tells us that we do not stand at all! We kneel! (*Ensign*, November 1981, p. 8.)

— *Neal A. Maxwell*

In the hearts of all mankind, of whatever race or station in life, there are inexpressible longings for something they do not now possess. This longing is implanted in man by a loving Creator. It is God's design that this longing of the human heart should lead to the one who alone is able to satisfy it. That fulness is found only in Jesus the Christ, the Son of our Eternal Father in Heaven. (*Ensign*, May 1982, p. 73.)

— *David B. Haight*

Jesus Christ is the *light* of the world because he is the source of the light that quickens our understanding, because his teachings and his example illuminate our path, and because his power persuades us to do good. . . .

The Lord Jesus Christ, our Savior and our Redeemer, is the *life* of the world because his resurrection and his atonement save us from both physical and spiritual death. (*Ensign*, November 1987, pp. 64-65.)

— *Dallin H. Oaks*

Jesus Christ was and is the *Lord God Omnipotent*. (See Mosiah 3:5.) He was chosen before He was born. He was the all-powerful Creator of the heavens and the earth. He is the source of life and light to all things.

His word is the law by which all things are governed in the universe. All things created and made by Him are subject to His infinite power.

Jesus Christ is the *Son of God*. (*Ensign*, November 1983, p. 6.)

— *Ezra Taft Benson*

Only Jesus Christ is uniquely qualified to provide that hope, that confidence, and that strength to overcome the world and rise above our human failings. (*Ensign*, November 1983, p. 6.)

— *Ezra Taft Benson*

The fundamental principles of our religion are the testimony of the Apostles and Prophets, concerning Jesus Christ, that He died, was buried, and rose again the third day, and ascended into heaven; and all other things which pertain to our religion are only appendages to it.

— Joseph Smith

One can still go to the Garden of Gethsemane, but the Lord Jesus cannot be found there, nor is He in the Garden Tomb. He is not on the road to Emmaus, nor in Galilee, nor at Nazareth or Bethlehem. He must be found in one's heart. (*Ensign,* November 1988, p.14.)

— James E. Faust

The greatest and most important of all requirements of our Father in heaven . . . is to believe in Jesus Christ, confess him, seek him, cling to him, make friends with him. Take a course to open a communication with your Elder Brother or file-leader—our Savior. (*JD,* 8:339.)

— Brigham Young

Let us consider some of the attributes of our Lord, as found in the Book of Mormon, that show that Jesus is the Christ. . . .

He is *Alive:* "The life of the world . . . a life which is endless" (Mosiah 16:9).

He is *Constant:* "The same yesterday, today, and forever" (2 Nephi 27:23).

He is the *Creator:* "He created all things, both in heaven and in earth" (Mosiah 4:9).

He is the *Exemplar:* He "set the example. . . . He said unto the children of men: Follow thou me" (2 Nephi 31:9,10).

He is *Generous:* "He commandeth none that they shall not partake of his salvation" (2 Nephi 26:24).

He is *Godly:* He is God (see 2 Nephi 27:23).

He is *Good:* "All things which are good cometh of God" (Moroni 7:12).

He is *Gracious:* "He is full of grace" (2 Nephi 2:6).

He is the *Healer:* The "sick, and . . . afflicted with all manner of diseases . . . devils and unclean spirits . . . were healed by the power of the Lamb of God" (1 Nephi 11:31).

He is *Holy:* "O how great the holiness of our God!" (2 Nephi 9:20).

He is *Humble:* "He humbleth himself before the Father" (2 Nephi 31:7).

He is *Joyful:* "The Father hath given" Him a "fullness of joy" (3 Nephi 28:10).

He is our *Judge:* We "shall be brought to stand before the bar of God, to be judged of him" (Mosiah 16:10).

He is *Just:* "The judgments of God are always just" (Mosiah 29:12).

He is *Kind:* He has "loving kindness . . . towards the children of men" (1 Nephi 19:9).

He is the *Lawgiver:* He "gave the law" (3 Nephi 15:5).

He is the *Liberator:* "There is no other head whereby ye can be made free" (Mosiah 5:8).

He is the *Light:* "The light . . . of the world; yea, a light that is endless, that can never be darkened" (Mosiah 16:9).

He is *Loving:* "He loveth the world, even that he layeth down his own life" (2 Nephi 26:24).

He is the *Mediator:* "The great Mediator of all men" (2 Nephi 2:27).

He is *Merciful:* There is a "multitude of his tender mercies" (1 Nephi 8:8).

He is *Mighty:* "Mightier than all the earth" (1 Nephi 4:1).

He is *Miraculous:* A "God of miracles" (2 Nephi 27:23).

He is *Obedient:* Obedient unto the Father "in keeping his commandments" (2 Nephi 31:7).

He is *Omnipotent:* He has "all power, both in heaven and in earth" (Mosiah 4:9).

He is *Omniscient:* "The Lord knoweth all things from the beginning" (1 Nephi 9:6).

He is our *Redeemer:* "All mankind were in a lost and in a fallen state, and ever would be save they should rely on this Redeemer" (1 Nephi 10:6).

He is the *Resurrection:* He brought to pass "the resurrection of the dead, being the first that should rise" (2 Nephi 2:8).

He is *Righteous:* "His ways are righteousness forever" (2 Nephi 1:19).

He is the *Ruler:* He rules "in the heavens above and in the earth beneath" (2 Nephi 29:7).

He is our *Savior:* "There is none other name given under heaven save it be this Jesus Christ . . . whereby man can be saved" (2 Nephi 25:20).

He is *Sinless:* He "suffereth temptation, and yieldeth not to the temptation" (Mosiah 15:5).

He is *Truthful:* "A God of truth, and canst not lie" (Ether 3:12).

He is *Wise:* "He has all wisdom (Mosiah 4:9). . . .

Let us read the Book of Mormon and be convinced that Jesus is the Christ. Let us continually reread the Book of Mormon so that we might more fully come to Christ, be committed to Him, centered in Him, and consumed in Him.

We are meeting the adversary every day. The challenges of this era will rival any of the past, and these challenges will increase both spiritually and temporally. We must be close to Christ, we must daily take His name upon us, always remember Him, and keep His commandments.

— *Ezra Taft Benson*

There is one God and Father of us all, one eternal plan of salvation, one way back to heaven. And Jesus Christ is the name given by the Father whereby men may be saved. His is the only name given under heaven—either now, or in ages past, or in eternities yet unborn—whereby salvation comes. (See D&C 18:23; Moses 6:52.) . . .

All true believers, all of the faithful from Adam to this hour, all those who through faith have wrought righteousness and gained salvation—all, without exception, have taken upon themselves his name and have followed him with full purpose of heart.

He is our God and he is the God of our fathers! (*Ensign*, November 1982, p. 33.)

— *Bruce R. McConkie*

The Healing Power of Christ
Jesus of Nazareth healed the sick among whom He moved. His regenerating power is with us today to be invoked through His holy priesthood. His divine teachings, His incomparable example, His matchless life, His all-encompassing sacrifice will bring healing to broken hearts, reconciliation to those who argue and shout, even peace to warring nations if sought with humility and forgiveness and love. (*Ensign*, November 1988, p. 59.)

— *Gordon B. Hinckley*

There was apparently nothing that the Savior could do that was acceptable in the eyes of the world; anything and almost everything he did was imputed to an unholy influence. When he cast out devils the people said he did it through the power of Beelzebub, the prince of devils; when he opened the eyes of the blind, the Pharisees and priests of the day told the man to "give God the glory; we know this man is a sinner." And so all his life through, to the day of his death upon the cross! There is something about all this that appears sorrowful; but it seemed necessary for the Savior to descend below all things that he might ascend above all things. (*JD*, 23:327.)

— *Wilford Woodruff*

We declare to the world that Jesus is the Christ. We abhor the doctrine that He is a myth or a creation of conspiring men in the world. We denounce the idea that He was just a great teacher. We testify of the divinity of Jesus of Nazareth, that He is the Son of God, the Savior of the world.

— *L. Tom Perry*

What do members of The Church of Jesus Christ of Latter-day Saints think of Christ?

Jesus Christ is the Only Begotten Son of God the Eternal Father. He is our Creator. He is our Teacher. He is our Savior. His atonement paid for the sin of Adam and won victory over death, assuring resurrection and immortality for all men.

He is all of these, but he is more. Jesus Christ is the Savior, whose atoning sacrifice opens the door for us to be cleansed of our personal sin so that we can be readmitted to the presence of God. He is our Redeemer. (*Ensign*, November 1988, p. 65.)

— *Dallin H. Oaks*

See also ATONEMENT, RESURRECTION, SACRAMENT

———— Joseph Smith ————

Few men have disturbed and annoyed the adversary more than Joseph; few have felt the combined powers of darkness more than he; and few have triumphed over Satan more nobly. (*Ensign*, May 1990, p. 63.)

— *Carlos E. Asay*

In 1830 I became intimately acquainted with the prophet Joseph Smith, and continued intimately acquainted with him until the day of his death. I had the great privilege . . . of boarding . . . at his house, so that I not only knew him as a public teacher, but as a private citizen, and as a husband and father. I witnessed his earnest and humble devotions, both morning and evening in his family. I heard the words of eternal life flow from his lips, nourishing and soothing and comforting his family, neighbors and friends. I saw his countenance lighted up as the inspiration of the Holy Ghost rested upon him, dictating the great and most precious revelations now printed for our guide. . . . I knew that he was a man of God. It was not a matter of opinion with me, for I received a testimony from the heavens concerning that matter.

I testify before God, angels and men that he was a good, honorable, and virtuous man, that his private and public character was irreproachable, and that he lived and died a man of God. ("Joseph Smith, Prophet of God," ms., talk delivered 12 December 1926, Salt Lake City, p. 13.)

— *Ezra C. Dalby*

Joseph Smith . . . claimed for himself no special sanctity, no faultless life, no perfection of character, no inerrancy for every word spoken by him. And as he did not claim these things for himself, so can they not be claimed for him by others. . . . Yet to Joseph Smith was given access to the mind of Deity, through the revelations of God to him. (*Comprehensive History*, 2:360-61.)

— *B.H. Roberts*

Joseph Smith holds the keys of this last dispensation, and is now engaged behind the veil in the great work of the last days. . . . No man or woman in this dispensation will ever enter into the celestial kingdom of God without the consent of Joseph Smith. . . . He holds the keys of that kingdom for the last dispensation—the keys to rule in the spirit-world; and he rules there triumphantly. (*JD,* 7:289-90.)

— *Brigham Young*

Many have belittled Joseph Smith, but those who have will be forgotten in the remains of mother earth, and the odor of their infamy will ever be with them, but honor, majesty, and fidelity to God, exemplified by Joseph Smith and attached to his name, will never die. (Quoted by Harold B. Lee, *CR,* October 1973, p. 166.)

— *George Albert Smith*

My older brother and I were going to school, near to the building which was known as Joseph's brick store. It had been raining the previous day, causing the ground to be very muddy, especially along that street. My brother Wallace and I both got fast in the mud, and could not get out, and of course, child-like, we began to cry, for we thought we would have to stay there. But looking up, I beheld the loving friend of children, the Prophet Joseph, coming to us. He soon had us on higher and drier ground. Then he stooped down and cleaned the mud from our little, heavy-laden shoes, took his handkerchief from his pocket and wiped our tear-stained faces. He spoke kind and cheering words to us, and sent us on our way to school rejoicing. Was it any wonder that I loved that great, good and noble man of God? (*Juvenile Instructor,* 15 January 1892, p. 67.)

— *Margarette McIntire Burgess*

No greater prophet than Joseph Smith ever lived on the face of the earth save Jesus Christ. (*JD,* 21:317.)

— *Wilford Woodruff*

Perhaps there are very few men now living who were so well acquainted with Joseph Smith the Prophet as I was. I was with him often times. I visited with him in his family, sat at his table, associated with him under various circumstances, and had private interviews with him for counsel. I know that Joseph Smith was a prophet of God; I know that he was an honorable man, a moral man, and that he had the respect of those who were acquainted with him. the Lord has shown me most clearly and completely that he was a prophet of God, and that he held the holy priesthood.

— *Lorenzo Snow*

President Joseph Smith was in person tall and well built, strong and active; of a light complexion, light hair, blue eyes, very little beard, and of an expression peculiar to himself, on which the eye naturally rested with interest, and was never weary of beholding. His countenance was ever mild, affable, beaming with intelligence and benevolence; mingled with a look of interest and an unconscious smile, or cheerfulness, and entirely free from all restraint or affectation of gravity; and there was something connected with the serene and steady penetrating glance of his eye, as if he would penetrate the deepest abyss of the human heart, gaze into eternity, penetrate the heavens, and comprehend all worlds.

He possessed a noble boldness and independence of character; his manner was easy and familiar; his rebuke terrible as the lion; his benevolence unbounded as the ocean; his intelligence universal, and his language abounding in original eloquence peculiar to himself—not polished—not studied—not smoothed and softened by education and refined by art; but flowing forth in its own native simplicity, and profusely abounding in variety of subject and manner. He interested and edified, while, at the same time, he amused and entertained his audience; and none listened to him that were ever weary with his discourse. I have even known him to retain a congregation of willing and anxious listeners for many hours together, in the midst of cold or sunshine, rain or wind, while they were laughing at one moment and weeping the next. Even his most bitter enemies were generally overcome, if he could once get their ears. (*Autobiography of Parley P. Pratt*, Salt Lake City: Deseret Book Co., 1938, pp. 45-46.)

— *Parley P. Pratt*

That Joseph Smith is beyond compare the greatest leader of modern times is a proposition that needs no comment. (Commencement Address, Brigham young University, August 19, 1983.)

— *Hugh Nibley*

There is not so great a man as Joseph standing in this generation. The gentiles look upon him and he is like a bed of gold concealed from human view. They know not his principles, his spirit, his wisdom, his virtues, his philanthropy, nor his calling. His mind, like Enoch's expands as eternity, and only God can comprehend his soul. (*Journal History of The Church of Jesus Christ of Latter-day Saints*, Salt Lake City: Historical Department, April 9, 1837.)

— *Wilford Woodruff*

This great and good man was led, before his death, to call the Twelve together from time to time and to instruct them in all things pertaining to the kingdom, ordinances and government of God. . . . Said he, "I know not why; but for some reason I am constrained to hasten my preparations, and to confer upon the Twelve all the ordinances, keys, covenants, endowments, and sealing ordinances of the priesthood, and so set before them a pattern in all things pertaining to the sanctuary and the endowment therein."

Having done this, he rejoiced exceedingly; "for," said he, "the Lord is about to lay the burden on your shoulders and let me rest awhile; and if they kill me," continued he, "the kingdom of God will roll on, as I have now finished the work which was laid upon me, by committing to you all things for the building up of the kingdom according to the heavenly vision, and the pattern shown me from heaven." With many conversations like this, he comforted the minds of the Twelve, and prepared them for what was soon to follow.

He proceeded to confer on Elder Young, the President of the Twelve, the keys of the sealing power, as conferred in the last days by the spirit and power of Elijah, in order to seal the hearts of the fathers to the children, and the hearts of the children to the fathers, lest the whole earth should be smitten with a curse. . . .

After giving them a very short charge to do all things according to the pattern, he quietly surrendered his liberty and his life into the hands of his blood-thirsty enemies, and all this to save the people for whom he had so long labored from threatened vengeance. (*MS*, 5:151.)

— *Parley P. Pratt*

Translating the Book of Mormon
I am satisfied that no man could have dictated the writing of the manuscripts unless he was inspired. For when [I acted] as his scribe, [Joseph] would dictate to me hour after hour; and when returning after meals or after interruptions, he would at once begin where he had left off, without either seeing the manuscript or having any portion of it read to him. . . . It would have been improbable that a learned man could do this, and for one so . . . unlearned as he was, it was simply impossible. (Quoted by Mark E. Petersen, *Ensign*, November 1977, p. 12.)

— *Emma Smith*

Who can justly say aught against Joseph Smith? I was as well acquainted with him as any man. I do not believe that his father and mother knew him any better than I did. I do not think that a man lives on the earth that knew him any better than I did; and I am bold to say that, Jesus Christ excepted, no better man ever lived or does live upon this earth. I am his witness. (*JD*, 9:332.)

— *Brigham Young*

Who will honor the name of Joseph Smith and accept the gospel restored through his instrumentality?

We answer: the same people who would have believed the words of the Lord Jesus and the ancient Apostles and prophets had they lived in their day.

If you believe the words of Joseph Smith, you would have believed what Jesus and the ancients said.

If you reject Joseph Smith and his message, you would have rejected Peter and Paul and their message. (*Ensign*, November 1981, p. 48.)

— *Bruce R. McConkie*

—— Journals ——

By now, in my own personal history, I have managed to fill seventy-eight large volumes, which are my personal journal. There have been times when I have been so tired at the end of a day that the effort could hardly be managed, but I am so grateful that I have not let slip away from me and my posterity those things which needed to be recorded. (*Ensign*, October 1980, p. 72.)

— *Spencer W. Kimball*

Every person should keep a journal and every person *can* keep a journal. It should be an enlightening one and should bring great blessings and happiness to the families. If there is anyone here who isn't doing so, will you repent today and change? (*Ensign*, May 1979, p. 84.)

— *Spencer W. Kimball*

I urge all of the people of this church to give serious attention to their family histories, to encourage their parents and grandparents to write their journals, and let no family go into eternity without having left their memoirs for their children, their grandchildren and their posterity. This is a duty and a responsibility, and I urge every person to start the children out writing a personal history and journal. (*Ensign*, May 1978, p. 4.)

— *Spencer W. Kimball*

Men should write down the things which God has made known to them. Whether things are important or not, often depends upon God's purposes; but the testimony of the goodness of God and the things he has wrought in the lives of men will always be important as a testimony. (*Wilford Woodruff*, Matthias F. Cowley, Salt Lake City: Bookcraft, 1964, p. 355.)

— *Wilford Woodruff*

See also HERITAGE

—— Joy ——

It was not intended that our lives should be a succession of confused, wearisome, frustrated days. Rather, it was intended that they should be orderly, fruitful days of true joy as we triumph over evil and rise above tribulation. This comes about as we approach our problems positively in the light of gospel teaching. (*A Woman's Reach*, Salt Lake City: Deseret Book Co., 1974, p. 121.)

— *Belle S. Spafford*

Pleasure is not the purpose of man's existence. Joy is. (*Gospel Ideals*, The Improvement Era, Salt Lake City: Deseret Book Co., 1976, p. 492.)

— *David O. McKay*

Pleasure usually takes the form of."me" and "now," while joy is "us" and "always." (*The Smallest Part*, Salt Lake City: Deseret Book Co., 1973, p. 23.)

— *Neal A. Maxwell*

The crowning attribute that leads to joy is love of God. (*Ensign*, November 1986, p. 69.)

— *Russell M. Nelson*

The gospel of Jesus Christ is true. It is the greatest joy, the only pure joy, we have in this life. (*Ensign*, May 1990, p. 43.)

— *Clinton L. Cutler*

Those who have died in Jesus Christ may expect to enter into all that fruition of joy when they come forth, which they possessed or anticipated here. (*TPJS*, p. 295.)

— *Joseph Smith*

——— **Judging** ———

Let no man judge his fellow being, unless he knows he has the mind of Christ within him. (*JD*, 1:339.)

— *Brigham Young*

Perhaps a supreme form of charity may be exhibited by one who withholds judgment of another's acts or conduct, remembering that there is only one who can look into the heart and know the intent—and know the honest desires found therein. There is only one whose right it is to judge the success of another's journey through life. (*Ensign*, May 1981, p. 81.)

— *H. Burke Peterson*

The discerning realize that it is not realistic to expect perfection in others when none of us is perfect. . . .

Meaningful progress can be made only when all of us can cast the motes out of our own eyes, leave judgment to our Father in Heaven, and lose ourselves in righteous living. (*Ensign*, November 1982, pp. 63-64.)

— *Marvin J. Ashton*

It is not for us to judge those who might be confused or who have not the strength to change. What they need is our understanding and support. (*Ensign*, May 1990, p. 26.)

— *Hans B. Ringger*

The faults and shortcomings we see in the members of our own war or branch are of less consequence to us than one of the smallest in ourselves. (*Ensign*, May 1983, p. 76.)

— *Jacob de Jager*

See also CRITICISM, FORGIVENESS, MERCY, TOLERANCE

——— Judgment ———

Evidence to the contrary, there are no successful sinners. All of us must one day stand before God and be judged according to our personal deeds done in the flesh. The burdens of the sinner will never be lighter than those of the saint. (*Ensign*, November 1990, p. 21.)

— *Marvin J. Ashton*

I am very thankful that it is not our province, in our present condition, to judge the world; if it were, we would ruin everything. We have not sufficient wisdom, our minds are not filled with the knowledge and power of God; the spirit needs to contend with the flesh a little more until it shall be successful in subduing its passions, until the whole soul is brought into perfect harmony with the mind and will of God. And we must also acquire the discretion that God exercises in being able to look into futurity and to ascertain and know the results of our acts away in the future, even in eternity, before we will be capable of judging. (*JD*, 19:7-8.)

— *Brigham Young*

It is not a matter of comparing individuals. We are not baptized collectively, nor will we be judged collectively. (*Ensign*, November 1985, p. 82.)

— *Boyd K. Packer*

Man will be held responsible in the life to come for the deeds that he has done in this life, and will have to answer for the stewardships entrusted to his care here, before the Judge of the quick and the dead, the Father of our spirits, and of our Lord and Master. This is the design of God, a part of his great purpose. (*GD*, p. 21.)

— *Joseph F. Smith*

On judgment day the Lord will mete out to us precisely as we have dealt with our fellowmen, unless we have fully repented. It is a staggering thought, and yet it is an integral factor in the Lord's method of judgment. Do we realize its broad significance? Do we see how we shall reap what we sow?

This principle, showing the manner by which God will judge us, puts a new light upon the commandment to love our neighbors as ourselves, and should persuade us to take that law seriously. (*Ensign*, May 1977, p. 74.)

— *Mark E. Petersen*

Resurrection is a free gift from Jesus Christ. There needs to be nothing done to receive it except to be born on the earth. However, those who are filthy, in the resurrection will be filthy still; and those who are righteous will be righteous still. In the words of the Master, the resurrection takes place so we can be judged. From this statement it appears that the Judgment requires the spirit and the body inseparably connected in order to receive a fullness of joy, meaning exaltation—or damnation. And what will be the basis of the Judgment? It will be according to the deeds done in the flesh—not what we did before we were born or what we do after we die, but what we do while we are here in mortality. (See Alma 5:15.) (*Ensign*, November 1985, p. 75.)

— *Hartman Rector, Jr.*

See also HAPPINESS, JUSTICE, REPENTANCE

Justice

We need not doubt the wisdom and intelligence of the Great Jehovah. . . . when the designs of God shall be made manifest, and the curtain of futurity be withdrawn, we shall all of us eventually have to confess that the Judge of all the earth has done right. (*TPJS*, p. 218.)

— *Joseph Smith*

I do not know that a spirit of malice has ever rested in my heart. I have asked the Lord to meet out justice to those who have oppressed us, and the Lord will take his own time and way for doing this. It is in his hands, and not mine, and I am glad of it, for I could not deal with the wicked as they should be dealt with. (*JD,* 10:297.)

— *Brigham Young*

Justice is usually pictured holding a set of scales and blindfolded against the possibility that she may be partial or become sympathetic. There is no sympathy in justice alone—only justice! . . . [But] there is a Redeemer, a Mediator, who stands both willing and able to appease the demands of justice and extend mercy to those who are penitent. (*Ensign,* May 1977, pp. 54, 56.)

— *Boyd K. Packer*

All too often, the justice of God seems to be relegated to the back burner, while the mercy of God seems to get the lion's share of attention. I presume this is true because we are all hoping for mercy and trying to avoid justice if at all possible. But it is a fact that God is just, and mercy cannot rob justice. Justice will have her due! (*Ensign,* November 1985, p. 76.)

— *Hartman Rector, Jr.*

See also JUDGMENT, MERCY

——— Kindness ———

Every kind act that we perform for one of our Father's children is but a permanent investment made by us that will bear eternal dividends. (*CR,* April 1914, p. 13.)

— *George Albert Smith*

It is indeed remarkable that the nature of our dealings with our fellowmen will determine, in large measure, our status in the kingdom of heaven. . . . We may attend to rites and rituals and yet overlook the weightier matters such as brotherly kindness, honesty, mercy, virtue, and integrity. Let us never forget that if we omit them from our lives we may be found unworthy to come into His presence. (*Ensign,* May 1977, p. 73.)

— *Mark E. Petersen*

One who is kind is sympathetic and gentle with others. He is considerate of others' feelings and courteous in his behavior. He has a helpful nature. Kindness pardons others' weaknesses and fault. Kindness is extended to all—to the aged and the young, to animals, to those low of stations as well as the high. (*Ensign*, November 1986, p. 47.)

— *Ezra Taft Benson*

Kindness has many synonyms—love, service, charity. But I like the word *kindness* because it implies action. It seems like something you and I can do. (*Ensign*, November 1990, p. 91.)

— *Betty Jo Jepsen*

Life is made up not of great sacrifices or duties, but of little things in which smiles and kindness and small obligations given habitually are what win and preserve the heart and secure comfort. (*CR*, October 1956, p. 6.)

— *David O. McKay*

So live, then, that each day will find you conscious of having wilfully made no person unhappy. ("Something Higher than Self," address, Brigham Young University, October 12, 1965.)

— *David O. McKay*

The greatest need of the human heart is encouragement. Let me whisper this secret in your ear: Every time you try to encourage someone else, your own soul will be flooded with a light and glow of peace and good cheer. Try it next time when the gloom is heavy and the load is barren. (*Relief Society Magazine*, September 1921.)

— *Susa Young Gates*

The measure of a man is not necessarily his title or his position, but rather how he treats others . . . (*Ensign*, November 1989, p. 76.)

— *Victor L. Brown*

We are made kind by being kind. (*Ensign*, November 1990, p. 91.)

— *Betty Jo Jepsen*

See also CHARITY, SERVICE

—— Kingdom of God ——

As Latter-day Saints we know no nationality; we belong to the kingdom of God. (*TLS*, p. 169.)

— *Lorenzo Snow*

In the midst of all the troubles, the uncertainties, the tumult and chaos through which the world is passing, almost unnoticed by the majority of the people of the world, there has been set up a kingdom, a kingdom over which God the Father presides, and Jesus the Christ is the King. That kingdom is rolling forward, . . . with a power and a force that will stop the enemy in its tracks while some of you live. (*CR*, October 1967, p. 115.)

— *Hugh B. Brown*

It has been asked . . . whether this kingdom will fail. I tell you in the name of Israel's God it will not fail. I tell you in the name of Israel's God it will roll forth, and that the things spoken of by the holy prophets in relation to it will receive their fulfillment. But in connection with this I will tell you another thing: A great many of the Latter-day Saints will fail, a great many of them are not now and never have been living up to their privileges, and magnifying their callings and their priesthood, and God will have a reckoning with such people, unless they speedily repent. (*Gospel Kingdom*, Salt Lake City: Bookcraft, 1964, p. 137.)

— *John Taylor*

May we be faithful in all of our labors, having the motto indelibly stamped upon our hearts, "The kingdom of God or nothing." (*CR*, April 1980, p. 82.)

— *Lorenzo Snow*

No unhallowed hand can stop the work from progressing; persecutions may rage, mobs may combine, armies may assemble, calumny may defame, but the truth of God will go forth boldly, nobly, and independent, till it has penetrated every continent, visited every clime, swept every country, and sounded in every ear, till the purposes of God shall be accomplished, and the Great Jehovah shall say the work is done. (*HC*, 4:540.)

— *Joseph Smith*

Now talk about this kingdom being destroyed! . . . why, you might as well try to pluck the stars from the firmament or the moon or the sun from its orbit! It can never be accomplished, for it is the work of the Almighty. I advise every man who has a disposition to put forth his hand against this work, to hold on and consider. Take the advice of Gamaliel the lawyer. Said he: "If this is the work of God, ye can do nothing against it; if it is not, it will come to naught." (*JD*, 14:307.)

— *Lorenzo Snow*

The heavenly Priesthood will unite with the earthly, to bring about those great purposes; and whilst we are thus united in the one common cause, to roll forth the kingdom of God, the heavenly Priesthood are not idle spectators, the Spirit of God will be showered down from above, and it will dwell in our midst. The blessings of the Most High will rest upon our tabernacles, and our name will be handed down to future ages; our children will rise up and call us blessed; and generations yet unborn will dwell with peculiar delight upon the scenes that we have passed through, the privations that we have endured; the untiring zeal that we have manifested; the all but insurmountable difficulties that we have overcome in laying the foundation of a work that brought about the glory and blessing which they will realize; a work that God and angels have contemplated with delight for generations past; that fired the souls of the ancient patriarchs and prophets; a work that is destined to bring about the destruction of the powers of darkness, the renovation of the earth, the glory of God, and the salvation of the human family. (*HC*, 4:610.)

— *Joseph Smith*

The kingdom of God is an order of government established by divine authority. It is the only legal government that can exist in any part of the universe. All other governments are illegal and unauthorized. God having made all beings and worlds, has the supreme right to govern them by his own laws, and by officers of his own appointment. (Quoted by Joseph Fielding Smith, *Seek Ye Earnestly*, Salt Lake City: Deseret Book Co., 1970, p. 22.)

— *Orson Pratt*

The kingdom of God is here to grow, to spread abroad, to take root in the earth, and to abide where the Lord has planted it by his own power and by his own word in the earth, never more to be destroyed nor to cease, but to continue until the purposes of the Almighty shall be accomplished, every whit that has been spoken of it by the mouths of the holy prophets since the world began. (*GD*, p. 76.)

— *Joseph F. Smith*

The law requires us to seek first the kingdom of God, and that our time, talent and ability must be held subservient to its interest. If this were not so, how could we expect hereafter, when this earth shall have been made the dwelling place of God and His Son, to inherit eternal lives and to live and reign with Him? (*Deseret News*, January 31, 1877.)

— *Lorenzo Snow*

The real power in the kingdom of God is not represented in outwardly observable things. Its strength is in the quality of the lives of its members. It is in the depth of their purity, their charity, their faith, their integrity, and their devotion to truth. (*Ensign*, November 1981, p. 25.)

— *Dean L. Larsen*

The strength of the Church is not in the numbers, nor in the amount of tithes and offerings paid by faithful members, nor in the magnitude of chapels and temple buildings, but because in the hearts of faithful members of the Church is the conviction that this is indeed the church and kingdom of God on the earth. (*CR*, April 1976, p. 70.)

— Harold B. Lee

What is the meaning of "thy kingdom come?" It means the rule of God. It means the law of God. It means the government of God. It means the people who have listened to and who are willing to listen to and observe the commandments of Jehovah. And it means that there is a God who is willing to guide and direct and sustain his people. Thy kingdom come, that thy government may be established, and the principles of eternal truth as they exist in the heavens may be imparted to men; and that, when they are imparted to men, those men may be in subjection to those laws and to that government, and live in the fear of God, keeping his commandments and being under his direction. Thy kingdom come, that the confusion, the evil, and wickedness, the murder and bloodshed that now exist among mankind may be done away, and the principles of truth and right, the principles of kindness, charity, and love as they dwell in the bosom of the gods, may dwell with us. (*JD*, 23:178.)

— John Taylor

When the wicked have power to blow out the sun, that it shines no more; when they have power to bring to a conclusion the operations of the elements, suspend the whole system of nature, and make a footstool of the throne of the Almighty, they may then think to check [the kingdom] in its course.

— John Taylor

Where there is a prophet, a priest, or a righteous man unto whom God gives his oracles, there is the kingdom of God. (*HC*, 5:256.)

— Joseph Smith

See also CHURCH, LATTER-DAY WORK

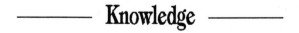

Knowledge

A little spiritual knowledge is a great deal better than mere opinions and notions and ideas, or even very elaborate arguments. (*JD*, 23:293.)

— Lorenzo Snow

A man is saved no faster than he gets knowledge. For if he does not get knowledge, he will be brought into captivity by some evil power in the other world, as evil spirits will have more knowledge, and consequently more power than many men who are on the earth. Hence it needs revelation to assist us, and give us knowledge of the things of God. (*HC*, 4:588.)

— *Joseph Smith*

How do men obtain a knowledge of the glory of God, his perfections and attributes? By devoting themselves to his service, through prayer and supplication incessantly strengthening their faith in him, until, like Enoch, the brother of Jared, and Moses, they obtain a manifestation of God to themselves.

— *Joseph Smith*

If I have learned something through prayer, supplication and perseverance in seeking to know the truth, and I tell it to you, it will not be knowledge unto you.

— *Joseph F. Smith*

In the acquisition of sacred knowledge, scholarship and reason are not alternatives to revelation. They are a means to an end, and the end is revelation from God.

— *Dallin H. Oaks*

It must eventually come to pass in the case of those who gain exaltation and become sons of God; that they must, in the eternities, reach the time when they will know all things. They must know mathematics; they must know all the principles of science; they must be prepared in all things—by learning, by study, by faith—to comprehend these principles of eternal truth, even as our Father in heaven comprehends them; and unless men will put themselves in harmony with him and his Spirit and seek the light which comes through the Spirit, they never will reach the goal of perfection in these things. It is, however, knowledge of the principles of the gospel that will save men in the kingdom of God.

— *Joseph Fielding Smith*

It requires striving—intellectual and spiritual—to comprehend the things of God—even the revealed things of God. In no department of human endeavor is the aphorism "no excellence without labor" more in force than in acquiring knowledge of the things of God. . . . Mental laziness is the vice of men, especially with reference to divine things. Men seem to think that because inspiration and revelation are factors in connection with the things of God, therefore the pain and stress of mental effort are not required. (*Seventy's Course in Theology*, Fifth Year, Deseret News Press, 1912, pp. 4-5.)

— *B.H. Roberts*

Knowledge comes through personal effort. Its acquisition involves labor. Exact and definite knowledge comes to us in exact ratio with the amount of diligence, moral courage, and perseverance we put into the active search for it.

— *David O. McKay*

Knowledge is of no value unless you put it into practice. (*IE*, 36:224.)

— *Heber J. Grant*

Knowledge is the handmaid of intelligence and priceless beyond words. (*CR*, April 1934, p. 93.)

— *J. Reuben Clark, Jr.*

Puzzlement, . . . is often the knob on the door of insight. The knob must be firmly grasped and deliberately turned with faith. (*Ensign*, May 1990, pp. 34-35.)

— *Neal A. Maxwell*

The knowledge explosion of which the world is so proud is not of man's creation. It is his discovery of portions of the unlimited knowledge and information which is part of God's knowledge. How we use it is determined by whether we are of the eternal Kingdom of God or a part of the temporary understanding of the world. (*Ensign*, January 1974, p. 55.)

— *Howard W. Hunter*

The most important knowledge in the world is gospel knowledge. It is a knowledge of God and his laws, of those things that men must do to work out their salvation with fear and trembling before the Lord. (*Ensign*, May 1971, p. 2.)

— *Joseph Fielding Smith*

The only way to gain spiritual knowledge is to approach our Father in Heaven through the Holy Spirit in the name of Jesus Christ. When we do this, and if we are spiritually prepared, we see things our eyes have not previously seen, and we hear things we may not have previously heard . . . . These things we receive through the Spirit. (*Ensign*, November 1981, p. 13.)

— *Howard W. Hunter*

This knowledge of "the only true God, and Jesus Christ" (John 17:3) is the most important knowledge in the universe; it is the knowledge without which the Prophet Joseph Smith said no man could be saved. The lack of it is the ignorance referred to in the revelation wherein it is written: "It is impossible for a man to be saved in ignorance." (D&C 131:6.) (*Ensign*, November 1981, p. 14.)

— *Marion G. Romney*

The philosophy of the heavens and the earth of the worlds that are, that were, and that are yet to come into existence, is all the Gospel that we have embraced. Every true philosopher, so far as he understands the principles of truth, has so much of the Gospel, and so far he is a Latter-day Saint, whether he knows it or not. Our Father, the great God, is the author of the sciences, he is the great mechanic, he is the systematizer of all things, he plans and devises all things, and every particle of knowledge which man has in his possession is the gift of God. (*DBY*, pp. 2-3.)

— *Brigham Young*

The principle of knowledge is the principle of salvation. This principle can be comprehended by the faithful and diligent; and everyone that does not obtain knowledge sufficient to be saved will be condemned. The principle of salvation is given us through the knowledge of Jesus Christ. (*TPJS*, p. 297.)

— *Joseph Smith*

See also EDUCATION, LEARNING, LIGHT OF CHRIST, TRUTH, WISDOM

———— Last Days ————

As the shutters of human history begin to close as if before a gathering storm, and as events scurry across the human scene like so many leaves before a wild wind—those who stand before the warm glow of the gospel fire can be permitted a shiver of the soul. Yet in our circle of certitude, we know, even in the midst of all these things, that there will be no final frustration of God's purposes. (*Ensign*, November 1981, p. 10.)

— *Neal A. Maxwell*

Be it remembered that tribulations lie ahead. There will be wars in one nation and kingdom after another. . . .

Peace has been taken from the earth, the angels of destruction have begun their work, and their swords shall not be sheathed until the Prince of Peace comes to destroy the wicked and usher in the great Millennium

There will be earthquakes and floods and famines. The waves of the sea shall heave themselves beyond their bounds, the clouds shall withhold their rain, and the crops of the earth shall wither and die.

There will be plagues and pestilence and disease and death. An overflowing scourge shall cover the earth and a desolating sickness shall sweep the land. Flies shall take hold of the inhabitants of the earth, and maggots shall come in upon them. . . .

Bands of Gadianton robbers will infest every nation, immorality and murder and crime will increase, and it will seem as though every man's hand is against his brother.

We need not dwell more upon these things. We are commanded to search the scriptures where they are recounted with force and fervor, and they shall surely come to pass. (*Ensign*, May 1979, p. 93.)

— *Bruce R. McConkie*

He who scattered Israel has promised to gather them; therefore inasmuch as you are to be instrumental in this great work, [the Lord] will endow you with power, wisdom, might, and intelligence, and every qualification necessary; while your minds will expand wider and wider, until you can circumscribe the earth and the heavens, reach forth into eternity, and contemplate the mighty acts of Jehovah in all their variety and glory. (*HC*, 4:128-129.)

— *Joseph Smith*

I prophesy, in the name of the Lord God of Israel, anguish and wrath and tribulation and the withdrawing of the Spirit of God from the earth await this generation, until they are visited with utter desolation. This generation is as corrupt as the generation of the Jews that crucified Christ; and if he were here today, and should preach to the same doctrine he did then they would put him to death.

— *Joseph Smith*

I saw men hunting the lives of their own sons, and brother murdering brother, women killing their own daughters, and daughters seeking the lives of their mothers. I saw armies arrayed against armies. I saw blood, desolation, fires. . . . These things are at our doors. They will follow the saints of God from city to city. Satan will rage, and the spirit of the devil is now enraged. I know not how soon these things will take place; but with a view of them, shall I cry peace? No! I will lift up my voice and testify of them. How long you will have good crops, and the famine be kept off, I do not know; when the fig tree leaves, know then that the summer is nigh at hand. (*HC*, 3:391.)

— *Joseph Smith*

In the last days, happily, the Church will grow extensively, with its membership being "scattered upon all the face of the earth" (1 Nephi 14:140. Nevertheless, its dominions will still be comparatively "small" because of "wickedness," which will close the ears of many to the gospel message (see 1 Nephi 14:12). (*Ensign*, May 1988, p. 8.)

— *Neal A. Maxwell*

It is my testimony that we are facing difficult times. We must be courageously obedient. My witness is that we will be called upon to prove our spiritual stamina, for the days ahead will be filled with affliction and difficulty. But with the assuring comfort of a personal relationship with the Savior, we will be given a calming courage. (*Ensign*, November 1976, p. 59.)

— *James E. Faust*

It may be, . . . that nothing except the power of faith and the authority of the priesthood can save individuals and congregations from the atomic holocausts that surely shall be. (*Ensign*, May 1979, p. 93.)

— *Bruce R. McConkie*

It will not be long until calamities will overtake the human family unless there is speedy repentance. It will not be long before those who are scattered over the face of the earth by millions will die like flies because of what will come. (*CR*, April 1950, p. 169.)

— *George Albert Smith*

Jesus warned that iniquities in the last days would become so great "that, if possible, they shall deceive the very elect, who are the elect according to the covenant" (Joseph Smith 1:22; Matt. 24:24). I understand this to mean that eventually even the most faithful of the Lord's covenant Saints will become contaminated and threatened by modern-day philosophies. I believe it is for this reason that unless these days are shortened none of us could long remain unaffected by such trends. (*Ensign*, May 1979, p. 72.)

— *Theodore M. Burton*

No man can contemplate the truth concerning the nations of the earth without sorrow, when he sees the wailing, the mourning, and death, that will come in consequence of judgments, plagues, and war. It has already begun, and it will continue to multiply and increase until the scene is ended, and wound up. . . .

Do I delight in the destruction of the children of men? No. Does the Lord? No. He gives them timely warning, and if they do not listen to his counsel, they must suffer the consequences of their wicked acts.

— *Wilford Woodruff*

Take away the Book of Mormon and the revelations, and where is our religion? We have none; for without Zion, and a place of deliverance, we must fall; because the time is near when the sun will be darkened, and the moon turn to blood, and the stars fall from heaven, and the earth reel to and fro. Then, if this is the case, and if we are not sanctified and gathered to the places God has appointed, with all our former professions and our great love for the Bible, we must fall;

we cannot stand; we cannot be saved; for God will gather out his saints from the Gentiles, and then comes desolation and destruction, and none can escape except the pure in heart who are gathered. (*HC*, 2:52.)

— *Joseph Smith*

There are events in the future, and not very far ahead, that will require all our faith, all our energy, all our confidence, all our trust in God, to enable us to withstand the influences that will be brought against us. . . . We cannot trust in our intelligence; we cannot trust in our wealth; we cannot trust to any surrounding circumstances with which we are enveloped; we must trust alone in the living God to guide us, to direct us, to lead us, to teach us and to instruct us. And there never was a time when we needed to be more humble and more prayerful; there never was a time when we needed more fidelity, self-denial, and adherence to the principles of truth, than we do this day.

— *John Taylor*

There comes a time when the general defilement of a society becomes so great that the rising generation is put under undue pressure and cannot be said to have a fair choice between the way of light and the way of darkness. When such a point is reached, the cup of iniquity is full; and the established order that has passed the point of no return and neither can nor will change its ways must be removed physically and forcibly if necessary from the earth, whether by war, plague, famine, or upheavals of nature. (*OAT*, p. 119.)

— *Hugh Nibley*

There is a cleansing [of the Church] coming. The Lord says that his vengeance shall be poured out "upon the inhabitants of the earth. . . . And upon my house shall it begin, and from my house shall it go forth, saith the Lord; First among those among you, saith the Lord, who have professed to know my name and have not known me. . . ." (D&C 112:24-26.) I look forward to that cleansing; its need within the Church is becoming increasingly apparent. . . . In our day the Lord has told us of the tares within the wheat that will eventually be hewn down when they are fully ripe. (*CR*, April 1969, pp. 10-12.)

— *Ezra Taft Benson*

There is more sin and evil in the world now than there has been at any time since the day of Noah, when the Lord felt disposed to destroy the world by a flood so that he could send his spirit children to earth in a better and more righteous environment.

This is the day in which Christ said that iniquity should abound. From the revelations he has given, we know that when the cup of iniquity is full, then cometh the destruction of the wicked, which is the end of the world; then cometh the day when the vineyard shall be cleansed by fire so that righteousness and peace may be in the hearts of all who remain to live on earth during the day of the great Millennium. (Baccalaureate Sermon, Ricks College, May 7, 1971.)

— *Joseph Fielding Smith*

There is an urgency in . . . [the Lord's] work. Time is getting short. This sense of urgency in promoting the Lord's kingdom in these last days does not arise out of panic, but out of a desire to move swiftly and surely to establish and strengthen his kingdom among all people who are seeking the light and truth of the gospel, which is God's plan of life for all his children.

God will hasten his work by opening the heavens and sending heavenly messengers to his prophets to warn his children to prepare themselves to receive their Lord at his second coming. (*Ensign*, November 1975, p. 49.)

— *Delbert L. Stapley*

There is rapidly coming something that will try you, perhaps as you have never been tried before. All, however, that is necessary for us to do now is to see where our faults and weaknesses lie, if we have any. If we have been unfaithful in the past, let us renew our covenants with God and determine, by fasting and prayer, that we will get forgiveness of our sins that the Spirit of the Almighty may rest upon us, that peradventure we may escape those powerful temptations that are approaching. The cloud is gathering in blackness. Therefore, take warning. (*Deseret Weekly*, 38:762-63.)

— *Lorenzo Snow*

The safety of the saints depends as much upon their fulfilling his commandments as the safety of Noah and Lot depended upon their obedience to the commands of God in their day. (*MS*, 6:3.)

— *Wilford Woodruff*

The sinner will slay the sinner, the wicked will fall upon the wicked, until there is an utter overthrow and consumption upon the face of the whole earth, until God reigns, whose right it is. (*JD*, 2:190.)

— *Brigham Young*

These are the *last days*. The last days of what? Neither we nor the outside world have ever bothered to explore or argue definitions about that—because the answer is obvious: it is the perennial message of the apocalyptic teaching which is now recognized as the very foundation of the Old and New Testaments. The last days are the last days of everything as we know it. (*OAT*, p. 35.)

— *Hugh Nibley*

We hear about living in perilous times. We are in perilous times, but I do not feel the pangs of the terror. It is not upon me. I propose to live so that it will not rest upon me. I propose to live so that I shall be immune from the perils of the world, if it be possible for me to so live, by obedience to the commandments of God. . . . I borrow no trouble nor feel the pangs of fear.

The Lord's hand is over all, and therein I acknowledge his hand. Not that men are at war, not that nations are trying to destroy nations, not that men are plotting against the liberties of their fellow creatures, not in those respects at all; but God's hand is not shortened. He will control the results that will follow, he will overrule them in a way that you and I, today, do not comprehend, or do not foresee, for ultimate good. (*GD*, p. 89.)

— *Joseph F. Smith*

We need to overcome fatalism. We know the prophecies of the future. We know the final outcome. We know the world collectively will not repent and consequently the last days will be filled with much pain and suffering. Therefore, we could throw up our hands and do nothing but pray for the end to come so the millennial reign could begin. To do so would forfeit our right to participate in the grand event we are all awaiting. We must all become players in the winding-up scene, not spectators. We must do all we can to prevent calamities, and then do everything possible to assist and comfort the victims of tragedies that do occur. (*Ensign*, November 1990, p. 8.)

— *Glenn L. Pace*

When I consider that soon the heavens are to be shaken, and the earth tremble and reel to and fro; and that the heavens are to be unfolded as a scroll when it is rolled up; and that every mountain and island are to flee away, I cry out in my heart. What manner of person ought we to be in all holy conversation and godliness! (*HC*, 1:442.)

— *Joseph Smith*

When I was a boy, fifty years ago, the kingdom of God had not been established among men; the angels of God had not visited the earth; the Lord Almighty had not clothed his servants with the priesthood and commanded them to go and warn the nations of the earth of the judgments which awaited them. There was not the wickedness then that there is today. The wickedness committed today in the Christian world in twenty-four hours is greater than would have been committed in a hundred years at the ratio of fifty years ago. And the spirit of wickedness is increasing, so that I no longer wonder that God Almighty will turn rivers into blood; I do not wonder that he will open the seals and pour out the plagues and sink great Babylon, as the angel saw, like a millstone cast into the sea, to rise no more forever. I can see that it requires just such plagues and judgments to cleanse the earth, that it may cease to groan under the wickedness and abomination in which the Christian world welters today.

> — *Wilford Woodruff*

When I was young I used to read about the day that should burn as an oven, and all the proud and they that do wickedly shall be as stubble. I then had an idea that a sheet of fire would come down from heaven and burn up the ungodly; . . . I look at things in another point of light now; I consider that the elements, the agents of destruction, are right here to accomplish that work, . . . That great day of burning is beginning; we have had a few drops before the shower; it will wax worse and worse, and men will continue to deceive and be deceived until the earth shall burn up. The word of the Lord is, "Come out from her, my people, that ye be not partakers of her sins and receive not of her plagues." (Rev. 18:4.) (JD, 11:154.)

> — *Orson Hyde*

Why is it that thrones will be cast down, empires dissolved, nations destroyed, and confusion and distress cover all people, as the prophets have spoken? Because the Spirit of the Lord will be withdrawn from the nations in consequence of their wickedness, and they will be left to their own folly. (JD, 6:24.)

> — *John Taylor*

You and I live in a day in which the Lord our God has set His hand for the last time, to gather out the righteous and to prepare a people to reign on this earth,—a people who will be purified by good works, who will abide the faith of the living God and be ready to meet the Bridegroom when He comes to reign over the earth, even Jesus Christ . . . and be prepared for that glorious event—the coming of the Son of Man—which I believe will not be at any great distant day. (MS, 36:220.)

> — *Joseph F. Smith*

See also LATTER-DAY WORK, MILLENNIUM, SECOND COMING

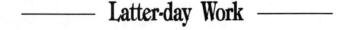

Latter-day Work

If I could speak so that the whole world would hear the utterance I would like to sound it in the ears of all mortal men—that there is no power that will ever be permitted to array itself, or to combine itself against this work of our God, to retard its onward progress from this time forward until the full consummation will be achieved—that is, if the Latter-day Saints themselves are faithful to God, if they will keep the commandments of God, if they will sanctify themselves and cleanse themselves from sin, and live pure and holy lives. If they will do this, then the success and the triumph and the continued growth and advancement of this kingdom . . . are assured unto us as a people. There is no doubt of it. I say in the name of Jesus Christ, that it will be so. (*JD*, 25:325.)

— *George Q. Cannon*

Here is the great trouble . . . : we forget that we are working for God; we forget that we are here in order to carry out certain purposes that we have promised the Lord that we would carry out. It is a glorious work that we are engaged in. It is the work of the Almighty, and he has selected the men and the women whom He knows from past experience will carry out His purposes.

— *Lorenzo Snow*

I need not remind you that this cause in which we are engaged is not an ordinary cause. It is the cause of Christ. It is the kingdom of God our Eternal Father. It is the building of Zion on the earth, the fulfillment of prophecy given of old and of a vision revealed in this dispensation. (*Ensign*, November 1989, p. 53.)

— *Gordon B. Hinckley*

I wish to testify that there are forces which will save us from the ever-increasing lying, disorder, violence, chaos, destruction, misery, and deceit that are upon the earth. Those saving forces are the everlasting principles, covenants, and ordinances of the eternal gospel of the Lord Jesus Christ. These same principles, covenants, and ordinances are coupled with the rights and powers of the priesthood of Almighty god. We of this church are the possessors and custodians of these commanding powers which can and do roll back much of the power of Satan on the earth. We believe that we hold these mighty forces in trust for all who have died, for all who are now living, and for the yet unborn. (*Ensign*, November 1987, p. 36.)

— *James E. Faust*

If we are to assist in moving forward the work of God, we must carry in our hearts a united conviction concerning the great basic foundation stones of our faith, including the truth and validity of the Book of Mormon as a voice speaking from the dust in testimony of Jesus the Christ, an ancient record written by inspired prophets and brought forth in this the dispensation of the fullness of times by the gift and power of God; of the reality and power of the priesthood which was restored under the hands of those who held it anciently . . . ; we must carry in our hearts a united conviction that the ordinances and covenants of this work are eternal and everlasting in their consequences; that this kingdom was established in the earth through the instrumentality of the Prophet Joseph Smith and that every man who has succeeded him in the office of President has been and is a prophet of the living God; and that there is incumbent upon each of us an obligation to live and teach the gospel as interpreted and taught by the prophet of our day. If we will be united in these basic and fundamental elements, this work will continue to grow in power and strength to touch for good the whole world. Of that I am satisfied and bear solemn testimony. (*Ensign*, November 1988, p. 48.)

— *Gordon B. Hinckley*

Let everyone labor to prepare himself for the vineyard, sparing a little time to comfort the mourners; to bind up the broken-hearted; to reclaim the backslider; to bring back the wanderer; to re-invite into the kingdom such as have been cut off, by encouraging them to lay to while the day lasts, and work righteousness, and, with one heart and one mind, prepare to help redeem Zion, that goodly land of promise, where the willing and obedient shall be blessed. Souls are as precious in the sight of God as they ever were; and the Elders were never called to drive any down to hell, but to persuade and invite all men everywhere to repent, that they may become the heirs of salvation.

— *Joseph Smith*

Let us go forward. If we will hold fast to the doctrine, if we will live with integrity, if we will cultivate love and charity in our homes, if we will build and sustain one another and move forward with faith, the Almighty, whose church this is, will bless us and his glorious work. . . . We are expected to give of our loyalty, our devotion, our hearts, minds, might, and strength to the on-rolling of this, the Lord's work. (See D&C 59:5.) (*Ensign*, May 1982, p. 46.)

— *Gordon B. Hinckley*

Our motives are not selfish; our purposes not petty and earthbound; we contemplate the human race—past, present, and yet to come—as immortal beings, for whose salvation it is our mission to labor; and to this work, broad as eternity and deep as the love of God, we devote ourselves, now and forever. (*CR*, April 1907, appendix, p. 16.)

— *The First Presidency*

The gospel breathes a new life and a new hope and a new and unknown holiness into a troubled world. This we see, and we see the work grow and increase and become more and more irresistible as it spreads like the gentleness of a sea that refreshes the shore upon which it flows. (*Ensign*, May 1988, p. 21.)

— *David B. Haight*

Looking ahead, we see the gospel preached in all nations and to every people with success attending.

We see the Lord break down the barriers so that the world of Islam and the world of Communism can hear the message of the restoration; and we glory in the fact that Ishmael—as well as Isaac—and Esau—as well as Jacob—shall have an inheritance in the eternal kingdom.

We see congregations of the covenant people worshipping their Lord in Moscow and Peking and Saigon. We see Saints of the Most High raising their voices in Egypt and India and Africa.

We see stakes of Zion in all parts of the earth; and Israel, the chosen people, gathering into these cities of holiness, as it were, to await the coming of their King. (*Ensign*, May 1980, p. 72.)

— *Bruce R. McConkie*

Now, brethren and sisters, I invite you to look beyond the narrow boundaries of your own wards and rise to the larger vision of this, the work of God. We have a challenge to meet, a work to do beyond the comprehension of any of us—that is, to assist our Heavenly Father to save His sons and daughters of all generations, both the living and the dead, to work for the salvation not only of those in the Church, but for those presently outside, wherever they may be. No body of people on the face of the earth has received a stronger mandate from the God of heaven than have we of this Church. (*Ensign*, May 1990, p. 97.)

— *Gordon B. Hinckley*

The great latter-day work of which we are a part shall be accomplished. Prophecies of the ages shall be fulfilled. "For with God all things are possible" (Mark 10:27). (*Ensign*, May 1988, p. 35.)

— *Russell M. Nelson*

Our great need, and our great calling, is to bring to the people of this world the candle of understanding to light their way out of obscurity and darkness and into the joy, peace, and truths of the gospel. (*Ensign*, February 1983, p. 5.)

— *Spencer W. Kimball*

The growth of this work has been a constantly unfolding miracle, and what an exciting and wonderful experience it is to be a part of it. Although storms of adversity have raged against it, it continues to move steadily forward along the course which the Almighty has outlined for it. It does so quietly, without great noise and fanfare, touching for good the lives of men and women across the earth. Its mission is not empire building. Its mission is to teach faith and repentance, and to bring truth and gladness to all who will listen and hearken to its message. (*Ensign*, May 1986, p. 46.)

— *Gordon B. Hinckley*

The mission of the Church is much more than a lofty ideal conceived at Church headquarters. It should be a part of the personal mission of every member. Each one of us should incorporated into our lives the practice of inviting all to come unto Christ by proclaiming the gospel, perfecting the Saints, and redeeming the dead. (*Ensign*, November 1988, p. 37.)

— *Joseph B. Wirthlin*

The mission of the Church is threefold: (1) To proclaim the gospel of the Lord Jesus Christ to every nation, kindred, tongue, and people; (2) To perfect the Saints by preparing them to receive the ordinances of the gospel and by instruction and discipline to gain exaltation; (3) To redeem the dead by performing vicarious ordinances of the gospel for those who have lived on the earth.

All three are part of one work—to assist our Father in Heaven and His Son, Jesus Christ, in Their grand and glorious mission "to bring to pass the immortality and eternal life of man." (Moses 1:39.) (*Ensign*, May 1981, p. 5.)

— *Spencer W. Kimball*

The work is demanding, the impact everlasting. This is no time for "summer soldiers" in the army of the Lord. (*Ensign*, November 1987, p. 41.)

— *Thomas S. Monson*

The world is our responsibility. We cannot evade it. (*Ensign*, May 1986, p. 42.)

— *Gordon B. Hinckley*

This is the day when the knowledge of the true Christ and of his everlasting gospel is being preached among men for the last time.

This is the day in which the Great God is sending forth his word to prepare a people for the second coming of the son of Man.

This is the day in which the Church of Jesus Christ has been organized anew and given the commission to administer that holy gospel by which salvation comes. (*Ensign*, November 1982, p. 34.)

— *Bruce R. McConkie*

With all my soul I testify that this work will go forward till every land and people have had opportunity to accept our message. Barriers will come down for us to accomplish this mission, and some of us will see this done. Our Heavenly Father will cause conditions in the world to change so that His gospel can penetrate every border. (*TETB*, p. 174.)

— *Ezra Taft Benson*

[In our premortal state] we agreed . . . to be not only saviors for ourselves but measurably, saviors for the whole human family. . . . The working out of the plan became then not merely the Father's work, and the Savior's work, but also our work. (*Utah Genealogical and Historical Magazine*, October 1934, p. 189.)

— *John A. Widtsoe*

See also CHURCH, MISSIONARY WORK, KINGDOM OF GOD

——— Laws ———

Does the law of gravity exist? Does it have effect in your life? If you jump from a high place, will your body not fall? Can you defy gravity? Can you step outside of its control?

Does the law of the gospel of Jesus Christ exist? Does it have effect in your life? If you disobey its limits and conditions, will your spirit not fall? Can you defy the law of the gospel of Jesus Christ? Can you step outside its control? (*Ensign*, November 1977, pp. 65-66.)

— *William R. Bradford*

Every process of nature is orderly. Chance, disorder, chaos are ruled out of the physical universe. If every condition involved in a system is precisely the same, the result, anywhere, everywhere, today or at any other time, will be the same. The sun does not rise in the east today and in the west tomorrow. That means that the phenomena of nature are products of law. The infinitely large or the infinitely small move in obedience to law. In man's earnest search for truth, no exception to this process has been found. (*Evidences and Reconciliations*, G. Homer Durham, ed., Salt Lake City: Bookcraft, 1960, p. 19.)

— *John A. Widtsoe*

If you and I ever get into the celestial kingdom, we have got to keep the law of that kingdom. Show me the law that a man keeps and I will tell you where he is going. (*MS*, July 1889, p. 596.)

— *Wilford Woodruff*

In scanning his works we learn that [God] is a being of order and law, and that all things are governed by law. Whether the minutest atoms . . . in the molecular world, that are scrutinized by the aid of the microscope, or whether we study the works of God in the vast unnumbered worlds that are rolling in the midst of the power of God, we find the same order. "All things are governed by law." (*JD*, 19:268.)

— *Erastus Snow*

It is not a matter of how many laws we keep and how many we do not keep. We keep the commandments because they are the laws that govern the Spirit. The Spirit in turn will sanctify us, condition us spiritually, and eventually prepare us to live in the kingdom where God is. (*Ensign*, May 1979, pp. 70-71.)

— *Loren C. Dunn*

Observance to law must become a rule in your life. Any rebellion against law is an evidence of weakness. Any observance of law—willing observance—is evidence of a willingness to be led and guided and protected as we were as little children. (Fireside Address, Brigham Young University, October 8, 1967.)

— *Hugh B. Brown*

One principle of the gospel that all . . . people of the Church should understand is this: God, our Heavenly Father, governs His children by law. He has instituted laws for our perfection. If we obey His laws, we receive the blessings pertaining to those laws. If we do not obey, we receive the consequences. (*Ensign*, May 1983, p. 53.)

— *Ezra Taft Benson*

The commandments found in the scriptures, both the positive counsel and the "shalt nots," form the *letter* of the law. There is also the *spirit* of the law. We are responsible for both. (*Ensign*, November 1990, p. 84.)

— *Boyd K. Packer*

The God of heaven, who created this earth and placed his children upon it, gave unto them a law whereby they might be exalted and saved in a kingdom of glory. For there is a law given unto all kingdoms, and all things are governed by law throughout the whole universe. Whatever law anyone keeps, he is preserved by that law, and he receives whatever reward that law guarantees unto him. It is the will of God that all his children should obey the highest law, that they may receive the highest glory that is ordained for all immortal beings. But God has given all his children an agency, to choose what law they will keep. (*The Discourses of Wilford Woodruff*, selected by G. Homer Durham, Salt Lake City: Bookcraft, 1946, p. 10.)

— *Wilford Woodruff*

The laws of God and the laws of nature and the laws of the land are made for the benefit of man—for his comfort, enjoyment, safety, and well-being. (*Ensign*, November 1977, p. 43.)

— *N. Eldon Tanner*

We have not got all yet, I expect higher laws will be revealed to us as we ascend nearer and nearer to our Father in heaven. Therefore we should prepare ourselves for this, and as fast as we can be willing to obey the laws that God reveals to us. . . . It has required faith to obey some laws that have been revealed in the past, and it will require faith to obey other laws that will yet be revealed. (*CR*, April 1900, p. 56.)

— *George Q. Cannon*

Without law all must certainly fall into chaos. (*HC*, 2:12.)

— *Joseph Smith*

See also BLESSINGS, COMMANDMENTS, OBEDIENCE

—— Leadership ——

Authoritative rule is not the proper rule by which to govern Saints, but rather seek to administer in the spirit of humility, wisdom, and goodness, teaching not so much by theory as by practice. Though one teach with the eloquence of an angel, yet one's good practice, good examples, one's acts constantly manifesting whole-heartedness for the interests of the people, teach much more. (*MS*, 13:362.)

— *Lorenzo Snow*

Holding the priesthood does not mean that a man is a power-broker, or that he sits on a throne, dictating in macho terms, or that he is superior in any way. Rather, he is a leader by authority of example. (*Ensign*, May 1988, p. 36.)

— *James E. Faust*

In the kingdom, the greater our responsibilities, the greater in our need to see ourselves as servants. (*Ensign*, May 1979, p. 107.)

— *Spencer W. Kimball*

It is your duty first of all to learn what the Lord wants and then . . . to so magnify your calling in the presence of your fellows that the people will be glad to follow you. (*Church News*, September 7, 1968, p. 15.)

— *George Albert Smith*

Leadership is the ability to encourage the best efforts of others in working toward a desirable goal. (*Ensign*, March 1976, p. 4.)

— *Spencer W. Kimball*

The personal nature of the Lord's ministry as the Master Shepherd should be the pattern for all who shepherd the flocks of Israel. The depth of His love, His willingness to give freely of Himself, His undeviating loyalty and devotion to the cause shared so completely with His Father, and His constant attention to the needs of the one stand as hallmarks of the true shepherd's calling. (*Ensign*, May 1988, p. 74.)

— *John R. Lasater*

Leaders on every level should be primarily interested in rendering compassionate caring for others. (*Ensign*, November 1987, p. 22.)

— *Marvin J. Ashton*

True shepherds nourish and care for each member of the flock and keep them in remembrance. They do not simply number them. Shepherds know and care for their flock. A shepherd cannot rest when even one of the flock is lost. (*Ensign*, May 1987, p. 75.)

— *Robert D. Hales*

We will find it very difficult to be significant leaders unless we recognize the reality of the perfect leader, Jesus Christ, and let him be the light by which we see the way! . . . If we would be eminently successful, here is our pattern. All the ennobling, perfect, and beautiful qualities of maturity, of strength, and of courage are found in this one person. (*Ensign*, August 1979, p. 7.)

— *Spencer W. Kimball*

Within the kingdom of God, *to lead is to serve.* (*Ensign*, May 1990, p. 27.)

— *Spencer J. Condie*

[Leadership] involves . . . a personal and sincere interest in the problems and concerns of those who are being led and, most importantly, a willingness to get on one's knees and seek for greater power than that which one naturally possesses. (*Ensign*, May 1983, p. 85.)

— *Gordon B. Hinckley*

See also EXAMPLE

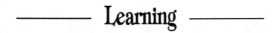

Learning

There is spiritual learning just as there is material learning, and the one without the other is not complete; yet, speaking for myself, if I could have only one sort of learning, that which I would take would be the learning of the Spirit, because in the hereafter I shall have opportunity in the eternities which are to come to get the other, and without spiritual learning here my handicaps in the hereafter would be all but overwhelming. (*CR*, April 1934, p. 94.)

— *J. Reuben Clark, Jr.*

Continuous education is our labor, our business and our calling. (*JD*, 6:268.)

— *Brigham Young*

How to Learn

I offer you five words that have evolved from a lifetime of teaching. . . . (1) *Read.* (2) *Listen.* (3) *Mark.* (To me *mark* means also copy, clip, assemble. . . . get it in an accessible form while you are thinking about it, . . .) (4) *Organize.* (Think and put things together. Get them cohesive, coherent.) (5) *Digest.* (As I understand it, that means getting the strength in your bloodstream, casting out the dross, and moving with energy.) (*Ensign*, July 1971, p. 63.)

— *Marion D. Hanks*

I shall not cease learning while I live, nor when I arrive in the spirit world; but shall there learn with greater facility; and when I again receive my body, I shall learn a thousand times more in a thousand times less time; and then I do not mean to cease learning, but shall still continue my researches. (*JD*, 8:10.)

— *Brigham Young*

It is a good thing to be a Saint. We are as children; we have to pass through the state of infancy, of childhood, and of youth, before we can arrive at manhood; and we have to learn by degrees. (*JD*, 5:314.)

— *Lorenzo Snow*

No matter where we begin, if we pursue knowledge diligently and honestly, our quest will inevitably lead us from the things of earth to the things of heaven. (*OAT*, p. 130.)

— *Hugh Nibley*

This restored gospel brings not only spiritual strength, but also intellectual curiosity and growth. Truth is truth. There is no clearly defined line of demarcation between the spiritual and the intellectual when the intellectual is cultivated and pursued in balance with the pursuit of spiritual knowledge and strength. (*Ensign*, May 1986, p. 48.)

— *Gordon B. Hinckley*

We should feel equally at home in the academy and in the temple. We should regard each as a center of learning. (*BYU Speeches 1981-82*, p. 132.)

— *Rex E. Lee*

We must gain learning, but we must apply it wisely. Otherwise, we have politics without principle, industry without morality, knowledge without wisdom, science without humanity! (*Ensign*, November 1984, p. 30.)

— *Russell M. Nelson*

We should seek learning by faith in God, the giver of revelation. I believe that many of the great discoveries and achievements in science and the arts have resulted from a God-given revelation. Seekers who have paid the price in perspiration have been magnified by inspiration.

— *Dallin H. Oaks*

When shall we cease to learn? Never, never. (*JD*, 3:203)

— *Brigham Young*

See also EDUCATION, KNOWLEDGE

——— Life ———

A universal question in the hearts and minds of men and women in all parts of the world is, "What is the purpose of life?"

The restored gospel of Jesus Christ answers this question. In modern revelation the Lord has told us, "If you keep my commandments and endure to the end you shall have eternal life, which gift is the greatest of all the gifts of God." (D&C 14:7.)

Therefore, in essence the purpose of life is to prepare us for the greatest gift of God, eternal life. (*Ensign*, May 1981, p. 50.)

— *Franklin D. Richards*

As far as you and I are concerned, at this time, this life is the most important part of all eternity. We have the light and knowledge and revelations of heaven. This life is the time for us to prepare to meet God, to keep the commandments of God, to hearken to counsels of the living oracles and to press forward in righteousness. (*CR*, April 1948, p. 51.)

— *Bruce R. McConkie*

Every normal individual should complete the full cycle of human life with all its joys and satisfactions in natural order—childhood, adolescence, youth, parenthood, middle age and the age of grandchildren. Each age has satisfaction which can be known only by experience. You must be born again and again in order to know the full course of human happiness. When the first baby is born, a mother is born and a father is born and grandparents are born. Only by birth can any of these come into being. Only by the natural cycle of life can the great progressive joys of mankind be reached.

Any social system which prevents the individual from pursuing the normal cycle of life, from marrying young, from rearing a family before the age of fifty or so and from obtaining the deep, peculiar joys of middle life and grandparenthood, defeats the divine order of the universe and lays the basis of all sorts of social problems. (*Ensign*, May 1976, p. 106.)

— *Spencer W. Kimball*

Existence is one thing; life is a great deal more. . . . there are persons that exist and manifest but little life. There are others that have life so far as it can be enjoyed in mortality to the full. . . . They are spiritually, intellectually, physically alive, and the power of increase is with them. (*CR*, October 1911, p. 53.)

— *Charles W. Penrose*

Life is a mission and not a career. (Quoted by Thomas S. Monson, *Ensign*, May 1988, p. 54.)

— *Stephen L Richards*

Life is an accumulation of every property and principle that is calculated to enrich, to ennoble, to enlarge, and to increase, in every particular, the dominion of individual man. (*JD*, 1:349.)

— *Brigham Young*

Life is God's greatest gift to man, and what we do with our life is our gift to God. (*CR*, April 1971, p. 38.)

— *Franklin D. Richards*

No matter what citizenship or race, whether male or female, no matter what occupation, no matter your education, regardless of the generation in which one lives, life is a homeward journey for all of us, back to the presence of God in his celestial kingdom. (*Ensign*, May 1987, p. 24.)

— *Boyd K. Packer*

The great test of life is obedience to God.
The great task of life is to learn the will of the Lord and then do it.
The great commandment of life is to love the Lord. (*Ensign*, May 1988, p. 4.)

— *Ezra Taft Benson*

The main purpose of earth life is to allow our spirits, which existed before the world was, to be united with our bodies for a time of great opportunity in mortality. The association of the two together has given us the privilege of growing, developing, and maturing as only we can with spirit and body united. With our bodies, we pass through a certain amount of trial in what is termed a probationary state of our existence. This is a time of learning and testing to prove ourselves worthy of eternal opportunities. It is all part of a divine plan our Father has for His children. (*Ensign*, May 1989, p. 14.)

— *L. Tom Perry*

The thoughts we think, the deeds we do, the lives we live influence not only the success of our earthly journey; they mark the way to our eternal goals. (*Ensign*, November 1988, p. 69.)

— *Thomas S. Monson*

The true purpose of life is the perfection of humanity through individual effort, under the guidance of God's inspiration. (*CR*, October 1963, p. 7.)

— *David O. McKay*

The whole mortal existence of man is neither more nor less than a preparatory state given to finite beings, a space wherein they may improve themselves for a higher state of being. (*JD*, 1:334.)

— *Brigham Young*

This life is worth as much to us as any life in the eternities of the gods. (*JD*, 9:170.)

— *Brigham Young*

We are here in mortality, and the only way to go is through; there isn't any around!

— *Neal A. Maxwell*

What is most important, then, is what we do with our lives. For faithful members of The Church of Jesus Christ of Latter-day Saints, the truth is not an end in itself. Our lives are a constant quest and example of a dynamic relationship between truth and knowledge, between living and being. (*Ensign*, May 1988, p. 26.)

— *Angel Abrea*

See also MAN, PLAN OF SALVATION, PROBATION, TODAY

———— Light of Christ ————

Every individual born to earth is given a detecting capability, a divinely appointed gift to distinguish truth from error. We call it our conscience. God calls it the Spirit of Christ. When we properly use this gift, we are naturally drawn to truth and repelled from error. (*Ensign*, November 1979, p. 70.)

— *Richard G. Scott*

If we falter and turn aside, our lamp will burn dim and finally go out, when lo, the Comforter, the source of revelation, will leave us, and darkness will take its place; then how great will be that darkness! (*JD*, 18:273.)

— *Joseph Smith*

There are three phases of the light of Christ that I want to mention.

The first one is the light which enlighteneth every man that cometh into the world (D&C 88:7,12; 84:45-46; Moro. 7:13-16);

The second phase is the gift of the Holy Ghost;

And the third is the more sure word of prophecy (D&C 131:5; 2 Pet. 1:10; D&C 88:3-4). (*Ensign*, May 1977, p. 43.)

— *Marion G. Romney*

There is a monitor in every person that would reign there triumphantly, if permitted so to do, and lead to truth and virtue.

— *Brigham Young*

[The light of Christ] strives with . . . men, and will continue to strive with them, until it brings them to a knowledge of the truth and the possession of the greater light and testimony of the Holy Ghost.

— *Joseph F. Smith*

We consider that God has created man with a mind capable of instruction, and a faculty which may be enlarged in proportion to the heed and diligence given to the light communicated from heaven to the intellect. (*TPJS*, p. 51.)

— *Joseph Smith*

We know that without physical light we cannot see the things around us or even where we are going; and without spiritual light we cannot have knowledge or understanding. . . . Reference has been made to the apostasy in the so-called Dark Ages. The Old Testament prophets repeatedly foretold the great apostasy and referred to a darkness that would cover the earth and the people. From the scriptures cited it is evident that only through the Spirit of Christ can we be enlightened and comprehend truth and that when the gospel was withdrawn from the earth, the progress of man was retarded. Since the restoration of the gospel, and the investiture once again of the power of God as given to man through the priesthood of God, it is remarkable to note the abundance in all fields of learning. All truth is discerned through the Spirit of Truth or the Light of Christ. (*Ensign,* November 1977, pp. 49, 50.)

— *N. Eldon Tanner*

See also INTELLIGENCE, KNOWLEDGE, REVELATION, TRUTH

Listening

As you develop your capacity to love unconditionally, remember that listening is a part of showing love. [Make] your home . . . a home where children are listened to, even when what they say doesn't seem important or you don't feel you have time, . . . Can we listen openly to a shocking experience without going into a state of shock ourselves, or without an immediate verbal overreaction? We all know there is a time to talk and a time to listen. To listen with patience to a young person's reasons for getting home late will bring you undying gratitude. Remember, you can listen to understand, not necessarily to agree. Ofttimes we do our best teaching when we listen. Husband-and-wife relationships are nourished and strengthened as we listen to each other more. Hearts are softened. (*Ensign,* May 1990, p. 84.)

— *H. Burke Peterson*

By listening emphatically, we often can help others find their own solutions. (*Ensign,* May 1983, p. 31.)

— *Marvin J. Ashton*

If I were a boy, what would I want my dad to be like? I'd probably wish he didn't preach to me so much, but rather, would listen to me more. Many dads spend too much time preaching and not enough time teaching. Sometimes great things happen inside a boy when he's listened to by his dad. He begins to think he is special—that he is not just another twelve-year old or sixteen-year-old. His self-image improves. One of our crying needs is to have young men who have a worthy self-image. These are the effective builders of the kingdom. In a father-son visit, who talks most? One successful father said, "Dads needs to give more ear and less lip to their sons." (*Ensign,* November 1982, p. 43.)

— *H. Burke Peterson*

Jesus was a listening leader. Because he loved others with a perfect love, he listened without being condescending. A great leader listens not only to others, but also to his conscience and to the promptings of God. (*Ensign*, August 1979, p. 5.)

— Spencer W. Kimball

———— Living the Gospel ————

A true measure of one's devotion to a principle is measured not by what he professes, but by what he manifests—day by day. (*CR*, October 1952, p. 55.)

— ElRay L. Christiansen

Each of us, whatever our knowledge of the gospel, can continue to learn. But learning is just the beginning. The fulness of blessings comes as we adopt the principles and live our lives by them. When we make them our way, when we live the principles, we are promised that they will be a light unto us. As we come to know that light, it will lead us through the mist of darkness, and as we begin to bring that light into our homes, it can become a beacon to our children, and to their children, and to theirs. (*Ensign*, November 1982, p. 85.)

— Barbara B. Smith

I leave you my testimony of the joy of living—of the joys of *full* gospel living and of going through the Refiner's fire and the sanctification process that takes place. As the Apostle Paul so well said, "We know that all things work together for good to them that love God." (Rom. 8:28.) (*Ensign*, November 1989, p. 8.)

— Ezra Taft Benson

It is one thing to talk about the gospel, but it is quite another to live it. It is one thing to preach about Christ, but it is another to follow in his footsteps. (*Ensign*, May 1984, p. 72.)

— Angel Abrea

Resolve to live the gospel of Jesus Christ in its entirety. "For you shall live by every word that proceedeth forth from the mouth of God." (D&C 84:44.) Many people live the gospel according to themselves. That is self-deception.

There is only one true gospel. . . . The menu has only one entree. To pick and choose which of God's precepts to live is satanic self-centeredness. (*Ensign*, May 1982, p. 13.)

— Hugh W. Pinnock

Security, *true* security, comes only by living the principles of the gospel. *Security is the fruit of righteous living.* (*Ensign*, May 1981, p. 90.)

— *Marion G. Romney*

In the final analysis, the gospel of God is written, not in the dead letters of the scriptural records, but in the lives of the Saints. (*CR*, October 1968, p. 135.)

— *Bruce R. McConkie*

Treasure up the Lord's word. Possess it, own it, make it yours by both believing it and living it. For instance: the voice of the Lord says that if men have faith, repent, and are baptized, they shall receive the Holy Ghost. It is not sufficient merely to know what the scripture says. One must treasure it up, meaning take it into his possession so affirmatively that it becomes a part of his very being; as a consequence, in the illustration given, one actually receives the companionship of the Spirit. Obviously such persons will not be deceived where the signs of the times and the Second Coming of the Messiah are concerned. (*Doctrinal New Testament Commentary*, Salt Lake City: Bookcraft, 1965-73, 1:662.)

— *Bruce R. McConkie*

We must take a positive approach to our religion and literally make it a way of life, a plan of daily action. We must reform ourselves day by day along gospel lines, for this is the time of our probation and it is now that we must prepare to meet our God. (See Alma 34:32.) (*Ensign*, May 1982, pp. 15-16.)

— *Mark E. Petersen*

See also ACTION, OBEDIENCE, PROCRASTINATION

———— **Loneliness** ————

There is no final solution to loneliness until you recognize that you need the resources which are in yourself to enjoy, within limits, being alone—being the kind of person that you like to be with, and reaching out to others, not in a grasping way, but in an attempt to be meaningful and loving and of service in their lives. (Fireside Address, Provo, Utah, 1980.)

— *Truman G. Madsen*

The key to overcoming aloneness and a feeling of uselessness for one who is physically able is to step outside yourself by helping others who are truly needy. We promise those who will render this kind of service that, in some measure, you will be healed of the loss of loved ones or the dread of being alone. The way to feel better about your own situation is to improve someone else's circumstances. (*Ensign*, November 1989, p. 6.)

— Ezra Taft Benson

The lord will never forsake or abandon anyone. You may abandon him, but he will not abandon you. You never need to feel that you are alone. (*Ensign*, November 1989, p. 75.)

— Joseph B. Wirthlin

——— Look to God ———

A man's mind should be single to the glory of God in everything that he starts to accomplish. We should consider that of ourselves we can do nothing. We are the children of God. We are in darkness, only as God enlightens our understanding. We are powerless, only as God helps us. The work that we have to do here is of that nature that we cannot do it unless we have the assistance of the Almighty. (*Deseret Weekly*, 48:638.)

— Lorenzo Snow

Everything is given by God. All talent, creativity, ability, insight, and strength comes from him. In our own strength we can do nothing. (*Ensign*, May 1990, p. 67.)

— Marvin J. Ashton

God knows the feelings in every human heart. He can soften sorrow and lead when there seems to be no light. Prayer can give guidance and confidence. It reminds us that no one need be alone in this world. If all else fails, remember: God and one other person can be a family. (*Ensign*, May 1988, p. 64.)

— Marvin J. Ashton

In life, . . . you should seek the help you need. Do not depend on your own strength alone. You have never done all you can to finish a task until you have sought help from the Lord. (*Ensign*, November 1989, p. 74.)

— Joseph B. Wirthlin

Through the years, the offices I have occupied have been decorated with lovely paintings of peaceful and pastoral scenes. However, there is one picture that always hangs on the wall which I face when seated behind my desk. It is a constant reminder of Him whom I serve, for it is a picture of our Lord and Savior, Jesus Christ. When confronted with a vexing problem or difficult decision, I always gaze at that picture of the Master and silently ask myself the question, "What would He have me do?" No longer does doubt linger, nor does indecision prevail. The way to go is clear, and the pathway before me beckons. (*Ensign*, November 1989, p. 69.)

— *Thomas S. Monson*

There is a gift available to all of us—the gift of looking to God for direction. Here is an avenue of strength, comfort, and guidance. . . .

"Look to God and live." This is the wonderful promise given so often in the scriptures. . . .

Our capacity to see and comprehend is increased only in proportion to our willingness to look. God becomes more approachable as we look to him. (*Ensign*, November 1987, p. 21.)

— *Marvin J. Ashton*

See also EYE SINGLE, TRUST IN GOD

——— Love ———

Eternal life, God's life, the life we are seeking, is rooted in two commandments. The scriptures say that "on these two commandments hang all the law and the prophets" (Matthew 22:40). Love God and love your neighbor. The two together; they are inseparable. In the highest sense they may be considered as synonymous. And they are commandments that each of us can live. (*Ensign*, November 1986, p. 34.)

— *Howard W. Hunter*

Knowing that we should love is not enough. But when knowledge is applied through service, love can secure for us the blessings of heaven. (*Ensign*, November 1982, p. 11.)

— *David B. Haight*

During the Great Depression, the homeless, the downtrodden, the unemployed "rode the rails" that passed not far from our home. On numerous occasions, there would be a soft knock on the back door. When I opened the door, there I would see a man, sometimes two, ill-clothed, ill-fed, ill-schooled. Generally, such a visitor held in his hand the familiar cap. His hair would be tousled, his face unshaven. The question was always the same: "Could you spare some food?" My dear mother invariably responded with a pleasant, "Come in and sit down at the table." She would then prepare a ham sandwich, cut a piece of cake, and pour a glass of milk. Mother would ask the visitor about his home, his family, his life. She provided hope and words of encouragement. Before leaving, the visitor would pause to express a gracious thank-you. I would note that a smile of content had replaced a look of despair. Eyes that were dull now shone with new purpose. Love, that noblest attribute of the human soul, can work wonders. (*Ensign*, May 1987, p. 68.)

— *Thomas S. Monson*

Impossible mountains are climbed by those who have the self-confidence that comes from truly being loved. Prisons and other institutions, even some of our own homes, are filled with those who have been starved for affection. (*Ensign*, May 1977, p. 69.)

— *H. Burke Peterson*

Love . . . [is] a lack of personal selfishness. (*Ensign*, May 1979, p. 72.)

— *Theodore M. Burton*

Love is like the Polar Star. In a changing world, it is a constant. It is of the very essence of the gospel. It is the security of the home. It is the safeguard of community life. It is a beacon of hope in a world of distress. (*Ensign*, May 1989, p. 66.)

— *Gordon B. Hinckley*

Love is the essence of the gospel and the guiding light for a Christlike life. It not only teaches us to look upward but also to look around us. (*Ensign*, May 1990, p. 26.)

— *Hans B. Ringger*

Nothing is so much calculated to lead people to forsake sin as to take them by the hand, and watch over them with tenderness. When persons manifest the least kindness and love to me, O what power it has over my mind, while the opposite course has a tendency to harrow up all the harsh feelings and depress the human mind. (*HC*, 5:23.)

— *Joseph Smith*

Someone has written, "Love is a verb." It requires doing—not just saying and thinking. The test is in what one does, how one acts, for love is conveyed in word and deed. (*Ensign*, November 1982, p. 12.)

— *David B. Haight*

The deepest expression of spirituality is love. (*CR*, October 1964, p. 94.)

— *Robert L. Simpson*

The person who has earned love the least needs it the most. (*Ensign*, May 1982, p. 70.)

— *F. Enzio Busche*

Much of our love is confined to mere lip service and dreams of good deeds accomplished, but true love must be expressed in unselfish acts of kindness that bring others closer to our Heavenly Father. (*Ensign*, May 1981, p. 60.)

— *Jack Goaslind, Jr.*

We must love one another. Only [by doing] so can our long years of toil and struggle reach full reward and we be crowned with life everlasting. (*Relief Society Magazine*, May 1921.)

— *Susa Young Gates*

Love should be a vehicle allowed to travel without limitations. (*Ensign*, May 1988, p. 64.)

— *Marvin J. Ashton*

We need to remember that though we make our friends, God has made our neighbors—everywhere. Love should have no boundary; we should have no narrow loyalties. (*Ensign*, November 1986, p. 35.)

— *Howard W. Hunter*

See also CHARITY, SERVICE, UNITY, ZION

——— Love God ———

A man filled with the love of God, is not content with blessing his family alone, but ranges through the whole world, anxious to bless the whole human race. (*HC*, 4:227.)

— *Joseph Smith*

Keeping the commandments of God is not a difficult burden when we do it out of love of him who has so graciously blessed us. (*Ensign*, November 1977, p. 21.)

— *Delbert L. Stapley*

He loves the Lord with all his heart who loves nothing in comparison of him, and nothing but in reference to him, who is ready to give up, do, or suffer anything in order to please and glorify him. He loves God with all his soul, or

rather with all his life, who is ready to give up life for his sake and to be deprived
of the comforts of the world to glorify him. He loves God with all this strength
who exerts all the powers of his body and soul in the service of God. He loves
God with all his mind who applies himself only to know God and his will, who
sees God in all things and acknowledges him in all ways. (*CR*, April 1965, p. 58.)

— Howard W. Hunter

If men and nations did reach up to God with all their hearts, war would cease.
If love of God were in the heart, a man would have no desire to destroy his
brother.

There would be no dishonesty if the love of God were in the heart. If God
came first in his life, a man would love his neighbor as himself, and instead of
taking from him, he would feel to give. (*Ensign*, November 1982, p. 27.)

— Rex C. Reeve

Love is a gift of God, and as we obey His laws and genuinely learn to serve
others, we develop God's love in our lives.

Love of God is the means of unlocking divine powers which help us to live
worthily and to overcome the world. (*Ensign*, November 1982, p. 12.)

— David B. Haight

Love the Lord thy God with all thy heart, and then speak evil of thy neighbor? No! No! Love the Lord thy God with all thy heart, and speak that which is
not true? No, oh, no! Love the Lord thy God with all thy heart, and seek after
riches of the world and forsake your religion? No! Love the Lord thy God with all
thy heart and take his name in vain, curse and swear? No, never! If the love of
God was really in the hearts of all who call themselves Latter-day Saints, there
would be no more speaking evil of one another, no more running after the gold
mines; nothing would be sought after, only to build up the kingdom of God.
(*JD*, 12:229.)

— Brigham Young

Of all the peoples in the world, we Latter-day Saints should have the greatest
love for God. We should love him more than anyone else loves him, because we
know so much more about him. (*Ensign*, September 1982, p. 3.)

— Marion G. Romney

The man who performs righteous acts for an erroneous reason lulls himself
into a false sense of security. He feels that the acts themselves will save him. But
when the rain descends and the flood comes and the wind blows and beats on the
house, it falls because it does not have the correct foundation. . . . Everything—the
heavens, the earth, and everything that in them is—is going to pass away, and if

you have tied your faith to any part of this frail existence—the earth, the heavens, or people on the earth—it is not going to stand. . . . Then love of the Lord becomes absolutely vital to salvation, because it forms the foundation of our motives for righteousness. (*CR*, October 1968, pp. 13-14.)

— *Hartman Rector, Jr.*

That man loves God most who puts his own life in harmony with him, and who serves his fellow men as though his life depends upon it, as indeed it does.

— *Sterling W. Sill*

The god of the world is gold and silver. The world worships this god. It is all-powerful to them, though they might not be willing to acknowledge it. . . . Latter-day Saints should show whether they have so far advanced in the knowledge, in the wisdom and in the power of God that they cannot be overcome by the god of the world. . . . We have got to love God more than we love the world, more than we love gold or silver, and love our neighbor as ourselves. (*TLS*, p. 130.)

— *Lorenzo Snow*

There is only one way you can pay the debt you owe . . . the Lord and that is to give service. The Lord has given you life. He has given you everything you have. You didn't earn it and you didn't buy it. So, when you think, "What could I do to repay?" . . . You could say, "I'm going to give You my life, all my years, all my effort." (*TSWK*, p. 252.)

— *Spencer W. Kimball*

To love God with all your heart, soul, mind, and strength is all-consuming and all-encompassing. It is no lukewarm endeavor. It is total commitment of our very being—physically, mentally, emotionally, and spiritually—to a love of the Lord. (*Ensign*, May 1988, p. 4.)

— *Ezra Taft Benson*

We live in a complex world. There are many forces calling out, "Love me." A sure way to set our guidelines for that which we choose to serve and learn to love is to follow the admonition of Joshua: "As for me and my house, we will serve the Lord." (Josh. 24:15.)

Let us look to our own lives. We serve that which we love. If we sacrifice and give our love for that which our Father in Heaven asks of us, it will help us set our footsteps upon the path of eternal life. (*Ensign*, May 1981, p. 24.)

— *Marvin J. Ashton*

Why should we not love him with all our heart and mind, and strength, since he has given us life, since he has formed us in his own likeness and image, since he has placed us here that we may become like unto his Only Begotten Son and to inherit the glory, exaltation and reward provided for God's own children? (*CR*, October 1914, p. 6.)

— *Joseph F. Smith*

See also EYE SINGLE, WILLINGNESS

—— Lying ——

Aspects of Lying
1. Satan is the father of lying and inaugurated the practice in this world when in the Garden of Eden he lied to Eve. (Moses 4:3-4.)
2. God cannot lie. (Eth. 3:9-12.)
3. God hates lying. (Prov. 6:16-17.)
4. Liars are classified with major transgressors. (Hos. 4:1-3.)
5. They languish in this world. (Acts 4:35; 5:1-11.)
6. All unrepentant liars "shall have their part in the lake which burneth with fire and brimstone: which is the second death. (Rev. 21:8.) (*Ensign*, November 1976, p. 38.)

— *Marion G. Romney*

No man can be at peace who is untrue to his better self. No man can have lasting peace who is living a lie. (*Ensign*, November 1985, p. 69.)

— *Marvin J. Ashton*

Nothing else is quite so despicable or cowardly as a lie, and it is an added iniquity to befoul another with an untruth. (Quoted by Marion G. Romney, *Ensign*, November 1976, p. 36.)

— *J. Reuben Clark, Jr.*

One teacher had her class repeat at the beginning of each day . . . "A lie is *any* communication given to another with the intent to deceive." . . . A lie can be effectively communicated without words ever being spoken. Sometimes a nod of the head or silence can deceive. Recommending a questionable business investment, making a false entry in a ledger, devious use of flattery, or failure to divulge all pertinent facts are a few other ways to communicate the lie. (*Ensign*, May 1982, p. 9.)

— *Marvin J. Ashton*

The world tempts us to lie and cheat and steal; to be shoplifters or worse; . . . What shall we do about that? We shall keep the Ten Commandments, avoiding dishonesty in all its forms. (*Ensign*, May 1981, p. 61.)

— *Mark E. Petersen*

See also HONESTY, INTEGRITY

—— Magnify Callings ——

I believe there is no place in God's service that is not bigger than we are, not greater than the talents we bring to bear on the assignment, whether as a home teacher, a secretary, a clerk, a visiting teacher, a teacher of any kind, a counselor, a bishop, or whatever, *if* we magnify our calling. (*Ensign*, July 1975, p. 5.)

— *Joe J. Christensen*

I remember reading an anecdote [about] a man who, through his wisdom and patriotism, had gained great renown. [The man] was, through envy, assigned to a position which was considered very degrading. On entering upon its duties it was said that he made this significant remark: "If the office does not honor me I will honor the office." Much difficulty would be avoided, and our condition and situation would be much more encouraging if we all honored the office in which we are called to act. (*Deseret News*, January 31, 1877.)

— *Lorenzo Snow*

If you do not magnify your calling, God will hold you responsible for those you might have saved, had you done your duty. (Quoted by Thomas S. Monson, *Ensign*, May 1986, pp. 37-38.)

— *John Taylor*

The Church is organized properly. We need to be sure that every man learns his duty and acts in the office in which he is appointed, in all diligence. (See D&C 107:99.) (*Ensign*, May 1986, p. 14.)

— *M. Russell Ballard*

What does it mean to magnify a calling? It means to build it up in dignity and importance, to make it honorable and commendable in the eyes of all men, to enlarge and strengthen it, to let the light of heaven shine through it to the view of other men. And how does one magnify a calling? Simply by performing the service that pertains to it. (*Ensign*, May 1986, p. 38.)

— *Thomas S. Monson*

While we magnify our callings, we honour our God; while we magnify our callings, we possess a portion of the Spirit of God; . . . while we magnify our calling, the Spirit of God flows through the proper channels by which and through which we receive our proper nourishment and are instructed in things pertaining to our welfare, happiness, and interest pertaining to this world and the world to come. (*JD*, 6:108.)

— John Taylor

See also CALLINGS, EXCELLENCE

Man

Man and God are of the same race, and it is within the power of a righteous man to become like his Father.

— Bruce R. McConkie

Man is a dual being, composed of the spirit which gives life, force, intelligence and capacity to man, and the body which is the tenement of the spirit and is suited to its form, adapted to its necessities, and acts in harmony with it, and to its utmost capacity yields obedience to the will of the spirit. The two combined constitute the soul. (*JD*, 23:169.)

— Joseph F. Smith

Man is a dual being, possessed of body and spirit, made in the image of God, and connected with him and with eternity. He is a God in embryo and will live and progress throughout the eternal ages, if obedient to the laws of the Godhead. (*JD*, 23:65.)

— John Taylor

Our body will not fulfill its purpose—it cannot—without that life—giving something within which is the offspring of Deity as eternal as [your] Father [in Heaven]. . . . That spirit within, . . . is the *real* you. What you make of yourself depends upon you. . . . You are in this world to choose the right or the wrong, to accept the right or yield to temptation. Upon that choice will depend the development of the spiritual part of you. (*CR*, April 1967, pp. 134-35.)

— David O. McKay

What is man in this boundless setting of sublime splendor? I answer you: Potentially now, actually to be, he is greater and grander, more precious according to the arithmetic of God, than all the planets and suns of space. For him were they created; they are the handiwork of God; man is his son. In this world man is given dominion over a few things; it is his privilege to achieve supremacy over many things. (August 9, 1931, quoted by Ted E. Brewerton, *Ensign*, November 1986, p. 31.)

— *James E. Talmage*

There is a divinity within ourselves that is immortal and never dies. Thousands and thousands of years hence we will be ourselves, and nobody else, so far as our individuality is concerned. That never dies from all eternity to all eternity. (*CR*, April 1898, p. 63.)

— *Lorenzo Snow*

We believe that we are the offspring of our Father in heaven, and that we possess in our spiritual organizations the same capabilities, powers and faculties that our Father possesses, although in an infantile state, requiring to pass through a certain course or ordeal by which they will be developed and improved according to the heed we give to the principles we have received. (*JD*, 14:300.)

— *Lorenzo Snow*

When we look to see the evidence of creation all around us, from a grain of sand to the majestic planets, we begin to realize that we are the greatest of all God's creations; we are created in his image. (*Ensign*, May 1988, p. 58.)

— *M. Russell Ballard*

[Man] had his being in the eternal worlds; he existed before he came here. He is not only the son of man, but he is the son of God also. He is a God in embryo and possesses within him a spark of that eternal flame which was struck from the blaze of God's eternal fire in the eternal world, and he is placed here upon the earth, that he may possess true intelligence, true light, true knowledge—that he may know himself; that he may know God; that he may know something about what he is destined to enjoy in the eternal worlds; that he may be fully acquainted with his origin, with his present existence, and with his future destiny; that he may know something about the strength and weakness of human nature; that he may understand the divine law, and learn to conquer his passions, and bring into subjection every principle that is at variance with the law of God; that he may understand his true relationship to God; and finally, that he may learn how to subdue, to conquer, subject all wrong, seek after, obtain, and possess every true, holy, virtuous, and heavenly principle; and, as he is only a sojourner, that he may fulfill the measure of his creation, help himself and family, be a benefit to the present and future generations, and go back to God, having accomplished the work he came here to perform. (*JD*, 8:3-4.)

— *John Taylor*

See also INDIVIDUALITY, LIFE, PLAN OF SALVATION

——— **Manhood** ———

A great deal of credit is due to our sisters. God has provided them as help-mates to their husbands, and it is the duty of the latter to cherish and protect those whom God has given unto them, . . . Teach them—our wives and daughters—the pure principles of the gospel that the daughters of Zion may be lovely and shine as the light and glory of the age in which we live. (*JD*, 19:142.)

— *John Taylor*

Brethren, your first and most responsible role in life and in the eternities is to be a righteous husband.

— *L. Tom Perry*

One of the duties of manhood is to safeguard womanhood. (*Ensign*, May 1988, p. 37.)

— *James E. Faust*

True men must reach out to show concern for boys. . . . Boys . . . need men to look up to, to love and follow. They need [true] men to teach them how to be men or they may learn, as so many do, from imitation men who themselves have it all wrong, who may have perverse ideas, who think that manhood rests in muscles or money, or crime or crudity, or cards or conquests. (*Ensign*, November 1977, p. 36.)

— *Marion D. Hanks*

We look to you to give righteous leadership in your home and families and, with your companions and the mothers of your children, to lead your families back to our Eternal Father. (Quoted by Joanne B. Doxey, *Ensign*, November 1987, p. 91.)

— *Ezra Taft Benson*

See also FATHERHOOD, MARRIAGE, PRIESTHOOD

——— **Marriage** ———

One day, those who are now anguished because they are unmarried will, if they are faithful, know the joys of being in the midst of a vast convocation of their posterity. The seeming deprivation which occurs in the life of a deserving single woman who feels she has no prospects of immediate marriage and motherhood, properly endured, foretells a delayed blessing. Some deprivation, therefore, is an excavation; it is the readying of a reservoir into which a generous God will later pour all that he hath. (*Ensign*, May 1983, p. 93.)

— *Neal A. Maxwell*

A husband should always try to treat his wife with the greatest courtesy and respect, holding her in the highest esteem. He should speak to her in a kind and a soft manner, showing his love by word and deed. As she feels this love and tenderness she will mirror it and return it tenfold. (*Ensign*, May 1988, p. 37.)

— *James E. Faust*

Alternatives to the legal and loving marriage between a man and a woman are helping to unravel the fabric of human society. That fabric, of course, is the family. These so-called alternative life-styles cannot be accepted as right because they frustrate God's commandment for a life-giving union of male and female within a legal marriage. If practiced by all adults, these life-styles would mean the end of family.

The scriptures clearly and consistently condemn all sex relations outside of legal marriage as morally wrong. Why is this so? It is so because God said so. It is so because we are made in the image of God, male and female. We are his spirit children. We were with him in the beginning. Bringing to pass our exaltation is his work and glory. We are directed to be the children of light. We are heirs to eternal life. The Spirit gives light to every man and woman who comes into the world. (*Ensign*, May 1987, p. 81.)

— *James E. Faust*

Divorces are increasing because in many cases the union lacks that enrichment which comes from the sanctifying benediction which flows from the keeping of the commandments of God. It is a lack of spiritual nourishment. (*Ensign*, November 1977, p. 11.)

— *James E. Faust*

Marriage is sustained by faith and knowledge of its divine establishment, and is sustained daily by the energy of love. (*Ensign*, May 1984, p. 14.)

— *David B. Haight*

Marriage . . . is without beginning of days or end of years; . . . it lays the foundation for worlds, for angels, and for the Gods; for intelligent beings to be crowned with glory, immortality, and eternal lives. In fact, it is the thread which runs from the beginning to the end of the holy Gospel of Salvation—of the Gospel of the Son of God; it is from eternity to eternity. (*DBY*, 195.)

— *Brigham Young*

Foundation Stones to a Secure Marriage

First: *faith,* the first principle of the gospel. It must be the first principle of your marriage—not only faith in God and in His beloved Son, not only in the living prophet, but, . . . also . . . in each other, ...

Second: *obedience,* often referred to as the first law of heaven. . . . Obedience to our covenants with the Lord is a prerequisite to peace and love within the family circle.

Third: *loyalty.* Loyalty to a companion through thick and thin will develop a basic character trait so strong that loyalty to the Church and true principles will follow just as naturally as the night follows the day. (*Ensign,* May 1982, p. 22.)
— *Robert L. Simpson*

Honorable marriage is more important than wealth, position, and status. As husband and wife, you can achieve your life's goals together. As you sacrifice for each other and your children, the Lord will bless you, and your commitment to the Lord and your service in His kingdom will be enhanced. (*Ensign,* May 1988, p. 53.)
— *Ezra Taft Benson*

Married people should be *best friends*; no relationship on earth needs friendship as much as marriage. . . .

Friendship in a marriage is so important. It blows away the chaff and takes the kernel, rejoices in the uniqueness of the other, listens patiently, gives generously, forgives freely. . . . It will not insist that both respond exactly the same in every thought and feeling, but it will bring to the union honesty, integrity. There will be repentance and forgiveness in every marriage . . . and respect and trust. (*Ensign,* November 1984, p. 36.)
— *Marion D. Hanks*

Marriage is a joint quest for the good, the beautiful, and the divine. (*Ensign,* November 1977, p. 11.)
— *James E. Faust*

Marriage is the way provided by God for the fulfillment of the greatest of human needs, based upon mutual respect, maturity, selflessness, decency, commitment, and honesty. Happiness in marriage and parenthood can exceed a thousand times any other happiness. (*Ensign,* November 1977, p. 11.)
— *James E. Faust*

Many new and enduring relationships spring into being with marriage—relationships all of which are vital to the happiness of the family.

For her, the words—sacred words—are wife, mother, homemaker, heart of a home; for him, husband, father, protector, provider, leader in his home in the warm spirit of the priesthood.

Together they enter a *partnership*, sharing and learning and growing. (*Ensign*, November 1984, pp. 36.)

— *Marion D. Hanks*

Men and women are of equal value before God and must be equally valuable in the eyes of each other. (*Ensign*, November 1984, p. 37.)

— *Marion D. Hanks*

One cannot degrade marriage without tarnishing other words as well, such words as *boy, girl, manhood, womanhood, husband, wife, father, mother, baby, children, family, home*. (*Ensign*, May 1981, p. 14.)

— *Boyd K. Packer*

One good yardstick as to whether a person might be the right one for you is this: in her presence, do you think your noblest thoughts, do you aspire to your finest deeds, do you wish you were better than you are?

— *Ezra Taft Benson*

Our natural affections are planted in us by the Spirit of God, for a wise purpose; and they are the very main-springs of life and happiness—they are the cement of all virtuous and heavenly society.

The fact is, God made man, male and female; he planted in their bosoms those affections which are calculated to promote their happiness and union. (*Writings of Parley Parker Pratt*, ed. Parker Pratt Robison, Salt Lake City: Deseret News Press, 1952, pp. 52-53.)

— *Parley P. Pratt*

Personally I would just as soon believe that death was a complete annihilation of both body and spirit as to think that I would have to live on forever and ever without a continuation of the love ties that bind my wife and me together. (*Ensign*, January 1974, p. 59.)

— *LeGrand Richards*

We believe in the eternal nature of the marriage relation, that man and woman are destined, as husband and wife, to dwell together eternally. We believe that we are organized as we are, with all these affections, with all this love for each other, for a definite purpose, something far more lasting than to be extinguished when death shall overtake us. We believe that when a man and woman are united as husband and wife, and they love each other, their hearts and feelings are one, that love is as enduring as eternity itself, and that when death overtakes them it will neither extinguish nor cool that love, but that it will brighten and kindle it to a purer flame, and that it will endure through eternity. (*JD*, 14:320.)

— George Q. Cannon

Remember constant courtship. The most important relationship upon this earth for you is between you and your sweetheart. Work at it, sacrifice for it, enjoy it. You can make your home a bit of heaven as you build for an eternity together. (*Ensign*, November 1986, p. 26.)

— George I. Cannon

The exalted view of marriage as held by this Church is given expressly in five words found in the 49th section of the Doctrine and Covenants, "Marriage is ordained of God" . . . . (*Gospel Ideals*, The Improvement Era, Salt Lake City: Deseret Book Co., 1976, p. 462.)

— David O. McKay

The lawful association of the sexes is ordained of God, not only as the sole means of race perpetuation, but for the development of the higher faculties and nobler traits of human nature, which the love-inspired companionship of man and woman alone can insure. (*IE*, June 1917, p. 739.)

— Joseph F. Smith

The secret of a happy marriage is to serve God and each other. The goal of marriage is unity and oneness, as well as self-development. Paradoxically, the more we serve one another, the greater is our spiritual and emotional growth. (*Ensign*, November 1982, p. 60.)

— Ezra Taft Benson

The very foundation of this basic unit of society [the family] is being undermined by infidelity, divorce, and total disregard of the sacred marriage vows. With such erosion come heartaches, untold suffering and distress, through the sins of adultery, fornication, and promiscuity when husbands and wives are unfaithful. Broken homes are one of the nation's great tragedies and are increasing in number every day.

Just imagine the reversal that would take place if full integrity were to rule in family life. There would be complete fidelity. Husbands would be faithful to wives, and wives to husbands. There would be no living in adulterous relationships in lieu of marriage. Homes would abound in love, children and parents would have respect for one another, and children would be reared in righteousness through *parental example*—the greatest teacher of all. (*Ensign*, May 1977, p. 16.)

— N. Eldon Tanner

True love is not so much a matter of romance as it is a matter of anxious concern for the well-being of one's companion. (*CR*, April 1971, p. 82.)

— *Gordon B. Hinckley*

Two of the most important principles anyone could know: that our Heavenly Father has provided that marriage and family ties may be established permanently, to endure forever; and that a marriage that we can joyfully look forward to eternally must be a good marriage here, a marriage that is the heart of a happy home and family. (*Ensign*, November 1984, p. 35.)

— *Marion D. Hanks*

We believe marriage was ordained by God for a wise, eternal purpose. The family is the basis of the righteous life. Divinely prescribed roles of father, mother, and children were given from the very beginning. (*Ensign*, May 1984, p. 6.)

— *Ezra Taft Benson*

When [men] kneel down in the presence of their wives and children they ought to be inspired by the gift and power of the Holy Ghost, that the husband may be such a man as a good wife will honor, and that the gift and power of God may be upon them continually. They ought to be one in their families, that the Holy Ghost might descend upon them, and they ought to live so that the wife through prayer may become sanctified, that she may see the necessity of sanctifying herself in the presence of her husband, and in the presence of her children, that they may be one together, in order that the man and the wife may be pure element, suitable to occupy a place in the establishment and formation of the kingdom of God, that they may breathe a pure spirit and impart pure instruction to their children, and their children's children. (*JD*, 4:155.)

— *Lorenzo Snow*

Without marriage the purposes of God would be frustrated, so far as this world is concerned, for there would be none to obey his other commands. (*Juvenile Instructor*, 37:400.)

— *Joseph F. Smith*

See also FAMILY, TEMPLE MARRIAGE

Mercy

How godlike a quality is mercy. It cannot be legislated. It must come from the heart. It must be stirred up from within. It is part of the endowment each of us receives as a son or daughter of God and partaker of a divine birthright. I plead for an effort among all of us to give greater expression and wider latitude to this instinct which lies within us. . . .

Mercy is of the very essence of the gospel of Jesus Christ. The degree to which each of us is able to extend it becomes an expression of the reality of our discipleship under Him who is our Lord and Master. (*Ensign*, May 1990, pp. 68, 69.)

— *Gordon B. Hinckley*

One cannot be merciful to others without receiving a harvest of mercy in return. (*Ensign*, May 1990, p. 70.)

— *Gordon B. Hinckley*

The nearer we get to our Heavenly Father, the more we are disposed to look with compassion on perishing souls; we feel that we want to take them upon our shoulders, and cast their sins behind our backs. If you would have God have mercy on you, have mercy on one another. (*HC*, 5:24.)

— *Joseph Smith*

While mercy cannot rob justice, mercy can satisfy the demands of justice, but only in the instance where we exercise faith in Jesus Christ unto repentance. (See Alma 34:14-16.) (*Ensign*, November 1985, p. 77.)

— *Hartman Rector, Jr.*

See also FORGIVENESS, JUDGMENT, JUSTICE

——— Millennium ———

Do you know what will be the main labor during the thousand years of rest? It will be that which we are trying to urge the Latter-day Saints to perform at the present time. Temples will be built all over this land, and the brethren and sisters will go into them and perhaps work day and night in order to hasten the work and accomplish the labors necessary before the Son of Man can present His kingdom to his Father. (*Deseret Weekly*, 50:738.)

— *Lorenzo Snow*

The Lord revealed to John that there shall be a thousand years' rest, a millennium or millennial era, when the earth shall rest from wickedness, and when knowledge shall cover it as waters cover the deep, and when one man shall not have to say to another, "Know ye the Lord?" but when, according to the words of the Prophet, "All shall know him, from the least even unto the greatest;"

when God's will shall be written in the hearts of the children of men, and they will understand his law. . . .

In that glorious period everything on the face of the earth will be beautiful; disease and crime, and all the evils that attend our present state of existence will be banished; and during that period, as God has revealed, the occupation of his people will be to lay a foundation for the redemption of the dead. (*JD*, 14:321-22.)

— *George Q. Cannon*

The millennium is dawning upon the world, we are at the end of the sixth thousand years; and the great day of rest, the millennium of which the Lord has spoken, will soon dawn and the Savior will come in the clouds of heaven to reign over his people on the earth one thousand years. (*JD*, 18:113.)

— *Wilford Woodruff*

The restored gospel plays a single tune for all the world to hear, and I know that the time *will* come when all the world will eagerly respond to that tune. Then, and only then, differences between nations and peoples will disappear, and the world will be one, when the Savior returns to rule and reign for a thousand years. (*Ensign*, May 1986, p. 72.)

— *Jacob de Jager*

The world has had a fair trial for six thousand years; the Lord will try the seventh thousand himself. (*HC*, 5:64.)

— *Joseph Smith*

We are living in the Saturday evening of time. . . . We are now at the end of the week, in the Saturday night of human history. Morning will break upon the Millennium; the thousand years of peace, the Sabbath of the world. (*CR*, October 1919, pp. 73-74.)

— *Orson F. Whitney*

We are living in the "Saturday Evening of Time." When the Lord says it is today until his coming, that, I think, is what he has in mind, for he shall come in the morning of the Sabbath, or seventh day . . . to inaugurate the millennial reign. (Quoted by Joseph Fielding Smith, *CR*, April 1935, p. 98.)

— *Orson F. Whitney*

See also SECOND COMING

——— **Mind** ———

All the minds and spirits that God ever sent into the world are susceptible of enlargement. (*TPJS*, p. 354.)

— *Joseph Smith*

Our minds can become veritable junk heaps with dirty, cast-off ideas that accumulate there little by little.

Years ago I put up some signs in my mind. They are very clearly printed and simply read: "No trespassing." "No dumping allowed."

. . . I do not want my mind to be a dumping place for shabby ideas or thoughts, for disappointments, bitterness, envy, shame, hatred, worry, grief, or jealousy. (*Ensign*, November 1977, pp. 59-60.)

— *Boyd K. Packer*

The greatest mystery a man ever learned, is to know how to control the human mind, and bring every faculty and power of the same in subjection to Jesus Christ; this is the greatest mystery we have to learn while in these tabernacles of clay.

— *Brigham Young*

The mind of man is the crowning creation of God, in whose express image man was made. The development of the mind is a companion responsibility to the cultivation of the spirit, as set forth in the revealed principles of the restored gospel of Jesus Christ. (*Ensign*, May 1986, p. 48.)

— *Gordon B. Hinckley*

A fanciful and flowery and heated imagination beware of; because the things of God are of deep import; and time, and experience, and careful and ponderous and solemn thoughts can only find them out. Thy mind, O man, if thou wilt lead a soul unto salvation, must stretch as high as the utmost heavens, and search into and contemplate the darkest abyss, and the broad expanse of eternity—thou must commune with God. How much more dignified and noble are the thoughts of God, than the vain imaginations of the human heart! (*HC*, 3:295.)

— *Joseph Smith*

See also KNOWLEDGE, THOUGHTS

—————— Miracles ——————

Everyday Miracles

Christ's many miracles were only reflections of those greater marvels which his Father had performed before him and continues to perform all around us. . . .

For example, the first miracle by Jesus recorded in the New Testament was the turning of water into wine at the marriage at Cana. But poor, indeed, was the making of the wine in the pots of stone, compared with its original making in the beauty of the vine and the abundance of the swelling grapes. No one could explain the onetime miracle at the wedding feast, but then neither could they explain the everyday miracle of the splendor of the vineyard itself.

It is most remarkable to witness one who is deaf made to hear again. But surely that great blessing is no more startling than the wondrous combination of bones and skin and nerves that let our ears receive the beautiful world of sound. Should we not stand in awe of the blessing of hearing and give glory to God for that miracle, even as we do when hearing is restored after it has been lost?

Is it not the same for the return of one's sight or the utterance of our speech, or even that greatest miracle of all—the restoration of life? The original creations of the Father constitute a truly wonder-filled world. Are not the *greatest* miracles the fact that we have life and limb and sight and speech in the first place? Yes, there will always be plenty of miracles if we have eyes to see and ears to hear. (*Ensign*, May 1989, p. 16.)

— *Howard W. Hunter*

They who doubt the possibility of miracles are indeed without the power to perform them. . . . Miracles are the fruits of faith. (*CR*, April 1925, p. 20.)

— *Orson F. Whitney*

We are miracles in our own right, every one of us, and the resurrected Son of God is the greatest miracle of all. He is, indeed, the miracle of miracles, and every day of his life he gave evidence of it. We should try to follow after him in that example. (*Ensign*, November 1989, p. 17.)

— *Howard W. Hunter*

When the Lord said, "Lengthen your stride, quicken your pace, heighten your reach, widen your vision, and stretch your capacity," he was in reality saying "expect a miracle," for these are the stuff from which miracles are made. (*Ensign*, May 1979, p. 31.)

— *Hartman Rector, Jr.*

———— Missionaries ————

Come, ye emperors and kings and state leaders, and turn the key. Our missionaries will be powerful ambassadors for your nation. They will bring you peace and joy and a happy, contented people. Please open your doors.
— *Spencer W. Kimball*

From now on, from this very moment, you are a trusted representative of your ward, of your parents, and of the Lord Jesus Christ. (*CR*, April 1950, p. 178.)
— *David O. McKay*

I commend the many couples who now go forth to serve. Leaving the comforts of home, the companionship of family, they walk hand in hand as eternal companions, but also hand in hand with God as His representatives to a faith-starved world. (*Ensign*, November 1987, p. 43.)
— *Thomas S. Monson*

Missionary Couples

Whenever I meet and talk with missionary couples, I am filled with love and respect for their humility . . . They regard their missions as one of the great opportunities to serve the Master in their lives. They always ask, "How many grandchildren have you?" Our response of eight is quickly overshadowed with "We have sixteen," or "twenty-seven," and almost always with "And there are two we haven't seen yet." They miss their family and grandchildren, but don't complain. Instead, they look forward to that great homecoming reunion. . . .

All these missionary couples are finding new purpose and fulfillment in their lives. . . .

I pray that couples whose families are grown may indeed listen to and obey the Spirit that prompts the call to prepare and serve the Lord in the mission field. (*Ensign*, November 1987, p. 24.)
— *Douglas J. Martin*

Missionaries go forward with the purest of intent, with no hidden agenda, and at great personal sacrifice. They are not out to destroy anyone's faith or to exert unrighteous pressure. They are teachers who invite those interested in their message to listen and determine for themselves if the message is true. They go forward not representing any government or political philosophy. . . .

They are not out to build any worldly kingdoms. They are, in the words of Mormon, "the peaceable followers of Christ." (Moro. 7:3.) The only kingdom which interests them is the kingdom of our Lord and Savior which He will establish at His return. Their only hope is to prepare us for that great day. (*Ensign*, November 1989, p. 71.)

— *L. Tom Perry*

Our missionaries are not salesmen with wares to peddle; rather, they are servants of the Most High God, with testimonies to bear, truths to teach, and souls to save. (*Ensign*, November 1987, p. 42.)

— *Thomas S. Monson*

Our missionaries, young men and women and older couples, are workers for world peace. . . . By inviting all to repent and come unto Christ, [they] are working for peace in this world by changing the hearts and behavior of individual men and women. (*Ensign*, May 1990, p. 73.)

— *Dallin H. Oaks*

See also MISSIONARY SUCCESS, MISSIONARY WORK, MISSIONS

——— Missionary Success ———

Get the Spirit of God before you go on your missions or anywhere else. Get the spirit of revelation with you. And when you get that you are safe, and you will do exactly what the Lord wants you to do. (*CR*, April 1898, p. 31.)

— *Wilford Woodruff*

Go in all meekness, in sobriety, and preach Jesus Christ and him crucified; not to contend with others on account of their faith, or systems of religion, but pursue a steady course. . . . Those who do, shall always be filled with the Holy Ghost. (*HC*, 2:431.)

—*Joseph Smith*

If God would grant me one wish—just one—it would be this: that each missionary felt and enjoyed the spirit of his calling. (Quoted by Carlos E. Asay, *Ensign*, November 1976, p. 41.)

— *Hugh B. Brown*

In missionary work, as in all else, preparation precedes power. (Regional Representatives Seminar, April 1987.)

— *Gordon B. Hinckley*

It is necessary for the missionaries who go out into the world to study the spirit of the gospel, which is the spirit of humility, the spirit of meekness and of true devotion. . . . Live so that the Spirit of God will have communion and be present with you to direct you in every moment and hour of your ministry, night and day. (*CR*, April 1915, p. 138.)

— *Joseph F. Smith*

Missionary WORK

One of the greatest secrets of missionary work is work. If a missionary works, he will get the Spirit; if he gets the Spirit, he will teach by the Spirit; and if he teaches by the Spirit, he will touch the hearts of the people; and he will be happy. There will be no homesickness, no worrying about families, for all time and talents and interests are centered on the work of the ministry. That's the secret—work, work, work. There is no satisfactory substitute, especially in missionary work. (Mission Presidents' Seminar, August 1982.)

— *Ezra Taft Benson*

No matter how gifted we may be, or how choice our language, it is the spirit of our Father that reaches the heart and brings conviction of the divinity of this work. (*CR*, October 1904, p. 66.)

— *George Albert Smith*

No matter how much an individual or family may sacrifice for a mission or anything else, unless missionaries choose obedience, consecrating all of their time, talents, and resources in the service of the Lord while they are in the mission field, they cannot fully realize all the great blessings the Lord has in store for them. (*Ensign*, May 1990, p. 41.)

— *Robert D. Hales*

Remember that "it is a day of warning, and not a day of many words." If they receive not your testimony in one place, flee to another, remembering to cast no reflections, nor throw out any bitter sayings. If you do your duty, it will be just as well with you, as though all men embraced the gospel. (*HC*, 1:468.)

— *Joseph Smith*

The first soul that anyone should bring to God is his own soul. (*CR*, April 1962, p. 13.)

— *Sterling W. Sill*

The Lord calls nobody to fail, but to succeed, and this the missionaries should understand fully.

— *Ezra Taft Benson*

The Lord never has, nor will He require things of His children which it is impossible for them to perform. [Missionaries] who expect to go forth to preach the gospel of salvation in the midst of a crooked and perverse generation, should cultivate this spirit especially. (*JD*, 20:192.)

— *Lorenzo Snow*

The men who have had the greatest success in converting souls to the Church of Jesus Christ of Latter-day Saints have been men who have been taught of God, who have been God-fearing, humble, and willing to give unto Him the honor and the glory for all they were able to accomplish. (*CR*, April 1975, p. 95.)

— *Ezra Taft Benson*

The missionaries who spend the least money and accept the simple hospitality of the people, accomplish the most work, develop the greatest faith and obtain the greatest results. (*CR*, October 1938, p. 96.)

— *Sylvester Q. Cannon*

The principles of the gospel . . . should be presented to men in humility, in the simplest forms of speech, without presumption or arrogance and in the spirit of the mission of Christ. . . . By earnestness and simplicity missionaries will establish themselves in the truth, [and their] testimonies will convince others. . . . They will touch the hearts of the people and will have the pleasure of seeing them come to an understanding of their message. The spirit of the gospel will shine forth from their souls and others will partake of their light and rejoice therein. (*CR*, April 1899, p. 40.)

— *Joseph F. Smith*

The question will arise, what am I here for? To sow the seeds of life in the hearts of [the people of the world]; and the prayer should arise in your heart, "O Lord, may it be so; may I have power through thy Spirit to touch the hearts of these thy people." That very short prayer is all that a missionary needs to make. "May I say something to save these souls." (*IE*, December 1899, p. 129.)

— *Lorenzo Snow*

There is a way to reach every human heart, and it is your business to find the way to the hearts of those to whom you are called on your mission. (*IE*, December 1899, p. 128.)

— *Lorenzo Snow*

There is one language that is understood by every missionary: the language of the Spirit. It is not learned from textbooks written by men of letters, nor is it acquired through reading and memorization. The language of the Spirit comes to him who seeks with all his heart to know God and to keep His divine commandments. Proficiency in this language permits one to breach barriers, overcome obstacles, and touch the human heart. (*Ensign*, May 1985, p. 68.)

— *Thomas S. Monson*

They who go forth in the name of the Lord, trusting in him with all their hearts, will never want for wisdom . . . to lead the people in the way of life and salvation. . . . Go in the name of the Lord, trust in the name of the Lord, lean upon the Lord, and call upon the Lord fervently and without ceasing, and pay no attention to the world. (*JD*, 12:34.)

— *Brigham Young*

We often hear it said that a missionary sacrifices two years of his life to serve the Lord. In the beginning he may think it a sacrifice, especially when the work becomes difficult and the disappointments are numerous; but the sooner the missionary learns to keep the commandments of the Lord, deny himself, as the Savior admonished his disciples, sacrifice his own desires for those of others for the building up of the kingdom of God, and lose himself in the work, then will he find true happiness in his missionary labors.

— *Adney Y. Komatsu*

When a man is called to go on a mission and a field of labor assigned him, he should say in his heart, not my will be done, but thine, O Lord. (*JD*, 25:100.)

— *Joseph F. Smith*

When missionaries rise to speak in the name of Israel's God, if they live in purity and holiness before Him, He will give them words and ideas of which they never dreamed before. (*JD*, 12:21.)

— *John Taylor*

You are going out on your mission, not merely to make friends for the Church, though that is important, but to properly convert and baptize the numerous people who are anxious and ready for the gospel. Brethren, the spirit of our work must be urgency, and we must imbue our missionaries and saints with this spirit of "Now." We are not justified in waiting for the natural, slow growth which would come with natural and easy proselyting. . . . We believe that we must put our shoulder to the wheel, lengthen our stride, heighten our reach, increase our devotion so that we can do the work to which we have been assigned. (Quoted by Bruce R. McConkie, Mission Presidents' Seminar, June 21, 1976.)

— *Spencer W. Kimball*

You might prove doctrine from the Bible till doomsday, and it would merely convince a people but would not convert them. . . . Nothing short of a testimony by the power of the Holy Ghost would bring light and knowledge to them—bring them in their hearts to repentance. Nothing short of that would ever do. (*JD*, 5:327.)

— *Brigham Young*

See also MISSIONARIES, MISSIONARY WORK, MISSIONS

——— Missionary Work ———

A man who is honest, full of integrity and love for the interest and happiness of mankind, . . . will not and cannot keep silent, but despite threats and opposition, however fierce and terrific, will boldly declare the glorious [gospel], spreading and multiplying this divine intelligence, and if so required, seal this testimony with his own life's blood. (*JD*, 26:376.)

— *Lorenzo Snow*

Begin on the man who lives next door by inspiring confidence in him, by inspiring love in him for you because of your righteousness, and your missionary work has already begun. (*CR*, October 1916, pp. 50-51.)

— *George Albert Smith*

Every member a missionary! (*CR*, April 1959, p. 122.)

— *David O. McKay*

I can attest that there is a lifting spirit associated with missionary service. I'm convinced that each time we walk our roads to Emmaus with nonmember friends, talking and opening up the scriptures to them, our eyes are opened to added truths and our hearts burn brighter. I'm convinced that each time we extend the right hand to the lame in body and spirit at our Gates Beautiful and lift people up, we walk a little straighter and praise God with greater fervor. I'm convinced that each time we visit our Jacob's wells and invite friends to drink of living waters, our thirst is quenched and we draw closer to the Savior of the world. (*Ensign*, November 1976, p. 43.)

— *Carlos E. Asay*

In the day of wickedness just preceding our Lord's return there is to be a great harvest of souls. We live in that day, the day when the harvest is ripe. We have deluded ourselves long enough with the thought that this is a day of gleaning only. This is not a day of gleaning, but of harvest. . . . Now, this work is going to succeed. This is absolutely guaranteed, it is the eternal decree of the Lord.

— *Bruce R. McConkie*

If we do not do our duty in regard to missionary service, then I am convinced that God will hold us responsible for the people we might have saved had we done our duty. (*Ensign*, October 1977, p. 5.)

— *Spencer W. Kimball*

Let's not use a sickle. Let's use a combine. (Quoted by David B. Haight, *Ensign*, November 1977, p. 58.)

— *Vaughn J. Featherstone*

Missionary work—the preaching of the gospel—has been the major activity of the true Church of Christ whenever the gospel has been upon the earth. (*IE*, June 1970, p. 95.)

— *Ezra Taft Benson*

More blessing comes to us in going forth to proclaim the gospel of Jesus Christ, and laboring for the salvation of the souls of men, than can possibly come to us by merely having a knowledge of the truth of our religion, and then remaining at home to mingle and labor in the ordinary affairs of life, and accumulate the wealth of this world that perishes with the using. (*Ensign*, May 1984, p. 80.)

— *L. Tom Perry*

Oh, our beloved Father in heaven, bring about the day when we may be able to bring in large numbers as Ammon and his brethren did, thousands of conversions, not dozens, not tens of fives or ones, thousands of conversions. The Lord promised it; He fulfills his promises.

Our Father, may we move forward with Jesus Christ as our advocate to establish the Church among the inhabitants of the earth. May Jacob flourish in the wilderness and blossom as the rose upon the mountains. May we merit the promise that the Lord will do things that we can hardly believe. May we improve the efficiency of our missionaries, each bringing thousands of converts into the Church. Please, Father, open the doors of the nations. I pray this in the name of Jesus Christ. (Regional Representatives Seminar, April 3, 1975.)

— *Spencer W. Kimball*

The missionary work of the Latter-day Saints is the greatest of all the great works in all the world. (*CR*, October 1921, p. 5.)

— *Heber J. Grant*

The very purpose of The Church of Jesus Christ of Latter-day Saints [is] to invite, encourage, and assist all of God's children, both living and dead, to come to Christ, and "lay hold upon every good gift" (Moroni 10:30), that "ye may receive a remission of your sins, and be filled with the Holy Ghost, that ye may be numbered with my people who are of the house of Israel" (3 Nephi 30:2).

That is why we do missionary work. (*Ensign*, November 1987, p. 25.)

— *Alexander B. Morrison*

Since baptism is essential there must be an urgent concern to carry the message of the gospel of Jesus Christ to every nation, kindred, tongue, and people. . . .

We accept the responsibility to preach the gospel to every person on earth. And if the question is asked, "You mean you are out to convert the entire world?" the answer is, "Yes. We will try to reach every living soul."

Some who measure that challenge quickly say, "Why that's impossible! It cannot be done!"

To that we simply say, "Perhaps, but we shall do it anyway." (*Ensign*, November 1975, p. 97.)

— *Boyd K. Packer*

The work of a missionary is everlasting in its consequences. Acceptance of the gospel at the hands of a true and dedicated teacher affects not only the recipient, but also generations who come after the recipient. (*Ensign*, May 1983, p. 85.)

— *Gordon B. Hinckley*

There are few things that invite the blessings of the Lord into our own lives . . . more powerfully than does missionary service—the broadening of knowledge of gospel principles, a deeper spirituality, strengthening of one's faith in the Lord, a greater understanding of the workings of the Spirit, and the expanding of one's talents, as promised by the Savior in the parable of the talents. (*Ensign*, November 1988, p. 85.)

— *David B. Haight*

We expect that approximately 245,000 converts will be baptized during 1988. This number is impressive; however, approximately that same number of people are being born in the world every day. (*Ensign*, November 1988, p. 28.)

— *M. Russell Ballard*

There is no joy that can compare with that of a missionary who has been made the instrument for the salvation of a soul. (*CR*, April 1918, p. 73.)

— *Orson F. Whitney*

There will arise from the performance of [missionary] duties honor, and glory and exaltation. (*Deseret Weekly*, 50:737-38.)

— *Lorenzo Snow*

We are the messengers, and we have the acceptable message.

— *Spencer W. Kimball*

We don't ask any people to throw away any good they have got; we only ask them to come and get more. (*HC*, 5:259.)

— *Joseph Smith*

We expect to have complete cooperation between the stake and full-time missionaries, and to involve the members of the Church generally in opening the gospel door to our Father's other children. . . .

I seemed to envision . . . thousands . . . prepared and anxious . . . for missionary service . . . until the army of the Lord's missionaries would cover the earth as the waters cover the mighty deep.

It is unrealistic to expect 19,000 or even 100,000 missionaries to cover the globe. . . . We call upon priesthood leaders to teach every family in the Church to assume its responsibilities. (Regional Representatives Seminar, April 4, 1974.)

— *Spencer W. Kimball*

When men go forth in the name of Israel's God, there is no power on earth that can overturn the truths they advocate. (*JD*, 12:396.)

— *John Taylor*

When men go forth possessing the truths of the everlasting gospel which God has revealed, they have a treasure within them that the world knows nothing about. They have the light of revelation, the fire of the Holy Ghost, and the power of the priesthood within them—a power that they know very little about even themselves, which, like a wellspring of life, is rising, bursting, bubbling, and spreading its exhilarating streams around. (*JD*, 12:22.)

— *John Taylor*

When you meet with an Arab, send him to Arabia; when you find an Italian, send him to Italy; and a Frenchman, to France; or an Indian, send him among the Indians. Send them to the different places where they belong. Send somebody to Central America and to all Spanish America; and don't let a single corner of the earth go without a mission. (*HC*, 5:368.)

— *Joseph Smith*

See also LATTER-DAY WORK, MISSIONARIES, MISSIONARY SUCCESS, MISSIONS, SHARING THE GOSPEL

——— Missions ———

A mission is not an expense. It is a great investment. (*Ensign*, May 1985, p. 97.)
— *Gordon B. Hinckley*

Every LDS male who is worthy and able should fill a mission. (*CR*, April 1974, p. 126.)
— *Spencer W. Kimball*

Every man who has a calling to minister to the inhabitants of the world was ordained to that very purpose in the Grand Council of heaven before this world was. (*HC*, 6:364.)
— *Joseph Smith*

Get into your hearts, young people, to prepare yourselves to go out into the world where you can get on your knees and draw nearer to the Lord than in any other labor. (*IE*, July 1936, p. 396.)
— *Heber J. Grant*

Missions are for missionaries. It is a marvelous gift of time, a time given when you can experience glimpses of heavenly life here on earth. It is a time of cleansing and refreshing. It is a special time when the Holy Ghost can seal upon you the knowledge of the great plan for your exaltation. It is one of your best opportunities to become a celestial candidate.

The teaching and conversion of others is the natural product of this process. To sanctify yourself you must serve others. The highest of all service to others is to teach them truth and bring them into the kingdom of God. (*Ensign*, November 1981, p. 51.)
— *William R. Bradford*

It is not an easy task . . . to be called out into the world, . . . but I say to you it will purchase for those who are faithful, for those who discharge that obligation as they may be required, peace and happiness beyond all understanding, and will prepare them that, in due time, when life's labor is complete, they will stand in the presence of their Maker, accepted of Him because of what they have done. (*CR*, April 1922, p. 53.)
— *George Albert Smith*

I know that our young men are under a great obligation to qualify themselves through education to fill positions of responsibility in the world. Their time is precious. But I do not hesitate to promise that the time spent in faithful and devoted service as a missionary declaring the Master will only add to their qualifications for positions of responsibility in the future. Regardless of the vocation they choose to pursue, they will be better qualified in their powers of expression, in their habits of industry, in the value they place on training, in the integrity of their lives, and in their recognition of a higher source of strength and power than that which lies within their native capacity. (*Ensign*, May 1983, p. 8.)

— *Gordon B. Hinckley*

Missionary service is not only a test of faith but a real test of character. (*CR*, April 1959, p. 13.)

— *ElRay L. Christiansen*

No finer example can be borne by parents to children or grandchildren, than through missionary service in their mature years. (*Ensign*, May 1987, pp. 60,61.)

— *David B. Haight*

Parents have the primary responsibility for preparing their sons to serve full-time missions, . . . Let me . . . say to every mother that her ambition should be that her newborn son will develop in cleanliness and worthiness to become part of the ranks to teach the gospel to the physical world and later to the spirit world, and then let every mother and father spend much of their time and effort in training that lad to fill his mission.

— *Spencer W. Kimball*

Serving a mission is like paying tithing; you're not compelled—you do it because it's right. We want to go on missions because it is the Lord's way. Now, when the Savior was up on the Mount of Olives, he never did say, "Now if it is convenient, I would like you to go." He did not say, "If somebody will give you the money to go , I would like you to go" He said to the Apostles, "Go ye into all the world, and preach the gospel to every creature." (Mark 16:15.) (Quoted by Rex D. Pinegar, *Ensign*, November 1976, p. 67.)

— *Spencer W. Kimball*

Should *every* young man fill a mission? The answer has been given by the Lord. It is *yes*. *Every* young man should fill a mission. (Regional Representative's Seminar, 4 April 1974.)

— *Spencer W. Kimball*

Some time ago, as the General Authorities met together on an upper floor of the temple, President Kimball stood and instructed us, saying: "Brethren, of late I have been concerned and troubled by the fact that we do not have sufficient missionaries proclaiming the message of the Restoration. I hear some parents say, 'We're letting our son make up his own mind regarding a mission,' or 'We hope our son fills a mission because it would be such a growing experience for him.'" He continued: "I have heard some young men say, 'I think I might serve a mission if I really want to go.'" President Kimball raised his voice, stood on tiptoe—as he is prone to do when anxious to communicate with power a special thought—and said: "It doesn't really matter whether Mother or Father thinks it might be nice for a son to serve a mission. It doesn't really matter whether or not John, Bill, and Bob want to go—they *must* go!" (*Ensign*, November 1984, p. 41.)

— *Thomas S. Monson*

The Lord has no better place to get acquainted with you than when you serve him in the mission field. When you are serving your mission, he will send you on errands to act in his name. He will give you experience with the power of the Holy Ghost. He will authorize you to teach, to convert, and then to perform the sacred ordinances of salvation in his name. He will come to know you. He will come to know that he can trust you and can rely on you. (*Ensign*, May 1985, p. 42.)

— *M. Russell Ballard*

The most important thing in this life is a testimony of the truth, and there is no place on earth where you can have the opportunity to get a testimony like the mission field. I know—I have been there time and time again. (*Ensign*, November 1984, p. 48.)

— *Ezra Taft Benson*

The two-fold nature of the purpose of missionary work: first, to sanctify the missionary himself, and second, to bring converts to a knowledge of the truths of the restored gospel of Jesus Christ and to baptism into His Church—which is the sure and natural product of a missionary who is in the process of sanctification. (*Ensign*, November 1981, p. 49.)

— *William R. Bradford*

The young man who goes into the world preaching the gospel of peace loses himself and saves himself. Missionary work is one of the great miracles of our time. (*Ensign*, May 1985, p. 96.)

— *Gordon B. Hinckley*

When a missionary is placed in a mission environment of order and discipline where all that is done is in harmony with the Spirit, the missionary experiences a great transformation. The heavens open. Powers are showered out. Mysteries are revealed. Habits are improved. Sanctification begins. Through this process the missionary becomes a vessel of light that can shine forth the gospel of Jesus Christ in a world in darkness. (*Ensign*, November 1981, p. 51.)

— *William R. Bradford*

This call to missionary service does not leave us any choice or option as to the course we should pursue. It is not merely a permissive invitation which allows us to spread the gospel message on a voluntary basis, or if we find it convenient to do so. The decree is mandatory. We have no choice about it, if we are to retain the favor of God. (*CR*, October 1960, p. 54.)

— *Bruce R. McConkie*

We now have more [missionaries] serving in the field than we have ever had, but we do not have enough. The world, with its four billion plus people, is a very large world. And while we do not have access to many millions of these, the numbers we are free to work with are still very large. Truly, the field is white and the laborers are few. (*Ensign*, May 1988, p. 92.)

— *Gordon B. Hinckley*

See also MISSIONARIES, MISSIONARY SUCCESS, MISSIONARY WORK

——— **Money** ———

Be prudent in all things, adopt the plan of keeping a strict account of all your expenses; by this you will not only understand what becomes of your money, but it will also induce . . . habits and methods and correctness in financial dealings in . . . life. (Quoted by H. Burke Peterson, *Ensign*, November 1977, p. 87.)

— *Brigham Young*

Five Guides to Money Management
1. Always pay your tithing.
2. Pay yourself something off the top.
3. Avoid using credit cards and charge accounts.
4. Budget your income and outgo.
5. Do not live beyond your means. (*Ensign*, May 1978, p. 57.)

— *O. Leslie Stone*

If you wish to get rich, save what you get. A fool can earn money; but it takes a wise man to save and dispose of it to his own advantage. (*JD*, 11:301.)

— *Brigham Young*

Interest

It is a rule of our financial and economic life in all the world that interest is to be paid on borrowed money. May I say something about interest?

Interest never sleeps nor sickens nor dies; it never goes to the hospital; it works on Sundays and holidays; it never takes a vacation; it never visits nor travels; it takes no pleasure; it is never laid off work nor discharged from employment; it never works on reduced hours; it never has short crops nor droughts; it never pays taxes; it buys no food; it wears no clothes; it is unhoused and without home and so has no repairs, no replacements, no shingling, plumbing, painting, or white-washing; it has neither wife, children, father, mother, nor kinfolk to watch over and care for; it has no expense of living; it has neither weddings nor births nor deaths; it has no love, no sympathy; it is as hard and soulless as a granite cliff. Once in debt, interest is your companion every minute of the day and night; you cannot shun it or slip away from it; you cannot dismiss it; it yields neither to entreaties, demands, nor orders; and whenever you get in its way or cross its course or fail to meet its demands, it crushes you. (*CR*, April 1938, pp. 102-3.)

— *J. Reuben Clark, Jr.*

Let us avoid debt as we would avoid a plague; where we are now in debt let us get out of debt; if not today, then tomorrow. Let us straitly and strictly live within our incomes, and save a little. (*CR*, April 1937, p. 26.)

— *J. Reuben Clark, Jr.*

Money in the lives of Latter-day Saints should be used as a means of achieving eternal happiness. (*Ensign*, July 1975, p. 73.)

— *Marvin J. Ashton*

The appetite for money grows upon a man, increases and strengthens unless he is careful, just as much as the appetite for whiskey. It gets possession of him, and he loves the money instead of loving it only for the good that he can do with it. He does not estimate properly the value of things. (*CR*, October 1911, p. 23.)

— *Heber J. Grant*

The body serves us best when we are least aware of it, and so with money.

— *Hugh Nibley*

The choice to serve God, worthily made, does not necessarily preclude a home or sufficient money or income, or the things of this world which bring joy and happiness, but it does require that we must *not* turn away from God and the teachings of Jesus Christ while in the pursuit of our temporal needs. (*Ensign*, June 1971, p. 11.)

— *N. Eldon Tanner*

The love of money is the root of many evils because it often involves selfishness. On the other hand, the wise use of money involves principles of righteousness. It involves sacrifice and discipline. It is the acid test of our faith.

— *James E. Faust*

There is nothing inherently evil about money. . . . The critical difference is the degree of spirituality we exercise in viewing, evaluating, and managing the things of this world and our experiences in it. (*Ensign*, November 1985, p. 63.)

— *Dallin H. Oaks*

See also DEBT, FINANCIAL STRENGTH, THRIFT, WEALTH

———— **Morality** ————

Adults and children need to know that public and private morality is not outmoded. We need to love our children enough to teach them that laws, policies, and public programs with a moral and ethical basis are necessary for the preservation of a peaceful, productive, compassionate, and happy society. Without the qualities and characteristics of integrity, honesty, commitment, loyalty, respect for others, fidelity, and virtue, a free and open society cannot endure. (*Ensign*, May 1987, p. 80.)

— *James E. Faust*

Growing numbers of people now campaign to make spiritually dangerous lifestyles legal and socially acceptable. Among them are abortion, the gay-lesbian movement, and drug addiction. They are debated in forums and seminars, in classes, in conversations, in conventions, and in courts all over the world. The social and political aspects of them are in the press every day.

The point I make is simply this: there is a *MORAL* and *SPIRITUAL* side to these issues which is universally ignored. For Latter-day Saints, morality is one component which must not be missing when these issues are considered—otherwise sacred covenants are at risk! (*Ensign*, November 1990, p. 84.)

— *Boyd K. Packer*

Keep your life clean—in thought and action. Immorality is Satan's most potent tool against us and leads to more unhappiness, grief, regret, and self-degradation than any other sin. It is deadly to our eternal progress. Avoid it like a plague. (*Ensign*, November 1987, p. 62.)

— *Robert L. Backman*

Little do we realize what we have brought upon ourselves when we have allowed our children to be taught that man is only an advanced animal. We have compounded the mistake by neglecting to teach moral and spiritual values. Moral laws do not apply to animals for they have no agency. Where there is agency, where there is choice, moral laws must apply. We cannot, absolutely cannot, have it both ways.

When our youth are taught that they are but animals, they feel free, even compelled, to respond to every urge and impulse. We should not be so puzzled at what is happening to society. We have sown the wind, and now we inherit the whirlwind. The chickens, so the saying goes, are now coming home to roost. (*Ensign*, November 1990, p. 85.)

— *Boyd K. Packer*

One of the great purposes of this work, as revealed by the Lord, is to fortify against moral sin. To the degree that we accept and follow these teachings we shall be a happy and blessed people. (*Ensign*, May 1986, p. 48.)

— *Gordon B. Hinckley*

One reason for the decline in moral values is that the world has invented a new, constantly changing, and undependable standard of moral conduct referred to as "situational ethics." Now, individuals define good and evil as being adjustable according to each situation; this is in direct contrast to the proclaimed God-given absolute standard: "Thou shalt not!" (*Ensign*, May 1987, p. 14.)

— *David B. Haight*

The earth cannot justify nor continue its life without marriage and the family. Sex without marriage, for all people, young or older, is an abomination to the Lord, and it is most unfortunate that many people have blinded their eyes to these great truths.

Husbands and wives should love and cherish their spouses. They must not break up their homes with divorce, and especially through infidelity and immorality. (*CR*, October 1974, p. 9.)

— *Spencer W. Kimball*

Would immorality be running rampant if people comprehended those precious words found in the first letter to the Corinthians where we learn that a person who commits fornication sins against his own body, which is the temple of the Holy Ghost, and that our bodies are not our own but have been bought through the sacrifice of Jesus. He bought our bodies and our spirits, and they belong to God. We surely are to take care of His possessions. (See 1 Cor. 6:15-20.) (*Ensign*, November 1984, p. 74.)

— *Hugh W. Pinnock*

The plaguing sin of this generation is sexual immorality. This, the Prophet Joseph said, would be the source of more temptations, more buffetings, and more difficulties for the elders of Israel than any other.

President Joseph F. Smith said that sexual impurity would be one of the three dangers that would threaten the Church within—and so it does. . . .

In the category of sins, the Book of Mormon places unchastity next to murder. (See Alma 39:5.) . . . We must forsake immorality and be clean. (*Ensign*, May 1986, p. 5.)

— *Ezra Taft Benson*

See also CHASTITY, VALUES, VIRTUE

——— Motherhood ———

Motherhood is the greatest potential influence for either good or ill in human life. The mother's image is the first that stamps itself on the unwritten page of the young child's mind. It is her caress that first awakens a sense of security; her kiss, the first realization of affection; her sympathy and tenderness, the first assurance that there is love in the world. (*IE*, May 1969, p. 3.)

— *David O. McKay*

A few years ago while I was presiding over the mission in Minneapolis, Minnesota, an interesting event took place. . . . A rather severe tornado hit the area. It was severe enough that it came to the attention of the nightly news broadcast over the national networks to California, Arizona, Utah, and Idaho. Before long, the telephone started ringing in our office there at the mission home. This went on for two or three hours, with parents calling from many areas wondering about their Johnny or Richard.

I recall later walking across the parking lot from the mission office to the mission home saying to myself, "You know these Mormon mothers. They just won't undo the apron strings. They just won't let their boys go." As I walked into the mission home, the phone again was ringing. I picked up the phone and guess who? My mother! She was wondering how her missionary was doing under these circumstances.

I learned a great and deep lesson. A mother's love and concern never ceases—nor should it. (*Ensign*, November 1988, p. 40.)

— *Monte J. Brough*

A mother has far greater influence on her children than anyone else, and she must realize that every word she speaks, every act, every response, her attitude, even her appearance and manner of dress affect the lives of her children and the whole family. It is while the child is in the home that he gains from his mother the attitudes, hopes, and beliefs that will determine the kind of life he will live and the contribution he will make to society. (*New Era*, January 1977, p. 33.)

— *N. Eldon Tanner*

A mother may pray with her children and call down the Lord's blessings upon them. She does not act by virtue of priesthood conferred upon her, but by virtue of her God-given responsibility to govern her household in righteousness. (*Ensign*, November 1974, p. 110.)

— *Spencer W. Kimball*

A mother's role is God-ordained. Mothers are to conceive, bear, nourish, love, and train. They are to be helpmates and are to counsel with their husbands. There is no inequality between the sexes in God's plan. It is a matter of division of responsibility. (*Ensign*, May 1984, p. 6.)

— *Ezra Taft Benson*

I do not believe that God's purposes on earth will ever be achieved without the influence, strength, love, support, and special gifts of the elect women of God. They are entitled to our deepest veneration, our fullest appreciation, and our most profound respect. I believe angels attend them in their motherly ministry. (*Ensign*, May 1988, p. 38.)

— *James E. Faust*

In the soft and gentle arms of a mother's love, children can come to know the voice of the Lord. (*Ensign*, November 1983, p. 87.)

— *Dwan J. Young*

Motherhood is near to divinity. It is the highest, holiest service to be assumed by mankind. (Quoted by James E. Faust, *Ensign*, May 1988, p. 38.)

— *The First Presidency*

Motherhood is the greatest potential influence either for good or ill in human life. (*Gospel Ideals*, The Improvement Era, Salt Lake City: Deseret Book Co., 1976, p. 452.)

— *David O. McKay*

Mothers are the moving instruments in the hands of Providence to guide the destinies of nations. (*JD*, 19:72.)

— *Brigham Young*

Mothers, will you be missionaries? We will appoint you a mission to teach your children their duty, and instead of ruffles and fine dresses to adorn the body, teach them that which will adorn their minds. Let what you have to clothe them with be neat and clean and nice. Teach them cleanness and purity of body and the principles of salvation. (*DBY*, pp. 210-11.)

— *Brigham Young*

No nobler work in this world can be performed by any mother than to rear and love the children with whom God has blessed her. (*CR*, April 1951, p. 81.)

— *David O. McKay*

The duty of the mother is to watch over her children and give them their early education, for impressions received in infancy are lasting. . . . Children have all the confidence in their mothers; and if mothers would take proper pains, they can instil in the hearts of their children what they please. (*JD*, 14:105.)

— *Brigham Young*

The spiritual rewards of motherhood are available to all women. Nurturing the young, comforting the frightened, protecting the vulnerable, teaching and giving encouragement need not—and should not—be limited to our own children. (*Ensign*, November 1987, pp. 87-88.)

— *Russell M. Nelson*

There is nothing more beautiful, no picture more lovely, than that of a mother with her daughters. (*Ensign*, November 1984, p. 90.)

— *Gordon B. Hinckley*

What mother, looking down with tenderness upon her chubby infant does not envision her child as the president of the Church or the leader of her nation! As he is nestled in her arms, she sees him a statesman, a leader, a prophet. Some dreams do come true! One mother gives us a Shakespeare; another a Michelangelo, and another a Joseph Smith. (*CR*, April 1960, p. 4.)

— *Spencer W. Kimball*

[Mothers in Zion,] we pray for you. We sustain you. We honor you as you bear, nourish, train, teach, and love for eternity. I promise you the blessings of heaven and "all that the Father hath" (see D&C 84:38) as you magnify the noblest calling of all. (Quoted by Joanne Doxey, *Ensign*, November 1987, p. 92.)

— *Ezra Taft Benson*

See also CHILD-REARING, CHILDREN, PARENTHOOD, WOMANHOOD

——— Music ———

As each of our religious services is opened by a hymn and a prayer, the spirit of worship is established and a beautiful feeling of fellowship is felt. . . .

In our Latter-day Saint hymns, we sing praises to the Lord, pray unto the Lord, recite great religious truths—in effect sermons—and our minds and spirits are elevated and spiritually stimulated. (*Ensign*, November 1982, p. 22.)

— *Franklin D. Richards*

Music has a very powerful and wonderful influence in establishing feelings and moods that can lift and elevate your thoughts and your actions. But because it is so powerful, it is cleverly used by the adversary to stimulate your thoughts, feelings, and moods, to pollute and poison your mind and cause you to do things you would not otherwise consider doing. (*Ensign*, November 1990, p. 94.)

— *Ardeth G. Kapp*

Music is one of the most forceful instruments for governing the mind and spirit of man. (Address, Brigham Young University, September 26, 1967.)

— *Boyd K. Packer*

Some of the greatest sermons that have ever been preached were preached by the singing of a song. There are many wonderful songs. . . . Sing them through. (New Zealand Area Conference Report, 20-22 February 1976, p. 27, quoted by Franklin D. Richards, *Ensign*, November 1982, p. 22.)

— *Spencer W. Kimball*

Sometimes . . . we get nearer to the Lord through music than perhaps through any other thing except prayer. (*CR*, October 1936, p. 111.)

— *J. Reuben Clark, Jr.*

There is no music in hell, for all good music belongs to heaven. (*JD*, 9:244.)

— *Brigham Young*

There is something in the spirit of song . . . an influence . . . and inspirational power . . . that fires the soul in a way that it can't otherwise be touched or fired. (*CR*, October 1917, p. 75.)

— *Charles W. Nibley*

Through music, man's ability to express himself extends beyond the limits of the spoken language in both subtlety and power. Music can be used to exalt and inspire or to carry messages of degradation and destruction. It is therefore important that as Latter-day Saints we at all times apply the principles of the gospel and seek the guidance of the Spirit in selecting the music with which we surround ourselves. (Quoted by Boyd K. Packer, *Ensign*, January 1974, p. 25.)

— The First Presidency

——— Obedience ———

God had decreed that all who will not obey His voice shall not escape the damnation of hell. What is the damnation of hell? To go with that society who have not obeyed His commands. (*TPJS*, p. 198.)

— Joseph Smith

I doubt not that when we know the reason for some of the things we do now on faith, the practical value of the actions will be so plain that we will wonder how we could have missed it, and then we shall be heartily glad that we did what we were told to do. (*OAT*, pp. 10-11.)

— Hugh Nibley

I made this my rule, "When the Lord commands, do it." (*HC*, 2:170.)

— Joseph Smith

If we do not obey, the power to obey is lessened. Our capability to recognize good is weakened. (*Ensign*, May 1981, p. 68.)

— Ted E. Brewerton

May we increase in faith until we can say, with Adam, "We keep the commandments because the Lord has given them."

— N. Eldon Tanner

Obedience is a powerful spiritual medicine. It comes close to being a cure-all. (*Ensign*, November 1977, p. 60.)

— Boyd K. Packer

Obedience is a requirement of heaven and is therefore a principle of the gospel. (*JD*, 19:193.)

— Joseph F. Smith

Obedience—that which God will never take by force—he will accept when freely given. And he will then return to you freedom that you can hardly dream of—the freedom to feel and to know, the freedom to do, and the freedom to *be*, at least a thousand fold more than we offer him. Strangely enough, the key to freedom is obedience. (*BYU Speeches of the Year*, Brigham Young University, 1971, pp. 1-7.)

— *Boyd K. Packer*

Let us be like little children, ready and willing to do as we are commanded by the powers that we should obey. Let us be obedient to the voice of truth, and ever be found in the path of duty; and there let us continue.

— *Lorenzo Snow*

Obedience is the first law of heaven, the cornerstone upon which all righteousness and progression rest.

— *Bruce R. McConkie*

Obey Local Leaders
It requires more energy and more strength of purpose in a man to follow out the counsel of one who is just above him than it does to follow a man that is a long way ahead of him. (*JD*, 5:315.)

— *Lorenzo Snow*

Rationalization is one of the real obstacles to obedience. (*Ensign*, November 1987, p. 88.)

— *Russell M. Nelson*

The gospel of Jesus Christ teaches us a way of life that, if followed, will help us avoid the stumbling blocks and the detours that draw us off course and beckon us to follow the ways of the world. Think of it! What a protection we have when we obey His laws such as the Word of Wisdom, the law of chastity, the law of tithing, and other commandments. (*Ensign*, November 1989, p. 90.)

— *Joanne B. Doxey*

The greatest single lesson we can learn in mortality is that when God speaks and a man obeys, that man will always be right. (*Ensign*, November 1988, pp. 46, 47.)

— *Thomas S. Monson*

The laws of nature are the laws of God, who is just; it is not God that inflicts penalties, they are the effects of disobedience to his law. The results of men's own acts follow them. (*CR*, October 1912, p. 9.)

— *Joseph F. Smith*

The people [of Israel] had been warned not to touch the ark, the symbol of the covenant. But when the oxen stumbled and the ark appeared to be falling, (see 1 Chronicles 13:7-10) Uzza stretched forth his hand to steady it and was immediately killed by the Lord. Uzza seemed justified, and today we think his punishment was very severe, but as President David O. McKay stated, this incident conveys a lesson of life: obedience—full obedience. (*Ensign*, May 1981, p. 69.)

— *Ted E. Brewerton*

The salvation of this people does not depend upon the great amount of teaching, instruction, or revelation that is given unto them, but . . . upon their obeying the commandments of God. (*JD*, 4:190.)

— *Wilford Woodruff*

Those who talk of blind obedience may appear to know many things, but they do not understand the doctrines of the gospel. There is an obedience that comes from a knowledge of the truth that transcends any external form of control. We are not obedient because we are blind, we are obedient because we can see. (*Ensign*, May 1983, p. 66.)

— *Boyd K. Packer*

We cannot justify ourselves in living by that particular part of the word that appeals to us, the part that we desire to obey, but must be willing to . . . "live by every word that proceeds from the mouth of God." (*CR*, October 1910, pp. 51-52.)

— *Albert E. Bowen*

We encourage families to have on hand [a] year's supply [of food], and we say it over and over and over and repeat over and over the scripture of the Lord where He says, "Why call ye me, Lord, Lord, and do not the things which I say?" How empty it is as they put their spirituality, so-called, into action and call him by his important names, but fail to do the things which he says. (*Ensign*, May 1976, p. 125.)

— *Spencer W. Kimball*

We shall never see the day in time nor eternity when it will not be obligatory, and when it will not be a pleasure as well as a duty for us, as his children, to obey all the commandments of the Lord . . . It is upon this principle that we keep in touch with God, and remain in harmony with his purposes. It is only in this way that we can consummate our mission, and obtain our crown and the gift of eternal lives, which is the greatest gift of God. Can you imagine any other way? (*CR*, April 1898, p. 68.)

— *Joseph F. Smith*

Whatever God requires is right, no matter what it is, although we may not see the reason thereof until all of the events transpire. (*HC*, 5:135.)

— *Joseph Smith*

Surely the Lord loves, more than anything else, an unwavering determination to obey his counsel. (*Ensign*, November 1982, p. 58.)

— *Howard W. Hunter*

When we keep the commandments, we are clean; and when we are clean in our thoughts, our words, and our actions, we can hear the whisperings of the Holy Ghost. In answer to your prayers, you will feel what is right and you will be able to discern between good and evil. (*Ensign*, November 1990, p. 94.)

— *Ardeth G. Kapp*

Whosoever will keep the commandments of God, . . . will rise and not fall, they will lead and not follow, they will go upward and not downward. God will exalt them and magnify them before the nations of the earth, and he will set the seal of his approval upon them, will name them as his own. This is my testimony to you. (*IE*, 6:501.)

— *Joseph F. Smith*

See also BLESSINGS, COMMANDMENTS, COVENANTS, LAWS, LIVING THE GOSPEL, PEACE

——— Obstacles ———

Too many of us seem to expect that life will flow ever smoothly, featuring an unbroken chain of green lights with empty parking places just in front of our destinations! (*Ensign*, November 1989, p. 82.)

— *Neal A. Maxwell*

Victories in life come through our ability to work around and over the obstacles that cross our path. We grow stronger as we climb our own mountains. (*Ensign*, May 1979, p. 67.)

— *Marvin J. Ashton*

See also ADVERSITY, CHALLENGES, OPPOSITION

———— Offerings ————

Clearly we are preparing for the day when the higher law, that of consecration, will again become the financial law of the Church through which we will properly take care of the poor. Until that time, it is our responsibility and blessing—as a matter of fact, our covenant—to give generously from our surplus to bless the poor. (*Ensign*, May 1981, p. 39.)

— *Victor L. Brown*

I am a firm believer that you cannot give to the Church and to the building up of the kingdom of God and be any poorer financially. . . . When Brother Ballard laid his hands on my head and set me apart to go on a mission, he said in that prayer of blessing that a person could not give a crust to the Lord without receiving a loaf in return. That's been my experience. If the members of the Church would double their fast-offering contributions, the spirituality in the Church would double. We need to keep that in mind and be liberal in our contributions. (Welfare Agricultural Meeting, 3 April 1971, p. 1, and quoted by L. Tom Perry, *Ensign*, May 1986, p. 32.)

— *Marion G. Romney*

I wonder sometimes if we appreciate what the few dollars we give to the Church for building the kingdom does for others. When I think of the great tithing contributions and other contributions that go to bless [Tonga], when I look at the homes that have been built because of the welfare program after their island was devastated because of a hurricane, my heart is filled with joy for a people who love the Lord, who are willing to give of their own means for the furthering of the kingdom of God. (*Ensign*, November 1984, p. 79.)

— *Philip T. Sonntag*

One of the important things the Lord has told us to do is to be liberal in our payment of fast offerings. I would like you to know that there are great rewards for so doing—both spiritual and temporal rewards. The Lord says that the efficacy of our prayers depends upon our liberality to the poor. (*Ensign*, May 1979, p. 95.)

— *Marion G. Romney*

President Heber J. Grant tells of a . . . reward that comes from trusting in the Lord. When he was a young man, he heard his bishop in a fast meeting make a strong appeal for donations. At that time President Grant had $50 in his pocket which he intended to deposit in the bank. But he was so impressed by his bishop's appeal that he tendered the whole $50 to the bishop. The bishop took $5 and handed him back $45, stating that $5 was his full share. Then President Grant replied, "Bishop Wooley, by what right do you rob me of putting the Lord in my debt? Didn't you preach here today that the Lord rewards fourfold? My mother is a widow and she needs two hundred dollars."

"My boy," queried the bishop, "do you believe that if I take this other forty-five dollars you will get your two hundred dollars quicker?"

"Certainly," replied President Grant.

Now here was an expression of trust in the Lord which the bishop could not withstand. He took the remaining $45.

President Grant testifies that on his way back to work "an idea popped" into his head, acting upon which he made $218.50. Speaking on this incident years later he said, "Someone will say that it would have happened anyway. I do not think it would have happened. I do not think I would have got the idea.

"I am a firm believer that the Lord opens up the windows of heaven when we do our duty financially and pours out blessings upon us of a spiritual nature, which are of far greater value than temporal things. But I believe He also gives us blessings of a temporal nature." (*Ensign*, November 1977, p. 41.)

— *Marion G. Romney*

Sometimes we have been a bit penurious and figured that we had for breakfast one egg and that cost so many cents and then we give that to the Lord. I think that when we are affluent, as many of us are, that we ought to be very, very generous . . . I think we should . . . give, instead of the amount saved by our two meals of fasting, perhaps much, much more—ten times more when we are in a position to do it. (*CR*, April 1974, p. 184.)

— *Spencer W. Kimball*

If we give a generous fast offering, we shall increase our own prosperity both temporally and spiritually.

— *Spencer W. Kimball*

While we await the redemption of Zion and the earth and the establishment of the United Order, we . . . should live strictly by the principles of the United Order insofar as they are embraced in present church practices, such as the fast offering, tithing, and the welfare activities. Through these practices we could as individuals, if we were of a mind to do so, implement in our own lives all the basic principles of the United Order. (*CR*, April 1966, p. 100.)

— *Marion G. Romney*

See also CHARITY, CONSECRATION, TITHING

─────── Opposition ───────

Can the people understand that it is actually necessary for opposite principles to be placed before them, or this state of being would be no probation, . . . Can they understand that we cannot obtain eternal life unless we actually know and comprehend by our experience the principle of good and the principle of evil, the light and the darkness, truth, virtue, and holiness—also vice, wickedness, and corruption? (*JD*, 7:237.)

— *Brigham Young*

In times of hurt and discouragement, it may be consoling . . . for all of us to recall that no one can do anything permanently to us that will last for eternity. Only we ourselves can affect our eternal progression. (*Ensign*, May 1984, p. 10.)

— *Marvin J. Ashton*

It was necessary and proper that there should be good and evil, light and darkness, sin and righteousness, one principle of right opposed to another of wrong, that man might have his free agency to receive the good and reject the evil, and by receiving the good . . . , [he] might be saved and exalted . . . while the disobedient would have to meet the consequences of their own acts. (*JD*, 22:301.)

— *John Taylor*

It was revealed to me in the commencement of this Church, that the Church would spread, prosper, grow and extend, and that in proportion to the spread of the Gospel among the nations of the earth, so would the power of Satan rise. (*JD*, 13:280.)

— *Brigham Young*

Jesus was not spared grief and pain and anguish and buffeting. No tongue can speak the unutterable burden he carried, nor have we the wisdom to understand the prophet Isaiah's description of him as "a man of sorrows." (Isa. 53:3.) His ship was tossed most of his life, and, at least to mortal eyes, it crashed fatally on the rocky coast of Calvary. We are asked not to look on life with mortal eyes; with spiritual vision we know something quite different was happening upon the cross.

Peace was on the lips and in the heart of the Savior no matter how fiercely the tempest was raging. May it so be with us—in our own hearts, in our own homes, in our nations of the world, and even in the buffetings faced from time to time by the Church. We should not expect to get through life individually or collectively without some opposition. (*Ensign*, November 1984, p. 35.)

— *Howard W. Hunter*

No saint could fully understand the power of God unless he learn the opposite. I am not myself acquainted with any happiness that I have not learned the opposite of. . . . I may say with safety, nearly all the blessings I enjoy and highly prize are most appreciated after I have learned their opposite; and I am of opinion that all saints sooner or later will have to partake of the bitter in order to properly appreciate the sweet, they will have to be impressed with pain that they may appreciate pleasure. (*JD*, 2:11.)

— *Jedediah M. Grant*

Opposition is evidence of the truth at work.

— *Mary Ellen Edmunds*

The Lord has often pushed the Saints into the water to make them swim; and when our own indolence, which is nothing less than disobedience, gets us into a jam, he lets us stew in our own juice until we do something about it. (*OAT*, p. 108.)

— *Hugh Nibley*

The work of the adversary may be likened to loading guns in opposition to the work of God. Salvos containing germs of contention are aimed and fired at strategic targets essential to that holy work. These vital targets include—in addition to the individual—the family, leaders of the Church, ad divine doctrine. (*Ensign*, May 1989, p. 69.)

— *Russell M. Nelson*

What can you know, except by its opposite? (*JD*, 8:28.)

— *Brigham Young*

Where there is no trial there can be no deliverance; where there is no temptation, the power of God cannot be made manifest. (*JD*, 5:323.)

— *Lorenzo Snow*

See also ADVERSITY, CHALLENGES, ENDURANCE

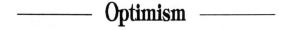

Optimism

There is no place in this Church or in any of our families for pessimism or negativism. We should be incurable optimists.

Irrespective of the condition of a person, he who is a cynic, a pessimist, or negative has the least progress, happiness, and prosperity.

On the other hand, the Lord's way is that the optimist with faith, who is positive, elevating, and edifying, is the individual in or out of the Church who is the most progressive, happy, and prosperous. (*Ensign*, May 1983, p. 73.)

— *Ted E. Brewerton*

Cultivate an attitude of happiness. Cultivate a spirit of optimism. Walk with faith, rejoicing in the beauties of nature, in the goodness of those you love, in the testimony which you carry in your heart concerning things divine. (*Ensign*, November 1984, p. 92.)

— *Gordon B. Hinckley*

Developing a cheerful disposition can permit an atmosphere wherein one's spirit can be nurtured and encouraged to blossom and bear fruit.

Being pessimistic and negative about our experiences will not enhance the quality of our lives. A determination to be of good cheer can help us and those around us to enjoy life more fully. (*Ensign*, November 1987, p. 96.)

— *Barbara W. Winder*

It seems to me that dwelling on negative thoughts and approaches is, in fact, working directly opposite of hope, faith, and trust—in the Lord, ourselves, and others—and causes continual feelings of gloom, while the positive lifts and buoys us up, encourages us to forge ahead, and is an attitude that can be developed, a habit that we can cultivate. (*Ensign*, May 1987, p. 74.)

— *Paul H. Dunn*

My father used to teach us that life is a journey, not a camp, and he indicated that too many people are camping. I'd like to challenge all of us, particularly the young people and young couples that are married, to see life as a whole and to enjoy the marvelous journey. (*Ensign*, November 1977, p. 24.)

— *Paul H. Dunn*

The optimist, as you probably know, is a person who, when he wears out his shoes, just figures he's back on his feet. (*Ensign*, May 1979, p. 29.)

— *Hartman Rector, Jr.*

The principles of the gospel of Jesus Christ will never change, but environment, circumstances, institutions, and cultural patterns do. Our challenge is to move forward in our present realms with commitment and enthusiasm. We must do our part to progress and enjoy life while we are in the process of meeting our situations. (*Ensign*, May 1984, p. 9.)

— *Marvin J. Ashton*

The spirit of the gospel is optimistic; it trusts in God and looks on the bright side of things. The opposite or pessimistic drags men down and away from God, looks on the dark side, murmurs, complains, and is slow to yield obedience. (*CR*, April 1917, p. 43.)

— *Orson F. Whitney*

With God's help, good cheer permits is to rise above the depressing present or difficult circumstances. . . . It is sunshine when clouds block the light. (*Ensign,* May 1986, p. 66.)

— *Marvin J. Ashton*

See also ATTITUDE, CHEERFULNESS, SELF-PITY

——— Ordinances ———
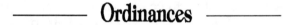

All men who become heirs of God and joint heirs with Jesus Christ will have to receive the fullness of the ordinances of the kingdom; and those who will not receive all the ordinances will come short of the fullness of that glory, if they do not lose the whole. (*HC*, 5:424.)

— *Joseph Smith*

External works, or outward ordinances . . . [are] inseparably connected with inward works, such as faith and repentance. . . . The Savior says, "Why call ye me, Lord, Lord, and do not the things which I say?" Again, He says, "He that heareth my words, and doeth them shall be likened unto a man that built his house upon a rock." And, "He that believeth and is baptized shall be saved." . . . These sayings of our Savior require men to perform external works in order to receive their salvation. (*TLS*, pp. 16-17.)

— *Lorenzo Snow*

Good conduct without the ordinances of the gospel will neither redeem nor exalt mankind. (*Ensign*, November 1985, p. 82.)

— *Boyd K. Packer*

Ordinances and covenants are an anchor to safety for the family, both here and hereafter. (*Ensign,* November 1987, p. 91.)

— *Joanne B. Doxey*

When ordinances are performed, blessings are received which give power to man, power that belongs to the everyday affairs of this life as to a future life. It is not merely knowledge; not merely consecration; not merely a labeling, so to speak; but the actual conferring of power that may be used every day. (*The Message of the Doctrine and Covenants*, ed. G. Homer Durham, Salt Lake City: Bookcraft, 1969, p. 161.)

— *John A. Widtsoe*

The covenants we make in the temple, like the other sacred ordinances in the kingdom, relate us to and center us in the life of the Lord Jesus Christ. (*Ensign*, November 1984, p. 37.)

— *Marion D. Hanks*

See also COVENANTS, PRIESTHOOD

—— Parenthood ——

After all the personal and social and economic reasons have been chalked up against childbearing and family rearing, there is still this to be said in its favor: that's the way we all got here! It is to be doubted if our coming were physically convenient for our mothers and economically convenient for our fathers. And yet the fact of our existence forces us to conclude that their sacrifice, if such it was, was something quite worthwhile. And our obligation to life is not removed until the next generation stands to our credit. (*IE*, October 1939, p. 608.)

— *Richard L. Evans*

Do not curtail the number of your children for personal or selfish reasons. Material possessions, social convenience, and so-called professional advantages are nothing compared to a righteous posterity. (*Ensign*, May 1987, p. 97.)

— *Ezra Taft Benson*

Have your families in a normal way; accept all the spirits the Lord sees fit to send you; do not delay your families; always be considerate of one another; have nothing to do with the sin of abortion. (Quoted by John H. Groberg, *Ensign*, November 1976, p. 45.)

— *Spencer W. Kimball*

I am convinced that having a child is the final and strongest pledge of a couple's love for each other. It is an eloquent testimony that their marriage is a complete one. It lifts their marriage from the level of selfish love and physical pleasure to that of devotion centered around a new life. It makes self-sacrifice rather than self-indulgence their guiding principle. It represents the husband's faith in his ability to provide the necessary security, and it demonstrates the wife's confidence in his ability to do so. The net result is a spiritual security which, more than any other power, helps to create material security as well. (*Ensign*, February 1972, p. 51.)

— *Harold B. Lee*

It is a grave responsibility and a transcendent blessing when a man and a woman make vows and covenants and receive the ordinances of marriage. When within the covenant of marriage a man and a woman invoke the great powers of creation, they literally become partners with God in creating new human life. (*Ensign*, May 1988, p. 38.)

— *James E. Faust*

Loving parent. What a noble title! There are no greater roles in life for a man than those of husband and father. Likewise, there are no greater roles for a woman than those of wife and mother. (*Ensign*, November 1989, p. 20.)

— *Russell M. Nelson*

Parental responsibility cannot go unheeded, nor can it be shifted to day-care centers, nor to the schoolroom, nor even to the Church. Family responsibility comes by divine decree. Parents may violate this decree only at the peril of their eternal salvation. (*Ensign*, January 1973, p. 67.)

— *A. Theodore Tuttle*

Parenthood should bring the greatest of all happiness. Men grow because as fathers they must take care of their families. Women blossom because as mothers they must forget themselves. We understand best the full meaning of love when we become parents. (*Ensign*, November 1977, p. 11.)

— *James E. Faust*

Parents have the glorious opportunity of being the most powerful influence, above and beyond any other, on the new lives that bless their homes. (*Ensign*, May 1989, p. 114.)

— *L. Tom Perry*

We should post ourselves regarding the prophecies which have been predicted. I will mention one in particular that was uttered by the Prophet Joseph Smith. He said the time would come when none but the women of the Latter-day Saints would be willing to bear children. (Quoted in 1890, *Young Women's Journal*, Vol. 2, p. 81.)

— *Lillie Tucket Freeze*

When He sends a child of His to earth, He gives to the parents that which is more precious than all the wealth of the worlds He has created. Sacred, indeed, is the trust, and great is the responsibility that is placed upon those who receive a child of His. (*CR*, October 1908, p. 36.)

— *Heber C. Iverson*

See also CHILD-REARING, FATHERHOOD, MOTHERHOOD

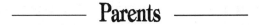

Parents

Children, remember your parents. After they have nurtured you through the tender years of your infancy and childhood, after they have fed and clothed and educated you, after having given you a bed to rest upon and done all in their power for your good, don't you neglect them when they become feeble and are bowed down with the weight of their years. Don't you leave them, but settle down near them, and do all in your power to minister to their comfort and well-being. (*IE*, December 1917, p. 105.)

— *Joseph F. Smith*

I would plead with you, . . . to honor your fathers and your mothers, . . . Be obedient and loving to them; and after they have climbed to the summit of the hill of life, perhaps through many a hard-fought struggle, and begin to descend, try to do all in your power to make the road smooth and pleasant for them. By their devotion to you and to your welfare they have proved themselves worthy of your affection, and God expects you to be loyal to them. He has honored them in the past, and will yet honor them more abundantly; but their joy will not be fully complete if their children disregard their wishes and are untrue to them and to God. . . .

Let your feet tread in the same path of advancement and progress as your parents; let your hearts beat in unison with theirs for the welfare of truth and righteousness, and by and by you will rejoice with them worlds without end. (*TLS*, p. 137.)

— *Lorenzo Snow*

In the divine wisdom of our Heavenly Father, each of you was born to parents who arrived on this earth a few years ahead of you. They have been over the ground you . . . are covering now. They have learned what leads to success and happiness and what leads to misery and sorrow. Seek their counsel, listen to them, and learn from them. (*Ensign*, November 1988, p. 34.)

— *Joseph B. Wirthlin*

It [is] one of the greatest earthly blessings to be blessed with . . . parents, whose mature years and experience render them capable of administering the most wholesome advice. (*HC*, 2:289.)

— *Joseph Smith*

Our parents deserve our honor and respect for giving us life itself. Beyond this they . . . made countless sacrifices as they cared for and nurtured us through our infancy and childhood, provided us with the necessities of life, and nursed us through physical illnesses and the emotional stresses of growing up. In many instances, they provided us with the opportunity to receive an education, and, in a measure, they educated us. Much of what we know and do we learned from their example. May we ever be grateful to them and show that gratitude. (*Ensign*, November 1989, p. 6.)

— *Ezra Taft Benson*

There is no righteous way to avoid the commandment "Honor thy father and thy mother." (Ex. 20:12.) (*Ensign*, May 1981, p. 83.)

— *H. Burke Peterson*

To honor parents . . . means to show love, kindness, thoughtfulness, and concern for them all of the days of their lives. It means to help them preserve their dignity and self-respect in their declining years. It means to honor their wishes and desires and their teachings both before and after they are dead. (*Ensign*, November 1986, p. 9.)

— *James E. Faust*

See also FAMILY, HERITAGE

——————— Patience ———————

If [God] deprives [his children] of any present blessing it is that he may bestow upon them greater and more glorious ones by and by. (*MS*, 25:634.)

— *George Q. Cannon*

Patience is learning to hide your impatience. (*Ensign*, May 1983, p. 76.)

— *Jacob de Jager*

Patience is another form of self-control. It is the ability to postpone gratification and to bridle one's passions. . . . Patience is composure under stress. A patient man is understanding others' faults. A patient man also waits on the Lord. We sometimes read or hear of people who seek a blessing from the Lord, then grow impatient when it does not come swiftly. Part of the divine nature is to trust in the Lord enough to "be still and know that [he is] God" (D&C 101:16). (*Ensign*, November 1986, p. 47.)

— *Ezra Taft Benson*

Patience is tied very closely to faith in our Heavenly Father. Actually, when we are unduly impatient, we are suggesting that we know what is best—better than does God. Or, at least, we are asserting that our timetable is better than his. Either way we are questioning the reality of God's omniscience. (*Ensign*, October 1980, p. 28.)

— *Neal A. Maxwell*

The Lord, Jesus Christ, is our perfect example of patience. Though absolutely unyielding in adherence to the truth, He exemplified patience repeatedly during His mortal ministry. He was patient with His disciples, including the Twelve, despite their lack of faith and their slowness to recognize and understand His divine mission. He was patient with the multitudes as they pressed about Him, with the woman taken in sin, with those who sought His healing power, and with little children. Finally, He remained patient through the suffering of His mock trials and His crucifixion. (*Hope*, Salt Lake City: Deseret Book Co., 1988, p. 156.)

— *Joseph B. Wirthlin*

There seems to be little evidence that the Creator of the universe was ever in a hurry. Everywhere, on this bounteous and beautiful earth, and to the farthest reaches of the firmament, there is evidence of patient purpose and planning and working and waiting. (*CR*, October 1952, p. 95.)

— *Richard L. Evans*

We do not have to worry about the patience of God, because he is the personification of patience, no matter where we have been, what we have done, or what we, to this moment, have allowed ourselves to think of ourselves. . . . God will not forsake [us]. (*Speeches of the Year, 1972-73*, Provo: Brigham Young University Press, 1973, p. 104.)

— *Marvin J. Ashton*

See also TOLERANCE

─── Patriarchal Blessings ───

I would encourage you . . . to receive a patriarchal blessing. Study it carefully and regard it as personal scripture to you—for that indeed is what it is. (*Ensign,* November 1986, p. 82.)

— *Ezra Taft Benson*

Patriarchal blessings contemplate an inspired declaration of the lineage of the recipient and, when so moved upon by the Spirit, an inspired and prophetic statement of the life mission of the recipient, . . . together with such blessings, cautions and admonitions as the patriarch may be prompted to give for the accomplishment of such life's mission, it being always made clear that the realization of all promised blessings is conditioned upon faithfulness to the gospel of our Lord, whose servant the patriarch is. (Letter to stake presidents, 28 June 1958, quoted by Thomas S. Monson, *Ensign,* November 1986, p. 65.)

— *The First Presidency*

The same Lord who provided a Liahona for Lehi provides for you and for me today a rare and valuable gift to give direction to our lives, to mark the hazards to our safety, and to chart the way, even safe passage—not to a promised land, but to our heavenly home. The gift to which I refer is known as your patriarchal blessing. Every worthy member of the Church is entitled to receive such a precious and priceless personal treasure. . . .

A patriarchal blessing is a revelation to the recipient, even a white line down the middle of the road, to protect, inspire, and motivate activity and righteousness. A patriarchal blessing literally contains chapters from your book of eternal possibilities. (*Ensign,* November 1986, pp. 65-66.)

— *Thomas S. Monson*

What does a patriarchal blessing say? Have you ever heard of one which says, "I am sorry—you're a loser. Do the best you can on earth, and we'll see you in about seventy years." Of course not! And you never will, because of the divine qualities each of God's children has inherited. A patriarchal blessing is like a road map, a guide, directing you in your walk through life. It identifies your talents and the good things that can be yours. (*Ensign,* November 1989, p. 87.)

— *Elaine L. Jack*

——— Patriarchal Order ———

Brethren, the priesthood, if magnified, is a stabilizing influence and a strength. It should be. Every wife and mother has a perfect right and responsibility to look to her husband who holds the priesthood for guidance, for strength, and for direction. And he has the responsibility of magnifying his priesthood so he might be able to give this direction, this security, this strength that is needed in the home. (*Seek Ye First the Kingdom of God*, Salt Lake City: Deseret Book Co., 1973, p. 177.)

— *N. Eldon Tanner*

I believe that of the two parties in a male-female relationship, the bearer of the priesthood has the greater duty to see that the commandments of God, the standards of the Church, and parental authority are honored. Likewise, when male and female violate these commandments, I believe the priesthood holder is generally more blameworthy because he has been entrusted with the great, righteous power to act in the name of God. (*Ensign*, May 1988, p. 37.)

— *James E. Faust*

The order of God's government, both in time and in eternity, is patriarchal; that is, it is a fatherly government. Each father who is raised from the dead and made a partaker of the celestial glory in its fullness will hold lawful jurisdiction over his own children and over all the families which spring of them to all generations, forever and ever. . . . We talk in this ignorant age, of children becoming of age . . . and we consider when they are of age they are free from the authority of their father. But no such rule is known in celestial law and organization, either here or hereafter. By that law a son is subject to his father forever and ever, worlds without end. (*MS*, 5:189.)

— *Parley P. Pratt*

The patriarchal system provides a basis for government in the kingdom of God. It places parents in a position of accountability for their own direct family, and it links these family kingdoms in a patriarchal order that lends cohesiveness to the greater kingdom of God of which they are a part. The patriarchal order has no relevance in the eternal worlds except for those husbands and wives and families who have entered into the covenant of eternal marriage.

— *Dean L. Larsen*

There is no higher authority in matters relating to the family organization, and especially when that organization is presided over by one holding the higher

Priesthood, than that of the father. . . . The patriarchal order is of divine origin and will continue throughout time and eternity. . . . In the home the presiding authority is always vested in the father, and in all home affairs and family matters there is no other authority paramount. (*GD*, pp. 286-87.)

— *Joseph F. Smith*

The very essence of divine government is fatherhood and the recognition of the family relationship. (*CR*, October 1966, p. 103.)

— *Hugh B. Brown*

This patriarchal order has its divine spirit and purpose, and those who disregard it . . . are out of harmony with the spirit of God's laws as they are ordained for recognition in the home. It is not merely a question of who is perhaps the best qualified. Neither is it wholly a question of who is living the most worthy life. It is a question largely of law and order. (*GD*, p. 287.)

— *Joseph F. Smith*

See also FATHERHOOD, PRIESTHOOD

Peace

For years it has been held that peace comes only by preparation for war; . . . [but] peace comes only by preparing for peace, through training the people in righteousness and justice, and seeking rulers who respect the righteous will of the people. There is only one thing that can bring peace into the world. It is the adoption of the gospel of Jesus Christ, rightly understood, obeyed and practiced by rulers and people alike. (*IE*, September 1914, pp. 1074-75.)

— *Joseph F. Smith*

It is very significant that when Jesus came forth from the tomb and appeared to his disciples, his first greeting was, "Peace be unto you." (Luke 24:36.) Peace—not passion, not personal possessions, not personal accomplishments nor happiness—is one of the greatest blessings a man can receive. (*Ensign*, November 1985, p. 69.)

— *Marvin J. Ashton*

Jesus Christ says, "my peace I give unto you: not as the world giveth, give I unto you." (John 14:27.) Wherever this peace exists, it leaves an influence that is comforting and refreshing to the souls of those who partake of it. It is like the morning dew to the thirsty plant. This peace is the gift of God alone, and it can be received only from him through obedience to his laws. If any man wishes to introduce peace into his family or among his friends, let him cultivate it in his own bosom; for sterling peace can only be had according to the legitimate rule and authority of heaven, and obedience to its laws. (*JD,* 1:228.)

— John Taylor

Men may yearn for peace, cry for peace, and work for peace, but there will be no peace until they follow the path pointed out by the Living Christ. (*CR,* October 1964, p. 5.)

— David O. McKay

Nations may rise, and nations may destroy each other in strife, but this gospel is here to stay, and we must preach it and proclaim it, that peace may come, for it is only through obedience to the gospel of Jesus Christ that peace will come permanently upon the earth. (*DFTP,* p. 353.)

— David O. McKay

No lasting peace can come to this world until a peace is based on the love of God for all peoples. (*CR,* October 1920, p. 173.)

— Levi Edgar Young

Peace is more than a spot of ink on a piece of paper or a sound upon our lips. it is the application of the teachings of the Prince of Peace in our daily lives. (*CR,* October 1964, p. 126.)

— John Longden

Peace will come and be maintained only through the triumph of the principles of peace, and by the consequent subjection of the enemies of peace, which are hatred, envy, illgotten gain, the exercise of unrighteous dominion of men. Yielding to these evils brings misery to the individual, unhappiness to the home, war among nations. (*IE,* 47:657.)

— David O. McKay

Peacemakers

The Lord has commanded us to love all men, including our enemies. He expects us to be peacemakers. He asks us to work out a reconciliation in a Christlike manner with those with whom we have difficulties or misunderstandings. It is his will that we should tolerate abuse rather than retaliate in a spirit of anger. It is better to turn the other cheek, to go the extra mile, to give our coat and our cloak also, than to offend. (*Ensign,* November 1974, p. 31.)

— O. Leslie Stone

It is a good thing to be at peace with God. (*CR,* October 1902, p. 87.)

— *Joseph F. Smith*

The formula for peace: keep the commandments of God. War and conflict are the result of wickedness; peace is the product of righteousness. . . . Each citizen furthers the cause of world peace when he or she keeps the commandments of God and lives at peace with family and neighbors. . . . What can one person do to promote world peace? The answer is simple: keep God's commandments, and serve his children. (*Ensign,* May 1990, p. 71.)

— *Dallin H. Oaks*

The only way to build a peaceful community is to build men and women who are lovers and makers of peace. Each individual, by that doctrine of Christ and His Church, holds in his own hands the peace of the world.

That makes me responsible for the peace of the world, and makes you individually responsible for the peace of the world. The responsibility cannot be shifted to someone else. It cannot be placed upon the shoulders of Congress of Parliament, or any other organization of men with governing authority. (*CR,* October 1943, p. 113.)

— *John A. Widtsoe*

See also OBEDIENCE, SERENITY, WAR

Perfection

Begin at a small point; can you not live to the Lord for one minute? Yes. Then can we not multiply that by sixty and make an hour, and live that hour to the Lord? Yes; and then for a day, a week, a month, and a year? Then, when the year is past, it has been spent most satisfactorily. (*JD,* 8:59-60.)

— *Brigham Young*

Godliness cannot be conferred but must be acquired. (*MS,* 13:362.)

— *Lorenzo Snow*

I do not expect that any of us will ever become in mortality quite so perfect as God is perfect; but in the spheres in which we are called to act, and according to the capacity and breadth of . . . talent, ability, and intelligence that God has given to us, we may become as perfect in our sphere as God is perfect in his higher and more exalted sphere. I believe that. (*CR,* April 1915, p. 140.)

— *Joseph F. Smith*

I never told you I was perfect; but there is no error in the revelations which I have taught. (*HC*, 6:366.)

— *Joseph Smith*

Man can transform himself and he must. Man has in himself the seeds of godhood, which can germinate and grow and develop. As the acorn becomes the oak, the mortal man becomes a god. It is within his power to lift himself by his very bootstraps from the plane on which he finds himself to the plane on which he should be. It may be a long, hard lift with many obstacles, but it is a real possibility. (*TSWK*, p. 28.)

— *Spencer W. Kimball*

No one professes to be perfect, but there is a spirit in this work and among this people that makes them better than they would be otherwise. (*Ensign*, November 1985, p. 10.)

— *Loren C. Dunn*

On the straight and narrow path, there are simply no corners to be cut. (*Ensign*, November 1988, p. 33.)

— *Neal A. Maxwell*

The nearer man approaches perfection, the clearer are his views, and the greater his enjoyments, till he has overcome the evils of his life and lost every desire for sin; and like the ancients, arrives at that point of faith where he is wrapped in the power and glory of his Maker and is caught up to dwell with Him. But we consider that this is a station to which no man ever arrived in a moment. (*TPJS*, p. 51.)

— *Joseph Smith*

Try, keep trying daily and hourly in all your avocations, in all your walks of life, in all your associations, to be perfect, even as our Father in Heaven is perfect. (*TLS*, p. 38.)

— *Lorenzo Snow*

We achieve perfection, . . . in the doing of many things, and can be perfect in our intent to do all things. (*Ensign*, May 1981, p. 10.)

— *James E. Faust*

When the saints of God chart a course of righteousness, when they gain sure testimonies of the truth and divinity of the Lord's work, when they keep the commandments, when they overcome the world, when they put first in their lives the things of God's kingdom: when they do all these things, and then depart this life—though they have not yet become perfect—they shall nonetheless gain eternal life in our Father's kingdom; and eventually they shall be perfect as God their Father and Christ His Son are perfect. (*Ensign*, November 1976, p. 107.)

— *Bruce R. McConkie*

When men correctly understand and have faith in the true and living God, they strive to develop within themselves his virtues. He becomes the lodestar of their lives. To emulate him is their highest aspiration. As they strive to "be . . . perfect, even as [their] Father which is in heaven is perfect" (Matt, 5:48), they actually become partakers of his divine nature. (*CR*, April 1970, pp. 67-68.)

— *Marion G. Romney*

"Be ye therefore perfect, even as your Father which is in heaven is perfect." (Matt. 5:48.) If the . . . passage I have quoted is not worded to our understanding, we can alter the phraseology of the sentence, and say: "Be ye perfect as ye can," for that is all we can do. When we are doing as well as we know how in the sphere and station which we occupy here, we are justified . . . The sin that will cleave to all the posterity of Adam and Eve is that they have not done as well as they know how. (*JD*, 2:129-30.)

— *Brigham Young*

See also PROGRESSION, PURITY, RIGHTEOUSNESS, WORTHINESS

Persecution

Always remember that if this were not the Lord's work, the adversary would not pay any attention to us. If this Church were merely a church of men and women, teaching only the doctrines of men, we would encounter little or no criticism or resistance—but because this is the Church of Him whose name it bears, we must not be surprised when criticisms or difficulties arise. With faith and good works, the truth will prevail. This is His work. There is none other like it. Let us, therefore, press forward, lengthening our stride and rejoicing in our blessings and opportunities. (*Ensign*, May 1981, p. 79.)

— *Spencer W. Kimball*

Those who desire to persecute and overthrow Mormonism, let them go on and do their work; that is for them to do. Our work is to grow in the knowledge of God, to keep the commandments of God, to be faithful and to continue to increase and to become more and more perfect as we advance in years.

— *Lorenzo Snow*

There are those who have made it the mission of their lives to try to destroy this, the work of God. It has been so from the beginning of the Church, and now, in recent times, we are seeing more of it with evil accusations, falsehoods, and innuendo designed to embarrass this work and its officers. A natural inclination is to fight back, to challenge these falsehoods and bring action against their perpetrators, But when these inclinations make themselves felt, there arise also the words of the Master healer who said:

"Ye have heard that it hath been said, Thou shalt love thy neighbor and hate thine enemy.

"But I say unto you, Love your enemies, bless them that curse you, do good to them that hate you, and pray for them which despitefully use you, and persecute you." (Matt. 5:43-44.) (*Ensign*, November 1988, pp. 54, 59.)

— *Gordon B. Hinckley*

Every time you kick "Mormonism" you kick it upstairs; you never kick it downstairs. The Lord Almighty so orders it. (*DBY*, p. 351.)

— *Brigham Young*

I will take shelter under the broad cover of the wings of the work in which I am engaged. It matters not to me if all hell boils over. (*HC*, 6:253.)

— *Joseph Smith*

There are those who mock our beliefs in the most uncharitable ways. And we will bear what they do with long-suffering, for it does not change truth. And in their own way they move our work along a little faster. (*Ensign*, November 1984, p. 69.)

— *Boyd K. Packer*

When the wicked have power to blow out the sun, that it shines no more; when they have power to bring to a conclusion the operations of the elements, suspend the whole system of nature, and make a footstool of the throne of the Almighty, they may then think to check "Mormonism" in its course, and thwart the unalterable purposes of heaven. (*JD*, 1:88.)

— *Brigham Young*

We surely have been warned and forewarned about our time, a period in which the compression of challenges may make a year seem like a decade. Members will be cleverly mocked and scorned by those in the "great and spacious building," representing the pride of the world. No matter, for ere long, He who was raised on the third day will raze that spacious but third-class hotel! (*Ensign*, May 1987, p. 71.)

— *Neal A. Maxwell*

Time is rapidly rolling on, and the prophecies must be fulfilled. The days of tribulation are fast approaching, and the time to test the fidelity of the Saints has come. Rumor with her ten thousand tongues is diffusing her uncertain sounds in almost every ear; but in these times of sore trial, let the saints be patient and see the salvation of God. Those who cannot endure persecution, and stand in the day of affliction, cannot stand in the day when the Son of God shall burst the veil, and appear in all the glory of his Father, with all the holy angels. (*HC*, 1:468.)

— *Joseph Smith*

See also ADVERSITY, APOSTASY, CRITICISM, ENEMIES

Perseverance

Brothers and sisters, the gospel is easy to live. All we have to do is stay everlastingly at it. (*Ensign*, November 1990, p. 78.)

— *Hartman Rector, Jr.*

History rests on the shoulders of those who accepted the challenge of difficulties and drove through to victory in spite of everything. (*CR*, October 1963, p. 87.)

— *Hugh B. Brown*

I believe that perseverance is vital to success in any endeavor, whether spiritual or temporal, large or small, public or personal. . . . All significant achievement results largely from perseverance. (*Ensign*, November 1987, p. 9.)

— *Joseph B. Wirthlin*

Perseverance is a positive, active characteristic. It is not idly, passively waiting and hoping for some good thing to happen. It gives us hope by helping us realize that the righteous suffer no failure except in giving up and no longer trying. . . . We must never give up, regardless of temptations, frustrations, disappointments, or discouragements. (*Ensign*, November 1987, p. 8.)

— *Joseph B. Wirthlin*

Perseverance is essential to us in learning and living the principles of the gospel. It will determine our progress as we strive to reach exaltation. . . . The ultimate example of perseverance is our Lord and Savior, Jesus Christ, who has and will overcome every obstacle in doing the will of our Heavenly Father. (*Ensign*, November 1987, pp. 9, 10.)

— *Joseph B. Wirthlin*

Where there are challenges, you fail only if you fail to keep trying! (*Ensign*, November 1980, p. 5.)

— *Spencer W. Kimball*

See also ACHIEVEMENT, ENDURANCE, PERSISTENCE, WORKS

Persistence

Only if you reach the boundary will the boundary recede before you. And if you don't, if you confine your efforts, the boundary will shrink to accommodate itself to your efforts. And you can only expand your capacities by working to the very limit (*OAT*, p. 130.)

— *Hugh Nibley*

Our task is to become our best selves. One of God's greatest gifts to us is the joy of trying again, for no failure ever need be final. (*Ensign*, May 1987, p. 68.)

— *Thomas S. Monson*

Personal, spiritual symmetry emerges only from the shaping of prolonged obedience. Twigs are bent, not snapped, into shape. (*Ensign*, May 1990, p. 34.)

— *Neal A. Maxwell*

That which we persist in doing becomes easier for us to do; not that the nature of the thing itself is changed, but that our power to do is increased. (*CR*, April 1901, p. 63.)

— *Often quoted by Heber J. Grant*

The strait and narrow path, though clearly marked, is a path, not a freeway nor an escalator. Indeed, there are times when the only way the strait and narrow path can be followed is on one's knees! And we are to help each other along the path. (*Ensign*, May 1982, p. 38.)

— *Neal A. Maxwell*

You remember the Duke of Wellington was talking of the Battle of Waterloo when he said that it was not that the British soldiers were braver than the French soldiers. It was just that they were brave five minutes longer.

And in our struggles sometimes that's all it takes—to be brave five minutes longer, to try just a little harder, to not give up on ourselves when everything seems to beg for our defeat. (*Ensign*, May 1979, p. 9.)

— *Paul H. Dunn*

See also CONSTANCY, DETERMINATION, VALIANCY

——— Perspective ———

Because we know we are living not just for this life, but for another, eternal one as well, we look at life's events differently. As you review the last year or the last ten years, what is the best day you remember? A person without hope centered in Christ may choose a day that was simply fun or easy. But the best day may really have been the one when life's events forced you to your knees to communicate with your Father with new intent; it may have been a day that wasn't convenient or even happy, but you became a bigger and better person when you faced a problem with courage. (_Ensign_, November 1986, p. 87.)

— _Dwan J. Young_

It is vital to know that there _really_ is a God, that there _really_ is a Savior, Jesus Christ, that there _really_ is impending immortality for all men, that there _really_ will be a judgment with genuine personal accountability, and that there _really_ is purpose in life and a divine plan of happiness for man.

When we know such basic truths as these, then we know what _really_ matters, how to approach life and how to view man in the universe. There is great power in perspective. Therefore, the adverb "really," as used by Jacob (Jacob 4:13), is deeply significant. (_Things As They Really Are_, Salt Lake City: Deseret Book Co., 1978, p. 4.)

— _Neal A. Maxwell_

Sometimes we focus too much of our attention and energy upon our temporal wants, not only to entertain ourselves and gratify our physical appetites, but also to gain recognition, position, and power. We can become so consumed by the pursuit of these things that we sacrifice the sweetness and enduring peace of mind that are found in spiritual well-being, in well-nurtured family relationships, and in the love and respect of friends and associates.

Too often we permit the narrow demands of our daily routine to dull our appreciation of the beauty of God's creations and the refining influences that are all about us. We fail to experience the fulfillment that comes from developing the gifts and talents with which we have been endowed. We do not draw close enough to the Lord to know him and feel of his redeeming love.

In today's complicated world with its diversity of demands and sometimes distracting voices, it is so important for us to deep our eyes upon the basic things that matter most and that will have the greatest eternal consequence for us. (_Ensign_, November 1987, p. 12.)

— _Dean L. Larsen_

We are looked upon by God as though we were in eternity; God dwells in eternity, and does not view things as we do. (*HC*, 6:313.)

— *Joseph Smith*

We see things not as they are, but as we are. (*CR*, April 1971, p. 153.)

— *Delbert L. Stapley*

When I take a small pebble and place it directly in front of my eye, it takes on the appearance of a mighty boulder. It is all I can see. It becomes all-consuming—like the problems . . . that affect our lives . . . . When the things you realistically can do . . . are done, leave the matter in the hands of the Lord and worry no more. . . . The Lord will take the pebble that fills your vision and cast it down among the challenges you will face in your eternal progress. It will then be seen in perspective. (*Ensign*, May 1988, p. 60.)

— *Richard G. Scott*

When we see things as they really were, really are, and really will be (see Jacob 4:13; D&C 93:24), dispensations are merely seasons, new friendships are but relationships resumed, and prophets sent forth on their errands from the Lord reflect associations which arc across the ages as they later rendezvous on mountaintops and hills, in woods, fields, groves, and even jails. (See Moses 1:1-2; Matt. 17:1-7; JS-H 1:14, 48-50; Acts 23:11.) (*Ensign*, May 1986, p. 36.)

— *Neal A. Maxwell*

With celestial sight, trials impossible to change become possible to endure. (*Ensign*, May 1988, p. 35.)

— *Russell M. Nelson*

See also BALANCE, PRIORITIES

———— Philosophies of Men ————

If, in the expediency of the moment, we set God aside to follow the teachings of men, we disown Him. (*Ensign*, May 1983, p. 18.)

— *Marion G. Romney*

One great reason why men have stumbled so frequently in many of their researches after philosophical truth is that they have sought them with their own wisdom, and gloried in their own intelligence, and have not sought unto God for that wisdom that fills and governs the universe and regulates all things. That is one great difficulty with the philosophers of the world, as it now exists, that man claims to himself to be the inventor of everything he discovers. Any new law and principle which he happens to discover he claims to himself instead of giving glory to God. (*The Gospel Kingdom,* Salt Lake City: Bookcraft, 1964, p. 47.)

— *John Taylor*

Sometimes people let their hearts get so set upon things and the honors of this world that they cannot learn the lessons they most need to learn. Simple truths are often rejected in favor of the much less demanding philosophies of men. (*Ensign,* May 1978, p. 77.)

— *Spencer W. Kimball*

The religion of the Latter-day Saints is not hostile to any truth, not to scientific search for truth. . . . A good motto for young people to adopt, who are determined to delve into philosophic theories, is to search all things, but be careful to hold on only to that which is true. (*IE,* 14:548.)

— *Joseph F. Smith*

We must cast aside the philosophies of men and the wisdom of the wise and hearken to that Spirit which is given to us to guide us into all truth. (*Ensign,* May 1985, p. 10.)

— *Bruce R. McConkie*

See also DISCERNMENT, FALSE DOCTRINE, KNOWLEDGE, LEARNING, TRUTH

——————— Plan of Salvation ———————

God had a purpose, therefore, in the organization of this earth, and in the placing of man upon it, he has never deviated one hair to the right or to the left in regard to man and his destiny from that time until the present. (*JD,* 17:370.)

— *John Taylor*

As Adam brought death, so Christ brought life; as Adam is the father of mortality, so Christ is the father of immortality.

And without both, mortality and immortality, man cannot work out his salvation and ascend to those heights beyond the skies where gods and angels dwell forever in eternal glory. (*Ensign,* May 1985, p. 10.)

— *Bruce R. McConkie*

In my judgment, the greatest motivator that we have in the Church is to have Church members understand the plan of salvation. (*Ensign*, May 1986, p. 15.)
— *M. Russell Ballard*

Because the centerpiece of the Atonement is already in place, we know that everything else in god's plan will likewise finally succeed. God is surely able to do His own work! (See 2 Ne. 27:20-21.) In His plans for the human family, long ago God made ample provision for all mortal mistakes. His purposes will all triumph and without abrogating man's moral agency. Moreover, all His purposes will come to pass in their time. (See D&C 64:32.) (*Ensign*, November 1990, p. 15.)
— *Neal A. Maxwell*

God's plan of salvation is the wrong thing to be wrong about!
No error could be more enormous or more everlasting in its consequences! (*Ensign*, May 1984, p. 22.)
— *Neal A. Maxwell*

It seems incredible to me, when we look into the works of nature, when we investigate the organism of man, the perfection of his body, the pulsation of his heart, the building and strengthening from childhood to manhood, then the gradual decline until this life is ended—that it is possible any of our Father's children can believe that human beings have been born into the world only to live, . . . and die, without some purpose in their having lived here. (*CR*, April 1905.)
— *George Albert Smith*

No man ever did or ever will obtain salvation, only through the ordinances of the gospel and through the name of Jesus. There can be no change in the gospel; all men that are saved from Adam to infinitum are saved by the one system of salvation. (*JD*, 10:217.)
— *Wilford Woodruff*

President Brigham Young said of a geographical destination, "This is the place." Of God's plan of salvation, with its developmental destination, it can be said, "This is the process!" (*Ensign*, November 1982, p. 67.)
— *Neal A. Maxwell*

The great plan of salvation is a theme which ought to occupy our strict attention, and be regarded as one of heaven's best gifts to mankind. (*HC*, 2:23.)
— *Joseph Smith*

There is no evidence to be found in the Bible that the gospel should be one thing in the days of the Israelites, another in the days of Christ and his apostles, and another in the 19th century, but, on the contrary, we are instructed that God is the same in every age, and that his plan of saving his children is the same . . . the plan of salvation is one, from the beginning of the world to the end thereof. (*JD*, 10:324.)

— Brigham Young

The Lord has not in view merely the salvation of a few people called Latter-day Saints, who have been or who may be gathered into these valleys, but the salvation of all men, the living and the dead. (*JD*, 23:338.)

— Lorenzo Snow

The object of man's taking a body is that through the redemption of Jesus Christ both the soul and body may be exalted in the eternal world, . . . and obtain a higher exaltation than he could be capable of doing without a body. (*MS*, 13:81.)

— John Taylor

The plan of salvation, . . . is a grand cooperative scheme, as expansive as the heavens and as wide as eternity; it penetrates through all time, extends through all ages, and reaches men in every position, living or dead. (*JD*, 17:374.)

— John Taylor

The grand object of our coming to this earth is that we may become like Christ, for if we are not like him, we cannot become the sons of God, and be joint heirs with Christ. (*JD*, 23:172-73.)

— Joseph F. Smith

We are not here [in this world] accidentally. We came here because we were willing to come, and because it was the wish of our Father in Heaven . . . . We undoubtedly saw very clearly that there was no other way for us to secure what the Father had in store for us. (*CR*, April 1901, p. 2.)

— Lorenzo Snow

What is man in this boundless setting of sublime splendor? I answer you: Potentially now, actually to be, he is greater and grander, more precious according to the arithmetic of God, than all the planets and suns of space. For him were they created; they are the handiwork of God; man is His son! In this world man is given dominion over a few things; it is his privilege to achieve supremacy over many things. . . .

Incomprehensibly grand as are the physical creations of the earth and space, they have been brought into existence as means to an end, necessary to the realization of the supreme purpose, which in the words of the Creator is thus declared:

"For behold, this is my work and my glory—to bring to pass the immortality and eternal life of man." (Moses 1:39) (Quoted by Joseph Anderson, *Ensign*, May 1978, p. 70.)

— James E. Talmage

You cannot find a compass on the earth that points so directly as the gospel plan of salvation. It has a place for everything and puts everything in its place. (*JD*, 3:96.)

— Brigham Young

See also AGENCY, DEATH, GOSPEL, LIFE, PROBATION, SALVATION

Poor

From [The Book of Mormon] we learn that care of the poor is an obligation that we take upon ourselves at the time of baptism. (See Mosiah 18:8-10.) . . . Ours is not to judge; ours is a covenantal obligation to care for the poor and the needy, to prepare for their rejoicing when the Messiah shall come again. (See D&C 56:18-19.) (*Ensign*, May 1986, pp. 26, 27.)

— Russell M. Nelson

If we neglect the poor, God will neglect us. (*CR*, April 1899, p. 5.)

— Rudger Clawson

Scriptures teach us that the poor—especially widows, orphans, and strangers—have long been the concern of God and the godly. . . . Few, if any, of the Lord's instructions are stated more often, or given greater emphasis, than the commandment to care for the poor and the needy. Our dispensation is no exception. (See D&C 35:15, 42:30-31, 44:6, 56:16.) (*Ensign*, May 1986, pp. 25, 26.)

— Russell M. Nelson

The Lord doesn't really need us to take care of the poor, but *we* need this experience; for it is only through our learning how to take care of each other that we develop within us the Christlike love and disposition necessary to qualify us to return to his presence. (*Ensign*, November 1981, p. 92.)

— Marion G. Romney

The prime duty of help to the poor by the Church is not to bring temporal relief to their needs, but salvation to their souls. (*CR*, October 1977, p. 118.)

— Marion G. Romney

——— Pornography ———

A person who becomes involved in obscenity soon acquires distorted views of personal conduct. He becomes unable to relate to others in a normal, healthy way. Like most other habits, an addictive effect begins to take hold of him. A diet of violence or pornography dulls the senses, and future exposures need to be rougher and more extreme. Soon the person is desensitized and is unable to react in a sensitive, caring, responsible manner, especially to those in his own home and family. Good people can become infested with this material and it can have terrifying, destructive consequences. (*Ensign*, November 1977, p. 71.)

— *Marvin J. Ashton*

Be as strong as Daniel in keeping distance between yourself and the evil practices and places of the world. Don't let the wrong kinds of books, pictures, and other reading material be near you to tempt you to take even the slightest glance. Such materials can intoxicate and destroy your mind just as surely as liquor and drugs can intoxicate and destroy your body.

Have the courage to turn off unfit television programs, and stay away from movies and videotapes that would fill your mind with thought of evil and violence. Remember, the scripture has said, "For as [a man] thinketh in his heart, so is he." (Prov. 23:7.) (*Ensign*, November 1985, p. 48.)

— *L. Tom Perry*

Let each of us resolve this day to keep our minds, our bodies, and our spirits free from the corrupting influence of pornography, including everything that is obscene and indecent. Let it have no place in our homes, our minds, or our hearts. (*Ensign*, November 1984, p. 72.)

— *David B. Haight*

Read only good books. Shun as deadly poison the "sexy" books. They only befoul your minds, lead to base and foul thoughts, and if persisted in, lead to sin and shame.

— *J. Reuben Clark, Jr.*

Teach your children to avoid smut as the plague it is. As citizens, join in the fight against obscenity in your communities. Do not be lulled into inaction by the pornographic profiteers who say that to remove obscenity is to deny people the rights of free choice. Do not let them masquerade licentiousness as liberty. (*Ensign*, November 1976, p. 4.)

— *Spencer W. Kimball*

Unfortunately, we live now in a sex-saturated society. Pornography comes at us from all sides, . . .

There is no way to blank it out entirely. But we can do something to offset its corrosive influence. We can expose our children to good reading. Let them grow with good books and good Church magazines around them. (*Ensign*, May 1982, p. 42.)

— *Gordon B. Hinckley*

We are surrounded by the promotional literature of illicit sexual relations on the printed page and on the screen. For your own good, avoid it. Pornographic or erotic stories and pictures are worse than filthy or polluted food. The body has defenses to rid itself of unwholesome food, but the brain won't vomit back filth. Once recorded it will always remain subject to recall, flashing its perverted images across your mind, and drawing you away from the wholesome things in life. (Quoted by N. Eldon Tanner, *Ensign*, January 1974, p. 7.)

— *Dallin Oaks*

We are unalterably opposed to sexual immorality and to all manner of obscenity. We proclaim in the strongest terms possible against the evil and wicked designs of men who would betray virtuous manhood and womanhood, enticing them to thought and actions leading to vice, the lowering of standards of clean living, and the breaking up of the home.

We call upon the members of the Church and all other right-thinking people to join in a concerted movement to fight pornography wherever it may be found. (*Church News*, February 26, 1966, p. 3.)

— *The First Presidency*

See also CHASTITY, ENTERTAINMENT

——— **Potential** ———

God will judge you by the way you make use of all your possibilities. (*Ensign*, November 1983, p. 62.)

— *Marvin J. Ashton*

In the private sanctuary of one's own conscience lies that spirit, that determination to cast off the old person and to measure up to the stature of true potential. (*Ensign*, May 1987, p. 69.)

— *Thomas S. Monson*

It is a denial of the divinity within us to doubt our potential and our possibilities. (*Ensign*, May 1986, p. 21.)

— *James E. Faust*

It is a happy day when we come to know that with God's help nothing is impossible for us. (*Ensign*, May 1979, p. 69.)

— *Marvin J. Ashton*

One of the great teachings of . . . the Lord Jesus Christ, was that you and I carry within us immense possibilities. In urging us to be perfect as our Father in Heaven is perfect, Jesus was not taunting us or teasing us. He was telling us a powerful truth about our possibilities and about our potential. It is a truth almost too stunning to contemplate. Jesus, who could not lie, sought to beckon us to move further along the pathway to perfection. (*Ensign*, August 1979, p. 7.)

— *Spencer W. Kimball*

Those who marched in Zion's Camp were not exploring the Missouri countryside but their own possibilities. (*Ensign*, November 1976, p. 14.)

— *Neal A. Maxwell*

We do not have to measure our potential for success by our known capabilities alone. We can count on the power of God and its expanding influence on our lives. We can know that our ability and strength can be magnified to meet any challenge that confronts us. (*Ensign*, November 1979, p. 71.)

— *Richard G. Scott*

What is our greatest potential? Is it not to achieve godhood ourselves? (*Ensign*, March 1976, p. 4.)

— *Spencer W. Kimball*

See also GREATNESS, INDIVIDUALITY, MAN, PROGRESSION, SELF-WORTH, TALENTS

──────── **Power** ────────

In knowledge there is power. God has more power than all other beings, because he has greater knowledge; and hence he knows how to subject all other beings to him. He has power over all. (*HC*, 5:340.)

— *Joseph Smith*

Power is never good except he be good that has it. (*CR*, October 1958, p. 67.)

— *Thorpe B. Isaacson*

Those who cling to power at the expense of principle often end up doing almost anything to perpetuate their power.

— *Spencer W. Kimball*

——— Prayer ———

A mammoth 747 jetliner, while flying over the Pacific, sustained a gigantic tear in its side, ejecting nine passengers to their deaths, and threatening the lives of all. When the pilot, Captain David Cronin, was interviewed, having brought the craft back safely to Honolulu, he was asked, "What did you do when the place ripped open? How did you cope?"
Captain Cronin replied, "I prayed, then went to work."
My brethren, this is an inspired plan for each of us to follow: Pray, and then go to work. (*Ensign*, May 1989, p. 44.)

— *Thomas S. Monson*

But is prayer only one-way communication? No! . . . At the end of our prayers, we need to do some intense listening—even for several minutes. We have prayed for counsel and help. Now we must "be still, and know the [he is] God" (Ps. 46:10.) . . .
Sometimes ideas flood our mind as we listen after our prayers. Sometimes feelings press upon us. A spirit of calmness assures us that all will be well. But always, if we have been honest and earnest, we will experience a good feeling—a feeling of warmth for our Father in Heaven and a sense of his love for us. (*Ensign*, October 1981, p. 5.)

— *Spencer W. Kimball*

Do not forget to pray. Don't suppose for a moment that you are as safe and secure in the favor of the Lord when you feel independent of Him as you will be if you feel your dependence upon Him all the day long. (*CR*, April 1915, p. 140.)

— *Joseph F. Smith*

I fear, as a people, we do not pray enough, in faith. We should call upon the Lord in mighty prayer and make all our wants known unto him. For if he does not protect and deliver us and save us, no other power will. (*MS*, 48:806.)

— *Wilford Woodruff*

If prayer is only a spasmodic cry at the time of crisis, then it is utterly selfish, and we come to think of God as a repairman or a service agency to help us only in our emergencies. (*Ensign*, November 1977, p. 52.)

— *Howard W. Hunter*

If prayer is to leave the public schools, let the ridicule of prayer leave also. (*Ensign*, September 1973, p. 38.)

— *Boyd K. Packer*

If we draw near to him, he will draw near to us if we seek him early, we shall find him. (*JD*, 13:312.)

— *Brigham Young*

If you find [anger] coming on you, go off to some place where you cannot be heard; let none of your family see you or hear you, while it is upon you, but struggle till it leaves you; and pray for strength to overcome. . . . if, when the time for prayer comes, you have not the spirit of prayer upon you, and your knees are unwilling to bow, say to them, "Knees, get down there," make them bend, and remain there until you obtain the Spirit of the Lord. (*JD*, 11:290.)

— *Brigham Young*

Let all persons be fervent in prayer until they know the things of God for themselves and become certain that they are walking in the path that leads to everlasting life. (*JD*, 9:150.)

— *Brigham Young*

Let every man and every woman call upon the name of the Lord, and that, too, from a pure heart, while they are at work as well as in their closet; while they are in public as well as while they are in private, asking the Father in the name of Jesus, to bless them, and to preserve and guide in, and to teach them, the way of life and salvation and to enable them so to live that they will obtain this eternal salvation that we are after. (*JD*, 15:63.)

— *Brigham Young*

No divine commandment has been more frequently repeated than the commandment to pray in the name of the Lord Jesus Christ. (*Ensign*, November 1979, p. 16).

— *Marion G. Romney*

Petitioning in prayer has taught me, again and again, that the vault of heaven with all its blessings is to be opened only by a combination lock. One tumbler falls when there is faith, a second when there is personal righteousness; the third and final tumbler falls only when what is sought is, in God's judgment—not ours— right for us. Sometimes we pound on the vault door for something we want very much and wonder why the door does not open. We would be very spoiled children if that vault door opened any more easily than it does. I can tell, looking back, that God truly loves me by inventorying the petitions He has refused to grant me. Our rejected petitions tell us much about ourselves but also much about our flawless Father. (*New Era*, April 1978, p. 6.)

— *Neal A. Maxwell*

Nothing is more simple than prayer. . . . If we have faith that our Heavenly Father lives and that we can commune with Him in a very direct way, then prayer becomes one of the most beautiful, lovely, simple acts that we can do. (*Ensign*, May 1988, p. 28.)

— *Glen L. Rudd*

Prayer is often difficult and strenuous—just plain hard work. If you really want to converse with the Lord, you must count on a mighty struggle. Receiving inspiration and revelation through prayer is one of the greatest achievements of man, and to expect that blessing without effort is contrary to the order of heaven. One has to break the prayer barrier by knocking and knocking. We should not be dismayed when much knocking at first seems to avail little. There are few exercises in faith greater than that of praying persistently, and the very act of knocking will capacitate us to accept, understand, and implement the new-found truths that may be revealed to us. Nothing teaches us how to pray more effectively than forcing ourselves to pray. However, as in skiing, the "learning how" can be exciting—the realization that we are participating in an effort that has brought most, if not all, celestial truths to the earth creates a sense of spiritual adventure second to none. (*JD*, 13:155.)

— *Brigham Young*

Prayer is the key which unlocks the door and lets Christ into our lives. (*Ensign*, May 1978, p. 50.)

— *Marion G. Romney*

Prayer is the passport to spiritual power. (*Ensign*, November 1990, p. 47.)

— *Thomas S. Monson*

Prayer is the way and means, given us by our Creator, whereby we can counsel and communicate with him. It is one of the chief cornerstones of pure and perfect worship. (*Ensign*, May 1984, p. 32.)

— *Bruce R. McConkie*

Prayer keeps man from sin, and sin keeps man from prayer. (Quoted by H. Burke Peterson, *Ensign*, January 1974, p. 19.)

— *Brigham Young*

Prayer is the instrument of miracles. (Quoted by Devere Harris, *Ensign*, November 1984, p. 27.)

— *Marion G. Romney*

Sincere praying implies that when we ask for any virtue or blessing we should work for the blessing and cultivate the virtue. (*True to the Faith*, Llewelyn R. McKay, comp., Salt Lake City: Bookcraft, 1966, p. 208.)

— *David O. McKay*

To learn to communicate with Him, to learn to pray effectively, requires diligence and dedication and desire on our part. I wonder sometimes of we are willing to pay the price for an answer from the Lord.

— *H. Burke Peterson*

To better understand prayer, I have listened to the counsel of others, pondered the scriptures, and studied the lives of prophets and others. Yet what seems most helpful is seeing in my mind a child approaching trustingly a loving, kind, wise, understanding Father, who wants us to succeed.

Don't worry about your clumsily expressed feelings. Just talk to your Father. He hears every prayer and answers it in His way. (*Ensign*, November 1989, pp. 30-31.)

— *Richard G. Scott*

To pray . . . may I suggest a process to follow: go where you can be alone, go where you can think, go where you can kneel, go where you can speak out loud to him. . . . Now picture him in your mind's eye. Think to whom you are speaking, control your thoughts—don't let them wander, address him as your Father and your friend. Now tell him things you really feel to tell him—not trite phrases that have little meaning, but have a sincere, heartfelt conversation with him. Confide in him, ask him for forgiveness, plead with him, enjoy him, thank him, express your love to him, and then listen for his answers. (*Ensign*, January 1974, p. 19.)

— *H. Burke Peterson*

We may say that our work drives us and that we have not time to pray, hardly time to eat our breakfasts. Then let the breakfasts go, and pray; . . . It matters not whether you or I feel like praying; when the time comes to pray, pray. . . . My doctrine is, it is your duty to pray. . . . Let no person give up prayer because he has not the spirit of prayer; neither let any earthly circumstance hurry you while in the performance of this important duty.

— Brigham Young

The first and most fundamental virtue in effective prayer is faith.

— David O. McKay

We must seek help from the great unseen world about us, from God and his messengers. We call that prayer. A man never finds perfect peace, never reaches afar unless he penetrates to some degree the unseen world, and reaches out to touch the hands, as it were, of those who live in that unseen world, the world out of which we came, the world into which we shall go. (*CR*, October 1938, p. 129.)

— John A. Widtsoe

When I was a boy, I couldn't always remember to say my prayers at night. I wanted to, but sometimes I would forget because I'd be too sleepy. When I got older, I had a great idea.

If I were you, I would go out in the field and find a rock about the size of your fist. I'd wash it clean and put it under my pillow. Then, when I would get in bed at night and drop my head on my pillow—crack! I would remember to get out of bed and kneel down by it. I would then put the rock on the floor by my bed and go to sleep. Then, in the morning, I would jump out of bed, and as my foot would come down on the rock—"Ouch!" And I would remember to kneel down and say my morning prayers. Sometimes we need reminders to form good habits. (*Ensign*, November 1981, p. 43.)

— H. Burke Peterson

When I was taught to pray, I learned that I was actually talking to God, in the name of Jesus Christ, through the power of the Holy Ghost. . . . I had been told that I was a son of God, a child of God, and that he was interested in me, that he knew me and knew best what was right for me. We were taught to pray at meals; we were taught to pray in the morning; we were taught to pray at night. And we were taught that our Father in Heaven was the one to whom we were talking.

I wonder how many of us know that we are spirit children of God; and when we are praying, whether it's over a meal, beginning or closing of a meeting, or at a baptism or confirmation, or the blessing of the bread and water in the sacrament, that we are actually talking to God. He is there, he hears our prayers, and he blesses us. (*Ensign*, May 1981, p. 50.)

— N. Eldon Tanner

See also HEAVENLY FATHER, REVELATION

Preexistence

All those salient truths which come home so forcibly to the head and heart seem but the awakening of the memories of the spirit. Can we know anything here that we did not know before we came? (*GD,* p. 13.)

— *Joseph F. Smith*

As a father, I put my arms around each of my boys as they left to serve their missions and whispered in their ears, "Return with honor." I can picture our Father in Heaven putting his arms around each of us as we left his presence and whispering, "Return with honor." (*Ensign,* May 1990, p. 41.)

— *Robert D. Hales*

Each one of us will be judged when we leave this earth according to his or her deeds during out lives here in mortality. Isn't it just as reasonable to believe that what we have received here in this earth life was given to each of us according to the merits of our conduct before we came here? (*Ensign,* January 1974, p. 5.)

— *Harold B. Lee*

I believe that every person who is called to do an important work in the kingdom of God, was called to that work and foreordained to that work before the world was. (*HC,* 6:364.)

— *Joseph Smith*

Jesus said there would be certain souls that would not be saved; and the devil said he could save them all, and laid his plans before the grand council, who gave their vote in favor of Jesus Christ. So the devil rose up in rebellion against God, and was cast down. (*TPJS,* p. 357.)

— *Joseph Smith*

The Prophet Joseph Smith, and . . . Hyrum Smith, Brigham Young, John Taylor, Wilford Woodruff, and other choice spirits who were reserved to come forth in the fullness of times to take part in laying the foundations of the great Latter-day work, . . . were also among the noble and great ones who were chosen in the beginning to be rulers in the Church of God. Even before they were born, they, with many others, received their first lessons in the world of spirits, and were prepared to come forth in the due time of the Lord to labor in his vineyard for the salvation of the souls of men. (*GD,* p. 475.)

— *Joseph F. Smith*

The War in Heaven

The war in heaven was not a war of bloodshed. It was a war of conflicting ideas—the beginning of contention. (*Ensign,* May 1989, p. 69.)

— *Russell M. Nelson*

There are many who were foreordained before the world was, to a greater state than they have prepared themselves for here. (*Ensign,* January 1974, p. 4.)

— *Harold B. Lee*

There is not a person here today but what is a son or a daughter of [God]. In the spirit world their spirits were first begotten and brought forth, and they lived there with their parents for ages before they came here. This, perhaps, is hard for many to believe, but it is the greatest nonsense in the world not to believe it. If you do not believe it, cease to call him Father; and when you pray, pray to some other character. (*JD,* 4:216.)

— *Brigham Young*

We are Joseph's spiritual heirs, called ages and ages ago—in the "there and then"—for the duties which await us "here and now!" (*Ensign,* May 1986, p. 36.)

— *Neal A. Maxwell*

We have forgotten! . . . But our forgetfulness cannot alter the facts. (*JD,* 7:315.)

— *Orson Hyde*

See also MAN, PLAN OF SALVATION

——— Preparedness ———

Family preparedness has been a long-established welfare principle. It is even more urgent today.

I ask you earnestly, have you provided for your family a year's supply of food, clothing, and, where possible, fuel? The revelation to produce and store food may be as essential to our temporal welfare today as boarding the ark was to the people in the days of Noah. (*Ensign,* November 1987, p. 49.)

— *Ezra Taft Benson*

For twenty-six years I was involved in the grocery industry. . . . I remember the effects that strikes, earthquakes, and rumors of war had on many very active Latter-day Saints. Like the five foolish virgins, they rushed to the store to buy food, caught in the panic of knowing that direction had been given by the prophet but not having followed that direction—fearful that maybe they had procrastinated until it was everlastingly too late.

It was interesting because only in Latter-day Saint communities did people seem to buy with abandon. It was not a few Latter-day Saints—it was a significant number. It caused great increases in sales. . . .

How foolish we can sometimes be! We have a living prophet; we have God's living oracles, the First Presidency and the Council of the Twelve Apostles. Let us follow the Brethren and be constant. We need have no fear if we are prepared. (*Ensign*, May 1976, p. 116.)

— Vaughn J. Featherstone

Great trials lie ahead. All of the sorrows and perils of the past are but a foretaste of what is yet to be. And we must prepare ourselves temporally and spiritually. (*Ensign*, May 1979, p. 92.)

— Bruce R. McConkie

I stand before the Church this day and raise the warning voice. . . . It is a voice calling upon the Lord's people to prepare for the troubles and desolations which are about to be poured out upon the world without measure.

For the moment we live in a day of peace and prosperity but it shall not ever be thus. Great trials lie ahead. All of the sorrows and perils of the past are but a foretaste of what is yet to be. And we must prepare ourselves temporally and spiritually. (*Ensign*, May 1979, p. 92.)

— Bruce R. McConkie

I wonder how many Saints will be able to withstand the disaster of their own personal flood by showing faith in the advice of modern prophets and building an ark of family preparedness. (*Ensign*, May 1981, p. 26.)

— Loren C. Dunn

Learn to sustain yourselves; lay up grain and flour, and save it against a day of scarcity. (*DBY*, p. 293.)

— Brigham Young

Let every head of every household see to it that he has on hand enough food and clothing, and, where possible, fuel also, for at least a year ahead. . . .

Cash is not food, it is not clothing, it is not coal, it is not shelter; and we have got to the place where no matter how much cash we have, we cannot secure those things in the quantities which we may need. . . . All that you can be certain you will have is that which you produce. (*CR*, April 1937, p. 26.)

— J. Reuben Clark, Jr.

Midnight is so late for those who have procrastinated. (*Faith Precedes the Miracle*, Salt Lake City: Deseret Book Co., 1978, p. 256.)

— *Spencer W. Kimball*

Spiritual Preparedness

Some reservoirs are to store water. Some are to store food, as we do in our family welfare program and as Joseph did in the land of Egypt during the seven years of plenty. There should also be reservoirs of knowledge to meet the future needs; reservoirs of courage to overcome the floods of fear that put uncertainty in our lives; reservoirs of physical strength to help us meet the frequent burdens of work and illness; reservoirs of goodness; reservoirs of stamina; reservoirs of faith. (*Ensign*, November 1977, p. 5.)

— *Spencer W. Kimball*

It is better to prepare and prevent than to repair and repent!

— *Ezra Taft Benson*

The counsel to have a year's supply of basic food, clothing, and commodities was given fifty years ago and has been repeated many times since. Every father and mother are the family's storekeepers. They should store whatever their own family would like to have in the case of an emergency. Most of us cannot afford to store a year's supply of luxury items, but find it more practical to store staples that might keep us from starving in case of emergency. Surely we all hope that the hour of need will never come. Some have said, "We have followed this counsel in the past and have never had need to use our year's supply, so we have difficulty keeping this in mind as a major priority." Perhaps following this counsel could be the reason why they have not needed to use their reserve. (*Ensign*, May 1986, p. 22.)

— *James E. Faust*

There are many very good people who keep most of the Lord's commandments with respect to the virtuous side of life, but who overlook His commandments in temporal things. They do not heed His warning to prepare for a possible future emergency, . . . To prepare for the future is part of God's eternal plan, both spiritually and temporally. To protect ourselves against reversals and hardships is only good sense. (*Ensign*, May 1981, p. 62.)

— *Mark E. Petersen*

We have had many calamities in this past period. It seems that every day or two there is an earthquake or a flood or a tornado or distress that brings trouble to many people. I am grateful to see that our people and our leaders are beginning to catch the vision of their self-help. . . . Now I think the time is coming when there will be more distresses, when there may be more tornadoes, and more floods, . . . more earthquakes. . . . I think they will be increasing probably as we come nearer to the end, and so we must be prepared for this. (*CR*, April 11974, pp. 183-84.)

— *Spencer W. Kimball*

We cannot progress without attending to our own personal and family preparedness on a regular basis. Preparedness is not something static, it is ever changing. I know of no situation in life where it is not necessary. (*Ensign*, November 1978, p. 84.)

— *H. Burke Peterson*

We will see the day when we live on what we produce. (*CR*, April 1975, p. 165.)

— *Marion G. Romney*

What a wonderful things it is to plant in the heart of a boy the compelling axiom—"be prepared." Be prepared for what? For tieing knots, yes. Knot tieing is Tenderfoot duty, but it is important. In one sense this whole business of living and doing is one of tieing knots, the kind of knots that will hold and not give under stress and strain. We see all around us the evidence of failure, of knots that slipped when they should have held. They are evident in career failures, in business failures, in professional failures, in marriage failures. To be able to tie the right knot for the right reason, for the right occasion, and to have it hold against every stress is a part of the process of being prepared. (Quoted by Vaughn J. Featherstone, *Ensign*, November 1987, pp. 28-29.)

— *Gordon B. Hinckley*

You do not need to go into debt . . . to obtain a year's supply. Plan to build up your food supply just as you would a savings account. Save a little for storage each paycheck. Can or bottle fruit and vegetables from your gardens and orchards. Learn how to preserve food through drying and possibly freezing. Make your storage a part of your budget. Store seeds and have sufficient tools on hand to do the job. If you are saving and planning for a second car or a TV set or some item which merely adds to your comfort or pleasure, you may need to change your priorities. We urge you to do this prayerfully and *do it now*. (*Ensign*, November 1980, p. 33.)

— *Ezra Taft Benson*

See also OBEDIENCE, SELF-SUFFICIENCY, TEMPORAL WELFARE

——— Pride ———

Being self-taught is no disgrace; but being self-certified is another matter. (*OAT*, p. 134.)

— *Hugh Nibley*

Fear of men's judgment manifests itself in competition for men's approval. The proud love "the praise of men more than the praise of God." (John 12:42-43.) . . . When pride has a hold on our hearts, we lose our independence of the world and deliver our freedoms to the bondage of men's judgment. The world shouts louder than the whisperings of the Holy Ghost. The reasoning of men overrides the revelations of God, and the proud let go of the iron rod. (*Ensign*, May 1986, p. 5.)

— *Ezra Taft Benson*

He whose obedience or humility is more for the gallery than for God, who seeks to exalt self and not Savior, is not acceptable to Him and shall be brought down. (*Ensign*, November 1976. p. 32.)

— *Marion D. Hanks*

It is impossible to pray sincerely to God the Father and live insincerely toward His children. It is inconsistent for a man to be humble toward God and be proud toward His children. (Address, Brigham Young University, February 22, 1966, p. 8.)

— *Stephen R. Covey*

One of Satan's greatest tools is pride: to cause a man or a woman to center so much attention on self that he or she becomes insensitive to their Creator or fellow beings. (*Ensign*, May 1979, p. 34.)

— *Ezra Taft Benson*

One of the most common of all sins among worldly people is relying on then boasting in the arm of flesh. This is a most serious evil. It is a sin born of pride, a sin that creates a frame of mind which keeps men from turning to the Lord and accepting his saving grace. When a man knowingly or unknowingly engages in self-exultation because of his riches, his political power, his worldly learning, his physical prowess, his business ability, or even his works of righteousness, he is not in tune with the Spirit of the Lord. (*Ensign*, May 1990, p. 67.)

— *Marvin J. Ashton*

Pride does not look up to God and care about what is right. It looks sideways to man and argues who is right. Pride is manifest in the spirit of contention.

Was it not through pride that the devil became the devil? Christ wanted to serve. The devil wanted to rule. Christ wanted to bring men to where He was. The devil wanted to be above men.

Christ removed self as the force in His perfect life. It was not *my* will, but *thine* be done.

Pride is characterized by "What do I want out of life?" rather than by "What would God have me do with my life?" It is self-will as opposed to God's will. It is the fear of man over the fear of God. (*Ensign*, May 1986, pp. 6-7.)

— *Ezra Taft Benson*

Pride is a very misunderstood sin, and many are sinning in ignorance.

— *Ezra Taft Benson*

Pride is the most deadly spiritual virus. (*Ensign*, May 1989, p. 59.)

— *Boyd K. Packer*

Pride is the universal sin, the great vice. . . . It was essentially the sin of pride that kept us from establishing Zion in the days of the Prophet Joseph Smith. It was the same sin of pride that brought consecration to an end among the Nephites.

Pride is the great stumbling block to Zion. I repeat: Pride *is* the great stumbling block to Zion. (*Ensign*, May 1989, pp. 6, 7.)

— *Ezra Taft Benson*

Sodom and Gomorrah and later Jerusalem were destroyed as a result of pride, selfishness, and the haughtiness of otherwise good people who refused to unite in the cause of righteousness. (*Ensign*, March 1971, p. 29.)

— *Theodore M. Burton*

Walk away from your investment in the penny stock of pride; it never pays dividends. (*Ensign*, May 1982, p. 39.)

— *Neal A. Maxwell*

What we read about in the Book of Mormon is the Nephite disease—and we have it! . . . [Their] doom was brought on them by pride which in turn was engendered by the riches of the earth. (*OAT*, p. 88.)

— *Hugh Nibley*

See also HUMILITY, WORLDLINESS

——— Priesthood ———

A priesthood holder acts as a type of mediator between the people and God, representing them officially in worship and in holy ordinances. Because he represents God, he cannot take this office to himself but must be called of God. In a special sense, a bearer of this priesthood power and authority delegated by God belongs to God. He must be holy and clean before Him. He represents the Lord and acts as His agent when officiating in or performing his priestly duties. Such priesthood rights are inseparably connected with the powers of heaven and can, therefore, be handled or utilized effectively only on the basis of personal righteousness. (D&C 121:36.) (*Ensign*, November 1985, p. 41.)

— *Rex D. Pinegar*

All of you, of course, are familiar with binoculars. When you put the lenses to your eyes and focus them, you magnify and in effect bring closer all within your field of vision. But if you turn them around and look through the other end, you diminish and make more distant that which you see.

So it is with our actions as holders of the priesthood. When we live up to our high and holy calling, when we show love for God through service to fellowmen, when we use our strength and talents to build faith and spread truth, we magnify our priesthood. When, on the other hand, we live lives of selfishness, when we indulge in sin, when we set our sights only on the things of the world rather than on the things of God, we diminish our priesthood. (*Ensign*, May 1989, p. 47.)

— *Gordon B. Hinckley*

By reason of our ordination to the priesthood, we are the most honored of all men. By the same token, we are charged with the greatest responsibility. We should diligently try—through prayer, study, and the faithful performance of our priesthood duties—to learn all we can about the priesthood. Even so, we will not be able, in mortal life, to fully comprehend it. (*Ensign*, May 1982, p. 43.)

— *Marion G. Romney*

High priests, seventies, and elders of Israel, . . . have you neglected qualifying yourselves in your holy callings, and let the cares of the world occupy your entire thoughts and attention, and your minds become dull, your spiritual armor rusty and but little room found in you for the Holy Ghost to abide?

Brethren, your eye should be single to the glory of God, to harkening to the counsel of the living prophet and to the building up of Zion; then your bodies would be filled with spirit, and your understandings with light, and your hearts with joy, and your souls would be quickened into eternal life with the power of the Holy Ghost. You would then become the depositories of that wisdom and knowledge which would qualify you to be saviors unto your brethren and your posterity. (*JD,* 4:154-55.)

— Lorenzo Snow

All those who receive the Melchizedek priesthood in this life were, as Alma teaches, "called and prepared from the foundation of the world according to the foreknowledge of God," because they were among the noble and great in that premortal sphere. (Alma 13:3.) (*CR,* April 1974, p. 102.)

— Bruce R. McConkie

I am of the persuasion that the greatest preparation we can make to relieve ourselves from fear of the future will not be the year's supply we accumulate in our basements, the savings accounts we build, or the stocks and bonds we store in our safety deposit boxes. As important as these are for the protection of our family, our real security, I believe, will be found in our understanding of the priesthood organization and in sound application of priesthood principles. (*Ensign,* November 1981, p. 39.)

— L. Tom Perry

If a man gets a fullness of the priesthood of God he has to get it in the same way that Jesus Christ obtained it, and that was by keeping *all* the commandments and obeying *all* the ordinances of the house of the Lord. (*TPJS,* p. 308.)

— Joseph Smith

In a priesthood blessing a servant of the Lord exercises the priesthood, as moved upon by the Holy Ghost, to call upon the powers of heaven for the benefit of the person being blessed. Such blessings are conferred by holders of the Melchizedek Priesthood, which has the keys of all the spiritual blessings of the Church (see D&C 107:18,67). (*Ensign,* May 1987, p. 36.)

— Dallin H. Oaks

No man, however great his intellectual attainments, however vast and far-reaching his service may be, arrives at the full measure of his sonship and the manhood the Lord intended him to have, without the investitures of the Holy Priesthood. (*CR,* October 1955, p. 88.)

— Stephen L Richards

One breaks the priesthood covenant by transgressing commandments—but also by leaving undone his duties. Accordingly, to break this covenant one needs only to do nothing. (*TSWK,* p. 497.)

— Spencer W. Kimball

One great privilege of the priesthood is to obtain revelations of the mind and will of God. (*HC*, 2:477.)

— *Joseph Smith*

Power in the priesthood, the power to bless and guide and teach, the power to forgive and forget, the power to give positive direction to a family . . . comes through righteousness. The laying on of hands we all received is not enough. Priesthood power comes to those prepared to receive it as a result of the righteous pattern of their lives. (*Ensign*, November 1982, p. 43.)

— *H. Burke Peterson*

Priesthood is power like none other on earth or in heaven. It is the very power of God himself, the power by which the worlds were made, the power by which all things are regulated, upheld, and preserved.

It is the power of faith, the faith by which the Father creates and governs. . . .

Faith and priesthood go hand in hand. Faith is power and power is priesthood. (*Ensign*, May 1982, p. 32.)

— *Bruce R. McConkie*

The Church is the organized Priesthood of God, the priesthood can exist without the Church, but the Church cannot exist without the priesthood.

— *J. Reuben Clark, Jr.*

The doctrine of the priesthood is known only by personal revelation. It comes, line upon line and precept upon precept, by the power of the Holy Ghost to those who love and serve God with all their heart, might, mind, and strength. (See D&C 98:12; D&C 121:45.) (*Ensign*, May 1982, p. 32.)

— *Bruce R. McConkie*

The fact that they hold the priesthood will be to many men a condemnation, because of the manner in which they have treated it, regarding it as though it were something very ordinary. Priesthood is a word as the titles apostle, prophet, are words and names that ought not to be repeated unnecessarily. We ought to honor these sacred names that bring to us the blessings when we understand.

— *George Albert Smith*

The holy priesthood is the channel through which God communicates and deals with man upon the earth; and the heavenly messengers that have visited the earth to communicate with man are men who held and honored the priesthood while in the flesh. (*Discourses of Wilford Woodruff*, selected by G. Homer Durham, Salt Lake City: Bookcraft, 1946, p. 64.)

— *Wilford Woodruff*

The Lord has made clear that they who receive his priesthood receive him. And I think that means more than just sitting in a chair and having somebody put his hands upon your head. I think when you receive it, you accept it. You do not just merely sit. "And he that receiveth my Father receiveth my Father's kingdom; therefore all that my Father hath shall be given unto him." Can you imagine anything greater? Shouldn't we be frightened, almost awed as we contemplate the honor we have and the responsibility we have that has come from the oath and the covenant. (*Stockholm Sweden Area Conference Report,* 1974, p. 100.)

— *Spencer W. Kimball*

The Lord has promised a guaranteed destiny for all who magnify the priesthood; and that destiny is eternal life. (*Ensign,* May 1987, pp. 40-41.)

— *Robert L. Simpson*

The Melchizedek Priesthood . . . is the channel through which all knowledge, doctrine, the plan of salvation and every important matter is revealed from heaven. (*HC,* 4:226-32.)

— *Joseph Smith*

The object of the priesthood is to make all men happy, to diffuse information, to make all partakers of the same blessings in their turn. (*JD,* 9:22.)

— *Lorenzo Snow*

The ordinances which we perform are administered in the name of Jesus Christ. This is something we should never forget and never overlook, for in the exercise of our priesthood, we are acting in behalf of God our Eternal Father and Jesus Christ, His Son. (*Ensign,* May 1988, p. 45.)

— *Gordon B. Hinckley*

The power of the priesthood is limitless but God has wisely placed upon each of us certain limitations. I may develop priesthood power as I perfect my life, yet I am grateful that even through the priesthood, I cannot heal all the sick. I might heal people who should die. I might relieve people of suffering who should suffer. I fear I would frustrate the purposes of God. (*Faith Precedes the Miracle,* Spencer W. Kimball, Salt Lake City: Deseret Book Co. 1978, p. 99.)

— *Spencer W. Kimball*

The priesthood cannot be conferred like a diploma. It cannot be handed to you as a certificate. It cannot be delivered to you as a message or sent to you in a letter. It comes only by proper ordination. An authorized holder of the priesthood has to be there. He must place his hands upon your head and ordain you. That is one reason why the General Authorities travel so much—to convey the keys of priesthood authority. Every stake president everywhere in the world has received his authority under the hands of one of the presiding brethren of the Church. There has never been one exception. (*Ensign,* November 1981, p. 32.)

— Boyd K. Packer

The priesthood in general is the authority given to man to act for God. Every man ordained to any degree of the priesthood, has this authority delegated to him.

But it is necessary that every act performed under this authority shall be done at the proper time and place, in the proper way, and after the proper order. The power of directing these labors constitutes the *keys* of the priesthood. (*IE,* 4:230.)

— Joseph F. Smith

The priesthood is . . . invulnerable because it is indivisible. As long as *one* true holder of the higher priesthood is on the earth the potentiality of the Church is there. It suggests the idea of cloning, that from one cell one can produce a whole organism. (*OAT,* p. 13.)

— Hugh Nibley

The priesthood is an everlasting principle, and existed wit God from eternity, and will, to eternity, without beginning of days or end of years. (*TPJS,* p. 157.)

— Joseph Smith

The priesthood is called an everlasting priesthood; it ministers in time and in eternity.

— John Taylor

The priesthood is the power and authority of God, delegated to man on earth, to act in all things for the salvation of men. (*Ensign,* November 1977, p. 33.)

— Bruce R. McConkie

The priesthood of the Son of God is the law by which the worlds are, were, and will continue forever and ever. It is that system that brings worlds into existence and peoples them, gives them their revolution—their days, weeks, months, years, their seasons and times and by which they are rolled up as a scroll, as it were, and go into a higher state of existence. (*JD,* 15:127.)

— Brigham Young

The priesthood will give you character, renown, wisdom, power and authority, and [will] build you up among the children of men. [It will] exalt you to peace and happiness, to thrones and dominions, even through countless eternities. (*MS,* 13:362.)

— Lorenzo Snow

The responsibility to perform [your] labor came to you from the Son of God. You are his servants. You will be held accountable to him for your stewardship. (*Seek Ye Earnestly* . . . , Salt Lake City: Deseret Book Co., 1970, pp. 235-36.)
— *Joseph Fielding Smith*

There is never a time, there never will come a time to those who hold the Priesthood . . . , when men can say of themselves that they have done enough. So long as life lasts, and so long as we possess ability to do good, to labor for the upbuilding of Zion, and for the benefit of the human family, we ought, with willingness, to yield with alacrity to the requirements made of us to do our duty, little or great. (*GD*, p. 188.)
— *Joseph F. Smith*

There is no exaltation in the kingdom of God without the fullness of the priesthood, and every man who receives the Melchizedek Priesthood does so with an oath and a covenant that he shall be exalted.

The covenant on man's part is that he will magnify his calling in the priesthood, and that he will live by every word that proceedeth forth from the mouth of God, and that he will keep the commandments.

The covenant on the lord's part is that if man does as he promises, then all that the Father hath shall be given unto him; and this is such a solemn and important promise that the Lord swears with an oath that it shall come to pass. (*Era*, June 1970, p. 66.)
— *Joseph Fielding Smith*

There is no new organization necessary to take care of the needs of this people. All that is necessary is to put the priesthood of God to work. (*CR*, October 1972, p. 124.)
— *Harold B. Lee*

There Must be Unity in the Priesthood
We of the priesthood are all part of the army of the Lord. We must be united. An army that is disorganized will not be victorious. It is imperative that we close ranks, that we march together as one. We cannot have division among us and expect victory. We cannot have disloyalty and expect unity. We cannot be unclean and expect the help of the Almighty. (*Ensign*, November 1986, p. 44.)
— *Gordon B. Hinckley*

Think what it means to hold keys of authority which—if exercised in wisdom and in righteousness—are bound to be respected by the Father, the Son, and the Holy Ghost. (*IE*, December 1917, p. 105.)
— *Joseph F. Smith*

We Can Make a Difference

As bearers of the priesthood, we have been placed on earth in troubled times. We live in a complex world with currents of conflict everywhere to be found. Political machinations ruin the stability of nations, despots grasp for power, and segments of society seem forever downtrodden, deprived of opportunity and left with a feeling of failure.

We who have been ordained to the priesthood of God can make a difference. When we qualify for the help of the Lord, we can build boys, we can mend men, we can accomplish miracles in His holy service. Our opportunities are without limit.

Though the task looms large, we are strengthened by the truth: "The greatest force in this world today is the power of God as it works through man." (*Ensign,* May 1988, p. 41.)

— *Thomas S. Monson*

There is no office growing out of this priesthood that is or can be greater than the priesthood itself. It is from the priesthood that the office derives its authority and power. No office gives authority to the priesthood. No office adds to the power of the priesthood. . . . If it were necessary, though I do not expect the necessity will ever arise, and there was no man left on earth holding the Melchizedek Priesthood, except an elder—that elder, by the inspiration of the Spirit of God and by the direction of the Almighty, could proceed, and should proceed, to organize the Church of Jesus Christ in all its perfection [and offices], because he holds the Melchizedek Priesthood. (*CR,* October 1903, p. 87.)

— *Joseph F. Smith*

We do not become the elect of God instantaneously by receiving the priesthood. Such honor will come only so far as we remember and perform according to the priesthood covenant. (*Ensign,* November 1985, p. 45.)

— *Carlos E. Asay*

We magnify our priesthood and enlarge our calling when we serve with diligence and enthusiasm is those responsibilities to which we are called by proper authority. I emphasize the words, "diligence and enthusiasm." This work has not reached its present stature through indifference on the part of those who have labored in its behalf. The Lord needs men, both young and old, who will carry the banners of His kingdom with positive strength and determined purpose. (*Ensign,* May 1986, pp. 48-49.)

— *Gordon B. Hinckley*

We mortals, in exercising the priesthood, do not do so in our own right as Jesus did. The priesthood we hold is a delegated power. We can only exercise it within the limits the Lord has set, upon the conditions he has specified, and in his name. But we can do many of the works which he did if we fully magnify our callings. (*Ensign*, May 1982, p. 43.)

— *Marion G. Romney*

What is the significance of a priesthood blessing? Think of a young man preparing to leave home to seek his fortune in the world. If his father gave him a compass, he might use this worldly tool to help him find his way. If his father gave him money, he could use this to give him power over worldly things. A priesthood blessing is a conferral of power over spiritual things. Though it cannot be touched or weighed, it is of great significance in helping us overcome obstacles on the path to eternal life. (*Ensign*, May 1987, p. 37.)

— *Dallin H. Oaks*

When a man holds the priesthood, he belongs to something bigger than himself. It is something outside himself to which he can make a complete commitment. It requires full dedication and loyalty. . . .

Membership in the priesthood magnifies the man and the boy. Wherever he is, whatever he does, no matter with whom he associates, he is expected to honor his priesthood. It is the commitment of his manhood to the highest standards of integrity. Attendance at quorum meetings on Sunday is but a part, even a small part, of his membership responsibilities. Through full activity in the priesthood every worthy desire may be achieved, every need of the man can be fulfilled. (*Ensign*, November 1980, p. 109.)

— *Boyd K. Packer*

When all priesthood holders of the Church are in step to march as the army of God in doing our duty, helping one another, looking after the Church, fellowshipping all mankind, then we will be accomplishing God's purposes and doing what he intended for us to do when he established his church.

— *N. Eldon Tanner*

When I was a young man in the Aaronic Priesthood, we boys used to stand in our quorum meetings and repeat in unison, "Priesthood means service. Bearing the priesthood, I will serve." This was our weekly pledge. It was part of every quorum meeting. Most of us began to understand that honoring the priesthood required our being active and serving in the Church. . . . No boy or man fully possesses the priesthood until he learns to serve others and the Lord. . . . Until we do something by way of service to others, the priesthood lies dormant within us and is little value. We must not fail to magnify the callings we receive. (*Ensign*, May 1988, p. 28.)

— *Glen L. Rudd*

You men who hold the priesthood will never get into the celestial kingdom, unless you honor your wives and your families and train them and *give them the blessings that you want for yourselves.*

— *George Albert Smith*

[Priesthood bearers represent Christ.] He preached the gospel; so can we. He spoke by the power of the Holy Ghost; so can we. He served as a missionary; so can we. He went about doing good; so can we. He performed the ordinances of salvation; so can we. He kept the commandments; so can we. He wrought miracles; such also is our privilege if we are true and faithful in all things.

We are his agents; we represent him; we are expected to do and say what he would do and say if he personally were ministering among men at this time. (*Ensign*, November 1977, pp. 33-34.)

— *Bruce R. McConkie*

See also AARONIC PRIESTHOOD, FATHERHOOD, PATRIARCHAL ORDER, PRIESTHOOD QUORUMS

——— Priesthood Quorums ———

I am confident that the Lord intended that a priesthood quorum should be far more than a class in theology on Sunday. . . . Each quorum must be a working brotherhood for every member if its purpose is to be realized.

. . . It will be a marvelous day, . . . a day of fulfillment of the purposes of the Lord—when our priesthood quorums become an anchor of strength to every man belonging thereto, when each such man may appropriately be able to say, "I am a member of a priesthood quorum of The Church of Jesus Christ of Latter-day Saints. I stand ready to assist my brethren in all of their needs, as I am confident they stand ready to assist me in mine. Working together, we shall grow spiritually as covenant sons of God. Working together, we can stand, without embarrassment and without fear, against every wind of adversity that might blow, be it economic, social, or spiritual." (*Ensign*, November 1977, p. 86.)

— *Gordon B. Hinckley*

I look forward to the time when the membership of our quorums will approach their quorum meetings in anticipation of that brotherhood and experience that fraternal feeling which strengthens the soul and which inspires all to render greater service to their fellow men. (*CR*, October 1929, p. 10.)

— *David O. McKay*

If his priesthood quorum functions properly, a man sustained by the brethren of his quorum, almost could not fail in any phase of life's responsibility. (Regional Representatives Seminar, October 1973.)

— *Boyd K. Packer*

The Priesthood of God on earth has been organized into quorums for the mutual good of the members, and for the advancement of the Church. A quorum which meets merely to study lessons, only partially accomplishes its purposes. . . . The spirit of brotherhood should be the directing force in all the plans and operations of the quorum. If this spirit be cultivated, wisely and persistently, no other organization will become more attractive to the man who holds the Priesthood. (Quoted by L. Tom Perry, *Ensign*, November 1981, p. 39.)

— *Rudger Clawson*

We as a people do not understand the quorum organization yet. When we do, we will find there will be a "power surge" through the Church that will electrify the world. The priesthood quorum is the Lord's organization for the brotherhood of men and brethren in the kingdom. The quorum is to function primarily to assist the quorum member in spiritual growth and development. The temporal welfare of every quorum member is also the responsibility of every other quorum member.

There is a holy brotherhood in a good quorum that draws the members together with bands stronger than steel. The quorum is a brotherhood of charity wherein the "pure love of Christ" prevails. (CR, October 1976.)

— *Vaughn J. Featherstone*

[The priesthood quorum] is an organized body of priesthood brethren who have the same office or calling. It is a Church agency that administers salvation to its members and their families. It is a local school of the prophets. (Regional Representatives Seminar, October 1973.)

— *Bruce R. McConkie*

———— Principles ————

I teach the people correct principles and they govern themselves. (*JD*, 10:57-8.)

— *Joseph Smith*

If all things are a matter of preference and nothing is a matter of principle, why not put Dracula in charge of the blood bank? (*Ensign*, July 1976, p. 72.)

— *Neal A. Maxwell*

It mattereth not whether the principle is popular or unpopular, I will always maintain a true principle, even if I stand alone in it. (*HC*, 6:223.)

— *Joseph Smith*

Programs blindly followed bring us to a *discipline* of doing good, but principles properly understood and practiced bring us to a *disposition* to do good. (*Ensign*, May 1986, p. 24.)

— *Glenn L. Pace*

See also COMMANDMENTS, GOSPEL PRINCIPLES, TRUTH, VALUES

—————— Priorities ——————

As a boy I was raised on a farm, where I remained until I went away to school. I had observed how a farmer on one side of the road was very successful, while one on the other side was almost a failure as a farmer. What made the difference? They received the same amount of sunshine and rain. They planted the same kind of seeds. But one had beautiful and bounteous crops, while the other had no harvest or a poor one.

I observed that the successful farmer worked at his job. He would do his plowing, discing, harrowing, seeding, and harvesting in the proper season and at the proper time, while his neighbor was procrastinating, or off hunting and fishing while the work was still to be done. We must learn to set our priorities straight. No one can be successful in his line of work unless he works at it in the proper season and plays in the proper season. (*Ensign*, May 1978, p. 44.)

— *N. Eldon Tanner*

In my career I have had many wonderful things happen to me, many more than I ever dreamed would ever happen. But I would like for you . . . to know that all that has happened to me in my chosen profession is a mere drop in the bucket compared to the truly important things in my life. The testimony of the gospel of Jesus Christ that I have, along with my wife and my family, are my most important possessions. (*Ensign*, November 1984, p. 46.)

— *LaVell Edwards*

Live the gospel every day, practice it, and study it regularly; do not let the affairs of the day that deal with the making of our temporal living crowd aside matters that pertain to the gospel. (*CR*, October 1943, p. 112.)

— *John A. Widtsoe*

Many things are only interesting and enticing, while other things are important. . . . The limits of time dictate that we must prioritize what we do. . . . As we make these choices, we might consider that the glitter and excitement of festive, fun-filled [service] projects are interesting, but the shut-ins, the lonely, the handicapped, the homeless, the latchkey kids, and the abandoned aged are important.

Worldly magazines, tabloids, and much of the multi-mass media mess of fast-track information we are receiving is interesting and enticing, but the scriptures are important.

The RVs and the TVs and retirement ease make it interesting to wander and play, but people's needs for selfless deeds are important. There is concern that "wander and play" have replaced "ponder and pray."

A focus on fashion and getting and spending and the accumulation of things for our enjoyment and comfort is interesting and enticing, but a focus on devoting one's means and time and one's very self to the cause of proclaiming the gospel is important.

The meetings and materials and planning are all interesting, but the doing is important. (*Ensign*, November 1987, p. 76.)

— *William R. Bradford*

Maybe each of us needs to stop amidst our busy, dashing, breathless lives . . . amidst our meetings and commitments . . . to really *see*: to see the way his eyes wrinkle when he laughs, see the tilt of her head as the light catches her hair, remember his dash of humor. Maybe when things get in the saddle and ride us, we need to step back for a moment of clarity. We need to remember why we are doing all of this—remember how much we love those we love. (*Ensign*, November 1977, pp. 24, 25.)

— *Paul H. Dunn*

Most men do not set priorities to guide them in allocating their time and most men forget that the first priority should be to maintain their own spiritual and physical strength; then comes their family; then the Church and then their professions. (Quoted by James E. Faust, *Ensign*, January 1974, p. 23.)

— *Harold B. Lee*

Pay attention to what the Lord requires of you and let the balance go. (*JD*, 3:159.)

— *Brigham Young*

Progress comes as we are able to give up something for something we want more. (*Ensign*, May 1979, p. 68.)

— *Marvin J. Ashton*

The problems of the world are, at root, all human problems, and the opportunities in the world are, at root, all human opportunities. Those who help solve the problems and make the most of the opportunities are those whose priorities are straight, who are mature and strong in character. (*Ensign*, November 1977, p. 36.)

— *Marion D. Hanks*

Think about your life and set your priorities. Find some quiet time regularly to think deeply about where you are going and what you will need to do to get there. Jesus, our exemplar, often "withdrew himself into the wilderness, and prayed" (Luke 5:16). We need to do the same thing occasionally to rejuvenate ourselves spiritually as the Savior did. (*Ensign*, May 1987, p. 14.)

— *M. Russell Ballard*

When earth life is over, and things appear in their true perspective, we shall more clearly see . . . that the fruits of the gospel are the only objectives worthy of life's full effort. (*CR*, October 1949, p. 39.)

— *Marion G. Romney*

When priorities are in place, one can more patiently tolerate unfinished business. (*Ensign*, November 1987, p. 88.)

— *Russell M. Nelson*

See also BALANCE, GOALS, PERSPECTIVE, STEWARDSHIP, TIME

——— Probation ———

I say to everyone within the sound of my voice, "Do not fail the Lord." We must accept the truth that the gospel principles are not on trial but that *we* are. (*Ensign*, May 1979, p. 7.)

— *Spencer W. Kimball*

My brethren, we are the sons of God. He has endowed us with his power, and he has called each of us to serve missions in a place called mortality. Our missions mean very much to him, and they should mean everything to us. In this mortal life, we are to prove ourselves worthy of his love and worthy of the inheritance he has offered.

What is that inheritance? It is all that he has, even eternal life. (*Ensign*, November 1985, p. 45.)

— *Carlos E. Asay*

Mortality is, in reality, a very, very short period. It is literally a snap of the fingers compared to an eternity. It is so short that we can do it. We can prevail. Why, you can stand your foot in a vise for a while if you know it's going to be released soon. . . . Yes, earthly probation is short compared to eternity, but so very much is riding on how we handle the trials and temptations of the flesh. (See D&C 121:7-8; 122:4.) (*Ensign*, November 1985, p. 76.)

— *Hartman Rector, Jr.*

May I say that this life never was intended to be easy. It is a probationary estate in which we are tested physically, mentally, morally, and spiritually. We are subject to disease and decay. We are attacked by cancer, leprosy, and contagious diseases. We suffer pain and sorrow and afflictions. Disasters strike; floods sweep away our homes; famines destroy our food; plagues and wars fill our graves with dead bodies and our broken homes with sorrow.

We are called upon to choose between the revealed word of God and the soul-destroying postulates of the theoretical sciences. Temptations, the lusts of the flesh, evils of every sort—all these are part of the plan, and must be faced by every person privileged to undergo the experiences of mortality. (*Ensign*, November 1976, p. 106.)

— *Bruce R. McConkie*

All of us on earth are winners because we chose to come to this mortal probation. (*Ensign*, May 1990, p. 39.)

— *Robert D. Hales*

The lifetime of man is a day of trial, wherein we may prove to God, in our darkness, in our weakness, and where the enemy reigns, that we are our Father's friends (*JD*, 8:61.)

— *Brigham Young*

We are now in a day of trial to prove ourselves worthy or unworthy of the life which is to come. (*DBY*, p. 345.)

— *Brigham Young*

We have reason to rejoice because the understanding that this life is a time for men to prepare to meet God has come to us while we still have time to consider the consequences of this message. We are still alive, and our probationary state is not yet over. (*Ensign*, May 1989, p. 73.)

— *F. Enzio Busche*

We must recognize that mortality has been granted to us as a probationary state where all physical appetites are to be mastered. It is far more difficult to

repent in the spirit world of sins which involve physical habits and actions. . . .
It is obvious we either discipline our lives here, or pay the price for the undisci-
plined life in the world to come.

— *Delbert L. Stapley*

The doctrine of probation is the inescapable choice between two ways,
everyone having a perfect knowledge of the way he *should* go. (*OAT*, p. 11.)

— *Hugh Nibley*

See also ADVERSITY, LIFE, PLAN OF SALVATION, TODAY, TRIALS

——— Problems ———

Every world problem may be solved by obedience to the principles of the
gospel of Jesus Christ. (*Gospel Ideals*, The Improvement Era, Salt Lake City: Deseret
Book Co., 1976, p. 5.)

— *David O. McKay*

It is not our situation or problems that make us unhappy; it is our failure to
properly resolve them. (*Ensign*, May 1984, p. 11.)

— *Marvin J. Ashton*

Problems form an important part of our lives. They are placed in our path for
us to overcome them, not to be overcome by them. We must master them, not let
them master us. Every time we overcome a challenge, we grow in experience, in
self-assuredness, and in faith. (*Ensign*, May 1990, p. 79.)

— *Horacio A. Tenorio*

Quit thinking that tomorrow your problems will go away and life will begin
in earnest. The Lord is waiting to help you cope today if you will lay your human-
size needs at his divine feet. (*Ensign*, May 1979, p. 9.)

— *Paul H. Dunn*

When you have a problem ,work it out in your own mind first. Ponder on it
and analyze it and meditate on it. Read the scriptures. . . . Measure the problem
against what you know to be right and wrong, and then make the decision. Ask
[the Lord] if the decision is right or if it is wrong. (*Ensign*, August 1975,
pp. 88, 89.)

— *Boyd K. Packer*

Often our own problems seem to diminish when we become aware of the challenges faced by others. When my wife was volunteering as a pink lady at one of our local hospitals, she noticed that some of the doctors in the area would encourage their patients who were depressed, sad, or emotionally ill to join the volunteer organization. That prescription often worked better than medicine to build self-image and restore health to those who found joy in helping others. (*Ensign*, May 1988, p. 64.)

— *Marvin J. Ashton*

See also CHALLENGES, DECISIONS, LOOK TO GOD, OBSTACLES, REVELATION

———— Procrastination ————

How wise and blessed we would be if we eliminated procrastination and made a decision to serve the Lord and accept His invitation to "Come, follow me." (Luke 18:22.) . . . How comfortable some of us become as we nestle in the web of procrastination. It is a false haven of rest for those who are content to live without purpose, commitment, or self-discipline. . . . It is an unwholesome blend of doubt and delay. (*Ensign*, May 1983, pp. 31-32.)

— *Marvin J. Ashton*

One of the most cruel games anyone can play with self is the "not yet" game—hoping to sin just a bit more before ceasing; to enjoy the praise of the world a little longer before turning away from the applause; to win just once more in the wearying sweepstakes of materialism; to be chaste, but not yet; to be good neighbors, but not now. (*CR*, October 1974, p. 16.)

— *Neal A. Maxwell*

Procrastination . . . is the thief of our self-respect. It nags at us and spoils our fun. It deprives us of the fullest realization of our ambitions and hopes. (Address, Brigham Young University, February 8, 1966.)

— *Thomas S. Monson*

There is nothing that steals man's time, his talents, his vigor, his energy, even his prospects of salvation, in greater degree than the crime of procrastination. (*CR*, October 1907, p. 58.)

— *Reed Smoot*

See also ACTION, INITIATIVE, PRIORITIES

—— Profanity ——

Profanity is filthiness. A person is known as much by his language as he is by the company he keeps. . . . Filthiness in any form is degrading and soul-destroying and should be avoided. (*Doctrines of Salvation*, Bruce R. McConkie, comp., Salt Lake City: Bookcraft, 1956, 1:13.)

— Joseph Fielding Smith

Stay out of the gutter in your conversation. Foul talk defiles the man who speaks it. . . . Don't swear. Don't profane. Avoid so-called dirty jokes. Stay away from conversation that is sprinkled with foul and filthy words. You will be happier if you do so, and your example will give strength to others. (*Ensign*, November 1987, pp. 47, 48.)

— Gordon B. Hinckley

Swearing is a vice that bespeaks a low standard of breeding. Blasphemous exclamations drive out all spirit of reverence. (*Gospel Ideals*, The Improvement Era, Salt Lake City: Deseret Book Co., 1967, p. 420.)

— David O. McKay

The names of the Father and the Son are used with authority when we reverently teach and testify of them, when we pray, and when we perform the sacred ordinances of the priesthood.

There are no more sacred or significant words in all of our language than the names of God the Father and his Son, Jesus Christ. . . .

Satan seeks to discredit the sacred names of God the Father and his Son, Jesus Christ, the names through which their work is done. He succeeds in a measure whenever he is able to influence any man or woman, boy or girl, to make holy names common and to associate them with coarse thoughts and evil acts. Those who use sacred names in vain are, by that act, promoters of Satan's purposes. (*Ensign*, May 1986, pp. 50-51.)

— Dallin H. Oaks

The nature and extent of profanity and vulgarity in our society is a measure of its deterioration. (*Ensign*, May 1986, p. 49.)

— Dallin H. Oaks

Though we are sure no boy can tell us any advantage that can arise from the abuse of God's holy name, yet we can tell him many evils that arise therefrom. To begin, it is unnecessary and consequently foolish; it lessens our respect for holy things and leads us into the society of the wicked; it brings upon us the disrespect of the good who avoid us; it leads us to other sins, for he who is willing to abuse his Creator is not ashamed to defraud his fellow creature; and also by so doing we directly and knowingly break one of the most direct of God's commandments. (*Juvenile Instructor*, September 27, 1873, p. 156.)

— *George Q. Cannon*

The habit . . . , which some young people fall into, of using vulgarity and profanity . . . is not only offensive to well-bred persons, but it is a gross sin in the sight of god, and should not exist among the children of the Latter-day Saints. (Quoted by Gordon B. Hinckley, *Ensign*, 1987, p. 46.)

— *The First Presidency*

We note the increasing coarseness of language and understand how Lot must have felt when he was, according to Peter, "vexed with the filthy conversation of the wicked." (2 Pet. 2:7.) We wonder why those of coarse and profane conversation, even if they refuse obedience to God's will, are so stunted mentally that they let their capacity to communicate grow more and more narrow. Language is like music; we rejoice in beauty, range, and quality in both, and we are demeaned by the repetition of a few sour notes. (*Ensign*, May 1978, p. 78.)

— *Spencer W. Kimball*

We should never lower our dignity by lowering our language. (*Ensign*, May 1983, p. 74.)

— *Ted E. Brewerton*

When I was a small boy in the first grade, I experienced what I thought was a rather tough day at school. I came home, walked in the house, threw my book on the kitchen table, and let forth an expletive that included the name of the Lord.

My mother was shocked. She told me quietly, but firmly, how wrong I was. She told me that I could not have words of that kind coming out of my mouth. She led me by the hand into the bathroom, where she took from the shelf a clean washcloth, put it under the faucet, and then generously coated it with soap. She said, "We'll have to wash out your mouth." She told me to open it, and I did so reluctantly. Then she rubbed the soapy washcloth around my tongue and teeth. I sputtered and fumed and felt like swearing again, but I didn't. I rinsed and rinsed my mouth, but it was a long while before the soapy taste was gone. In fact, whenever I think of that experience, I can still taste the soap. The lesson was worthwhile. I think I can say that I have tried to avoid using the name of the Lord in vain since that day. I am grateful for that lesson. (*Ensign*, November 1987, p. 46.)

— *Gordon B. Hinckley*

See also WORDS

——— Progression ———

A commitment to improve on a daily basis should be a high priority in the lives of those who would move in the right direction. . . . It is a fact of life that the direction in which we are moving is more important than where we are. (*Ensign,* May 1987, pp. 66, 67.)

— *Marvin J. Ashton*

A truly wise person will constantly move forward, striving for self-improvement, knowing that daily repentance is needed for progress. He will realize the good life is simply conforming to a standard of right and justice. The joys of happiness can only be realized by living lofty principles. (*Ensign,* November 1986, p. 15.)

— *Marvin J. Ashton*

As we improve and advance, and develop the attributes of deity within us, God will remove from our path the impediments and obstacles to our progress that are found therein.

— *Lorenzo Snow*

Gospel living is a process of continuous individual renewal and improvement until the person is prepared and qualified to enter comfortably and with confidence into the presence of God. (*Ensign,* November 1984, p. 65.)

— *Ronald E. Poelman*

I am convinced of the fact that the speed with which we head along the straight and narrow path isn't as important as the direction in which we are traveling. (*Ensign,* May 1989, p. 21.)

— *Marvin J. Ashton*

If there was a point where man in his progression could not proceed any further, the very idea would throw a gloom over every intelligent and reflecting mind. God himself is still increasing and progressing in knowledge, power, and dominion, and will do so worlds without end. It is just so with us. (*JD,* 6:120.)

— *Wilford Woodruff*

If we are striving, if we are working, if we are trying, to the best of our ability, to improve day by day, then we are in the line of our duty. (*CR,* April 1909, p. 111.)

— *Heber J. Grant*

It is not intended that we shall accomplish everything in this life, but that we are expected to be progressive beings, growing toward our final destiny. But that principle in no way excuses us from doing the best we can or from acquiring all the knowledge that we have capacity and opportunity to assimilate as we go along. (*CR*, April 1951, p. 122.)

— *Albert E. Bowen*

Let us "be of good cheer" (D&C 78:18), for the Lord will, as he has promised, lead us along and show us the way. He will help us as we decide from day to day on the allocation of our time and talent. We will move faster if we hurry less. We will make more real progress if we focus on the fundamentals. We will even come to know more as we serve more, for as we learn to *bear* more we are made ready to *hear* more. (*Ensign*, May 1979, p. 83.)

— *Spencer W. Kimball*

On this journey of life you are . . . headed for immortality and eternal life and eternal increase. When I mention eternal increase I am referring not only to increase of posterity, but to increase of knowledge and the power that comes with knowledge when it is set on fire. I am referring to the increase of wisdom, which is a proper use of knowledge; the increase of intelligence, which is the glory of God, and will be the glory of man. (Fireside Address, Brigham Young University, October 8, 1967.)

— *Hugh B. Brown*

Progress is not created by contented people. (*Ensign*, November 1984, p. 23.)

— *Russell C. Taylor*

Progress or perish.

— *B.H. Roberts*

Salvation does not come all at once; we are commanded to be perfect even as our Father in heaven is perfect. It will take us ages to accomplish this end, for there will be greater progress beyond the grave, and it will be there that the faithful will overcome all things, and receive all things, even the fullness of the Father's glory. (*Doctrines of Salvation*, Bruce R. McConkie, comp., Salt Lake City: Bookcraft, 1956, 2:18-19.)

— *Joseph Fielding Smith*

There is no such thing as principle, power, wisdom, knowledge, life, position, or anything that can be imagined, that remains stationary—they must increase or decrease.

— *Brigham Young*

Those who continually prefer to stir up waters find that they create only a whirlpool and are carried around in circles rather than progressing straightway. (*Ensign*, May 1983, p. 31.)

— *Marvin J. Ashton*

We should labor for perfection so far as possible, and seek to go onward. There is no man or woman who can stand still . . . . In this path over which we are moving we are very likely to go backward if we undertake to stand still or act indifferently. We must push forward, because the Church moves on . . . . Latter-day Saints should not permit themselves to stand still. (*CR*, April 1898, p. 12.)

— *Lorenzo Snow*

When you climb up a ladder, you must begin at the bottom, and ascend step by step, until you arrive at the top; and so it is with the principles of the Gospel—you must begin with the first, and go on until you learn all the principles of exaltation. But it will be a great while after you have passed through the veil before you will have learned them. (*TPJS*, 348.)

— *Joseph Smith*

"For behold, this is my work and my glory—to bring to pass the immortality and eternal life of man." (Moses 1:39.) This tremendous scripture summarizes in one sentence the sum and substance, the purpose, of all creation.

When I was young, I always assumed it would be impossible for God to participate further in the great process of eternal progression. After all, he was perfect. All knowledge was his. He had indeed overcome all things. But understanding this scripture, I now know that he is capable of further glorification or exaltation. Indeed, he is added upon through the success of his children. Your failure or my failure diminishes his possibilities. Our success in righteous endeavors adds further glory to his name. Should not that be the perfect motivation? It is perfect because it is without selfish interest. (*Ensign*, March 1977, p. 65.)

— *Robert L. Simpson*

See also ETERNAL LIFE, GOODNESS, PLAN OF SALVATION

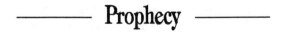

Prophecy

It is truly a strange thing for prophets to speak of future events as though they were present before their seeric eyes. It is truly a wondrous thing for earthbound eyes to pierce the fogs and darkness of our planet and see within the gates of heaven. It is marvelous, almost beyond belief, that mere mortals can begin to comprehend him who is eternal, can know of a surety of things past, present, and future, . . .

But strange or not, so it is. (*Ensign*, November 1978, p. 60.)

— *Bruce R. McConkie*

Prophecy is but history in reverse—a divine disclosure of future events. (*CR*, October 1973, p. 89.)

— *Ezra Taft Benson*

Prophecy is the most sure way of knowing what is to happen—and Isaiah said that the Lord had declared the end from the beginning (see Isa. 46:10)—it's all there when we understand it. (*Ensign*, May 1978, p. 74.)

— *LeGrand Richards*

The greatest events that have been spoken of by all the holy prophets will come along so naturally as the consequence of certain causes, that unless our eyes are enlightened by the Spirit of God, and the spirit of revelation rests upon us, we will fail to see that these are the events predicted by the holy prophets. (*JD*, 21:266-267.)

— *George Q. Cannon*

We also believe in prophecy, in tongues, in visions, and in revelations, in gifts, and in healing; and that these things cannot be enjoyed without the gift of the Holy Ghost. We believe that the holy men of old spake as they were moved by the Holy Ghost, and that holy men in these days speak by the same principle. (*TPJS*, p. 243.)

— *Joseph Smith*

See also PROPHETS, REVELATION

——— **Prophets** ———

A revealing characteristic of a true prophet is that he declares a message from God. He makes no apology for the message, nor does he fear for any social repercussions which may lead to derision and persecution. (*Ensign*, November 1981, p. 61.)

— *Ezra Taft Benson*

Always keep your eye on the President of the Church, and if he ever tells you to do anything, and it is wrong, and you do it, the Lord will bless you for it. . . .

But you don't need to worry. The Lord will never let his mouthpiece lead the people astray. (Quoted by Marion G. Romney, *CR*, October 1960, p. 78.)

— *Heber J. Grant*

I do not believe members of this church can be in full harmony with the Savior without sustaining his living prophet on the earth, the President of the Church. If we do not sustain the living prophet, whoever he may be, we die spiritually. (*Ensign*, November 1989, p. 9.)

— *James E. Faust*

I say, in the deepest of humility, but also by the power and force of a burning testimony in my soul, that from the prophet of the Restoration to the prophet of our own year, the communication line is unbroken, the authority is continuous, and light, brilliant and penetrating, continues to shine. The sound of the voice of the Lord is a continuous melody and a thunderous appeal. For nearly a century and a half there has been no interruption.

Man never needs to stand alone. . . . the Lord definitely calls prophets today and reveals his secrets unto them as he did yesterday, he does today, and will do tomorrow: that is the way it is. (*Ensign*, May 1977, p. 78.)

— *Spencer W. Kimball*

If I can be remembered for anything (and I hope that somehow, somewhere I can), I would settle for [being known as] one who is willing to give allegiance to and follow a prophet of God. And if that can be my lot, then I feel I will have accomplished the thing the Lord has sent me to do.

It's not the program, it's not the activities, but in the final analysis it is our loyalty to him whom God has called and the offering of our prayers on his behalf. (*Ensign*, May 1983, p. 30.)

— *Loren C. Dunn*

If you want to know what the Lord has for this people at the present time, I would admonish you to get and read the discourses that have been delivered at this conference; for what these brethren have spoken by the power of the Holy Ghost is the mind of the Lord, the will of the Lord, the voice of the Lord, and the power of God unto salvation. (*CR*, April 1973, p. 176.)

— *Harold B. Lee*

In response to a contention that to follow [the Prophet] is tantamount to surrendering one's "moral agency," suppose a person were in a forest with his vision limited by the denseness of the growth about him. Would he be surrendering his agency in following the directions of one who stands on a lookout tower commanding an unobstructed view? To me, our leaders are true watchmen on the towers of Zion, and those who follow their counsel are exercising their agency just as freely as would be the man in the forest. For I accept as *fact*, without reservation, that this Church is headed by the Lord Jesus Christ, and that He, through the men whom He chooses and appoints to lead his people, gives it active direction. I believe that He communicates to them his will, and that they, enjoying his Spirit, counsel us.

— *Marion G. Romney*

If you will follow the admonitions of the Lord and heed the counsel of His chosen servants in their callings as prophets, seers, and revelators, I promise you that love at home and obedience to parents will increase; faith will be developed in the hearts of the youth of Israel and they will gain power and strength to combat the evil influences and temptations which beset them. Each of our homes may veritably become a little heaven on earth. (*Children's Friend*, April 1957, p. 26.)

— *Ezra Taft Benson*

Key statements made by latter-day prophets are not trite cliches. They are vital counsel to us from the Lord through his prophets. We should ponder and act upon such statements. (*Ensign*, November 1988, p. 37.)

— *Joseph B. Wirthlin*

One who rationalizes that he or she has a testimony of Jesus Christ but cannot accept direction and counsel from the leadership of His church is in a fundamentally unsound position and is in jeopardy of losing exaltation. (*Ensign*, May 1982, p. 64.)

— *Ezra Taft Benson*

President Marion G. Romney sometimes wonders out loud, "How many tellings does it take—how many repetitions of counsel? How many individual corrections must be given?"

As parents may pose these questions to their children, Heavenly Father may also wonder the same about *his* sons and daughters. How many of us turn a deaf ear to the admonitions from our modern-day prophets and stay passive, uninvolved, as when we half-listen to the radio? (*Ensign*, May 1986, p. 71.)

— *Jacob de Jager*

So often the prophets have been rejected because they first rejected the wrong ways of their own society. . . . The prophets have always been free from the evil of the times, free to be divine auditors who will still call fraud, fraud; embezzlement, embezzlement; and adultery, adultery.

— *Spencer W. Kimball*

The devil never did care how many dead prophets the people believed in, and he does not care today. But he does care if they believe in the living prophets. (*CR*, October 1901.)

— *Ben E. Rich*

The Lord knows whom He wants to preside over His Church, and he never makes a mistake. (Quoted by Heber J. Grant, *CR*, April 1938, p. 120.)

— *Joseph F. Smith*

The Lord never had—and never will have to the end of time—a church on the earth without prophets, apostles, and inspired men. Whenever the Lord had a people on the earth that he acknowledged as such, that people were led by revelation. (*JD*, 24:240.)

— *Wilford Woodruff*

The only safety and security there is in this Church is in listening to the words that come from the prophets of the Lord, as if from the mouth of the Lord himself. . . . We have the prophets today telling us what our responsibility is here and now. God help us not to turn deaf ears but to go out while the harvest is yet possible and build on a foundation such that when the rains descend, and the floods come, and the winds blow and beat on the house our house will have stone walls.

— *Harold B. Lee*

There are some of our members who practice selective obedience. A prophet is not one who displays a smorgasbord of truth from which we are free to pick and choose. However, some members become critical and. suggest the prophet should change the menu. A prophet doesn't take a poll to see which way the wind of public opinion is blowing. He reveals the will of the Lord to us. The world is full of deteriorating churches who have succumbed to public opinion and have become more dedicated to tickling the ears of their members than obeying the laws of God. (*Ensign*, May 1989, p. 26.)

— *Glenn L. Pace*

Those who profess to accept the gospel and who at the same time criticize and refuse to follow the counsel of the prophet are assuming an indefensible position. (*Ensign*, May 1983, p. 17.)

— *Marion G. Romney*

We have some tight places to go before the Lord is through with this church and the world in this dispensation, which is the last dispensation, which shall usher in the coming of the Lord. . . . The power of Satan will increase; we see it in evidence on every hand. . . .

Now the only safety we have as members of this church is to . . . give heed to the words and commandments that the Lord shall give through his prophet, "as he receiveth them, walking in all holiness before me; . . . as if from mine own mouth, in all patience and faith." (D&C 21:4-5.) There will be some things that take patience and faith. You may not like what comes from the authority of the Church. . . . But if you listen to these things, as if from the mouth of the Lord himself, with patience and faith, the promise is that "the gates of hell shall not prevail against you; yea, and the Lord God will disperse the powers of darkness from before you, and cause the heavens to shake for your good, and his name's glory." (D&C 21:6.) (*CR*, October 1970, p. 152.)

— *Harold B. Lee*

Today the Lord is revealing his will to all the inhabitants of the earth, and to members of the Church in particular, on the issues of this our day through the living prophets, with the First Presidency at the head. What they say as a presidency is what the Lord would say if he were here in person. This is the rock foundation of Mormonism. If it ever ceases to be that fact, this will be an apostate Church . . . so I repeat again, what the presidency say as a presidency is what the Lord would say if he were here, and it is scripture. It should be studied, understood, and followed, even as the revelation in the Doctrine and covenants and other scriptures. Those who follow this course will not interpret what they say as being inspired by political bias or selfishness; neither will they say that the brethren are uninformed as to the circumstances of those affected by their counsel; or that their counsels cannot be accepted because they are not prefaced by the quotation, "Thus saith the Lord."

— *Marion G. Romney*

What we need today is not more prophets. We have the prophets. But what we need is more people with listening ears. That is the great need of our generation. (*CR*, October 1948, p. 82.)

— *J. Reuben Clark, Jr.*

Therefore, O Israel, we must sustain the living prophets. The dead we honor, but the living are chosen, ordained, appointed and sustained, and it is to the living we look for counsel, reproof, and instruction.

— *J. Golden Kimball*

You may not like what comes from the authority of the Church. It may contradict your political views. It may contradict your social views. It may interfere with some of your social life. But if you listen to these things, as if from the mouth of the Lord himself, with patience and faith, the promise is that "the gates of hell shall not prevail against you; yea, and the Lord God will disperse the powers of darkness from before you, and cause the heavens to shake for your good, and his name's glory." (D&C 21:6.)

— Harold B. Lee

When the enemy is near, and when the stormy clouds arise, and the war clouds approach, even then we can feel free and quiet, and be satisfied that all is right in Israel. It is only for us to be ready to do our duty, to serve our President with all our heart, with all our might, with all our feelings, with all our property and energies, and with all things that the Lord has put into our hands. (*JD*, 5:314.)

— Lorenzo Snow

When there are no prophets, there is no divine direction, and without such guidance the people walk in darkness.

— Mark E. Petersen

[People] in all ages search for happiness; they desire social and domestic peace; and when they think of the vast future, they desire to participate in the blessings that are spoken of as pertaining to that state of existence; but they know not how to obtain them, except a servant of God comes along and points out the way of life. (*JD*, 9:163.)

— Wilford Woodruff

See also RESTORATION, REVELATION

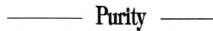

Purity

Purity [is] the condition one attains unto, when, through faith in the Lord Jesus Christ, repentance, baptism by immersion, and baptism by fire and the Holy Ghost, he receives forgiveness of sins which works in him a spiritual rebirth, a birth through which he comes back into harmony with, and is sensitive and alive to, the things of the Spirit. *Healed* is the term frequently used in the scriptures to denote the state of such an one. (*Look to God and Live*, Salt Lake City: Deseret Book Co., 1975, p. 261.)

— Marion G. Romney

The strength of this Church lies in the purity of the thoughts and lives of its members, then the testimony of Jesus abides in the soul, and strength comes to each individual to withstand the evils of the world.

— David O. McKay

I will put my own definition to the term of sanctification, and say it consists in overcoming every sin and bringing all into subjection to the law of Christ. God has placed in us a pure spirit; when this reigns predominant, without let or hindrance, and triumphs over the flesh and rules and governs and controls as the Lord controls the heavens and the earth, this I call the blessing of sanctification. (*JD*, 10:173.)

— *Brigham Young*

Sanctification . . . consists in overcoming every sin and bringing all into subjection to the law of Christ. (*JD*, 10:173.)

— *Brigham Young*

This whole probation that we are undergoing in mortality, is to permit us to cleanse and perfect and purify our souls. It is to permit us to take evil and iniquity and carnality and everything that leads away from God out of our souls. (*CR*, October 1950, p. 17.)

— *Bruce R. McConkie*

We believe that these bodies are to be well cared for, that they are to be looked upon as something belonging to the Lord, and that each may be made, in very truth, the temple of the Holy Ghost, the place into which the Spirit of God shall enter and where he shall delight to dwell, if he shall find there cleanliness and order and purity and uprightness of thought and conduct.

— *James E. Talmage*

What could inspire one to purity and worthiness more than to possess a spiritual confirmation that we are the children of God? What could inspire a more lofty regard for oneself, or engender more love for mankind?

This thought does not fill me with arrogance. It fills me with overwhelming humility. Nor does it sponsor any inclination to worship oneself or any man.

The doctrine we teach has no provision for lying or stealing, for pornography, immoralities, for child abuse, for abortion, or murder. We are bound by the laws of His church, *as sons and daughters of God*, to avoid all of these and every other unholy or impure practice. (*Ensign*, November 1984, p. 69.)

— *Boyd K. Packer*

See also PERFECTION, RIGHTEOUSNESS

——— Reactivation ———

Eight Considerations in the Work of Reactivation
A *first* step is to recognize, where known, the causes of inactivity . . . .
Second, recognize that his work takes time; it does interrupt our regular routine. . . . Some wounds require more than a quick Band-Aid.
A *third* step to be overseen by priesthood executive committees and ward correlation councils, is the careful matching of person to person. Organized love is better than generalized concern. . . .
Fourth, provide such individuals with a fresh opportunity to serve, because they are genuinely needed. . . .
Fifth, provide the needed teaching. *Activation requires conversion.* . . .
A *sixth* step is to remember the Lord's hand is in this work. He can bring about those circumstances in which such souls are "in a preparation to hear the word." (Alma 32:6.)
Seventh, prevention is always better than rehabilitation. . . . (*Ensign*, May 1982, pp. 37-38.)

— *Neal A. Maxwell*

Here is a great key to reactivation of many of those who have fallen by the wayside. Each has a talent that can be employed. It is the task of leaders to match those talents with needs, and then to offer a challenge. (*Ensign*, November 1982, p. 8.)

— *Gordon B. Hinckley*

It is exciting to see the servants of the Lord, the leaders and members, prepare as vessels of the Spirit of God to identify the families who have been distracted or have transgressed and are now less active and then to touch the hearts of these wonderful families. Yes, thousands of families are returning to the Lord. They have received in love the invitation to return, have understood the humble, loving plea, "Please come back!" They have been searched out by servants of the Lord, then have been sought out by the Spirit of the Lord and brought back as they have remembered once again the word spoken through the Lord's servants. (*Ensign*, November 1986, p. 28.)

— *Gardner H. Russell*

It is my hope and my belief that the Lord never permits the light of faith wholly to be extinguished in any human heart, however faint the light may glow. The Lord has provided that there shall still be there a spark which, with teaching, with the spirit of righteousness, with love, with tenderness, with example, with living the Gospel, shall brighten and glow again, however darkened the mind may have been. And if we shall fail so to reach those among us of our own whose faith has dwindled low, we shall fail in one of the main things which the Lord expects at our hands. (*CR*, October 1936, p. 114.)

— *J. Reuben Clark, Jr.*

People who drift away from the true doctrine usually know in their hearts something is missing. The kernel of truth, though small, remains—never to be replaced with fame or money or worldly pleasures. (*Ensign*, November 1981, p. 59.)

— *David B. Haight*

This work of reactivation is done a soul at a time, quietly and with dignity . . . and if some bristle a bit, then let us learn how to pat a porcupine. (*Ensign*, May 1982, p. 37.)

— *Neal A. Maxwell*

Those that stray need a friend—but they need one who knows the Shepherd. Seldom do people cease coming to Church because of doctrine; they are waiting for a show of genuine love and friendly fellowship to heal their hurts or doubts. (*Ensign*, November 1981, p. 60.)

— *David B. Haight*

See also FELLOWSHIPPING, HOME TEACHING

———— Reading ————

I have always read with my pen, marking every idea, every phrase, every quote, and every other thing that I think will help me. And then I put these thoughts into my notebooks. One of my most valuable possessions in the world is my collection of 25 notebooks. . . . I have 7,500 pages of notes. I think of my reading as a combine harvester sweeping across a field of wheat. It cuts everything before it, but throws out the weeds and the chaff and the straw and puts the wheat in the sack.

— *Sterling W. Sill*

The reading habit is most valuable in life. I mean by that the practice of using a little time, say half an hour a day, in the systematic reading of worthwhile literature. The mind is opened to precious fields of thought; the achievements of the ages become ours; even the future takes form. As the mind and spirit are fed by well chosen reading, comfort, peace and understanding come to the soul. Those who have not tried it, have missed a keen and easily accessible joy. (*CR*, April 1939, p. 21.)

— *John A. Widtsoe*

In addition to reading fairy tales to our children, we should build a consistent, planned program of introducing the principles of the gospel through Bible and Book of Mormon stories, stories of our current-day prophets, and also of our family histories, which bring a heritage of gospel living into the lives of our children. (*Ensign*, November 1988, p. 74.)

— *L. Tom Perry*

Reading is one of the true pleasures of life. In our age of mass culture, when so much that we encounter is abridged, adapted, adulterated, shredded, and boiled down, it is mind-easing and mind-inspiring to sit down privately with a congenial book. (*Ensign*, November 1988, p. 70.)

— *Thomas S. Monson*

You know that your children will read. They will read books and they will read magazines and newspapers. Cultivate within them a taste for the best. While they are very young, read to them the great stories which have become immortal because of the virtues they teach. Expose them to good books. Let there be a corner somewhere in your house, be it ever so small, where they will see at least a few books of the kind upon which great minds have been nourished. (*Ensign*, November 1975, p. 39.)

— *Gordon B. Hinckley*

See also EDUCATION, LEARNING

Relief Society

Grateful indeed we should be to live in a period of time when the gospel is upon the earth to show us the way. Favored are we to mingle with sisters who believe as we believe, who share experiences and who are comforted and sustained by the Spirit of the Lord and by the wisdom and love of one another. (*A Woman's Reach*, Salt Lake City: Deseret Book Co., 1974, p. 121.)

— *Belle S. Spafford*

Service in the Relief Society magnifies and sanctifies each individual sister. Your membership in Relief Society should be ever with you. When you devote yourself to the Relief Society and organize it and operate it and participate in it, you sustain the cause that will bless every woman who comes within its influence. . . . The Relief Society might be likened to a refuge—the place of safety and protection—the sanctuary of ancient times. You will be safe within it. It encircles each sister like a protecting wall. (*Ensign*, November 1980 p. 110.)

— *Boyd K. Packer*

Service in the Relief Society magnifies and sanctifies each individual sister. Your membership in Relief Society should be ever with you. When you devote yourself to the Relief Society and organize it and operate it and participate in it, you sustain the cause that will bless every woman who comes within its influence. . . . The Relief Society might be likened to a refuge—the place of safety and protection—the sanctuary of ancient times. You will be safe within it. It encircles each sister like a protecting wall. (*Ensign*, November 1980 p. 110.)

— *Boyd K. Packer*

Oh, how powerful the tender, tempering teachings and the disarming wisdom of our sisters can be. I found the spirit of Relief Society—the whole of it—in the quiet reply of one of your number.

Someone ridiculed her determination to gather her year's supply. She had stored enough for herself and her husband, with some to spare for her young married children who were without the means or the space to provide much for themselves. She told him she did it because the prophets had counseled us to do it. He chided her, "In the crunch you won't have it anyway. What if your leaders call everything in? You'd have to share it with those who didn't prepare. What will you think then?"

"If that should happen," she said, "at least I will have something to bring." (*Ensign*, November 1980, p. 111.)

— *Boyd K. Packer*

The mission of the Relief Society is to succor the distressed, to minister to the sick and feeble, to feed the poor, to clothe the naked, and to bless all the sons and daughters of God. No institution was ever founded with a nobler aim. Its basis is true charity, which is the pure love of christ, and that spirit has been manifested in all the ministrations of the Society among the people. . . . I can testify that there are no purer and more God-fearing women in the world than are to be found within the ranks of the Relief Society.

— *Lorenzo Snow*

This organization offers relief from spiritual and intellectual ignorance, relief from poverty and suffering, relief from sorrow and loneliness, relief from the evils of the world, relief from cynicism and doubt.

But most important is the continuing gift of discernment which the inspiration of heaven provides to us through Relief Society. We can see more clearly today than ever before how great the challenge is for us to build strong homes and provide loving care for the children who come to our care. It really is not now and never has been a question of either a rich and full life for women or a strong and loving home. A Relief Society home must meet the challenge of both positions. (*Ensign*, May 1982, p. 111.)

— *Barbara B. Smith*

The work of Relief Society is focused on the pure and simple part of the gospel, to develop faith and bear testimony; to render compassionate service as we care for the needy; to strengthen our families here and in eternity, and to work with our "hearts knit together in unity and love one towards another." (Mosiah 18:21.) (*Ensign*, May 1990, p. 76.)

— *Barbara W. Winder*

This great organization is devoted wholeheartedly to the interests of women. It is the Lord's organization especially provided for them.

I remind you that the program of the Church is the plan of salvation and that Relief Society is a part of that plan. It is God-given. It is inspired. It will lift everyone who participates in it. It is part and parcel of the Lord's program for the Church, and therefore every woman should come within its divine influence. (*Ensign*, March 1976, p. 74.)

— *Mark E. Petersen*

Visiting Teachers

To be successful, . . . a visiting teacher would wish to have high purpose, . . . great vision, a terrific enthusiasm that cannot be worn down, a positive attitude, of course, and a great love. (Address, Salt Lake Monument Park Stake, September 16, 1958.)

— *Spencer W. Kimball*

We ask our sisters of the Relief Society never to forget that they are a unique organization in the whole world, for they were organized under the inspiration of the Lord. . . . No other woman's organization in all the earth has had such a birth.

This divinely inspired origin brings with it a corresponding responsibility, in consecration to service, and in the loftiest loyalty to the Priesthood of God and to one another. The members should permit neither hostile nor competitive interests of any kind to detract from the duties and obligations, the privileges and honors, the opportunities and achievements of membership in this great Society. (Quoted by Boyd K. Packer, *Ensign*, November 1980, p. 110.)

— *The First Presidency*

When Joseph Smith turned the keys in behalf of women in Nauvoo there was a door of great significance opened for womankind. Light and knowledge from heaven began to flow down upon women not only in the Church, but everywhere; and the wheels of progress provided women with more and more opportunities to take the responsibility for their own lives, and thus work out their own salvation and make contributions to the work of society. (*Ensign*, May 1983, p. 90.)

— *Barbara B. Smith*

See also CHURCH PROGRAMS

——— Religion ———

No religion made by man can do for men that which must be done. (*CR*, October 1948, p. 94.)

— *Levi Edgar Young*

Pure religion is learning the gospel of Jesus Christ and then putting it into action. Nothing will ever be of real benefit to us until it is incorporated into our own lives. (*Ensign*, November 1982, p. 63.)

— *Marvin J. Ashton*

Religion as a purely human product, valuable as it is to human life and progress, has not the inner vigor to retain a place of commanding power. Religion requires revelation. (*CR*, April 1950, p. 65.)

— *Levi Edgar Young*

Religion is not a thing apart from life. It is not principles and ordinances or missionary work or leadership as an end in themselves. It is manifested by the kind of people we are, by our relationship with our Heavenly Father and his Son and all of the commandments, by the measure in which we qualify for the approval of our own Spirit-guided conscience, and by the way we treat other people. (*Ensign*, November 1988, p. 62.)

— *Marion D. Hanks*

See also GOSPEL

——— Remorse ———

Almighty God has promised to forgive, forget, and never mention the sins of which we have truly repented. But he has given us the gift of remorse to help *us* remember them constructively, thankfully, and humbly. (*Ensign*, May 1979, p. 76.)

— *Marion D. Hanks*

Search your hearts, and see if you are like God. I have searched mine, and feel to repent of all my sins. (*HC*, 4:588.)

— *Joseph Smith*

Sin will always, *always*, result in suffering. It may come sooner, or it may come later, but it will come. The scriptures state that you will "stand with shame and awful guilt before the bar of God" (Jacob 6:9) and that you will experience "a lively sense of . . . guilt, and pain, and anguish." (Mosiah 2:38.) (*Ensign*, November 1990, p. 36.)

— *M. Russell Ballard*

There may be some who feel so burdened with guilt over transgressions of the past that they have lost hope; . . . . To everyone the gospel plan gives encouragement and hope . . . through the principle of repentance. (*Ensign*, November 1978, p. 49.)

— *N. Eldon Tanner*

Undoubtedly it is too much the case with some that they consider and fear the publicity of the wrong they commit more than committing the wrong itself; they wonder what people will say when they hear of it.

— *Lorenzo Snow*

You have an alarm system built into both body and spirit. In your body it is pain; in your spirit it is guilt—or spiritual pain. While neither pain nor guilt is pleasant, and an excess of either can be destructive, both are a protection, for they sound the alarm "Don't do that again!" (*Ensign*, May 1989, pp. 54, 59.)

— *Boyd K. Packer*

See also REPENTANCE

Repentance

Ellen was a young girl who really gained an understanding of repentance. While at the store, she took an item without paying for it. But when she got home, she felt miserable. She confided in her mother: "I'm so sorry I took it; will you take it back for me?"

Her mother said, "I can't repent for you, Ellen. You must repent yourself. *You* will have to take it back and say you are sorry."

It was hard, but she did it. "This is my first repentance," Ellen said. "I'm glad I know how to make things right."

Repentance makes it possible to return to the straight and narrow path and become as pure as we were at baptism. (*Ensign*, November 1984, p. 95.)

— *Dwan J. Young*

I am convinced that repentance is about 90 percent from the Lord and about 10 percent from man. Nephi goes still further and says, " . . . for we know that it is by grace that we are saved, after all we can do" (2 Ne. 25:23.) However, man's part is the most urgent and vital part because it must be first, and full, and sincere. An ancient Hebrew writing declares, "There must be a stirring below before there is a stirring above." This means that repentance must begin with us, with mortals. Many times we say we are waiting on the Lord, when as a matter of fact, the Lord is waiting on us. (CR, April 1970, p. 141.)

— *Hartman Rector, Jr.*

I readily confess that I would find no peace, neither happiness nor safety, in a world without repentance. I do not know what I should do if there were no way for me to erase my mistakes. The agony would be more than I could bear. (*Ensign*, May 1988, p. 71.)

— *Boyd K. Packer*

If punishment is the price repentance asks, it comes at bargain price. Consequences, even painful ones, protect us. So simple a thing as a child's cry of pain when his finger touches fire can teach us that. Except for the pain, the child might be consumed. (*Ensign*, May 1988, p. 71.)

— *Boyd K. Packer*

If you, through poor judgment, were to cover your shoes with mud, would you leave them that way? Of course not. You would cleanse and restore them. Would you then gather the residue of mud and place it in an envelope to show others the mistake that you made? No. Neither should you continue to relive forgiven sin. Every time such thoughts come into your mind, turn your heart in gratitude to the Savior, who gave His life that we, through faith in Him and obedience to His teachings, can overcome transgression and conquer its depressing influence in our lives. (*Ensign*, May 1986, p. 12.)

— *Richard G. Scott*

If we could feel or were sensitive even in the slightest to the matchless love of our Savior and his willingness to suffer for our individual sins, we would cease procrastination and "clean the slate," and repent of all our transgressions. (*Ensign*, May 1988, p. 23.)

— *David B. Haight*

If you and I and all who profess to be the followers of the Lord Jesus will bow down before him with humble hearts, each of us with a broken heart and contrite spirit, what will be the effect? Why, we will confess our faults to him, because they will be plain in our sight, we will see ourselves in the light of the Spirit of God, and the spirit of repentance will rest down upon us. (*JD*, 20:289.)

— *George Q. Cannon*

If your life is in disarray and you feel uncomfortable and unworthy to pray because you are not clean, don't worry. He already knows about all of that. He is waiting for you to kneel in humility and take the first few steps. Pray for strength. Pray for others to be led to support you and guide you and lift you. Pray that the love of the Savior will pour into your heart. Pray that the miracle of the Atonement will bring forgiveness because you are willing to change. I know that those prayers will be answered, for God loves you. His Son gave his life for you. I know they will help you. (*Ensign*, November 1988, p. 77.)

— *Richard G. Scott*

Repentance involves recognition of our imperfections, remorse for having strayed, restitution where appropriate, and resolve that the transgression will never be repeated. (*Ensign*, May 1989, p. 97.)

— *Royden G. Derrick*

Repentance is indispensable to the growing life, since in all growth there is constant adjustment, taking on and sloughing off. We cannot replace a bad life with a good one by any single word or act; there must be a continuing process of replacing error and wrongdoing with truth and right doing; of going from bad to good and from good to better. (*Eternal Quest*, Charles Manley Brown, ed., Salt Lake City: Bookcraft, 1956, p. 99.)

— *Hugh B. Brown*

Repentance is not a free gift. Just as faith without works is dead (see James 2:17)—so repentance, too, demands much. It is not for the fainthearted or the lazy. It requires a complete turning away from wrongdoing and a set of new works or doings which produce a new heart and a different man. Repentance means work. (*Ensign*, May 1983, p. 60.)

— *F. Burton Howard*

Repentance is not that superficial sorrow felt by the wrongdoer when "caught in the act" —a sorrow not for sin, but for sin's detection. Chagrin is not repentance. (*DFTP*, p. 381.)

— *Orson F. Whitney*

Repentance is the key with which we can unlock the prison from inside. We hold that key within our hands, and agency is ours to use it. (*Ensign*, May 1988, p. 71.)

— *Boyd K. Packer*

Repentance means turning the heart and the will to God. It denotes a change of mind, a fresh view about God, about oneself, and about the world. It is a cleansing process. It *is* the way back. (*Ensign*, November 1989, p. 88.)

— *Elaine L. Jack*

Sin is like cancer in the body. It will never heal itself. It will become progressively worse unless cured through the medicine of repentance. You can be made completely whole, new, purified, and clean every whit, through the miracle of repentance. (*Ensign*, May 1989, p. 36.)

— *Richard G. Scott*

Some people have an idea that because they have entered the waters of baptism and repented of their sins then that is an end of it. What a mistake! We need to have this spirit of repentance continually; we need to pray to God to show us our conduct every day. Every night before we retire to rest we should review the thoughts, words, and acts of the day and then repent of everything we have done that is wrong or that has grieved the Holy Spirit. Live this way every day and endeavor to progress every day. (*Gospel Truth*, Jerreld L. Newquist, ed., Salt Lake City: Deseret Book Co., 1987, p. 129.)

— *George Q. Cannon*

The enlarging of the soul requires not only some remodeling, but some excavating. (*Ensign*, May 1990, p. 34.)

— *Neal A. Maxwell*

The essence of the miracle of forgiveness is that it brings peace to the previously anxious, restless, frustrated, perhaps tormented soul.

— *Spencer W. Kimball*

The fatal symptom of our day is not that men do wrong—they always have . . . , but that they have *no intention of repenting,* while God has told us that the first rule that he has given the human race is that all men everywhere must repent. (*OAT,* p. 113.)

— *Hugh Nibley*

The heaviest load we feel is often from the weight of our unkept promises and our unresolved sins, which press down relentlessly upon us. In any genuine surrendering to God, one says, "I will give away all my sins to know thee." (Alma 22:18.) To Whom shall we give our sins? Only Jesus is both willing and able to take them! (*Ensign,* November 1989, p. 85.)

— *Neal A. Maxwell*

There is a . . . process whereby men and women are purified. The misuse of their lives is forgotten, and they are renewed and changed. This principle, of course, is repentance. When accompanied by authorized baptism, it provides not only an initial cleansing but an ongoing remission of sin as well. (*Ensign,* May 1983, p. 58.)

— *F. Burton Howard*

Treat one another aright. Have you sinned against another? Then go and make restitution. Have you defrauded another? Go and make it right. Have you spoken unkindly to your brother or sister? Then go and acknowledge your wrong and ask to be forgiven, promising to do better in the future. . . . How much better and how much more in keeping with the calling of a saint of God such a course would be than to harbor hard feelings in the heart. (*JD,* 21:99.)

— *John Taylor*

True repentance does not permit repetition.

— *Spencer W. Kimball*

We Must Learn to Judge Ourselves

The Lord does not want us to become aware of our state of nothingness and misery only at the Day of Judgment. Now and every day in our mortal lives, He wants to sharpen our awareness, that we may become our own judges, as he calls us to a continuous process of repentance.

After Alma had spoken about repentance and desires of righteousness until the end of life, he said, "They . . . are redeemed of the Lord; . . . for behold, they are their own judges." (Alma 41:7.) The Apostle Paul also explained, as stated in 1 Corinthians 11:31: "For if we would judge ourselves, we should not be judged."

It seems that we can only effectively go through the process of continuous repentance if we literally learn to become our own judges. (*Ensign*, May 1989, p. 72.)

— *F. Enzio Busche*

What a sweet, personal victory it is to recognize misdirection in one's own life and to pay the price that then lets us walk in His paths. (*Ensign*, May 1979, p. 69.)

— *Marvin J. Ashton*

When we disobey the laws of God, justice requires that compensation be made—a requirement which we are incapable of fulfilling. But out of his divine love for us, our Father has provided a plan and a Savior, Jesus Christ, whose redeeming sacrifice satisfies the demands of justice for us and makes possible repentance, forgiveness, and reconciliation with our Father. (*Ensign*, May 1982, p. 28.)

— *Ronald E. Poelman*

You know, the devil is very cunning in his approach, and when a boy or girl has done something wrong he whispers in their ears, "Now you have committed an unpardonable sin, there's no hope for you in the future." And he tells them that they might as well go on sinning, because they have taken the first step and there is no turning back. I want to say to you, . . . that is a lie from the champion of all liars. God wants you to be forgiven. He wants you to change your course. He wants you to call for help, and He stands ready and willing to help. (Fireside Address, Brigham Young University, October 8, 1967.)

— *Hugh B. Brown*

See ATONEMENT, FORGIVENESS, JUDGMENT, REMORSE, SACRAMENT, SIN, SPIRITUAL REBIRTH

Restoration

Be it known to all men, let it be proclaimed by the very trump of God, let angelic choirs sing of its wonders and glory, let all the hosts of men stand in awe as the voice from heaven declares that God has in these last days restored the fullness of his everlasting gospel.

Let every eye see, every ear hear, every heart be penetrated—for the voice of God is heard again. Angels again are coming from the courts of glory to declare eternal truths to mortal men. The gift of the Holy Ghost is being poured out upon the faithful, and thousands again shout praises to the Holy One of Israel. (*Ensign,* November 1984, p. 83.)

— *Bruce R. McConkie*

I bear witness to the world today that more than a century and a half ago the iron ceiling was shattered; the heavens were once again opened, and since that time revelations have been continuous. . . . Never again will the sun go down; never again will all men prove totally unworthy of communication with their Maker. Never again will God be hidden from his children on the earth. Revelation is here to remain. (*Ensign,* May 1977, p. 77.)

— *Spencer W. Kimball*

I think we all understand that this great latter-day kingdom has been set up for the last time, never again to be destroyed, and that never again will the necessity arise for another and future restoration. . . . With the opening of the heavens and the revealing of the gospel in our day, there came the positive unqualified assurance that the gospel was to remain on earth; that the kingdom was to be secure; that the Church of Jesus Christ of Latter-day Saints was to remain among men to prepare a people for the second coming of the Son of man. (*CR,* October 1958, p. 115.)

— *Bruce R. McConkie*

Mormonism, a nickname for the real religion of the Latter-day Saints, does not profess to be a new thing, except to this generation. It proclaims itself as the original plan of salvation, instituted in the heavens before the world was, and revealed from God to man in different ages. That Adam, Enoch, Noah, Abraham, Moses, and other ancient worthies had this religion successively, in a series of dispensations, . . . To us, the gospel taught by the Redeemer in the meridian of time was a restored gospel, of which, however, He was the author, . . . Mormonism, in short, is the primitive christian faith restored, the ancient gospel brought back again—this time to usher in the last dispensation, introduce the Millennium, and wind up the work of redemption as pertaining to this planet. (*MS,* 64:1-2.)

— *Lorenzo Snow*

The fact that I was not born in the times of spiritual darkness in which the heavens were silent and the Spirit withdrawn fills my soul with gratitude. Truly, to be without the word of the Lord to direct us is to be as wanderers in a vast desert who can find no familiar landmarks, or in the dense darkness of a cavern with no light to show us the way to escape. (*Ensign,* September 1976, p. 4.)

— *Spencer W. Kimball*

The message of the Restoration includes three great truths, truths which must be accepted by all mankind if they are to save themselves. These are, first, the divine Sonship of Christ; second, the divine mission of the Prophet Joseph Smith; and third, the truth and divinity of The Church of Jesus Christ of Latter-day Saints. (*Ensign*, November 1981, p. 46.)

— *Bruce R. McConkie*

The restoration of the wondrous truths known to Adam, Enoch, Noah, and Abraham has scarcely commenced. The sealed portion of the Book of Mormon is yet to be translated. . . . The greatness of the era of restoration is yet ahead. (*Ensign*, October 1073, pp. 78-83.)

— *Bruce R. McConkie*

You may take up Isaiah and all the prophets, and you will find that they refer to this latter-day dispensation, when the kingdom of God should be established on the earth. There never was a prophet, from Adam down, whose records we have, but had his eye upon this great dispensation of the last days. (*JD*, 13:324.)

— *Wilford Woodruff*

See also APOSTASY, JOSEPH SMITH, KINGDOM OF GOD

——— Resurrection ———

Against the medals and monuments of centuries of men's fleeting victories stands the only monument necessary to mark the eternal triumph—an empty garden tomb. (*Ensign*, May 1986, p. 15.)

— *Howard W. Hunter*

All our losses and sufferings will be made up to us in the resurrection. (*Ensign*, November 1976, p. 108.)

— *Bruce R. McConkie*

I want to impress . . . the fact that the resurrection will prove to be just as natural as birth; that the coming together of those particles that belong to us and belong to one another, each in a distinct organization, although similar in many respects to others, and the formation or reformation of our own personality, is just as sure as that we lay down our lives. As we rise in the morning from our night's rest, so it will be with us in the resurrection. (*Ensign*, November 19, 22:754.)

— *Charles W. Penrose*

In coming back from the dead, Moroni was a physical being of literal, corporeal, material reality. He held those heavy gold plates in his hands. A block of metal measuring seven-by-seven-by-eight inches could weigh anywhere from thirty to fifty pounds. But Moroni held them in his hands and turned over the pages with his fingers. His were flesh-and-bone hands, resurrected hands.

Then the Book of Mormon, as a physical, material, tangible object, also becomes evidence of the resurrection of the dead. (*Ensign*, May 1978, p. 63.)

— *Mark E. Petersen*

It seems there is good news and bad news about the resurrection. The good news is that everyone will be resurrected. All will live again! And all who have been righteous will be righteous still. The bad news is that he that is filthy shall be filthy still. (*Ensign*, November 1990, p. 76.)

— *Hartman Rector, Jr.*

What makes people repent? As near as I have been able to determine, once a person has sufficient faith in the Lord Jesus Christ that he believes Christ has paid for his sins, then he will repent. (*Ensign*, November 1990, p. 76.)

— *Hartman Rector, Jr.*

Jesus our Lord and Savior died for all, and all will be resurrected—good and bad, white and black, people of every race, whether sinners or not; and no matter how great their sins may be, the resurrection of their bodies is sure. Jesus has died for them, and they all will be redeemed from the grave through the atonement which he has made. (*Juvenile Instructor*, 35:124.)

— *George Q. Cannon*

Joseph Smith declared that the mother who laid down her little child, being deprived of the privilege, the joy, and the satisfaction of bringing it up to manhood or womanhood in this world, would, after the resurrection, have all the joy, satisfaction and pleasure, and even more than it would have been possible to have had in mortality, in seeing her child grow to the full measure of the stature of its spirit. (*MS*, 57:389.)

— *Joseph F. Smith*

Man is an eternal being, both in regard to his material organization and his mind and affections. The resurrection from the dead restored him to life with all his bodily and mental powers and faculties, and (if quickened by the celestial glory) consequently associates him with his family, friends, and kindred, as one of the necessary links of the chain which connects the great and royal family of heaven and earth in one eternal bond of kindred affection and association. (*The Prophet*, Parley P. Pratt, New York City, 1845.)

— *Parley P. Pratt*

Of all the victories in human history, none is so great, none so universal in its effect, none so everlasting in its consequences as the victory of the crucified Lord who came forth in the Resurrection that first Easter morning.

We laud the captains and the kings, we praise the nations that are victorious against oppressors. We appropriately build monuments to remember their sacrifices and their triumphs over the forces of oppression. But great and important as are these achievements, none can compare with the victory of the lonely, pain-racked figure on Calvary's cross who triumphed over death and brought the gift of eternal life to all mankind. (*Ensign*, May 1988, p. 66.)

— *Gordon B. Hinckley*

Resurrection is the reuniting of the body and the spirit. As Jesus was resurrected, eventually every person who was ever born into this world will be resurrected, whether he wants to be or not. When a person is resurrected, he receives immortality, which is to live forever in the resurrected state. Likewise, every person who was ever born into this world will receive immortality regardless of his or her behavior in this life. Thus, *resurrection* and *immortality* are synonymous. They are not a reward—they are a gift—for we have rendered no service nor attained any accomplishment to warrant these as a reward. The gift is from the Savior; it comes through His atoning sacrifice. (*Ensign*, May 1989, p. 76.)

— *Royden G. Derrick*

So plain was the vision, that I actually saw men, before they had ascended from the tomb, as though they were getting up slowly. They took each other, "My father, my son, my mother, my daughter, my brother, my sister." And when the voice calls for the dead to arise, suppose I am laid by the side of my father, what would be the first joy of my heart? To meet my father, my mother, my brother, my sister; and when they are by my side, I embrace them and they me. (*TPJS*, pp. 295-96.)

— *Joseph Smith*

The Savior did not have a fulness at first, but after he received his body and the resurrection all power was given to him both in heaven and in earth. Although he was a God, even the Son of God, with power and authority to create this earth and other earths, yet there were some things lacking which he did not receive until after his resurrection. In other words he had not received the fulness until he got a resurrected body. (*Doctrines of Salvation*, Bruce R. McConkie, comp., Salt Lake City: Bookcraft, 1956, 1:33.)

— *Joseph Fielding Smith*

We know that in the future, after we have passed through this life, we will then have our wives and our children with us. We will have our bodies glorified, made free from every sickness and distress, and rendered most beautiful. There is nothing more beautiful to look upon than a resurrected man or woman. There is nothing grander that I can imagine that a man can possess than a resurrected body. (*CR*, October 1900, p. 4.)

— *Lorenzo Snow*

To whom did the Lord first appear after His resurrection? . . .

Before anyone else saw Him, He made known His victory over death to this devoted and humble woman, whose name was Mary. She was the first one on earth to see a resurrected person, the first to greet the risen Lord as He emerged from the tomb—the first of all mankind, this lovely woman.

All the hosts of heaven had looked forward to this great event. The ancient prophets had spoken of it and yearned for it. But who was favored to see it first? A woman—a faithful, believing woman, Mary—there in the garden, near the tomb, where the angels spoke to her. (*Ensign*, May 1982, pp. 98-99.)

— *Mark E. Petersen*

We believe that Christ . . . was crucified upon the cross, that he died, his spirit leaving his body, and was buried and was on the third day resurrected, his spirit and body re-uniting, . . . That he is a resurrected being, and that in his pattern every man, woman, and child that ever lived shall come forth from the grave a resurrected being, even as Christ is a resurrected being. (*MS*, 99:395-96.)

— *Heber J. Grant*

When we speak of Jesus being resurrected, we mean that his premortal spirit, which animated his mortal body from his birth in the manger until he died on the cross, reentered that body; and the two, his spirit body and his physical body, inseparably welded together, arose from the tomb an immortal soul.

Our belief is, and we so testify, that Jesus not only conquered death for himself and brought forth his own glorious resurrected body, but that in so doing he also brought about a universal resurrection. (*Ensign*, May 1982, p. 6.)

— *Marion G. Romney*

Without the Resurrection, the gospel of Jesus Christ becomes a litany of wise sayings and seemingly unexplainable miracles—but sayings and miracles with no ultimate triumph. No, the ultimate triumph is in the ultimate miracle: for the first time in the history of mankind, one who was dead raised himself into living immortality. He *was* the Son of God, the Son of our immortal Father in Heaven, and his triumph over physical and spiritual death is the good news every Christian tongue should speak. (*Ensign*, May 1986, p. 16.)

— *Howard W. Hunter*

See also DEATH, JESUS CHRIST

——— Revelation ———

Changes in organization or procedures are a testimony that revelation is ongoing. While doctrines remain fixed, the methods or procedures do not. . . .

There will be changes made in the future as in the past. Whether the Brethren make changes or resist them depends entirely upon the instructions they receive through the channels of revelation which were established in the beginning.

The doctrines will remain fixed, eternal; the organization, programs, and procedures will be altered as directed by Him whose church this is. (*Ensign*, November 1989, pp. 15, 16.)

— *Boyd K. Packer*

Even the least Saint may know all things as fast as he is able to bear them. (*TPJS*, p. 149.)

— *Joseph Smith*

Every Church member has the opportunity, right, and privilege to receive a personal witness regarding gospel principles and Church practices. Without such a witness, one may feel confused and perhaps even burdened by what may appear to be simply institutional requirements of the Church.

We should obey the commandments and counsel of Church leaders; but also through study, through prayer, and by the influence of the Holy Spirit, we should seek and obtain an individual, personal witness that the principle or counsel is correct and divinely inspired. Then we can give enlightened, enthusiastic obedience, utilizing the Church as a means through which to give allegiance, time, talent, and other resources without reluctance or resentment. (*Ensign*, November 1984, p. 65.)

— *Ronald E. Poelman*

Every man or woman that has ever entered into the church of God and been baptized for the remission of sins has a right to revelation, a right to the Spirit of God, to assist them in their labors, in their administrations to their children, . . . and those over whom they are called upon to preside. (*MS*, 51:548.)

— *Wilford Woodruff*

I am more afraid that this people have so much confidence in their leaders that they will not inquire for themselves of God whether they are led by Him. I am fearful they settle down in a state of blind self-security, trusting their eternal destiny in the hands of their leaders with a reckless confidence that in itself would thwart the purposes of God in their salvation, and weaken that influence they could give to their leaders, did they know for themselves, by the revelations of Jesus, that they are led in the right way. Let every man and woman know, by the whispering of the Spirit of God to themselves, whether their leaders are walking in the path the Lord dictates, or not. (*JD*, 9:150.)

— *Brigham Young*

God hath not revealed anything to Joseph, but what He will make known unto the Twelve, and even the least Saint may know all things as fast as he is able to bear them, for the day must come when no man need say to his neighbor, Know ye the Lord; for all shall know Him (who remain) from the least to the greatest. (*TPJS*, p. 149.)

— *Joseph Smith*

How this confused world of today needs revelation from God. With war and pestilence and famine, with poverty, desolation, with more and more graft, dishonesty, and immorality, certainly the people of this world need revelation from God as never before. How absurd it would be to think that the Lord would give to a small handful of people in Palestine and the Old World his precious direction through revelation and now, in our extremity, close the heavens. (*Ensign*, May 1977, p. 76.)

— *Spencer W. Kimball*

How to Get Personal Revelation
1.   Search the Scriptures.
2.   Keep the Commandments.
3.   Ask in Faith.

Any person who will do this will get his heart so in tune with the infinite that there will come into his being, from the "still small voice," the eternal realities of religion. And as he progresses and advances and comes nearer to God, there will be a day when he will entertain angels, when he will see visions, and the final end is to view the face of God. (*Speeches of the Year*, Provo: Brigham Young University Press, 1967, p. 8.)

— *Bruce R. McConkie*

It is not a call to a special office that opens the windows of revelation to a truth seeker. Rather it is personal righteousness. (*CR*, October 1969, p. 82.)

— *Bruce R. McConkie*

It is the sad truth that if prophets and people are unreachable, the Lord generally does nothing for them. . . . The Lord will not force himself upon people, and if they do not believe, they will receive no revelation. . . . Remember: If there be eyes to see, there will be visions to inspire. If there be ears to hear, there will be revelations to experience. If there be hearts which can understand, know this: that the exalting truths of Christ's gospel will no longer be hidden and mysterious, and all earnest seekers may know God and his program. (*IE*, December 1966, p. 1105.)

— *Spencer W. Kimball*

Just as prayer is the means by which men address the Lord, so revelation is the means by which God communicates to men. (*Ensign*, May 1978, p. 50.)

— *Marion G. Romney*

Men and women who obey the principles of life and salvation, sincerely repent of their sins, and as sincerely strive to live in accordance with the principles of the gospel, are guided and inspired by the Holy Ghost, and are shown things to come. I testify that that guidance is with this Church and has been since the Prophet Joseph Smith established it. (*CR*, October 1929, p. 15.)

— *David O. McKay*

One minute's instruction from personages clothed with the glory of God coming down from the eternal worlds is worth more than all the volumes that were ever written by uninspired men. (*JD*, 12:354.)

— *Orson Pratt*

Personal revelation to the individual is the strength of the church of Jesus Christ in any age. (*Ensign*, May 1977, p. 23.)

— *Delbert L. Stapley*

Prophecy is the most sure way of knowing what is to happen. . . . It's all there when we understand it. (*Ensign*, May 1978, p. 74.)

— *LeGrand Richards*

Reading the experience of others, . . . can never give *us* a comprehensive view of our condition and true relation to God. Knowledge of these things can only be obtained by experience through the ordinances of God set forth for that purpose. Could you gaze into heaven five minutes, you would know more than you would by reading all that ever was written on the subject. (*TPJS*, p. 324.)

— *Joseph Smith*

Revelation continues with us today. The promptings of the Spirit, the dreams, and the visions and the visitations, and the ministering of angels all are with us now. And the still, small voice of the Holy Ghost "is a lamp unto [our] feet, and a light unto [our] path." (Ps. 119:105.) Of that I bear witness. (*Ensign*, November 1989, p. 16.)

— *Boyd K. Packer*

Revelation is a superlative spiritual endowment . . . which sets the Latter-day Saints apart from the world and makes them a peculiar people. It is a gift which the Lord always gives to his people which identifies them as the chosen of God.

— *Bruce R. McConkie*

Revelation is nontransferable. (*OAT*, p. 137.)

— *Hugh Nibley*

Revelation: Pure, perfect, personal revelation—this is the rock! (*Ensign*, May 1981, p. 77.)

— *Bruce R. McConkie*

Salvation cannot come without revelation; it is in vain for anyone to minister it. No man is a minister of Jesus Christ without being a prophet. No man can be a minister of Jesus Christ except he has the testimony of Jesus; and this is the spirit of prophecy. (*TPJS*, p. 160.)

— *Joseph Smith*

Since the establishment of the divine order on earth could come only by revelation, so its continuation is no less dependent upon the continuation of revelation. (*OAT*, p. 16.)

— *Hugh Nibley*

The foundation upon which The Church of Jesus Christ of Latter-day Saints is built is the rock of revelation—upon the rock that Jesus said He would build His church, and the gates of hell should not prevail against it. We have not received this knowledge through flesh and blood, . . . but through the operations of the Holy Ghost, . . . You cannot take this knowledge from us by imprisonment or any kind of persecution. We will stand by it unto death. (*JD*, 20:332.)

— *Lorenzo Snow*

The Melchizedek Priesthood holds the mysteries of the revelations of God. Wherever that priesthood exists, there also exists a knowledge of the laws of God; and wherever the gospel has existed, there has always been revelation. (*JD*, 13:231.)

— *John Taylor*

The Spirit of Revelation is in connection with these blessings. A person may profit by noticing the first intimation of the spirit of revelation; for instance, when you feel pure intelligence flowing into you, it may give you sudden strokes of ideas, so that by noticing it, you may find it fulfilled the same day or soon; those things that were presented unto your minds by the Spirit of God, will come to pass; and thus by learning the Spirit of God and understanding it, you may grow into the principle of revelation, until you become perfect in Christ Jesus. (*TPJS*, p. 151.)

— *Joseph Smith*

We are entitled to receive revelation. . . . Every member of the Church, independent of any position that he may hold, is entitled to get revelation from the Holy Ghost; he is entitled to entertain angels; he is entitled to view the visions of eternity; and . . . he is entitled to see God the same way that any prophet in literal and actual reality has seen the face of Deity. (Address, Brigham Young University, October 11, 1966.)

— *Bruce R. McConkie*

We require a living tree—a living fountain—living intelligence, proceeding from the living priesthood in heaven, through the living priesthood on earth. . . . And from the time that Adam first received a communication from God, to the time that John, on the Isle of Patmos, received his communication, or Joseph Smith had the heavens opened to him, it always required new revelations, adapted to the peculiar circumstances in which the churches or individuals were placed. Adam's revelation did not instruct Noah to build his ark; nor did Noah's revelation tell Lot to forsake Sodom; nor did either of these speak of the departure of the children of Israel from Egypt. These all had revelations for themselves, and so had Isaiah, Jeremiah, Ezekiel, Jesus, Peter, Paul, John, and Joseph. And so must we, or we shall make a shipwreck. (*MS*, 9:323-24.)

— *John Taylor*

Whenever the Lord had a people on the earth that He acknowledged as such, that people were led by revelation. (*JD*, 24:240.) . . . This power is in the bosom of Almighty God, and he imparts it to his servants the prophets as they stand in need of it day by day to build up Zion. (*JD*, 14:33.)

— *Wilford Woodruff*

While much must be taken on faith alone, there is individual revelation through which we may know the truth. "There is a spirit in man: and the inspiration of the Almighty giveth them understanding." (Job 32:8.) What may be obscure in the scriptures can be made plain through the gift of the Holy Ghost. We can have as full an understanding of spiritual things as we are willing to learn. (*Ensign*, November 1984, p. 66.)

— *Boyd K. Packer*

See also HOLY GHOST, INSPIRATION, PROPHETS, SPIRITUAL STRENGTH

———— **Revenge** ————

It is reported that President Brigham Young once said that he who takes offense when no offense was intended is a fool, and he who takes offense when offense *was* intended is usually a fool. It was then explained that there are two courses of action to follow when one is bitten by a rattlesnake. One may, in anger, fear, or vengefulness, pursue the creature and kill it. Or he may make full haste to get the venom out of his system. If we pursue the latter course we will likely survive, but if we attempt to follow the former, we may not be around long enough to finish it. (*Ensign*, January 1974, p. 21.)

— *Marion D. Hanks*

None of us can afford to pay the price of resenting or hating, because of what it does to us. (*CR*, October 1973, p. 16.)

— *Marion D. Hanks*

The spirit of revenge, of retaliation, of bearing a grudge, is entirely foreign to the gospel of the gentle, forgiving Jesus Christ. (*Miracle of Forgiveness*, Salt Lake City: Bookcraft, 1969, p. 265.)

— *Spencer W. Kimball*

Some years ago a group of teenagers from the local high school went on an all-day picnic into the desert on the outskirts of Phoenix. . . . These young people were picnicking and playing, and during their frolicking, one of the girls was bitten on the ankle by a rattlesnake. As is the case with such a bite, the rattler's fangs released venom almost immediately into her bloodstream.

This very moment was a time of critical decision. They could immediately begin to extract the poison from her leg, or they could search out the snake and destroy it. Their decision made, the girl and her young friends pursued the snake. It slipped quickly into the undergrowth and avoided them for fifteen or twenty minutes. Finally, they found it, and rocks and stones soon avenged the infliction.

Then they remembered: their companion had been bitten! . . . By then, the venom was well into its work of destruction. . . . The tissue in her limb had been destroyed by the poison, and a few days later it was found her leg would have to be amputated below the knee.

It was a senseless sacrifice, this price of revenge. How much better it would have been if, after the young woman had been bitten, there had been an extraction of the venom from the leg in a process known to all desert dwellers.

There are those today who have been bitten—or offended, if you will—by others. What can be done? What will you do when hurt by another? The safe way, the sure way, the right way is to look inward and immediately start the cleansing process. The wise and the happy person removes first the impurities from within. The longer the poison of resentment and unforgiveness stays in a body, the greater and longer lasting is its destructive effect. . . . The poison of revenge, or of unforgiving thoughts or attitudes, unless removed, will destroy the soul in which it is harbored. (*Ensign*, November 1983, p. 59.)

— *H. Burke Peterson*

Suppose one should injure me in person, or estate, and I should overlook it, and show mercy to the individual, it would cause him to reflect upon his conduct, and show him the true bearings of his unjust act, and make him ashamed of it much better than if I retaliated. If I were to pay him back in his own coin, I should render myself worthy of what I have received. If I bear an insult with meek patience, and do not return the injury, I have a decided advantage over my adversary. (*JD*, 2:93.)

— *Brigham Young*

See also FORGIVENESS, JUDGING, MERCY

—————— Reverence ——————

In the process of moral decline, reverence is one of the first virtues to disappear, and there should be serious concern about that loss in our times. (*Ensign*, November 1977, p. 52.)

— *Howard W. Hunter*

It is not enough to behave reverently; we must feel in our hearts reverence for our Heavenly Father and our Lord, Jesus Christ. Reverence flows from our admiration and respect for Deity. Those who are truly reverent are those who have paid the price to know the glory of the Father and His Son. (*Ensign*, November 1990, p. 70.)

— *L. Tom Perry*

One who has profound reverence for the Lord loves him, trusts in him, prays to him, relies upon him, and is inspired by him. (*Ensign*, September 1982, p. 3.)

— *Marion G. Romney*

Reverence is the atmosphere of heaven.

— *Howard W. Hunter*

Reverence is the soul of true religion. Its seedbed is sincerity. Its quality is determined by the esteem in which one holds the object of his reverence as evidenced by his behavior toward that object. When that object is *God*, the genuinely reverent person has a worshipful adoration coupled with a respectful behavior toward him and all that pertains to him. (*Ensign*, October 1976, p. 2.)

— *Marion G. Romney*

Reverence may be defined as a profound respect mingled with love and awe. Other words that add to our understanding of reverence include *gratitude, honor, veneration,* and *admiration.* The root word *revere* also implies an element of fear. Thus, reverence might be understood to mean an attitude of profound respect and love with a desire to honor and show gratitude, with a fear of breaking faith or offending. (*Ensign*, May 1988, p. 57.)

— *M. Russell Ballard*

The temple where Jesus taught and worshipped in Jerusalem was built in such a way as to establish respect for and devotion to the Father. Its very architecture taught a silent but constant lesson of reverence. Every Hebrew was privileged to enter into the outer courts of the temple, but only one particular class of men could enter into the inner court or holy place. Into the innermost sanctuary, the Holy of Holies, only one man was permitted to make his way, and this was limited to only one special day each year. In this way a great truth was taught: that God must be approached carefully, respectfully, and with great preparation. (*Ensign*, November 1977, p. 52.)

— *Howard W. Hunter*

Three influences in home life awaken reverence in children and contribute to its development in their souls. These are gentle guidance, courtesy by parents to each other and to children, and prayer in which children participate.

— *David O. McKay*

See also WORSHIP

Righteousness

God admires the men and women today who pursue a course of rectitude and who, notwithstanding the powers of Satan that are arrayed against them, can say, Get thee behind me Satan, and who live a righteous, a godly life, and such people have influence with God and their prayers avail much. (*JD*, 23:191.)

— *Lorenzo Snow*

If we can pattern our life after the Master, and take his teaching and example as the supreme pattern for our own, we will not find it difficult to be consistent and loyal in every walk of life, for we will be committed to a single, sacred standard of conduct and belief. (*Ensign*, May 1990, p. 60.)

— *Howard W. Hunter*

It matters not what our nationality, our race, our culture, our academic degree, or our political or social standing, we build security and strength in our lives by living the gospel. (*Ensign*, January 1974, p. 121.)

— *James A. Cullimore*

Live so your memories can bless the full length of your life. (*Ensign*, May 1981, p. 41.)

— *David B. Haight*

Perfection is our ultimate destination. Righteousness, or goodness, is the chariot to carry us there. (*Ensign*, November 1988, p. 92.)

— *Michaelene P. Grassli*

Righteousness is living a life that is in harmony with the laws, principles, and ordinances of the gospel. (*Ensign*, May 1988, p. 81.)

— *Joseph B. Wirthlin*

The challenging conditions we find in the world today should be no surprise to us. As we approach the time of the Savior's return, wickedness will increase. There will be more temptations in our daily lives, and they will become more intense. It will become more acceptable in the world to break the laws of God or to disregard them altogether. The stigma attached to immoral, dishonest behavior will disappear.

In this difficult environment we will be expected to steer our own course in an upward direction. As President Kimball has warned us, it will neither be acceptable nor safe to remain on the plateaus where our present conduct has kept us. Abrupt downward forces, represented by increasing wickedness in the world, can only be offset by forces that move correspondingly upward. Our lives must be better than they have ever been before. (*Ensign*, May 1983, p. 34.)

— *Dean L. Larsen*

There are two influences ever present in the world. One is constructive and elevating and comes from our Heavenly Father; the other is destructive and debasing and comes from Lucifer. We have our agency and make our own choice in life subject to these unseen powers. There is a division line well defined that separates the Lord's territory from Lucifer's. If we live on the Lord's side of the line, Lucifer cannot come there to influence us, but if we cross the line into his territory, we are in his power. By keeping the commandments of the Lord we are safe on His side of the line, but if we disobey His teachings we voluntarily cross into the zone of temptation and invite the destruction that is ever present there. Knowing this, how anxious we should always be to live on the Lord's side of the line. (*IE*, 38:278.)

— *George Albert Smith*

Righteous living is a shield, a protector, an insulation, a strength, a power, a joy, a Christlike trait. (*Ensign*, November 1986, p. 14.)

— *Marvin J. Ashton*

We cannot condone a separation of our religious beliefs from our daily living. Righteousness must prevail in our lives and in our homes. (*Ensign*, May 1979, p. 7.)

— *Spencer W. Kimball*

The whole armor of God will keep the divine light of Jesus Christ inside and the darkness of evil outside. (*Ensign*, January 1974, p. 118.)

— *Bernard P. Brockbank*

We would say to the brethren, seek to know God in your closets, call upon him in the fields. Follow the directions of the Book of Mormon, and pray over, and for your families, your cattle, your flocks, your herds, your corn, and all things that you possess; ask the blessing of God upon all your labors, and everything that you engage in. Be virtuous and pure; be men of integrity and truth; keep the commandments of God; and then you will be able more perfectly to understand the difference between right and wrong—between the things of God and the things of men; and your path will be like that of the just, which shineth brighter and brighter unto the perfect day. (*TPJS*, p. 247.)

— *Joseph Smith*

See also OBEDIENCE, PERFECTION, PROGRESSION, PURITY

——— Sabbath ———

How we observe the Sabbath indicates our feelings toward our Father in Heaven. (*Ensign*, November 1990, p. 13.)

— *LeGrand R. Curtis*

A sacred Sabbath is not going out on excursions on Sunday. A sacred Sabbath is to attend to our meetings and to read the Scriptures, to supplicate God, and to have our minds set upon the things that are calculated to save us in this life and in the life to come. (*IE*, 24:874.)

— *Heber J. Grant*

It's all right to pull the cow out of the mud on Sunday, provided that you don't push him in on Saturday night. (Quoted by Eldred G. Smith, *Ensign*, January 1974, p. 63.)

— *Harold B. Lee*

The Lord's plan is perfect, his commandments have in view the salvation of the body as well as the spirit, for it is the soul that will be redeemed from the grave and glorified. God has commanded us to care for the spirit, as well as for the body, and give it food in due season, and He set aside the Sabbath day that man might rest from his temporal labors and go to the house of the Lord and be fed with that holy influence which nourishes the spirit of man. That is why we meet together on the Sabbath day. Our spirits need their food, the same as do our bodies and if we neglect them, they will starve and dwindle and die upon the same principle that the body will die when deprived of its proper nourishment. (*Liahona: The Elders' Journal*, 7:530.)

— *Orson F. Whitney*

The Sabbath has become the play-day of this great nation—the day set apart by thousands to violate the commandment that God gave long, long ago, and I am persuaded that much of the sorrow and distress that is afflicting and will continue to inflict mankind is traceable to the fact that they have ignored his admonition to keep the Sabbath day holy. (*CR*, October 1935, p. 120.)

— *George Albert Smith*

The small island kingdom of Tonga lies immediately next to the international date line, so it is the first country in the world to greet the Sabbath day. It is a small country and, in the counting of the world, a poor country. But years ago a wise Tongan king decreed that the Sabbath would be kept holy in Tonga forever.

Modern civilization has come in many ways to Tonga. If one goes to the capital of Nuku'alofa on a weekday, he finds the usual heavy traffic of trucks and cars and the bustle of thousands of shoppers making their regular purchases from well-stocked stores and markets. One sees people line up to view the latest movies and to rent videos. One can watch modern buses whisk tourists off to catch their jet planes, or observe the speed and clarity of a satellite call to the United States. The streets are crowded and business is good. You might wonder, "What is so different about this town from hundreds of others like it throughout the world?"

But when Sunday dawns on the kingdom of Tonga, a transformation takes place. If one goes downtown, he sees deserted streets—no taxis or buses or crowds of people. All the stores, all the markets, all the movie theaters, all the offices are closed. No planes fly, no ships come in or out, no commerce takes place. No games are played, The people go to church. Tonga is remembering to keep the Sabbath day holy.

It is significant that the first country in the world to greet the holy Sabbath keeps the Sabbath holy.

Has the Lord blessed them? Maybe the world cannot see his blessings, but in the ways that really count, he has blessed them abundantly. He has blessed them with the gospel of Jesus Christ, and a larger percentage of the population there belongs to the Church than in any other country. (*Ensign*, November 1984, pp. 79-80.)

— *John H. Groberg*

There is power in keeping the Sabbath day holy—power to help others as well as ourselves. If we would have God's blessings and protection as individuals, as families, as communities, and as nations, we must keep His Sabbath day holy. . . . I further testify that when we eventually see things through the proper perspective of eternal truth, we will be amazed at how much we were blessed in important—though often unperceived—ways through keeping the Sabbath holy. (*Ensign*, November 1984, pp. 80-81.)

— *John H. Groberg*

There seems to be an ever-increasing popularity in disregarding the centuries-old commandment to observe and respect the Sabbath day. For many it has become a holiday rather than a holy day of rest and sanctification. . . .

The Lord's commandment about the Sabbath day has not been altered, nor has the Church's affirmation of the commandment to observe the Sabbath day. Those who violate this commandment in the exercise of their agency are answerable for losing the blessings which observance of this commandment would bring. (*Ensign*, November 1986, p. 9.)

— *James E. Faust*

See also COMMANDMENTS, WORSHIP

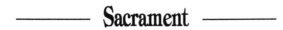

Sacrament

Order, reverence, attention to divine promises—the promise to enter into the fold of Christ, to cherish virtues mentioned in the gospel of Christ, to keep them ever in mind, to love the Lord wholeheartedly, and to labor, even at the sacrifice of self, for the brotherhood of man—these and all kindred virtues are associated with the partaking of the Lord's Supper. (*CR*, October 1929, p. 15.)

— *David O. McKay*

As we worthily partake of the sacrament, we will sense those things we need to improve in and receive the help and determination to do so. No matter what our problems, the sacrament always gives hope. (*Ensign*, May 1989, p. 38.)

— *John H. Groberg*

It is . . . necessary for our spiritual body that we should partake of this sacrament, and by it obtain spiritual food for our souls. If we were given our physical food only on stated occasions and at specified places we would all be there . . . .

How can we have spiritual hunger? Who is there among us that does not wound his spirit by word, thought, or deed, from Sabbath to Sabbath? We do things for which we are sorry, and desire to be forgiven, or we have erred against someone and given injury. If there is a feeling in our hearts that we are sorry for what we have done; if there is a feeling in our souls that we would like to be forgiven, then the method to obtain forgiveness is not through rebaptism . . . but it is to repent of our sins, to go to those against whom we have sinned or transgressed and obtain their forgiveness, and then repair to the sacrament table, where, if we have sincerely repented and put ourselves in proper condition, we shall be forgiven, and spiritual healing will come to our souls. . . .

Ordinarily we will be our own judges. If we are properly instructed, we know that it is not our privilege to partake of the emblems of the flesh and blood of the Lord in sin, in transgression, or having injured and holding feelings against our brethren and sisters. No man goes away from this Church and becomes an apostate in a week, nor in a month. It is a slow process. The one thing that would make for the safety of every man and woman would be to appear at the sacrament table every Sabbath day. We would not get very far away in one week, not so far away that, by the process of self-investigation, we could not rectify the wrongs we may have done. If we should refrain from partaking of the sacrament, condemned by ourselves as unworthy to receive these emblems, we could not endure that long, and we would soon, I am sure, have the spirit of repentance. *The road to the sacrament table is the path of safety for Latter-day Saints.* (*IE*, October 1919, pp. 1025-1028.)

— *Melvin J. Ballard*

The partaking of the Sacrament is one of the most sacred ordinances of the Church of Jesus Christ of Latter-day Saints. Associated with it are the principles fundamental in character-building and essential to man's advancement and exaltation in the kingdom of God. . . . In the partaking of the Sacrament, there is danger of people's permitting formality to supersede spirituality, but he who partakes of the Sacrament worthily and sincerely is truly an acceptable follower of the Son of God. (*IE*, 64:214.)

— *David O. McKay*

The Lord instituted the sacrament, as we know it today, during what we commonly call the Last Supper. In one sense, it was the last supper, but in another, it was the first supper—the beginning of many spiritual feasts. (*Ensign*, May 1989, p. 38.)

— *John H. Groberg*

The Sacrament Covenant

Who can measure the responsibility of such a covenant? How far reaching! How comprehensive! It excludes from man's life, profanity, vulgarity, idleness, enmity, jealousy, drunkenness, dishonesty, hatred, selfishness, and every form of vice. It obligates him to sobriety, to industry, to kindness, to the performance of every duty in church and state. He binds himself to respect his fellowmen, to honor the Priesthood, to pay his tithes and offerings and to consecrate his life to the service of humanity. (*MS*, 85:778.)

— *David O. McKay*

We want every Latter-day Saint to come to the sacrament table because it is the place for self-investigation, for self-inspection, where we may learn to rectify our course and to make right our own lives, bringing ourselves into harmony with the teachings of the Church and with our brethren and sisters. (*Sermons and Missionary Services of Melvin Joseph Ballard*, Salt Lake City: Deseret Book Co., 1949, p. 150.)

— *Melvin J. Ballard*

What a strength there would be in this Church if next Sunday every member who partakes of the sacrament would sense the significance of the covenant made in that ordinance; if every member were willing to take upon him the name of the Son, to be a true Christian, to be proud of it, and always to remember him in the home, in business, in society, always remember him and keep his commandments that he has given them. How comprehensive the blessing, and how significant the covenant we make each Sabbath day. (Quoted by Delbert L. Stapley, Address, Brigham Young University, May 8, 1956.)

— *David O. McKay*

[When partaking] of the sacrament of the Lord's Supper, . . . we should endeavor to draw away our feelings and affections from things of time and sense.

For in partaking of the sacrament we not only commemorate the death and sufferings of our Lord and Savior Jesus Christ, but we also shadow forth the time when he will come again and when we shall meet and eat bread with him in the kingdom of God. When we are thus assembled together, we may expect to receive guidance and blessings from God.

— *John Taylor*

You will find first that the sacrament is a memorial of Christ's life and death. . . .

A second significance or a second principle associated with the administering of the sacrament is the bond of brotherhood. . . . We meet in the brotherhood of Christ, all on the same level, each expressing confidence in the other and all in one another. Oh, the strength of brotherhood! Sin divides us. Righteousness unites.

The partaking of the sacrament indicates also how communion with Christ may be secured. It cannot be obtained by Sunday righteousness and weekday indulgence. It implies that we will remember Christ always. . . .

And the fourth great significance is the promise that it is a means of receiving divine guidance. If a friend is one who summons us to our best, then is not Jesus Christ our best friend and should we not think of the sacrament as one of the chief appeals to us to be our best? The Lord's Supper looks not back to our past with a critical eye, but to our future with a helpful one. (*CR*, October 1929, pp. 10-15.)

— *David O. McKay*

It is said of President Wilford Woodruff that while the sacrament was being passed, his lips could be observed in silent motion as he repeated to himself over and over again. "I do remember thee, I do remember thee." (*Ensign*, October 1976, p. 3.)

— *Marion G. Romney*

The solemn moments of thought while the sacrament is being served have great significance. They are moments of self-examination, introspection, self-discernment—a time to reflect and to resolve. (*Ensign*, May 1977, p. 25.)

— *Howard W. Hunter*

See also AARONIC PRIESTHOOD, ATONEMENT, JESUS CHRIST, REPENTANCE

Sacrifice

A religion that does not require the sacrifice of all things never has power sufficient to produce the faith necessary unto life and salvation; for from the first existence of man, the faith necessary unto the enjoyment of life and salvation never could be obtained without the sacrifice of all earthly things. (*Lectures on Faith*, Lecture 6.)

— *Joseph Smith*

Celestial glory is worth all we possess; if it calls for every dollar we own and our lives into the bargain, if we obtain an entrance into the celestial kingdom of God it will amply repay us. (*JD*, 17:250.)

— *Wilford Woodruff*

I would not give the ashes of a rye straw for any religion that was not worth living for and . . . dying for; and I would not give much for the man that was not willing to sacrifice his all for the sake of his religion. (*JD*, 23:155.)

— *Lorenzo Snow*

I [am] persuaded of one great truth: Whenever the Lord has a great blessing for one of his children, he puts that son or daughter in the way to make a great sacrifice.

— *Harold B. Lee*

If we are to walk in the steps of the Savior, we cannot do it without personal sacrifice and sincere involvement. It is rarely convenient; but love extends beyond convenience for those who have conditioned themselves to look for opportunities to serve. (*Ensign*, November 1981, p. 82.)

— *J. Richard Clarke*

Surely, in the work of the Lord, it is what we do after we think we have done enough that really counts with him, for that's when the blessings flow. . . . If you would have a blessing from the Lord, put something upon the altar. Make a sacrifice. (*Ensign*, May 1979, p. 30.)

— *Hartman Rector, Jr.*

The Lord requires sacrifice, meaning something above and beyond the minimum. The Master spoke of the "second mile" and told us to go there (see Matt. 5:41). Why? Because he wants to bless us [and] he put all the blessings in the second mile. (*Ensign*, May 1979, p. 30.)

— *Hartman Rector, Jr.*

There can be no true worship without sacrifice, and there can be no true sacrifice without a cause. The cause that earns our love and priority is the cause of Jesus Christ. (*Ensign*, November 1984, p. 32.)

— *Russell M. Nelson*

We must lay on the altar and sacrifice whatever is required by the Lord. We begin by offering a "broken heart and a contrite spirit." We follow this by giving our best effort in our assigned fields of labor and callings. We learn our duty and execute it fully. Finally we consecrate our time, talents, and means as called upon by our leaders and as prompted by the whisperings of the Spirit. (*Ensign*, May 1978, p. 81.)

— *Spencer W. Kimball*

See also CONSECRATION, EYE SINGLE, SELFLESSNESS

Saints

A saint is a believer in Christ, and knows of His perfect love. The giving saint shares in a true spirit of that love, and the receiving saint accepts in a true spirit of gratitude. A saint serves others, knowing that the more one serves, the greater the opportunity for the Spirit to sanctify and purify.

A saint is tolerant, and is attentive to the pleading of other human beings, . . .

A saint "refrain[s] from idleness" (Alma 38:12) and seeks learning by study, and also by faith. . . .

A saint is honest and kind, paying financial obligations promptly and fully, treating others as she or he would want to be treated.

A saint is an honorable citizen, . . .

A saint resolves any differences with others honorably and peacefully and is constant in courtesy . . . .

A saint shuns that which is unclean or degrading and avoids excess even of that which is good.

Perhaps above all, a saint is reverent. Reverence for the Lord, for the earth He created, for leaders, for the dignity of others, for the law, for the sanctity of life, for chapels and other buildings, are all evidences of saintly attitudes.

A reverent saint loves the Lord and gives highest priority to keeping His commandments. Daily prayer, periodic fasting, payment of tithes and offerings are privileges important to a faithful saint.

Finally, a saint is one who receives the gifts of the Spirit that God has promised to all His faithful sons and daughters. (See Joel 2:28-29; Acts 2:17-18.) (*Ensign*, May 1990, pp. 16-17.)

— *Russell M. Nelson*

A saint is one who follows Christ in holiness and devotion with a view fixed on *eternal* life. (*Ensign*, May 1987, p. 11.)

— *William Grant Bangerter*

Let the winds and the storms beat and pound upon . . . faithful Saints; they will overcome the world—not vice versa. Let others falter; these will not! Let others pout and doubt; these will not! . . . To a world spiritually illiterate, [they] give great lessons in the grammar of the gospel. (*Ensign*, May 1983, p. 11.)

— *Neal A. Maxwell*

The word *saint* does not mean that any of us is perfect. What is does mean is that we are all trying, all serving, and all vowing to stand firm in the faith. (*Ensign*, May 1987, p. 17.)

— *Howard W. Hunter*

We do not become Saints automatically by entering the waters of baptism. We become saints, in the true sense of the word, as we live saintly lives and cultivate Christlike attributes. (*Ensign*, November 1985, p. 45.)

— *Carlos E. Asay*

See also DISCIPLESHIP, PERFECTION, PROGRESSION, RIGHTEOUSNESS

——— Salvation ———

As there is only one God and one Savior, so there is only one salvation, one strait and narrow path leading to eternal life, one way in which the grace of God can be poured out upon us mortals in full measure.

To gain salvation all men everywhere must have faith in the Lord Jesus Christ. They must repent of their sins and be baptized by a legal administrator who has power to seal on earth and in heaven. They must receive the gift of the Holy Ghost, be sanctified by the power of the Spirit, and keep the commandments of God all their days. (*Ensign*, November 1984, p. 83.)

— *Bruce R. McConkie*

I cannot get my heart upon anything else, only salvation for the people. All nations are going to share in these blessings; all are incorporated in the redemption of the Savior. He has tasted death for every man; they are all in his power, and he saves them all, as he says, . . ; and the Father has put all the creations upon this earth in his power. The earth itself, and mankind upon it, the brute beasts, the fish of the sea, and the fowls of heaven, the insects, and every creeping thing with all things pertaining to this earthly ball—all are in the hands of the Savior, and he has redeemed them all. (*JD*, 6:296-297.)

— *Brigham Young*

May I suggest a formula for bringing forth good fruit and helping one to gain eternal salvation? (1) have faith in the Lord Jesus Christ and in yourself, (2) study eternal truths, (3) ponder and pray for understanding, (4) strive to incorporate principles of truth into daily living, and (5) exercise integrity in all that you do, and (6) strive to do everything you do to a standard of excellence. (*Ensign*, November 1984, p. 63.)

— *Royden G. Derrick*

Offering salvation to [all of his children] . . . is the Lord's self-imposed duty, this great labor his highest glory. Likewise, it is man's duty, self-imposed, his pleasure and joy, his labor, and ultimately his glory. (*The Utah Genealogical and Historical Magazine*, October 1934, p. 189.)

— *John A. Widtsoe*

Salvation is administered on the same terms and conditions in all ages. Men must have faith in him, repent of their sins, be baptized in his name, receive the gift of the Holy Ghost, and remain steadfast to gain life eternal. (*Ensign*, May 1988, p. 22.)

— *David B. Haight*

Salvation is nothing more nor less than to triumph over all our enemies and put them under our feet. And when we have power to put all enemies under our feet in this world, and a knowledge to triumph over all evil spirits in the world to come, then we are saved, as in the case of Jesus, who was to reign until He had put all enemies under His feet, and the last enemy was death. (*TPJS*, p. 297.)

— *Joseph Smith*

There is only one way provided by the Lord for man to gain salvation and eternal life in the kingdom of God and that is by and through the living, personal Jesus Christ, and by knowing and living his commandments. (*Ensign*, May 1977, p. 27.)

— *Bernard P. Brockbank*

See also ETERNAL LIFE, EXALTATION, JESUS CHRIST, PLAN OF SALVATION

Satan

God does not fight Satan: a word from him and Satan is silenced and banished. There is no contest there; in fact we are expressly told that all the power which Satan enjoys here on earth is granted him by God. "We will allow Satan, our common enemy, to try man and to tempt him." It is man's strength that is being tested—not God's. (*OAT*, p. 7.)

— *Hugh Nibley*

All beings who have bodies have power over those who have not. the devil has no power over us only as we permit him. The moment we revolt at anything which comes from God, the devil takes power. (*TPJS*, p. 181.)

— *Joseph Smith*

God loves us; the devil hates us. God wants us to have a fullness of joy as He has. The devil wants us to be miserable as he is. God gives us commandments to bless us. The devil would have us break these commandments to curse us. (*Ensign*, May 1988, p. 6.)

— *Ezra Taft Benson*

He may try to *discourage*. . . . He may *tempt* towards disobedience and sin. He may try to *frighten* by displays of power, or to *deceive* by revelations or visions or impressions that are false and damning. He will use his logic to *confuse* and his rationalizations to *destroy*. He will shade meanings, open doors an inch at a time, and,lead from purest white through all the shades of gray to the darkest black. (*Faith Precedes the Miracle,* Spencer W. Kimball, Salt Lake City: Deseret Book Co., 1978.)

— *Spencer W. Kimball*

It was revealed to me in the commencement of this Church, that the Church would spread, prosper, grow and extend, and that in proportion to the spread of the gospel among the nations of the earth, so would the power of Satan rise. (*JD*, 13:280.)

— *Brigham Young*

Satan . . . was more concerned with credit than with results. (*CR*, October 1975, p. 115.)

— *N. Eldon Tanner*

Satan has the power to transform himself into an angel of light; he can give visions and revelations as well as spiritual manifestations. (*MS*, 19:197.)

— *John Taylor*

Satan sows selfishness, unbelief, fear, doubt, greed, spiritual instability, and a general concern for self into men's hearts. He is a master builder of spiritual detours to waste time, divert attention from that which is good, and diminish spiritual receptivity. Satan especially desires to deceive the Latter-day Saints, those who know the truth about him, those who can particularly influence others in their teaching and living of the gospel in the home, in the classroom, from the pulpit, and in the world. In these days of increasing deception, and more to come, one must be aware of Satan's spiritual snares and be sure of his own discernment. (*Ensign*, May 1982, p. 26.)

— Gene R. Cook

The desire and work of Satan is to mislead and corrupt. He seeks to frustrate the gospel plan by which God has provided the opportunity of eternal life for His children. (*Ensign*, May 1986, p. 51.)

— Dallin H. Oaks

Lucifer in clever ways manipulates our choices, deceiving us about sin and consequences. He, and his angels with him, tempt us to be unworthy, even wicked. But he cannot, in all eternity he cannot, with all his power he cannot completely destroy us; not without our own consent. (*Ensign*, May 1988, p. 71.)

— Boyd K. Packer

The men and women who desire to obtain seats in the celestial kingdom will find that they must battle with the enemy of all righteousness every day. (*JD*, 11:14.)

— Brigham Young

The priesthood in the Church is a mighty bulwark against the advance of evil. There is no power on earth that can withstand the thrust of the adversary except a body of righteous men who honor their priesthood in their homes. (*Ensign*, July 1972, p. 120.)

— A. Theodore Tuttle

We talk about Satan being bound. Satan will be bound by the power of God; but he will be bound also by the determination of the people of God not to listen to him, not to be governed by him. (*CR*, October 1897, p. 65.)

— George Q. Cannon

There is an ample shield against the power of Lucifer and his hosts. This protection lies in the spirit of discernment through the gift of the Holy Ghost. This gift comes undeviatingly by personal revelation to those who strive to obey the commandments of the Lord and to follow the counsel of the living prophets.

This personal revelation will surely come to all whose eyes are single to the glory of God, for it is promised that their bodies will be "filled with light, and there shall be no darkness" in them (D&C 88:67). Satan's efforts can be thwarted by all who come unto Christ by obedience to the covenants and ordinances of the gospel. (*Ensign*, November 1987, pp. 35-36.)

— *James E. Faust*

It is interesting that Satan, who voted for "no opposition," has become the main source of it!

— *Mary Ellen Edmunds*

[Satan] is working under such perfect disguise that many do not recognize either him or his methods. There is no crime he would not commit, no debauchery he would not set up, no plague he would not send, no heart he would not break, no life he would not take, no soul he would not destroy. He comes as a thief in the night; he s a wolf in sheep's clothing. (*IE*, 45:761.)

— *The First Presidency*

See also DECEPTION, EVIL, OPPOSITION, WICKEDNESS

——— Scripture Study ———

Always remember, there is no satisfactory substitute for the scriptures and the words of the living prophets. These should be your original sources. Read and ponder more what the Lord has said, and less about what others have written concerning what the Lord has said. (Address to educators, Salt Lake City, September 17, 1976.)

— *Ezra Taft Benson*

Brothers and sisters, you don't have to be a natural student to read the scriptures; you just need to love the Lord. (*Ensign*, November 1982, p. 15.)

— *J. Richard Clarke*

Do not wonder at your sons and daughters going astray and losing the faith, when they do not read the word of God. (*CR*, October 1897, p. 40.)

— *George Q. Cannon*

Do you read the scriptures, my brethren and sisters, as though you were writing them a thousand, two thousand, or five thousand years ago? Do you read them as though you stood in the place of the men who wrote them? If you do not feel thus, it is your privilege to do so, that you may be as familiar with the spirit and meaning of the written word of God as you are with your daily walk and conversation, or as you are with your workmen or with your households. You may understand what the Prophets understood and thought—what they designed and planned to bring forth to their brethren for their good.

When you can thus feel, then you may begin to think that you can find out something about God, and begin to learn who he is. (*JD*, 7:333.)

— *Brigham Young*

Family Scripture Study

Families need to teach the gospel to each other *in the language of God,* our Heavenly Father. In the home, when direction is needed, When a problem or misunderstanding arises, I pray that we may open the scriptures with our youth beside us and find the law irrevocably decreed upon which blessings are predicated. Reading the will of God in the language of God builds reverence and witness and commitment, and we will all live more purely. (*Ensign*, May 1984, p. 26.)

— *Elaine A. Cannon*

I admonish you, O Israel, search the Scriptures; read them in your homes; teach your families what the Lord has said; let us spend less of our time reading the unimportant and often harmful literature of the day and go to the fountain of truth and read the word of the Lord. (*CR*, October 1917, p. 41.)

— *George Albert Smith*

I am going to give more time and attention to the study and pondering of the scriptures themselves, rather than to the commentaries and criticisms that others have written about them. In doing this, I am going to be as open as I can be to the Spirit of the Lord so that I can understand these things for myself. (*Ensign*, November 1987, p. 12.)

— *Dean L. Larsen*

The scriptures that are never read will never help us. (*Ensign*, May 1985, p. 23.)

— *L. Tom Perry*

If you pray for an angel to visit you, you know what he'll do if he comes. He'll just quote the scriptures to you—so you know you're wasting your time waiting for what we already have. I'm quite serious about that. (*OAT*, p. 42.)

— *Hugh Nibley*

I don't know much about the gospel other than what I've learned from the standard works. When I drink from a spring I like to get the water where it comes out of the ground, not down the stream after the cattle have waded in it. . . . I appreciate other people's interpretation, but when it comes to the gospel we ought to be acquainted with what the Lord says. . . . You ought to read the Book of

Mormon and the Doctrine and Covenants; and . . . all the scriptures with the idea of finding out what's in them and what the meaning is and not to prove some idea of your own. Just read them and plead with the Lord to let you understand what he had in mind when he wrote them. (Address delivered at Coordinators' Convention, Seminaries and Institutes of Religion, 13 April 1973, quoted by J. Richard Clarke, *Ensign*, November 1982, p. 15.)

— *Marion G. Romney*

If we immerse ourselves daily in the scriptures, particularly the Book of Mormon, we will have increased discernment. We will have power to do good and to resist evil, and our ability to solve problems will be expanded. Messages to help us in our day were foreseen by the Lord and were divinely placed on the pages of the scriptures to assist us and our families. (*Ensign*, November 1989, pp. 89-90.)

— *Joanne B. Doxey*

In the final analysis there is no way, absolutely none, to understand any scripture except to have the same spirit of prophecy that rested upon the one who uttered the truth in its original form. Scripture comes from God by the power of the Holy Ghost. It does not originate with man. It means only what the Holy Ghost thinks it means. To interpret it, we must be enlightened by the power of the Holy Spirit. It takes a prophet to understand a prophet, and every faithful member of the Church should have "the testimony of Jesus" which "is the spirit of prophecy." (Rev. 19:10.) (*Ensign*, October 1973, p. 82.)

— *Bruce R. McConkie*

Knowledge received from studying the scriptures assists us in making correct decisions in all areas of life's activities and helps us to know God and understand his purposes. (*Ensign*, May 1981, p. 51.)

— *Franklin D. Richards*

One cannot receive eternal life without becoming a "doer of the word" (see James 1:22) and being valiant in obedience to the Lord's commandments. And one cannot become a "doer of the word" without first becoming a "hearer." And to become a "hearer" is not simply to stand idly by and wait for chance bits of information; it is to seek out and study and pray and comprehend. Therefore the Lord said, "Whoso receiveth not my voice is not acquainted with my voice, and is not of me." (D&C 84:52.) (*Ensign*, September 1976, p. 2.)

— *Spencer W. Kimball*

Pondering is a progressive mental pursuit. It is a great gift to those who have learned to use it. . . .

By pondering, we give the Spirit an opportunity to impress and direct. Pondering is a powerful link between the heart and the mind. As we read the scriptures, our hearts and minds are touched. If we use the gift to ponder, we can take these eternal truths and realize how we can incorporate them into our daily actions. . . .

We find understanding, insight, and practical application if we will use the gift of pondering. (*Ensign*, November 1987, p. 20.)

— *Marvin J. Ashton*

Search the scriptures—search the revelations which we publish, and ask your Heavenly Father, in the name of his Son Jesus Christ, to manifest the truth unto you, and if you do it with an eye single to his glory, nothing doubting, he will answer you by the power of his Holy Spirit. You will then know for yourselves and not for another. You will not then be dependent on man for the knowledge of God; nor will there be any room for speculation. . . . For when men receive their instruction from Him that made them, they know how He will save them. . . . Again we say: Search the Scriptures, search the Prophets and learn what portion of them belongs to you. (*TPJS*, pp. 11-12.)

— *Joseph Smith*

Study the scriptures. They offer one of the best sources we have to keep in touch with the Spirit of the Lord. One of the ways I have gained my sure knowledge that Jesus is the Christ is through my study of the scriptures. (*Ensign*, May 1987, p. 15.)

— *M. Russell Ballard*

Studying and searching the scriptures is not a burden laid upon [us] by the Lord, but a marvelous blessing and opportunity. (*Ensign*, May 1986, p. 81.)

— *Ezra Taft Benson*

There is a special power in the scriptures. Scripture study, combined with daily, purposeful prayer, can provide much of the resolution that is necessary today to offset the influences so prevalent in the world that lead us into forbidden ways. (*Ensign*, November 1989, p. 63.)

— *Dean L. Larsen*

We have the Bible, the Book of Mormon, the Doctrine and Covenants, and the Pearl of Great Price. There are in these four books a total of 1579 chapters. I think it would not be too much to say that we could with propriety, day in and day out, consistently, read three chapters in one or the other of these works; and if we pursued such a course, we would read all of the Gospels in less than a month. We would read the entire New Testament in three months, We would read the Old

Testament in ten months, and the whole Bible in thirteen months. We would go through the Book of Mormon in two and two-thirds months, the Doctrine and Covenants in a month and a half, and the Pearl of Great Price in five days. Taken altogether, we would read all the standard works in less than eighteen months and be ready to start over again. (*CR,* October 1959, p. 51.)

— *Bruce R. McConkie*

There is so much we can learn from the example of the young Prophet Joseph Smith, whose persistent, prayerful study of the Holy Bible compelled him to seek the God of Heaven for divine guidance. This brought him to the threshold of the greatest revelation ever given to man since the mortal ministry of the Savior Himself. Throughout the Prophet's life, he continued to probe and ponder until he gained a mastery of the scriptures. (*Ensign,* November 1982, p. 13.)

— *J. Richard Clarke*

We live and will one day die. And when we do, we will know our Savior, for we will have searched the holy scriptures and felt His nearness as He walks with us on our journey home. (*Ensign,* November 1985, p. 95.)

— *Ardeth G. Kapp*

We must search the scriptures, accepting them as the mind and will and voice of the Lord and the very power of God unto salvation. (*Ensign,* May 1985, p. 10.)

— *Bruce R. McConkie*

See also SCRIPTURES

——— Scriptures ———

Buildings and budgets, and reports and programs and procedures are very important. But, by themselves, they do not carry that essential spiritual nourishment and will not accomplish what the Lord has given us to do. . . . The right things, those with true spiritual nourishment, are centered in the scriptures. (Meeting with Stake Presidents and Regional Representatives, 2 April 1982, pp. 1-2, quoted by Ezra Taft Benson, *Ensign,* May 1986, p. 81.)

— *Boyd K. Packer*

I fear that many of us rush about from day to day taking for granted the holy scriptures. We scramble to honor appointments with physicians, lawyers, and businessmen. Yet we think nothing of postponing interviews with Deity— postponing scripture study. Little wonder we develop anemic souls and lose our direction in living. How much better it would be if we planned and held sacred fifteen or twenty minutes a day for reading the scriptures. Such interviews with Deity would help us recognize his voice and enable us to receive guidance in all of our affairs.

We must look to God through the scriptures. (*Ensign*, November 1978, pp. 53, 54.)

— *Carlos E. Asay*

Can you imagine being away from home and receiving a letter from your parents and not bothering to open it or read it? This is what happens when we don't read these precious records. The holy scriptures are like letters from home telling us how we can draw near to our Father in Heaven. He tells us to come as we are. No one will be denied. He loves everyone. (See 3 Ne. 9:14, 17-18.) (*Ensign*, November 1985, p. 94.)

— *Ardeth G. Kapp*

From the holy scriptures, heaven-sent lift will be found for heaven-sent duties. (*Ensign*, May 1988, p. 34.)

— *Russell M. Nelson*

However talented men may be in administrative matters; however eloquent they may be in expressing their views; however learned they may be in the worldly things—they will be denied the sweet whisperings of the Spirit that might have been theirs unless they pay the price of studying, pondering, and praying about the scriptures. (Regional Representatives' Seminar, 2 April 1982, pp. 1-2, quoted by Ezra Taft Benson, *Ensign*, May 1986, p. 81.)

— *Bruce R. McConkie*

I am convinced that each of us, at least some time in our lives, must discover the scriptures for ourselves—and not just discover them once, but rediscover them again and again. . . .

The Lord is not trifling with us when he gives us these things, for "unto whomsoever much is given, of him shall be much required." (Luke 12:48.) Access to these things means responsibility for them. We must study the scriptures according to the Lord's commandment (see 3 Ne, 23:1-5); and we must let them govern our lives. (*Ensign*, September 1976, pp. 3-5.)

— *Spencer W. Kimball*

I feel strongly that we must all of us return to the scriptures . . . and let them work mightily within us, impelling us to an unwavering determination to serve the Lord.

— *Spencer W. Kimball*

I find that when I get casual in my relationships with divinity and when it seems that no divine ear is listening and no divine voice is speaking, that I am far, far away. If I immerse myself in the scriptures, the distance narrows and the spirituality returns. (Quoted by James E. Faust, *Ensign,* November 1976, p. 58.)

— *Spencer W. Kimball*

I have reached the stage where I have nothing more to say. As far as I am concerned the scriptures say it all. (*OAT,* p. 42.)

— *Hugh Nibley*

Let us . . . seek to read and understand and apply the principles and inspired counsel found within the [scriptures]. If we do so, we shall discover that our personal *acts* of righteousness will also bring *personal revelation or inspiration* when needed into our own lives. (*Ensign,* September 1975, p. 4.)

— *Spencer W. Kimball*

Read your Scriptures, read them early and read them late, read them in your youth and do not abandon them when you get older. (Fireside Address, December 11, 1960.)

— *J. Reuben Clark, Jr.*

Recently, a young man purchased a used computer but could not get it to work properly. Soon he became discouraged. His temper grew short and he threatened the inanimate object with painful destruction unless its performance improved. A wise father intervened and took his son to a local vendor, where they obtained an instruction manual. After all, who would know more about a complex computer than the person or company that created it? Who would know most about its capacity and potential? Who would better know the safeguards required to avoid damaging or ruining this fine instrument? Soon the boy enjoyed the full potential of his computer by working within the guidelines given in the instruction book provided by its creator.

Likewise in our lives, he who knows most about us, our potential, and our eternal possibilities has given us divine counsel and commandments in his instruction manuals—the holy scriptures. When we understand and follow these instructions, our lives have purpose and meaning. We learn that our Maker loves us and desires our happiness. (*Ensign,* May 1988, pp. 58-59.)

— *M. Russell Ballard*

Spiritual development is tied very closely to a knowledge of the scriptures, where the doctrines are taught.

— *Boyd K. Packer*

Success in righteousness, the power to avoid deception and resist temptation, guidance in our daily lives, healing of the soul—these are but a few of the promises the Lord has given to those who will come to His word. . . . However diligent we may be in other areas, certain blessings are to be found only in the scriptures, only in coming to the word of the Lord and holding fast to it as we make our way through the mists of darkness to the tree of life. (*Ensign*, May 1986, p. 82.)

— *Ezra Taft Benson*

The Bible, the Book of Mormon, the book of Doctrine and Covenants contain the words of eternal life unto this generation, and they will rise in judgment against those who reject them. (*JD*, 22:335.)

— *Wilford Woodruff*

The holy scriptures represent mankind's spiritual memory. And when man's connection with scripture is severed, mortals are tragically deprived of an awareness of spiritual history, blinding the eyes of faith. . . .

Without this precious, spiritual perspective, the human family is seldom more than one generation away from deep doubt and even disbelief. (*Ensign*, November 1986, p. 52.)

— *Neal A. Maxwell*

The truest source of divine wisdom is the word of the Lord in . . . the standard works of the Church. Here is found the doctrine to which we must hold fast if this work is to roll forth to its divinely charted destiny. (*Ensign*, May 1982, p. 45.)

— *Gordon B. Hinckley*

This is an answer to the great challenge of our time. The word of God, as found in the scriptures, in the words of living prophets, and in personal revelation, has the power to fortify the Saints and arm them with the Spirit so they can resist evil, hold fast to the good, and find joy in this life. (*Ensign*, May 1986, p. 80.)

— *Ezra Taft Benson*

We have recommended that so far as possible all the children have their own scriptures and learn to use them. (*Ensign*, November 1977, p. 4.)

— *Spencer W. Kimball*

[The scriptures] . . . are like a lighthouse in the ocean or a fingerpost which points out the road we should travel. Where do they point? To the fountain of light. . . . By them we can establish the doctrine of Christ. (*JD*, 8:129.)

— *Brigham Young*

What mattereth it though we understand Homer and Shakespeare and Milton, and I might enumerate all the great writers of the world, if we have failed to read the scriptures we have missed the better part of this world's literature. (*CR*, October 1917, p. 43.)

— *George Albert Smith*

[Speaking of a book of scriptures:] He who reads it oftenest will like it best. (*TPJS*, p. 56.)

— *Joseph Smith*

See also BIBLE, BOOK OF MORMON, DOCTRINE AND COVENANTS, SCRIPTURE STUDY

——— Second Coming ———

He comes! The earth shakes, and the tall mountains tremble; the mighty deep rolls back to the north as in fear, and the rent skies glow like molten brass. He comes! The dead Saints burst forth from their tombs, and "those who are alive and remain" are "caught up" with them to meet him. The ungodly rush to hide themselves from his presence, and call upon the quivering rocks to cover them. He comes! with all the hosts of the righteous glorified. The breath of his lips strikes death to the wicked. His glory is a consuming fire. The proud and rebellious are as stubble; they are burned and "left neither root nor branch." He sweeps the earth "as with the besom of destruction." He deluges the earth with the fiery floods of his wrath, and the filthiness and abominations of the world are consumed. Satan and his dark hosts are taken and bound—the prince of the power of the air has lost his dominion, for He whose right it is to reign has come, and "the kingdoms of this world have become the kingdoms of our Lord and of his Christ." (*MS*, September 10, 1859, p. 583.)

— *Charles W. Penrose*

I will prophesy that the signs of the coming of the Son of Man are already commenced. One pestilence will desolate after another. We shall soon have war and bloodshed. The moon will be turned into blood. I testify of these things and that the coming of the Son of Man is nigh, even at your doors. (*HC*, 3:390.)

— *Joseph Smith*

Let us be sure we thoroughly understand the most important things we can do to prepare ourselves for our Lord's second coming to earth and, by our obedience and faithfulness, escape his punishment. . . . We must set our lives and homes in order. This means a searching of our souls, an admittance of wrongdoing, and repentance where needed. It means keeping all of God's commandments. It means loving our neighbor. . . . It means being good husbands and wives. It means teaching and training our children in the ways of righteousness. It means being honest in all our doings, in business and at home. It means spreading the gospel of Jesus Christ to all the peoples of the world. (*Ensign*, January 1974, p. 129.)

— *Delbert L. Stapley*

Having bled at every pore, how red His raiment must have been in Gethsemane, how crimson that cloak!

No wonder, when Christ comes in power and glory, that he will come in reminding red attire (see D&C 133:48), signifying not only the winepress of wrath, but also to bring to our remembrance how He suffered for each of us in Gethsemane and on Calvary. (*Ensign*, May 1987, p. 72.)

— *Neal A. Maxwell*

In the not distant future he will come again, with ten thousand of his angels, in all the glory of his Father's kingdom, to usher in his personal reign of righteousness and peace. When he comes he will slay the wicked and judge the world; and every corruptible thing will be destroyed by the glory of his presence. (*Ensign*, May 1977, p. 14.)

— *Bruce R. McConkie*

Jesus Christ never did reveal to any man the precise time that he would come. Go and read the scriptures, and you cannot find anything that specifies the exact hour he would come; and all that say so are false teachers. (*HC*, 6:254.)

— *Joseph Smith*

Jesus has been upon the earth a great many more times than you are aware of. When Jesus makes his next appearance upon the earth, but few of this Church and kingdom will be prepared to receive him and see him face to face and converse with him. (*JD*, 7:142.)

— *Brigham Young*

Jesus is coming to reign, and all you who fear and tremble because of your enemies, cease to fear them and learn to fear to offend God, fear to transgress his laws, fear to do any evil to your brother, or to any being upon the earth, and do not fear Satan and his power, nor those who have only power to slay the body, for God will preserve His people. (*JD*, 10:250.)

— *Brigham Young*

Jesus will come by and by, and appear in our midst, as he appeared upon the earth among the Jews, and He will eat and drink with us and talk to us, and explain the mysteries of the kingdom, and tell us things that are not lawful to talk about now. (*CR*, April, 1898, p. 14.)

— *Lorenzo Snow*

Deliberately and advisedly the actual time of his coming has been left uncertain and unspecified, so that men of each succeeding age shall be led to prepare for it as though it would be in their mortal lives. (Quoted by J. Richard Clarke, *Ensign*, May 1978, p. 84.)

— *Bruce R. McConkie*

One of the most compelling concepts in the gospel is that the Savior will come again. And he counsels, "Behold, I come quickly." (Rev. 3:11.) We must live with constant anticipation of his coming. Being ready to receive him is the position of our greatest strength. Let this be our bulwark against temptation or slothfulness. Let it cause us to read the Savior's words, to search our hearts, and to try to live every principle of righteousness he taught. This will require us to love as he loves. Then, we are told, when he comes we shall know him, for we shall be like him. (See 1 Jn. 3:2.) (*Ensign*, November 1983, p. 85.)

— *Barbara B. Smith*

The hour and day of the Lord's future advent is withheld from the knowledge of both men and angels; yet the signs, so definitely specified as harbingers of His coming, are multiplying apace. The prevailing unrest among men and nations, the fury of the elements, widespread destruction by land and sea, the frequency and intensity of volcanic and earthquake disturbances—all tell to the well-tuned and listening ear that the gladsome yet terrible day of the Lord is nigh—aye, even at the doors! (*MS*, 91:34.)

— *Heber J. Grant*

The Lord Jesus, the Everlasting Christ, the Savior who was and is and is to be, shall soon come again.

Just as surely as the son of Mary came to dwell among his fellowmen, so shall the Son of God come, in all the glory of his Father's kingdom, to rule among the sons of men.

In that dread day the world that now is shall end; wickedness will cease; every corruptible thing will be consumed, and the glory of the Lord will shine daily upon all men from the rising of the sun until it sinks in the western sky. (*Ensign*, November 1982, p. 34.)

— *Bruce R. McConkie*

We are required to carry the gospel of Jesus Christ to every nation of the world. The Lord commanded it in these words:

"Send forth the elders of my church unto the nations which are afar off; unto the islands of the sea; send forth unto foreign lands; call upon all nations, first upon the Gentiles, and then upon the Jews." (D&C 133:8.)

This commission to take the gospel to every nation, kindred, tongue, and people is one of the signs by which believers will recognize the nearness of the Savior's return to earth. Concerning this sign of His second coming, Jesus prophesied:

"And this gospel of the kingdom shall be preached in *all the world* for a witness unto *all* nations; and then shall the end come." (Matt. 24:14; italics added.) (*Ensign*, May 1984, p. 43.)

— *Ezra Taft Benson*

We believe that Jesus Christ will descend from heaven to earth again even as he ascended into heaven. . . . He will come to receive His own and rule and reign King of Nations as he does King of Saints; . . . He will banish sin from the earth and its dreadful consequences, tears shall be wiped from every eye and there shall be nothing to hurt or destroy in all God's holy mountain. (*JD*, 11:123-24.)

— *Brigham Young*

We do not know when the calamities and troubles of the last days will fall upon any of us as individuals or upon bodies of the Saints. The Lord deliberately withholds from us the day and hour of his coming and of the tribulations which shall precede it—all as part of the testing and probationary experiences of mortality. He simply tells us to watch and be ready.

We can rest assured that if we have done all in our power to prepare for whatever lies ahead, he will then help us with whatever else we need. . . .

And so we raise the warning voice and say: Take heed; prepare; watch and be ready. There is no security in any course except the course of obedience and conformity and righteousness. (*Ensign*, May 1979, p. 93.)

— *Bruce R. McConkie*

When he comes again, he will not come as he did when the Jews rejected him; neither will he appear first at Jerusalem when he makes his second appearance on the earth; but he will appear first on the land where he commenced his work in the beginning, and planted the Garden of Eden, and that was done in the land of America. (*JD*, 11:279.)

— *Brigham Young*

You and I live in a day in which the Lord our God has set his hand for the last time, to gather out the righteous and to prepare a people to reign on this earth—a people who will be purified by good works, who will abide the faith of the living God and be ready to meet the Bridegroom when he comes to reign over the earth, even Jesus Christ . . . and be prepared for that glorious event—the coming of the Son of Man—which I believe will not be at any great distant day. (*MS*, 36:220.)

— Joseph F. Smith

See also LAST DAYS, MILLENNIUM

Selfishness

It is all good, the air, the water, the gold and silver; the wheat, the fine flour, and the cattle upon a thousand hills are all good. . . . But the moment that men seek to build up themselves . . . and seek to hoard up riches it proves that their hearts are weaned from their God; and their riches will perish in their fingers, and they with them. (*JD*, 1:272.)

— Brigham Young

It is selfishness which is the cause of most of our misery. (*Ensign*, November 1988, p. 54.)

— Gordon B. Hinckley

Man's earthly existence is but a test as to whether he will concentrate his efforts, his mind, his soul upon things which contribute to the comfort and gratification of his physical nature or whether he will make as his life's purpose the acquisition of spiritual qualities. (*Relief Society Magazine*, June 1941, p. 364.)

— David O. McKay

Of all influences that cause men to choose wrong, selfishness is undoubtedly the strongest. Where it is, the Spirit is not. (*Ensign*, November 1987, p. 76.)

— William R. Bradford

Selfishness is much more than an ordinary problem because it activates all the cardinal sins! It is the detonator in the breaking of the Ten Commandments. (*Ensign*, November 1990, p. 14.)

— Neal A. Maxwell

Selfishness is the great unknown sin. No selfish person ever thought himself to be selfish. (*Ensign*, May 1985, p. 66.)

— H. Burke Peterson

Selfishness is one of the more common faces of pride. "How everything affects me" is the center of all that matters—self-conceit, self-pity, worldly self-fulfillment, self-gratification, and self-seeking. (*Ensign*, May 1986, p. 6.)

— *Ezra Taft Benson*

Selfishness is the canker that drives out peace and love. Selfishness is the root on which grow argument, anger, disrespect, infidelity, and divorce. (*Ensign*, May 1982, p. 45.)

— *Gordon B. Hinckley*

Shun those who would build themselves by destroying others. (*Ensign*, May 1988, p. 63.)

— *Marvin J. Ashton*

There are two spirits striving with all men—one telling them what to do that is right, and one telling them what to do that will please themselves, that will gratify their own pride and ambition. (*CR*, April 1938, p. 12.)

— *Heber J. Grant*

True love is the exact opposite of the present philosophy of selfishness which seems to permeate the world. Selfish interests color people's dealings with each other and even color person-to-person contact within the family. . . .

It may well be that the present attitude of personal selfishness is the cause of most of the unhappiness with life among the people of the world. (*Ensign*, May 1979, p. 72.)

— *Theodore M. Burton*

Unchecked selfishness . . . stubbornly blocks the way for developing all of the divine qualities: love, mercy, patience, long-suffering, kindness, graciousness, goodness, and gentleness. Any tender sprouts from these virtues are sheared off by sharp selfishness. Contrariwise, brothers and sisters, I cannot think of a single gospel covenant the keeping of which does not shear off selfishness from us! (*Ensign*, November 1990, p. 15.)

— *Neal A. Maxwell*

Unless overcome by serving others, selfishness leads to serious sin, with its depressing feelings and binding chains. It is the crowbar Satan uses to open a heart to temptation in order to destroy agency. He would bind mind and body through crippling habits and separate us from our Father in Heaven and His Son by cultivating selfishness. (*Ensign*, May 1989, p. 36.)

— *Richard G. Scott*

When life-style takes the form of "me" and "now" rather than "us" and "always," apparent consequences are inevitable. (*Ensign*, October 1974, p. 70.)
— *Neal A. Maxwell*

Where selfishness and transgression flourish, the Spirit of the Lord can't enter your life to bless you. To succeed, you must conquer your selfishness. When your beacon is focused on self, it does little more than blind your vision. When turned outward through acts of kindness and love, it will light your path to happiness and peace. (*Ensign*, May 1990, p. 74.)
— *Richard G. Scott*

See also SELFLESSNESS, SERVICE, WEALTH

——— Selflessness ———

A selfless person is one who is more concerned about the happiness and well-being of another than about his or her own convenience or comfort, one who is willing to serve another when it is neither sought for nor appreciated, or one who is willing to serve even those whom he or she dislikes. A selfless person displays a willingness to sacrifice, a willingness to purge from his or her mind and heart personal wants, and needs, and feelings. Instead of reaching for and requiring praise and recognition for himself, or gratification of his or her own wants, the selfless person will meet these very human needs for others. (*Ensign*, May 1985, p. 66.)
— *H. Burke Peterson*

I am convinced that when we give unconditional love; when our interest is first in serving, building, edifying, strengthening without thought of self; . . . when we are not concerned about what we will receive or what others will say or whether our own burdens will be diminished, . . . the miracle of the power of the gospel is released in our lives. (*Ensign*, November 1983, p. 71.)
— *Richard G. Scott*

"And he said to them all, If any man will come after me, let him deny himself, and take up his cross daily, and follow me." (Luke 9:23.) Wise self-denial shrinks our sense of entitlement. (*Ensign*, May 1989, p. 64.)
— *Neal A. Maxwell*

Selflessness is righteousness. It embraces the true spirit of companionship. It is the very essence of friendship. It is the portrayer of true love and oneness in humanity. Its reward is the freeing of the soul, a nearness to divinity, a worthiness for the companionship of the Spirit. Every requirement that God's plan for our salvation places upon us is based on the giving of oneself.

The only way under the heavens whereby a person can be sanctified is in selfless service. (*Ensign*, November 1987, p. 76.)

— *William R. Bradford*

To deny oneself of all ungodliness (see Moro. 10:32) is to come to Christ by ordinances and covenants, to repent of any sins which prevent the Spirit of the Lord from taking precedence in our lives. To deny oneself of all ungodliness is to "offer a sacrifice unto the Lord thy God. . . , even that of a broken heart and a contrite spirit" (D&C 59:8). (*Ensign*, May 1979, p. 32.)

— *Ezra Taft Benson*

See also CHARITY, SELFISHNESS, SELF-MASTERY, SERVICE

——— Self-Mastery ———

A person's reaction to his appetites and impulses when they are aroused gives the measure of that person's character. (*CR*, April 1964, p. 4.)

— *David O. McKay*

I would mention, then, as one of the definite controlling factors of all life, self-discipline—that which a man uses when he is tempted by someone or something to do something or say something that he knows he ought not to do or say. When he gets the courage and the stamina to say no and mean it, then he can take charge of his life and go forward. (Fireside Address, Brigham Young University, October 8, 1967.)

— *Hugh B. Brown*

If we are not able to build into ourselves and our families the brakes of self-restraint and self-discipline, we are apt, unwittingly, to create tyranny in our government or anarchy in our citizenry. If we push onto the government the management not only of our economy, but also the management of our morals, the civil servants of the future will be neither civil nor servants.

— *Neal A. Maxwell*

It's not enough just to grow. Even the weeds and the biblical tares can do that. It is expected of us that we . . . will successfully negotiate the bumps and curves by enlarging upon our talents, by disciplining ourselves, so that our mortal experience brings us toward greater and greater mastery of those characteristics which make us worthy of association with the Divine. (*Ensign*, May 1982, pp. 93-94.)

— *Dwan J. Young*

Man is a spiritual being, a soul, and at some period of his life everyone is possessed with an irresistible desire to know his relationship to the infinite. He realizes that he is not just a physical object that is to be tossed for a short time from bank to bank, only to be submerged finally in the everflowing stream of life. There is something within him which urges him to rise above himself, to control his environment, to master the body and all things physical and live in a higher and more beautiful world. (*CR*, October 1928, p. 37.)

— *David O. McKay*

Most of us don't mind doing what we *ought* to do when it doesn't interfere with what we *want* to do, but it takes discipline and maturity to do what we ought to do whether we want to or not. Duty is too often what one expects from others and not what one does. (*Ensign*, November 1980, p. 69.)

— *Joseph B. Wirthlin*

No man is safe unless he is master of himself; and there is no tyrant more merciless or more to be dreaded than an uncontrollable appetite or passion. We will find that if we give way to the groveling appetites of the flesh and follow them up, that the end will be invariably bitter, injurious and sorrowful, both to the individual and society. (*DFTP*, p. 414.)

— *Joseph F. Smith*

Now brethren, can we fight against and subdue ourselves? That is the greatest difficulty we ever encountered, and the most arduous warfare we ever engaged in. (*JD*, 6:315.)

— *Brigham Young*

One of the great tragedies we witness almost daily is the tragedy of men of high aim and low achievement. Their motives are noble. Their proclaimed ambition is praiseworthy. Their capacity is great. But their discipline is weak. They succumb to indolence. Appetite robs them of will. (*Ensign*, May 1979, p. 65.)

— *Gordon B. Hinckley*

The spirit within us is more powerful than the body, and we can use that spirit to commit ourselves to righteous actions. We *can* control the body and its bodily appetites. It is fallacious to say that we were created with propensities and appetites we cannot control. It is simply not true that people are born with such powerful appetites and passions that they are powerless to control them. God would not be a righteous God if man were created with drives he could not control. (*Ensign*, May 1981, p. 30.)

— *Theodore M. Burton*

Our first enemy we will find within ourselves. It is a good thing to overcome that enemy first and bring ourselves into subjection to the will of the Father, and into strict obedience to the principles of life and salvation which he has given to the world for the salvation of me.. (*CR*, October 1914, p. 128.)

— *Joseph F. Smith*

The man who yields to every appetite and every desire of the flesh cannot receive exaltation, because he does not prepare himself for and make himself worthy of it. (*CR*, April 1933, p. 24.)

— *Joseph Fielding Smith*

Unless you control the passions that pertain to fallen nature—make all your faculties subservient to the principles God has revealed, you will never arrive at that state of happiness, glory, joy, peace, and eternal felicity that you are anticipating. (*JD*, 8:116.)

— *Brigham Young*

We did not come on earth to love ourselves, to appease our tempers, to satisfy our desires, lusts, longings. We came to subjugate the flesh—to make our minds and bodies do the things which the spirit knows are best in the long run. (*Miracle of Forgiveness*, Salt Lake City: Bookcraft, 1969.)

— *Spencer W. Kimball*

We have a great mission to perform—we have to try to govern ourselves according to the laws of the kingdom of God, and we find it one of the most difficult tasks we ever undertook, to learn to govern ourselves, our appetites, our dispositions, our habits, our feelings, our lives, our spirits, our judgment, and to bring all our desires into subjection to the law of the kingdom of God and to the spirit of truth. (*JD*, 9:12.)

— *John Taylor*

We must be master of our beings and control ourselves, and not be controlled by some habit or by someone else. We must be lifters and not leaners. (*Ensign*, November 1986, p. 30.)

— *Ted E. Brewerton*

You may have heard the expression "mind over matter." I would like to . . . phrase it a little differently: "spirit over body." That is self-mastery. (*Ensign,* November 1985, p. 30.)

— *Russell M. Nelson*

See also HABITS, PERFECTION, PROGRESSION, THOUGHTS

Self-Pity

A life can never be happy that is focused inward. So if you are miserable now, forget your troubles. March right out your door, and find someone who needs you. (*Ensign,* November 1985, p. 13.)

— *Robert L. Backman*

Don't live your life in despair, feeling sorry for yourself because of the mistakes you have made. Let the sunshine in by doing the right things—now. (See 1 Ne. 22:26.) . . . Pick up the scriptures and immerse yourself in them. Look for favorite passages. Lean on the Master's teachings, . . . Refresh your parched soul with the word of God. (See 2 Ne. 4:15-16.) (*Ensign,* May 1990, pp. 74-75.)

— *Richard G. Scott*

It is generally good medicine to sympathize with others, but not with yourself. (*Ensign,* May 1988, p. 63.)

— *Marvin J. Ashton*

Spare yourselves from the indulgence of self-pity. It is always self-defeating. Subdue the negative and emphasize the positive. Count your blessings and not your problems. (*Ensign,* November 1985, p. 86.)

— *Gordon B. Hinckley*

Too often we allow incidents to contribute to our stagnation when we permit ourselves to feel ignored, unwanted, or unworthy. How damaging sympathy is when it is self-administered. (*Ensign,* May 1979, p. 68.)

— *Marvin J. Ashton*

Yielding to the pains of tragedy and grief deters self-development and takes away the opportunity for triumph over trying obstacles. (*Ensign,* May 1979, p. 69.)

— *Marvin J. Ashton*

See also DISCOURAGEMENT, ENDURANCE

——— Self-Reliance ———

All we have been trying to do is make our people self-reliant, because the more self-reliant one is, the more able to serve he becomes, and the more he serves, the greater his sanctification. (Quoted by Glenn L. Pace, *Ensign*, May 1986, p. 23.)

— *Marion G. Romney*

It is entirely appropriate to depend upon others for some of what we need. There is no substitute for loving and supportive parents, priesthood and auxiliary leaders, skilled doctors, dedicated teachers, and expert auto mechanics. Turning to these people for help is not wrong. But what is wrong is expecting others to do what we can and should do for ourselves. (*Ensign*, May 1989, p. 10.)

— *Hugh W. Pinnock*

Let us be self-reliant. Salvation is an individual matter. There will be no mass salvation. (*Ensign*, May 1979, p. 94.)

— *Marion G. Romney*

Man is commanded of God to live by the sweat of *his* brow, not someone else's. (*Ensign*, November 1976, p. 34.)

— *Ezra Taft Benson*

Members of the Church [are] to use their own gifts and abilities, their financial and personal resources in becoming temporally self-reliant and then reaching out to help others to gain that same capacity for self-reliance.

We should strive for self-reliance physically, emotionally, financially, and, most important of all, spiritually. (*Ensign*, May 1983, p. 84.)

— *J. Thomas Fyans*

No true Latter-day Saint, while physically or emotionally able will voluntarily shift the burden of his own or his family's well-being to someone else. So long as he can, under the inspiration of the Lord and with his own labors, he will supply himself and his family with the spiritual and temporal necessities of life. (Quoted by Spencer W. Kimball, *Ensign*, May 1978, p. 79.)

— *The Presiding Bishopric*

Spiritual self-reliance is the sustaining power in the Church. . . . When you are discouraged and feel that you cannot solve a problem on your own, you may be right, but at least you are obligated to try. . . . You, through prayer, can solve your

problems without endlessly going to those who are trying so hard to help others.
. . . This Church relies on individual testimony. Each must earn his own testimony.
It is then that you can stand and say, as I can say, that I know that God lives . . .
I know that he is close, that we can go to him and appeal, and then, if we will be
obedient and listen and use every resource, we will have an answer to our
prayers. (*Ensign*, August 1975, pp. 87, 88, 89.)

— *Boyd K. Packer*

Self-reliance comes by complying so completely with the principles of the
gospel that each individual and family are added upon by the Lord's strength,
making them able to stand strong against the blows of adversity and the changing
winds of time and growth. (*Ensign*, November 1981, p. 85.)

— *Barbara B. Smith*

The Lord's real storehouse is indeed in the homes and the hearts of His
people. As the members of the Church follow the counsel to become self-reliant,
they represent an immense pool of resources, knowledge, skills, and charity
available to help one another. (*Ensign*, May 1986, p. 29.)

— *Robert D. Hales*

The obligation to sustain one's self was divinely imposed upon the human
race at its beginning. "In the sweat of thy face shalt thou eat bread, till thou return
unto the ground." (Gen. 3:19) (Quoted by Boyd K. Packer, *Ensign*, August 1975,
p. 85.)

— *Marion G. Romney*

The responsibility for each member's spiritual, social, emotional, physical, or
economic well-being rests first, upon himself, second, upon his family, and third,
upon the Church. Members of the Church are commanded by the Lord to be self-
reliant and independent to the extent of their ability.

— *The Presiding Bishopric*

Without self-reliance one cannot exercise innate desires to serve. How can we
give if there is nothing there? Food for the hungry cannot come from empty
shelves. Money to assist the needy cannot come from an empty purse. Support
and understanding cannot come from the emotionally starved. Teaching cannot
come from the unlearned. And most important of all, spiritual guidance cannot
come from the spiritually weak. (*Ensign*, November 1982, p. 93.)

— *Marion G. Romney*

See also INITIATIVE, PREPAREDNESS, WORK

Self-Sufficiency

I am shocked as I become aware that in so many homes, many of the children do not know how to make a bed, care for their clothing, squeeze a tube of toothpaste to conserve, turn off the lights, set a proper table, mow a lawn, or care for a vegetable garden. These simple acts of cleanliness, order, and conservation will bless their lives every day that they live and prepare them to become self-sufficient when they reach an age when they must be out on their own. Teach them the basic knowledge that the earth is the Lord's. He has a marvelous system of replenishment and renewal so long as we care for, conserve, and waste not. (*Ensign*, November 1988, p. 74.)

— *L. Tom Perry*

I hope that we understand that, while having a garden, for instance, is often useful in reducing food costs and making available delicious fresh fruits and vegetables, it does much more than this. Who can gauge the value of that special chat between daughter and Dad as they weed or water the garden? How do we evaluate the good that comes from the obvious lessons of planting, cultivating, and the eternal law of the harvest? And how do we measure the family togetherness and cooperating that must accompany successful canning? Yes, we are laying up resources in store, but perhaps the greater good is contained in the lessons of life we learn as we live providently and extend to our children their pioneer heritage. (*Ensign*, November 1977, p. 78.)

— *Spencer W. Kimball*

Ye Latter-day Saints, learn to sustain yourselves, produce everything you need to eat, drink or wear; and if you cannot obtain all you wish for today, learn to do without that which you cannot purchase and pay for; and bring your minds into subjection that you must and will live within your means. (*JD*, 12:231.)

— *Brigham Young*

See also PREPAREDNESS, SELF-RELIANCE, TEMPORAL WELFARE

Self-Worth

A righteous self-respect [is] defined as belief in one's own worth, worth to God, and worth to man. (*Ensign*, January 1974, p. 4.)

— *Harold B. Lee*

As we mature spiritually under the guidance of the Holy Ghost, our sense of personal worth, of belonging, and of identity increases. (*Ensign*, May 1989, p. 33.)

— *James E. Faust*

Ask yourself, are the comparisons you may make of yourself and others based on the model of the Savior's life, or do they come from trying to fit your life into the pattern of others' lives? (*Ensign*, November 1990, p. 89.)

— *Ardeth G. Kapp*

Certainly what we are is more important than what we have or what is said of us. (*Ensign*, May 1979, p. 68.)

— *Marvin J. Ashton*

He who was thrust down in the first estate delights to have us put ourselves down. Self-contempt is of Satan; there is none of it in heaven. We should, of course, learn from our mistakes, but without forever studying the instant replays as if these were the game of life itself. (*Ensign*, November 1976, p. 14.)

— *Neal A. Maxwell*

I am certain our Heavenly Father is displeased when we refer to ourselves as "nobody." . . . We do ourselves a great injustice when we allow ourselves, through tragedy, misfortune, challenge, discouragements, or whatever the earthly situation, to so identify ourselves. No matter how or where we find ourselves, we cannot with any justification label ourselves "nobody."

As children of God we are somebody. He will build us, mold us, and magnify us if we will but hold our heads up, our arms out, and walk with him. What a great blessing to be created in his image and know of our true potential in and through him! What a great blessing to know that in his strength we can do all things! (*CR*, April 1973, p. 21.)

— *Marvin J. Ashton*

I testify that as we mature spiritually under the guidance of the Holy Ghost, our sense of personal worth, of belonging, and of identity increases.

— *James E. Faust*

If one has a vivid sense of his own divinity, he will not easily be persuaded to deprave his mind, debauch his body, or sell his freedom for temporary gain. (*CR*, October 1969, p. 106.)

— *Hugh B. Brown*

Now, this is the truth. We humble people, we who feel ourselves sometimes so worthless, so good-for-nothing, we are not so worthless as we think. There is not one of us but what God's love has been expended upon. There is not one of us that he has not cared for and caressed. There is not one of us that He has not desired to save and that He has not devised means to save. There is not one of us that He has not given His angels charge concerning. We may be insignificant and contemptible in our own eyes and in the eyes of others, but the truth remains that we are children of God and that He has actually given His angels . . . charge concerning us, and they watch over us and have us in their keeping. (*Ensign*, May 1989, p. 21.)

— *George Q. Cannon*

If we love God, do His will, and fear His judgment more than men's, we will have self-esteem.

— *Ezra Taft Benson*

In God's eyes, nobody is a nobody. We should never lose sight of what we may become and who we are. (*Ensign*, May 1988, p. 63.)

— *Marvin J. Ashton*

Self-esteem is different than conceit—conceit is the weirdest disease in the world. It makes everyone sick except the one who has it. (*Ensign*, May 1979, p. 29.)

— *Hartman Rector, Jr.*

Spiritual self-esteem begins with the realization that each new morning is a gift from God. Even the air we breathe is a loving loan from him. He preserves us from day to day and supports us from one moment to another (see Mosiah 2:21.) (*Ensign*, November 1986, p. 68.)

— *Russell M. Nelson*

The least, the most inferior person now upon the earth . . . is worth worlds. (*JD*, 9:124.)

— *Brigham Young*

The world would have you believe that you are of worth only if you have money, a certain physical appearance, stylish clothes, or social position. The gospel assures you that your value is not dependent on your looks or material possessions. . . . Part of what it means to be a Latter-day Saint is to know within your soul your eternal worth, who you rally are, and why you are here on earth. (*Ensign*, November 1989, p. 88.)

— *Elaine L. Jack*

There is a natural, probably a mortal, tendency to compare ourselves with others. Unfortunately, when we make these comparisons, we tend to compare our weakest attributes with someone else's strongest. . . . Obviously these kinds of comparisons are destructive and only reinforce the fear that somehow we don't measure up. (*Ensign*, May 1989, 20.)

— *Marvin J. Ashton*

The most realistic self-image of all is to conceive of yourself as made in the image of God. You cannot sincerely hold this conviction without experiencing a profound new sense of strength and power.

— *Thomas S. Monson*

True personal worth comes from a secure relationship with Heavenly Father. Individual worth is intrinsic; it is internal; it is eternal. It is something that cannot be taken from us when the blossom of youth fades, when economic conditions leave us desolate, when sickness or handicaps befall us, or when prominence and visibility are obscured. (*Ensign*, November 1987, p. 91.)

— *Joanne B. Doxey*

See also MAN, POTENTIAL, TALENTS

——— Serenity ———

I acknowledge with great gratitude the peace and contentment we can find for ourselves in the spiritual cocoons of our homes, our sacrament meetings, and our holy temples. In these peaceful environments, our souls are rested. We have the feeling of having come home. (*Ensign*, May 1990, p. 86.)

— *James E. Faust*

Sweet serenity is found in fervent prayer. Then, we forget ourselves and remember the reaching hands of the Savior, who said, "Come unto me, all ye that labour and are heavy laden, and I will give you rest." (Matt. 11:28.) As our burdens are shared with Him, they do become lighter. (*Ensign*, November 1989, p. 22.)

— *Russell M. Nelson*

The Holy Ghost is the greatest guarantor of inward peace in our unstable world. . . . It will calm nerves; it will breathe peace to our souls. (*Ensign*, May 1989, pp. 32-33.)

— *James E. Faust*

There are depths in the sea which the storms that lash the surface into fury never reach. They who reach down into the depths of life where, in the stillness, the voice of God is heard, have the stabilizing power which carries them poised and serene through the hurricane of difficulties. (*Ensign*, January 1974, p. 17.)

— *Spencer W. Kimball*

See also PEACE

Service

A dear sister had been incapacitated for the past eight years—she could not walk or talk and was confined to bed. About six years ago, she and her husband were assigned a faithful home teacher. He asked if his wife could come over to their house every Sunday morning and stay with the invalid woman while her husband attended priesthood meeting. For six years, every Sunday this home teacher would bring his wife over to stay with the invalid sister while her husband went to his meeting. And every Sunday the home teacher's wife would bring with her some baked goods or something special that she had made for this older couple.

Finally, this sister who had been ill passed away. When her daughter tried to express her deep love and appreciation to this loving home teacher and his wife for what they had done over the years, the wife said, "Oh, don't thank us. It was our *privilege* to visit with your sweet mother. What am I going to do now? The hour and a half on Sunday Morning will now be, for me, the loneliest hour and a half in the week." (*Ensign*, November 1981, p. 81.)

— *J. Richard Clarke*

Almost everyone can do or be something for someone else in need. (*Ensign*, May 1989, p. 75.)

— *Joy F. Evans*

God does notice us, and he watches over us. But it is usually through another person that he meets our needs. (*Ensign*, December 1974, p. 5.)

— *Spencer W. Kimball*

Great women and men are always more anxious to serve than to have dominion. (*Ensign*, November 1979, p. 104.)

— *Spencer W. Kimball*

It is by serving that we learn how to serve. When we are engaged in the service of our fellowmen, not only do our deeds assist them, but we put our own problems in a fresher perspective. When we concern ourselves more with others, there is less time to be concerned with ourselves. In the midst of the miracle of serving, there is the promise of Jesus, that by losing ourselves, we find ourselves. (*Ensign*, December 1974, p. 2, 5.)

— Spencer W. Kimball

I know sanctification comes not with any particular calling, but with genuine acts of service, often for which there is no specific calling. (*Ensign*, May 1985, p. 78.)

— Neal A. Maxwell

If you would be loved, love another. If you would be understood, show understanding to another. If you would find peace, harmony, and happiness, lift another. (*Ensign*, November 1983, p. 71.)

— Richard G. Scott

It has been wisely said, "Service is the rent we pay for our own room on earth." We should know that the rent is due on a daily basis and know that the receipt is never stamped "paid in full," because the rent, service in God's kingdom, is again due today and due tomorrow. (*Ensign*, November 1984, p. 23.)

— Russell C. Taylor

Jesus washed the feet of his disciples, feet that were hot, sweaty, and soiled with dust and dirt. He washed not their hands or face; he washed their feet. He who is the greatest shall be the least—he it is who learns to serve. (*Ensign*, November 1984, p. 24.)

— Russell C. Taylor

Peace can come to both the giver and the receiver as we follow the promptings of the Spirit to serve one another. (*Ensign*, November 1985, p. 96.)

— Barbara W. Winder

Loving service anonymously given may be unknown to man—but the gift and the giver are known to God. (*Ensign*, May 1983, p. 57.)

— Thomas S. Monson

Service is the virtue that has distinguished the great of all times and which they will be remembered by. It places a mark of nobility upon its disciples. It is the dividing line which separates the two great groups of the world—those who help and those who hinder, those who lift and those who lean, those who contribute and those who only consume. How much better it is to give than to receive. Service in any form is comely and beautiful. To give encouragement, to impart sympathy, to show interest, to banish fear, to build self-confidence and awaken hope in the hearts of others, in short to love them and to show it, is to render the most precious service. (*New Era,* June 1975, p. 14.)

— *Bryant S. Hinckley*

Love without service, like faith without works, is *DEAD!*

— *Mary Ellen Edmunds*

One sister continued to serve as a visiting teacher supervisor when she was ill and homebound. Her Relief Society president reported that, with much effort, this sister put on one of her prettiest dresses before doing the telephoning each month, feeling that this act gave her service importance and dignity as she filled this assignment for the Lord. (*Ensign,* November 1977, p. 89.)

— *Barbara B. Smith*

Ten Ways Service Increases Spirituality
1. Service helps us establish true values and priorities by distinguishing between the worth of material things that pass, and those things of lasting, even eternal, value.
2. Service helps us establish a righteous tradition. This is so necessary, particularly among young people. Wise parents will provide service opportunities in the home for their children from an early age.
3. Service helps us overcome selfishness and sin.
4. Service . . . helps to recompense for sin. (Ezek. 33:16; James 5:20.)
5. Service helps us generate love and appreciation. We come to know people by serving them—their circumstances, their challenges, their hopes and aspirations.
6. Service is the principal way of showing gratitude to the Savior. (Matt. 25:40.)
7. Service channels our desires and energies into righteous activity.
8. Service helps us cleanse ourselves and become purified and sanctified.
9. Charitable service helps us do as the Savior did, for was not His whole ministry one of reaching out and helping, lifting and blessing, loving and caring?
10. Service helps us to get to know the Savior, for "how knoweth a man the master whom he has not served?" (Mosiah 5:13.) As we immerse ourselves in the service of others, we find our spiritual selves and come unto Him. (*Ensign,* May 1990, p. 13.)

— *Derek A. Cuthbert*

Service opens windows in your life instead of just mirrors that always reflect yourself.

— *Russell C. Taylor*

Sisters, put away from you the vanities and frivolities of the world, administer to the poor and the afflicted. The sisters know how to sympathize with and administer to those who are poor, afflicted, and downcast; and let the brethren help them in their kindly ministrations. (*JD*, 19:142.)

— John Taylor

The Elements of Service Shown by the Good Samaritan

First, the Samaritan "had compassion." He had the urge to help, for he felt sympathetic to the wounded man's problem. This kindly affection is brought forth in the heart of anyone who has been touched by the Spirit of the Lord. . . .

Second, the Samaritan "went to him." He did not wait to be approached by the one in need, but rather perceived the need and stepped forth . . . In that great hymn "A Poor Wayfaring Man of Grief," . . . we sense that the high reward promised by the Savior came not just because acts of kindness were performed, but also because they were done spontaneously, consistently, and selflessly.

Third, the Samaritan "bound up his wounds, pouring in oil and wine." He provided medical attention and refreshed the sufferer's thirst. This *immediate relief* may well have saved the man's life.

Fourth, the Samaritan "set him on his own beast"—that is, he provided transportation and "brought him to an inn," a place of rest and care. By providing this appropriate accommodation he ensured the proper conditions for healing to take place.

Fifth, the Samaritan "took care of him." Notice that during the critical stages of healing, the Samaritan did not turn the care of the wounded man over to others, but sacrificed of his own time and energy to perform the healing service *himself.* . . .

Sixth, the Samaritan "on the morrow . . . took out two pence, and gave them to the host." He took of his own money, not someone else's, and paid for the services he could not render himself. He thus consecrated of his means for the care of the poor and the needy.

Seventh, the Samaritan, needing to continue earning his own living, told the innkeeper to "take care of him." In this way he enlisted *others—resource persons—*to help and to continue the care.

Eighth, the Samaritan then promised that "whatsoever thou spendest more, when I come again, I will repay thee." Here the ultimate in compassion is shown! He puts no limit on the extent to which he will help. And, perhaps even more significant, he does not drop it there and forget it, but commits himself to return and ensure that all that could be done has been done.

This seems to be the consummate story of service [Luke 10:25-37]. (*Ensign,* November 1977, pp. 91-92.)

— N. Eldon Tanner

The more we serve our fellowmen in appropriate ways, the more substance there is to our souls. We become more significant individuals as we serve others. We become more substantive as we serve others—indeed, it is easier to "find" ourselves because there is so much more of us to find! (*Ensign*, December 1974, p. 2.)

— *Spencer W. Kimball*

The most worthy calling in life . . . is that in which man can serve best his fellowman. (*The Instructor*, March 1961, pp. 73-74.)

— *David O. McKay*

Those we serve, we love. (*Ensign*, November 1985, p. 14.)

— *Robert L. Backman*

Those who labor unselfishly in behalf of others, with no thought of remuneration, will be physically and spiritually refreshed and renewed. (*Ensign*, May 1990, p. 25.)

— *David B. Haight*

To measure the goodness of life by its delights and pleasures is to apply a false standard. The abundant life does not consist of a glut of luxury. It does not make itself content with commercially produced pleasure, mistaking it for joy and happiness.

To find real happiness, we must seek for it in a focus outside ourselves. No one has learned the meaning of living until he has surrendered his ego to the service of his fellowmen. Service to others is akin to duty, the fulfillment of which brings true joy. (*Ensign*, May 1990, p. 92.)

— *Thomas S. Monson*

We . . . tend to evaluate others on the basis of physical, outward appearance: Their "good looks," their social status, their family pedigrees, their degrees, or their economic situations. The Lord, however, has a different standard by which he measures a person. . . . When the Lord measures an individual, He does not take a tape measure around the person's head to determine his mental capacity, nor his chest to determine his manliness, but He measures the heart as an indicator of the person's capacity and potential to bless others. (*Ensign*, November 1988, p. 15.)

— *Marvin J. Ashton*

We need to look around us, and if we cannot see poverty, illness, and despair in our own neighborhood or ward, then we have to look harder. And remember, we cannot be afraid to go beyond our own social and cultural circles. We have to rid ourselves of religious, racial, or social prejudices and expand the boundaries of our service. Service should never discriminate and is hardly ever easy. (*Ensign,* May 1990, p. 26.)

— *Hans B. Ringger*

We lose our life by serving and lifting others. By so doing we experience the only true and lasting happiness. Service is not something we endure on this earth so we can earn the right to live in the celestial kingdom. Service is the very fiber of which an exalted life in the celestial kingdom is made. (*Ensign,* November 1982, p. 93.)

— *Marion G. Romney*

We must never ignore or pass by the prompting of the Spirit to render service to one another. (*Ensign,* May 1990, p. 8.)

— *M. Russell Ballard*

We should be involved in quiet acts of selfless service.

— *Spencer W. Kimball*

When someone asked how he was doing, my father simply stated, "I'm lonely, but I'm not lonesome." Do you know what he meant? Though he was now without his sweetheart, he was so busy assisting family and friends, he had replaced sorrow with service and had displaced self-pity with selfless love. He had found joy in following the timeless example of the Master. (*Ensign,* November 1985, p. 32.)

— *Russell M. Nelson*

Where there is a need, I personally have a responsibility to help. There is little use asking who is my neighbor; *I am neighbor* to my neighbor in need. (*Ensign,* November 1976, p. 32.)

— *Marion D. Hanks*

See also BROTHERHOOD, CHARITY, DISCIPLESHIP, LOVE, TEMPORAL LAW, WELFARE, ZION

——— Sharing the Gospel ———

After all that has been said, the greatest and most important duty is to preach the gospel. (*TPJS,* p. 113.)

— *Joseph Smith*

After conversion comes the desire to share—not so much out of a sense of duty, even though that responsibility falls on the priesthood, but out of a sincere love and appreciation for that which has been received. When such a "pearl of great price" comes into our lives, we cannot be content just to admire it by ourselves. It must be shared! And here is the great joy and happiness of the gift! (*Ensign*, May 1984, p. 79.)

— *L. Tom Perry*

As a member of the Church, do you realize that, as a member-missionary, you have a sacred responsibility to share the gospel with friends and family? The Lord needs every member of the Church having the faith and the courage to set a date to have someone prepared to be taught by the missionaries. Would each member of the Church prayerfully consider this sacred challenge? (*Ensign*, May 1988, p. 84.)

— *Ezra Taft Benson*

As disciples of Christ, we need to feel genuine charity for one another. As we do, new light will come into our own lives. This charity is essential in missionary work, but we must never allow ourselves to treat our neighbors only as potential converts. We have had the sad experience of seeing members of the Church who attempted to convert their neighbors and friends and, when they did not respond, withdrew their friendship and neighborliness. We must not be so anxious to share the gospel that we become insensitive to the feelings of others. . . .

If [nonmember friends] are not interested in the gospel, we should show unconditional love through acts of service and kindness, and never imply that we see an acquaintance only as a potential convert. (*Ensign*, November 1988, p. 30.)

— *M. Russell Ballard*

Brethren and sisters, never be ashamed of the gospel of Jesus Christ. Never apologize for the sacred doctrines of the gospel.

Never feel inadequate and unsettled because you cannot explain them to the satisfaction of all who might inquire of you.

Do not be ill at ease or uncomfortable because you can give little more than your conviction.

Be assured that, if you will explain what you know and testify of what you feel, you may plant a seed that will one day grow and blossom into a testimony of the gospel of Jesus Christ. (*Ensign*, November 1985, p. 83.)

— *Boyd K. Packer*

Every missionary and every member of the Church has the right—yes, even the obligation—to bear testimony of Jesus Christ to his friends, family, and neighbors in mildness and in meekness. (*Ensign*, May 1979, p. 77.)

— *Robert D. Hales*

It is not necessary for you to be called to go into the mission field in order to proclaim the truth. Begin on the man who lives next door by inspiring confidence in him, by inspiring love in him for you because of your righteousness, and your missionary work has already begun. (*CR*, October 1916, p. 49.)

— *George Albert Smith*

My understanding is that the most important mission that I have in this life is: first, to keep the commandments of God, as they have been taught to me; and next, to teach them to my Father's children who do not understand them. (*CR*, October 1916, p.50.)

— *George Albert Smith*

The day for carrying the gospel to ever more places and people is here and now. We must come to think of our obligation to share the message rather than of our own convenience. Calls from the Lord are seldom convenient. The time is here when sacrifice must become an even more important element in the Church. (*Ensign*, November 1982, p. 5.)

— *Spencer W. Kimball*

The first great commandment was to love the Lord our God with all our hearts, might, mind and strength; and the second was like unto it, to love our neighbors as ourselves. And the best way in the world to show our love for our neighbor is to go forth and proclaim the gospel of the Lord Jesus Christ, of which He has given us an absolute knowledge concerning its divinity. (*CR*, April 1927, p. 176.)

— *Heber J. Grant*

The Gospel of Jesus Christ was not intended just for a contingent or a segment of the earth. The gospel is intended for every soul that walks the earth, they are all the children of God. Our responsibility is to bring to the world the message of truth, to show the world that within the teachings of the gospel of Jesus Christ are to be found the solutions to every problem that affects mankind. (*Church News*, July 15, 1972, p. 4.)

— *Harold B. Lee*

We are commanded by God to take this gospel to all the world. That is the cause that must unite us today. Only the gospel will save the world from the calamity of its own self-destruction. Only the gospel will unite men of all races and nationalities in peace. Only the gospel will bring joy, happiness, and salvation to the human family. (*TETB*, p. 167.)

— *Ezra Taft Benson*

The Lord has told us that our sins will be forgiven more readily as we bring souls unto Christ and remain steadfast in bearing testimony to the world, and surely every one of us is looking for additional help in being forgiven of our sins. (*Ensign*, October 1977, p. 5.)

— *Spencer W. Kimball*

The more I am involved in this work, the more I realize that Satan would have you and me believe that we cannot succeed in sharing the gospel. He lies to us. In fact, he is the father of all lies. Do not listen to him. Listen to the prompting of the Holy Ghost, and then act in faith in sharing the gospel. (*Ensign*, November 1986, p. 33.)

— *M. Russell Ballard*

We can give the saving ordinances of the gospel to others when we allow the Lord to help us with someone we know and love. Sharing our feelings about God and religion should be easy since most Latter-day Saints are loving, sharing, and trusting people. With a relationship of trust established and with help from the Lord, we generally can feel comfortable moving beyond the realm of friendship and can invite our friends to learn more about the Church. (*Ensign*, November 1986, p. 33.)

— *M. Russell Ballard*

We cannot receive the beneficent favor of our Heavenly Father that is bestowed upon us, the knowledge of eternal life, and selfishly retain it, thinking that we may be blessed thereby. It is not what we receive that enriches our lives, it is what we give. (*CR*, April 1935, p. 46.)

— *George Albert Smith*

We have some excellent information which shows that, generally, the number of converts in a geographical area is more related to the number of Church members than to the number of full-time missionaries. Of all the things we can do to lift dramatically the number of convert baptisms, more effective involvement of Church members in missionary work tops the list. (*Ensign*, May 1979, p. 104.)

— *Howard W. Hunter*

When the Spirit is present, people are not offended when you share your feelings about the gospel. (*Ensign*, November 1986, p. 33.)

— *M. Russell Ballard*

[The] light of truth sparks a desire to share. When our minds are expanded by new knowledge, we want others to know; when our spirits are elevated by heavenly influence, we want others to feel; and when our lives are filled with goodness, we want others, particularly those whom we love, to enjoy similar experiences. (*Ensign*, November 1976, p. 41.)

— *Carlos E. Asay*

When we live outside ourselves and attempt to share the gospel, we invite the presence of a beautiful spirit—a spirit which accompanies fervent testimony, scripture reading, and a genuine concern for the souls of men. (*Ensign*, November 1976, p. 43.)

— *Carlos E. Asay*

When we partake of the sacrament, we covenant that we are willing to take upon us the name of Jesus Christ and that we will always remember Him and keep His commandments. Is there any better way that you and I can demonstrate to the Lord our love for Him than to share His gospel? (*Ensign*, November 1984, p. 16.)

— *M. Russell Ballard*

See also FELLOWSHIPPING, LATTER-DAY WORK, MISSIONARY WORK

——— Signs of the Times ———

A sure indication of the great event [second coming of Christ] as specified by the Lord himself, was and is that the gospel of the kingdom shall be preached in all the world. The missionary service of The Church of Jesus Christ of Latter-day Saints attests the progressive fulfillment of this prediction. (*MS*, 91:34.)

— *Heber J. Grant*

And so it goes: all sects, parties, and denominations acclaim a Christ molded to fit their diverse theological idiosyncrasies. And as we know, this very babble of voices crying out that salvation comes through Christ according to this or that system, is itself one of the signs of the times. (*CR*, April 1977, p. 15.)

— *Bruce R. McConkie*

God has held the angels of destruction for many years, lest they should reap down the wheat with the tares. But I want to tell you now, that those angels have left the portals of heaven, and they stand over this people and this nation now, and are hovering over the earth waiting to pour out the judgments. And from this very day they shall be poured out. Calamities and troubles are increasing in the earth, and there is a meaning to these things. (*IE*, October 1914, p. 1165.)

— *Wilford Woodruff*

For many in our day, the profane has become commonplace and the vulgar has become acceptable. Surely this is one fulfillment of the Book of Mormon prophecy that in the last days "there shall be great pollutions upon the face of the earth." (Morm. 8:31.) (*Ensign*, May 1986, p. 49.)

— *Dallin H. Oaks*

I say to you, as I stand with you and see the moving hand of the Lord in the affairs of the nations of the world today, we are seeing the signs of our times as foretold by the prophets and by the Master himself, and we see what is happening and the things transpiring before us in our day. In the Church, we have been witnessing some of the most dramatic things. (*Ensign*, January 1974, p. 128.)

— *Harold B. Lee*

I testify that wickedness is rapidly expanding in every segment of our society. (See D&C 1:14-16; 84:49-53.) It is more highly organized, more cleverly disguised, and more powerfully promoted than ever before. Secret combinations lusting for power, gain, and glory are flourishing. A secret combination that seeks to overthrow the freedom of all lands, nations, and countries is increasing its evil influence and control over America and the entire world. (See Ether 8:18-25.)

I testify that the church and kingdom of God is increasing in strength. Its numbers are growing, as is the faithfulness of its faithful members. It has never been better organized or equipped to perform its divine mission.

I testify that as the forces of evil increase under Lucifer's leadership and as the forces of good increase under the leadership of Jesus Christ, there will be growing battles between the two until the final confrontation. As the issues become clearer and more obvious, all mankind will eventually be required to align themselves either for the kingdom of God or for the kingdom of the devil. As these conflicts rage, either secretly or openly, the righteous will be tested. God's wrath will soon shake the nations of the earth and will be poured out on the wicked without measure. (See JS-H 1:45; D&C 1:9.) But God will provide strength for the righteous and the means of escape; and eventually and finally truth will triumph. (See 1 Ne. 22:15-23.)

I testify that it is time for every man to set in order his own house both temporally and spiritually. (*Ensign*, November 1988, p. 87.)

— *Ezra Taft Benson*

Political changes have occurred recently in many countries. Previous restrictions of personal liberties have been relieved. The shell of spiritual confinement has been shattered. Swelling shouts of freedom fill the air. Surely the hand of the Lord is apparent. He said, "I will hasten my work in its time" (D&C 88:73), and that time of hastening is now. (*Ensign*, May 1990, p. 17.)

— *Russell M. Nelson*

In America two great civilizations, the Jaredite and the Nephite, were completely annihilated because of their rejection of the laws of righteousness which God revealed unto them.

In both cases, the Lord, through His prophets, pointed out their iniquities, warned them, and predicted their destruction if they did not repent. This they did not do. Consequently they were totally destroyed.

We today are approaching the close of a similar cycle. (*Ensign,* November 1977, pp. 14-15.)

— *Marion G. Romney*

Jesus warned us that one of the principal characteristics of the last days would be that love among the people would gradually die. . . .We are living in the last days. It is a day when love is waxing cold. . . . Jesus Christ will soon come in power and glory. When he comes only those will be spared who have learned to love God and one another with all their heart, might, mind, and strength. (*Ensign,* May 1979, p. 74.)

— *Theodore M. Burton*

Samuel the Lamanite sets forth the interesting rule that when the economy becomes the main and engrossing concern of a society—or in the routine Book of Mormon phrase, when "they begin to set their hearts upon their riches"—the economy will self-destruct. . . . Note well that sequence of folly: first we are well-pleased with ourselves because of our wealth, then comes the game of status and prestige, leading to competitive maneuvers, hatred, dirty tricks and finally the ultimate solution. Where wealth guarantees respectability, principles melt away as the criminal element rises to the top. (*OAT,* p. 127.)

— *Hugh Nibley*

The Lord Jesus Christ is coming to reign on earth. The world may say that He delays His coming until the end of the earth. But they know neither the thoughts nor the ways of the Lord. The Lord will not delay His coming because of their unbelief, and the signs both in heaven and earth indicate that it is near. The fig trees are leafing in sight of all the nations of the earth, and if they had the Spirit of God they could see and understand them. (*JD,* 16:35.)

— *Wilford Woodruff*

There are four portentous danger signals in the Book of Mormon, three internal and one external. . . . The external threat is of course the Lamanites; the internal danger signals are: (1) the accumulation of wealth, (2) the appearance on the scene of ambitious men, and (3) the presence in the society of "secret combinations to get power and gain." . . . I have always thought in reading the Book of Mormon, "Woe to the generation that understands this book!" . . . With every passing year this great and portentous story becomes more and more familiar and more frighteningly like our own. (*OAT*, pp. 88, 89-90.)

— *Hugh Nibley*

The signs of the times, and the rapid approach of scenes that will try the hearts of the Latter-day Saints and their integrity, demand that we now seek earnestly the Spirit of God, and divine assistance, for it will certainly be needed in the scenes now rapidly approaching. . . . If we have needed the Holy Spirit in the past, we may truly understand that it will be needed in the future. (*Deseret Weekly*, 38:762.)

— *Lorenzo Snow*

This is a gloomy day of sorrow and sadness. The heavens gather blackness; men's hearts are failing them for fear (see Luke 21:26); nations are perplexed and know not where to turn to find peace and security.

This is a day in which mad men in high places can, in an instant, suddenly, unleash such fearful weapons that millions can be slain between the rising and the setting of the sun.

There has never been such a dire day as this. Iniquity abounds; all the perversions and evils of Sodom have their devotees. And the revealed word assures us that conditions will get worse, not better, until the coming of the Son of Man. (*Ensign*, November 1981, p. 46.)

— *Bruce R. McConkie*

We are living in a troublous age. Many people in the Church, as millions in the world, are stirred with anxiety; hearts are heavy with feelings of foreboding. For the third time in half a century lowering war clouds threaten world peace. O foolish man! Will he never profit by the experiences of the past! . . . It is the duty of the members of the Church to hold aloft true spiritual standards. Then we shall be better prepared for any eventuality. (*CR*, April 1948, pp. 64-65.)

— *David O. McKay*

We live in the day of the smooth and subtle sins, the fashionable immoralities, the clever compromises, the routine treason, with evil on the rampage. (Regional Representatives Seminar, Salt Lake City, Utah, September 30, 1977.)

— *Ezra Taft Benson*

We trace the hand of the Almighty and we see His Spirit moving in all communities for their good, restraining and encouraging, establishing governments and nations, inspiring men to take a course that shall most advance His purposes until the set time shall come when He shall work more fully and effectually for the accomplishment of His designs, and when sorrow, wickedness, evil, crime, bitter disappointments, vexation, distress, and poverty shall cease and be no more known, and the salvation and happiness of His children be secured, when the earth shall be rolled back into its pristine purity and the inhabitants thereof dwell upon it in perfect peace and happiness.

— *Lorenzo Snow*

You will see that the wisdom of the wise among the nations will perish and be taken from them. They will fall into difficulties, and they will not be able to tell the reason, not point a way to avert them . . . . They can fight, quarrel, contend and destroy each other, but they do not know how to make peace. So it will be with the inhabitants of the earth. (*JD*, 10:315.)

— *Brigham Young*

See also LAST DAYS

Sin

All sin is selfish, whether it be lying, cheating, stealing, immorality, covetousness, or idleness. Sin is for one's own ends, not another's—certainly not for the Lord's ends. (*Ensign*, May 1990, p. 12.)

— *Derek A. Cuthbert*

Sin is sin because it destroys instead of saves; it tears down instead of builds; it causes despair instead of hope. (*Ensign*, May 1986, p. 53.)

— *Jack H. Goaslind*

Not being perfect, are we not all sinners? (*Ensign*, May 1990, p. 13.)

— *Derek A. Cuthbert*

As we go through life, we ofttimes build a rock wall between ourselves and heaven. This wall is built by our unrepented sins. For example, in our wall there may be stones of many different sizes and shapes. There could be stones because we have been unkind to someone. Criticism of leaders or teachers may add another stone. A lack of forgiveness may add another. Vulgar thoughts and actions may add some rather large stones in this wall. Dishonesty will add another; selfishness another; and so on.

In spite of the wall we build in front of us, when we cry out to the Lord, he still sends his messages from heaven; but instead of being able to penetrate our hearts, they hit the wall that we have built up and bounce off. His messages don't penetrate, so we say, "He doesn't hear," or "He doesn't answer." Sometimes this wall is very formidable, and the great challenge of life is to destroy it, or, if you please, to cleanse ourselves, purifying this inner vessel so that we can be in tune with the Spirit. (*Ensign*, June 1981, p. 73.)

— *H. Burke Peterson*

Decadence . . . is no friend of liberty. . . . Far from freeing those involved, sin is an admission of surrender to the herd. It is a capitulation to the carnal in man and a rejection of joy and beauty in this life and in the world to come. (*Ensign*, May 1978, p. 78.)

— *Spencer W. Kimball*

God's gift and commitment to agency never will include a tolerance of sin. (*Ensign*, November 1990, p. 20.)

— *Marvin J. Ashton*

In the arithmetic of heaven, several commendables do not cancel out one inexcusable! (*Ensign*, November 1988, p. 33.)

— *Neal A. Maxwell*

It is painful to be the victim. But have you not yet learned how much more painful it is to be the offender? (*Ensign*, November 1987, p. 17.)

— *Boyd K. Packer*

One of the philosophers has said: "The greatest treason is to do the right thing for the wrong reason." Of course, this isn't strictly true. Obviously it is greater treason to do the wrong thing for any reason. (*CR*, October 1968, p. 13.)

— *Hartman Rector, Jr.*

Sin can stun the conscience as a blow on the head can stun the physical senses. (*Gospel Ideals*, The Improvement Era, Salt Lake City: Deseret Book Co., 1978, p. 146.)

— *David O. McKay*

Sin is co-eternal with righteousness, for it must needs be that there is an opposition in all things. (*JD*, 10:3.)

— *Brigham Young*

Sin is the only real tragedy! (*Ensign*, May 1983, p. 11.)

— *Neal A. Maxwell*

Sin is waste. It is doing one thing when you should be doing other and better things for which you have the capacity. Hence, there are no innocent idle thoughts. That is why even the righteous must repent, constantly and progressively, since all fall short of their capacity and calling. (*OAT*, p. 109.)

— *Hugh Nibley*

Sin may result from activities that begin innocently or that are perfectly legitimate in moderation, but in excess, they can cause us to veer from the straight and narrow path to our destruction. (*Ensign*, November 1990, p. 65.)

— *Joseph B. Wirthlin*

Since the beginning there has been in the world a wide range of sins. Many of them involve harm to others, but every sin is against ourselves and God, for sins limit our progress, curtail our development, and estrange us from good people, good influences, and from our Lord. (*Ensign*, November 1980, p. 94.)

— *Spencer W. Kimball*

The heaviest burden one may have to bear in this life is the burden of sin. (*Ensign*, November 1977, p. 30.)

— *Ezra Taft Benson*

There is no happiness is sin, and when we depart from the path of righteousness we begin to do those things which will inevitably lead us to unhappiness and misery and loss of freedom. (*Ensign*, May 1977, p. 17.)

— *N. Eldon Tanner*

Too many of our young people have the idea that limited sin is not really wrong because it will be forgiven easily with no consequences. We see young people who are guilty of moral sins but are not overly concerned because they expect to repent quickly, thinking all is well. The idea that any sin is unimportant is false; it comes from the devil. "The Lord cannot look upon sin with the least degree of allowance." (D&C 1:31.)

— *Joseph B. Wirthlin*

When you are overtaken in a fault, or commit an act unthinkingly; when you are full of evil passion, and wish to yield to it, then stop and let the spirit, which God has put into your tabernacle, take the lead. If you do that, I will promise that you will overcome all evil, and obtain eternal lives. (*JD*, 2:255-56.)

— *Brigham Young*

See also EVIL, REPENTANCE, WICKEDNESS

———— Sorrow ————

Almighty God has promised to forgive, forget, and never mention the sins of which we have truly repented. But he has given us the gift of remorse to help *us* remember them constructively, thankfully, and humbly . . . (*Ensign*, May 1979, p. 76.)

—*Marion D. Hanks*

Sorrow can actually enlarge the mind and heart in order to "give place," expanded space for later joy. (*Ensign*, May 1990, p. 34.)

—*Neal A. Maxwell*

There are many kinds of sorrow and suffering: self-inflicted suffering; suffering from infirmities of our mortal bodies and sorrow from separation by death; suffering that tries and tests us; suffering to develop our spiritual strength; suffering to humble us and lead us to repentance; the Savior's suffering and atoning sacrifice, the most important event in the history of the world.

But if our sorrow and suffering strengthen our faith in our Savior, Jesus Christ, "[our] sorrow shall be turned to joy." (John 16:20.) (*Ensign*, November 1983, p. 65.)

—*Robert D. Hales*

We are commanded to be joyful because He has borne our sorrows. He was a man of sorrows and acquainted with grief so that we need not be. Our own sins and limitations are the things that make us sad. He had no sins and limitations: he was not sad for his sake, but wholly for ours. Only one could suffer for others who did not deserve to suffer for himself.

If we remain gloomy after what he did for us, it is because we do not accept what he did for us. If we suffer, we deserve to suffer because there is no need for it if we only believe in him. (*OAT*, p. 6.)

—*Hugh Nibley*

We have been sent into the world to do good to others; and in doing good to others we do good to ourselves. . . . When you find yourselves a little gloomy, look around you and find somebody that is in a worse plight than yourself; go to him and find out what the trouble is, then try to remove it with the wisdom which the Lord bestows upon you; and the first thing you know, your gloom is gone, you feel light, the Spirit of the Lord is upon you, and everything seems illuminated. (*CR*, April, 1899, pp. 2-3.)

—*Lorenzo Snow*

You never saw a true Saint in the world that had sorrow, neither can you find one. If persons are destitute of the fountain of living water, or the principles of eternal life, then they are sorrowful. If the words of life dwell within us, and we have the hope of eternal life and glory, and let that spark within us kindle to a flame, to the consuming of the least and last remains of selfishness, we never can walk in darkness and are strangers to doubt and fear. (*DBY*, p. 235.)

—*Brigham Young*

See also ADVERSITY, DISCOURAGEMENT, JOY

——— Spirit of the Lord ———

During my travels in the southern country last winter I had many interviews with President Young, and with Heber C. Kimball, and George A. Smith, and Jedediah M. Grant, and many others who are dead. They attended our conference, they attended our meetings. And on one occasion, I saw Brother Brigham and brother Heber ride in a carriage ahead of the carriage in which I rode when I was on my way to attend conference; and they were dressed in the most priestly robes. When we arrived at our destination I asked President Young if he would preach to us. He said, "No, I have finished my testimony in the flesh; I shall not talk to this people any more. But I have come to see you; I have come to watch over you, and to see what the people are doing. I want you to teach the people—and I want you to follow this counsel yourself—that they must labor and so live as to obtain the Holy Spirit, for without this you cannot build up the kingdom; without the spirit of God you are in danger of walking in the dark, and in danger of failing to accomplish your calling as apostles and as elders in the church and kingdom of God. (*JD*, 21:317-18.)

—*Wilford Woodruff*

Every man and woman in this Church should labor to get that Spirit. We are surrounded by these evil spirits that are at war against God and against everything looking to the building up of the kingdom of God; and we need this Holy Spirit to enable us to overcome these influences. (*Deseret Weekly*, November 7, 1896, p. 643.)

—*Wilford Woodruff*

Some years ago, as a pilot, I was taken by an instructor up in an airplane. By turning the airplane at less than two degrees at a time, the instructor succeeded in turning the airplane completely upside down. My inner ear could not detect the transition because he kept positive gravity upon us at all times. Therefore, I did not know that, when he gave the airplane to me, it was upside down. Everything on the airplane, every instrument, was exactly right except for the landing gear, which was upside down; and every reaction I made had an opposite reaction from what I thought it would have. This is called vertigo, and it taught me a great lesson.

I would like to talk for a moment about spiritual vertigo. Although we know of the atoning sacrifice of Jesus Christ, of His obedience, of His willingness to serve and to be an example to us, and of His message to "come, follow me," there are times when we get off course, less than a degree at a time, and do not know that we turn totally upside down. . . .

When we go into the waters of baptism, we take upon us His name and promise that we will always be obedient. . . . For that obedience, we are told that we will always have His Spirit to be with us. We will always have the spiritual gyroscope that will guide us so that we will never have to encounter spiritual vertigo and that we will never be off course. (*Ensign*, November 1985, p. 21.)

—*Robert D. Hales*

The Spirit does not get our attention by shouting or shaking us with a heavy hand. Rather, it whispers. It caresses so gently that if we are preoccupied we may not feel it at all. . . .

Occasionally it will press just firmly enough for us to pay heed. But most of the time, if we do not heed the gentle feeling, the Spirit will withdraw and wait until we come seeking and listening and say in our manner and expression, like Samuel of ancient times, "Speak, Lord, for Thy servant heareth." (1 Samuel 3:9-10.) (New Mission Presidents' Seminar, June 25, 1982.)

—*Boyd K. Packer*

When men stop praying for God's Spirit, they place confidence in their own unaided reason, and they gradually lose the Spirit of God, just the same as near and dear friends, by never writing to or visiting with each other, will become strangers. (*IE*, 47:481.)

—*Heber J. Grant*

[In February, 1847, Brigham Young had a dream in which the Prophet Joseph Smith appeared to him and gave this message:]

"Tell the brethren to be humble and faithful and be sure to keep the Spirit of the Lord, that it will lead them aright. Be careful and not turn away the still, small voice; it will teach them what to do and where to go; it will yield the fruits of the kingdom. Tell the brethren to keep their hearts open to conviction, so that when the Holy Ghost comes to them, their hearts will be ready to receive it.

"They can tell the Spirit of the Lord from all other spirits—it will whisper peace and joy to their souls; it will take malice, hatred, strife and all evil from their hearts, and their whole desire will be to do good, bring forth righteousness, and build up the kingdom of God . . .

"Tell the people to be sure to keep the Spirit of the Lord and follow it and it will lead them just right." (Quoted by Marion G. Romney, *CR*, April 1944, pp. 140-41.)

—Brigham Young

See also HOLY GHOST, REVELATION

—— Spirit World ——

Here, we are continually troubled with ills and ailments of various kinds . . . in the spirit world we are free from all this and enjoy life, glory, and intelligence; and we have the Father to speak to us, Jesus to speak to us, and angels to speak to us, and we shall enjoy the society of the just and the pure who are in the spirit world until the resurrection. (*JD*, 14:231.)

—Brigham Young

I believe that those who have been chosen in this dispensation and in former dispensations, to lay the foundation of God's work in the midst of the children of men, . . . will not be deprived in the spirit world from looking down upon the results of their own labors, . . . So I feel quite confident that the eye of Joseph the Prophet, and of the martyrs of this dispensation, and of Brigham, and John, and Wilford, and those faithful men who were associated with them in their ministry upon the earth, are carefully guarding the interests of the kingdom of God in which they labored and for which they strove during their mortal lives. I believe they are as deeply interested in our welfare today, if not with greater capacity, with far more interest, behind the veil, than they were in the flesh . . . they see us, they are solicitous for our welfare, they love us now more than ever. (*CR*, April 1916, pp. 2-3.)

—Joseph F. Smith

Where is the spirit world? It is incorporated within this celestial system. Can you see it with your natural eyes? No. Can you see spirits in this room? No. Suppose the Lord should touch your eyes that you might see, could you then see the spirits? Yes, . . . If the Lord would permit it, and it was his will that it should be done, you could see the spirits that have departed from this world as plainly as you now see bodies with your natural eyes. (*JD*, 3:368.)

—Brigham Young

Spiritual Guidance

God . . . has conferred upon us His Holy Spirit, which is an unerring guide, standing, as an angel of God, at our side, telling us what to do, and affording us strength and succor when adverse circumstances arise in our way. (*JD*, 20:191.)

—*Lorenzo Snow*

I am convinced that one of the greatest and one of the best things in all the world to keep a man true and faithful in the gospel of the Lord Jesus Christ is to supplicate God secretly in the name of Jesus Christ for the guidance of His Holy Spirit. (*CR*, October 1923, p. 7.)

—*Heber J. Grant*

It matters very little what we are engaged in, it is impossible for us to do right without the guidance of the Almighty. (*JD*, 13:221.)

—*John Taylor*

Never proceed to do anything until you go and labor in prayer and get the Holy Spirit. Wherever the Spirit dictates you to go or to do, that will be right; and, by following its dictates, you will come out right. (*JD*, 5:85.)

—*Wilford Woodruff*

The Lord gives to many of us the still, small voice of revelation. It comes as vividly and strongly as though it were with a great sound. It comes to each man, according to his needs and faithfulness, for guidance in matters that pertain to his own life. . . . This certain knowledge which we have that the guiding influence of the Lord may be felt in all the ways of life, according to our needs and faithfulness, is among the greatest blessings God grants unto men. With this blessing comes the responsibility to render strict obedience to the "still small voice." (*IE*, December 1938, p. 712.)

—*Heber J. Grant*

See also HOLY GHOST, INSPIRATION, REVELATION, SPIRIT OF THE LORD

Spiritual Rebirth

The Son of God came into the world to redeem it from the fall. But except a man be born again, he cannot see the kingdom of God. This eternal truth settles the question of all men's religion. A man may be saved, after the judgment, in the terrestrial kingdom, or in the telestial kingdom, but he can never see the celestial kingdom of God, without being born of water and the Spirit. (*TPJS*, p. 12.)

—Joseph Smith

Being born again, comes by the Spirit of God through ordinances. (*TPJS*, p. 162.)

—Joseph Smith

I then fell asleep, and beheld in vision something infinitely sublime. In the distance I beheld a beautiful white city. Though far away, yet I seemed to realize that trees with luscious fruit, shrubbery with gorgeously-tinted leaves, and flowers in perfect bloom abounded everywhere. The clear sky above seemed to reflect these beautiful shades of color. I then saw a great concourse of people approaching the city. Each one wore a white flowing robe, and a white headdress. Instantly my attention seemed centered upon their Leader, and though I could see only the profile of his features and his body, I recognized him at once as my Savior! The tint and radiance of his countenance were glorious to behold! There was peace about him which seemed sublime—it was divine!

The city, I understood, was his. It was the City Eternal; and the people following him were to abide there in peace and eternal happiness.

But who were they?

As if the Savior read my thoughts, he answered by pointing to a semicircle that then appeared above them, and on which were written in gold the words: *"These Are They Who Have Overcome The World—Who Have Truly Been Born Again!"*

When I awoke, it was breaking day. (*Cherished Experiences*, Clare Middlemiss, comp., Salt Lake City: Deseret Book Company, 1955, pp. 101-02.)

—David O. McKay

Out of the refiner's fire can come a glorious deliverance. It can be a noble and lasting rebirth. The price to become acquainted with God will have been paid. There can come a sacred peace. There will be a reawakening of dormant, inner resources. A comfortable cloak of righteousness will be drawn around us to protect us and to keep us warm spiritually. Self-pity will vanish as our blessings are counted. (*Ensign*, May 1979, p. 59.)

—James E. Faust

Under the influence of this Spirit [the Holy Ghost] they become new creatures. They are born again. Their hearts are changed. The old desires and feelings that they have had are either changed or brought into subjection to the will of God.

If this change does not take place, it is because the person who has been baptized and who has had the laying on of the hands for the gift of the Holy

Ghost has not sought for these blessings with diligence. Everyone who submits to the ordinances of the Gospel with sincerity and determination to serve God will undergo this change. (*Gospel Truth*, Jerreld L. Newquist, ed., Salt Lake City: Deseret Book Co., 1987)

—*George Q. Cannon*

The Lord works from the inside out. The world works from the outside in. The world would take people out of the slums. Christ takes the slums out of people, and then they take themselves out of the slums. The world would mold men by changing their environment. Christ changes men, who then change their environment. The world would shape human behavior, but Christ can change human nature. . . .

Yes, Christ changes men, and changed men can change the world. (*Ensign*, November 1985, p. 6.)

—*Ezra Taft Benson*

We need to break free of our old selves—the provincial, constraining, and complaining selves—and become susceptible to the shaping of the Lord. But the old self goes neither gladly nor quickly. Even so, this subjection to God is really emancipation. (*Ensign*, May 1985, p. 71.)

—*Neal A. Maxwell*

See also CONVERSION, PURITY, REPENTANCE

——— Spiritual Strength ———

As the time of repentance is procrastinated, the ability to repent grows weaker; neglect of opportunity in holy things develops inability.

—*James E. Talmage*

Every individual must get a testimony for himself and be guided by the Spirit entirely on his own; then, and only then, as Brigham Young so often and so emphatically declared, can the people of God be led by revelation. In the light of such a doctrine, whether Joseph Smith ever made mistakes or not becomes completely irrelevant. . . . What mortals have ever been more keenly aware of their weaknesses and shortcomings than the prophets? (*OATS*, pp. 14-15.)

—*Hugh Nibley*

Men and women should become settled in the truth, and founded in the knowledge of the gospel, depending upon no person for borrowed or reflected light, but trusting only upon the Holy Spirit, who is ever the same, shining forever and testifying to the individual and the priesthood, who live in harmony with the laws of the gospel, of the glory and the will of the Father. They will then have light everlasting which cannot be obscured. By its shining in their lives, they shall cause others to glorify God; and by their well-doing put to silence the ignorance of foolish men, and show forth the praises of him who hath called them out of darkness into his marvelous light. (*GD*, pp. 87-88.)

—*Joseph F. Smith*

In speaking of these wondrous things [the Atonement] I shall use my own words, though you may think they are the words of scripture, words spoken by other Apostles and prophets.

True it is they were first proclaimed by others, but they are now mine, for the Holy Spirit of God has borne witness to me that they are true, and it is now as though the Lord had revealed them to me in the first instance. I have thereby heard his voice and know his word. . . .

I testify that he is the Son of the Living God and was crucified for the sins of the world. He is our Lord, our God, and our King. This I know of myself independent of any other person. (*Ensign*, May 1985, pp. 9, 11.)

—*Bruce R. McConkie*

Just as exercise, proper nourishment, and rest are essential to our physical well-being, so are such things as regular prayer, scripture study, Sabbath worship, partaking of the sacrament, and service to others necessary for our spiritual vigor. (*Ensign*, November 1989, p. 62.)

—*Dean L. Larsen*

Our temporal bodies would soon become emaciated, if we fed them only once a week, or twice, as some of us are in the habit of feeding our spiritual and religious bodies. (*IE*, 7:135.)

—*Joseph F. Smith*

The Lord has clearly indicated that His purifying and sifting judgment would begin *first* at the house of God and then proceed outward to the world. (See 1 Pet. 4:17; D&C 112:25.) Just what this sifting will consist of is not now clear, what special pressures—combined with the ongoing and demanding rigors of "taking up the cross daily"—we know not. (See Luke 9:23.) We do know that the tempter's triad of tools, identified by Jesus as temptation, persecution, and tribulation, will be relentlessly used. (See Matt. 13:21; Luke 8:13.) . . .

Much sifting will occur because of lapses in righteous behavior which go unrepented of. A few will give up instead of holding out to the end. A few will be deceived by defectors. Likewise, others will be offended, for sufficient unto each dispensation are the stumbling blocks thereof! A few will stumble because, in their preoccupation with the cares of the world, they do not have oil in their lamps. And, again and again, those who refuse to eat their spiritual spinach will come off second when they wrestle with the world. Some, because of the scorn of the world, will grow ashamed and let go of the iron rod. (See 1 Ne. 8:28.) A few who have not been Saints, but merely tourists passing through, will depart from the path. A few, failing to be of good cheer, will even charge God foolishly. (See Job 1:22.)

Surely, brothers and sisters, already too many Church members have broken hearts and broken homes because of broken covenants and broken promises. Society's increasing slide towards pleasure-seeking brings our so-called civilization comparatively closer to Sodom than to Eden.

In our striving to be prepared, therefore, let us be careful to rely on parents, priesthood, and principles—and on scriptures, and temples, and leaders who lead—to see us through. Let us not mistake program scaffolding for substance. (*Ensign*, November 1982, p. 68.)

—*Neal A. Maxwell*

The men and the women who are honest before God, who humbly plod along, doing their duty, paying their tithing, and exercising that pure religion and undefiled before God and the Father, which is to visit the fatherless and the widows in their afflictions and to keep oneself unspotted from the world, and who help look after the poor; and who honor the holy Priesthood, who do not run into excesses, who are prayerful in their families, and who acknowledge the Lord in their hearts, they will build up a foundation that the gates of hell cannot prevail against; and if the floods come and the storms beat upon their house, it shall not fall, for it will be built upon the rock of eternal truth. (*CR*, April 1900, p. 42.)

—*Joseph F. Smith*

The time is come when it behooves every man and every woman to know for themselves in relation to the foundation on which they stand. We should all strive to get a little nearer to the Lord. (*MS*, 49:244.)

—*Lorenzo Snow*

The time is when each of you must stand on your own feet. Be converted, because no one can endure on borrowed light. You will have to be guided by the light within yourself. If you do not have it, you will not stand. (*New Era*, February 1971, p. 4.)

—*Harold B. Lee*

To meet the difficulties that are coming, it will be necessary for you to have a knowledge of the truth of this work for yourselves. The difficulties will be of such a character that the man or woman who does not possess this personal knowledge or witness will fall. If you have not got the testimony, live right and call upon the Lord and cease not till you obtain it. If you do not you will not stand. . . .

The time will come when no man nor woman will be able to endure on borrowed light. Each will have to be guided by the light within himself. . . .

If you don't have it you will not stand; therefore seek for the testimony of Jesus and cleave to it, that when the trying time comes you may not stumble and fall. (*Life of Heber C. Kimball*, Orson F. Whitney, Salt Lake City: Bookcraft, 1945, p. 450.)

—*Heber C. Kimball*

See also HOLY GHOST, REVELATION, SPIRITUALITY, TESTIMONY

——— **Spirituality** ———

A person who has developed spirituality may suffer deeply and know frustration; but yet he is able to continue in showing forth kindness and love because of a power that rises up from his spiritual base that governs his actions and urges him to "speak with a new tongue" (2 Nephi 31:14), as Nephi said, and to be his best despite obstacles and setbacks. (*Ensign*, May 1988, pp. 21-22.)

—*David B. Haight*

All that we do must be measured by its ultimate spiritual uplift.

—*Marion G. Romney*

Every person can and must make spiritual progress. The gospel of Jesus Christ is the divine plan for that spiritual growth eternally. It is more than a code of ethics. It is more than an ideal social order. It is more than positive thinking about self-improvement and determination. The gospel is the saving power of the Lord Jesus Christ with his priesthood and sustenance and with the Holy Spirit. With faith in the Lord Jesus Christ and obedience to his gospel, a step at a time improving as we go, pleading for strength, improving our attitudes and our ambitions, we will find ourselves successfully in the fold of the Good Shepherd. (*Ensign*, May 1979, p. 26.)

—*Howard W. Hunter*

Qualities of spirituality do not come without effort. Like any other talent with which we are blessed, they must be constantly practiced. (*Ensign*, November 1988, p. 88.)

—*Barbara W. Winder*

Spirituality comes by faith, repentance, baptism, and reception of the Holy Ghost. One who has the companionship of the Holy Ghost is in harmony with God. He is, therefore, spiritual. Spirituality is sustained by so living as to keep that companionship. (*Ensign*, November 1979, p. 15.)

—*Marion G. Romney*

Spirituality, our true aim, is the consciousness of victory over self, and of communion with the Infinite. Spirituality impels one to conquer difficulties and acquire more and more strength. To feel one's faculties unfolding, and truth expanding in the soul, is one of life's sublimest experiences. (*Pathways to Happiness*, David O. McKay, Salt Lake city: Bookcraft, 1957, p. 246.)

—*David O. McKay*

The development of our spiritual nature should concern us most. Spirituality is the highest acquisition of the soul, the divine in man; "the supreme, crowning gift that makes him king of all created things." It is the consciousness of victory over self and of communion with the infinite. It is spirituality alone which really gives one the best in life. (*CR*, October 1936, p. 103.)

—*David O. McKay*

The Lord sent sea gulls to help those early Saints. Sea gulls are not the answer for us today. But *spirituality* is. We live in a world where many voices and influences are attempting to deceive youth and adults. You might honestly wonder, "How can I know for sure? Some things that are so enticing seem so innocent at first."

There is a sure way to know. Just as the Lord sent the sea gulls to destroy the crickets, He has provided safety and protection for you and me. Spirituality allows us to have the Spirit of the Lord with us, and when we do, we will never be deceived. (*Ensign*, November 1990, p. 94.)

—*Ardeth G. Kapp*

The source of our spiritual power is the Lord! The ultimate source of spiritual power is God our Father. The messenger of this power is the Holy Ghost. This power differs from electrical power. An electrical appliance *consumes* power. The use of His spiritual power *replenishes* our power. (*Ensign*, November 1984, p. 31.)

—*Russell M. Nelson*

The spiritual nature within us should not be dominated by the physical. It behooves each of us to remember who he or she is and what God expects him or her to become. (*Ensign*, May 1987, p. 67.)

—*Thomas S. Monson*

Things of the Spirit need not—indeed, should not—require our uninterrupted time and attention. Ordinary work-a-day things occupy most of our attention. And that is as it should be. We are mortal beings living in this physical world.

Spiritual things are like leavening. By measure they may be very small, but by influence they affect all that we do. Continuing revelation is fundamental to the gospel of Jesus Christ. (*Ensign*, November 1989, p. 14.)

—*Boyd K. Packer*

We have been taught to store a year's supply of food, clothing, and, if possible, fuel—at home. There has been no attempt to set up storerooms in every chapel. We know that in the crunch our members may not be able to get to the chapel for supplies.

Can we not see that the same principle applies to inspiration and revelation, the solving of problems, to counsel, and to guidance? We need to have a source of it stored in every home, not just in the bishop's office. (*Ensign*, May 1978, p. 9.)

—*Boyd K. Packer*

We seek spirituality through faith, repentance, and baptism; through forgiveness of one another; through fasting and prayer; through righteous desires and pure thoughts and actions. We seek spirituality through service to our fellow men; through worship; through feasting on the word of God, in the scriptures and the teachings of the living prophets. We attain spirituality through making and keeping covenants, through conscientiously trying to keep all the commandments of God. Spirituality is not acquired suddenly. It is the consequence of a succession of right choices. It is the harvest of a righteous life. (*Ensign*, November 1985, p. 63.)

—*Dallin H. Oaks*

With all my soul, I plead with members of the church, and with people everywhere, to think more about the gospel; more about the development of the spirit within; to devote more time to the real things of life, and less time to those things which will perish. (*CR*, April 1968, p. 144.)

—*David O. McKay*

You can't store spirituality. It's like manna—it has to be gathered daily and the only way is through prayer.

—*A. Theodore Tuttle*

See also RIGHTEOUSNESS, SPIRITUAL STRENGTH

—— Stewardship ——

In the Church a stewardship is a sacred spiritual or temporal trust for which there is accountability. Because all things belong to the Lord, we are stewards over our bodies, minds, families, and properties. A faithful steward is one who exercises righteous dominion, cares for his own, and looks to the poor and needy. (*Ensign*, November 1977, p. 78.)

—Spencer W. Kimball

Let me assure you, Brethren, that some day you will have a personal Priesthood interview with the Savior, Himself. If you are interested, I will tell you the order in which He will ask you to account for your earthly responsibilities.

First, He will request an accountability report about *your relationship with your wife*. Have you actively been engaged in *making her happy* and ensuring that *her needs* have been met as an individual?

Second, He will want an accountability report about *each of your children* individually. He will not attempt to have this for simply a family stewardship, but will request information about your relationship *to each and every child*.

Third, He will want to know what you personally have done with the *talents* you were given in the pre-existence.

Fourth, He will want a *summary of your activity in your church assignments*. He will not be necessarily interested in what assignments you have had, for in His eyes the home teacher and a mission president are probably equals, but He will request a summary of how you have been of service to your fellowmen in your church assignments.

Fifth, he will have *no* interest in how you earned your living, but if you were honest in all your dealings.

Sixth, He will ask for an accountability on what you have done to contribute in a positive manner to your community, state, country, and the world. (Address to employees of the Physical Facilities Dept. of the Church, Hotel Utah, June 1965.)

—David O. McKay

The Lord claims the earth as his, that it is not yours and mine to own and manage independently of him. No matter how many stocks and bonds or how much land and other properties we possess, they are not wholly ours. They are the Lord's. He further says that he owns and gives to us all the blessings we have and that he makes us stewards over them, responsible to him. (*Ensign*, May 1979, p. 95.)

—Marion G. Romney

Whatever you have, it is the Lord's. You own nothing, I own nothing. . . . The Lord has placed what I have in my hands, to see what I will do with it. . . . I have neither wife nor child, . . . they are only committed to me, to see how well I treat them. If I am faithful, the time will come when they will be given to me. (*JD*, 10:298.)

—*Brigham Young*

When the Master in the Savior's parable of the stewards called his servants before him he gave them several talents to improve on while he should tarry abroad for a little season, and when he returned, he called for an accounting. So it is now. Our Master is absent only for a little season, and at the end of it he will call each to render an account; and where the five talents were bestowed, ten will be required; and he that has made no improvement will be cast out as an unprofitable servant, while the faithful will enjoy everlasting honors. Therefore we earnestly implore the grace of our Father to rest upon you, through Jesus Christ his Son, that you may not faint in the hour of temptation, nor be overcome in the time of persecution. (*HC*, 2:23-24.)

—*Joseph Smith*

See also PRIORITIES

——— Success ———

A man who so lives that those who know him best, love him most, and whom God loves, is entitled to be crowned with the wreath of success although he might die in poverty. (*CR*, April 1932, p. 12.)

—*Heber J. Grant*

Success results when preparation meets opportunity. (*Ensign*, November 1989, p. 74.)

—*Joseph B. Wirthlin*

I assert with confidence that the law of success, here and hereafter, is to have a humble and a prayerful heart, and to work, work, WORK. (*IE*, 3:195.)

—*Heber J. Grant*

There are daily evidences of a growing tendency among the masses . . . to regard success in life purely from the standpoint of material advancement. The man who has a beautiful home and a large income is looked upon as a successful man. . . . One's success must be determined more by the eternal needs of man, than by temporary standards which men erect in pursuance of the spirit of the age in which they live. Certainly nothing is more fatal to our well being than the notion that our present and eternal welfare is founded upon the wealth and honors of this world. . . . The standard of success as declared by the word of God is the salvation of the soul. The greatest gift of god is eternal life. (*GD*, pp. 123-125.)

—*Joseph F. Smith*

If you wish to achieve financial success, if you wish to be happy, if you wish to be healthy, if you would be morally clean, if you wish to find religious peace of mind, there is only one sure way, and that is the straight and narrow path—the way of honor, the way of industry, of moderation, simplicity, and virtue. (*CR*, April 1975, p. 112.)

—*N. Eldon Tanner*

In my estimation, the Master's great success formula . . . is—First, *believe* you can do it. . . . Second, *look to the Lord for your blessings.* . . . Third, *make the sacrifice.* . . . Fourth, *expect a miracle.* . . . And fifth, *receive the miracle with great humility.* . . . I bear witness that this formula is effective in the Lord's work, and I am persuaded it works everywhere else too. (*Ensign,* May 1979, p. 31.)

—*Hartman Rector, Jr.*

Personal revelation, consecration of performance, attention to detail, and dependency on God—with these qualities you cannot fail. (*TETB*, p. 464.)

—*Ezra Taft Benson*

Success should not necessarily be gauged by always reaching the goal set, but by progress and attainment. (Regional Representatives Seminar, April 3, 1975.)

—*Spencer W. Kimball*

The whole world admires success. But how each of us defines success and how we seek it is crucial to our happiness. (*Ensign,* May 1982, p. 48.)

—*James E. Faust*

The secret of succeeding comes from doing the right thing at the right time and in the right way, and God will show you the way. (*CR,* April 1933, p. 127.)

—*Melvin J. Ballard*

The success of this life is not measured at the end of it by what we have, but rather by what we are. (*CR,* October 1912, p. 25.)

—*Rulon S. Wells*

The gospel of Jesus Christ is the formula for success. Every principle of the gospel, when lived, has a positive influence over your choice of an occupation and on what you will achieve. . . . Living the gospel will give you a perspective and an inspiration that will see you successful however ordinary your work may be or however ordinary your life may seem to others. (*Ensign,* May 1982, p. 87.)

—*Boyd K. Packer*

Remember this: there is no one great thing that you can do which will determine your happiness or success in life. Life is a series of little things—how you do your work from day to day, personal honesty in your everyday contacts, a smile and a handshake, courtesy and kindness—these are the "little things" that become the sum of your character. (*TETB,* p. 462.)

—*Ezra Taft Benson*

There is a course for every person to pursue in which there will be no failure. It will apply to temporal as well as spiritual matters. . . . "If your eye be single to my glory, your whole bodies shall be filled with light, and there shall be no darkness in you; and that body which is filled with light comprehendeth all things. Therefore, sanctify yourselves that your minds become single to God." That is the key by which a person can always be successful. (*Deseret Weekly,* 48:637.)

—*Lorenzo Snow*

To be a success regardless of your situation, . . . I recommend that you come to know your Father in Heaven. Come to love Him, and always remember that He loves you and will give you guidance and support if you will but give Him the chance. Include Him in your decision-making. Include Him when you take inventory of your personal worth. (*Ensign,* May 1984, p. 11.)

—*Marvin J. Ashton*

We . . . struggle through life, perhaps missing both fame and fortune, to finally learn one day that one can, indeed, succeed without possessing either. Or we may, one day, have both and learn that neither has made us happy; neither is basic to the recipe for true success. (*Ensign,* November 1980, p. 21.)

—*Boyd K. Packer*

See also EXCELLENCE, GREATNESS

Suffering

Being human we would expel from our lives, sorrow, distress, physical pain, and mental anguish and assure ourselves of continual ease and comfort. But if we closed the doors upon such, we might be evicting our greatest friends and benefactors. Suffering can make saints of people as they learn patience, long-suffering and self-mastery. (*IE*, March, 1966, p. 178.)

—*Spencer W. Kimball*

I find in tracing out the scriptures, that from the beginning there have existed two powers—the powers of light and the powers of darkness; that both these things existed in the heavens before they came here, that the powers of darkness were cast out, and thus became the devil and his angels. This antagonism, then, existed before, and it is necessary it should exist. It is necessary men should be tried and purged and purified and made perfect through suffering. (*JD*, 20:305.)

—*John Taylor*

Men and women who have suffered, . . . bring forth the riches of their sympathy and condolences as a blessing to those now in need. Could they do this had they not suffered themselves?

. . . Is not this God's purpose in causing his children to suffer? He wants them to become more like himself. God has suffered far more than man ever did or ever will, and is therefore the great source of sympathy and consolation. (*IE*, November 1918, p. 7.)

—*Orson F. Whitney*

Men have to suffer that they may come upon Mount Zion and be exalted above the heavens. (*HC*, 5:556.)

—*Joseph Smith*

Take it individually or take it collectively, we have suffered and we shall have to suffer again; and why? Because the Lord requires it at our hands for our sanctification. (*JD*, 5:323.)

—*Lorenzo Snow*

While most of our suffering is self-inflicted, some is caused by or permitted by God. This sobering reality calls for deep submissiveness, especially when God does not remove the cup from us. In such circumstances, when reminded about the premortal shouting for joy as this life's plan was unfolded (see Job 38:7), we can perhaps be pardoned if, in some moments, we wonder what all the shouting was about. (*Ensign*, May 1985, p. 72.)

—*Neal A. Maxwell*

See also ADVERSITY

——— Talents ———

Every man and woman who has talent and hides it will be called a slothful servant. Improve day by day upon the capital you have. In proportion as we are capacitated to receive, so it is our duty to do. (*JD*, 7:7.)

— *Brigham Young*

Once an English writer with a great respect for titles wrote a letter to Brigham Young. He addressed it this way: "To His Excellency, Brigham Young, Governor of the Territory of Utah, President of the Church of Jesus Christ of Latter-day Saints. Indian Agent of the Territory."
When they met, President Young told the man he'd omitted one of his titles.
"Do you mean the generalship, Governor?" the writer asked.
"No, no. I mean, Brigham Young, master cabinetmaker, painter, and glazier," said the Church President. (As told by Steve Hale, *Ensign*, May 1971, p. 47.)

— *Neal A. Maxwell*

The gross size of our talent inventories is less important than the net use of our talents. (*Ensign*, July 1975, p. 7.)

— *Neal A. Maxwell*

Your entire life is a mission and each new phase of it can be richly rewarding as you magnify your talents and take advantage of your opportunities. (*Ensign*, May 1988, p. 51.)

— *Ezra Taft Benson*

I respect the man occupying the humblest position, if he is faithful in the sphere in which he acts, and is truly an honest man; I deem him just as honorable as any person who may act in a higher position. The Lord does not require so much of the man who possesses but one talent, as of him who possesses more than one; but, according to that which he hath, so shall it be required of him. (*Deseret News*, January 31, 1877.)

— *Lorenzo Snow*

One of the great tragedies of life, it seems to me, is when a person classifies himself as someone who has no talents or gifts. When, in disgust or discouragement, we allow ourselves to reach depressive levels of despair because of our demeaning self-appraisal, it is a sad day for us and a sad day in the eyes of God. For us to conclude that we have no gifts when we judge ourselves by stature, intelligence, grade-point average, wealth, power, position, or external appearance is not only unfair but unreasonable. . . .

God has given each of us one or more special talents. . . . It is up to each of us to search for and build upon the gifts which God has given. We must remember that each of us is made in the image of God, that there are no unimportant persons. (*Ensign*, November 1987, p. 20.)

— *Marvin J. Ashton*

See also GIFTS OF THE SPIRIT

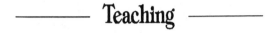

——— Teaching ———

I have learned that I can receive and treasure up but little knowledge at a time, and I have learned that this is the case with others. If the people had the whole catalogue of the law to govern them spiritually and temporally repeated to them today, they would need it repeated to them again next week. It is necessary to constantly teach the people. (*JD*, 10:314.)

— *Brigham Young*

In the home, the school, or the house of God, there is one teacher whose life overshadows all others. He taught of life and death, of duty and destiny. He lived not to be served, but to serve; not to receive, but to give; not to save his life, but to sacrifice it for others. He described a love more beautiful than lust, a poverty richer than treasure. It was said of this teacher that he taught with authority and not as do the scribes. In today's world, when many men are greedy for gold and for glory, and dominated by a teaching philosophy of "publish or perish," let us remember that this teacher never wrote—once only he wrote on the sand, and the wind destroyed forever his handwriting. His laws were not inscribed upon stone, but upon human hearts. I speak of the master teacher, even Jesus Christ, the Son of God, the Savior and Redeemer of all mankind. (*Ensign*, May 1973, p. 29.)

— *Thomas S. Monson*

My plea to the teachers of the Church is to study, ponder, and pray for guidance in your preparation. Use the scriptures and the approved curriculum materials, teaching with the objective to bless and inspire the lives of those assigned to you. (*Ensign*, May 1983, p. 70.)

— *M. Russell Ballard*

No greater responsibility can rest upon any man, than to be a teacher of God's children. (*CR*, October 1916, p. 57.)

— *David O. McKay*

No man, no matter what his office may be, . . . has the right to teach the people unless he does it my the light of the Holy Ghost, by the power of God. He should not attempt to teach the people that which he may have framed in his own heart to say to them. On the contrary, he should treasure up, as God has said, continually the words of life, and it shall be given unto him what to say, even that which shall be suited to the circumstances of the people and of each individual. (*JD*, 23:366.)

— George Q. Cannon

Please take a particular interest in strengthening and improving the quality of teaching in the Church. . . . I fear at times that all too often many of our members come to church, sit through a class or meeting, and then return home having been largely uninformed. . . . We all need to be touched and nurtured by the Spirit, and effective teaching is one of the most important ways this can happen. (*Ensign*, May 1981, p. 45.)

— Spencer W. Kimball

Study the life of the Master. You do not have to have a college degree to be an efficient teacher. But you do have to become acquainted with the life and teachings of the Master to be an effective teacher in the Church. (*CR*, April 1959, p. 85.)

— A. Theodore Tuttle

The gospel is one of harmony, unity, and agreement. It must be presented in love, and with glad tidings, by those who are calm. (*Ensign*, November 1987, p. 22.)

— Marvin J. Ashton

There is no greater responsibility in the world than the training of a human soul. (Quoted by Vaughn J. Featherstone, *Ensign*, November 1976, p. 103.)

— David O. McKay

We are individually responsible and will be held accountable for . . . the breaking of covenants by others for whom we are responsible insofar as such breaking is the result of our failure to teach them. (*Ensign*, November 1975, p. 73.)

— Marion G. Romney

We have no interest in teaching by the wisdom or learning or according to the precepts of men. We want to teach the gospel the way the Lord would have us teach it, and to do it under the power and influence of the Holy Ghost. If we will do that, we will teach sound doctrine. It will be the truth. It will build faith and increase righteousness in the hearts of men, and they will be led along that path which leads to the celestial world.

But if we teach without the Spirit of the Lord, if we are not guided by the Holy Ghost, we will be teaching at our peril. It is a serious thing to teach false doctrine, to teach that which is not true, to teach that which does not build faith in the hearts of men. (*CR*, October 1946.)

— *Bruce R. McConkie*

What should be the source for teaching the great plan of the Eternal God? The scriptures, of course—particularly the Book of Mormon. This should also include the other modern-day revelations. These should be coupled with the words of the Apostles and prophets and the promptings of the Spirit. (*Ensign*, May 1987, p. 85.)

— *Ezra Taft Benson*

You're to teach the doctrines, not so plainly that they can just understand, but you must teach the doctrines of the Church so plainly that no one can misunderstand. (*Charge to Religious Educators*, Salt Lake City: The Church of Jesus Christ of Latter-day Saints, 1981-82, p. 64.)

— *Harold B. Lee*

See also EDUCATION, EXAMPLE, LEADERSHIP

———— Temple Endowment ————

If we go into the temple we raise our hands and covenant that we will serve the Lord and observe his commandments and keep ourselves unspotted from the world. If we realize what we are doing then the endowment will be a protection to us all our lives—a protection which a man who does not go to the temple does not have. I have heard my father say that in the hour of trial, in the hours of temptation, he would think of the promises, the covenants that he made in the House of the Lord, and they were a protection to him . . . This protection is what these ceremonies are for, in part. They save us now and exalt us hereafter, if we will honor them. I know that this protection is given, for I, too, have realized it, as have thousands of others who have remembered their obligations. (*Utah Genealogical and Historical Magazine*, 21:104.)

— *Joseph Fielding Smith*

The endowment which was given by revelation can best be understood by revelation; and to those who seek most vigorously, with pure hearts, will the revelation be the greatest. (*Utah Genealogical and Historical Magazine*, April 1921, p. 63.)

— *John A. Widtsoe*

It is a wonderful thing to come into the Church but you cannot receive an exaltation until you have made the covenants in the House of the Lord and received the keys and authorities that are there bestowed and which cannot be given in any other place on the earth today. . . .

Abraham wrote of these things and sealed them up that they cannot be read. They cannot be revealed unto the world, but they are to be had in the holy temple of God. (*Doctrines of Salvation*, Bruce R. McConkie, comp., Salt Lake City: Bookcraft, 1956, 3:225.)

— *Joseph Fielding Smith*

The endowment in the temple is a necessary and sacred blessing as essential for the members of the Church as baptism. (*Ensign*, May 1982, p. 71.)

— *W. Grant Bangerter*

The endowment you are so anxious about, you cannot comprehend now, . . . but strive to be prepared in your hearts, be faithful in all things, that when we meet in the solemn assembly, . . . we must be clean every whit . . . . You need an endowment, brethren, in order that you may be prepared and able to overcome all things, and those that reject your testimony will be damned. (*HC*, 2:309.)

— *Joseph Smith*

The environment in the temple is intended to provide the worthy member of the Church with the power of enlightenment, of testimony, and of understanding. The temple endowment gives knowledge that, when acted upon, provides strength and conviction of truth. (*Ensign*, November 1990, p. 61.)

— *David B. Haight*

The temple endowment . . . is the step-by-step ascent into the eternal Presence. If [we] could but glimpse it, it would be the most powerful spiritual motivation of [our] lives.. (Quoted by Truman G. Madsen, Ten-Stake Fireside Address, Brigham Young University, March 5, 1972.)

— *David O. McKay*

We live in a world of symbols. No man or woman can come out of the temple endowed as he should be, unless he has seen, beyond the symbol, the mighty realities for which the symbols stand. (*Utah Genealogical and Historical Magazine*, 12:62.)

— *John A. Widtsoe*

Your endowment is, to receive all those ordinances in the House of the Lord, which are necessary for you, after you have departed this life, to enable you to walk back to the presence of the Father, passing the angels who stand as sentinels, being enabled to give them the key words, the signs and tokens, pertaining to the holy priesthood, and gain your eternal exaltation in spite of earth and hell. (*DBY*, p. 416.)

— *Brigham Young*

When you enter a holy temple, you are by that course gaining fellowship with the saints in God's eternal kingdom, where time is no more. In the temples of your God you are endowed not with a rich legacy of worldly treasure, but with a wealth of eternal riches that are above price.

The temple ceremonies are designed by a wise heavenly father who has revealed them to us in these last days as a guide and a protection throughout our lives, that you and I might not fail to merit exaltation in the celestial kingdom where God and Christ dwell. (*IE*, June 1967, p. 144.)

— *Harold B. Lee*

See also COVENANTS, TEMPLES

——— Temple Marriage ———

I believe that no worthy young Latter-day Saint man or woman should spare any reasonable effort to come to a house of the Lord to begin life together. The marriage vows taken in these hallowed places and the sacred covenants entered into for time and all eternity are proof against many of the temptations of life that tend to break homes and destroy happiness. (*IE*, 39:198.)

— *Heber J. Grant*

I picture you coming to the temple to be sealed for time and for all eternity, and I yearn to talk to you about the sacred sealing ordinance, but this we do not do outside those sacred walls. The transcendent nature of all that is conferred upon us at the marriage alter is so marvelous it is worth all the waiting and all the resisting . . .

But this is not the fulfillment of the story of love. In the book or play, on the stage, the curtain comes down here. But it is not so in real love. This is not the conclusion—only the beginning. (*Eternal Love*, Provo: Brigham Young University Press, 1963, pp. 15-16.)

— *Boyd K. Packer*

If someone wants to marry you outside the temple, whom will you strive to please—God or a mortal? If you insist on a temple marriage, you will be pleasing the Lord and blessing the other party. Why? Because that person will either become worthy to go to the temple—which would be a blessing—or will leave—which could also be a blessing—because neither of you should want to be unequally yoked (see 2 Corinthians 6:14). (*Ensign*, May 1988, p. 5.)

— Ezra Taft Benson

No one can enter into a temple marriage until he or she has been to the temple previously to receive his or her own blessings. Two who desire an eternal marriage cannot establish that relationship until each has personally made sacred covenants with the Lord. These covenants center in principles that are basic in a truly Christian life and in the foundation of a good marriage and family. (*Ensign*, November 1984, p. 37.)

— Marion D. Hanks

The blessings and promises that come from beginning life together, for time and eternity, in a temple of the Lord cannot be obtained in any other way, and worthy young Latter-day Saint men and women who so begin life together find that their eternal partnership under the everlasting covenant becomes the foundation upon which are built peace, happiness, virtue, love, and all of the other eternal verities of life, here and hereafter. (*IE*, 39:199.)

— Heber J. Grant

The most important single thing that any Latter-day Saint ever does in this world is to marry the *right* person in the *right* place by the *right* authority. (Quoted by Ezra Taft Benson, *Ensign*, May 1988, p. 51.)

— Bruce R. McConkie

Understand that temple marriage is essential to your salvation and exaltation. (*Ensign*, May 1988, p. 51.)

— Ezra Taft Benson

When two Latter-day Saints are united together in marriage, promises are made to them concerning their offspring that reach from eternity to eternity. They are promised that they shall have the power and the right to govern and control and administer salvation and exaltation and glory to their offspring worlds without end. . . . What else could [they] wish? A man and a woman in the other life, having celestial bodies, free from sickness and disease, glorified and beautified beyond description, standing in the midst of their posterity, governing and controlling them, administering life, exaltation and glory, worlds without end. (*DFTP*, p. 318.)

— Lorenzo Snow

See also MARRIAGE, TEMPLE

———— Temple Work ————

A temple recommend is one of the highest accolades we may receive. To use it regularly permits us to participate in the choicest gifts within the keeping of the Church. Those who attend feel a special spirit there. Peace comes. I know that their service there assists a departed one to gain exaltation. And I know that they in turn qualify for blessings from the other side of the veil. And I know that blessings will follow you home from the temple. (*Ensign*, May 1982, p. 66.)

— *A. Theodore Tuttle*

As surely as Christ offered Himself a vicarious service in behalf of *all* mankind, so we can engage in vicarious service in behalf of *some* of mankind, thus affording them the opportunity to move forward on the road of immortality and eternal life. Great is this work of love which goes on in these holy houses. Legion are the men and women who, with total unselfishness, labor day and night in this work which speaks of divinity. (*Ensign*, May 1989, p. 66.)

— *Gordon B. Hinckley*

Concerning the work of the dead, the Prophet Joseph Smith said that in the resurrection those who had been worked for would fall at the feet of those who had done their work, kiss their feet, embrace their knees and manifest the most exquisite gratitude. (Quoted by Vaughn J. Featherstone, *Ensign*, November 1987, p. 28.

— *Wilford Woodruff*

Dr. Krister Stendahl, bishop of the Lutheran Church in Stockholm, expressed this profound sentiment about our temple in Sweden:"Isn't it wonderful!" he said. "Only the Mormons are extending the blessings of the atonement of Jesus Christ to those beyond the grave." He is right. The blessings of the Atonement do extend beyond the grave. Jesus suffered and died to preserve and unify our Father's family. (*Ensign*, May 1989, p. 60.)

— *J. Richard Clarke*

I believe that the busy person on the farm, in the shop, in the office, or in the household, who has his worries and troubles, can solve his problems better and more quickly in the house of the Lord than anywhere else. If he will . . . [do] the temple work for himself and for his dead, he will confer a mighty blessing upon those who have gone before, and . . . a blessing will come to him; for, at the most unexpected moments, in or out of the temple will come to him, as a revelation, the solution of the problems that vex his life. That is the gift that comes to those who enter the temple properly. (*The Utah Genealogical and Historical Magazine*, April 1921, pp. 63-64.)

— *John A. Widtsoe*

I was impressed by the testimony of a single adult in Washington, D.C., who, as a recent convert, found herself suddenly immersed in the pursuit of her family history. After her first sacred experience of participating in the temple ordinance work for several of her kindred family, she expressed her feelings with tears of joy. "Now," she exclaimed, "I am no longer the only member of the Church in my family!" (*Ensign*, May 1989, p. 61.)

— *J. Richard Clarke*

It is no more incredible that God should *save* the dead, than that he should *raise* the dead. (*HC*, 4:425.)

— *Joseph Smith*

It takes just as much to save a dead man as a living man. (*The Discourses of Wilford Woodruff*, selected by G. Homer Durham, Salt Lake City: Bookcraft, 1946, p. 160.)

— *Wilford Woodruff*

May we always remember that we perform the temple ordinances for people and not for names. Those we call "the dead" are alive in the spirit and are present in the temple. (*Ensign*, May 1982, p. 72.)

— *W. Grant Bangerter*

Temple and genealogy work are visible testimonies of our belief in the resurrection and atonement of the Lord Jesus Christ. (*Ensign*, May 1987, p. 25.)

— *Boyd K. Packer*

When we go back into the other life and find our dead friends living there, if we have not performed the labor that is necessary for their exaltation and glory we shall not feel very happy and it will not be a very pleasant meeting. (*Deseret Weekly*, 50:738.)

— *Lorenzo Snow*

The duty of temple work has been laid upon this people. But it is more than a duty. It is a blessing. I am satisfied that if our people would attend the temple more, there would be less selfishness in their lives. There would be less absence of love in their relationships. There would be more fidelity on the part of husbands and wives. There would be more love and peace and happiness in the homes of our people. There would come into the minds of the Latter-day Saints an increased awareness of their relationship to god our Eternal Father and of the need to work a little harder at the matter of living as sons and daughters of God. (*Ensign*, May 1984, p. 99.)

— *Gordon B. Hinckley*

The great and important work of teaching the gospel of Christ to the people of the world is incomplete, at best, if it does not also provide for that teaching to those in another sphere and making available to them those gospel ordinances required of all if they are to move forward on the way of eternal life.

These temples are there to be used, and those who use them will reap a blessing of harmony in their lives. They will draw nearer unto the Lord, and He will draw nearer unto them. (*Ensign*, November 1985, p. 60.)

— *Gordon B. Hinckley*

The Saints have not too much time to save and redeem their dead, and gather together their living relatives, that they may be saved also, before the earth will be smitten, and the consumption decreed falls upon the world.

I would advise all the saints to go with their might and gather together all their living relatives . . . that they may be sealed and saved. (*TPJS*, p. 330.)

— *Joseph Smith*

Whoever seeks to help those on the other side receives help in return in all the affairs of life. (Quoted by Joanne B. Doxey, *Ensign*, November 1987, p. 92.)

— *John A. Widtsoe*

Why did [the Lord] call [Joseph Smith] unto the spirit world? Because he held the keys of this dispensation, . . . He held the keys of past generations—of the millions of people who dwelt on the earth in the fifty generations that had passed and gone who had not the law of the gospel, who never saw a prophet, never saw an apostle, never heard the voice of any man who was inspired of God and had the power to teach them the gospel of Christ, and to organize the church of Christ on earth. He went to unlock the prison doors of these people, as far as they would receive his testimony, and the saints of God who dwell in the flesh will build temples and perform certain ordinances for the redemption of the dead. This was the work of Joseph the Prophet in the spirit world. (*CR*, April 1880, p. 8.)

— *Wilford Woodruff*

See also GENEALOGY, PLAN OF SALVATION, TEMPLES

——— Temples ———

A temple is a retreat from the vicissitudes of life, a place of prayer and meditation of life, a place of prayer and meditation providing an opportunity to receive inner peace, inspiration, guidance, and, frequently, solutions to the problems that vex our daily lives.

A temple is a place where . . . the infinite in man, can seek the infinite in God. (*Ensign*, November 1986, p. 71.)

— *Franklin D. Richards*

A temple is more than chapel or church, more than a synagogue or cathedral; it is a structure erected as the house of the Lord, sacred to the closest communion between the Lord himself and the holy priesthood, and devoted to the highest and most sacred ordinances characteristic of the age or dispensation to which the particular temple belongs. . . .

The latin *templum* was the equivalent of the hebrew *beth elohim* and signified the abode of deity; hence, as associated with divine worship, it meant literally the House of the Lord. (*The House of the Lord*, James E. Talmage, Salt Lake City: Deseret Book Co., 1976. pp. 14, 1.)

— *James E. Talmage*

How far is heaven? It is not very far: in the temples of God, it is right where you are. (*Ensign*, November 1986, p. 99.)

— *Thomas S. Monson*

A watchman employed on Temple Square gave me this note:

"One morning not so long ago I was sitting at the desk of the temple gate house reading when my attention was drawn to a knock on the door. There stood two little boys, aged about seven or eight years. As I opened the door, I noticed that they were poorly dressed and had been neither washed nor combed. They appeared as if they had left home before father or mother had awakened that morning. As I looked beyond these little fellows, I saw two infants in pushcarts. In answer to my question as to what they wanted, one of the boys pointed to his little brother in the cart and replied: 'His name is Joe. Will you shake hands with little Joe? It is little Joe's birthday—he is two years old today, and I want him to touch the temple so when he gets to be an old man he will remember he touched the temple when he was two years old.'

"Pointing to the other little boy in the other cart, he said this: 'This is Mark, he's two years old, too.' Then, with a solemn, reverent attitude rare in children so young, he asked, 'Now can we go over and touch the temple?' I replied: 'Sure you can.' They pushed their little carts over to the temple and lifted the infants up, and placed their hands against that holy building. Then as I stood there with a lump in my throat, I heard the little boy say to his infant brother, 'Now, Joe, you will always remember when you was two years old you touched the temple.' They thanked me and departed for home." (*Ensign*, February 1971, p. 35.)

— *Harold B. Lee*

I am grateful to the Lord for temples. It is in temples where we obtain God's greatest blessings. . . . As we serve [therein], the veil may become very thin between this world and the other. It is not too important which side we are working on as long as we serve with all our hearts and strength.

We will not fail in this work. The Lord will not permit us to fail. (*Ensign*, November 1987, pp. 104, 105.)

— *Ezra Taft Benson*

It is at the Temple that all things are bound together. The ancient word for the Temple was "The Binding Point of Heaven and Earth." (How Firm a Foundation: What Makes It So," Lecture, Brigham Young University, September 20, 1979.)

— *Hugh Nibley*

Our temples are testaments of our faith in the everlasting family. (*Ensign*, May 1987, p. 81.)

— *James E. Faust*

Prayers are answered, revelation occurs, and instruction by the Spirit takes place in the holy temples of the Lord. (*Ensign*, May 1988, p. 85.)

— *Ezra Taft Benson*

The main object was to build unto the Lord a house whereby he could reveal unto his people the ordinances of his house and the glories of his kingdom, and teach the people the way of salvation; for there are certain ordinances and principles that, when they are taught and practiced, must be done in a place or house built for that purpose. (*HC*, 4:24.)

— *Joseph Smith*

The preparation to enter the temple lies in the gospel. Nothing is said or done in the temple which does not have its foundation in the scriptures. (*Ensign*, May 1982, p. 72.)

— *W. Grant Bangerter*

When we go to the temple because we want to go and not because it is an obligation; when we go with an attitude of worship and a reverence for God and for His son Jesus Christ, and with gratitude for the Savior's sacrifice, when we spend sufficient time to leave the cares of the world outside, wonderful things happen which cannot be described. The Spirit of the Lord distills upon one's soul in these holy houses, truly the most sacred places on earth. A new perception comes into focus of who we are, of what this life is really about, of the opportunities of eternal life, and of our relationship with the Savior. (*Ensign,* November 1989, p. 77.)

— *Victor L. Brown*

The temple is the house of the Lord. Our attendance there blesses the dead and also blesses us, for it is a house of revelation. (*Ensign,* May 1986, p. 78.)

— *Ezra Taft Benson*

The temple is the only "university" for men to prepare spiritually for their graduation to eternal life. (*Ensign,* May 1989, p. 71.)

— *F. Enzio Busche*

See also COVENANTS, ORDINANCES, TEMPLE ENDOWMENT, TEMPLE MARRIAGE, TEMPLE WORK

—————— Temporal Law ——————

It is written that "It is not given that one man should possess that which is above another." Of course, there is some allowance to be made for this expression. A man who has ability superior to another man, and who is able to manage and control larger affairs than another, may possess far more than another who is not able to control and manage as much as he. But if they each had what they were capable of managing and of using wisely and prudently, they would each have alike. It is like the quart and the pint measures. You cannot put a quart into a pint measure; but you can put a pint into a quart measure, and then you can duplicate it. If the pint measure is full, that is all it has capacity to hold; if the quart measure is full, it can hold no more; and they are equal, so far as their capacity is concerned. . . . I expect to see every man a steward over his inheritance, and I expect to see every man manage his inheritance according to the light and wisdom that he possesses and in accordance with his capacity for managing. If his capacity is greater than another's he will have more than another, because he cannot be curtailed in his liberties or rights to do good and to magnify, to enlarge, to increase, to be greater and better, because there is another that cannot be as great or as good as he. What is meant then by this passage which says that it is not given that one man should possess that which is above another? I take it that in part at least it means this: It is not right for one man because of superior advantages that he may possess in a social or financial way, or in any other way, to take advantage of another and to deprive him of that which naturally and rightfully belongs to him. I understand too that it is not right for men to combine together in order to oppress their fellow beings and to take advantage of them. The Spirit of the Lord forbids this, and commands that it shall not be in the midst of the Latter-day Saints. Furthermore, the Lord requires that when men have abundance they shall be as humble, as economical and as prudent in the management of their abundance as the man who possesses much less is expected to be prudent and economical in the management of that which is given to him. (*CR,* October 1898, pp. 23-24.)

— *Joseph F. Smith*

When wealth multiplies, the people get lifted up in the pride of their hearts, and they look down on their poor brethren and despise them, because they are better educated, have better manners, and speak better language—in a word, because they have advantages which their poor brethren and sisters have not. There is sin in this, and God is angry with a people who take this course. He wants us to be equal in earthly things, as we are in heavenly. He wants no poor among his people; he does not want the cry of the oppressed to ascend from the midst of the Latter-day Saints, and God forbid that it ever should! God forbid that the cry of any should ever ascend from the midst of the Latter-day Saints because of oppression or because of the lack of any blessing necessary for comfort! God wants us to feed the hungry, clothe the naked, and impart our substance for their support. God wants us to build each other up in righteousness. He wants us to love one another and to seek one another's benefit. This is the spirit of the gospel of Jesus Christ. He has revealed it unto us, and we must cultivate it. (*JD*, 15:156.)

— *George Q. Cannon*

You must continue to bear in mind that the temporal and the spiritual are blended. They are not separate. One cannot be carried on without the other, so long as we are here in mortality.

The Latter-day Saints believe not only in the gospel of spiritual salvation, but also in the gospel of temporal salvation. . . . We do not feel that it is possible for men to be really good and faithful Christian people unless they can also be good, faithful, honest and industrious people. Therefore, we preach the gospel of industry, the gospel of economy, the gospel of sobriety. (*GD*, pp. 208-9.)

— *Joseph F. Smith*

See also CHARITY, CONSECRATION, SERVICE, STEWARDSHIP, TEMPORAL WELFARE, UNITY, WEALTH, ZION

──────── # Temporal Welfare ────────

Every individual should be in a position to add something to the wealth of the whole. Everyone should be increasing, improving, and advancing in some way, and accomplishing something for his or her good and for the good of the whole. (*CR*, October 1898. p. 23.)

— *Joseph F. Smith*

It has always been a cardinal teaching with the Latter-day Saints that a religion that has not the power to save people temporally and make them prosperous and happy here cannot be depended upon to save them spiritually and to exalt them in the life to come.

— *Joseph F. Smith*

It has always been the disposition of the true disciples of Christ, as they reached higher degrees of spirituality, to look after the needy. (*Ensign*, May 1978, p. 83.)

— *J. Richard Clarke*

It is our duty to seek the welfare of all God's children. We must warn them, teach them, lift them; we must build their faith, cause them to repent and forsake sin, help them overcome evil habits and filth, and move them up to a higher level of living. Through the cleansing of body and soul, our brothers and sisters may be privileged to bask in the companionship of the Holy Spirit and draw claim upon all of the blessing of the atonement. (Mission Presidents' Seminar, June 22, 1979.)

— *Carlos E. Asay*

It is the aim of the Church to help the Saints to care for themselves and, where need be, to make food and clothing and other necessities available, lest the Saints turn to the doles and evils of Babylon. (*Ensign*, May 1979, p. 93.)

— *Bruce R. McConkie*

Relief is only temporary, but welfare is eternal. (*Ensign*, November 1981, p. 85.)

— *Barbara B. Smith*

Spiritual Objectives of Welfare Services
The real long-term objective of the welfare plan is the building of character in the members of the Church, givers and receivers, rescuing all that is finest down deep in the inside of them, and bringing to flower and fruitage the latent richness

of the spirit, which after all is the mission and purpose and reason for being of this Church. (Meeting of stake presidencies, October 2, 1936.)

— *J. Reuben Clark, Jr.*

The following seven Welfare [Services] principles are essential to our happiness and spiritual development:
1. The welfare plan is an integral part of the plan of salvation.
2. The scriptures provide the spiritual framework for the welfare plan.
3. The welfare plan builds faith in the Lord Jesus Christ.
4. By living welfare principles, we can develop self-reliance.
5. The welfare plan builds love and compassion for our fellowmen.
6. The welfare plan sanctifies both the giver and the receiver.
7. The welfare plan builds a Zion People. (*Ensign*, May 1986, p. 28.)

— *Robert D. Hales*

We have a keen responsibility to care for the poor and the needy. Welfare is not restricted to a farm. Welfare is only encompassed or restricted by our vision and by our understanding and by our inspiration. (*Ensign*, May 1984, p. 101.)

— *Thomas S. Monson*

Welfare Services
Our primary purpose was to set up, in so far as it might be possible, a system under which the curse of idleness would be done away with, the evils of a dole abolished, and independence, industry, thrift and self-respect be once more established amongst our people. The aim of the Church is to help the people to help themselves. (*CR*, October 1936, p. 3.)

— *Heber J. Grant*

Welfare Services is nothing more nor less than the gospel in action. (*Ensign*, May 1979, p. 100.)

— *Spencer W. Kimball*

See also CHARITY, POOR, PREPAREDNESS, SELF-SUFFICIENCY, SERVICE, TEMPORAL LAW, UNITY, ZION

——— Temptation ———

A total commitment to anxiously serve the Lord and others is the surest way to overcome temptations of the adversary. (*Ensign*, May 1979, p. 61.)

— *James M. Paramore*

Enduring temptation is one of the greatest challenges. Jesus endured temptation but yielded not. (See Mosiah 15:5.) Christ withstood because He gave "no heed" to temptations. (D&C 20:22.) You and I tend to dally over and dabble in temptations, entertaining them for a while, even if we later evict them. However, to give temptations any heed can set the stage for later succumbing. (*Ensign*, May 1990, p. 34.)

— *Neal A. Maxwell*

I have seen men tempted so sorely that finally they would say, "I'll be damned if I'll stand it any longer." Well, you will be damned if you do not. So you had better bear it and go to the Lord and say: "O God, I am sorely tempted; Satan is trying to destroy me, and things seem to be combined against me. O Lord, help me! Deliver me from the power and grasp of the devil. Let they Spirit descend upon me that I may be enabled to surmount this temptation and to ride above the vanities of this world." This would be far better than giving way to sin, and proving yourself unworthy of the association of the good and pure. (*JD*, 22:318.)

— *John Taylor*

If we don't want temptation to follow us, we shouldn't act as if we are interested. No one ever fell over a precipice who never went near one. (*CR*, April 1970, p. 16.)

— *Richard L. Evans*

If we entertain temptations, soon they begin entertaining us! (*Ensign*, May 1987, p. 71.)

— *Neal A. Maxwell*

It is important that we make up our minds early in life as to what we will do and what we will not do. Long before the moment of temptation comes we should have determined that we will resist . . . anything that will keep us from enjoying the companionship of the Spirit of the Lord. (*Ensign*, May 1979, p. 45.)

— *N. Eldon Tanner*

Men are mortal and beset by human frailties. They are enticed by the pressures of immediate . . . desire to depart from the high standards of the perfect law. When they are under the influence of an exalted occasion, they make high resolves. They firmly determine to avoid past mistakes and to do better. But gone out from under the spell of that influence and absorbed in the complicated pursuits of life, they find difficulty in holding fast to their noble purposes. . . . So it is essential that they come again, and frequently, under the influence which kindles anew the warmth of spirit in which good resolutions are begotten, that they may go out fortified to withstand the pressures of temptation which lure them into false ways. Happily, if they refresh themselves frequently enough under ennobling influences, the spirit of repentance will be at work with them, and they will make conquest of some temptations—rise above them—and advance thus far toward their final goal. (*CR*, October 1949, p. 139.)

— *Albert E. Bowen*

One of Satan's clever tactics is to tempt us to concentrate on the present and ignore the future. . . . He tempts us with the transitory pleasures of the world so that we will not focus our minds and efforts on the things that bring eternal joy. The devil is a dirty fighter, and we must be aware of his tactics. (*Ensign*, November 1990, p. 36.)

— *M. Russell Ballard*

Real disciples absorb the fiery darts of the adversary by holding aloft the quenching shield of faith with one hand, while holding to the iron rod with the other. There should be no mistaking; it will take both hands! (*Ensign*, May 1987, p. 70.)

— *Neal A. Maxwell*

So soon as we discover ourselves in a fault, we should repent of that wrongdoing and as far as possible repair or make good the wrong we may have committed. By taking this course we strengthen our character, we advance our own cause, and we fortify ourselves against temptation. (*JD*, 23:192.)

— *Lorenzo Snow*

When temptation comes your way, name that boastful, deceitful giant "Goliath" and do with him as David did to the Philistine of Gath! (*Ensign*, May 1983, p. 51.)

— *Gordon B. Hinckley*

[Jesus] suffered all manner of temptations, yet He "gave no heed unto them" (D&C 20:22). Unlike some of us, He did not fantasize, reconsider, or replay temptations. How is it that you and I do not see that while initially we are stronger and the temptations weaker, dalliance turns things upside down? (*Ensign*, May 1989, p. 64.)

— *Neal A. Maxwell*

See also ADVERSITY, OPPOSITION, SATAN, SIN

——— Testimony ———

A testimony comes when the Holy Ghost gives the earnest seeker a witness of the truth. A moving testimony vitalizes faith; that is, it induces repentance and obedience to the commandments. (*IE,* December 1963, p. 1066.)

— *Marion G. Romney*

A testimony is fragile. It is as hard to hold as a moonbeam. It is something you have to recapture every day of your life. (*Church News,* July 15, 1972, p. 4.)

— *Harold B. Lee*

A testimony is one of the few possessions we may take with us when we leave this life. (*Ensign,* May 1982, p. 62.)

— *Ezra Taft Benson*

Each member of the Church, to be prepared for the millennial reign, must receive a testimony, each for himself, of the divinity of the work established by Joseph Smith. (*CR,* October 1956, p. 62.)

— *Harold B. Lee*

I do not believe that a member of the Church can have an active, vibrant testimony of the gospel without keeping the commandments. A testimony is to have current inspiration to know the work is true, not something we receive only once. The Holy Ghost abides with those who honor, respect, and obey God's laws. And it is that Spirit which gives inspiration to the individual. (*Ensign,* May 1983, p. 54.)

— *Ezra Taft Benson*

I suggest that we plant in our hearts the seed of testimony, a firm unwavering conviction of the truth and divinity of the gospel that we can share freely with power and persuasion. Humble, fervent testimonies borne as prompted by the Spirit can have far-reaching effects.

— *Joseph B. Wirthlin*

It is not by marvelous manifestation unto us that we shall be established in the truth, but it is by humility and faithful obedience to the commandments and laws of God. When I as a boy first started out in the ministry, I would frequently go out and ask the Lord to show me some marvelous thing, in order that I might receive a testimony. But the Lord withheld marvels from me, and showed me the truth, line upon line, precept upon precept, here a little and there a little, until he made me to know the truth from the crown of my head to the soles of my feet, and until doubt and fear had been absolutely purged from me. He did not have to send an angel from the heavens to do this, nor did he have to speak with the trump of an archangel. By the whisperings of the still small voice of the Spirit of the living God, he gave to me the testimony I possess. (*CR*, April 1900, pp. 40-41.)

— *Joseph F. Smith*

Testifying is the purest form of human communication. The deepest meaning, the deepest conviction of one's soul is being given to another through the medium of the Holy Spirit. (*Ensign*, October 1977, p. 53.)

— *Stephen R. Covey*

Testimony, like the widow's cruse of oil, will not fail (see 1 Kgs. 17:14), neither be diminished as it is shared; rather, it will be enlarged at its base and renewed at its source. (*Ensign*, May 1985, p. 26.)

— *F. Arthur Kay*

To hold his testimony, one must bear it often and live worthy of it. (*CR*, October 1944, p. 45.)

— *Spencer W. Kimball*

We should be patient in developing and strengthening our testimonies. Rather than expecting immediate or spectacular manifestations, though they will come when needed, we should pray for a testimony, study the scriptures, follow the counsel of our prophet and other Church leaders, and live the principles of the gospel. Our testimonies then will grow and mature naturally, perhaps imperceptibly at times, until they become driving forces in our lives. (*Ensign*, May 1987, p. 32.)

— *Joseph B. Wirthlin*

What does it mean to bear testimony? A testimony is an open declaration or confession of one's faith. To bear is to give or bring forward. So as I bear testimony, I am giving a declaration of my faith. (*Ensign*, November 1988, p. 25.)

— *John K. Carmack*

Who can argue with a testimony? Unbelievers may contend about our doctrine. They may wrest the scriptures to their destruction. They may explain away this or that from a purely intellectual standpoint, but they cannot overpower a testimony. (*Ensign*, April 1979, p. 24.)

— *Bruce R. McConkie*

There is nothing a man can possess in this world which will bring more comfort, more hope and faith, than a testimony of the existence of a Heavenly Father who loves us, or of the reality of Jesus Christ, his Only Begotten Son, that those two heavenly personages appeared to the Prophet Joseph Smith and established the Church of Jesus Christ, and that men are officially authorized to represent Deity. (*Man May Know for Himself,* Clare Middlemiss, comp., Salt Lake City: Deseret Book Co., 1967, p. 12.)

— *David O. McKay*

See also CONVERSION, HOLY GHOST, SPIRITUAL STRENGTH

Thoughts

Each of us must learn self-control of his thoughts. We must learn to control our thoughts, or someone or something else will control them. Untrained, unemployed thoughts are soon enslaved. (Address, Brigham Young University, September 26, 1967, p. 3.)

— *Boyd K. Packer*

How could a person possibly become what he is *not* thinking? Nor is any thought, when persistently entertained, too small to have its effect. The "divinity that shapes our ends" is indeed ourselves. (*Miracle of Forgiveness,* Salt Lake City: Bookcraft, 1969, p. 105.)

— *Spencer W. Kimball*

If you first gain power to check your words you will then begin to have power to check your judgment, and at length actually gain power to check your thoughts and reflections. (*JD,* 6:98.)

— *Brigham Young*

No good thought is ever lost. No turn of the mind, however brief or transitory or elusive, if it is good, is ever wasted. No thought of sympathy, nor of forgiveness, no reflection on generosity or of courage or of purity, no meditation on humility or gratitude or reverence is ever lost. The frequency with which they are experienced is the measure of you. The more constant they become, the more you are worth, or in scriptural terms, the more you are worthy. Every clean thought *becomes* you. Every clean thought becomes *you.*

— *Boyd K. Packer*

The evil purpose, thought, or desire, is of itself essentially sin; and such a case, therefore, presents no phenomenon of abstract guilt, but actual and individual offense; for the thinker of evil is a sinner.

— *James E. Talmage*

It is throwing your life away to think of the wrong things.

— *Hugh Nibley*

The thought in your mind at this moment is contributing, however infinitesimally, almost imperceptibly to the shaping of your soul, even to the lineaments of your countenance . . . even passing and idle thoughts leave their impression. (Quoted by Ezra Taft Benson, *Ensign*, April 1984, p. 10.)

— *David O. McKay*

Thoughts lead to acts, acts lead to habits, habits lead to character—and our character will determine our eternal destiny. (*Ensign*, April 1984, p. 9.)

— *Ezra Taft Benson*

You will be held accountable for your thoughts, because when your life is completed in mortality, it will be the sum of your thoughts. That one suggestion has been a great blessing to me all my life, and it has enabled me upon many occasions to avoid thinking improperly, because I realize that I will be, when my life's labor is complete, the product of my thoughts. (*DFTP*, p. 416.)

— *George Albert Smith*

See also MIND, SELF-MASTERY

Thrift

If a man is worth millions of bushels of wheat . . . , he is not wealthy enough to . . . sweep a single kernel of it into the fire; let it be eaten by something and pass again into the earth, and thus fulfil the purpose for which it grew. Remember it, do not waste anything, but take care of everything. (*JD*, 1:253.)

— *Brigham Young*

If you cannot obtain all you wish for today, learn to do without. (*DBY*, p. 293.)

— *Brigham Young*

There is a wise old saying: "Eat it up, wear it out, make it do, or do without." Thrift is a practice of not wasting anything. Some people are able to get by because of the absence of expense. They have their shoes resoled, they patch, they mend, they sew, and they save money. They avoid installment buying and make purchases only after saving enough to pay cash, thus avoiding interest charges. *Frugality* means to practice careful economy. (*Ensign*, May 1986, p. 20.)

— James E. Faust

Live within your income. Be frugal and wise. Pay your obligations to the Lord, your country, and yourself, and then live on what is left. (*Ensign*, November 1986, p. 26.)

— George I. Cannon

Never let anything go to waste. Be prudent, save everything. (*JD*, 1:250.)

— Brigham Young

The practice of thrift is not outdated. We must discipline ourselves to live within our incomes even if it means going without or making do. The wise person can distinguish between basic needs and extravagant wants. Some find budgeting extremely painful, but I promise you, it is never fatal. (*Ensign*, November 1981, p. 90.)

— Marvin J. Ashton

See DEBT, FINANCIAL STRENGTH, MONEY

Time

I have told you many times: the property which we inherit from our Heavenly Father is our *time*, and the power to *choose* in the disposition of the same. This is the real capital that is bequeathed unto us by our Heavenly Father. (*Ensign*, May 1990, p. 90.)

— Brigham Young

Jesus taught us how important it is to use our time wisely. . . . Time cannot be recycled. When a moment has gone, it is really gone. Wise time management is really wise management of ourselves. (*Ensign*, August 1979, p. 6.)

— Spencer W. Kimball

Time is numbered only to man. God has your eternal perspective in mind. (*Ensign*, November 1988, p. 97.)

— Ezra Taft Benson

Leisure Time

Proper use of leisure requires discriminating judgment. Our leisure provides opportunity for renewal of spirit, mind, and body. It is a time for worship, for family, for service, for study, for wholesome recreation. It brings harmony into our life. (*Ensign*, May 1982, p. 78.)

— *J. Richard Clarke*

Money alone does not lift the burdens of our fellowmen, . . . The world is in need of time, and if we have but one hour to spare, we are wealthy. It takes time to listen and to comfort, it takes time to teach and to encourage, and it takes time to feed and to clothe. We all have the gift to lift each other's burdens and to make a difference in somebody's life. (*Ensign*, May 1990, p. 26.)

— *Hans B. Ringger*

Spare minutes are the gold-dust of time; the portions of life most fruitful in good or evil; the gaps through which temptations enter. (*IE*, June 1966, p. 511.)

— *John Longden*

Time is one of our most valuable possessions. Use it wisely. Remind yourselves often that things that matter most should not be left to the mercy of things that matter the least. (*Ensign*, May 1978, p. 57.)

— *O. Leslie Stone*

Use your spare time wisely. If we waste thirteen minutes each day, it is the equivalent of two weeks a year without pay. (*Ensign*, May 1982, p. 78.)

— *J. Richard Clarke*

See also PRIORITIES, TODAY

——— Tithing ———

If you desire the Spirit of God be honest in keeping the commandments of God. If you desire prosperity, and at the same time the testimony of the gospel, pay all your obligations to God and you shall have it. If you are not honest with God, you may prosper and you may be blessed with the things of this world, but they will crowd out from your heart the spirit of the gospel; and you will become covetous of your own means and lose the inspiration of Almighty God. (*CR*, October 1899, p. 20.)

— *Heber J. Grant*

If you don't pay tithing, you are stealing from the Lord (see Mal. 3:8), and that's contrary to the eighth commandment, and no one has ever prospered doing that. On the other hand, when we pay our tithes and offerings, the Lord gives it all back to us "good measure, pressed down, and shaken together, and running over." (Luke 6:38.) How is that for a promise? (*Ensign*, November 1990, p. 77.)

— *Hartman Rector, Jr.*

A part of a tithing is no tithing at all, no more than immersing only part of a person's body is baptism. (*TLS*, pp. 155-156.)

— *Lorenzo Snow*

Now, do not get me wrong. I am not here to say that if you pay an honest tithing you will realize your dream of a fine house, a Rolls Royce, and a condominium in Hawaii. *The Lord will open the windows of heaven according to our need, and not according to our greed.* (*Ensign*, May 1982, p. 40.)

— *Gordon B. Hinckley*

Paying tithing is discharging a debt to the Lord. . . .

If we obey this commandment, we are promised that we will "prosper in the land." This prosperity consists of more than material goods—it may include enjoying good health and vigor of mind. It includes family solidarity and spiritual increase. (*Ensign*, November 1979, p. 81.)

— *N. Eldon Tanner*

Personally, I have always considered tithing to be the law of inheritance in the land of Zion, for the Lord said when he gave the law that all those who gathered to Zion should observe it or they should not be worthy to abide among the inhabitants of that land (see D&C 119:5). (*Ensign*, May 1979, p. 41.)

— *Marion G. Romney*

Prosperity comes to those who observe the law of tithing; and when I say prosperity I am not thinking of it in terms of dollars and cents alone . . . ; but what I count as real prosperity, . . . the growth in a knowledge of God, a testimony, and the power to live the gospel and to inspire our families to do the same. That is prosperity of the truest kind. (*CR*, April 1925, p. 10.)

— *Heber J. Grant*

The time has now come for every Latter-day Saint, who calculates to be prepared for the future and to hold his feet strong upon a proper foundation, to do the will of the Lord and to pay his tithing in full. (*MS*, 61:533.)

— *Lorenzo Snow*

There has been laid upon the Church a tremendous responsibility. Tithing is the source of income for the Church to carry forward its mandated activities. The need is always greater than the availability. God help us to be faithful in observing this great principle which comes from him with his marvelous promise. (*Ensign,* May 1982, p. 41.)

— *Gordon B. Hinckley*

Pay your tithing monthly or weekly as you are paid. Never be in debt to the Lord. (*Ensign,* May 1981, p. 42.)

— *David B. Haight*

Those who pay tithing will have roots and branches at the last day, and those who do not will have neither roots nor branches. (See Mal. 3 & 4.) Now what are our roots? Alex Haley wrote a book about roots. Obviously our roots are our ancestors. And what are our branches? They are our children. Then those who walk in holiness before the Lord, which includes the payment of tithing, will have an eternal family at the last day. And those who do not pay tithing will have none. (*Ensign,* May 1983, p. 27.)

— *Hartman Rector, Jr.*

Tithing . . . is one of the bedrock foundation principles of exaltation. And as it turns out, when a man pays tithing, the Lord opens the windows of heaven and rebukes the devourer so that it doesn't cost him anything, but really puts him far more ahead than he ever could have been if he had not paid it. It is a principle of great promise and brings eternal joy and happiness. (*Ensign,* May 1983, p. 27.)

— *Hartman Rector, Jr.*

We *can* pay our tithing. This is not so much a matter of money as it is a matter of faith. I have yet to find a faithful tithe payer who cannot testify that in a very literal and wonderful way the windows of heaven have been opened and blessings have been poured out upon him or her. (*Ensign,* November 1985, p. 85.)

— *Gordon B. Hinckley*

[After quoting D&C 64:23-24:] What does that mean? Does it mean that if man will not pay his tithing, that the Lord is going to send a ball of fire down from heaven and burn him up? No. The Lord does not do [it] that way. The Lord works on natural principles. This is what it means, . . . : a man who ignores the express command of the Lord, by failing to pay his tithing, it means that the Spirit of the Lord will withdraw from him; it means that the power of the priesthood will withdraw from that man, if he continues in the spirit of neglect to do his duty. He will drift away into darkness, gradually but surely, until finally he will lift up his eyes among the wicked. That is where he will finally land; and then when the destruction comes and when the burning comes, he will be among the wicked, and will be destroyed; while those who observe the law will be found among the righteous, and they will be preserved. There is a God in heaven, and he has promised to shield and protect them. I tell you there is a day of burning, a day of destruction coming upon the wicked. And where will we be? Will we be with the wicked, or with the righteous? (*CR*, October 1913, p. 59.)

— *Rudger Clawson*

When you are in doubt as to just how you should calculate your tithes, reverse the terms as we sometimes do in solving complex mathematical problems, and suppose for the time being that the Lord had said this; let us postulate this is an assumed law given to the Church: "In order to show my love for my people, the faithful members of my Church, it is my will, saith the Lord, that each one shall receive from my storehouse, the storehouse of my Church, at regular intervals during the year, an amount equal to one-tenth of his income." Now my dear brother, sit down and calculate how much the Lord owes you under that kind of law, and then go pay it to your bishop. (*CR*, October 1928, p. 119.)

— *James E. Talmage*

See also CONSECRATION, FINANCIAL STRENGTH, OFFERINGS

Today

Each one of us must live with himself through the eternity and each one is now working on the kind of man he will have this eternal association with—I say that now is the time to act; it is neither too early nor too late. (*MS*, 126:51.)

— *Hugh B. Brown*

It is our privilege to say every day in our lives, "that is the best day I ever lived." Never let a day so pass that you will have cause to say, "I will live better tomorrow," and I will promise you, in the name of the Lord Jesus, that your lives will be as a well of water springing up to everlasting life. You will have his spirit to dwell in you continually, and your eyes will be open to see, your ears to hear, and your understanding to comprehend. (*JD*, 8:140.)

— *Brigham Young*

Let us this very day begin anew, and now say, with all our hearts, we will forsake our sins and be righteous. (*TPJS*, p. 364.)

— *Joseph Smith*

Life is for us, and it is for us to receive it today, and not wait for the millennium. Let us take a course to be saved today, and, when evening comes, review the acts of the day, repent of our sins, if we have any to repent of, and say our prayers; then we can lie down and sleep in peace until the morning, arise with gratitude to God, commence the labors of another day, and strive to live the whole day to God and nobody else.

— *Brigham Young*

My fatherly counsel is to remind you of the importance of today. This is the time in which the work of this life is to be done. Be a participant. See that things happen. Make commitments to yourself and the Lord. Live outside yourself with love. A Hindu proverb says, "Help thy brother's boat across, and lo, thine own has reached the shore." (*Ensign*, November 1986, p. 25.)

— *George I. Cannon*

The present is the outcome of the past; and it is the great hook upon which the future hangs. (*CR*, April 1916, p. 64.)

— *Orson F. Whitney*

There is only one day that you and I have to live and that's today. There is nothing we can do about yesterday except repent, and there may be no tomorrows. The thing for us to do when we arise from our beds as God gives us a new day, is to pray that whatever comes to our hands, we will do it to the best of our ability.

— *Harold B. Lee*

"Choose you this day whom ye will serve; . . . but as for me and my house, we will serve the Lord." (Josh. 24:15.) Not tomorrow, not when we get ready, not when it is convenient—but "this day," straightway, choose whom you will serve. (*Ensign*, May 1983, p. 30.)

— *Marvin J. Ashton*

See also LIFE, PROBATION, TIME

Tolerance

Shall we deny the existence of that which we do not understand? If we do, we would want to keep an iron bedstead to measure every person according to our own measurement and dimensions; and if persons were too long we would cut them off, and if too short draw them out. But we should discard this principle, and our motto should be, we will let every one believe as he pleases and follow out the convictions of his own mind. (*JD,* 14:131.)

— *Brigham Young*

Of course, there will be differences in the personal standards and social activities of faithful Latter-day Saints and members of other groups. But these differences are no excuse for ostracism, arrogance, or unkindness by LDS people. (*Ensign,* May 1988, p. 32.)

— *Dallin H. Oaks*

Some people say that we are illiberal because we do not admit that all other churches are what they profess to be, when their profession is based on facts. Now when we say that the Lord is not pleased with those churches, we do not mean that he is not pleased with the members thereof. We hold that God is no respecter of persons, but, on the contrary, that he will acknowledge good in any soul, no matter whether that person belongs to a church or not.

— *James E. Talmage*

The teachings of the Lord breathe a spirit of forbearance, tolerance, even love for those who differ from us in beliefs, standards, and actions. We recognize free agency as a law of God, and we respect tolerance as a part of gospel teachings. But this in no way involves emulation or acceptance of that which is counter to that which we profess as Latter-day Saints. (*A Woman's Reach,* Salt Lake City: Deseret Book Co., 1974, p. 127.)

— *Belle S. Spafford*

Tolerance may be a virtue, but it is not *the* commanding one. There is a difference between what one *is* and what one *does.* What one is may deserve unlimited tolerance; what one does, only a measured amount. (*Ensign,* November 1990, p. 85.)

— *Boyd K. Packer*

See also JUDGING

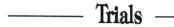

Trials

All intelligent beings who are crowned with crowns of glory, immortality, and eternal lives must pass through every ordeal appointed for intelligent beings to pass through, to gain their glory and exaltation. Every calamity that can come upon mortal beings will be suffered to come upon the few, to prepare them to enjoy the presence of the Lord. If we obtain the glory that Abraham obtained, we must do so by the same means that he did . . . we must pass through the same experience and gain the knowledge, intelligence, and endowments that will prepare us to enter into the celestial kingdom of our Father and God . . . . Every trial and experience you have passed through is necessary for your salvation. (*DBY*, 345.)

— *Brigham Young*

God hath said that He would have a tried people, that He would purge them as gold. (*TPJS*, p. 135.)

— *Joseph Smith*

I thank the Lord that I may have passed some of the tests, but maybe there will have to be more before I shall have been polished to do all that the Lord would have me do.

Sometimes when the veil has been very thin, I have thought that if the struggle had been still greater that maybe then there would have been no veil. (*CR*, October 1973, p. 170.)

— *Harold B. Lee*

It matters not that giants of tribulation torment you. Your prayerful access to help is just as real as when David battled his Goliath (see 1 Samuel 17). (*Ensign*, May 1988, p. 35.)

— *Russell M. Nelson*

At a recent stake conference the stake president called a young father, who had just been ordained an elder, from the audience to bear his testimony. The father had been active in the Church as a boy, but during his teenage years had veered somewhat from his childhood pattern. After returning from the military service he married a lively girl and presently children blessed their home. Without warning an undisclosed illness overcame their little four-year-old daughter. Within a very short time she was on the critical list in the hospital. In desperation and for the first time in many years the father went to his knees in prayer—asking that her life be spared. As her condition worsened and he sensed that she would not live, the tone of the father's prayers changed—he no longer asked that her life be spared—but rather for a blessing of understanding—"Let thy will be done," he said. Soon the child was in a coma, indicating her hours on earth were few. Now, fortified with understanding and trust, the young parents asked for one more favor of the Lord. Would he allow her to awaken once more that they might hold her closely. The little one's eyes opened, her frail arms outstretched to her mother and then to her daddy for a final embrace. When the father laid her on the pillow to sleep till another morning, he knew their prayers had been answered—a kind, understanding Father in heaven had filled their needs as he knew them to be. His will had been done—they had gained understanding—they were determined now to live that they might live again with her. (*Ensign*, January 1974, p. 18.)

— *H. Burke Peterson*

Every Latter-day Saint who gains a celestial glory will be tried to the uttermost. If there is a point in our character that is weak and tender, you may depend upon it that the Lord will reach after that and we will be tried at that spot, for the Lord will test us to the utmost before we can get through and receive that glory and exaltation which he has in store for us as a people.

— *George Q. Cannon*

God never bestows upon his people, or upon an individual, superior blessings without a severe trial to prove them—to prove that individual, or that people, to see whether they will keep their covenants with him, and keep in remembrance what he has shown them. Then the greater the vision, the greater the display of the power of the enemy. (*JD*, 3:205.)

— *Brigham Young*

I used to think, if I were the Lord, I would not suffer people to be tried as they are. But I have changed my mind on that subject. Now I think I would, if I were the Lord, because it purges out the meanness and corruption that stick around the saints, like flies around molasses. (*JD*, 5:115.)

— *John Taylor*

No pain that we suffer, no trial that we experience is wasted. It ministers to our education, to the development of such qualities as patience, faith, fortitude, and humility. All that we suffer and all that we endure, especially when we endure it patiently, builds up our characters, purifies our hearts, expands our souls, and makes us more tender and charitable, more worthy to be called the children of God . . . and it is through sorrow and suffering, toil and tribulation, that we gain the education that we come here to acquire and which will make us more like our Father and Mother in heaven. (Quoted by Howard W. Hunter, *Ensign*, November 1987. p. 60.)

— *Orson F. Whitney*

Our trials and sufferings give us experience, and establish within us principles of godliness.

— *Lorenzo Snow*

Sometimes the tests and trials of those who have received the gospel far exceed any imposed upon worldly people. Abraham was called upon to sacrifice his only son. Lehi and his family left their lands and wealth to live in a wilderness. Saints in all ages have been commanded to lay all that they have upon the altar, sometimes even their very lives. (*Ensign,* November 1976, p. 106.)

— *Bruce R. McConkie*

The Latter-day Saints have done wonders; but they cannot cease from doing wonders in the future. There will be greater things demanded of the latter-day Saints than have ever been demanded since the organization of the Church. The Lord has determined in His heart that He will try us until He knows what He can do with us. . . . He will try us, and continue to try us, in order that He may place us in the highest positions in life and put upon us the most sacred responsibilities. (*TPJS,* p. 93.)

— *Lorenzo Snow*

Let us remember—trials are an evidence of a Father's love. They are given as blessings to his children. They are given as opportunities for growth. (*CR,* October 1973, p. 12.)

— *H. Burke Peterson*

The people of the Most High God must be tried. It is written that they will be tried in all things, even as Abraham was tried. If we are called to go upon mount Moriah to sacrifice a few of our Isaacs, it is no matter; we may just as well do that as anything else. I think there is a prospect for the Saints to have all the trials they wish for, or can desire. (*DBY,* p. 345.)

— *Brigham Young*

The Saints will be put to tests that will try the integrity of the best of them. The pressure will become so great that the more righteous among them will cry unto the Lord day and night until deliverance comes. (Quoted by Ezra Taft Benson, *Ensign,* May 1978, p. 32.)

— *Heber C. Kimball*

We are not required to go through [Jesus'] trials, but we are required to be *willing* to go through them. To prove that we are willing to do so, we must go through our own trials and remain faithful. (*Ensign,* May 1989, p. 77.)

— *Royden G. Derrick*

We should understand that a life filled with problems is no respecter of age or station in life. Challenges come to the young and to the aged—to the rich and to the poor—to the struggling student or the genius scientist—to the farmer, carpenter, lawyer, or doctor. Trials come to the strong and to the weak—to the sick and to the healthy. Yes, even to the simplest child as well as to a prophet of God. (*Ensign*, January 1974, p. 18.)

— *H. Burke Peterson*

See also ADVERSITY, CHALLENGES, ENDURANCE, PROBATION, PROBLEMS, SUFFERING

———— Trust ————

It is better to trust and sometimes be disappointed than to be forever mistrusting and be right occasionally. (Address, Brigham Young University, October 26, 1976.)

— *Neal A. Maxwell*

Let us . . . live so as to create confidence in all men with whom we deal and come in contact; and treasure up each particle of confidence we obtain as one of the most precious possessions mortals can possibly possess. When by my good actions I have created confidence in my neighbor towards me, I pray that I may never do anything that will destroy it. (*JD*, 11:256.)

— *Brigham Young*

That person who never forsaketh his trust, should ever have the highest place of regard in our hearts. (*TPJS*, p. 31.)

— *Joseph Smith*

To be trusted is a greater compliment than to be loved. Love is the sweetest thing in the world, but to be trusted throws upon him who receives that trust an obligation that he must not fail to discharge. (*CR*, October 1934, p. 91.)

— *David O. McKay*

Trust is to human relationships what faith is to gospel living. It is the beginning place, the foundation upon which more can be built. Where trust is, love can flourish. (*Ensign*, November 1981, p. 83.)

— *Barbara B. Smith*

———— Trust in God ————

Do not fear the challenges of life, but approach them patiently, with faith in God. He will reward your faith with power not only to endure, but also to overcome hardships, disappointments, trials, and struggles of daily living. Through diligently striving to live the law of God and with faith in Him, we will not be diverted from our eternal course. (*Ensign*, November 1982, p. 26.)

— *Rex D. Pinegar*

How ill-qualified we were one year ago to pass through the scenes through which we have been led with success. From which let us realize the folly of an over-anxiety to pry into the scenes that are lying before us, inasmuch as God will prepare a way by a gradual process, step by step, and leading us forward in a manner that will prove easy as we pass along, but which, if presented to our view at once, would seem insurmountable. (Quoted by Dean L. Larson, *Hope*, Salt Lake City: Deseret Book Co., 1988, p. 200.)

— *Lorenzo Snow*

If you seek His help, be sure your life is clean, your motives are worthy, and you're willing to do what He asks—for He *will* answer your prayers. He is your loving Father; you are His beloved child. He loves you perfectly and wants to help you. (*Ensign*, November 1989, p. 32.)

— *Richard G. Scott*

It is not in the economy of the Almighty to permit His people to be destroyed. If we will do right and keep His commandments, He will surely deliver us from every difficulty. (*JD*, 23:293.)

— *Lorenzo Snow*

It is only by yielding to God that we can begin to realize His will for us. And if we truly trust God, why not yield to His loving omniscience? After all, He knows us and our possibilities much better than do we. (*Ensign*, May 1985, p. 72.)

— *Neal A. Maxwell*

Men and women who turn their lives over to God will find out that He can make a lot more out of their lives than they can. He will deepen their joys, expand their vision, quicken their minds, strengthen their muscles, lift their spirits, multiply their blessings, increase their opportunities, comfort their souls, raise up friends, and pour out peace. Whoever will lose his life to God will find he has eternal life. (Christmas Devotional, Salt Lake City, Utah, December 7, 1986.)

— *Ezra Taft Benson*

The world is like a jungle, with dangers that can harm or mutilate your body, enslave or destroy your mind, or decimate your morality. It was intended that life be a challenge, not so that you would fail, but that you might succeed through overcoming. You face on every hand difficult but vitally important decisions.

There is an array of temptations, destructive influences, and camouflaged dangers, the like of which no previous generation has faced. I am persuaded that today no one, no matter how gifted, strong, or intelligent, will avoid serious problems without seeking the help of the Lord. . . .

Trust in the Lord. He knows what He is doing. He already knows of your problems. And He is waiting for you to ask for help. (*Ensign,* May 1989. p. 36.)
— *Richard G. Scott*

There is no place for fear among men and women who place their trust in the Almighty, who do not hesitate to humble themselves in seeking divine guidance through prayer. Though persecutions arise, though reverses come, in prayer we can find reassurance, for God will speak peace to the soul. That peace, that spirit of serenity, is life's greatest blessing. (*Ensign,* May 1977, p. 34.)
— *Ezra Taft Benson*

There is no place for fear among men and women who place their trust in the Almighty, who do not hesitate to humble themselves in seeking divine guidance through prayer. Though persecutions arise, though reverses come, in prayer we can find reassurance, for God will speak peace to the soul. That peace, that spirit of serenity, is life's greatest blessing. (*Ensign,* May 1977, p. 34.)
— *Ezra Taft Benson*

To turn to the Lord and to trust him through revelation will help any individual, at any time, in any part of the world, understand and interpret correctly and righteously life's experiences from the only true perspective, which is the Lord's perspective revealed to man. To turn to the Lord and to trust his revelations is to live in such a way as to resist the floods and the winds of doubt and uncertainty. (*Ensign,* May 1987, p. 27.)
— *Charles Didier*

We can afford the luxury of trusting our fellow-man only because we trust in God, who has assured us that if others let us down, he will make it up to us. (*OAT,* p. 12.)
— *Hugh Nibley*

Whom the Lord calls, the Lord qualifies. (*Ensign,* May 1988, p. 43.)
— *Thomas S. Monson*

You will win only by trust in the Lord, . . . and by doing faithfully that which you have in hand. (Quoted by H. Burke Peterson, *Ensign,* November 1977, p. 87.)
— *Brigham Young*

See also FAITH, LOOK TO GOD

——— Truth ———

A declaration of our faith reads: "If there is anything virtuous, lovely, or of good report or praiseworthy, we seek after these things." (A of F 1:13.) This embraces the truth of science, the truth of philosophy, the truth of history, the truth of art. I emphasize the word *truth*. It is a principle set forth in our scripture that "the glory of God is intelligence, or, in other words, light and truth." (D&C 93:36.) (*Ensign*, May 1986, p. 48.)

— *Gordon B. Hinckley*

All truths are not of the same value. The saving truths of salvation are of greatest worth. (*Ensign*, November 1985, p. 36.)

— *Ezra Taft Benson*

As a Church, we encourage gospel scholarship and the search to understand all truth. Fundamental to our theology is belief in individual freedom of inquiry, thought, and expression. Constructive discussion is a privilege of every Latter-day Saint. (*Ensign*, September 1985, p. 5.)

— *Gordon B. Hinckley*

As a general thing men love lies better than truth. (*JD*, 12:396.)

— *John Taylor*

God, our Heavenly Father—Elohim—lives. That is an absolute truth. . . . All the people on the earth might deny him and disbelieve, but he lives in spite of them. . . . In short, opinion alone has no power in the matter of an absolute truth. He still lives. And Jesus Christ is the Son of God, the Almighty, the Creator, the Master of the only true way of life—the gospel of Jesus Christ. The intellectual may rationalize him out of existence and the unbeliever may scoff, but Christ still lives and guides the destinies of his people. That is an absolute truth; there is no gainsaying. (*Ensign*, September 1978, pp. 3-4.)

— *Spencer W. Kimball*

Gospel truths and testimony are received from the Holy Ghost through reverent personal study and quiet contemplation.

— *Dallin H. Oaks*

Hell is truth seen too late. (Address, Brigham Young University, March 3, 1964, p. 3.)

— *Sterling W. Sill*

Help dispel gloom. Bring the light of truth. Do it through your senses, through your reason, and most significantly through the Spirit. It does not matter who you are or what you are currently doing with your life. The light of truth is there waiting to be discovered, and, being discovered, waiting to illuminate the life of each child of God. (*Ensign*, November 1981, p. 101.)

— *Barbara B. Smith*

If any man has truth that we have not, we say, "Let us have it." I am willing to exchange all the errors and false notions I have for one truth, and should consider that I had made a good bargain. We are not afraid of light and truth. Our religion embraces every truth in heaven, earth or hell; it embraces all truth, the whole gospel and plan of salvation, and the fulfillment of the whole volume of revelation that God has ever given. (*JD*, 18:117.)

— *Wilford Woodruff*

No man can disprove a truth. (*JD*, 8:132.)

— *Brigham Young*

The best way to obtain truth and wisdom is not to ask it from books, but to go to God in prayer and obtain divine teaching. (*TPJS*, p. 191.)

— *Joseph Smith*

The definition of truth given in 1833 about things "as they are," "as they were," and "as they are to come" (D&C 93:24) is related to another scripture: ". . . for the Spirit speaketh the truth and lieth not. Wherefore, it speaketh of things as they really are, and of things as they really will be . . . plainly, for the salvation of our souls." (Jac. 4 :13.) Note the presence of that powerful adverb *really*. The gospel of Jesus Christ and The Church of Jesus Christ of Latter-day Saints deal plainly with realities—"things as they really are," and "things as they really will be." (*Ensign*, October 1974, p. 71.)

— *Neal A. Maxwell*

The truth can only make him free who hath it and will continue in it.

— *Joseph F. Smith*

The heavens are full of truth and of everything that is good and noble, and many things are revealed to the servants of God which they are commanded not to reveal to the people. . . . Joseph had things revealed to him that he did not make known. . . . Paul, we are told, saw things that were unutterable. When the Lord visited the Nephites they had things shown to them, and their little children spoke things which could not be written. So it is now. The heavens are full of knowledge. . . . We think we have taken a great stride when we have obeyed baptism and had hands laid upon us and received the Holy Ghost. We think, Oh! what a wonderful thing has come to us! Well, it is wonderful. But, my brethren and sisters, that is just the beginning of what there is in the future. The heavens are full of light and intelligence, and a little of it has been communicated to us. (CR, April 1900.)

— *George Q. Cannon*

The two great gifts to this Church are the gifts of truth and authority. (*CR*, April 1921, p. 38.)

— *John A. Widtsoe*

There are no dogmas nor theories extant in the world that we profess to listen to, unless they can be verified by the principles of eternal truth. We carefully scan, investigate, criticize, and examine everything that presents itself to our view, and so far as we are enabled to comprehend any truths in existence, we gladly hail them as part and portion of the system with which we are associated. (*JD*, 14:337-338.)

— *John Taylor*

There is no other armor so strong as truth, none other that will turn aside the shafts of envy, hatred, malice, and all the rest of that great horde of iniquities, as will the simple unadorned truth. (Quoted by Marion G. Romney, *Ensign*, November 1976, p. 38.)

— *J. Reuben Clark, Jr.*

There is no truth but what belongs to the Gospel. (*JD*, 11:375.)

— *Brigham Young*

To be good, one must seek after truth, for truth is the ingredient which, when inculcated into our lives, changes us for good. (*Ensign*, November 1984, p. 61.)

— *Royden G. Derrick*

Truth—pure diamond truth—truth unmixed with error, truth and truth alone can lead a soul to salvation. (*Ensign*, November 1984, p. 83.)

— *Bruce R. McConkie*

We are after the truth. We commenced searching for it, and we are constantly in search of it, and so fast as we find any true principle revealed by any man, by God, or by holy angels, we embrace it and make it part of our religious creed. (*JD*, 14:341.)

— *John Taylor*

We believe in all truth, no matter to what subject it may refer. No sect or religious denomination in the world possesses a single principle of truth that we do not accept or that we will reject. . . . No man's faith, no man's religion, no religious organization in all the world, can ever rise above the truth. The truth must be at the foundation of religion, or it is in vain and it will fail of its purpose. I say that the truth is at the foundation, at the bottom and top of, and it entirely permeates this great work of the Lord that was established through the instrumentality of Joseph Smith, the prophet. (*CR*, April 1909, p. 7.)

— *Joseph F. Smith*

When attacked by error, truth is better served by silence than by a bad argument.

— *Dallin H. Oaks*

See also DOCTRINE, KNOWLEDGE, PHILOSOPHIES OF MEN

Unity

I firmly believe that activities and practices, even traditions that do not adhere to gospel standards, can be changed. . . . There is great power to change when there is unity—in families, in wards and stakes, in neighborhoods and schools—especially when motivated by righteous principles. (*Ensign*, November 1990, p. 94.)

— *Ardeth G. Kapp*

If as a people we will build and sustain one another, the Lord will bless us with the strength to weather every storm and continue to move forward through every adversity. The enemy of truth would divide us and cultivate within us attitudes of criticism which, if permitted to prevail, will only deter us in the pursuit of our great divinely given goal. We cannot afford to permit it to happen. We must close ranks and march shoulder to shoulder, the weak helping the strong, those with much assisting those with little. No power on earth can stop this work if we shall so conduct ourselves. (*Ensign*, May 1982, p. 46.)

— *Gordon B. Hinckley*

In His church we are always home—home in the things we believe, the standards we hold dear, the spirit we need, and the help, security, and belonging that are there. . . . Latter-day Saints everywhere open their hearts, their homes, their purses, their lives, in service and love to others. This is not done by constraint, but by the love and joy they feel from God and for each other. Indeed, this is the essence of the gospel as the Savior lived and taught it. Remember his word: "Be one; and if ye are not one ye are not mine." (D&C 38:27.) (*Ensign*, May 1983, p. 28.)

— *James M. Paramore*

Only a united people, keeping god's commands, can expect the protection which he alone can give when the floods come, and the rains descend, and the winds blow, and beat upon our house. (See Matt. 7:25.) (*Ensign*, May 1983, p. 18.)

— *Marion G. Romney*

Within each of us there is an intense need to feel that we belong. This feeling of unity and togetherness comes through the warmth of a smile, a handshake, or a hug, through laughter and unspoken demonstrations of love. It comes in the quiet, reverent moments of soft conversation and in listening. It comes from a still, small voice reminding us that we are brothers and sisters, the children of a Heavenly Father.

— *William R. Bradford*

The gospel binds together the hearts of all its adherents; it makes no difference, it knows no difference between the rich and the poor; we are all bound as one individual to perform the duties which devolve upon us.

— *Lorenzo Snow*

The sacrament meeting which was given of the Lord by revelation is designed specifically to promote unity. We are even admonished not to partake of the sacrament if we entertain unkindly feelings in our hearts toward others.

— *Stephen L. Richards*

The way to unity is for us to learn the will of the Lord and then to do it. . . . The power of the Church for good in the world depends upon the extent to which we, the members thereof, observe this principle. . . .

We of this Church can come to a unity and a oneness which will give us strength beyond anything we have yet enjoyed if we will obtain a sounder understanding of the principles of the gospel and come to a unity in our interpretations of present world conditions and trends. . . .

If we will study the word of the Lord as it comes to us through the standard works and through the instructions of the living prophet and not harden our hearts, but humble ourselves and develop a real desire to understand its application to us in our own peculiar circumstances, and then ask the Lord in faith, believing that we shall receive (see D&C 18:18), all the while being diligent in keeping the commandments of the Lord, surely the path we should follow will be made known unto us, and we will be able to face the world as a solid unit.

Surely we need this unity and this strength in this day in which we live. We have a great opportunity, the opportunity to rise heavenward, to gain the spirit of the gospel as we have never enjoyed it before. This we can do by developing among us that unity required by the laws of the celestial kingdom. (*Ensign*, May 1983, pp. 17-18.)

— *Marion G. Romney*

Unity is power. (*HC*, 6:198.)

— *Joseph Smith*

Unity is the hallmark of the true church of Christ. It is felt among our people throughout the world. As we are one, we are his. (*Ensign*, November 1983, p. 5.)

— *Gordon B. Hinckley*

We could progress a great deal faster, and could prosper a thousand times more than we do if we would be one in carrying out the counsels given us by the Lord through his servants.

— *John Taylor*

Could we all come together with one heart and one mind in perfect faith the veil might as well be rent today as next week, or any other time.

— *Joseph Smith*

We should go to work with a united faith like the heart of one man; and whatever we do should be performed in the name of the Lord, and we will then be blessed and prospered in all we do. We have a work on hand whose magnitude can hardly be told.

— *Brigham Young*

You and I would like to know how to control our wants and increase our gratitude and generosity. We are going to need that change. Someday, in our families and as a people, we will live as one, seeking each other's good. (*Ensign*, November 1989, p. 11.)

— *Henry B. Eyring*

See also BROTHERHOOD, FELLOWSHIP, LOVE, ZION

Valiancy

Having received the light of the everlasting gospel, and partaken of the good things of the kingdom, and being of the seed of Israel and heirs to great and glorious promises, we should labor with fidelity and diligence to accomplish what God has designed to do through us. We should be men and women of faith and power as well as good works; and when we discover ourselves careless or indifferent in the least, it should be sufficient for us to know it in order to mend our ways and return to the path of duty.

— *Lorenzo Snow*

God is weaving his tapestry according to his own grand design. All flesh is in his hands. . . .

We have no need to fear. We have no need to worry. . . . Our imperative need is to be found doing our duty. . . . (*Ensign*, May 1983, p. 6.)

— *Gordon B. Hinckley*

God judges men according to the use they make of the light which he gives them.

— *Joseph Smith*

Only the valiant are saved. Members of the Church who are not valiant in the testimony of Jesus, not valiant in the cause of Christ, not valiant in defense of his prophets and in preaching his word are not heirs of the celestial kingdom. (*Ensign*, November 1984, p. 85.)

— *Bruce R. McConkie*

The Lord will have a people to carry on his purposes who will obey and serve him . . . Those who have got oil in their lamps are men who live their religion, pay their tithing, pay their debts, keep the commandments of God, and do not blaspheme his name; men and women who will not sell their birthright for a mess of pottage or for a little gold or silver; these are those that will be valiant in the testimony of Jesus Christ.

— *Wilford Woodruff*

There has never been more expected of the faithful in such a short period of time as there is of us. . . . Each day we personally make many decisions that show where our support will go. The final outcome is certain—the forces of righteousness will finally win. What remains to be seen is where each of us personally, now and in the future, will stand in this fight—and how tall we will stand. Will we be true to our last-days, foreordained mission? (Quoted by Marvin J. Ashton, *Ensign*, November 1989, pp. 36-37.)

— *Ezra Taft Benson*

There is but one path of safety and that is the path of duty. It is not a testimony; it is not a marvelous manifestation; it is not knowing the gospel is true—it is not actually knowing that the Savior is the Redeemer; but it is the keeping of the commandments of God, living the life of a Saint.

> — *Heber J. Grant*

To be valiant . . . is to take the Lord's side on every issue. (*CR*, October 1974, p. 46.)

> — *Bruce R. McConkie*

The summer patriot and the sunshine saint retreat when the battle wages fiercely around them. Theirs is not the conqueror's crown. (*CR*, October 1974, p. 44.)

> — *Bruce R. McConkie*

We have been warned by our prophet that the "forces of evil increase under Lucifer's leadership and the forces of good increase under the leadership of Jesus Christ." (Ezra Taft Benson, *Ensign*, November 1988, p. 87.) The heat of that great confrontation is becoming more intense. Sooner or later, either privately or publicly, we will all be tested. We must be prepared to defend our values, our standards, our commitments, and our covenants to stand as a witness of God at all times, in all things, and in all places. (*Ensign*, November 1990, p. 93.)

> — *Ardeth G. Kapp*

[Be] true when you are tempted, [be] true when you don't want to be, [be] true when it means standing alone from the rest of the world. (*Ensign*, November 1990, p. 79.)

> — *Ruth B. Wright*

See also COURAGE, ENDURANCE, PERSISTENCE, RIGHTEOUSNESS

——— Values ———

God is the same yesterday, today, and forever, and his covenants and doctrines are unchanging. Old values are upheld by the Church, not because they are old, but rather because through the ages they have proved right. (Quoted by N. Eldon Tanner, *Ensign*, November 1976, p. 82.)

> — *Spencer W. Kimball*

Teaching the next generation is not easy in a society where many fundamental beliefs are disappearing. Deadly mass marketing challenges almost every cherished human value. Excessive permissiveness under the banner of individual freedom is one driving force behind this. Reaching a public consensus on what values should be taught to the next generation is almost impossible. People strongly disagree about almost everything. Social restraints are weakened.

This means we will have to teach our children a life-style of our own and provide moral anchors in the sea of self-indulgence, self-interest, and self-service in which they float. (*Ensign*, May 1987, p. 80.)

— *James E. Faust*

Just forty years ago, President J. Reuben Clark, Jr., a member of the First Presidency, gave an address titled "Slipping from Our Old Moorings." He described how we have slipped away from living the Ten Commandments (see *Church News*, 8 March 1947, pp. 1,8-9). If we had slipped away then, where are we forty years later? In 1947, television and computers were in their infancies. We had no satellite broadcasts or videotapes and no computer fraud. Certainly our moral standards of decency and propriety have slipped from where they were in 1947. The obscenity, nudity, and other forms of pornography that would have made us blush and turn away in shame in 1947 are now thrust at us openly in printed and audiovisual material. They are even paraded through our homes unless we are careful to keep them out. As a people, we are slipping further from our old moorings today because we are not following our prophets. (*Ensign*, May 1987, p. 30.)

— *Joseph B. Wirthlin*

The continued survival of a free and open society is dependent upon a high degree of divinely inspired values and moral conduct.

— *David B. Haight*

To some it may seem old-fashioned to speak of virtue and chastity, honesty, morality, faith, character, but these are the qualities which have built great men and women and point the way by which one may find happiness in the living of today and eternal joy in the world to come. These are the qualities which are the anchors to our lives, in spite of the trials, the tragedies, the pestilences, and the cruelties of war. (*Ensign*, January 1974, p. 2.)

— *Harold B. Lee*

We live in a critical time in the world's history. Satan and his forces are busy. His temptations are relentless, deceiving many, sometimes even the very elect. He would lead us to believe that gospel standards which we know to be good—virtue, honesty, morality, courtesy, industry, cleanliness of mind and body—are no longer important. Let me reaffirm that the Lord's eternal values are still true. The ways of the world may have changed, but the commandments of our Heavenly

Father, given for our welfare, are still in force, and true joy comes only from doing his will.

— *Barbara W. Winder*

See also MORALITY, PRINCIPLES

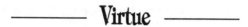

Virtue

How glorious is he who lives the chaste life. He walks unfearful in the glare of the noon-day sun, for he is without moral infirmity. He can be reached by no shafts of base calumny, for his armor is without flaw, his virtue cannot be challenged by any just accuser, for he lives above reproach. His cheek is never blotched with shame, for he is without sin. He is honored and respected by all mankind, for he is beyond their censure. He is loved by the Lord, for he stands without blemish. The exaltations of eternities await his coming. (Message of the First Presidency, 3 October 1942.)

— *The First Presidency*

There is no strength that is greater than the strength of virtue. There is no other nobility equal to the nobility of virtue. There is no quality so becoming, no attire so attractive. (*Ensign,* November 1984, p. 91.)

— *Gordon B. Hinckley*

Virtue is akin to holiness—an attribute of godliness. (*Ensign,* November 1983, p. 42.)

— *Ezra Taft Benson*

See also CHASTITY, PURITY

War

Let mothers of any nation teach their children not to make war, and the children would not grow up and enter into it. (*JD*, 19:72.)

—*Brigham Young*

Alas, though we are asked to be peacemakers, we do live in a time when peace has been taken from the earth. (See D&C 1:35.) War has been the almost continuing experience of modern man. There have been 141 wars, large and small, just since the end of World War II in 1945. As the American Civil War was about to begin, the Lord declared there would be a succession of wars poured out upon all nations, resulting in the "death and misery of many souls." (D&C 87:1.)

Moreover, that continuum of conflict will culminate in "a full end of all nations." (D&C 87:6.) Meanwhile, let mortals, if they choose, put over-reliance upon mortal arms. As for us, we shall "put on the whole armour of God!" (Eph. 6:11.) And in the midst of such affliction, if we are righteous and we die, we die unto Him; and if we live, we live unto Him. (See D&C 42:44.) (*Ensign*, November 1982, p. 67.)

—*Neal A. Maxwell*

I hate war, with all its mocking panoply. It is a grim and living testimony that Satan, the father of lies, the enemy of God, lives. War is earth's greatest cause of human misery. It is the destroyer of life, the promoter of hate, the waster of treasure. It is man's costliest folly, his most tragic misadventure. (*Ensign*, March, 1971, p. 20.)

—*Gordon B. Hinckley*

The Lord says *he has decreed wars*. Why? Because of the hatred in the hearts of men, because of the wickedness in the hearts of men, because they will not repent. (*Doctrines of Salvation*, Bruce R. McConkie, comp., Salt Lake City: Bookcraft, 1956, 3:42.)

—*Joseph Fielding Smith*

We are dismayed by the growing tensions among the nations, and the unrestricted building of arsenals of war, including huge and threatening nuclear weaponry. Nuclear war, when unleashed on a scale for which the nations are preparing, spares no living thing within the perimeter of its initial destructive force, and sears and maims and kills wherever its pervasive cloud reaches.

While recognizing the need for strength to repel any aggressor, we are enjoined by the word of God to "renounce war and proclaim peace." We call upon the heads of nations to sit down and reason together in good faith to resolve their differences. If men of good will can bring themselves to do so, they may save the world from a holocaust, the depth and breadth of which can scarcely be imagined. We are confident that when there is enough of a desire for peace and a will to bring it about, it is not beyond the possibility of attainment. (*Church News*, December 20, 1980. p. 3.)

—*The First Presidency*

There are, . . . two conditions which may justify a truly Christian man to enter—mind you, I say *enter, not begin*—a war: (1) An attempt to dominate and to deprive another of his free agency, and, (2) Loyalty to his country. Possibly there is a third, viz., Defense of a weak nation that is being unjustly crushed by a strong, ruthless one. (*CR*, April 1942, p. 72.)

—*David O. McKay*

See also ADVERSITY, CONTENTION, OPPOSITION, PEACE, PROBLEMS

——— Weaknesses ———

Some of us are inclined to look to the weaknesses and shortcomings of others in order to expand our own comfort zone. (*Ensign*, May 1988, p. 63.)

—*Marvin J. Ashton*

At the perfect day, we will see that we have been a part of things too wonderful for us. Part of the marvel and the wonder of God's "marvelous work and a wonder" will be how perfect Divinity mercifully used us—imperfect humanity. (*Ensign*, November 1984, p. 11.)

—*Neal A. Maxwell*

Faultfinding is easy. It takes a true disciple of the Master to look beyond the weaknesses we all have and find the threads of gold that are always there. (*Ensign*, November 1982, p. 43.)

—*H. Burke Peterson*

I can fellowship the President of the Church if he does not know everything. . . . I saw the . . . imperfections in [Joseph Smith] . . . I thanked God that He would put upon a man who had those imperfections the power and authority He placed upon him . . . for I knew that I myself had weakness, and I thought there was a chance for me . . . I thanked God that I saw these imperfections. (Quoted by Neal A. Maxwell, *Ensign*, November 1984, p. 10.)

—*Lorenzo Snow*

Our weaknesses are like dogs, you see. If we walk toward them, they will run away from us. But if we run away from them they'll chase us. (*OAT*, p. 111.)

—*Hugh Nibley*

We do notice each other's weaknesses. But we should not celebrate them. Let us be grateful for the small strides that we and others make, rather than rejoice in the shortfalls. And when mistakes occur, let them become instructive, not destructive. (*Ensign*, May 1982, p. 39.)

—*Neal A. Maxwell*

See also FORGIVENESS, JUDGING

——— Wealth ———

Are we not wealthy if the Lord has blessed us with something we can share with others? (*Ensign*, November 1985, p. 74.)

—*Howard W. Hunter*

For those of us who have worldly riches, it does not mean that we cannot enjoy the commodities of life for which we work. But it means that we use them to do good and that we share them with those in need. (*Ensign*, May 1990, p. 26.)

—*Hans B. Ringger*

God recognizes only one justification for seeking wealth, and that is with the express intent of helping the poor. (*OAT*, p. 125.)

—*Hugh Nibley*

In many respects, the real test of a man is his attitude towards his earthly possessions. A person who places earthly possessions in the scales against the things of God evidences little understanding of eternal values. (*Ensign*, May 1979, p. 39.)

—*Franklin D. Richards*

The right to own and control private property is not only a human right; it is a divine right. We will largely be judged, if I understand the Savior's teachings correctly (see Matt. 25), by how we use our property voluntarily for the blessings and benefits of our Father's other children. (Address, Brigham Young University, March 8, 1966.)

—*Howard W. Hunter*

The worst fear that I have about this people is that they will get rich in this country, forget God and His people, wax fat, and kick themselves out of the Church and go to hell. This people will stand mobbing, robbing, poverty, and all manner of persecution, and be true. But my greater fear for them is that they cannot stand wealth. (*The Faith of Our Pioneer Fathers*, Bryant S. Hinckley, Salt Lake City: Deseret Book Co., 1956, p. 13.)

—*Brigham Young*

Seek after wisdom rather than . . . material things and pleasures. . . . Frequently, when we seek after wisdom rather than riches, the Lord blesses us with wisdom *and* riches as he did King Solomon. When this occurs, we have the great opportunity and responsibility to use our material wealth in the building up of the kingdom of God. (*Ensign*, May 1976 pp. 35-36.)

—*Franklin D. Richards*

See also CHARITY, CONSECRATION, MONEY, OFFERINGS, TEMPORAL LAW

——— Wickedness ———

Lehi's vision of the tree of life is appropriate for our day. In that vision, he saw a great and spacious building, which represents the pride and temptations of the world: . . .

To those of you who are inching your way closer and closer to that great and spacious building, let me make it completely clear that the people in that building have absolutely nothing to offer except instant, short-term gratification inescapably connected to long-term sorrow and suffering. The commandments you observe were not given by a dispassionate God to prevent you from having fun, but by a loving Father in Heaven who wants you to be happy while you are living on this earth as well as in the hereafter.

Compare the blessings of living the Word of Wisdom to those available to you if you choose to party with those in the great and spacious building. Compare the joy of intelligent humor and wit to drunken, silly, crude, loud laughter. Compare our faithful young women who still have a blush in their cheeks with those who, having long lost their blush, try to persuade you to join them in their loss. Compare lifting people up to putting people down. Compare the ability to receive personal revelation and direction in your life to being tossed to and fro with every wind of doctrine. Compare holding the priesthood of God with anything you see going on in that great and spacious building. . . .

When all of the evidence is in, the world's graduate school of hard knocks will teach what you . . . were taught in the kindergarten of your spiritual training, "Wickedness never was happiness" (Alma 41:10). (*Ensign*, November 1987, p. 40.)

—*Glenn L. Pace*

My brothers and sisters, there seems to be a general state of wickedness in the world in these perilous yet crucially momentous days. . . . It seems that iniquity abounds on all sides, with the Adversary taking full advantage of the time remaining to him in this day of his power. The leaders of the Church continually cry out against that which is intolerable in the sight of the Lord: against pollution of mind and body and our surroundings; against vulgarity, stealing, lying, cheating, false pride, blasphemy, and drunkenness; against fornication, adultery, homosexuality, abortion; and all other abuses of the sacred power to create; against murder and all that is like unto it; against all manner of degradation and sin.

As Latter-day Saints we must ever be vigilant. The way for each person and each family to guard against the slings and arrows of the Adversary and to prepare for the great day of the Lord is to hold fast to the iron rod, to exercise greater faith, to repent of our sins and shortcomings, and to be anxiously engaged in the work of His kingdom on earth, which is The Church of Jesus Christ of Latter-day Saints. Herein lies the only true happiness for all our Father's children. (*Ensign*, November 1982, pp. 4-5.)

—*Spencer W. Kimball*

Once the carnal in man is no longer checked by the restraints of family life and real religion, there comes an avalanche of appetites which gathers momentum that is truly frightening. As one jars loose and begins to roll down hill, still another breaks loose, whether it is an increase in homosexuality, corruption, drugs, or abortion. Each began as an appetite that needed to be checked but which went unchecked. Thus misery achieves a ghastly monument. (*Ensign*, May 1978, p. 78.)

—*Spencer W. Kimball*

There is no bravery in evil, no true courage in behavior that can only result in deep disappointment. (*Ensign*, November 1986, p. 13.)

—*Marion D. Hanks*

Those who freely deny God with their amoral and agnostic practices will one day find that He may just as freely deny them! (See 3 Ne. 28:34.) (*Ensign*, November 1984, p. 31.)

—*Russell M. Nelson*

What is wrong is wrong, and trends do not make something right which is at variance with the laws of God. (*Ensign*, May 1978, p. 78.)

—*Spencer W. Kimball*

You cannot do wrong and feel right. It is impossible! (*Ensign*, November 1977, p. 30.)

—*Ezra Taft Benson*

Our society maintains the fiction that the display of such things as adultery, pornography, nudity, and licentiousness should be kept from the young people. Of course it should, but to set an age limit is pure hypocrisy. Perhaps greater corruption is being administered to the older and married generation. They are those who commit the adulteries. They are those who destroy the homes and violate the sanctity of families. The married ones obtain the divorces, break the covenants, cheat their spouses, and become dishonest in their commitments. (*Ensign*, May 1984, p. 27.)

—*William Grant Bangerter*

See also EVIL, RIGHTEOUSNESS, SIN

——— Willingness ———

A willing heart describes one who desires to please the Lord and to serve His cause first. He serves the Lord on the Lord's terms, not his own. There are no restrictions to where or how he will serve. (*Ensign*, November 1988, p. 16.)

—*Marvin J. Ashton*

It is not enough to serve God with all of our *might and strength*. He who looks into our hearts and knows our minds demands more than this. In order to stand blameless before God at the last day, we must also serve him with all our *heart and mind*. (*Ensign*, November 1984, p. 15.)

—*Dallin H. Oaks*

Obedience must be voluntary; it must not be forced; there must be no coercion. Men must not be constrained against their will to obey the will of God; they must obey it because they know it to be right, because they desire to do it, and because it is their pleasure to do it. God delights in the willing heart. (*JD*, 25:59.)

— *Joseph F. Smith*

We must seek the ability . . . to sanctify our motives, desires, feelings and affections, that they may be pure and holy, and our will in all things be subservient to the will of God, and have no will of our own except to do the will of our Father. (*JD*, 20:189.)

— *Lorenzo Snow*

The submissive soul will be led aright, enduring some things well while being anxiously engaged in setting other things right—all the time discerning the difference. (*Ensign*, May 1985, p. 71.)

—*Neal A. Maxwell*

We need to learn the will of the Lord for us and then do it, . . . His will is made manifest through the standard works, His anointed servants, and personal revelation. (*Ensign*, May 1986, p. 78.)

—*Ezra Taft Benson*

Whatever I am, whatever I need to overcome, I will be one upon whom the Lord can count. We can all use our agency this way—to be one upon whom the Lord can count.

Let's do it! (*Ensign*, November 1983, p. 89.)

—*Elaine Cannon*

Yes, to Caesar we owe taxes. But to God, in whose image we are minted, we owe ourselves! (*Ensign*, November 1988, p. 31.)

—*Neal A. Maxwell*

See also EYE SINGLE, HUMILITY, OBEDIENCE

Wisdom

All true wisdom that mankind have they have received from God, whether they know it or not. There is no ingenious mind that has ever invented anything beneficial to the human family but what he obtained it from that One Source. . . . There is only one source from whence men obtain wisdom, and that is God, the fountain of all wisdom; and though men may claim to make their discoveries by their own wisdom, by meditation and reflection, they are indebted to our Father in heaven for all. (*JD*, 13:148.)

—*Brigham Young*

Being learned is not always the same thing as being wise. (*Ensign*, October 1974, p. 71.)

—*Neal A. Maxwell*

Men may be very good, and yet they may not be very wise, nor so useful as they might be; but the gospel is given to make us wise, and to enable us to get those things in our minds that are calculated to make us happy. (*JD*, 9:22.)

—*Lorenzo Snow*

The fear of the Lord is the beginning of great wisdom. (*CR*, April 1952, p. 17.)

—*Thorpe B. Isaacson*

Wisdom is not to be proclaimed or exhibited, but rather, it is to be sought, to be treasured; we need to pray for it and then express it by living a worthy life, according to the knowledge we have obtained. (*Ensign*, May 1988, p. 26.)

—*Angel Abrea*

The way to get along in any important matter is to gather unto yourselves wise men, experienced and aged men, to assist in council in all times of trouble. Handsome men are not apt to be wise and strong-minded men; but the strength of a strong-minded man will generally create coarse features, like the rough, strong bough of the oak. You will always discover in the first glance of a man, in the outlines of his features something of his mind. (*HC*, 5:389.)

—*Joseph Smith*

See also INTELLIGENCE, KNOWLEDGE

—— Womanhood ——

A beautiful, modest, gracious woman is creation's masterpiece. (*Gospel Ideals*, The Improvement Era, Salt Lake City: Deseret Book Co., 1976, p. 449.)

—*David O. McKay*

A wise woman renews herself. In proper season, she develops her talents and continues her education. She musters the discipline to reach her goals. She dispels darkness and opens windows of truth to light her way. (*Ensign*, November 1989, p. 21.)

—*Russell M. Nelson*

A woman's role in a man's life is to lift him, to help him uphold lofty standards, and to prepare through righteous living to be his queen for all eternity. (*Ensign*, November 1981, p. 107.)

—*Ezra Taft Benson*

Before the world was created, in heavenly councils the pattern and role of women were prescribed. You were elected by God to be wives and mothers in Zion. Exaltation in the celestial kingdom is predicated on faithfulness to that calling. (*Ensign*, November 1981, p. 105.)

—*Ezra Taft Benson*

No greater heroine lives in today's world than the woman who is quietly doing her part. (*Ensign*, November 1990, p. 89.)

—*Elaine L. Jack*

Brethren, we cannot be exalted without our wives. There can be no heaven without righteous women. (*Ensign*, November 1979, p. 37.)

—*Spencer W. Kimball*

Each of you is an elect lady. You have come out of the world as partakers of the restored gospel of Jesus Christ. You have made your election, and if you are living worthy of it, the Lord will honor you in it and magnify you. (*Ensign*, November 1984, p. 91.)

—*Gordon B. Hinckley*

There are adversities to be overcome, not a few of them. There are trials to be endured. There is much of evil in the world and too much of harshness, even in the home. Do what you can to rise above all of this. Stand up. Speak out against evil and brutality. Safeguard against abuse. Keep out of your homes the filthiness of the world, which can lead to such abuse. Rise up in the stature of your divine inheritance. God bless you, you wonderful girls, you strong and able young women, you older women of faith and integrity, you mothers in Zion. (*Ensign*, November 1989, p. 98.)

—*Gordon B. Hinckley*

The average woman today would do well to appraise her interests, evaluate the activities in which she is engaged, and then take steps to simplify her life, putting things of first importance first, placing emphasis where the rewards will be greatest and most enduring, and ridding herself of the less rewarding activities. The endless enticements and demands of life today require that we determine priorities in allocating our time and energies if we are to live happy, poised, productive lives. (*A Woman's Reach*, Salt Lake City: Deseret Book Co., 1974, p. 23.)

—*Belle S. Spafford*

Sisters, do not allow yourselves to be made to feel inadequate or frustrated because you cannot do everything others seem to be accomplishing. Rather, each should assess her own situation, her own energy, and her own talents, and then choose the best way to mold her family into a team, a unit that works together and supports each other. Only you and your Father in Heaven know your needs, strengths, and desires. Around this knowledge your personal course must be charted and your choices made. (*Ensign*, May 1984, p. 10.)

—*Marvin J. Ashton*

I love being a mother, a wife, a daughter, a sister, a woman in these latter days. The Lord knows us and loves each of us and desires to bless us in our important work. We must be willing to come unto him; to accept his will over our own wants; to bring souls unto him; to feed his lambs and his sheep, so that at that great day when we meet him face to face he will say, "Come unto me ye blessed, for behold, your works have been the works of righteousness" (Alma 5:16). (*Ensign*, November 1987, p. 92.)

—*Joanne B. Doxey*

From [early times] until now woman has comforted and nursed the Church. She has borne more than half the burdens, she has made more than half the sacrifices, she has suffered the most of the heartaches and sorrows. (*CR*, April 1940, p. 21.)

—*J. Reuben Clark, Jr.*

God has given the women of this church a work to do in building his kingdom. That concerns all aspects of our great triad of responsibility—which is, first, to teach the gospel to the world; second, to strengthen the faith and build the happiness of the membership of the church; and, third, to carry forward the great work of salvation for the dead. . . .

Know that you are daughters of God, children with a divine birthright. Walk in the sun with your heads high, knowing that you are loved and honored, that you are a part of his kingdom, and that there is for you a great work to be done which cannot be left to others. (*Ensign*, November 1983, p. 84.)

—*Gordon B. Hinckley*

Happiness lies in keeping the commandments. For a Latter-day Saint woman . . . who observes them, there is the promise of a crown, a queenly crown for each daughter of God, a crown of righteousness and eternal truth. (*Ensign*, November 1984, p. 92.)

—*Gordon B. Hinckley*

I stress again the deep need each woman has to study the scriptures. . . . As you become more and more familiar with the truths of the scriptures, you will be more and more effective. . . . After all, who has any greater need to "treasure up" the truths of the gospel than do women and mothers who do so much nurturing and teaching. (*Ensign*, November 1979, p. 102.)

—*Spencer W. Kimball*

If our good women are to continue in their primary roles as nurturers, teachers, homemakers, and managers, they will need more support and help in order for them to find time to give compassionate service to their families and others. If this help is withheld, our lives, our homes, the Church, and the world will be the poorer, for so much love, gentleness, and understanding will be lost. (*Ensign*, May 1988, p. 38.)

—*James E. Faust*

Man is at his best when complemented by a good woman's natural influence. (*Woman*, Salt Lake City: Deseret Book Co., 1979, p. 69.)

—*Ezra Taft Benson*

In the pioneering days of this church when men grubbed the sagebrush and broke the sod so that crops might be planted to sustain life, many a wife and mother planted a few flowers and a few fruit trees to add beauty and taste to the drabness of pioneer life. . . . Beauty is a thing divine. The cultivation of it becomes an expression of the divine nature within you. (*Ensign*, November 1989, p. 98.)

—*Gordon B. Hinckley*

It is according to our natures, sisters, to have feelings of charity and benevolence. It isn't always easy to put these feelings into action. But as women, we should pray for charitable desires and opportunities and then work to foster these godlike attributes. (*Ensign*, November 1988, p. 89.)

—*Barbara W. Winder*

Marvelous is the power of women of faith. It has been demonstrated again and again in the history of this church. It goes on among us today. I think it is part of the divinity within you.

Sisters, rise to the stature of that divinity. (*Ensign*, November 1989, p. 97.)

—*Gordon B. Hinckley*

Much of the major growth that is coming to the Church in the last days . . . will happen to the degree that the women of the Church reflect righteousness and articulateness in their lives and to the degree that [they] are seen as distinct and different—in happy ways—from the women of the world. (*Ensign*, November 1979, pp. 103-4.)

—*Barbara W. Winder*

Perhaps the Church does more to enlighten understanding about and to lift the cause of women than any other institution on earth. It provides the path to her eternal destiny. . . . To all faithful Saints He has promised thrones, kingdoms, principalities, glory, immortality, and eternal lives. (See Rom. 2:7; D&C 75:5; 128:12, 23; 132:19.) That is the potential for women in The Church of Jesus Christ of Latter-day Saints. It is exalting, everlasting, and divine. (*Ensign*, November 1989, pp. 20, 22.)

—*Russell M. Nelson*

Someday, when the whole story of this and previous dispensations is told, it will be filled with courageous stories of our women, of their wisdom and their devotion, their courage; for one senses that perhaps, just as women were the first at the sepulchre of the Lord Jesus Christ after his resurrection, our righteous women have so often been instinctively sensitive to things of eternal consequence. (*Ensign*, May 1978, p. 5.)

—*Spencer W. Kimball*

Study the scriptures. Thus you may gain strength through the understanding of eternal things. . . . We want our sisters to be scholars of the scriptures as well as our men. (*Ensign,* November 1978, p. 102.)

—*Spencer W. Kimball*

The word and law of God are as important for women who would reach wise conclusions as they are for men; and women should study and consider the problems of this great latter-day work from the standpoint of God's revelations, and as they may be actuated by his Spirit, which it is their right to receive through the medium of sincere and heartfelt prayer.

—*Joseph F. Smith*

Surely the secret citadel of women's inner strength is their spirituality. In this they equal and even surpass men, as they do in faith, morality, and commitment when truly converted to the gospel. They have "more trust in the Lord [and] more hope in his word" (*Hymns,* 1985, no. 131). (*Ensign,* May 1988, p. 37.)

—*James E. Faust*

The Lord loves you for being His partner in His plan. Be of good cheer as you perform your divinely ordained task of guiding the destiny of this generation, that they may then pass the baton of righteousness on to generations yet unborn. (*Ensign,* November 1989, p. 91.)

—*Joanne B. Doxey*

The true spirit of the Church of Jesus Christ of Latter-day Saints gives to woman the highest place of honor in human life. (Quoted by James E. Faust, *Ensign,* May 1988, pp. 36-37.)

—*The First Presidency*

The world is making butterflies out of women and a prison out of home. (*CR,* October 1951.)

—*Stephen L Richards*

There are a few women in the Church who complain because they do not hold the priesthood. I think the Lord would say to you, "murmur not because of the things which are not given thee."

This is his work. Joseph did not set the rule about not showing the plates to others. He was instructed concerning it. Nor have we set the rule concerning those who should receive the priesthood. That was established by him whose work this is, and he alone could change it. (*Ensign,* November 1984, p. 91.)

—*Gordon B. Hinckley*

There are people fond of saying that women are the weaker instruments, but I don't believe it. Physically they may be, but spiritually, morally, religiously, and in faith, what man can match a woman who is really converted to the gospel! Women are more willing to make sacrifices than are men, more patient in suffering, more earnest in prayer. They are the peers and often superior to men in resilience, in goodness, in morality, and in faith. (Relief Society Conference, September 29, 1965.)

—*Hugh B. Brown*

There is no sister so isolated, and her sphere so narrow but what she can do a great deal towards establishing the kingdom of God upon the earth. (*Women's Exponent*, 15 September 1873, p. 62.)

—*Eliza R. Snow*

Without the wonderful work of the women, I realize that the Church would have been a failure. (*Gospel Standards*, Salt Lake City: Improvement Era, 1942, p. 150.)

—*Heber J. Grant*

There is no surer way for a man to show his lack of character . . . than for him to show lack of respect for a woman or to do anything that would discredit or degrade her. (*Ensign*, January 1974, p. 10.)

—*N. Eldon Tanner*

There is nothing so sacred as true womanhood. (*Gospel Ideals*, The Improvement Era, Salt Lake City: Deseret Book Co., 1976, p. 353.)

—*David O. McKay*

This is a wonderful world for women. The richness, the hope, the promise of life today, are exciting beyond belief. Nonetheless, we need stout hearts and strong characters; we need knowledge and training; we need organized effort to meet the future—a future pregnant with unborn events, big with possibilities, stupendous in its demands, and challenging in its problems. (*A Woman's Reach*, Salt Lake City: Deseret Book Co., 1974, p. 27.)

—*Belle S. Spafford*

To help another human being reach one's celestial potential is part of the divine mission of woman. As mother, teacher, or nurturing Saint, she molds living clay to the shape of her hopes. In partnership with God, her divine mission is to help spirits live and souls be lifted. This is the measure of her creation. It is ennobling, edifying, and exalting. (*Ensign*, November 1989, p. 22.)

—*Russell M. Nelson*

We are accustomed to focusing on the men of God because theirs is the priesthood and leadership line. But paralleling that authority line is a stream of righteous influence reflecting the remarkable women of God who have existed in all ages and dispensations, including our own. (*Ensign*, May 1978, p. 10.)

—*Neal A. Maxwell*

You cannot become great women if you are not also good women. . . . Great women respond generously to their instincts to do good. With your very being held still, listen to the whisperings of the Holy Spirit. Follow those noble, intuitive feelings planted deep within your soul by Deity. By responding thus to the Holy Spirit of God, you will be sanctified by truth and you will be eternally honored and loved. (*Ensign*, September 1986, p. 20.)

—*James E. Faust*

[Sisters,] your foes in a sordid society demean the sacredness of women and the sanctity of motherhood. Your world, sickened by unchastity and plagued with sexually transmitted disease, needs your righteous example. . . .

Beloved sisters, let your lives be committed to your Father in Heaven, to his Only Begotten Son, and to his church. (*Ensign*, November 1987, p. 89.)

—*Russell M. Nelson*

You sisters, I suppose, have read that poem which my sister composed years ago, and which is sung quite frequently now in our meetings [O my Father]. It tells us that we not only have a Father in "that high and glorious place," but that we have a Mother too; and you will become as great as your Mother, if you are faithful. (*TLS*, pp. 7-8.)

—*Lorenzo Snow*

Women are not just cooks, stewards of our homes, or servants. They are much more. They are the enrichment of humanity. (*Ensign*, May 1988, p. 36.)

—*James E. Faust*

Young women, mothers, leaders, let us all be filled—filled with the light, the strength, the faith that comes from prayer, scripture study, and obedience to God's commandments each day of our lives. Let us stand united together, shoulder to shoulder, heart to heart, and hand in hand, bonded together by that light that never grows dim. We'll hold our torches high that Christ's true light through us will shine, His name to glorify.

God is our Father, and we are His daughters. (*Ensign*, November 1988, p. 95.)

—*Ardeth G. Kapp*

We are in a time when the swift changes of our social structure are thrusting enormous challenges upon us. We must remember that the work of women is important and still must be done. The spirit children of God must have the experience of mortality, and that means babies must be wanted, nurtured, loved, and cared for. The Lord has given women a primary responsibility in the establishment of good homes and well-cared-for families. No matter what the challenges are, we must find ways to accomplish this life-giving and eternal work. (*Ensign*, November 1983, p. 84.)

—*Barbara B. Smith*

See also MOTHERHOOD

Word of Wisdom

I know that if we keep the Word of Wisdom, the destroying angel will spare us. God has counseled us not to use alcoholic beverages, tea, or coffee, and has told us not to use tobacco [or] any substance which is habit-forming and harmful to the body. The word of the Lord is enough to guide me in my life. I urge you, then, to listen carefully to these words of warning, not only to avoid the use of those things which are harmful to your bodies, but also to use those foods recommended by the Lord with prudence and thanksgiving. The Lord has spoken. (*Ensign*, May 1976, p. 29.)

—*Theodore M. Burton*

Conspiring, evil men want to make money by selling drugs, alcohol, and tobacco. They don't care how much death and pain come as a result. Beware of these merchants of death. Say no to those mind- and body-destroying drugs and chemicals that are ravaging the youth throughout the world. Why indulge when you know they destroy and promise nothing but sorrow? . . . Live the Word of Wisdom. (*Ensign*, May 1989, p. 42.)

—*Russell C. Taylor*

Drugs are not a "quick fix." They are a quick exit through a door which too often swings only one way—toward heartache and self-destruction. (*Ensign*, November 1986, p. 15.)

—*Marvin J. Ashton*

I am fully convinced that the Lord in His mercy, when He gave us the Word of Wisdom, gave it to us, not alone that we might have health while we live in the world, but that our faith might be strengthened, that our testimony of the divinity of the mission of our Lord and Master might be increased, that thereby we might be better prepared to return to His presence when our labor here is complete. (*CR*, April 1907, p. 19.)

—*George Albert Smith*

In faith, modern Israel is commanded to obey the Word of Wisdom. It becomes our token of a covenant with the Lord—a spiritual separator of covenant Israel from the rest of the world. (*Ensign,* November 1986, p. 69.)

—*Russell M. Nelson*

We *can* observe that Word of Wisdom. We receive numerous letters inquiring whether this item or that item is proscribed by the Word of Wisdom. If we will avoid those things which are definitely and specifically defined, and beyond this observe the spirit of that great revelation, it will not involve a burden. It will, rather, bring a blessing. Do not forget: it is the Lord who has made the promise. (*Ensign,* November 1985, p. 85.)

—*Gordon B. Hinckley*

Approximately 5,000 people a day quit smoking, and another 1,000—every single day—die from cigarette smoking, or one in every ninety seconds, in the United Sates alone. This means that each day 6,000 people either kick the habit or kick the bucket. . . .

I had my own comment printed and pasted on all cigarette advertising in the magazines of my medical office waiting room. It sates:

"Many of the ads in this magazine are misleading, deceptive, and are a rip-off. For example, smoking does not make one glamorous, macho, or athletic. It does make one sick, poor, and dead." (*Ensign,* May 1990, pp. 44-45.)

—*Malcolm S. Jeppsen*

I am grateful to understand that my physical body is an eternal, non-evil component of my eternal soul, and that I have, therefore, a duty to honor and respect and care for it, and to refrain from knowingly imposing upon it any treatment or substances deleterious to it. While I could not choose nor govern the condition of the body into which I came, I have the responsibility to give it the best care I can, and if I do not I am acting in derogation of a great gift of God.

—*Marion D. Hanks*

See also DRUG ABUSE, HEALTH

—————— Words ——————

If we are not most careful with our thoughts and speech, the words we use will use us. Language has its own ethics, and one who communicates truth is like a bright light in the darkness. (*Ensign*, May 1983, p. 73.)

—*Ted E. Brewerton*

Wise is the man who says what needs to be said, but not all that could be said. (*Ensign*, November 1976, p. 86.)

—*Marvin J. Ashton*

We will be held accountable for all that we say. The Savior has warned "that every idle word that men shall speak, they shall give account thereof in the day of judgment." (Matt. 12:36.) This means that no communication shall be without consequence. This includes the slight slips of the tongue, the caustic communications that canker the soul, and the vain, vulgar, and profane words which desecrate the name of Deity. (*Ensign*, November 1988, p. 23.)

—*L. Lionel Kendrick*

Members of the Church, young or old, should never allow profane or vulgar words to pass their lips. The language we use projects the images of our hearts, and our hearts should be pure. (*Ensign*, May 1986, p. 51.)

—*Dallin H. Oaks*

See also PROFANITY

—————— Work ——————

Daily toil, however humble it may be, is our daily duty, and by doing it well, we make it a part of our daily worship.

—*Brigham Young*

The "W" Formula: Work will win when wish-washy wishing won't. (*CR*, October 1973, p. 97.)

—*Thomas S. Monson*

The first recorded instruction given to Adam after the Fall dealt with the eternal principle of work. The Lord said: "In the sweat of thy face shalt thou eat bread." (Gen. 3:19.) Our Heavenly Father loves us so completely that he has given us a commandment to work. This is one of the keys to eternal life. He knows that we will learn more, grow more, achieve more, serve more, and benefit more from a life of industry than from a life of ease.

—Howard W. Hunter

It is the eternal, inescapable law that growth comes only from work and preparation, whether the growth be material, mental, or spiritual. Work has no substitute. (*CR*, April 1933, p. 103.)

—J. Reuben Clark, Jr.

Let us . . . realize that the *privilege* to work is a gift, that [the] *power* to work is a blessing, that *love* [of] work is success. (*True to the Faith*, Llewelyn R. McKay, comp., Salt Lake City: Bookcraft, 1966, p. 287.)

—David O. McKay

We are here on earth to work—to work long, hard, arduous hours, to work until our backs ache and our tired muscles knot, to work all our days. This mortal probation is one in which we are to eat our bread in the sweat of our faces until we return to the dust from whence we came.

Work is the law of life; it is the ruling principle in the lives of the Saints. (*Ensign*, May 1979, p. 93.)

—Bruce R. McConkie

We must open our eyes to the fact that to serve God is the greatest career in the world. (*Ensign*, January 1974, p. 111.)

—Mark E. Petersen

We should never be discouraged in those daily tasks which God has ordained to the common lot of man. Each day's labor should be undertaken in a joyous spirit and with the thought and conviction that our happiness and eternal welfare depend upon doing well that which we ought to do, that which God has made it our duty to do. (*GD*, p. 285.)

—Joseph F. Smith

Work brings happiness, self-esteem, and prosperity. It is the means of all accomplishment; it is the opposite of idleness. Work should be the ruling principle in the lives of our Church membership. (*Ensign*, November 1977, p. 77.)

—Spencer W. Kimball

Work is a spiritual necessity as well as an economic necessity. (*Ensign*, May 1981, p. 80.)

—Spencer W. Kimball

Work is, after all, not a busy running back and forth in established grooves, though that is the essence of our modern business and academic life, but the supreme energy and disciplined curiosity required to cut *new* grooves. (*OAT*, p. 116.)

—*Hugh Nibley*

Work is honorable. It is good therapy for most problems. It is the antidote for worry. It is the equalizer for deficiency of native endowment. Work makes it possible for the average to approach genius. What we may lack in aptitude, we can make up for in performance. . . .

In the broader sense, work is the means to achieve happiness, prosperity, and salvation. When work and duty and joy are commingled, then man is at his best. (*Ensign*, May 1982, pp. 77-78, 79.)

—*J. Richard Clarke*

Working for what we receive is a cardinal, timeless principle of self-respect. (*Ensign*, May 1982, p. 48.)

—*James E. Faust*

See also CAREERS, IDLENESS, SELF-RELIANCE, TEMPORAL WELFARE

Worldliness

As far as I am concerned, . . . I would rather walk barefoot from here to the celestial kingdom and . . . into the presence of my Heavenly Father, if I can get there, than to let the things of this world keep me out.

—*N. Eldon Tanner*

Babylon and Zion cannot mix in any degree. A Zion that makes concessions is no longer Zion. (*OAT*, p. 124.)

—*Hugh Nibley*

Cease to mingle with the wicked. Many of our elders seem to believe that Christ and Baal can yet be made friends. How many times elders of Israel try to make me fellowship the devil, or his imps, or his servants; also try to make you fellowship your enemies, to amalgamate the feelings of the saints and the ungodly! It cannot be done; it never was done, and never can be accomplished. Christ and Baal never can be friends. (*JD*, 8:325.)

—*Brigham Young*

Christ taught that we should be in the world but not of it. Yet there are some in our midst who are not so much concerned about taking the gospel into the world as they are about bringing worldliness into the gospel. They want us to be in the world and of it. They want us to be popular with the worldly even though a prophet has said that this is impossible, for all hell would then want to join us. (*IE*, 72:43.)

—*Ezra Taft Benson*

I fear that the Latter-day Saints, in many cases, are blinded by . . . their desire to be what the world is; and we have been told in such plain language by our Heavenly Father that we cannot live as the world lives and enjoy His Spirit. (*CR*, April 1929, p. 30.)

—*George Albert Smith*

I like this little poem:
> All the water in the world
> No matter how it tried
> Could never sink the smallest ship
> Unless it got inside.
> All the evil of the world
> And every kind of sin
> Could never damn a human soul
> Unless we let it in.

We can live in the world, . . . without letting the world into us. We have the gospel message that can carry men and women buoyantly through the "mist of darkness" (1 Ne. 8:23) to the source of all light. We can raise children who have been taught to discern and to make personal righteous decisions.

The Lord does not need a society that hides and isolates itself from the world. Rather, he needs stalwart individuals and families who live exemplary lives *in* the world and demonstrate that joy and fulfillment come not of the world but through the spirit and the doctrine of Jesus Christ. (*Ensign*, May 1989, p. 80.)

—*M. Russell Ballard*

Conscience warns us not to sink our cleats too deeply in mortal turf, which is so dangerously artificial. (*Ensign*, November 1987, p. 32.)

—*Neal A. Maxwell*

Many people spend most of their time working in the service of a self-image that includes sufficient money, stocks, bonds, investment portfolios, property, credit cards, furnishings, automobiles, and the like to *guarantee* carnal security throughout, it is hoped, a long and happy life. Forgotten is the fact that our assignment is to use these many resources in our families and quorums to build up the kingdom of God—to further the missionary effort and the genealogical and temple work; to raise our children up as fruitful servants unto the Lord; to bless others in every way, that they may also be fruitful. Instead, we expend these blessings on our own desires, and as Moroni said, "Ye adorn yourselves with that which hath no life, and yet suffer the hungry, and the needy, and the naked, and the sick and the afflicted to pass by you, and notice them not." (Morm. 8:39.)

As the Lord himself said in our day, "They seek not the Lord to establish his righteousness, but every man walketh in his own way, and after the image of his own God, whose image is in the likeness of the world, and *whose substance is that of an idol*, which waxeth old and shall perish in Babylon, even Babylon the great, which shall fall." (D&C 1:16; italics added.) (*Ensign,* June 1976, pp. 4-5.)

—*Spencer W. Kimball*

If . . . we as a community do not stand in that high relationship to God that we could wish, the fault is not in the Lord, it is not for the lack of information placed before us, but that lack is in ourselves; it arises from our ignorance or neglect, or from a desire, peradventure, to serve the spirit of the world instead of the Spirit of God. (*CR,* April 1880, p. 80.)

—*Lorenzo Snow*

Do not be caught up in materialism, one of the real plagues of our generation—that is, acquiring things, fast-paced living, and securing career success. (*Ensign,* May 1988, p. 53.)

—*Ezra Taft Benson*

If we are faithful in keeping the commandments of God, His promises will be fulfilled to the very letter. . . . The trouble is, the adversary of men's souls blinds their minds. He throws dust, so to speak, in their eyes, and they are blinded with the things of this world. (*Gospel Standards,* Salt Lake City: Improvement Era, 1942, pp. 44-45.)

—*M. Russell Ballard*

If you are worshipping false gods—such as football, baseball, golf, tennis, or money or technology or automobiles or houses or gold or silver—and you can tell what a man worships by what he does on Sunday—repent and start worshipping the true and living God, the maker of heaven and earth and all things that in them are. (*Ensign,* November 1990, p. 78.)

—*Hartman Rector, Jr.*

Materialism, which gives priority to material needs and objects, is obviously the opposite of spirituality. (*Ensign,* November 1985, p. 62.)

—*Dallin H. Oaks*

In this very material world where the acquisition of things assumes an importance that too often overshadows the pursuit of everything else, it is too easy for families to pursue other gods.

—Elliot D. Landau

It is written that we must love the Lord with all our hearts, and our neighbor as we love ourselves. When we reach this point, we shall not be liable to the accusation of loving the world more than we love God.

—Joseph F. Smith

No, my friends, the Book of Mormon does not exaggerate either the relentless efficiency or the speed with which wealth corrupts all those who set their hearts upon riches and the things of the world. (*OAT*, p. 127.)

—Hugh Nibley

No stone wall separates the members of the Church from all of the seductions of the world. Members of the Church, like everyone else, are being surfeited with deceptions, challenges, and temptations. However, to those of enduring faith, judgment, and discernment, there is an invisible wall which they choose never to breach. (*Ensign*, November 1985, p. 8.)

—James E. Faust

Some among us have become "unpeculiar" and have too often modeled our lives after the worldly among whom we live.

—Elliot D. Landau

The worldly fountain does not breed spiritual depth. (Address, Brigham Young University, February 22, 1966, p. 8.)

—Stephen R. Covey

The cares of the world are so many and so entangling, even very good people are diverted from following the truth because they care too much for the things of the world. (*Ensign*, May 1978, p. 77.)

—Spencer W. Kimball

The great criterion of success in the world is that men can make money. But I want to say to you Latter-day Saints that to do this is not true success. As a man grows and increases in the things of this world, if he is not careful, he will lose the Spirit of the Lord, and he will set his heart upon the things of this world. (*CR*, October 1911, p. 23.)

—George Albert Smith

The Lord . . . is sending forth his voice . . . unto the hearts of his people, crying unto them: "Stop! Stop your course! Cease to bring and build up Babylon in your midst!" (*JD*, 17:37.)

—Brigham Young

One of the greatest accomplishments of Satan in these last days is his success in turning men's affection towards the destructive, the fleeting, or the worldly. . . .

If our top priorities are constantly directed toward the acquisition of more and better worldly goods, it will not take long to increase our love in those directions. The purchase of a larger house or a nicer car or a more expensive boat may cause us to sacrifice our resources and develop an unwise love for these symbols of success and pleasure. We learn to love that which we serve, and we serve that which we love. (*Ensign*, May 1981, pp. 23-24.)

—Marvin J. Ashton

This is my Scripture: They who long and lust after the fashions of the world are destitute of the Spirit of God. (*JD*, 14:18.)

—Brigham Young

To "seek ye first financial independence and all other things shall be added," is . . . a rank *per*version of the scriptures and an immoral *in*version of values. (Commencement Address, Brigham Young University, August 19, 1983.)

—Hugh Nibley

Why do we insist on taking ourselves so seriously? Because we are frightened to death of being found out. Men have turned their backs on the atonement of Jesus Christ to make for themselves a world of humbug. To lend dignity and authority to the pretentious fraud, they have invented the solemn business and drudgery of everyday life. To avoid answering questions, we pretend to be very busy—my, how busy! (*OAT*, p. 109.)

—Hugh Nibley

We have been warned against the things of this world . . . But exactly what are the things of the world? An easy and infallible test has been given us in the well-known maxim "You can have anything in this world for money." If a thing is of this world, you can have it for money; if you cannot have it for money, it does not belong to this world. (Commencement Address, Brigham Young University, August 19, 1983.)

—Hugh Nibley

We know that the world will go on in wickedness until the end of the world, which is the destruction of the wicked. We shall continue to live in the world, but

with the Lord's help we shall not be of the world. We shall strive to overcome carnality and worldliness of every sort and shall invite all men to flee from Babylon, join with us, and live as becometh Saints. (*Ensign,* May 1979, p. 93.)
—*Bruce R. McConkie*

Too frequently Latter-day Saints of all ages yield to the temptation to explore and sample forbidden things of the world. Often this is not done with the intent to embrace these things permanently, but with the knowing decision to indulge in them momentarily, as though they hold a value of some kind too important or too exciting to pass by. While some recover from these excursions, an increasingly large number of tragedies occur that bring a blight and a despair into many lives. (*Ensign,* November 1981, pp. 26-27.)
—*Dean L. Larsen*

We will become increasingly different from those around us whose lives follow the world's way. . . . But we must clearly understand that it is not safe to move in the same direction the world is moving, . . . Such a course will eventually lead us to the same problems and heartaches. It will not permit us to perform the work the Lord has chosen us to do. It would disqualify us from his blessing and his protecting care. . . .
We must recognize . . . that it is not enough to be a Latter-day Saint in name only. It is not enough to simply declare that we are a chosen people of the Lord. We must keep the trust he has given us. We must qualify for his blessing by the way we remain different from the world in our obedience to his laws. Otherwise, we have no promise, and our fate will be the fate of the world. (*Ensign,* May 1983, p. 34.)
—*Dean L. Larsen*

Whether you can see it or not, I know that this people are more or less prone to idolatry; for I see that spirit manifested every day, and hear it from nearly every quarter. (*JD,* 6:19.)
—*Brigham Young*

See also HYPOCRISY, SELFISHNESS, WEALTH

——— Worry ———

All this trouble and vexation of mind is but a matter of the present; and if we keep the light of the Spirit within us, we can so walk in the gospel that we can measurably enjoy happiness in this world; and while we are traveling onward, striving for peace and happiness that lie in our path, we shall have a peace of mind that none can enjoy but those who are filled with the Holy Spirit. (*JD,* 5:313.)

—*Lorenzo Snow*

Somewhere there is a message in the protest of a man who said: "You can't tell me worry doesn't help. The things I worry about never happen." (*Ensign,* November 1977, p. 60.)

—*Boyd K. Packer*

There is no necessity for Latter-day Saints to worry over the things of this world. They will all pass away. Our hearts should be set on things above; to strive after that perfection which was in Christ . . . . Why should we fret and worry over temporal things when our destiny is so grand and glorious?

—*Lorenzo Snow*

We have no cause to worry. Live the gospel, keep the commandments. Attend to your prayers night and morning . . . .Maintain the standard of the Church. Try and live calmly and cheerfully. The Lord has said, "Ask and ye shall receive." (*TETB,* p. 342.)

—*Ezra Taft Benson*

See also FEAR, SERENITY, SORROW, TRUST IN GOD

——— **Worship** ———

If men are no longer awed by the thought of a holy God and are, as Mormon said of the people of his day, "without principle, and past feeling" (Moro. 9:20), then we face a fearful time. . . .

Prayer, reverence, worship, devotion, respect for the holy—these are basic exercises of our spirit and must be actively practiced in our lives or they will be lost.

. . . The Lord said, "Speak unto all the congregation of the children of Israel, and say unto them, Ye shall be holy; for I the Lord your God am holy." (Lev. 19:2.) (*Ensign,* November 1977, p. 54.)

—*Howard W. Hunter*

When we . . . meet to worship God, I like to see us worship him with all our hearts. I think it altogether out of place on such occasions to hear people talk about secular things; these are times, above all others, when our feelings and affections should be drawn out towards God. If we sing praises to God, let us do it in the proper spirit; if we pray, let every soul be engaged in prayer, doing it with all our hearts, that through our union our spirits may be blended in one, that our prayers and our worship may be available with God, whose Spirit permeates all things and is always present in the assemblies of good and faithful saints. (*JD*, 22:226.)

—John Taylor

Let me assure you . . . if there is anything in our hearts that interferes with our complete love of God and our reverence for him and his word, we shall have to banish it, or sooner or later we shall lose our standing in the Church of God; for he wants a people who will render implicit obedience to his laws and the requirements of his gospel, and who will love him better that any earthly thing, and place a higher value on the gifts of the Spirit than on worldly possessions or even life itself.

—George Q. Cannon

The Lord is saying to us, "Here is how you worship. You worship by emulation. You worship by imitation. You worship by patterning your life after mine. You worship by magnifying me and my course, by doing what I have done." (*Speeches of the Year*, Provo: Brigham Young University Press, 1971, p. 6.)

—Bruce R. McConkie

There is something essential about joining together with other believers to worship, to sing, to pray, to learn of God's will for us, and to acknowledge his goodness to us. He has commanded that this should be so. (*Ensign*, November 1989, p. 63.)

—Dean L. Larsen

We do not go to Sabbath meetings to be entertained or even solely to be instructed. We go to worship the Lord. If the service is a failure to you, you have failed. No one can worship for you; you must do your own waiting upon the Lord. (*TSWK*, p. 220.)

—Spencer W. Kimball

See also SABBATH

——— Worthiness ———

As we live the commandments of God, we can look forward with joyful anticipation to the second coming of the Lord Jesus Christ and know that through our efforts we are worthy, with our loved ones, to dwell in His presence for all eternity. Surely nothing is too hard to gain this great goal. (Tokyo Japan Area Conference, August 10, 1975.)

—*Ezra Taft Benson*

We give our hopes, our time, our talent, our thoughts, our words, our actions, to the temporalities of life, and once in a while, we think of God. We come before him in that pitiful form of unworthiness to crave his blessings and his favors. Do you wonder that we are often denied that which we ask for, and fail to receive that which we desire? It is because we do not ask aright. When we approach God in this way, we are not in a condition to ask aright, nor are we in a condition to receive that which we ask for, for God is not likely to bestow upon his children gifts and blessings of which they are not worthy. (*CR*, October 1913, p. 7.)

—*Joseph F. Smith*

We need to remove *unworthy* from our vocabulary and replace it with *hope* and *work*. (*Ensign*, May 1989, p. 22.)

—*Marvin J. Ashton*

Worthiness is a process, and perfection is an eternal trek. We can be worthy to enjoy certain privileges without being perfect. (*Ensign*, May 1989, p. 20.)

—*Marvin J. Ashton*

See also PERFECTION, PURITY

——— Young Men ———

Give me a young man who has kept himself morally clean and has faithfully attended his Church meetings. Give me a young man who has magnified his priesthood and has earned the Duty to God Award and is an Eagle Scout. Give me a young man who is a seminary graduate and has a burning testimony of the Book of Mormon. Give me such a young man, and I will give you a young man who can perform miracles for the Lord in the mission field and throughout his life. (*Ensign*, May 1986, p. 45.)

— *Ezra Taft Benson*

Honor Young Women
When you boys become priests and elders and begin to date, you need to know that the best place to date is at Church and Church-related activities. As you date, you will be entrusted by a girl's parents with their most cherished blessing.

You will have the responsibility to protect not only her well-being, but also her honor, even above your own safety. (*Ensign*, May 1986, p. 45.)

— *James E. Faust*

In these latter days when keeping the commandments of God is unimportant to many, you young men have a greater challenge to honor the priesthood than any who have held it at any other time. This is true because Lucifer is on the prowl. He knows that his days are numbered. He has learned how to destroy people, especially the youth. He seeks to find any chink in the armor of each person. He knows our weaknesses and knows how to exploit them if we allow him to do so. We can defend ourselves against his attacks and deceptions only by understanding the commandments and by fortifying ourselves each day through praying, studying the scriptures, and following the counsel of the Lord's anointed. (*Ensign*, November 1988, p. 35.)

— *Joseph B. Wirthlin*

My beloved Aaronic Priesthood brethren, with all you are learning as you progress toward virile manhood, I pray that you will get understanding of the vital truth that chastity is the ultimate and perfect standard underlying all spiritual progression.

Righteousness is happiness. . . .

I challenge you to be *clean*, be *worthy*, be *strong*, be *happy!* (*Ensign*, November 1989, p. 38.)

— *Robert L. Backman*

President Spencer W. Kimball said: "When I read Church history, I am amazed at the boldness of the early brethren as they went out into the world. They seemed to find a way. Even in persecution and hardship, they went and opened doors which evidently had been allowed to sag on their hinges and many of them to close. . . .

"These men of valor began to walk the earth with dignity and honor, with mantles on their shoulders, and keys in their hands and love in their hearts."

My faithful young friends, you can match their boldness stride for stride. You can walk with equal dignity and honor, with the mantle on your shoulders, and keys in your hands, and love in your hearts. (*Ensign*, November 1987, p. 30.)

— *Vaughn J. Featherstone*

To you wonderful young men of the Church, turn your hearts to the Lord, put Him first in your lives. The finest thing each of you can do for the Lord and for yourself and your family is to prepare yourself to serve as a missionary. (*Ensign*, November 1982, p. 28.)

— *Rex C. Reeve*

I remind you young men that regardless of your present age, you are building your life; it will be cheap and shoddy or it will be valuable and beautiful; it will be full of constructive activities or it can be destructive; it can be full of joy and happiness, or it can be full of misery. It all depends upon you and your attitudes, for your altitude, or the height you climb, is dependent upon your attitude or your response to situations. (*Ensign*, November 1974, p. 80.)

— *Spencer W. Kimball*

Remember, my young friends, you are somebody! You are a child of promise. You are a man of might. You are a son of God, endowed with faith, gifted with courage, and guided by prayer. Your eternal destiny is before you. The Apostle Paul speaks to you today as he spoke to Timothy long years ago: "Neglect not the gift that is in thee. . . . O Timothy, keep that which is committed to thy trust." (1 Tim. 4:14; 6:20.) (*Ensign*, May 1989, p. 43.)

— *Thomas S. Monson*

In schools where in reality only a few students are using drugs, drinking alcohol, or smoking, non-users commonly believe that most of their fellow students are doing it.

Everyone is *not* doing it. You don't! And you influence your friends. And others watch you. You help set the standard.

Young men, you are a royal brotherhood—not because you're better than anyone else—but because the Lord has blessed you with special privileges and responsibilities. . . .

You are one of his spirit sons, singled out with a special calling. And we know that he loves you. You have the gift of the Holy Ghost. You can discern good from evil. And with the power of the priesthood, you have the authority to represent your Heavenly Father. (*Ensign*, November 1986, pp. 37-38.)

— *David B. Haight*

You, my fine young men, must not be just average. Your lives must be clean and free from all kinds of evil thoughts or acts—no lying, no theft, no anger, no faithlessness, no failure to do that which is right, no sexual sins of any kind, at any time.

You know what is right and what is wrong. you have all received the Holy Ghost following your baptism. You need no one to brand the act or thought as wrong or right. You know by the Spirit. You are painting your own picture, carving your own statue. It is up to you to make it acceptable.

May God bless you, our beloved young men. I know your Heavenly Father is your true friend. Everything he asks you to do is right and will bring blessings to you and make you manly and strong. (*Ensign*, November 1974, p. 83.)

— *Spencer W. Kimball*

Young men, I do not believe that you are here upon the earth at this time by accident. I believe you qualified in the premortal life to come into mortality at a time when great things would be required of you. . . . You have come to the earth when the foundation has been laid for this great work. The gospel has been restored for the last time. The Church has been established in almost every part of the world. The stage is set for the final dramatic scenes to be enacted. You will be the principal players. You are among the last laborers in the vineyard. This is the yoke that is set upon your necks. This is the service for which you are chosen. (*Ensign*, May 1983, p. 33.)

— *Dean L. Larsen*

Young men of the Aaronic Priesthood, you have been born at this time for a sacred and glorious purpose. It is not by chance that you have been reserved to come to earth in this last dispensation of the fullness of times. Your birth at this particular time was foreordained in the eternities.

You are to be the royal army of the Lord in the last days. You are "youth of the noble birthright." (*Hymns*, 1985, no. 255.) (*Ensign*, May 1986, p. 43.)

— *Ezra Taft Benson*

Young men, listen to the counsel of your brethren. Live near to God; pray while young; learn to pray; learn to cultivate the Holy Spirit of God; link it to you and it will become a spirit of revelation unto you, inasmuch as you nourish it. (Quoted by Gordon B. Hinckley, *Ensign*, May 1988, p. 46.)

— *Wilford Woodruff*

See also AARONIC PRIESTHOOD, MISSIONARY WORK, YOUTH

———— Young Women ————

A young man in Michigan several years ago fell in love with an LDS girl. He was told forthrightly and with great love that she wanted the power of the priesthood in her home and the blessings of an eternal family, and she would only marry someone who could give her those blessings. The teachings she had received had taken root, and the seeds of faith, knowledge, and choice had grown, and she knew that they were true. The young man felt her spirit and agreed to be taught the gospel.

And after he had learned that the gospel was true, his father would not approve his baptism. A great shepherd, a bishop of the young girl went to the father and helped him to see the value of that young woman, her standards, the Church, and the really truly important things in life. The father was touched that day as he attended the baptism and saw about twenty young men and women of the Church. Following the service, he asked that the missionaries come teach him. A young woman had taken on the divine nature and was able to share the priceless truths with others. (*Ensign*, May 1988, p. 11.)

— *James M. Paramore*

Love the Scriptures

Through prayer and study you can know the scriptures are true. I am so anxious for you to know and love the scriptures so they can provide answers during your teenage years when the climb is steep and scary and risky and you need inspiration as you make important choices every day. As you become more and more familiar with the scriptures, they can eventually become your favorite stories, easy to read; and they will help you have determination to stand firm for righteousness, even when it's hard. (*Ensign*, November 1985, p. 95.)

— *Ardeth G. Kapp*

Of all the creations of the Almighty there is none more beautiful, none more inspiring than a lovely daughter of God who walks in virtue, with an understanding of why she should do so, who honors and respects her body as a thing sacred and divine, who cultivates her mind and constantly enlarges the horizon of her understanding, who nurtures her spirit with everlasting truth. (*Ensign*, May 1988, p. 92.)

— *Gordon B. Hinckley*

What hopes I have for you young sisters! What hopes our Father in Heaven has for you!

You have been born at this time for a sacred and glorious purpose. It is not by chance that you have been reserved to come to earth in this last dispensation of the fullness of times. Your birth at this particular time was foreordained in the eternities.

You are to be the royal daughters of the Lord in the last days. You are "youth of the noble birthright" (*Hymns*, 1985, no. 255). (*Ensign*, November 1986, p. 81.)

— *Ezra Taft Benson*

You lovely young women of the Church, put the Lord first in your lives, turn your hearts to Him. He has placed such trust and confidence in you as His daughters. Prepare to marry in the temple. Work and plan to this end. It will not only bless your own lives, but the lives of many others will be blessed by your desire and example. Put the Lord first in your lives and hearts. (*Ensign*, November 1982, p. 28.)

— *Rex C. Reeve*

Women are endowed with special traits and attributes that come trailing down through eternity from a divine mother. Young women have special God-given feelings about charity, love, and obedience. Coarseness and vulgarity are contrary to their natures. They have a modifying, softening influence on young men. Young women were not foreordained to do what priesthood holders do. Theirs is a sacred, God-given role, and the traits they received from heavenly mother are equally as important as those given to the young men. (*Ensign*, November 1987, p. 28.)

— Vaughn J. Featherstone

Yes, give me a young woman who loves home and family, who reads and ponders the scriptures daily, who has a burning testimony of the Book of Mormon. Give me a young woman who faithfully attends her church meetings, who is a seminary graduate, who has earned her Young Womanhood Recognition Award and wears it with pride! Give me a young woman who is virtuous and who has maintained her personal purity, who will not settle for less than a temple marriage, and I will give you a young woman who will perform miracles for the Lord now and throughout eternity. (*Ensign*, November 1986, p. 84.)

— Ezra Taft Benson

Young women, we call upon you to increase your spirituality by living righteously. Raise your standards high, that others might follow. You are the promise of tomorrow, the hope of Israel. (*Ensign*, November 1990, p. 95.)

— Ardeth G. Kapp

Young women, you are needed. Never before in the history of the Church has there been such a need for young women who are willing to sacrifice popularity if necessary, suffer loneliness if required, even be rejected if needed, to defend the gospel of Jesus Christ.

When you keep the commandments and follow the Savior's example, it's like holding up a light. Your good example helps others to find their way in a darkening world. (*Ensign*, November 1988, p. 94.)

— Ardeth G. Kapp

See also WOMANHOOD

——— Youth ———

For nearly six thousand years, God has held you in reserve to make your appearance in the final days before the Second Coming. Every previous gospel dispensation has drifted into apostasy, but ours will not. . . . God has saved for the final inning some of his strongest children, who will help bear off the kingdom triumphantly. And that is where you come in, for you are the generation that must be prepared to meet your God. . . . Make no mistake about it—you are a marked generation. (*Ensign*, April 1987, p. 73.)

— *Ezra Taft Benson*

Be a light unto the world, a standard to others. You can live in the world and not partake of the sins of the world. You can live life joyously, beautifully, unmarred by the ugliness of sin. This is our confidence in you. (*New Era*, June 1986, p. 8.)

— *Ezra Taft Benson*

Beloved youth, you will have your trials and temptations through which you must pass, but there are great moments of eternity which lie ahead. You have our love and our confidence. We pray that you will be prepared for the reins of leadership. We say to you, "Arise and shine forth" (D&C 115:5) and be a light unto the world, a standard to others. (*New Era*, June 1986, p. 8.)

— *Ezra Taft Benson*

Beloved youth, you will have your trials and temptations through which you must pass, but there are great moments of eternity which lie ahead. . . . You can live in the world and not partake of the sins of the world. You can live a life joyously, beautifully, unmarred by the ugliness of sin. This is our confidence in you. (*Ensign*, November 1977, p. 32.)

— *Ezra Taft Benson*

God bless you young women and young men who struggle through the worrisome teenage years. Some of you may not yet have found yourselves, but you are *not* lost, for Jesus is the Christ, the Son of God, our Savior and Redeemer. (*Ensign*, May 1989, p. 59.)

— *Boyd K. Packer*

I have little or no fear for the young man or the young woman, who honestly and conscientiously supplicates God twice a day for the guidance of His Spirit. I am sure that when temptation comes they will have the strength to overcome it by the inspiration that shall be given to them. Supplicating the Lord for the guidance of His Spirit places around us a safeguard, and if we earnestly and honestly seek the guidance of the Spirit of the Lord, I can assure you that we will receive it. (*Gospel Standards*, Salt Lake City: Improvement Era, 1942, p. 26.)

— *Heber J. Grant*

God loves you as He loves each and every one of His children, and His desire and purpose and glory is to have you return to Him pure and undefiled, having proven yourselves worthy of an eternity of joy in His presence.

Your Father in heaven is mindful of you. He has given you commandments to guide you, to discipline you. He has also given you your agency—freedom of choice—"to see if [you] will do all things whatsoever [He] shall command." His kingdom here on earth is well organized, and your leaders are dedicated to helping you. May you know that you have our constant love, our concern, and prayers. (*Ensign,* November 1977, p. 30.)

— *Ezra Taft Benson*

I challenge youth to cooperate with parents who are concerned about your reading and your viewing. Be concerned yourself about what you take into your mind. Young people, you would never eat a meal of spoiled or contaminated food if you could help it, would you? Select your reading and your viewing carefully and in good taste. (*Ensign,* November 1977, p. 72.)

— *Marvin J. Ashton*

If you will listen to the promptings of your best self, your clearest judgement, the whisperings of your own true heart, you will learn this lesson: That self-mastery during youth and the compliance with the single standard of morality is (1) the source of virile manhood; (2) the crown of beautiful womanhood; (3) the foundation of a happy home; and (4) the contributing factor to the strength and perpetuity of the race! (*IE,* 4:1139.)

— *David O. McKay*

In our society, young people often see parents as the past and friends as the future. Magazines, movies, and music made for teenagers often emphasize going your own way and dismissing parents as naive. Avoid that kind of thinking; it is false. Your parents are wise. They have a maturity that comes only from experience. The Lord has given them the fundamental task of teaching, guiding, and caring for you and helping you prepare for the challenges that are necessary for your growth and progress. (*Ensign,* November 1988, p. 34.)

— *Joseph B. Wirthlin*

It's okay that your parents aren't perfect; no one's are. And it's okay that they didn't have any perfect children either; no one's are.

You see, our whole purpose is to strive together in righteousness, overcoming our weaknesses day by day. Don't ever give up on each other. (*Ensign,* November 1984, p. 97.)

— *Ardeth G. Kapp*

Oh, if our young people could learn this basic lesson—to always keep good company, to never be found with those who tend to lower their standards! (*Ensign*, November 1976, pp. 27-28.)

— *Spencer W. Kimball*

Our most precious possession is the youth of the land, and to instruct them to walk uprightly and to become worthy citizens in the kingdom of God is our greatest obligation. (Conference address reprint, *Ensign*, October 1972, p. 31.)

— *David O. McKay*

Our young people are among the most blessed and favored of our Father's children. They are the nobility of heaven, a choice and chosen generation who have a divine destiny. Their spirits have been reserved to come forth in this day when the gospel is on earth, and when the Lord needs valiant servants to carry on his great latter-day work.

May the Lord bless you, the youth of Zion, and keep you true to every covenant and obligation, cause you to walk in paths of light and truth, and preserve you for the great labors ahead. (*IE*, June 1970, p. 3.)

— *Joseph Fielding Smith*

Do I know God lives? Do I know the devil lives? I want to tell you young people there is a constant war between the two, and the war is over you and your soul. The adversary would take you and destroy you if God would permit it. He has many devices, many means of attack, many avenues of approach, and you must be on guard. . . .

I want to say to you young people . . . the eyes of the whole Church are upon you, expecting you to stand firm, to have faith and fortitude and courage, and keep yourselves absolutely clean from the center of your heart to the ends of your fingers and toes. . . . Beware of the approaches of the adversary and know always that God stands ready to help. (Ten-Stake Fireside Address, Brigham Young University, October 8, 1967.)

— *Hugh B. Brown*

Young women, you are the mothers of tomorrow. Young men, you are the fathers. Together, you are the parents, the teachers, and the advisers who will help nurture and feed young lambs and lead them home. Prepare yourselves now for that sacred responsibility. Study the scriptures. Develop your God-given talents. Learn all you can about the world around you that is clean and good. Prepare yourselves to enter the temple of the Lord and be worthy to receive the ordinances and blessings by living, teaching, and sharing the gospel. (*Ensign*, November 1989, p. 79.)

— *Jayne B. Malan*

You know that palm trees do not grow from acorns—only oaks come from acorns. The reason is that somehow oaks are involved in acorns, and that which is involved can evolve. Now, young people, God is your Father—in a very real and genuine sense he is your Father, and therefore he is involved in you. If you will conduct yourselves properly you may evolve into something like him. But again I say, if we yield to the temptations to do what we ought not to do and continue to yield, then we will not develop and grow and unfold into our possibilities. That which is involved can evolve, and God is involved in *you*. (Fireside Address, Brigham Young University, October 8, 1967.)

— *Hugh B. Brown*

Somehow, my dear young friends, we will stem the tide of untruth and immorality that is sweeping the earth. It will be accomplished by you, the youth of the Church, through your faith and strength. Don't be discouraged at seemingly overwhelming odds in your desire to live and to help others live God's commandments. At times it may seem like David trying to fight Goliath. But remember, David did win. (*Ensign*, November 1977, p. 58.)

— *David B. Haight*

The youth of the Church are one of the most powerful forces for good on the earth today.

It is not difficult to understand why the great God in heaven has reserved these special spirits for the final work of the kingdom prior to his millennial reign.

My heart, like Enoch's, seems to swell "wide as eternity" (Moses 7:41) as I consider what our youth and those being born in this time will accomplish. This generation will face trials and troubles that will exceed those of their pioneer forebears. Our generation has had some periods of respite from the foe. The future generation will have little or none. But their great faith in the Lord will give them needed strength. (*Ensign*, November 1987, pp. 27-28.)

— *Vaughn J. Featherstone*

Though the world is becoming more wicked, the youth of Christ's Church can become more righteous if they understand who they are, understand the blessings available, and understand the promises God has made to those who are righteous, who believe, who endure. (*CR*, October 1973, p. 42.)

— *David B. Haight*

To the Youth

You have a heritage: Honor it. *You will meet sin:* Shun it. *You have the truth:* Live it. *You have a testimony:* Share it. (*Ensign*, November 1990, p. 47.)

— *Thomas S. Monson*

To Youth

You are a child of God. He is the father of your spirit. Spiritually you are of noble birth, the offspring of the King of Heaven. Fix that truth in your mind and hold to it. However many generations in your mortal ancestry, no matter what race or people you represent, the pedigree of your spirit can be written on a single line. You are a child of God! (*Ensign*, May 1989, p. 54.)

— *Boyd K. Packer*

Today our youth are faced with tremendous challenges—and what do they need most?

They need sound knowledge, sensible understanding, a guiding hand. They need real homes that are maintained in a clean and orderly manner. They need fathers who are really fathers and mothers who are mothers in the true sense of the word. They need more than mere progenitors or landlords. They are in need of loving, understanding parents, who give fatherly and motherly care, who put their families first in their lives, and who consider it their fundamental and most important duty to save their own children, to so orient them and their thinking that they will not be swayed by every wind of persuasion which happens to blow in their direction. (*Ensign*, November 1976, p. 61.)

— *O. Leslie Stone*

What a wonderful time to be young. You will see events in your lifetime that will test your courage and extend your faith. If you will face the sunlight of truth, the shadows of discouragement and sin and error will fall behind you. You must never give up! (*Ensign*, May 1989, p. 59.)

— *Boyd K. Packer*

Young people, your parents, with their maturity of years and experience you have not had, can provide wisdom, knowledge, and blessings to help you over life's pitfalls. You may find, that life's sweetest experiences come when you go to Mom and Dad for help. (*Ensign*, November 1977, p. 31.)

— *Ezra Taft Benson*

Young people. . . , God wants us to be victorious. He wants you to triumph over all of your foes. Stalwart and brave we must stand. God is at the helm. There is no reason for defeat. (*Ensign*, November 1989, p. 37.)

— *Marvin J. Ashton*

See also YOUNG MEN, YOUNG WOMEN

——— Zion ———

As much virtue can be gained in progressing toward Zion as in dwelling there. It is a process as well as a destination. (*Ensign*, May 1986, p. 30.)

— *Robert D. Hales*

Every step in the direction of increasing one's personal holdings is a step away from Zion. . . . In Zion you labor, to be sure, but not for money, and not for yourself (see 2 Ne. 26:31), which is the exact opposite of our present version of the work ethic. (*OAT*, pp. 125, 126.)

— *Hugh Nibley*

It is the mission of the Church of this last dispensation to develop another people who shall live the gospel in its fulness. This people are to become "pure in heart," and they shall flourish and be blessed upon the mountains and upon the high places. They shall be the Lord's people. They shall walk with God because they shall be of one heart and one mind, and they shall dwell in righteousness, and there shall be no poor among them. (*Ensign*, November 1981, p. 93.)

— *Marion G. Romney*

Establish the principles of Zion inside your hearts, and then you will be worthy to receive Zion outside.

— *Lorenzo Snow*

My greatest desire is to see Zion established according to the revelations of God, to see her inhabitants industrious and self-sustaining, filled with wisdom and the power of God, that around us may be built a wall of defense, a protection against the mighty powers of Babylon; and while the disobedient of our Father's family are contending, and filling up their cup of iniquity, even to the brim, and thus preparing themselves for the burning, we who are the acknowledged children of the kingdom, being filled with the righteousness and knowledge of God, may be like the wise virgins, clothed in our wedding garments, and properly prepared for the coming of our Lord and Savior. (*JD*, 18:376.)

— *Lorenzo Snow*

The Zion of God. What does it mean? The pure in heart in the first place. In the second place those who are governed by the law of God—the pure in heart who are governed by the law of God. (*JD*, 26:109.)

— *John Taylor*

Not long ago a man asked me, "Does your church still believe that when Christ comes you will be living as one, the way they did in the city of Enoch?" He put a spin on the word *still*, as if we might not believe such a thing anymore. I said, "Yes, we do." And then he said, "You are the people who could do it." (*Ensign*, November 1989, p. 13.)

— *Henry B. Eyring*

The redemption of Zion is more than the purchase or recovery of lands, the building of cities, or even the founding of nations. It is the conquest of the heart, the subjugation of the soul, the sanctifying of the flesh, the purifying and ennobling of the passions. (*The Life of Heber C. Kimball*, 2d ed., Salt Lake City: Stevens & Wallis, 1945, p. 65.)

— *Orson F. Whitney*

The building up of Zion is a cause that has interested the people of God in every age; it is a theme upon which prophets, priests and kings have dwelt with peculiar delight; they have looked forward with joyful anticipation to the day in which we live; and fired with heavenly and joyful anticipations they have sung and written and prophesied of this our day; but they died without the sight; we are the favored people that God has made choice of to bring about the Latter-day glory; it is left for us to see, participate in and help to roll forward the Latter-day glory, "the dispensation of the fullness of times," when God will gather together all things that are in heaven, and all things that are upon the earth, . . . when the Saints of God will be gathered in one from every nation, and kindred, and people, and tongue, when the Jews will be gathered together into one, the wicked will also be gathered together to be destroyed, as spoken of by the prophets; the Spirit of God will also dwell with His people, and be withdrawn from the rest of the nations, and all things whether in heaven or on earth will be in one, even in Christ. (*HC*, 4:609-610.)

— *Joseph Smith*

The gospel gives us glimpses of the far horizon, revealing a glow from the lights of the City of God. It is a place of happy countenances, where justice and mercy as well as righteousness and truth are constant companions. Herein gentleness and generosity prevail, "without compulsory means." (D&C 111:46.) Coarseness and selfishness are unknown, belonging to a previous and primitive place. Here envy would be a sure embarrassment. Neighbors are esteemed as self. This city, where all the residents keep the first and second great commandments, is a community of striking individuals of one heart and of one mind. (*Ensign*, May 1986, p. 36.)

— *Neal A. Maxwell*

On the last night of a play the whole cast and stage crew stay in the theater until the small or not-so small hours of the morning striking the old set. If there is to be a new opening soon, as the economy of the theater requires, it is important that the new set should be in place and ready for the opening night. All the while the old set was finishing its usefulness and then being taken down, the new set was rising in splendor to be ready for the drama that would immediately follow.

So it is with this world. It is not our business to tear down the old set—the agencies that do that are already hard at work and very efficient. The set is coming down all around us with spectacular effect. Our business is to see to it that the new set is well on the way for what is to come—and that means a different kind of politics, beyond the scope of the tragedy that is now playing its closing night. We are preparing for the establishment of Zion. (*OAT,* p. 128.)

— *Hugh Nibley*

There is not one thing wanting in all the works of God's hands to make a Zion upon the earth when the people conclude to make it. (*DBY,* p. 182.)

— *Brigham Young*

We can make Zion, or we can make Babylon, just as we please. We can make just what we please of this place. The people can make Zion: they can make a heaven within themselves. When people gather here, they should come with a determination to make Zion within themselves, with the resolution that "I will carry myself full of the Spirit of Zion wherever I go . . ." and do you not see that such a course will make Zion? (*JD,* 5:4.)

— *Brigham Young*

We are here to build up the church of God, the Zion of God, and the kingdom of God, and to be on hand to do whatever God requires—first to purge ourselves from all iniquity, from covetousness and evil of every kind, to forsake sin of every sort, cultivate the Spirit of God, and help to build up his kingdom; to beautify Zion and have pleasant habitations, and pleasant gardens and orchards, until Zion shall be the most beautiful place there is on the earth. . . . Zion shall yet become the praise and the glory of the whole earth. (*Gospel Kingdom,* G. Homer Durham, ed., Salt Lake City: Bookcraft, 1943, p. 221.)

— *John Taylor*

We cannot build up Zion except upon the principle of righteousness. Men must forsake their wickedness, their lusts, covetousness, greed, and love of the pleasures of the world, and bring themselves under the law of God, or they never will partake of the blessings and glory of Zion. (*CR,* April 1880, p. 35.)

— *Joseph F. Smith*

We ought to have the building up of Zion as our greatest object. (*HC*, 3:390.)

— *Joseph Smith*

When Zion descends from above, Zion will also ascend from beneath, and be prepared to associate with those from above. The people will be so perfected and purified, ennobled, exalted, and dignified in their feelings and so truly humble and most worthy, virtuous and intelligent that they will be fit, when caught up, to associate with that Zion that shall come down from God out of heaven. (*JD*, 10:147.)

— *John Taylor*

Zion can be built up only among those who are the pure in heart, not a people torn by covetousness or greed, but a pure and selfless people. Not a people who are pure in appearance, rather a people who are pure in heart. Zion is to be in the world and not of the world, not dulled by a sense of carnal security, nor paralyzed by materialism. No, Zion is not things of the lower, but of the higher order, things that exalt the mind and sanctify the heart. (*Ensign*, May 1978, p. 81.)

— *Spencer W. Kimball*

Zion is a constant in time and place. It belongs to the order of the eternities. We're not making Zion here, but we're preparing the ground to receive it. . . . We must be prepared to receive this glory; we don't produce it ourselves. We must be ready, so that we won't die of shock when we get it. (*OAT*, p. 121.)

— *Hugh Nibley*

Zion is a name given by the Lord to his covenant people, who are characterized by purity of heart and faithfulness in caring for the poor, the needy, and the distressed. This highest order of priesthood society is founded on the doctrines of love, service, work, self-reliance, and stewardship, all of which are circumscribed by the covenant of consecration. (*Ensign*, November 1977, p. 78.)

— *Spencer W. Kimball*

Zion will extend, eventually, all over this earth. There will be no nook or corner upon the earth but what will be in Zion.

— *Brigham Young*

See also CONSECRATION, PURITY, TEMPORAL LAW, TEMPORAL WELFARE, UNITY

Index

Index

Index